THE CAMBRIDGE COMPANION TO
# RAWLS

Each volume of this series of companions to major philosophers contains specially commissioned essays by an international team of scholars, together with a substantial bibliography, and will serve as a reference work for students and
nonspecialists. One aim of the series is to dispel the intimi-
dation such readers often feel when faced with the work of a
difficult and challenging thinker.

John Rawls is the most significant and influential political and moral philosopher of the twentieth-century. His
work has profoundly shaped contemporary discussions of
social, political, and economic justice in philosophy, law,
political science, economics, and other social disciplines. In
this exciting collection of new essays, many of the world's
leading political and moral theorists discuss the full range
of Rawls's contribution to the concepts of political and economic justice, democracy, liberalism, constitutionalism, and
international justice. There are also assessments of Rawls's
controversial relationships with feminism, utilitarianism,
and communitarianism.

New readers will find this the most convenient and accessible guide to Rawls currently available. Advanced students
and specialists will find a conspectus of recent developments
in the interpretation of Rawls.

Samuel Freeman is Professor of Philosophy and Law at the
University of Pennsylvania.

*The Cambridge Companion to*
# RAWLS

Edited by
Samuel Freeman
*University of Pennsylvania*

CAMBRIDGE UNIVERSITY PRESS
Cambridge, New York, Melbourne, Madrid, Cape Town, Singapore,
São Paulo

Cambridge University Press
40 West 20th Street, New York, NY 10011-4211, USA

www.cambridge.org
Information on this title: www.cambridge.org/9780521651677

First published 2003
Reprinted 2003, 2004, 2005

Printed in the United States of America

*A catalog record for this publication is available from the British Library.*

*Library of Congress Cataloging in Publication Data*

The Cambridge companion to Rawls / edited by Samuel Freeman.
  p.  cm. – (Cambridge companions to philosophy)
Includes bibliographical references and index.
ISBN 0-521-65167-0 (hardback) – ISBN 0-521-65706-7 (pbk.)
1. Rawls, John 1921 – Contributions to philosophy. 2. Justice.
3. Liberalism. I. Freeman, Samuel Richard. II. Series.
JC251 .R32C35 2002
320.51′092 – dc21                                 2002022267

ISBN-13   978-0-521-65167-7 hardback
ISBN-10   0-521-65167-0 hardback

ISBN-13   978-0-521-65706-8 paperback
ISBN-10   0-521-65706-7 paperback

# CONTENTS

vii

# CONTRIBUTORS

JOSHUA COHEN is Professor of Philosophy and Political Science and Goldberg Professor of the Humanities at MIT. He writes on democratic theory, is coauthor of *On Democracy* and *Associations and Democracy*, and has written numerous articles on the theory and practice of deliberative democracy. Cohen is editor-in-chief of *Boston Review* and associate editor of *Philosophy and Public Affairs*.

NORMAN DANIELS is Professor of Ethics and Population Health, School of Public Health, Harvard University. His main work in ethics and political philosophy includes *Reading Rawls* (ed., 1975), *Just Health Care* (1985), *Am I My Parents' Keeper?* (1988), *Seeking Fair Treatment* (1995), *Justice and Justification* (1996), *Benchmarks of Fairness for Health Care Reform* (with Don Light and Ronald Caplan, 1996), *From Chance to Choice* (with Allen Buchanan, Dan Brock, and Dan Wikler, 2000), *Is Inequality Bad for Our Health?* (with Bruce Kennedy and Ichiro Kawachi, 2000), and *Setting Limits Fairly* (with James Sabin, 2002).

BURTON DREBEN was Professor of Philosophy at Harvard University and at Boston University until his death in 1999. He is the author of several essays on the history of logic and analytic philosophy, as well as (with Warren Goldfarb) *The Decision Problem: Solvable Classes of Unsolvable Formulas*.

SAMUEL FREEMAN is Steven F. Goldstone Term Professor of Philosophy and Law at the University of Pennsylvania. He has written numerous articles in political, moral, and legal philosophy on such subjects as liberalism and libertarianism, deliberative democracy, utilitarianism and deontology, constitutional interpretation, contractualism, and Rawls and social contract theory. He edited John Rawls's *Collected Papers* (1999).

AMY GUTMANN is Provost and Laurance S. Rockefeller University Professor of Politics at Princeton University. She is the author of *Democratic Education* and *Liberal Equality* and of the forthcoming *Identity Groups in Democracy: A Humanist View*; coauthor of *Democracy and Disagreement* and *Color Conscious: The Political Morality of Race*; and editor of eight books, including *Democracy and the Welfare State, Multiculturalism,* and *Freedom of Association.*

CHARLES LARMORE is Chester D. Tripp Professor in the Humanities at the University of Chicago. His books include *Patterns of Moral Complexity* (1987), *The Morals of Modernity* (1996), and *The Romantic Legacy* (1996). He is currently completing a book (in French) on the nature of self, entitled *Les Pratiques du Moi.*

FRANK I. MICHELMAN is Robert Walmsley University Professor, Harvard University, where he has taught since 1963. He is the author of *Brennan and Democracy* (1999) and has published widely in the fields of constitutional law and theory, property law and theory, local government law, and jurisprudence.

STEPHEN MULHALL is Fellow and Tutor in Philosophy at New College, Oxford. His research interests include political philosophy, philosophy of religion, Wittgenstein, Heidegger, and Kierkegaard. His most recent books are *Inheritance and Originality* (OUP: 2001) and *On Film* (Routledge: 2001).

THOMAS NAGEL is Professor of Philosophy and Fiorello LaGuardia Professor of Law at New York University and author of *Equality and Partiality, The Last Word, The View from Nowhere,* and *The Possibility of Altruism.*

MARTHA C. NUSSBAUM is Ernst Freund Distinguished Service Professor of Law and Ethics at the University of Chicago with appointments in the Law School, Philosophy Department, and the Divinity School. She is on the Board of the Center for Gender Studies. Her most recent books are *Women and Human Development* (2000) and *Upheavals of Thought: The Intelligence of Emotions* (2001).

ONORA O'NEILL is Principal of Newnham College, Cambridge. She has written widely on Kant's practical philosophy, on international justice, and on ethics. Her recent books include *Bounds of Justice* (CUP 2000) and *Autonomy and Trust in Bioethics* (CUP 2002).

T.M. SCANLON is Professor of Philosophy at Harvard University. His writings in moral and political philosophy include many articles and a book, *What We Owe to Each Other*.

SAMUEL SCHEFFLER is Professor of Philosophy and Law at the University of California, Berkeley. He is the author of *The Rejection of Consequentialism, Human Morality*, and *Boundaries and Allegiances*.

ADAM SWIFT is Fellow in Politics and Sociology at Balliol College, Oxford. He coauthored *Liberals and Communitarians* (2nd ed., Blackwell 1996) and *Against the Odds? Social Class and Social Justice in Industrial Societies* (OUP 1997) but wrote *Political Philosophy: A Beginner's Guide for Students and Politicians* (Polity 2001) on his own.

PHILIPPE VAN PARIJS directs the Hoover Chair of economic and social ethics at the Catholic University of Louvain (Belgium). His books in English include *Evolutionary Explanation in the Social Sciences* (1981), *Arguing for Basic Income* (1992), *Marxism Recycled* (1993), *Real Freedom for All* (1995), and *What's Wrong with a Free Lunch?* (2001). He is currently working on the relationships between linguistic diversity, justice, and democracy.

# Introduction
## John Rawls – An Overview

## I. PRELIMINARIES

John Rawls's published works extend over fifty years from the middle of the twentieth century to the present.[1] During this period his writings have come to define a substantial portion of the agenda for Anglo–American political philosophy, and they increasingly influence political philosophy in the rest of the world. His primary work, *A Theory of Justice* (*TJ*), has been translated into twenty-seven languages.[2] Only ten years after *Theory* was published, a bibliography of articles on Rawls listed more than 2,500 entries.[3] This extensive commentary indicates the widespread influence of Rawls's ideas as well as the intellectual controversy his ideas stimulate.

From the outset Rawls's work has been guided by the question, "What is the most appropriate moral conception of justice for a democratic society?" (*TJ*, p. viii/xiii rev.).[4] In *Theory* he pursued this question as part of a more general inquiry into the nature of social justice and its compatibility with human nature and a person's good. Here Rawls aimed to redress the predominance of utilitarianism in modern moral philosophy. As an alternative to utilitarianism, Rawls, drawing on the social contract tradition, developed a conception of justice "that is highly Kantian in nature" (*TJ*, p. viii/xviii rev.). According to this conception, justice generally requires that basic social goods – liberty and opportunity, income and wealth, and the bases of self-respect – be equally distributed, unless an unequal distribution is to everyone's advantage (*TJ*, p. 62/54 rev.). But under favorable social conditions a special conception, "justice as fairness," applies; it requires giving priority to certain liberties and opportunities via the institutions of a liberal constitutional democracy. Rawls's two principles of justice require that certain important liberties be provided equally for all, that these "basic" liberties have priority over aggregate social welfare and perfectionist values, that "fair" (not just "formal") opportunities be provided equally for all citizens, and that differences in income and wealth and in social positions be structured so as to maximally benefit the worst-off members of society.

*Theory* depicts justice as fairness as a universal moral ideal to be aspired to by all societies. Over two decades after *Theory* Rawls published *Political Liberalism* (*PL*). Here, because of the demands of liberalism itself, Rawls revises the argument for justice as fairness to limit its applicability. No longer does Rawls take issue directly with utilitarianism, perfectionism, or other general moral conceptions. Political liberalism instead addresses the culture of a constitutional democracy. Its guiding question is, What is the most just and feasible arrangement of basic social institutions that realizes the core democratic values of freedom and equality for all citizens?

To appreciate the development of Rawls's views it is essential to understand that all along he has sought to work out a realistic ideal of justice (a "realistic utopia"[5]). His conception is *ideal* insofar as it is designed for the ideal conditions of a "well-ordered society," where reasonable persons who are free and equal all accept the same conception of justice. Rawls's account of justice is *realistic* since it is designed to apply neither to moral saints or perfect altruists on the one hand, nor to natural sinners or rational egoists on the other, but to what humans at their best are capable of, given their nature, under normal conditions of social life.[6] To situate Rawls's realistic ideal in terms of the predecessors that most influenced him: Akin to Kant, Rawls seeks to discover the fundamental moral principles that regulate reasoning and judgments about justice. These principles he presumes to be deeply implicit in ordinary moral awareness and are evidenced by our most considered moral judgments. But Rawls rejects Kant's dualisms;[7] he does not suppose principles of justice are a priori or based in "pure practical reason" alone. Human nature and the fixed empirical conditions within which practical reason is normally exercised are relevant to discovering and justifying principles of justice. Rawls here moves some way toward the more "sentimental" and "naturalistic" accounts suggested by Rousseau and Hume. He conditions the justification of principles of justice on certain psychological tendencies of human nature and our capacities for sociability.[8] This explains Rawls's emphasis on the "stability" or feasibility of a moral conception of justice. A conception of justice is stable when its realization would foster in people a steadfast will to do justice and a disposition to uphold just institutions (as that conception defines them). It is because of his concern for the stability of justice as fairness that Rawls is led eventually to make the modifications that lead to political liberalism.

In what follows I discuss some of the main features of justice as fairness, as presented both in *Theory* (Section II) and in *Political Liberalism* (Section III). In Section IV, I briefly discuss Rawls's recent account of international justice in *The Law of Peoples*. I aspire not to a comprehensive overview but to emphasize certain crucial ideas to aid the reader in understanding Rawls and the contributions to this volume.

## II. *A THEORY OF JUSTICE*: JUSTICE AS FAIRNESS

### A. The Principles of Justice

Rawls describes *Theory* as an attempt "to generalize and carry to a higher order of abstraction the traditional theory of the social contract as represented by Locke, Rousseau, and Kant" (*TJ*, p. viii/xviii rev.). This tradition's main idea is that the political constitution and the laws are just when they *could* be agreed to by free rational persons from a position of equal right and equal political jurisdiction. Rawls applies the idea of a hypothetical social agreement to argue for principles of justice. These principles apply in the first instance to decide the justice of the institutions that constitute *the basic structure of society*. Individuals and their actions are just insofar as they conform to the demands of just institutions. The basic structure is the interconnected system of rules and practices that define the political constitution, legal procedures and the system of trials, the institution of property, the laws and conventions which regulate markets and economic production and exchange, and the institution of the family (which is primarily responsible for the reproduction of society and the care and education of its new members). These institutions can be individually organized and jointly combined in several different ways. How they are specified and integrated into a social system deeply affects people's characters, desires and plans, and their future prospects, as well as the kinds of persons they aspire to be. Because of the profound effects of these institutions on the kinds of persons we are, Rawls says the basic structure of society is "the primary subject of justice" (*TJ*, p. 7/6 rev.).

The significance of the basic structure comes out especially in Rawls's treatment of economic rights of property and freedom of contract. Rawls takes a "holistic" approach to these rights and to distributive justice more generally.[9] This means that we cannot decide what economic rights and duties people have without first determining the effects of various systems of economic rights and practices on others – particularly on others' capacities to exercise their basic rights and liberties. Rawls's principle of distributive justice is then closely aligned with his principle of equal basic liberties (as explained at the end of this Section A). We will begin then with the first principle of justice.

Rawls's first principle, the principle of equal basic liberties, parallels J.S. Mill's principle of liberty in that it is conceived as defining constitutional limits on democratic government. Rawls sees certain liberties as "basic." These include liberty of conscience and freedom of thought, freedom of association, and the rights and liberties that define the freedom and integrity of the person (including freedom of movement, occupation, and choice of careers, and a right to personal property); also included for Rawls are equal political rights of participation and the rights and liberties that maintain the rule of law.[10] To call these liberties "basic" means (in part) that they are more important than others. Most people would readily admit that it is far more important that people be free to speak their minds, practice their faiths or lack thereof, choose their careers, and marry, befriend, or associate with people they choose than that they be free to harass others, drive recklessly and as fast as they please, or walk the streets naked and relieve themselves in public view. Few would call laws restricting these latter actions restrictions on a person's freedom at all. Most any purported liberal would agree with these restrictions and with the greater significance of Rawls's basic liberties. But what makes Rawls's list of basic liberties more important than other normally permissible liberties many people argue for, such as freedom to enter contracts of all kinds, to own weapons, or to accumulate, use, and dispose of productive resources as one pleases?

Rawls calls the liberties of the first principle "basic" since they are morally more significant to the freedom of democratic citizens than are the "nonbasic" liberties just mentioned. This means, first, that the basic liberties are necessary for pursuing a wide range of conceptions of the good. Second, the basic liberties are essential to the exercise and development of the two *moral powers* that define the conception of the person implicit in Rawls's constructivist view.[11] The two moral powers are the capacity for a sense of justice (to understand, apply, and act on and for the sake of principles of justice) and the capacity for a conception of the good (to form, revise, and rationally pursue a rational plan of life). In *Theory* Rawls sees the moral powers in Kantian terms; as the powers of practical reasoning in matters of justice, they are the essential capacities for moral and rational agency. By virtue of these capacities we see ourselves and each other as free and responsible agents. As such the moral powers are the grounds for *full autonomy*. Subsequently, in *Political Liberalism*, the moral powers are characterized in less ambitious terms; they are the capacities that anyone needs if he or she is to occupy the role of citizen and engage in, benefit from, and comply with the demands of social cooperation in a democratic society.

Because of their role in defining the conception of moral persons that underlies Rawls's view, justice as fairness assigns the basic liberties strict priority over other social goods. This means basic liberties can be limited only for the sake of maintaining other basic liberties. They cannot be compromised to promote greater aggregate happiness in society, to increase national wealth, or to promote perfectionist values of culture. The basic liberties cannot be limited even for the sake of better realizing the purposes of Rawls's difference principle. That the worst off may be willing to give up some of their basic liberties (such as their right to vote) in exchange for added income supplements is of no political consequence. For the first priority of justice for Rawls is to maintain equal freedom and respect for persons in their capacity as democratic citizens. This indicates the way justice as fairness is grounded in an ideal of persons as free and equal citizens who exercise their capacities for justice and rationality (the two moral powers) as they jointly govern public matters and freely pursue their conceptions of a good life.[12] The political liberties, besides being necessary to a person's sense of self-respect, are also essential to the full development of the capacity for a sense of justice that partly defines this ideal of citizens. It is because the basic liberties are essential to the exercise of the moral powers that they are *inalienable*: there is no right to give up or trade away the liberties needed to define a citizen's status as a free and equal person. This is one of several ways justice as fairness differs from libertarianism. The unrestricted freedoms of contract and transfer that are defining features of libertarianism are not basic or even protected liberties according to Rawls's liberal view.

Now let us turn to Rawls's second principle and particularly the question of distributive justice. For Rawls economic rights of property and contract are institutional but not conventional. To say property is an *institution* means in part that it consists in a system of social (mainly legal) rules and practices that specify exclusive rights and duties with regard to the use and control of things. To say property is *conventional* means that the institutional rights of property people have are specified exclusively by existing legal rules and institutions and that these rules are valid only so long as they are effective and enforced. In the conventional view then, people have no claim to property independent of existing legal rules and institutional arrangements. Justice in distribution is simply enforcing current property conventions, thereby giving each person his or her due. Hobbes and Hume held such a view. Rawls does not.

Natural rights theory was designed to combat the conventional view. The idea of a state of nature emphasizes that certain rights are not conventional but are moral and apply to persons whatever their social circumstances. So Locke contends that governments have no authority to prohibit freedom of religious association, for this is an inalienable right people have independent of political society. Similarly, if the Crown confiscates people's property, an injustice has been done since they have arbitrarily been denied their livelihood and means of independence. Now Rawls says that because of the first principle, "justice as fairness has the characteristic marks of a natural rights theory" (*TJ*, p. 506n/443n). But he denies the account of "natural" or presocial property argued for by libertarians and Lockeans.

The idea of natural, presocial property effectively deals with the problem of oppressive confiscations by governments. But the idea of natural property is inadequate when used to address questions of the kinds of property rights and distributions that ought to exist in modern industrialized and democratic societies. In the isolated state of nature, where natural property claims hypothetically originate, people need not be so concerned with the effects on others of possessing and exercising their rights, for few are around to be adversely affected. When this conception of presocial property is applied to social conditions, it implies that people may accumulate, use, transfer, and exchange their possessions as if they were in an isolated state of nature, and no matter what the effects or how badly off others might be made as a result of a system of institutionalized natural property.[13] Surely there must be some other way to argue that people can be morally entitled to their possessions without relying on a presocial state of nature.

Rawls, like natural property advocates, distinguishes between conventional property and the property rights people ought to have. But Rawls does not derive the property rights people ought to have from a preinstitutional state of nature. He refers instead to an ideal of social cooperation where institutions are designed to benefit everyone on a basis of *reciprocity*. They benefit everyone, not in the weak sense that all are made better off than in an apolitical state of nature, but in the strong sense that all are made better off than they would be in a state of equality and where no one benefits at the expense of the poorest. The role of Rawls's difference principle is to define this ideal of reciprocity.[14] The institution of property is justly ordered when it is part of a social and economic system that specifies property relations so as to make the worst-off class better off than they could be under the institutions of any feasible alternative economic system (subject to the conditions that equal basic liberties and fair equality of opportunities are always maintained). It is the responsibility of political institutions to structure economic and property relations so that, over a lifetime, the economic prospects of the worst-off class (which might be defined as the average wage of unskilled workers, or in some other way) are as favorable as they can be.[15]

Here it should be emphasized that "worst off" is defined in terms of certain resources that Rawls calls "primary social goods" with special focus on income and wealth. From the standpoint of justice the worst off are the poorest among us. They are not necessarily the unhappiest (as in welfarist views) or the most disabled physically or mentally (as in Sen's capability approach).[16] Rawls's reasons for eschewing happiness or welfare as a basis for interpersonal comparisons is connected with his (Kantian) emphasis on freedom and responsibility. Agency requires that people see themselves as acting freely and as responsible for their ends. Because of our capacities to reflect critically on our desires and rationally structure our ends into a coherent plan of life, we normally do not see ourselves as saddled with desires and ends we can do nothing about. To encourage this self-conception and the development and exercise of these capacities for rational (and moral) agency, Rawls contends that a conception of justice should not simply take as given whatever desires people happen to have and distribute welfare as if people's ends were imposed on them. Instead, people should be held responsible for their ends and expected to adjust their desires to the fair share of resources they can legitimately expect. What individuals may fairly and legitimately expect is specified by the difference principle, which is itself geared towards providing resources adequate for realizing everyone's capacities for free and responsible agency.

It is because of his (Kantian) conception of agency that Rawls treats severe mental and physical handicaps as a special case. He abstracts from such handicaps in the initial argument for principles of justice, leaving special principles to be worked out for them to the legislative stage of his "four-stage sequence" (*Restatement*, pp. 171–76). This does not mean that such problems are unimportant or that the disabled are not due special consideration because of their handicaps. But it does imply that for Rawls justice is not primarily about redressing inequalities imposed by nature or misfortune. Rather justice is primarily about providing each person with resources that are sufficient to their realizing their "moral powers" of free, responsible, and rational agency. As a result, Rawls (unlike Sen) does not give the naturally handicapped absolute priority in decisions of justice.[17] He treats their situation similar to problems of partial compliance. Principles of justice are initially chosen for the ideal case of a well-ordered society, where it is assumed all have the capacities for cooperation and that there will be "strict compliance." Just as the parties in the original position assume that the members of a well-ordered society have an effective sense of justice and normally will not violate just laws, they assume that members are normal cooperating members of society over a complete life who have the capacities needed for social cooperation (the moral powers). These are idealizations (like the assumption of perfect competition in price theory). Rawls says these idealizations present a more tractable problem of choice and provide a basis for dealing with less than ideal circumstances, such as partial compliance or the special problems of the disabled.[18] But what primarily underlies these assumptions is a view about the bases of social justice. It is an ideal of a society of free and equal citizens who take responsibility for their ends and cooperate with one another on a basis of reciprocity and mutual respect. It is this ideal, not the ideal of redressing undeserved inequalities of welfare, resources, or luck, that is at the foundation of Rawls's view.

This raises again the question of the relationship between the difference principle and the equal basic liberties. Rawls believes the two principles of justice cannot be appreciated or justified in isolation from one another. To be a liberal conception it is not enough to recognize basic liberties and assign them priority. A liberal conception of justice also recognizes a *social minimum*, a basic social entitlement to enabling resources, particularly income and wealth. For without a social minimum, the basic liberties are merely formal protections and are worth little to people who are impoverished and without the means to take advantage of their liberties. So, Rawls contends, any liberal view provides some kind of social minimum to guarantee the worth of the basic liberties (*PL*, p. 6, 156f.). What distinguishes justice as fairness is its egalitarianism: it defines the social minimum in terms of the difference principle.[19] Now the difference principle has a distinct relationship to the principle of equal basic liberties. It permits inequalities in income and wealth in order to maximally promote the effective exercise of the equal basic liberties by the worst off:

Taking the two principles together, the basic structure is to be arranged to maximize the worth to the least advantaged of the complete scheme of equal liberty shared by all. This defines *the end of social justice*. (*TJ*, p. 205/179 rev., emphases added)

The "end of social justice" is not simply that everyone's equal freedoms be formally protected but that the basic liberties be effectively exercisable by all to the degree that the worth of freedom to the worst off is maximal. Its guarantee of the maximal worth of equal liberties provides one of the more compelling reasons for Rawls's difference principle.[20] In every other economic system, the value of liberty to the least advantaged is less than in justice as fairness. For Rawls this means that the effective freedom of the least fortunate is being compromised for the sake of those better off. Only the difference principle achieves reciprocity in the sense that gains to those better off are not achieved at the expense of the poorest members of society (*Restatement*, pp. 123–24).

## B. The Argument from the Original Position

Appeal to a hypothetical agreement – of what people could or would agree to under certain conditions – is characteristic of social contract doctrine. None of the major historical proponents of contractarianism (Hobbes, Locke, Rousseau, and Kant) saw the existing status quo as the appropriate perspective from which to achieve agreement on laws and social institutions. For even supposing agreement were achievable under current conditions, it would presuppose the validity of existing distributions of rights, bargaining advantages, and the very laws and institutions whose justice is to be decided by the social contract. In order to abstract from the influence of existing conditions, Hobbes and Locke assume that general agreement takes place in the prepolitical (and for Hobbes, presocial) circumstances of a hypothetical state of nature. Now a state of nature is *historical* in the following sense: Its inhabitants have knowledge of their circumstances and interests; they know everything about themselves that any historically situated individual might know about prevailing circumstances. So like any other contract, a social contract in a state of nature would be affected by its parties' access to information about themselves and others' situations.

One respect in which awareness of one's historical situation affects the resulting distribution of political power is evident from Locke's justification of passive citizenship. For Locke a political constitution is just only if free persons could agree to it via a series of agreements starting from a state of nature wherein each person has equal political jurisdiction. But while Locke's contracting parties begin with equal political rights, their knowledge of their circumstances in the state of nature leads to the peculiar consequence that the majority of free persons could agree to alienate their equal political status in exchange for other benefits. For Locke political rights are alienable in a way that freedom of conscience and the "right of private judgment" are not. So Locke does not envision that women, or even the majority of men (those who do not satisfy property qualifications) retain their political rights under the constitution.

This is a peculiar result for a view that assumes equal political rights are a defining feature of our natural condition. If not in Locke's day, it conflicts now with our considered convictions of justice.[21] For why should gender or property ownership affect one's having the right to vote or hold office, or one's status as an equal citizen? It is only because the occupants of Locke's state of nature know their particular characteristics and social circumstances that the class of affluent men are in a position to take advantage of their privileged position and persuade others to give up the equal political status all originally have in exchange for enjoying the benefits of political society. But a person's gender or wealth, even if relevant to certain kinds of contracts, is not morally relevant to agreement on principles of justice for the basic structure of society. So Rawls imposes a *veil of ignorance* on the parties, depriving them of knowledge of this information, as well as any other information that might advantage or disadvantage the parties in their discussions and agreement. Decision on principles of justice is then rendered ahistorical to make the decision strictly impartial with respect to peoples' social status, natural characteristics and abilities, and even their conceptions of the good.

The veil of ignorance rules out information that, Rawls contends, is morally irrelevant to decision on principles of justice.[22] Philosophers of course disagree about the moral relevance of information to deciding principles of justice. Libertarians will say that knowledge of one's property rights and bargaining position is relevant to any contract so long as one is entitled to them according to libertarian principles. They would then reject the idea of an ahistorical hypothetical agreement on principles of justice.[23] So do utilitarians and contemporary Hobbesians, but for different reasons.

According to many utilitarians, the appropriate solution to problems of partiality and people's taking advantage of their position in making moral decisions is to impose a "thin" veil of ignorance: allow the parties to an original position full historical information, including knowledge of everyone's desires and interests, and simply deprive them of knowledge of their identity in society. People are then not in a position to take advantage of knowledge of their particular situations and conceptions of the good.[24] Under this more modest impartiality condition, parties still have knowledge of existing desires and interests. Surely, utilitarians argue, this information is relevant, for what could the end of justice be if not promoting existing human interests?

One problem with this proposal is that it still does not entirely remedy the problem of partiality towards dominant interests. Though parties may not know their situation in society, a thinly veiled initial position still leads them to play the odds in hopes that they are among those who endorse the dominant majority position and values. Moreover, the initial condition of knowing particular social facts while ignorant of one's social position still does not address the crucial question of the justice of existing background conditions that led to the status quo. People's desires are consequently taken as given no matter what the conditions of their origin or how unreasonable they are; these desires are then allowed to influence and even determine final agreement on principles of justice. For example, to impose only a thin veil of ignorance on a racially segregated society or (to emphasize the point) on a slave society still leaves people open to assume that there is nothing unjust about racism and apartheid, or even about owning slaves, so long as it is rational to take a chance on entering society as a free member of the dominant class. But why should we take such clearly unjust circumstances and the unreasonable desires they generate as a relevant touchstone for deciding the justice of social institutions and the reasonableness of expectations? To remedy this problem, it will not suffice to rule out such "antisocial" desires as the desire to own slaves or the desire to live apart from racial minorities.[25] This proposed solution, even if it works in this instance, only addresses the more extreme examples of a general problem. Should we impose only a thin veil over the inhabitants of a traditional hierarchical society, where the overwhelming majority are satisfied with the status quo and would gladly deny themselves and others freedom of religion and speech or the right to vote? Some communitarians and utilitarians may think so, for on the basis of their views information about existing conditions and conceptions of the good is relevant to deciding basic principles of justice.

In ruling out knowledge of all historical information, Rawls's "thick" veil of ignorance ensures that principles of justice are not contoured to the conditions of any particular social situation or designed to promote or especially favor any particular conception of the good. This does not mean the original position is "neutral" among conceptions of the good, for it is not. The principles chosen in the original position clearly render certain conceptions impermissible (e.g., racist and other intolerant doctrines) and others difficult to achieve under conditions of a well-ordered society (e.g., traditionalist religions requiring conditions of minimal education and widespread social conformity for their success). But it is not as if neutrality among conceptions of the good were a desirable goal to begin with – what's the point, after all, of being neutral towards racist or other intolerant doctrines which deny the values of fairness or equal freedom? Instead of aiming to be neutral among desires or fair to conceptions of the good, Rawls's original position seeks fairness to *persons*, conceived as equals with the capacities to critically reflect on, adopt, and pursue their conceptions of the good.[26] In this regard the original position assigns importance, not to existing ends but to people's freedom and moral powers to shape and amend their ends. Consequently, the original position's conditions encourage a diversity of conceptions of the good. In this regard, the original position necessarily results in distinctly liberal principles that guarantee equality of basic liberties.

There are many objections to Rawls's original position and to his argument from this perspective for the principles of justice. Here I can only consider one of the more prominent objections. This should provide a better idea how Rawls sees the original position's connection with the principles of justice and differentiate his account from ostensibly similar views.

Consider first Rawls's account of the rationality of the parties in the original position (*TJ*, Sec. 25). They are rational in the thin sense used in the social sciences insofar as they choose principles solely to promote their interests. The parties are assigned no moral motivations, and with respect to one another's welfare and position they are indifferent under the special circumstances of the original position. Now it would be a mistake to say, as many do, that Rawls's parties are purely self-interested, like rational egoists. They are not egoists any more than chess players who play to win or buyers who shop for the lowest price are egoists. Just as chess players and ordinary consumers usually have all sorts of moral convictions and motives as well as benevolent affections for others, so the parties in the original position are assumed to have them too. Indeed, their moral interests and benevolent concerns are among the interests they aim to protect in their choice among principles of justice. Moreover, the parties are assumed to be distinctly nonegoistical since they have a capacity for an effective sense of justice – a desire to act not just according to, but also for the sake of, justice. This moral motivation in the end proves crucial to Rawls's argument for the principles of justice and their stability. But for purposes of this particular decision – namely, deciding on principles of justice for the basic structure of society – the parties do not act from their benevolent affections and moral sentiments. They "take no interest in one another's interest" as contracting agents but are concerned only with promoting their own interests.[27] The idea of the original position is to devise a choice situation where *rational decision is subject to reasonable (moral) constraints* imposed by the conditions on choice in the original position. Rawls believes this way of proceeding promotes greater clarity and that the alternative method of assigning moral motivations to the parties would not result in the definite choice of a conception of justice (*TJ*, pp. 148–9/128–9 rev.; 584/512 rev.).

Describing the parties as strictly rational agents whose choice is subject to moral constraints allows Rawls to invoke the theory of rational choice and decision under conditions of uncertainty. In decision theory it is standard practice under conditions of uncertainty to assign probability estimates to alternatives based on the limited knowledge that one has. According to Bayesian decision theory, where there is no such limited knowledge upon which to base judgments of probability, rational choosers would assign an equal probability to each outcome they confront. Now assume that a rational chooser seeks to maximize individual utility. The economist John Harsanyi has argued that, confronted with a thin veil of ignorance which allows complete knowledge of society and everyone's preferences in it but ignorance of his or her own identity, a rational chooser would assign an equal likelihood to being each person in society. To maximize individual utility, the rational chooser would sympathetically identify with the preferences of each person, and ask, How much utility would I experience if I had the preferences of this individual $i$ under conditions C? Multiplying the utility that the rational chooser would experience under C if he or she were $i_1$, $i_2$, $i_3 \ldots i_n$, by $1/n$ (according to the equiprobability assumption), and adding up the results, the rational chooser achieves a measure of the expected utility if outcome X or Y under C is chosen. That is:

$$U_{\text{rational chooser}} = 1/nUi_1 + 1/nUi_2 + 1/nUi_3 \ldots + 1/nUi_n.$$

In maximizing his or her utility behind a thin veil of ignorance it is as if the rational chooser were applying the principle of average utility.

What now about the maximin rule of choice that Rawls has the parties apply in his original position? Harsanyi contends that the absurdity of maximin is easy to demonstrate. For example, suppose you have the opportunity to choose between two bets, (1) and (2), each of which has two outcomes, A and B. You have no knowledge of the likelihood of outcomes A and B, but you do know the bets' respective payoffs:

|      | A      | B           |
|------|--------|-------------|
| (1)  | $1     | $2          |
| (2)  | $ .10  | $1,000,000  |

It is clear by looking at these examples that a rational person would not hesitate to choose alternative (2). Following the equiprobability rule suggests this too.[28] The maximin strategy, however, since it requires that we focus on the worst-off position, requires choice of (1) (since if circumstances A prevail, you avoid the worst outcome, namely ten cents.) But by choosing (1) you give up the chance of enormous gains for the sake of assuring yourself an additional 90 cents. This seems clearly irrational. So Harsanyi says, "Rawls makes the technical mistake of basing his analysis on a highly irrational decision rule, the maximin principle, which [has] absurd practical implications."[29]

No doubt maximin is an irrational strategy under most circumstances of uncertainty. Rawls admits this.[30] But simply because it is most often irrational does not mean that it is *never* rational to follow maximin. Suppose, in the preceding example, you need $1 immediately to save your child's life? Or suppose a tycoon as rich as Bill Gates derives perverse pleasure from giving people the opportunity to play Russian roulette in hopes of gaining his enormous wealth. You know nothing about the gun(s) he uses. Whether or not you are inclined to play, it would not be rational to base your decision on the assumption of an equal probability of becoming the world's richest person or being shot, or on any assumption about the makeup of the weapon used. The tycoon's gun(s) may have only two chambers and one bullet, or, if you are lucky, six chambers and one bullet. They may also have six chambers and five bullets; or he may play with 10,000 guns and pick at random from 9,999 that are fully loaded and one six-shooter that has five bullets. You have no basis for knowing anything about these facts. Under these dire circumstances, one does not have to be risk averse to make no probability assumptions whatsoever and prudently refuse the tycoon's wager.

Now consider a decision problem more like the one envisioned by Rawls (though still involving factual information his original position does not allow). Consider the following game of chance. You are confronted with the following choices and schedule of payoffs:

|  |  | States of World | | Sum expected utility assuming equal probability |
|---|---|---|---|---|
|  |  | A | B |  |
|  | (1) | −100 | 500 | = 200 |
| Choices |  |  |  |  |
|  | (2) | 100 | 200 | = 150, |

where (1) and (2) are two potential choices, and A and B represent two states of the world that may occur. The numbers represent potential payoffs, what you receive if you choose alternative (1) or (2) and state of the world A or B transpires. These payoffs may be winnings (in dollars) from bets, or the average utilities experienced (over a lifetime) by individuals in different social classes A and B in societies (1) and (2), respectively.

Now assume that you have no knowledge whatsoever about the likelihood of either alternative, A or B. Bayesians say that, ignorant of probabilities of A or B we are to apply the principle of insufficient reason: We are to calculate the expected utilities of choices (1) and (2) as if the probability of A and B were each .5 and then pick the course of action whose expected utility is maximal. Therefore, we should choose (1) over (2) (since the expected utility of (1) $[-100(.5) + 500(.5) = 200]$ exceeds the expected utility of (2) $[100(.5) + 200(.5) = 150]$.

But now assume that, unbeknownst to you the chooser, 90% of choosers end up in Class A, and 10% in Class B. Given accurate information we can say then that the real likelihood of A is .9 and of B is .1. Then the expected utility of choosing (1) is −40 [−100(.9) + 500(.1) = −40], while the expected utility of choosing (2) is 110 [100(.9) + 200(.1) = 110]. That is,

| | States of World | | | Sum expected utility |
| | A | B | | given accurate information |
|---|---|---|---|---|
| (1) | −100 | 500 | = | −40 |
| (2) | 100 | 200 | = | 110 |

Depending on what is at stake, forming expectations according to the principle of insufficient reason can result in a minor setback or complete ruin. If all that is involved in choosing between (1) and (2) is a choice between bets on horses or voting on some minor piece of legislation, insufficient reason might be the rational strategy if you are ignorant of relevant information, for you will have the opportunity to play again and recoup your losses. If, however, a person's life is at stake, or all future prospects, then it seems a different matter entirely. Suppose you are choosing which society to enter: (1) is libertarian laissez-faire capitalism, while (2) is Social Democracy that provides a social minimum. There are two classes in each society, A and B, which represent the unfortunates (A) and the well off (B) in each society. Given that the risk of being an unfortunate is .9, it would be most unfortunate indeed to assume otherwise, choose according to the principle of insufficient reason, and end up in A, the worst-off class in a libertarian society.

Strict Bayesians contend that the principle of insufficient reason is the rational strategy to adopt under complete uncertainty no matter what is at stake. But in what sense can it be rational to risk one's future, or life itself, on a strategy (namely insufficient reason) unsupported by evidence and which one otherwise has no reason to adopt? The principle of insufficient reason says that if there is no reason for assigning one set of probabilities rather than another, then we ought to assign equal probability to each outcome.[31] But if there is insufficient reason for one set of probabilities rather than another, it should follow that there is no reason to assign equal probability either. If every probability assignment is groundless, then perhaps the rational thing to do is to assign no probability at all,[32] at least under life and death circumstances or when one's life prospects are at stake and there is an acceptable alternative.

This roughly represents the reasoning behind Rawls's argument against adopting the principle of insufficient reason in the original position.[33] But by itself the rejection of the equiprobability assumption under conditions of complete uncertainty does not necessarily speak in favor of adopting the maximin strategy. Two other conditions need to hold to make maximin rational. These conditions are, first, that the choice singled out by following a maximin strategy is an acceptable alternative we can live with. There is little point in following maximin if it results in an unacceptable worst outcome that is only marginally better than some other possible worst outcome. When this condition is satisfied, then every position is acceptable no matter what the outcome. Second, all the other alternatives have (worst) outcomes that we could not live with and accept (so if some other alternative has a worst outcome you could live with and accept, then maximin may not be an appropriate strategy).[34]

Rawls contends these three conditions for following the maximin strategy are satisfied in the original position when choice is made between the principles of justice and different versions of the principle of utility. Because all one's future prospects are at stake in the original position, and there is no hope of renegotiating the outcome, a rational person would agree to the principles of justice instead of the principle of utility (average or aggregate). For the principles of justice imply that no matter what position you occupy in society, you will have the rights and resources needed to enable you to exercise your rational capacities to pursue a wide range of conceptions of the good. With the principle of utility there is no such guarantee. Of course, by choosing the principles of justice, there is no guarantee that everyone will be in a position to pursue his or her current conception of the good either. A rich plutocrat, for example, may no longer enjoy his privileged position. But neither the principle of utility nor any other traditional moral conception would guarantee the rights and resources the plutocrat currently enjoys. Almost all moral theories agree that justice is not simply a Pareto improvement on existing conditions, for the status quo itself may be unjust. At least with justice as fairness all persons have the necessary freedoms, opportunities, and resources to freely pursue a wide range of conceptions of the good. This is not guaranteed under the principle of utility.

Controversies surrounding the rationality of maximin choice in the original position have obscured three other arguments Rawls relies on to support justice as fairness (all in Section 29 of *Theory*). Each of these depends on the concept of a "well-ordered society." Since two of them also rely on the idea of the stability of a well-ordered society, they will be discussed in the next section. The first of Rawls's three arguments proceeds from the idea that choice in the original position is an agreement and as such involves certain "strains of commitment."[35] As background to this argument, consider the frequent objection that there is no genuine agreement among persons in the original position because of the veil of ignorance. The parties in effect are described in the same way since they know nothing distinctive about themselves, and so there is no basis for bargaining to begin with. But if not, there is no point in describing their decision as a contract or agreement. The original position really involves the rational choice of one person.[36]

The objection assumes that all contracts are like economic contracts in that they must involve bargaining based on conflicting interests. But none of the major historical contractarians – Locke, Rousseau, Kant, or even Hobbes – conceived of their social contracts on the order of an economic bargain.[37] Underlying their appeals (and Rawls's) to a social contract is the idea that every member of society should be able to accept the same terms of cooperation because they achieve certain interests everyone has. The *mutual acknowledgment* of principles involved here warrants the term "agreement," and the *mutual precommitment* involved might just as well be called a "contract." For each agrees only on condition others do too, and all tie themselves into social and political relations permanently to achieve certain common purposes as well as their individual interests.[38] Marriage contracts are just one example of a mutual precommitment that is not a bargain or based in a conflict of interests but which assumes common purposes.

To understand the original position in this way indicates why it may be said to involve a contract or agreement. By mutual accord and on condition that others do too, all the parties commit themselves in advance to certain principles in perpetuity. Their precommitment is reflected in the fact that once these principles become embodied in institutions, no means would allow one or more persons to depart from the terms of their commitment. The result is that the parties have to take seriously the legal obligations and social pressures they will incur by their agreement, for there is no going back to the initial situation. So if they do not sincerely believe that they can accept the requirements of a conception of justice and conform their actions and life plans to it, then these are strong reasons to avoid choosing those principles. It would not be rational for a party to take risks, falsely assuming that if it turns out badly, he or she can violate the terms of agreement and later recoup the situation.

Rawls gives special poignancy to this precommitment require-ment by making it a condition that the parties cannot choose and agree to principles in bad faith; they have to be able, not just to live with, but also to endorse the principles of justice once in society. Essential to Rawls's argument is the assumption of *willing compli-ance* with requirements of justice. This is what he means by "the strains of commitment." The parties are choosing principles for a well-ordered society (discussed in the next section), where everyone is assumed to have a sense of justice: they accept the principles of justice and want to act as these principles demand. Given this re-striction, the parties can only choose principles they believe they will be able to accept and comply with come what may. A party, then, cannot take risks with principles he or she knows it will be difficult to comply with. That would be making an agreement in bad faith, and this is ruled out by the conditions of the original position.

Rawls contends that these "strains of commitment" created by the agreement strongly favor the principles of justice over the princi-ples of utility and other consequentialist views. For it is much more difficult for those who end up worse off in a utilitarian society to willingly accept their situation. Given what we know about human nature, the person is rare who can freely and without resentment sacrifice his or her life prospects so that those who are better off can have even greater comforts, honors, and enjoyments. This is too much to demand of our capacities for human benevolence. Besides, why should we want to encourage such subservient dispositions and the accompanying lack of self-respect? The principles of justice, by contrast, conform better with our desire for self-respect and natural moral capabilities to reciprocally recognize and respect others' le-gitimate interests while freely promoting our own good. The strains of commitment incurred by agreement in the original position pro-vide strong reasons for the parties to choose the principles of justice and reject the risks involved in choosing the principles of average or aggregate utility.

## C. The Good of Justice and the Stability of a Well-Ordered Society

Rawls's strains of commitment argument indicates a rarely noted feature of his account: it involves in effect two social contracts. First, hypothetical agents situated equally in the original position unanimously agree to principles of justice. This agreement has attracted the most attention from Rawls's critics, especially the argument from the maximin criterion. But hypothetical agreement in the original position itself is patterned on the general acceptability and feasibility of a conception of justice among the members of society.[39] There must be a genuine possibility that real persons, given human nature, can agree and act on principles of justice. Rawls's argument for *stability* has attracted little commentary. But it is crucial to understanding Rawls's argument for justice as fairness.

Rawls expresses this second contractarian requirement via the condition that principles of justice are to be agreed to in the original position only if they can be generally acknowledged within and remain stable under conditions of a "well-ordered society." This is a central idea in Rawls's theory.[40] It provides a way for testing whether moral conceptions of justice are consistent with psychological and social theory. In a *well-ordered society*, (1) everyone accepts the same public conception of justice, and their general acceptance is public knowledge; (2) society consistently realizes the generally accepted conception in its institutions; and (3) everyone has an effective sense of justice, which leads them to want to do what justice requires of them. A well-ordered society is an ideal social world.[41] For it is desirable that people know and freely accept the principles of justice regulating their basic social institutions.

The stability requirement says that the parties in the original position are to choose principles that will be feasible and enduring within a well-ordered society. It bears emphasizing that Rawls is not concerned with Hobbesian stability or peace and tranquillity for their own sake. The stability of a grossly unjust society is worth little or nothing by itself, particularly if its destabilization will result in a more just situation without great loss of life. Rawls's concern is with the stability of a presumptively *just* (or "well-ordered") society, which depends on its members having certain moral motives. A conception of justice is *stable* when "those taking part in [just] arrangements acquire the corresponding sense of justice and desire to do their part in maintaining them" (*TJ*, p. 454/398 rev.). One conception of justice is relatively more stable than another when people are more willing to observe its requirements under conditions of a well-ordered society. The stability question raised in *Theory* is, Which conception of justice is more likely to engage our moral sensibilities and our sense of justice? This requires an inquiry into moral psychology and the human good.

Rawls initially appeals to stability in the two remaining arguments (in *TJ*, Sec. 29) from the original position to argue against utilitarianism and perfectionism. Briefly, Rawls first contends that these and other "teleological" conceptions are not likely to be practically feasible when made *public* under the conditions of a well-ordered society.[42] A feature of a well-ordered society is that its regulative principles of justice are publicly known and regularly are appealed to as a basis for deciding and justifying laws and basic institutions. Rawls contends that under this *publicity condition* justice as fairness remains more stable than utilitarianism.[43] For public knowledge that reasons of maximum average (or aggregate) utility determine the distribution of benefits and burdens understandably would lead those worse off to resent their situation. After all, their well-being and interests are being sacrificed for the greater good of those more fortunate, and it is too much to expect of human nature that people should freely acquiesce in and embrace such terms of cooperation.[44] The principles of justice, by contrast, are designed to advance reciprocally everyone's position in society, and those who are better off do not achieve their gains at the expense of the less advantaged. "Since everyone's good is affirmed, all acquire inclinations to uphold the scheme" (*TJ*, p. 177/155 rev.).

The publicity condition is also crucial to Rawls's second stability argument for the principles of justice (*TJ*, pp. 178–82/155–9 rev.). These principles, when publicly known, give greater support to citizens' sense of self-respect than do utilitarian and perfectionist views. Of self-respect Rawls says it is "perhaps the most important primary good" (*TJ*, p. 440/386 rev.), since few things seem worth doing if people have little sense of their own value or no confidence in their abilities. The parties in the original position will then aim to choose principles that best secure their sense of self-respect. Now justice as fairness, by protecting the priority of equal basic liberties, secures the status of each as equal citizens; there are no "passive citizens" who must depend on others to protect their interests politically. Moreover, the second principle secures fair opportunities and adequate resources for all to make everyone's equal basic liberties worthwhile. The aim is to make all citizens socially and economically independent so that no one need be subservient to the will of another. Citizens then can respect one another as equals and not as masters or subordinates. Equal basic liberties and political and economic independence are primary among the bases of self-respect in a democratic society. For in the absence of a generally accepted religion or other shared system of beliefs, people confront one another mainly as citizens. The parties in the original position should then choose the principles of justice over utilitarianism and other teleological views both to guarantee their equal status as citizens and secure their sense of self-respect, and to procure the same for others, thereby guaranteeing greater overall stability.[45]

Rawls relies substantially on the publicity condition to argue against utilitarianism and perfectionism. He says the publicity condition "arises naturally from a contractarian standpoint" (*TJ*, p. 133/115 rev.). His point ultimately is that giving people knowledge of the moral bases of coercive laws is a condition of fully acknowledging and respecting them as responsible agents. People then have knowledge of the reasons for their social and political relations and the formative influences of the basic structure of society on their characters, plans, and prospects.[46] Moreover, when made public, principles of justice can serve agents as bases for their practical reasoning and for political argument and justification. These considerations underlie Rawls's contention that having knowledge of the principles that determine the bases of social relations is a precondition of individuals' freedom.[47]

Now we turn to Part III of *Theory* to examine in more detail Rawls's argument for stability and the good of justice. The stability problem for Rawls requires showing how a conception of justice is realistically possible given human nature and certain fixed conditions of social life. To do so, Rawls assumes the ideal case of a well-ordered society. If a conception of justice is not workable there, then it is not feasible under less than ideal conditions. In this regard a conception is utopian and thus it is not rational to seek to achieve it.

There are two parts to the stability argument in Part III. In the first Rawls undertakes to show how citizens in a well-ordered society of justice as fairness can come to acquire a *sense of justice*, a disposition to act not simply according to, but also for the sake of justice, as defined by the principles of justice and the legal and social norms that satisfy them. The relevant question here is whether justice as fairness is compatible with human nature. The moral psychology of *Theory*, Chapter VIII, assumes that moral motives are real and are not grounded ultimately in self-interests. Rawls contends that by virtue of our nature we are inclined to appreciate and develop sincere attachments towards persons and institutions that affirm our good. He offers three "reciprocity principles" that develop this basic idea. The third says that it is a psychological law that, once attitudes of love and trust, and of friendly feeling and mutual confidence, have been generated in the course of moral development, "then the recognition that we and those whom we care for are the beneficiaries of an established and enduring just institution tends to engender in us the corresponding sense of justice" (*TJ*, pp. 473–4/415 rev.). If so, then it should be a normal part of citizens' development in a well-ordered society of justice as fairness that they will acquire a desire to support and maintain its laws and institutions. For justice as fairness itself is built upon an ideal of reciprocity: basic institutions are to be designed to promote reciprocally everyone's good as measured from a baseline of equality.

The second stage of Rawls's stability argument in *Theory* builds on the first, for it assumes that citizens already have an effective sense of justice and want to do what is right and just for its own sake. The question now is, Is exercise and development of the sense of justice compatible with the human good, or is having this disposition contrary to our interests and something which undermines our good? The primary purpose of Chapter IX of *Theory* is to show how exercise of a sense of justice is not only compatible with, but can also promote, and realize the human good.

For Rawls the concept of the 'good' is formally characterized in terms of certain rational principles of choice and rationally formed desires. A person's good is what is rational for that person to want, assuming that he or she has full and accurate information and has critically reflected on his or her ends, made them consistent, and decided on effective means for realizing them. Rawls defines the good in terms of the plan of life that a person would choose under such ideal conditions of deliberative rationality (*TJ*, Sec. 64). The idea here is that everyone has primary ends and commitments which (if they are not already apparent) are discoverable upon careful thought under conditions conducive to reflective deliberation. These aims and commitments can be arranged in terms of importance and consistently scheduled according to rational principles of choice (enumerated in *TJ*, Sec. 63) to yield a plan of life suitable for each person. There may be several desirable plans each of us can imagine. The plan of life that a person would choose under ideal deliberative conditions of full information, imaginative appreciation of the options, and so on, is most rational for that person and specifies his or her objective good (*TJ*, Sec. 64).

To provide content to this formal account of a person's good, Rawls appeals to another psychological law, the *Aristotelian principle* (*TJ*, Sec. 65). "Other things equal, human beings enjoy the exercise of their realized capacities (their innate or trained abilities), and this enjoyment increases the more the capacity is realized, or the greater its complexity" (*TJ*, p. 426/374 rev.). This principle implies that we are not just moved by the desire for pleasurable sensations and the pressures to satisfy bodily needs and achieve its comforts. Instead, we desire to engage in more complex and demanding activities so long as they are within our reach. If so, then it will generally be rational for people (when given the opportunity) to realize and train their mature capacities and incorporate certain "higher activities" (J.S. Mill's terms) into their plans of life (*TJ*, p. 428/376 rev.). Otherwise, life becomes monotonous and boring.

The question raised by the *congruence* argument (*Theory*, Chap. IX) for stability is as follows: Is it rational in a well-ordered society to exercise and develop the sense of justice, as defined by justice as fairness, and incorporate this virtue into one's conception of the good? That is, from the point of view of deliberative rationality, is it rational to choose a plan of life in which one is steadfastly predisposed to take up the impartial standpoint of justice and act on the principles that would be chosen from this (original) position? If so, then choice from these two ideal perspectives coincide, and the right and the good are congruent.

Rawls advances two main arguments to show that justice as fairness is congruent with the human good. The first invokes the good

of participation in community and develops the idea of a just society as a "social union of social unions" (*TJ*, Sec. 79).[48] This argument and the second congruence argument (*TJ*, Sec. 86) both invoke the Aristotelian principle and also (particularly in the second)
the *Kantian Interpretation of Justice as Fairness* (*TJ*, Sec. 40). In the
Kantian interpretation Rawls seeks to give specific content to Kant's
notion of autonomy, understood as reason giving a law to itself. "The
original position may be viewed...as a procedural interpretation of
Kant's conception of autonomy and the categorical imperative" (*TJ*,
p. 256/cf. 226 rev.). Rawls's thought here roughly is this: We are capable of autonomy by virtue of "our nature as free and equal rational
beings" (*TJ*, p. 252/222 rev.). Our nature as free rational moral agents
consists in the two moral powers mentioned earlier, the capacity for
a sense of justice and the capacity for a conception of the good. These
are, in effect, the capacities for practical reasoning as applied to justice. They are essential to our being free self-governing agents who
have a conception of our good and who can take responsibility for
our actions and ends and participate in social life. Now the Kantian
interpretation says that the conditions of the original position can be
construed as a "procedural interpretation" of the conception of free
and equal rational beings. The original position "models" this conception of the person (in ways Rawls explains in detail in subsequent
works).[49] When the original position is construed as "modeling" the
moral powers, then the principles chosen there can be interpreted
as principles that we give to ourselves out of our nature as free and
equal rational beings. If so, then to act on and from these principles
is to act autonomously in Kant's sense: it is to act for the sake of
principles that express our nature as free and equal rational beings.[50]

Against this background Rawls argues that it is rational (in the
"thin" sense discussed above and in *TJ*, Sec. 64) and thus part of
their good, for the members of a well-ordered society to realize their
nature as free and equal rational beings. To argue for the rationality of
justice Rawls relies on the Aristotelian principle – the psychological
law that, given appropriate conditions, we prefer ways of life that
engage our higher faculties – to contend that the development and
exercise of the moral powers is a good for people generally. Without
going here into the details of this argument for congruence,[51] the
main point is that, if it is indeed rational for people generally to
develop and exercise their sense of justice in a well-ordered society,

then there should be no concerns regarding its stability. For then it is normally in people's interests to do what justice as fairness requires of them. Rawls's congruence argument ambitiously aims to show that justice is rational in the strongest way. It is not simply instrumental (as Hobbes tried to show) to each person's good to do what just laws require; instead, acting on justice is an intrinsic and supremely regulative good, for it enables each to realize his or her nature as a morally and rationally autonomous being.

The Kantian interpretation provides the subsequent basis for Rawls's Kantian constructivism.[52] *Constructivism* in moral philosophy is an account of the validity and objectivity of moral statements and principles. It denies both realism as well as the skeptical thesis that moral statements do not possess a truth value or objective validity. Constructivism says that, while moral statements are not true in the realist's sense that they represent an independent order of (moral) facts existing prior to moral reasoning, they nonetheless possess a kind of validity that is appropriate to the distinct subject matter of moral theory. Moral statements are correct when they accord with reasonable moral principles, and moral principles are reasonable when they are the product of a reasoning procedure that incorporates all the relevant requirements of practical reason. *Kantian constructivism* begins from a conception of the person and of practical reason, the ideal of free and equal moral persons who are both reasonable and rational. It "represents" or "models" this conception in a "procedure of construction," (in Kant, the categorical imperative procedure, and in Rawls, the original position.)[53] The principles chosen by the parties to this procedure are objective so long as all who employ it reach the same or similar conclusions and the procedure incorporates all relevant requirements of practical reason. In this regard, moral principles are said by Rawls to be "constructed" from a conception of the person and of practical reason.

Rawls offers Kantian constructivism as an alternative account of the objective validity of moral claims in contrast to "rational intuitionism." The traditional realist account of moral correctness (endorsed by Plato, the Rationalists, Sidgwick, G.E. Moore, and many others) says that moral principles are objective insofar as they are true, and they are true only insofar as they represent a prior and independent order of (nonnatural) facts accessible to rational intuition. The problem with this account from a Kantian perspective is not simply that it posits a peculiar domain of nonnatural facts and a special faculty of reason with access to them. Rather, intuitionism, if correct, undermines the Kantian idea of moral autonomy – that reason provides most basic moral principles out of its own resources. Kantian constructivism attempts to retain and make sense of Kant's obscure idea of autonomy by depicting moral principles of justice as the product of an objective procedure of deliberation that is designed to capture the main features of practical reasoning. According to constructivism, objectivity of judgment (conceived as judgment according to universal rules) precedes the notion of moral validity or truth. Moral statements are sound or true, not in representing a prior order of moral facts but when they accord with principles that could or would be accepted by fully rational persons in an objective procedure of practical reasoning.[54] For Rawls, the procedure that bestows objective status on judgments of justice is the original position.

## III. POLITICAL LIBERALISM

### A. Problems with Rawls's Argument for Stability

*Political liberalism* is seen by many as the result of Rawls's coming to terms with his critics, especially communitarians.[55] But these criticisms had little to do with Rawls's development of his ideas. Instead, political liberalism results from certain tensions implicit within Rawls's argument for stability in *Theory*, which became only more noticeable in Kantian constructivism (cf. *PL*, p. xvii/xix pb. ed.).

The Kantian conception of the person Rawls invokes in *Theory* embodies a philosophical view of moral agency: We are free responsible agents by virtue of the moral powers for practical reasoning. Upon this basis Rawls develops accounts of autonomy as self-realization (*TJ*, Sec. 40), of the intrinsic good justice possesses by its relation to moral autonomy (*TJ*, Sec. 86), and of the epistemic objectivity of judgments of justice (*TJ*, Sec. 78). Rawls's 1980 Dewey Lectures on Kantian constructivism work out the details of these philosophical theses and mark a further stage in the development of justice as fairness as part of a general moral theory.

But Kantian constructivism proves to be a transitional stage in Rawls's thought. Already in the Dewey Lectures Rawls says a conception of justice must have a "practical role" in a well-ordered society: It should provide a basis for "public justification" among persons who have different and conflicting conceptions of the good. "Because its principles are to serve as a shared point of view among citizens with opposing religious, philosophical and moral convictions, as well as diverse conceptions of the good, this point of view needs to be appropriately impartial among those differences." So, the kinds of reasons that can be invoked to justify and apply the conception of justice must be limited to "part of the truth, and not the whole." "Justice as fairness tries to construct a conception of justice that takes deep and unresolvable differences on matters of fundamental significance as a permanent condition of human life."[56]

But surely (one might argue) there will be deep and unresolvable differences in a well-ordered society of justice as fairness about the nature of morality and moral justification – even about the justification and truth of the shared public conception of justice governing society. So, too, we might expect that there will be fundamental differences regarding the good of autonomy. Imagine a liberal Catholic who accepts the principles and duties of justice as fairness but who sees them as natural laws, part of divine law willed by God to enable rational beings to achieve the *summum bonum*, the contemplation and glorification of God. According to the liberal Thomist, principles of justice are divinely ordained and are knowable, some perhaps as self-evident truths, by the natural light of reason. This denies Kantian constructivism's position that moral principles originate in practical reason. Rejecting the constructivist view of justification and objectivity, the liberal Thomist also rejects the Kantian conception of autonomy that underpins the congruence argument. Recall that the aim of the Kantian congruence argument is to show that justice is a supremely rational good for each in a well-ordered society. The argument depends on showing that the sense of justice is the same as the desire to realize our nature as free and equal rational beings and thereby become morally autonomous. But the liberal Thomist denies this identification of desires. The sense of justice is a desire to conform to God's natural laws, not a desire to express our nature as the author of these laws. Not only is autonomy not an intrinsic good; to think so is a conceit of human reason that comes from rejecting the divine source of morality.

So we have a peculiar situation: There will be reasonable citizens[57] in a well-ordered society of justice as fairness who can endorse the principles of justice and the institutions they authorize, but yet, because of their religious views, cannot accept its public justification. Significantly, this problem is not peculiar to orthodox Catholics and other religious believers. It is typical of anyone who accepts liberal principles of justice on grounds at odds with Kantian constructivism. Nothing about a well-ordered society ensures against there being significant numbers who accept the public principles of justice for utilitarian, perfectionist, or pluralist reasons; others may accept these principles and yet endorse moral relativism or skepticism about moral truth. Given basic liberties of freedom of thought, conscience, and association it is predictable that these and other moral and philosophical doctrines will gain adherents. This means that the public conception of justice Rawls envisions for a well-ordered society incorporates premises that starkly conflict with many citizens' conscientious beliefs. Consequently this conception, far from ensuring a shared basis for justification and stabilizing the social system, is likely to have destabilizing consequences. It can adversely affect the sense of self-respect of those who hold non-Kantian philosophical and ethical views and even undermine their allegiance and support for just institutions.

Do these problems mean that justice as fairness is unworkable? It may be unworkable as initially conceived. But Rawls believes justice as fairness still can serve as a publicly shared conception of justice that provides a common basis for justification if certain features are altered or relinquished. In *Political Liberalism* Rawls surrenders the Kantian congruence argument for stability – the claim that moral autonomy and therewith justice are supremely rational goods in a well-ordered society. Given Rawls's account of goodness in terms of rational desire, this claim appears untrue for many reasonable persons – not just liberal Catholics and members of other faiths, but liberal utilitarians, perfectionists, pluralists, and others too.

Second, Rawls gives up the comprehensive constructivist position that says (a) that there is no moral order apart from the activity of practical reason, and (b) that moral objectivity and the validity of judgments are to be understood only in terms of correct judgment from a suitably constructed social point of view.[58] These philosophical claims, even if true, cannot gain widespread agreement as part of a public conception of justice because they conflict with other not unreasonable views about the nature of morality and moral objectivity and validity.

Third, the Kantian conception of the person (as free, equal, reasonable, and rational) is retained but not without modification. It is no longer presented as part of a "comprehensive doctrine" that grounds morality in the conditions of moral agency and the powers of practical reason. Rather "the idea of the person as having moral personality with the full capacity of moral agency is transformed into that of the citizen" (*PL*, pb. ed., p. xlv). This "political conception of the person" provides the basis for a "freestanding" conception of justice. As discussed in the next section, a political conception is not to be committed to any particular philosophical doctrine but is to have its basis in ideas implicit in democratic thought and culture.

Before proceeding, something should be said about the idea of *reasonableness* that figures prominently in Rawls's later works. While Rawls relied on a distinction between reasonable and rational in *Theory*, the distinction is not made explicit. There the concept of rationality was used to characterize the good and what is to a person's advantage.[59] Reasonableness concerned the concept of the right, particularly the ideas of fairness and willingness to moderate one's demands out of respect for others and their legitimate claims.[60] Beginning with "Kantian constructivism," Rawls explicitly marks a distinction between "the Reasonable" and "the Rational."[61] But he still does not ever try to define the concept of 'reasonableness'. This can be frustrating for the reader, since this concept is so crucial to Rawls's argument and is used by him in several different ways. To some it may seem that the idea is so obscure that it explains little, and its recurrent usage only masks the lack of a proper argument.

On Rawls's behalf, it should be said that there should be no presumption that a list of necessary and sufficient conditions can exhaust the meaning of this rich concept.[62] At best, what 'reasonable' means may be revealed only by its uses, which we might then try to clarify and explicate by other concepts and principles. These explications of 'reasonable' can then be applied to clarify other moral concepts and to develop these and other ideas into a political conception of justice. Rawls contends that proceeding in this way is necessary, since "the content of the reasonable" can only be "specified by the content of a reasonable political conception" of justice

(*PL*, p. 94). If this is correct, then there seems something misguided or at least premature about the most common objections to Rawls's (and Scanlon's) use of 'reasonable', namely, that the concept lacks a precise definition, or that people mean different things by the concept, or that they find different actions or persons reasonable and unreasonable. The very point of developing a conception of justice for Rawls is to discover more precisely our understanding of what is reasonable and unreasonable in matters of justice. This crucial moral concept can be properly understood in no other way. If this is correct, then whatever objections one has to the idea of reasonableness should be directed to the theory that explicates it and to the way the theory elucidates and develops the idea through moral principles. The criticism that our ordinary concept is too vague to be of any consequence in moral philosophy otherwise has no force.

Rawls begins to elucidate the concept of (political) reasonableness by elaborating primary features of the idea of a reasonable person. Reasonable persons in Rawls's account recognize and accept that (because of the "burdens of judgment") other reasonable persons inevitably will affirm comprehensive doctrines different from their own.[63] Moreover, reasonable persons desire to cooperate with other reasonable persons holding different reasonable doctrines according to terms that all of them can reasonably accept.[64] So reasonable persons are not simply tolerant of other (reasonable) doctrines. They also accept a criterion of reciprocity: They want to be able to live with others according to principles other reasonable persons can acknowledge and policies they can endorse; moreover, they want to be able to *justify* laws and political policies to people holding different reasonable doctrines with reasons that reasonable persons recognize and can reasonably accept as well. Being reasonable then requires a willingness to address others in terms of *public reasons* (discussed below in Section C).

## B. A Freestanding Political Conception and Overlapping Consensus

Because of problems with the stability argument in *Theory*, Rawls is led to rethink the justification for justice as fairness. This rethinking leads Rawls in *Political Liberalism* to focus on a more general problem. If agreement on a comprehensive moral or philosophical doctrine is no more likely in a well-ordered society than agreement on religion, then not only is the stability of justice as fairness jeopardized, but so too is the general acceptance and stability of most any liberal conception. This casts doubt on the possibility of a just and stable society in which there is general agreement among reasonable and rational citizens on a liberal conception of justice. But if such a well-ordered society is not realistically possible under real-world conditions, liberalism as an ideal is not realizable, and in this regard it is utopian.[65] Liberalism on the basis of Rawls's account involves an ideal of mutual respect and reciprocity among free and equal citizens and their toleration of one another's diverse reasonable religious, philosophical, and moral views. If free and equal citizens cannot agree on a conception of justice to regulate their relations and serve as a basis for public argument, criticism, and agreement, then inevitably coercive force will have to be applied to reasonable persons for reasons which they cannot reasonably accept. This, in an important regard, would be a denial of their freedom.

The more general aim of *Political Liberalism* is to show how a just and stable society among reasonable and rational persons who conceive of themselves as free and as equals is realistically possible. To do this Rawls introduces and develops three main ideas that revise or go beyond the account found in *Theory*: the idea of a political conception of justice, the idea of an overlapping consensus on this political conception among reasonable comprehensive doctrines, and the idea of public reason (*PL*, p. 44). These three ideas specify sufficient conditions for a well-ordered liberal society that is "stable for the right reasons."

1. A POLITICAL CONCEPTION OF JUSTICE. The first condition for a just and stable democratic society is that it be regulated by a political conception of justice. What primarily distinguishes a political conception of justice is that it is "freestanding" or independent and without grounding in premises peculiar to metaphysical, epistemological, and general moral conceptions. A freestanding conception aims to "bracket" or avoid philosophical questions of the original source of moral principles, how we ultimately come to know them, and even the question of their ultimate truth. In *Political Liberalism* Rawls reconstructs justice as fairness as a political conception so that it may be understood in a metaphysically, epistemologically,

and morally neutral way. The main step Rawls takes is to construe the underlying account of free and equal moral persons as a "political conception of the person." It is now said to be implicit in our aware- ness of ourselves, not as moral agents and in whatever we do, but in the more circumscribed role we occupy as democratic citizens.[66] As democratic citizens – and for some people, perhaps only for these purposes – we see ourselves as free and equal. Outside political life many people may not see themselves this way, but in some other moral capacity (as children of God, for example, or as bundles of per- ceptions). In political constructivism there is no longer the implica- tion that the moral powers constitute our nature as moral beings, or are necessary conditions of moral agency, or that realizing these powers enables us to realize the supreme human good of autonomy. The moral powers rather are presented as empirical conditions for our gaining the benefits of social cooperation. Without them, we could not take advantage of the rights, or comply with the duties, of democratic citizens. For these reasons, it is rational for citizens to want to realize the moral powers whatever their conception of the good; they have a "higher-order interest" in the exercise and develop- ment of their moral powers in addition to their higher-order interest in realizing their conception of the good. This conception of citizens and their interests provides the foundation for political liberalism.

That a political conception of justice can be made "freestanding" of "comprehensive" philosophical, religious, and moral doctrines rests on Rawls's assumption that there are certain deeply entrenched ideas and principles that citizens share in a constitutional democ- racy, whatever their conceptions of the good. Even in *Theory* Rawls assumed that all reasonable and rational persons share certain "considered convictions of justice." But he underestimated the de- gree of diversity in the philosophical and religious foundations rea- sonable persons entertain for their considered moral views. Because of the conditions of a liberal democracy, there is no realistic likeli- hood that the members of even a well-ordered society will ever come to agree on the foundations of justice, a philosophical conception of agency, or on any particular intrinsic good.[67] So if the role of a con- ception of justice is to be practically conceived – as aiming to supply a basis for public argument all can accept, and for publicly criticizing and justifying laws and institutions – then other bases for agreement must be found.

Now in most moral conceptions (utilitarianism for example, or even Kant's view) the capacity of a conception of justice to stand up to public scrutiny under real world conditions, no matter how ideal, might be seen as irrelevant to its justification. Why should the justification of a conception of justice depend on the philosophical beliefs of those to whom this conception is to apply? People's beliefs, some say, are at most relevant to the application of a moral conception, not to its justification.[68] People who disagree about the philosophical bases of justice cannot all be correct. By seeking to accommodate a conception of justice to citizens' conflicting philosophical and religious views, the false as well as the true, it might seem Rawls is pushing the idea of respect for persons too far (further than Kant would). But Rawls is not trying to accommodate false philosophical views; instead he is trying to avoid them. Moreover, for it to be justified a political conception has to serve as a publicly acceptable basis for justification, not in just any democratic society but only under the ideal circumstances of a well-ordered society. Rawls's idea here seems to be that if moral and philosophical disagreement about the foundations of justice are inevitable even under free conditions where all can, in spite of their differences, still agree on principles of justice, then respect for persons as free democratic citizens requires that metaphysical and epistemological questions of the foundations of justice be avoided in public reasoning about justice. They should be avoided to maintain the full freedom of conscience of citizens and to provide citizens with justifying reasons for the use of coercive force that all can reasonably accept.

Liberalism, then, needs an argument for itself and for the public conception of justice that is to regulate liberal society framed in terms of ideas and reasons accessible to people in their capacity as free and equal citizens. This argument must appeal to ideas implicit in the culture of a constitutional democracy and avoid ideas peculiar to any particular comprehensive view. In this respect a political conception of justice differs from the conception of justice argued for in *Theory*, which invoked the Kantian interpretation to account for the good of justice.

2. OVERLAPPING CONSENSUS. The independence of a political conception from comprehensive views is essential to understanding the idea of overlapping consensus. Some have argued that Rawls seeks a

conception of justice whose content is adjusted to accommodate all reasonable comprehensive views – as if a political conception were designed as a compromise, or were tailored with all comprehensive views in mind and based on ideas implicit in them. But this cannot be right, since if Rawls were to attempt it, his political conception could not be freestanding.

Overlapping consensus does not have to do with the argumentative bases of a political conception of justice. In the development of its principles, a political conception does not attend at all to the premises and principles of reasonable comprehensive views; it draws rather from ideas implicit in democratic culture. Once the principles and ideas of a political conception are fully developed, the idea of overlapping consensus is invoked to explain how the political conception can be stable in the face of reasonable pluralism. How is it possible for the freestanding political conception to be supported by disparate conceptions of the good so that people who affirm these conceptions can be rationally motivated to do what the political conception requires? Having given up the argument for the congruence of justice with each person's rational good, Rawls needs an account of why people should be sufficiently motivated to do what justice requires according to a liberal political conception like justice as fairness. Since many do not accept the good of autonomy, we cannot expect all citizens to endorse the public conception of justice to affirm their nature as autonomous agents. The idea of overlapping consensus is based in the conjecture that reasonable citizens in a well-ordered society still can affirm the freestanding political conception for reasons peculiar to their comprehensive views. Different comprehensive doctrines should be able to accept the political conception since it can be justified according to reasons already affirmed within each comprehensive view. So while Kantians may affirm a liberal political conception for reasons of autonomy (as congruence suggests), reasonable utilitarians might affirm a liberal conception if they believe that it indirectly promotes overall utility; moreover, reasonable Catholics may affirm the same political conception on grounds that it expresses God's natural laws, and pluralists can endorse it on grounds that the reasons it provides are sufficient for purposes of justification without the need to appeal to some more abstract comprehensive view.

Overlapping consensus then envisions a two-part justification for a liberal political conception. First, it is assumed that reasonable citizens can understand and accept the justification of the political conception in terms of public reason, the reasons and ideas implicit in democratic political culture. The political conception of justice best expresses their political conception of themselves as free and equal and their interests as citizens. Second, it is conjectured that reasonable citizens also can accept the political conception on the basis of nonpublic reasons stemming from their different comprehensive views. The political conception should be compatible with each reasonable person's self-conception as a moral agent and fit with the other moral, religious, and philosophical ideas and values that constitute his or her comprehensive view. If all the reasonable comprehensive doctrines satisfy this second stage, then there is an overlapping consensus. The key assumption underlying Rawls's conjecture here is that, because of the reciprocity of the principles of justice, over time the public political culture and the benefits of a well-ordered society will lead all reasonable persons holding reasonable comprehensive views to accommodate their own comprehensive accounts of justice and morality to the public view. In effect Rawls extends the account in *Theory* of the development of the sense of justice – that we accept and support persons and institutions that support our good – to account for the evolution of comprehensive doctrines in a well-ordered society. Reasonable comprehensive doctrines, in response to the benefits of justice they all enjoy in a well-ordered society, should evolve there so as to incorporate a liberal political conception into their values and principles. Moreover, Rawls conjectures, the circumstances of a well-ordered liberal society should not be such as to give rise to such a preponderance of unreasonable illiberal doctrines as to undermine its stability. Assuming that these two speculative conjectures are true in a well-ordered society, then there will be an overlapping consensus on the political conception, and this conception will be stable.

### C. Public Reason

3. LIBERAL LEGITIMACY AND THE IDEA OF PUBLIC REASON. One way to understand the idea of public reason is to see it as a development

of the publicity condition within justice as fairness and as following from the practical aim of a political conception.[69] If a conception of justice is to serve as a public basis for justification then it must be interpreted and applied according to methods of reasoning and rules of evidence accessible to the common reason of democratic citizens. The idea of public reason also might be explained as implied by a moral requirement on any liberal and democratic society. It stems from a *liberal principle of legitimacy*:

Our exercise of political power is fully proper only when it is exercised in accordance with a constitution the essentials of which all citizens as free and equal may reasonably be expected to endorse in the light of principles and ideals acceptable to their common human reason.[70]

From the principle of liberal legitimacy follows a moral duty:

*the duty of civility* – to be able to explain to one another on those fundamental questions how the principles and policies they advocate and vote for can be supported by the political values of public reason. (*PL*, p. 217 emphasis added)

Since explanation in terms of public reason is here described as a requirement of political legitimacy, some remarks on legitimacy are in order before discussing public reason. In any society there are always going to be disagreements about the laws, and everyone will think at least some of the laws are bad or unjust. What is to make the coercive enforcement of these and other laws legitimate in the eyes of citizens? In political theory legitimacy is often construed as popular acceptance of political power and laws. But for Rawls not just any popularly accepted law or exercise of political power can be legitimate (laws denying basic liberties to minorities are not, for example). For Rawls a condition of laws' legitimacy is that they stem from a just, or at least nearly just, democratic constitution. But legitimacy is not the same as justice. For laws can be just and still not be legitimate. Just laws for Rawls accord with principles and a constitution that would be agreed to by hypothetical parties in the original position and the ensuing four-stage sequence (cf. *TJ*, Sec. 31). But just laws (so defined) are not legitimate within a particular democratic society until they have been duly enacted by its citizens according to a constitution all may reasonably be expected to endorse. (For example, universal health care may be required by justice but has not yet been legitimately enacted in the United States). Moreover, laws can be legitimate in the way just described and still not be just. No constitutional procedure, no matter how just, always yields just laws or the just adjudication and administration of just laws. No matter how sincere and conscientious, legislators, judges, and administrators will make mistakes about what justice requires in particular situations. Any existing political procedure exhibits "imperfect procedural justice." Still, Rawls contends it is a requirement for the stability of a democratic society that citizens obey legitimate laws, even when they are unjust (provided they do not exceed certain limits of injustice). This, too, is a requirement of the duty of civility (*TJ*, p. 355/312 rev.). No democratic political system could survive for long if its citizens believed that they had a right to violate any laws or decrees they believed to be less than just.[71]

Liberal legitimacy requires that laws be enacted according to a constitution whose "essentials" are acceptable to public reason; moreover laws themselves must be supportable by the "political values of public reason." What is public reason? It concerns the kinds of reasons appropriate for government decisions and political argument and justification addressed to the public. An idea of public reason is suggested in the social contract views of Rousseau and Kant. They assume that for laws and the constitution to be acceptable to everyone, they must be justified for reasons they can accept too.[72] A narrow way to construe this phrase –"justifiable to all for reasons they can accept" – is that it means we can justify laws with one argument for the Catholics, different arguments for Protestants and for Jews, and then other arguments directed to nonbelievers, and so on. But the idea of public reason implies that all should be able to accept the constitution and laws for the same reasons. Public reason presupposes a kind of political community that is unified by shared beliefs and ideas. But not just any political community of shared moral beliefs is guided by public reason. Even were all subjects of Iran to publicly affirm the political priority of the Koran, this would not make Islamic religious doctrine part of public reason. The idea of public reason is defined against a background of democratic institutions, and it assumes toleration of different religious, philosophical, and ethical positions. Moreover, public reason is reason addressed to persons *as* democratic citizens and not in their capacity as economic agents or as endorsers of a particular religion or other comprehensive conception of the good. There is a need to address the members of a democratic society purely as citizens since they affirm such different philosophical and religious doctrines and values. Because of these differences citizens differ in the reasons they will accept in any other capacity or position they occupy. It is because of these differences that an idea of public reason is needed to regulate argument and deliberation in public political life. Public reason, like the ideas of a political conception of justice and overlapping consensus, responds to this *fact of reasonable pluralism.*

Reasonable pluralism, not pluralism per se, defines the parameters and the reach of public reason. This means, first, that public reason does not seek to address unreasonable persons or unreasonable doctrines in its efforts to justify laws and public policies. So (to mention views Rawls's critics have suggested) there is no presumption that Social Darwinists, fundamentalists, neo-Nazis, or Southern slaveholders would be amenable to public reason; nor should any effort be made to address or accommodate their views. These doctrines either are unreasonable, or they could not be affirmed by reasonable citizens who want to justify their social and political relations by reasons that other free and equal citizens can reasonably accept.

A second way reasonable pluralism defines the parameters of public reason is that public reason must rely on principles, values, and methods of reasoning and assessing evidence shared by reasonable doctrines under conditions of a free democratic society. Some of these values and principles are explicitly affirmed by any reasonable comprehensive doctrine. All reasonable doctrines reject slavery and forced servitude and affirm the integrity of human life, freedom of movement, freedom of conscience, and some degree of freedom of association and occupation. Reasonable doctrines also affirm the abstract values of justice and the common good. These and other common values provide shared reasons for a variety of measures such as laws prohibiting violence, maintaining public order and public health, and so on. But other basic values and principles have to be uncovered. Earlier I said public reason is reason addressed to free and equal persons in their capacity as democratic citizens. The values shared by reasonable doctrines are presumed to be political values. The *political values of public reason* are responsive to the way reasonable persons think of themselves politically: of their status and role as citizens, their political rights and duties, their relations to other citizens, and the proper exercise of political power. A working assumption of political liberalism is that reasonable persons holding reasonable comprehensive doctrines in a well-ordered democratic society all conceive of themselves for political purposes as free and equal citizens. They should be able to recognize, then, that they have fundamental political interests in maintaining their "moral powers," the powers of reason and volition that enable them to take advantage of, and to be cooperating members of, democratic society. Now the conception of the person as free, equal, reasonable, and rational and with interests in maintaining his or her moral and rational powers provides a basis for thinking about the political values of public reason. The reasons that are public and shared in a constitutional democracy will in some way respond to political values, which themselves are in turn related to the conditions needed for realizing this ideal conception of democratic citizens.[73]

A controversial feature of public reason is that it does not claim that the reasons and principles it provides are true. To make such claims, public reason would have to subscribe to an account of the nature and conditions of moral truth. Any such account is bound to be controversial – the reasonable moral skeptic, among others, would disagree. This would put public reason in contention with reasonable comprehensive doctrines, each of which affirms one or another metaphysical doctrine of truth. It is for this reason (and not because public reason might be false) that it cannot be said within public reason that the reasons and moral principles public reason provides are true. What can be said, however, (and this should satisfy even the reasonable moral skeptic) is (a) that the moral principles of public reason are the most reasonable principles for free and equal democratic citizens to order their political relations, and (b) that insofar as any of the reasonable comprehensive doctrines that affirm the political values and principles of public reason are true in a well-ordered society, then the reasons offered by public reason, and the conception of justice that provides content to public reason, are also true.

Recall now that the practical aim of a political conception is to provide a basis for public justification acceptable to free and equal citizens. Rawls says public reasoning in a democracy seeks a *shared public basis* for deliberation, justification, and agreement. Even though free and equal citizens can agree on political values of public reason, without a shared basis for justification and agreement public reasoning is not only contentious but inconclusive and incomplete. Citizens will still disagree, even if they abstract from their personal interests, agree on the political values of public reason, and vote the common good as they see it. In the absence of a more secure basis for deliberation, they will assign importance to the political values of public reason according to the demands of their particular comprehensive views. This is a breakdown of public reasoning, for laws are ultimately decided according to the particular reasons of comprehensive views which many democratic citizens cannot reasonably be expected to endorse. Consequently, the powers of government are exercised against citizens on grounds that they do not find reasonable and which they also cannot endorse as free and equal citizens.

One significant role of a political conception of justice is to address this problem. It supplies "the content of public reason."

A citizen engages in public reason when he or she deliberates within a framework of what he or she sincerely regards as the most reasonable political conception of justice, a conception that expresses political values that others, as free and equal citizens might also reasonably be expected reasonably to endorse.[74]

To engage in public reason, then, is not just to reason in terms of public political values while assigning them weight or significance according to one's conception of the good. Let us consider the most prominent case: in deliberating about the political permissibility of abortion, a legislator, judge, or citizen who on religious grounds assigns absolute weight to the political value of respect for the integrity of human life while assigning little or no weight to other relevant political values (women's freedom to control their procreation, the equality of women as equal citizens, and society's interest in the ordered reproduction of society over time) is not engaged in public reasoning. Rather he or she is interpreting the political values of public reason in terms of a comprehensive view. The same is true of those who assign absolute weight to women's freedom and equality on grounds of rational autonomy while assigning no weight to respect for the integrity of human (fetal) life.[75]

Democratic citizens' recognition of a political conception of justice is then needed for them fully to engage in public reasoning. Public reasoning involves ascertaining and reflecting on political values, clarifying their obscurities, assigning their respective degrees of significance, and applying them to decide the laws and to resolve constitutional issues. A political conception of justice is needed for these purposes to provide "the content of public reason" and to make public reason "complete." For public reason to be complete requires that the meaning and relative importance of competing political values be decided according to a political conception, and not (simply) according to citizens' or officials' own philosophical, moral, and religious views. When judges, legislators, and citizens appeal to comprehensive views to make political decisions that are not supportable by a reasonable political conception, other citizens are subjected to coercive political power for reasons they could not accept on the basis of their own particular values or from their shared perspective as democratic citizens. Citizens are then treated as subjects and not as equals who are free.

Public reason aims for a basis for public deliberation in order to achieve public justification and agreement. A reasonable political conception of justice is needed for these purposes to provide content to public reason. Rawls says three main features characterize reasonable political conceptions. First, a list of basic rights, liberties, and opportunities; second, an assignment of special priority to these rights, liberties, and opportunities with respect to claims of the general good, economic efficiency, and perfectionist values; and third, measures ensuring all citizens the all-purpose means to make effective use of their freedoms.[76] These three features imply that a reasonable political conception will be liberal. Several conceptions of justice can satisfy these liberal requirements and the criterion of reciprocity. Justice as fairness is not the only one. There is a "family of political conceptions" that are reasonable and which can provide the content of public reason in a deliberative democracy. Accordingly, "the forms of permissible public reason are always several."[77]

But libertarianism would not be among the reasonable political conceptions according to Rawls's criteria. It cannot then provide content to public reason. This should not be surprising, since Libertarians normally reject democracy altogether.[78] The ideal of the person and society that underlies libertarianism is not that of free and equal citizens cooperating on a basis of reciprocity but free individuals who are absolute owners of themselves and their external assets and whose cooperative interactions are based in private contracts. For Rawls, libertarianism is not reasonable because it has no place for ensuring each citizen the means to make effective use of his or her freedoms and opportunities. Not having a place for equal opportunity or a guaranteed social minimum, libertarianism cannot satisfy the limiting condition of a political conception, the *criterion of reciprocity*.[79] We cannot reasonably expect everyone (especially the worse off) to reasonably accept political terms of cooperation that assign rights to income and wealth only according to libertarian entitlement principles.

## IV. THE LAW OF PEOPLES

Rawls's account of the Law of Peoples is easily misunderstood. He is not asking such abstract questions as, What are the nature and conditions of global justice? or What is the ideal composition of the cosmopolitan order? Kant, Rawls's model in many respects, did address these questions. Kant rejected a world-state since he thought it would degenerate into either global despotism or a fragile empire torn by civil wars in which regions and peoples would seek to gain their political autonomy. He held that an ideal cosmopolitan order consists of an international society of politically independent and autonomous peoples, each having a republican constitution. A republican constitution, Kant says, affirms the sovereignty of the people as that entity or legal person that "possesses the highest political authority." It guarantees each member the status of free and equal citizen and gives them the "civil rights" of citizens.[80] Rawls follows Kant in rejecting a world government as utopian.[81] Rawls's Law of Peoples also endorses the independence and autonomy of different peoples. But Rawls does not incorporate Kant's requirement that every government should be republican and guarantee all the civil rights of free and equal citizens. What is behind this surprising conclusion? It may seem as if Rawls no longer endorses the position implicit in *Theory* – that a well-ordered democratic society is an ideal of justice to be aspired to by all societies and that the guarantee of equal rights of political participation is morally required once a society achieves the requisite social and economic conditions for democracy.[82]

What explains this otherwise surprising position is that Rawls's *The Law of Peoples* addresses a more modest question than Kant and other theorists concerned with the questions of global justice raised at the beginning of the previous paragraph. Assume (as Rawls himself would acknowledge) a less than perfect international order consisting of both liberal and nonliberal governments. How are liberal peoples to relate to nonliberal peoples, and in particular to nonliberal peoples who are decent, if not wholly just by the standards of a well-ordered constitutional democracy?

Rawls's Law of Peoples is developed within political liberalism as an extension of a liberal political conception of justice. A liberal political conception, such as justice as fairness, pertains to domestic justice. Still needed are principles of foreign policy to regulate a constitutional democracy's interaction with other societies, liberal and nonliberal (*LP*, pp. 10, 83). As expected Rawls maintains that a liberal society should cooperate on fair terms with other liberal societies, recognizing their independence and respecting them as equals. The primary question is, Should liberal societies tolerate and cooperate with nonliberal societies that are not just according to (political) liberalism, and if so, how far should toleration and cooperation extend? Or should liberal societies seek to shape in their own image all societies not yet liberal or democratic, intervening in their internal affairs and applying sanctions whenever effective?

To address these questions Rawls distinguishes a just society from a decent society (and then distinguishes both from indecent or "outlaw" societies). Respect for human decency is a condition of justice, but not all decent societies are just (in a liberal democratic sense). A "decent hierarchical society" Rawls defines as one that (a) is peaceful and nonexpansionist; (b) is guided by a common-good conception of justice that affirms the good of all of its members; (c) has a "just consultation hierarchy," which represents each major segment of society and which is seen as legitimate in the eyes of its people; and (d) honors the basic human rights that respect the human decency of its members (*LP*, pp. 64–7). The basic human rights that are a condition of a decent society are, Rawls says, those protecting the life and integrity of the person (including the right to life and security of the person, and minimum rights to means of subsistence – a decent people does not let its members starve); rights to liberty of the person (including freedom of movement, freedom from forced work and occupation, and the right to hold personal property); formal equality and guaranteed protections of the rule of law (due process, fair trials, right against self-incrimination, and so on); and some degree of liberty of conscience, freedom of thought, and freedom of association (*LP*, pp. 65, 78–81). It is not a condition of a decent society that it affirm the equality of its members, or give them equal political rights (it may afford them no political rights at all), or even that it provide for equality of all basic human rights. For example, a decent society may have a state religion and reject separation of church and state as long as it provides a degree of freedom to practice dissenting religions. Also a decent society must respect the human rights of women and represent their interests in its just consultation hierarchy (LP, pp. 75, 110).[83]

Perhaps no existing societies satisfy Rawls's description of a decent hierarchical society (just as no existing societies satisfy his account of a well-ordered liberal society). So what is his point? Rawls's primary aim in The Law of Peoples is to define the limits of liberal people's toleration of nonliberal peoples. The idea of a decent hierarchical society is a theoretical construct developed for this purpose. Rawls contends that liberal societies should not tolerate dictatorial, tyrannical, and other "outlaw" regimes. But what about nonliberal societies that are not so unjust as to be indecent? Is it reasonable to expect unjust but nonetheless decent societies to conform to all the egalitarian norms of a constitutional democracy as a condition of peaceable coexistence and cooperation with them? Rawls contends that it is unreasonable for free and equal peoples to refuse to cooperate with decent nonliberal regimes and require, as a matter of foreign policy or international law, that they be liberal and democratic. To insist that the *only* bases for cooperation with a people is that they provide their members with the full rights and benefits of liberal–democratic citizens is an unreasonable view. A liberal society is to respect other societies organized by nonliberal, nondemocratic comprehensive doctrines provided that their political and social institutions meet conditions of decency.

Given that the alternative is a standing intention to intervene in, if not destabilize, all nonliberal regimes, Rawls's position makes good sense. His position does not imply that political liberalism endorses decent hierarchical societies as just and beyond criticism. Liberal citizens and associations have full rights (perhaps even duties according to their comprehensive views) to publicly criticize the illiberal or undemocratic character of other societies. But critical assessment by liberal citizens is different from their government's hostile criticisms, sanctions, and other forms of coercive intervention.[84] The Law of Peoples says that liberal peoples, *as peoples* represented by their governments, have a duty to cooperate with, and not seek to undermine, decent nonliberal societies. This means that liberal peoples have certain moral duties to decent nonliberal peoples, and their relations are not defined in purely strategic terms. Among the duties they have is a duty to respect the territorial integrity of decent peoples, as well as their political independence and autonomy (within the limits of decency).[85]

Now turn to Rawls's account of human rights. Rawls distinguishes human rights from the liberal democratic rights required by political liberalism. Human rights are conceived as a special class of rights that specify the minimum standards of decent political institutions. To deny people the right to vote or freedom of artistic expression seriously infringes liberal justice, but it is not as egregious as denying them the right to life, torturing or enslaving them, or persecuting them for their religion. Rawls says human rights are the rights that are necessary for any system of cooperation (*LP*, p. 68). He means that people denied human rights are not cooperating in any sense but are compelled or coerced (as under a slave system). They are not seen as independent agents with a good that is worthy of respect or consideration. The role of the idea of human rights within political liberalism is, first, to set limits to a government's internal autonomy – no government can claim sovereignty as a defense against its violation of the human rights of those subject to its authority. Second, human rights restrict the reasons for war and its conduct: War can only be waged in self-defense, or to protect the human rights of other peoples when violated by their own or another government. Also, within war the human rights of enemy noncombatants are to be respected; noncombatants are not to be targeted for attack, and measures should be taken to protect them and their property from injury. Because of the special role Rawls assigns to human rights within the law of peoples, he does not include among them all the moral rights of persons as such. Peoples and governments which afford only human rights are simply decent; they are not ideal or just from the point of view of many comprehensive doctrines. But for Rawls decency is an important political category in the law of peoples, since it is sufficient for a people's enjoying rights to noninterference and self-determination that they afford all under their authority human rights and meet the four conditions of decency listed previously in this section.

The implication is that an international order of independent peoples can be just without all of its members being just (in the liberal–democratic sense) towards their own people. It is the business of all peoples, as corporate bodies represented by their governments, to ensure basic human rights to all peoples, as well as to assist them in meeting basic human needs. But it is not the task of a society of peoples to enforce the rights of democratic citizens among all peoples. Achieving democratic justice is to be left up to the self-determination of each independent people. This implies that, in Rawls's account, the duties of justice that governments and citizens owe to their own people are more extensive than the duties of justice they owe to other peoples. Many find this peculiar, since it appears to rest on nothing more than the arbitrariness of national boundaries. Why should we have duties to promote the political rights and economic interests of people in San Diego and not owe similar duties to those in worse positions across the border in Tijuana?

Existing territories within which a people reside are indeed arbitrary; most often they have resulted from aggression by distant forebears. But historical arbitrariness of existing boundaries does not mean that it is arbitrary whether or not a people has a territory to reside in and control which is respected by others. (In general, the moral arbitrariness of a situation does not mean we can morally ignore it; for example, the arbitrariness of blindness does not entitle the blind to someone else's eye.) Arbitrary boundaries are morally important since residing in and politically controlling a territory is normally needed for a people to exist. Nor do arbitrary boundaries imply that special duties to the members of one's society are arbitrary. Just as families could not exist without family members owing duties to one another that are not owed to others, so too a people could not exist without its members owing special duties to one another. Moreover, most individuals identify with those with whom they share political and social relationships, and their being a member of a particular people is a good and as much a part of their self-conception as are their family relationships (cf. *LP*, p. 111).

This goes some way towards explaining why Rawls does not globally extend the difference principle, as some have suggested[86] (*LP*, pp. 113–20). Instead he argues that independent peoples have a duty to assist "burdened societies" in meeting their basic needs so that they can become independent members in the society of well-ordered peoples (*LP*, pp. 106–113).[87] To clarify, we can distinguish two ways to support the claim that a people does not have a general duty to equally support the disadvantaged everywhere. One view argues that a people has a moral entitlement to all that they produce by their labor or acquire by voluntary gift or exchange (adding that they are also entitled to natural resources within their territory by natural right of acquisition, though this provision is not necessary). This entitlement approach resembles Robert Nozick's theory but applied to nations instead of individuals. It supports the claim that a people has no duty of justice to assist other peoples. Any assistance to be afforded others is charitable. This resembles the way nation-states today conceive of international assistance.

This is not Rawls's view. Just as individuals have no property entitlements independent of the circumstances of other persons (recall the opening remarks in Section I), so a people has no property entitlements (claims to a territory, its natural resources, and the output produced from them) independent of the circumstances of other peoples. Claims to territory made by a people require some justification other than initial acquisition and appropriation for use. The justification Rawls gives is not that the world's worst off are maximally benefitted.[88] It is that a people having political control over a territory serves the important function of ascribing to identifiable peoples responsibility to care for that territory and its resources and so mitigates deterioration of the environment and waste of its resources, which is in the interest of all peoples and all their members (*LP*, pp. 38–9). (This functional argument does not justify existing boundaries, nor is it intended to. That is a separate issue altogether.)

Now the question arises, assuming that all peoples and their members can benefit from independent peoples enjoying territorial independence, what rights and duties do a liberal people have with respect to their resources and what they produce? They do not have a right to hoard them exclusively for their own use. But do they have a general duty to equally support the disadvantaged everywhere? Rawls, in effect, argues that a self-sufficient people has a general duty to support disadvantaged peoples so they may become self-sufficient, but it has a special duty to its own people – and particularly to the disadvantaged members of its own society (at least if it is a liberal society). This special duty to provide for the disadvantaged of one's own (liberal) society stems not from conjectured psychological laws that national sentiments are stronger than the sentiment for humanity or that a people more closely identifies with its own disadvantaged than with the disadvantaged of some other people. It is based rather in the special cooperative relations among a people that exist by virtue of their shared basic structure. Because the members of a society stand in cooperative relationships with one another that they do not have with other peoples, relationships that are defined and mediated by shared basic social institutions, the duties of justice that they owe one another are different and more stringent than those owed to other peoples. They are defined by a conception of fairness and reciprocity in Rawls's account of liberal and democratic domestic justice. It is by appealing to the idea of reciprocity among members who share co-operative relations (political, legal, social, and economic) within the same basic structure that provides Rawls with the main argument for his difference principle.

This is one way to understand Rawls's difference principle from a global perspective. (I do not contend it is the way he understands it.) Assume that all peoples have a general duty, and that all individual persons have a natural duty, to disadvantaged people everywhere. Assume also that all persons benefit from being a member of an independent, self-governing society and its people. If the integrity of the basic structure of a society is to be maintained, then special duties to meet the basic needs of the disadvantaged of one's own society are justified over and above general duties owed to the disadvantaged everywhere (just as if the institution of the family is to be maintained, special duties must be owed to one's family members that are not owed to others). The difference principle is designed to apply to the special cooperative relations existing by virtue of the shared political, legal, and economic institutions that constitute the basic structure of a democratic society. It is not designed to apply on a global level to the more fluid and inchoate collaborative relations among world inhabitants. To apply it at the global level (just as to apply it at the level of the family) is to misunderstand its function of specifying the special cooperative relations of reciprocity that define a democratic people.

There is also a more practical problem. By virtue of their political institutions a people has the power to shape the basic structure of their society – a power they do not have with respect to other people's basic institutions. Can a people reasonably be expected to exercise this power to structure their own institutions in such a way that maximizes the life prospects of the least advantaged persons in the world? How could they do this if they have little control over the life prospects of the least advantaged of other nations? Nothing short of assuming political control over other societies would be required. This would deprive a people of their political institutions and their powers of self-determination. Moreover, it would require something on the order of a world-state to enforce, which Rawls rejects as utopian (*LP*, p. 36). As in his account of domestic justice, his account of the law of peoples is conditioned by a view of what is practicably possible given human nature.

These are controversial issues. For many, the most pressing problems of justice pertain to wealthy nations' relations to peoples in much less favored parts of the world on whose efforts and labor wealthy nations rely. Critics of Rawls do not find that the kind of cooperative relations that exist among people within a society are qualitatively different from the cooperative relations (especially economic relations) they have with other peoples in the world – not so different as to justify applying different criteria of distributive justice. For these critics, Rawls's duty of assistance to enable a people to reach economic self-sufficiency will not be enough to satisfy requirements of global justice. Clearly more needs to be said on Rawls's behalf than has been said here to respond adequately to these and other objections.

## V. OUTLINE OF VOLUME

The papers presented here critically elucidate many of the main features of Rawls's account of justice set forth in *A Theory of Justice* and in *Political Liberalism*.[89] The volume begins with discussions of Rawls's understanding of and contribution to liberalism (Nagel) and to democratic thought (Cohen). The next nine contributions focus on particular features of Rawls's theory. Chapter 3 (Scanlon) takes up Rawls's views on justification and discusses the roles of reflective equilibrium, the original position, and public reason. Chapters 4 through 7 deal primarily with central ideas in *A Theory of Justice*. Chapter 4 (Gutmann) discusses the first principle of justice and emphasizes the basic liberties' dual foundation in both liberal and democratic principles. Rawls's account of economic justice and the difference principle is critically assessed in Chapter 5 (van Parijs). Chapter 6 (Daniels) discusses how justice as fairness is egalitarian and defends Rawls against some of his more (and less) egalitarian critics. Chapter 7 (Freeman) takes up Rawls's argument for stability and the good of justice and therewith discusses Kant's influence on Rawls's views. The next four papers, Chapters 8 through 11, focus on *Political Liberalism*.⁹⁰ Chapter 8 (Dreben) discusses the philosophical background to political liberalism, emphasizing the fundamental differences with Rawls's earlier view. Chapter 9 (O'Neill) discusses Rawls's political constructivism and critically compares it with Kant's constructivist view. A discussion of publicity and public reason and their relation to equal respect follows in Chapter 10 (Larmore). Then, Chapter 11 (Michelman) provides a survey of Rawls's positions on liberal constitutionalism and the role of the courts in a constitutional democracy. The volume concludes with three discussions of Rawls's relations to some of his critics. Chapter 12 (Scheffler) shows that Rawls has important affinities as well as fundamental differences with utilitarianism. Chapter 13 (Mulhall and Swift) discusses communitarianism and how it has affected Rawls's view. The volume closes with a critical discussion in Chapter 14 (Nussbaum) of Rawls's relationship to feminist thought.

ENDNOTES

1   For his early and later papers, see John Rawls, *Collected Papers*, ed. Samuel Freeman (Cambridge, MA: Harvard University Press, 1999).

2   John Rawls, *A Theory of Justice* (Cambridge, MA: Harvard University Press, 1971; revised edition, 1999). The revised edition was completed in 1976 for the German translation and has provided the basis for all subsequent translations. In the text references will be made either to *Theory* or to "TJ" followed by page numbers. Page numbers refer to the 1971 edition first and then to the 1999 revised edition (as in "TJ, p. 100/93 rev.").

3   *John Rawls and His Critics – An Annotated Bibliography*, eds. J.H. Wellbank, Dennis Snook, and David T. Mason (New York: Garland Press, 1982).

4   See also, *Political Liberalism* (New York: Columbia University Press, 1993; revised paperback edition, 1996), p. 3, where a similar question is said to be fundamental to his inquiry. The abbreviation "PL"

will be used in the text with page references to this work. Except for the prefaces, the pagination of the 1996 paperback edition of *Political Liberalism* is the same as the first edition.

5 A term Rawls uses in *The Law of Peoples* (Cambridge, MA: Harvard University Press, 1999), pp. 4, 5–6, 11–12.

6 These are "the circumstances of justice" defined as moderate scarcity and restricted altruism in *Theory*, Sec. 22, to which Rawls adds "the fact of reasonable pluralism" in *Political Liberalism*.

7 Cf. Rawls, "Kantian Constructivism in Moral Theory," in *Collected Papers*, p. 304.

8 This empirical turn is not entirely unrelated to Kant. A reasonable interpretation of Kant's dictum, "ought implies can" is that, to be valid and applicable to us, moral principles must be within the capacities of human nature and compatible with the human good. Otherwise, a moral conception is not realizable under the normal conditions of human life and is utopian. This relates to Rawls's concern for stability.

9 See Samuel Scheffler in this volume on this feature of Rawls's work.

10 See *Political Liberalism*, Lecture VIII, p. 291 for Rawls's list of basic liberties. It develops the list initially set forth in *TJ*, p. 61/53 rev.

11 On the conception of moral persons and its relation to constructivism, see "Kantian Constructivism in Moral Theory," in *Collected Papers*, Chap. 16, and "Political Constructivism," Lecture III of *Political Liberalism*. Rawls introduces the moral powers in *Theory*, Sec. 77, to explain the bases for equality of persons. They are also essential to his argument for the good of justice and the congruence of the right and the good. See *Theory*, Sections 40, 86, also pp. 478, 514, 515, 563/418–19, 451, 452, 493 rev.

12 Compare here Rawls's claim that justice as fairness, rather than being a "rights-based" view grounded in a right of equal respect is instead an "ideal-based" conception built on an ideal of the person and of social cooperation. "Justice as Fairness: Political, not Metaphysical," in Rawls, *Collected Papers*, pp. 400–401n.

13 Robert Nozick's *Anarchy, State, and Utopia* (New York: Basic Books, 1974) states the libertarian case for absolute property most forcefully. The only limitation on accumulation and exercise of property rights he recognizes is the "Lockean Proviso" that people cannot be made worse off than they would be in a hypothetical state of nature. Id. pp. 178–82.

14 See *Theory of Justice*, Sections 13 and 49, and pp. 102–105/88–90 rev. The sense of reciprocity Rawls relies on is illustrated by Figure 6, Section 13, with its rising contribution curve, where gains to the most advantaged are accompanied by gains to the least advantaged, and vice versa. See Rawls, *Justice as Fairness: A Restatement* (Cambridge,

MA: Harvard University Press, 2001) Sec. 18, pp. 61–66. (Referred to hereafter as 'Restatement.')

15   See *TJ*, Sections 13 and 41–43 on the difference principle and its application. See also, *Restatement*, Secs. 17–22, pp. 57–79. For critical discussions, see the chapters by Philippe van Parijs and Norman Daniels in this volume (Chapters 5 and 6, respectively).

16   See Amaryta Sen, *Inequality Re-Examined* (Cambridge, MA: Harvard University Press, 1992).

17   See Amartya Sen, *Development as Freedom* (New York: Random House, 1999), pp. 54ff. For Rawls's response to Sen see *Restatement*, Sec. 51, 168–76.

18   For example, just as we have to know for what purpose we are punishing offenders to decide what sanctions are due, we need to know what the ideal case of free and equal persons cooperating on a basis of mutual respect and reciprocity requires to decide what the handicapped are due as a matter of justice as opposed to what ought to be done on their behalf as a matter of public benevolence. These remarks address the frequent complaint that Rawls's omitting consideration of problems of the handicapped in the original position is "ad hoc" or unfair to them. See works by Brian Barry and A. Sen, for example, in the bibliography and van Parijs (Chapter 5) in this volume.

19   Rawls says two other ways the view is egalitarian is the first principle's requirement that the *fair value* of equal political liberties be guaranteed and the second principle's requirement of fair equality of opportunity. See *Political Liberalism*, p. 6. See also, *Restatement*, pp. 132–32. On Rawls's egalitarianism, see Norman Daniels' chapter in this volume (Chapter 6).

20   See Joshua Cohen, "Democratic Equality," *Ethics* 99 (1989): 727–51, who clarifies the relationship between the difference principle, the basic liberties, and the bases of self-respect. See also the chapter by Amy Gutmann in this volume (Chapter 4). See also *Restatement*, pp. 148–52.

21   Rawls discusses the relevance of considered moral judgments and the related account of reflective equilibrium, at *TJ*, pp. 19–21/17–19 rev. and *TJ*, pp. 47–52/40–45 rev. For a discussion, see Section I of T.M. Scanlon's contribution to this volume (Chapter 3). On the historical nature of Locke's social contract, see *Restatement*, pp. 16, 52–54.

22   "The idea here is simply to make vivid to ourselves the restrictions that it seems reasonable to impose on arguments for principles of justice, and therefore on these principles themselves" ( *TJ*, p. 18/16 rev.). Rawls contends that the "conditions embodied in the description of the original position are ones that we do in fact accept. Or if we do not, then

perhaps we can be persuaded to do so by philosophical reflection" ( *TJ*, p. 21/19 rev.).

23   See Robert Nozick, *Anarchy, State and Utopia*, pp. 198–204 for a libertarian criticism of the original position.

24   See, for example, the references to J. Harsanyi and K. Binmore in the bibliography to this volume, and in Note 25.

25   This is suggested by John Harsanyi, "Morality and the Theory of Rational Behavior," in *Utilitarianism and Beyond*, A. Sen and B. Williams, eds. (Cambridge, UK: Cambridge University Press, 1982), p. 56, as a remedy to similar problems raised by his thin veil of ignorance.

26   See Rawls, "Fairness to Goodness," in *Collected Papers*, esp. pp. 270–1; also see *Political Liberalism*, pp. 191–4 on liberalism and neutrality.

27   It is partly in order to avoid suggesting that the assumption of mutual disinterest implies the parties are egoistic that Rawls, since *Theory*, has come to speak of the parties as "representatives" of moral persons in a well-ordered society and that the parties act in a fiduciary capacity to further the interests of the persons they represent. *Restatement*, pp. 84–5.

28   Since the expected utility of (2) is $500,000 [= ($.10 \times .5) + ($1,000,000 \times .5)]$, whereas the expected utility of (1) is only $1.50 [= $1 \times .5) + ($2 \times .5)]$.

29   See Harsanyi, "Morality and the Theory of Rational Behavior," p. 47.

30   For Rawls's own example of the irrationality of maximin under most circumstances, see *TJ*, p. 157/136 rev.

31   Harold Jeffreys writes:

> If there is no reason to believe one hypothesis rather than another, the probabilities are equal ... *to say that the probabilities are equal is a precise way of saying that we have no good grounds for choosing between the alternatives.* ... The rule that we should take them equal is not a statement of any belief about the actual composition of the world, nor is it an inference from previous experience; it is merely the formal way of expressing ignorance. [Jeffreys' emphases]

*Theory of Probability*, 3rd ed. (Oxford, UK: Clarendon Press, 1961), pp. 33–4, quoted in Mark Kaplan, *Decision Theory as Philosophy* (Cambridge, UK: Cambridge University Press, 1996), p. 26n.

32   See Rawls, *TJ*, Section 28; see also Michael Resnick, *Choices*, (Minneapolis: University of Minnesota Press, 1987) p. 37; and Kaplan, id., p. 27.

33   Here it should be kept in mind that, unlike the examples in the text, in Rawls's original position the parties do not even know potential payoffs resulting from choosing between alternatives.

34   Rawls's argument is that maximin is a rational strategy under conditions that exhibit three features: first, "the situation is one where knowledge of probabilities is impossible, or at best extremely insecure"; second,

"the person choosing has a conception of the good such that he cares very little, if anything, for what he might gain above the minimum stipend that he can, in fact, be sure of by following the maximin rule"; and third, "the rejected alternatives have outcomes that one can hardly accept" ( *TJ*, p. 154–5/134 rev.). Rawls argues that the original position exhibits all three of these features. Rawls's critics normally focus on the first condition alone and usually ignore the other conditions Rawls imposes on the rationality of using maximin.

Many economists and philosophers reject Rawls's use of maximin strategy. See Brian Barry, *Theories of Justice*, p. 224. See also Ken Binmore, *Playing Fair*, Volume I, *Game Theory and the Social Contract* (Cambridge, MA: MIT Press, 1995), p. 331, who concedes that Rawls's thick veil of ignorance may justify the use of maximin.

35  See *TJ*, 176–7/153–4 rev. see also Rawls, *Collected Papers*, pp. 250–2 for further discussion of the strains of commitment. See also, *Restatement*, pp. 103–4.

36  David Gauthier and Jean Hampton, among others, raise this objection (see bibliography references). Actually the parties are not described the same way. They have different conceptions of the good, for example. That they do not know the specifics of their conceptions of the good, or any other distinguishing facts about themselves, does not imply they are the same person any more than that a group of mathematicians, all intently focused on proving the same theorem while abstracting from their personal features and differences, are the same person.

37  For Hobbes the social contract is a mutual authorization agreement whereby all authorize the sovereign as their agent to exercise whatever powers are needed to enforce the Laws of Nature.

38  In Hobbes all authorize a sovereign to achieve their common interests in peace and prosperity (the background conditions for effectively pursuing their individual interests). Locke calls the state of nature a "natural community" since all recognize and are assumed to have a common interest in the moral Laws of Nature. In Rousseau and Kant, all parties have an interest in freedom and equality. And in Rawls, it is assumed that all have an interest in justice and living with one another on terms of mutual respect.

39  See Rawls, *Collected Papers*, p. 250: "The reason for invoking the concept of a contract in the original position lies in its correspondence with the features of a well-ordered society [which] require, for example, that everyone accepts, and knows that the others accept, the same principles of justice."

40  The centrality of the idea is evident from Rawls's assertion, "The comparative study of well-ordered societies is, I believe, the central

theoretical endeavor of moral theory" ("The Independence of Moral Theory," in Rawls, *Collected Papers*, p. 294).

41 See *TJ*, Section 69. The idea of a well-ordered society occupies a position akin to Kant's Realm of Ends. Cf. Rawls's remarks on Kant's Realm of Ends in his *Collected Papers*, pp. 505–6, 508, 526; also Rawls, *Lectures on the History of Moral Philosophy*, pp. 203–11, 311–13, 321–22.

42 A teleological moral conception, as Rawls defines it (*TJ*, p. 24/21–2 rev.), includes most, but not all, the conceptions more commonly know as "consequentialist." See Samuel Freeman, "Utilitarianism, Deontology, and the Priority of Right," *Philosophy and Public Affairs*, 23, n. 4 (Fall 1994): 313–16 on this topic. See also the contribution by Samuel Scheffler in this volume (Chapter 12).

43 See *TJ*, pp. 177–8/154–5 rev. The publicity condition is introduced at *TJ*, p. 133/115 rev.

44 For this and other reasons, Henry Sidgwick said that the principle of utility may be better satisfied when it is a nonpublic or "esoteric morality." The implication is that people should be misled to believe that some other principle provides standards for right and justice. See Sidgwick, *Methods of Ethics* (7th ed.), pp. 489–90.

45 For a thorough discussion of Rawls's argument from self-respect, see Joshua Cohen, "Democratic Equality," *Ethics* 99 (July 1989): 727–51.

46 See "The Independence of Moral Theory," in Rawls, *Collected Papers*, p. 293.

47 See, "Kantian Constructivism in Moral Theory," in *Collected Papers*, pp. 325–6. See also p. 293, where Rawls indicates a further reason for publicity is that it educates people to the Kantian conception of the person as a "free and equal rational being."

48 For a discussion of Rawls's argument from social union, see Joshua Cohen, "Democratic Equality."

49 Particularly in "Kantian Constructivism in Moral Theory," *Collected Papers*, pp. 303–58.

50 Cf. Kant, *Groundwork of the Metaphysics of Morals*, Ak. 432–3, on the "principle of the autonomy of the will."

51 For detailed discussion of the congruence argument, see Chapter 7 in this volume by Samuel Freeman.

52 See "Kantian Constructivism in Moral Theory," in *Collected Papers*, Chap. 16.

53 See Rawls, *Collected Papers*, Chap. 23, pp. 510–16, for Rawls's account of Kant's moral constructivism; also Rawls, *Lectures in the History of Moral Philosophy*, Chap. VI.

54 See Rawls, *TJ*, Sec. 78, "Autonomy and Objectivity"; also *Collected Papers*, Chap. 16, Lecture III, "Construction and Objectivity," pp. 340–58;

and *Political Liberalism*, Lecture III, "Political Constructivism," pp. 89–129. On Kant's and Rawls's constructivisms, see the contribution by Onora O'Neill in this volume (Chapter 9).

55 See particularly Michael Sandel, *Liberalism and the Limits of Justice*. Rawls denies the influence of communitarian criticisms in *Political Liberalism*, pp. xvii/xix pb. ed., n. 6. See the essay by Stephen Mulhall and Adam Swift in this volume on Rawls and communitarianism (Chapter 13).

56 Rawls, *Collected Papers*, p. 329.

57 "Reasonable" persons or citizens have an effective sense of justice and so desire to abide by fair terms of cooperation. They also recognize a duty of mutual respect and so want to justify their actions and institutions to others on grounds all could reasonably accept. And they recognize the burdens of judgment and accept their consequences. See *Political Liberalism*, pp. 48–9, and 49n.

58 See Rawls, *Collected Papers*, pp. 354 and 356, respectively, for these two claims.

59 See Chapter VII of *Theory*, "Goodness as Rationality."

60 The most noticeable use of the idea of reasonableness is in Rawls's description of the restrictions on rational choice in the original position. See for example, *TJ*, pp. 17–20/14–18 rev.

61 See *Collected Papers*, Chap. 16., pp. 316–17.

62 On this point, see the discussion by Burton Dreben in this volume (Chapter 8).

63 See *Political Liberalism*, pp. 54–8 on the burdens of judgment that account for reasonable disagreement.

64 Two additional features of reasonable persons Rawls mentions are (1) they want to be seen as fully cooperating members of society by others; (2) they have a "reasonable moral psychology." Feature (2) implies reasonable persons are capable of acting for the sake of a conception of justice (*Political Liberalism*, pp. 81–2).

65 Rawls states the general question addressed in *Political Liberalism* in this way: "How is it possible for there to exist over time a just and stable society of free and equal citizens, who remain profoundly divided by reasonable religious, philosophical, and moral doctrines?" (p. 4). In the 1995 preface to the paperback edition Rawls slightly revises the question so that it addresses the possibility of a just society that is "stable for the right reasons." A society in which people were deceived about the bases of society might be stable but not "for the right reasons." On this, see Section II of T.M. Scanlon's contribution to this volume (Chapter 3).

66 On the political conception of the person, see *Political Liberalism*, Lect. I, Sec. 5, pp. 29–35, and Lect. II, "The Powers of Citizens and Their Representation."

67   Some have maintained that there is no realistic likelihood that citizens will ever agree on substantive principles of justice either and advocate a more procedural conception of justice. In effect their arguments deny that a well-ordered society is possible. See the 1994 reviews by Stuart Hampshire and Jeremy Waldron referred to in the bibliography under 'Political Liberalism'.

68   Habermas raises a similar objection in "Reconciliation through the Public Use of Reason," in his *The Inclusion of the Other* (Cambridge, MA: MIT Press, 1999).

69   See Charles Larmore on the idea of public reason in his contribution to this volume (Chapter 10). See also, Section III of T.M. Scanlon on public reason in Chapter 3 of this volume, and Burton Dreben in Chapter 8. My discussion here draws on a fuller discussion of the idea of public reason in my "Deliberative Democracy: A Sympathetic Comment," *Philosophy and Public Affairs* 29 (no. 4. Fall 2000): 371–418 at 396ff.

70   *Political Liberalism*, p. 137. See also *PL*, p. 217. See *PL*, pp. 393–94 (paperback edition) on legitimacy.

71   See *TJ*, Sec. 53, "The Duty to Comply with an Unjust Law." Still Rawls insists on the proper role of civil disobedience and conscientious refusal to respond to injustices in a nearly just society. See *TJ*, Secs. 55–9.

72   Rousseau says of the magistrate that "his own reason ought to be suspect to him, and the only rule he should follow is the public reason." "Discourse on Political Economy," par. 6, in *On the Social Contract and Discourses* (Indianapolis: Hackett, 1983), p. 165. See also Rousseau's reference to "the precepts of public reason" in par. 19, p. 169. For Kant see "What is Enlightenment?" in Immanuel Kant, *Perpetual Peace and Other Essays*, Ted Humphrey, trans. (Indianapolis: Hackett, 1983), p. 42/Ak. VIII: 37. Public reason is contrasted with one's "own reasons" (by Rousseau), with "private reason" (by Kant), and with "nonpublic reasons" (by Rawls).

73   Exploring the relationships between the political values of public reason, the idea of reasonableness, and the democratic conception of citizens is a complicated matter. All that can be done here is to suggest that these ideas are interconnected. This may alleviate some of the commonly expressed concerns that the idea of public reason is too obscure to perform any real service.

74   "The Idea of Public Reason Revisited," in *Collected Papers*, p. 581.

75   Cf. *Political Liberalism*, p. 243nf. for Rawls's discussion of abortion and public reason. I do not mean to imply there is no argument within public reason against abortions. For example, one may argue that all abortions should be prohibited because of a "slippery slope": Namely, even if fetuses are not persons, they are nonetheless a form of human life; and if we start down the path of destroying unborn human life, this

will reduce respect for mature human lives, leading to more killings and greater disrespect for persons. This argument appeals only to political values to justify a strict prohibition on abortion. It may not be a good argument, but it is an admissible one within public reason. Thanks to Sanford Kadish for this example.

76    Rawls, *Collected Papers*, p. 582.

77    Ibid. p. 583. Here Rawls mentions specifically Habermas's discourse conception of legitimacy, as well as Catholic views of the common good, as permissible forms of public reason so long as they are expressed in terms of political values and not in terms of the comprehensive doctrines they are part of. See also *Political Liberalism* (paperback ed.), pp. lii–liii.

78    As Robert Nozick says, democracy is "ownership of the people, by the people, for the people." See pp. 268–71 of his *Anarchy, State and Utopia* for his argument against democracy.

79    On the criterion of reciprocity, see "The Idea of Public Reason Revisited," in Rawls, *Collected Papers*, pp. 578–9.

80    See Kant's essay "Perpetual Peace," in *Perpetual Peace and Other Essays*, trans. Ted Humphrey (Indianapolis: Hackett, 1983), pp. 112–8, 124–5.

81    See Rawls, *The Law of Peoples* (cited as *LP*), pp. 36, 48.

82    For a different reading of the relationship between Rawls and Kant on this issue, see the chapter by Onora O'Neill in this volume (Chapter 9).

83    Rawls's account of a decent society differs in some ways from Avishai Margalit's account in *The Decent Society* (Cambridge, MA: Harvard University Press, 1996). For Margalit the main feature of a decent society is that it "is one in which the institutions do not humiliate people" (p. 1). Margalit also says a decent society's institutions accord respect to those under its authority (p. 3), but, unlike Rawls, he holds that "the concept of a decent society is not necessarily connected with the concept of rights" (ibid., p. 2). Margalit says a decent society may differ from Rawls's account of a just society, which may be humiliating for some (e.g., aliens and the poor) subject to its authority (ibid., pp. 272–81). A crucial omission from Margalit's account of Rawlsian justice is the natural duty of mutual respect, which implies a duty not to humiliate others. See *TJ*, rev. ed., pp. 156, 297, 447.

84    More troublesome is Rawls's suggestion that it is not reasonable for liberal governments even to provide incentives, such as subsidies, to decent regimes to reform their societies. Rawls says it is "more important" that subsidies be used to assist peoples burdened by unfavorable conditions. Here it helps to keep in mind that Rawls is engaged in ideal theory and so is referring to decent well-ordered societies, where people generally

accept the hierarchal system as legitimate and endorse its conception of justice. Under these conditions, incentives to become more liberal are likely to cause resentment within the society of peoples and also compromise the self-determination of nonliberal societies. See *Law of Peoples*, p. 85.

85   Some object to Rawls's duty of noninterference since it seems to imply a duty not to come to the assistance of democratic liberation movements. But the duty of noninterference only prohibits assisting democratic liberation movements in decent hierarchical regimes, not in tyrannical and other indecent regimes. A decent nonliberal society should be deemed capable of the eventual self-imposition of democracy; otherwise, Rawls implies, its members are not likely to sustain democratic rule that is imposed upon them.

86   See Brian Barry, *The Liberal Theory of Justice*, pp. 128–33; Charles Beitz, *Political Theory and International Relations* (Princeton, NJ: Princeton University Press, 1979), pp. 127–69, and Thomas Pogge, "An Egalitarian Law of Peoples," *Philosophy and Public Affairs* 23, n. 3 (Summer 1994).

87   This is the "target" of the duty of assistance; unlike a global distribution principle, it has a cut-off point and no longer applies once a society achieves political autonomy and economic self-sufficiency. In view of the independence and self-determination of a people who take responsibility for their political culture, and for their rate of savings and investment, Rawls sees little justification for a global distribution principle (like the difference principle) that applies continuously without end ( *LP* 117). Citing Japan, Rawls says once unjust political causes are removed and a people achieves independence, its wealth is largely determined by its political culture and industriousness, not its level of natural resources.

88   In earlier drafts of *LP*, Rawls said that the contention that the justification of boundaries must rest in the difference principle begs the issue for its global application.

89   Because *The Law of Peoples* was not near completion when this volume was planned in 1996, an essay on the law of peoples was not commissioned.

90   On political liberalism, see also Sections II and III of Scanlon's chapter in this volume (Chapter 3) containing a discussion of overlapping consensus and public reason, Gutmann's chapter (Chapter 4) on liberalism and democracy (especially Section 6 on public reason), and Section V of Freeman's chapter on overlapping consensus (Chapter 7).

# 1   Rawls and Liberalism

## I

"Liberalism" means different things to different people. The term is currently used in Europe by the left to castigate the right for blind faith in the value of an unfettered market economy and insufficient attention to the importance of state action in realizing the values of equality and social justice. (Sometimes this usage is marked by the variants "neoliberalism" or "ultraliberalism.") In the United States, on the other hand, the term is used by the right to castigate the left for unrealistic attachment to the values of social and economic equality and the too ready use of government power to pursue those ends at the cost of individual freedom and initiative. Thus, American Republicans who condemn the Democrats as bleeding-heart liberals are precisely the sort of people who are condemned as heartless liberals by French Socialists.

Both of these radically opposed pejorative uses have some basis in the broad tradition of liberalism as a group of political movements and political ideas, sharing certain convictions and disagreeing about others. It is a significant fact about our age that most political argument in the Western world now goes on between different branches of that tradition. Its great historical figures are Locke, Rousseau, Constant, Kant, and Mill, and, in our century, its intellectual representatives have included Dewey, Orwell, Hayek, Aron, Hart, Berlin, and many others. With the recent spread of democracy, liberalism has become politically important in countries throughout the world.

Rawls occupies a special place in this tradition. He has explored and developed its philosophical foundations to an unprecedented depth – and thereby transformed the subject of political theory in our time – and he has defended a distinctive, strongly egalitarian view that is at odds with many others in the liberal camp, although he sees it as following the basic ideas of liberalism to their logical conclusion.

One indication of the importance of a political theory is the vehemence with which it is attacked and the need its opponents feel to explain their disagreements and situate themselves in relation to it. Rawls has been attacked relentlessly, and from many directions, because his theory of justice has the kind of real substance that arouses strong disagreement. Though the style of presentation is always accommodating rather than challenging, the views themselves are highly controversial. They do not, for example, represent the main stream of liberal opinion in the United States today.

In brief, what Rawls has done is to combine the very strong principles of social and economic equality associated with European socialism with the equally strong principles of pluralistic toleration and personal freedom associated with American liberalism, and he has done so in a theory that traces them to a common foundation. The result is closer in spirit to European social democracy than to any mainstream American political movement.

Rawls's theory is the latest stage in a long evolution in the content of liberalism that starts from a narrower notion, exemplified by Locke, which focused on personal freedom and political equality. The evolution has been due above all to recognition of the importance of social and economic structures, equally with political and legal institutions, in shaping people's lives and a gradual acceptance of social responsibility for their effects. When the same moral attention was turned on these as had earlier been focused on strictly political institutions and uses of political power, the result was an expansion of the liberal social ideal and a broadened conception of justice. Indeed, the use of the terms "just" and "unjust" to characterize not only individual actions and laws but entire societies and social or economic systems is a relatively recent manifestation of this change of outlook. Rawls's liberalism is the fullest realization we have so far of this conception of the justice of a society taken as a whole whereby all institutions that form part of the basic structure of society have to be assessed by a common standard.

The original impulse of the liberal tradition, found in Locke and Kant, is the idea of the moral sovereignty of each individual. It implies limitations on the ways in which the state can legitimately restrict the liberty of individuals even though it must be granted a monopoly of force in order to serve their collective interests and preserve the peace among them. Freedom of religion, of speech, of association, and of the conduct of private life and the use of private property form the core of the protected liberties. Mill gave a different, rule-utilitarian justification to these limits on the authority of the state over the individual. They have remained central to liberalism through continuing arguments both about their moral foundation and about their proper scope and interpretation.

The other great moral impulse of liberalism, a hostility to the imposition by the state of inequalities of status, overlaps at its point of origin with the protection of liberty since both of them mean that slavery, serfdom, and caste are ruled out. But opposition to inequality extends gradually to more positive requirements such as equal citizenship for all groups, universal suffrage, the right to hold office, the abolition of hereditary political authority – in short, political and legal equality as a general feature of public institutions.

What has led to the development of modern forms of egalitarian liberalism of the kind that Rawls defends is the recognition that a society may impose inequalities of status on its members in many ways other than by making them legally explicit. The entire system of social and economic institutions – partly made possible by laws, such as the laws of contract and property, but really shaped by conventions and patterns that are the sum of countless transactions and choices by individuals acting in this framework over time – offers very unequal life chances and opportunities to different persons, depending on where they are situated in it by fate.

Consciousness of the hereditary inequalities of class led, of course, to other political movements besides liberalism, but it expanded the concerns of liberalism, through a natural extension of the opposition to inequality, from inequality that was deliberately imposed to inequality that was foreseeable and preventable but tolerated. This has led to a great expansion of what liberalism can demand of the state because it is not just a prohibition but a positive requirement – the requirement that the state use its power to prevent certain severe social inequalities from arising or from having their worst effects.

But the egalitarian impulse in liberalism, as opposed to movements farther to the left, has always been strictly tied to the limits on state power imposed by each individual's sovereignty over himself. However much is required of the state in a positive direction to curb the development of deep institutional and structural inequalities, it may not violate the basic rights to liberty of individual citizens when carrying out this charge. Putting these impulses together in a coherent theory is not always easy, and the task has resulted in familiar disagreements within the liberal camp.

Rawls's theory is remarkable for the distance to which he has followed both of these moral impulses and for the way he connects them. Rawls interprets both the protection of pluralism and individual rights and the promotion of socioeconomic equality as expressions of a single value – that of equality in the relations between people through their common political and social institutions. When the basic structure of society deviates from this ideal of equality, we have societally imposed unfairness, hence the name "justice as fairness." A society fails to treat some of its members as equals whether it restricts their freedom of expression or permits them to grow up in poverty.

It is the very strong interpretation he gives to the requirements of justice for all of the basic institutions of society that makes Rawls's liberalism so controversial. It is very different from the liberalism of Mill with its dominant insistence on limits to government action. Mill was aware of the egalitarian appeal of socialism and responded to it in his posthumously published "Chapters on Socialism."[1] His doubts about the economic and psychological viability of a system of that type were of the kind that have persisted and proven valid. But the egalitarian impulse also persisted and eventually had its effect on the development of the liberalism of the welfare state. How extensive that effect will be remains uncertain; the question is very much under current political debate in all broadly liberal regimes.

The other big difference from Mill is that Rawls's account of the individual rights central to liberalism is not instrumental. He does not think they are good because of the results they will bring about; he thinks they are good in themselves. Or rather, he holds that they are principles of right and that the right is prior to the good. The protection of certain mutual relations among free and equal persons, giving each of them a kind of inviolability, is a condition of a just society that cannot, in Rawls's view, be explained by its tendency to promote the general welfare. It is a basic, underived requirement.

This noninstrumental conception of individual rights is also supported by Rawls's rejection of the utilitarian method of aggregating advantages and disadvantages across persons and choosing the system that maximizes the total. The importance for morality of the distinctness of persons also accounts for the special form he gives to the social contract as a foundation for political theory. But the details would take us too far from the topic of this essay.

## II

The relation of Rawls's theory to other views will show up clearly if we examine his two principles of justice in detail. We will then see how his choices among alternatives express a specific moral position and what other positions would have been expressed by other choices. The two principles, in their latest formulation in *Political Liberalism*, are as follows:

> a. Each person has an equal claim to a fully adequate scheme of equal basic rights and liberties, which scheme is compatible with the same scheme for all; and in this scheme the equal political liberties, and only those liberties, are to be guaranteed their fair value.
>
> b. Social and economic inequalities are to satisfy two conditions: first, they are to be attached to positions and offices open to all under conditions of fair equality of opportunity; and second, they are to be to the greatest benefit of the least advantaged members of society.[2]

The first principle (equal rights and liberties) has priority over the second, and the first part of the second principle (fair equality of opportunity) has priority over the second part (the difference principle).

Note that the first principle is a principle of strict equality, and the second a principle of permissible inequality. The first applies roughly to the constitutional structures and guarantees of the political and legal systems, and the second to the operation of the social and economic systems, particularly insofar as they can be affected by tax policies and various approaches to social security, employment, disability compensation, child support, education, medical care, and so forth. The strict priority of individul rights and liberties over the reduction of social and economic inequalities is the true core of liberalism, and it has attracted the scorn of the radical left over a long period. This ideological battle is not over, as we see from the denigration of "Western values" by the latest generation of non-Western despots.

However, the issue of what to include in the required scheme of rights and liberties marks an important division among liberals. There are those who believe that the core rights are connected with the protection of the democratic process and the prevention of political oppression – such rights as freedom of speech, freedom of association, due process of law, the right to vote and hold office, and freedom of religion. On this view, purely personal and cultural liberties, such as those involved in disputes over the legal enforcement of sexual morality or the legality of abortion, do not have the same status. On these issues Rawls's interpretation of the scope of basic rights tends to be broader for reasons having to do with the foundations of those rights and with the ways in which a just society must accept pluralism, reasons that will be discussed below.

On the other hand, there is one significant kind of right that Rawls excludes from the full protection of the first principle, namely, property rights. Those who give significant moral weight to property rights – not just to the right to possess some personal property, which Rawls includes, but significant rights of accumulation and disposition of private property – belong to the libertarian branch of liberalism. Even if strict libertarians are rare, the high valuation of economic freedom is a significant element in the outlook of those who retain a Lockean sympathy for the natural right of individuals to enjoy the fruits of their labor and their gains from other uncoerced economic transactions.

Rawls will have none of this. Entitlement to what one has earned or otherwise legally acquired has a completely different status in his theory from free speech, freedom of worship, or freedom to choose one's employment. Economically significant property rights are valued not as an essential part of individual liberty but as indispensable features of the economic system without which the reliable expectations and security that are essential for long-term planning, investment, production, and capital accumulation would not be possible. Reliance on contract, salary agreements, the payment of dividends, and so forth is economically essential, and it is only the justification of the whole system that provides the moral support for an individual's entitlement to what he earns or otherwise acquires through the actions he and others take in accordance with its rules. What he is entitled to is determined by the rules, and what the rules should be, including the rules of taxation and redistribution, is determined by which overall system would be most just in its results, taken as a whole. In Rawls's theory individual property rights are the consequence, and not the foundation, of the justice of economic institutions. In theories of a libertarian tendency the reverse is the case.

This rejection of economic freedom as a value in itself is one feature of Rawls's view that has attracted opposition along with the closely related rejection of individual desert as a fundamental political value. For the purposes of political theory, at least, Rawls holds that people deserve the product of their efforts only in the sense that if they are entitled to it under the rules of a just system, then they have a legitimate expectation that they will get it. This view is, I think, more uncompromising than would be accepted even by most of those who would describe themselves as liberals. There are certainly those who would maintain that, even preinstitutionally, people deserve what they gain by their own efforts and that this should be allowed to have some effect on the form of a just economic system. That might be expressed by some modification in the interpretation of Rawls's first principle, to admit a measure of economic freedom as a protected right.

If we move now to the second principle, the first thing to observe is that the inclusion of any such principle at all, limiting the inequalities that can be permitted by a just state to arise through the free choices of individuals acting under a regime of adequate and fully protected individual rights and liberties, marks the difference between laissez-faire liberalism and welfare state liberalism. The second principle expresses the recognition that class stratification and the resulting inequality of chances in life are social evils bearing on the justice of a society.

To begin with the first part of the second principle: Equal opportunity has come to be a central tenet of most liberal positions, but it is open to two very different interpretations, negative and positive. Negative equality of opportunity means the absence of barriers to competition for places in the social and economic hierarchy, so that anyone can rise to a position for which he is qualified. This is what

Rawls calls the principle of "careers open to talents." Positive equality of opportunity, or what Rawls calls "fair equality of opportunity," requires more: It requires that everyone, whatever his starting place in life, have the same opportunity to develop his natural talents to the level of which he is capable so that he can compete for a position, when the time comes, without handicaps that are due to a deprived background. The second interpretation, enabling everyone to realize his potentialities, demands much more state action than the first, making sure the doors are open to anyone who qualifies.

Attachment to negative equality of opportunity – condemning the deliberate exclusion of anyone on grounds of race, class, sex, or religion from an equal chance to compete – is now nearly uncontroversial.[3] And to some degree the value of fair or positive equality of opportunity, or equality of chances, is more and more widely recognized. The obligation of an affluent society to ensure access to education through the university level to all who are willing and able to benefit from it and some obligation to see that children receive adequate nourishment and medical care, however poor their parents may be, are accepted by most segments of the political spectrum in broadly liberal societies. The disagreements are over the degree to which inequalities of opportunity ought to be evened out.

Such inequalities cannot be eliminated entirely because differences between families have a big effect on children that state action cannot completely override. But there is room for disagreement over how much has to be done. Some of that disagreement may be due to differences of opinion about how powerful the effect of class is on people's options. Some parties claim that anyone can succeed by hard work, whereas others point out how much more difficult it is if you start at the bottom rather than at the top. But most of the disagreement, I suspect, is due to a difference of moral focus. Those who are inclined to regard the competitive advantages children get from the luck of having been born to prosperous parents as unobjectionable probably focus on the fact that they result from normal and irreproachable family affection. Others, who think those advantages and the corresponding disadvantages of those born poor are unfair, probably focus on the fact that their recipients have done nothing to deserve them.

Still, the debate over the proper form of equal opportunity is much less divisive than that over whether a just society should go beyond this to strive for equality of results. That brings us finally to the second part of the second principle – the difference principle – which is Rawls's most strikingly egalitarian requirement and one of his most contested claims. It says, to repeat, that social and economic inequalities "are to be to the greatest benefit of the least advantaged members of society." One can conceive of an even more egalitarian principle, one which favored greater equality even if it would lower everyone's level of welfare, including that of the worst off. But this does not hold much appeal outside the tradition of utopian socialism and is in any case probably the reflection of something else – the idea that strict equality of possessions would promote a universal level of self-esteem and mutual respect that is impossible in a socially and economically stratified society. That is the appeal of the perennial fantasy of the abolition of all hierarchy. But Rawls's difference principle is still very egalitarian, and it can be contrasted with several alternatives that command support within the spectrum of liberal views.

First there is the view that the only equality required for justice is equality of opportunity and that since the inequalities that arise under a regime of equal opportunity are the result of what people make of their opportunities, they are not unjust. Somewhat more egalitarian is the view that certain forms of misfortune, including disability, serious illness, and particularly low earning capacity due to lack of skills or overwhelming parental responsibilities, should not be allowed to render their victims helpless and destitute. The provision of some kind of social safety net is widely favored to deal with such cases, although there is disagreement over how high the net should be – what level of social minimum it should guarantee. This view is perhaps best interpreted not as a fundamentally egalitarian one but rather as the consequence of something else: the judgment that certain absolute forms of deprivation are particularly bad and that no decent society should tolerate them if it has the resources to prevent them.

Another view that has egalitarian consequences, although it is not fundamentally egalitarian, is utilitarianism, the position that the maximization of total welfare should be a social goal. Destitution seriously brings down the total, and the diminishing marginal utility of resources means that transferring some of them from the rich to the poor, if it can be done without too much loss, will increase total welfare. It seems likely that most support for moderate policies of assistance to the disadvantaged is due to moral positions like these rather than to the much more deeply rooted egalitarianism that Rawls defends.

Rawls's difference principle is based on the intuitively appealing moral judgment that all inequalities in life prospects dealt out to people by the basic structure of society and for which they are not responsible are prima facie unfair; these inequalities can only be justified if the institutions that make up that structure are the most effective available in achieving an egalitarian purpose – that of making the worst-off group in the society as well off as possible. This is an egalitarian aim because it blocks the pursuit of further equality only if that would make everyone worse off.

This may be a radical position, but it should be kept in mind that it applies only to deep structural inequalities that affect statistically large numbers of people in the different social categories. It does not apply to the countless inequalities among individuals that will inevitably arise as people make choices and interact, and succeed or fail in their efforts, in the context of any socioeconomic structure, however just. If the broad structure of society satisfies the principles of justice in its large-scale statistical effects on the life prospects of different groups, then, according to Rawls, any individual inequalities that emerge from its operation will be ipso facto just. That is what he means by calling it a system of pure procedural justice: The broad design of the system confers legitimacy on the specific outcomes, whatever they are.

Nevertheless, the difference principle means that the broad design of the system is supposed to be evaluated by its success in eliminating those inequalities that are not needed to provide maximum benefit to the worst off. And this imperative depends on the moral claim that it is unfair if people suffer or benefit differentially because of differences between them that are not their fault. A society that does not try to reduce such differentials is not just, and that applies whether the differences in question are racial, sexual, or religious or disparities in the fortunes of birth, such as being born rich or poor, or being born with or without unusual natural abilities.

It is this last point, the unfairness of society's systematically rewarding or penalizing people on the basis of their draw in the natural or genetic lottery, that underpins the difference principle. Even under ideal conditions of fair equality of opportunity, such inequalities will arise from the normal operation of a competitive market economy in which there is bidding for scarce productive skills. According Rawls those inequalities are unjust unless supplemental policies ensure that the system works to the maximum benefit of the worst off. People do not deserve their place in the natural lottery any more than they deserve their birthplace in the class structure, and they therefore do not automatically deserve what "naturally" flows from either of those differences.

One other point about the second principle deserves attention: the priority of the first of its conditions over the second. Rawls holds that fair equality of opportunity may not be sacrificed even if this would benefit the worst-off group in a society. It may be difficult to imagine how that might be so, but I mentioned earlier in this section the deviation from equality of opportunity represented by affirmative action, and it is perhaps possible that, even in the absence of the historical legacy of slavery or a caste system, someone might favor an ongoing program of preference in assignment of desirable positions to the less talented, or perhaps some randomization of assignment, in order to prevent the development of a hereditary meritocracy. That kind of reversal of priority between equality of opportunity and equality of results would represent a more radically egalitarian position than Rawls's, and also one that was in a sense more anti-individualistic.

This brief survey of the alternatives shows that in putting forward his two principles of justice, Rawls has not only expressed a distinctive position but provided a framework for identifying the morally crucial differences among a whole range of views on the main questions of social justice. I now want to go more deeply into the justifications for the most controversial features of his view – its pluralism and its egalitarianism.

## III

An important element in Rawls's conception of liberty is the requirement that a just state refrain, so far as possible, from trying to impose on its members a single conception of the ends and meaning of life. This is most straightforward in the requirement of freedom of religion, and Rawls assigns great importance to the historical descent of ideas of toleration from the seventeenth-century wars of religion and their aftermath. But he applies the principle much more widely to cover all deep differences in fundamental conceptions of the good. Toward these, he believes a just society should adopt an attitude of toleration and the expectation of pluralism and should leave people free to pursue their ultimate aims provided they do not interfere with the other requirements of justice.

What this position opposes, in particular, is one or another form of perfectionism based on commitment to a particular contested idea of the ends of life and insistence that it is the proper role of a political community to guide its members in that direction by coercion, education, the exclusion of other options, and control of the cultural environment. Rawls opposes perfectionism not merely because the contest for religious or cultural hegemony has divisive results and is potentially dangerous for all parties. That would be to accept pluralism and toleration as a mere modus vivendi, necessary for practical reasons though falling short of the ideal. Rawls believes, on the contrary, that pluralism and toleration with regard to ultimate ends are conditions of mutual respect between citizens that our sense of justice should lead us to value intrinsically and not instrumentally. In the original position, this ideal receives formal expression through the fact that parties to the hypothetical contract are supposed not to know their own full conception of the good – so they have to choose principles of justice based on a thin, purely formal conception that they know would be consistent with any of the thicker conceptions that might be their actual one. This feature of the veil of ignorance, like not knowing one's race or class background, is required because Rawls holds that equal treatment by the social and political systems of those with different comprehensive values is an important form of fairness.

The distinction between comprehensive values and more narrowly political values is discussed extensively in *Political Liberalism*, and Rawls suggests that in *A Theory of Justice* he failed adequately to attend to this difference.[4] This is a rather subtle matter. I myself think that the aim of making the theory of justice independent of any particular comprehensive view was already implicitly present in the earlier book, though the later discussion is very important in working out how Rawls believes this can coherently be accomplished. In any case, the questions whether it is possible, and if so whether it is desirable, have generated a great deal of attention. Rawls himself points to others in the liberal tradition, such as Kant and Mill, who take it for granted that political liberalism should be derived from a comprehensive moral conception. That outlook still has many adherents. And since Rawls has raised the issue, a number of skeptics have argued that it is impossible to ground a political theory of justice on a much narrower base, as he wishes to do – that the kind of neutrality or abstinence that he requires of us when thinking about justice is unavailable and incapable of sustaining the moral commitment to principles of tolerance and antiperfectionism.[5]

This corresponds to a heated dispute that arises again and again in public debate: Do the typical liberal demands for tolerance and individual liberty with respect to religion, sexual conduct, pornography, abortion, assisted suicide, and so forth really depend on the requirement of state impartiality toward deep and contested personal convictions, or are those demands in reality based on the quite specific contested convictions of those very liberals, convictions which they think it politically inadvisable to invoke directly – religious skepticism, sexual libertinism, and moral endorsement of abortion and assisted suicide? Alternatively, the charge may be that the true basis of all liberal positions is a comprehensive belief that the best thing for each person is to live his life in accordance with his own autonomous choices, whatever they are, and that that is what a just society should make possible so far as it can be managed for people with widely varying preferences and commitments. This is an important issue both theoretically and substantively; the appropriate form of liberal toleration turns on it.

It is true that with respect to any issue of individual rights, such as homosexuality, two very different arguments can be offered on the side of liberty. The first is that there is nothing wrong with homosexuality, so it should not be prohibited. The second is that, whether or not homosexuality is morally wrong, sex is one of those highly personal matters that should not be controlled by a society on the basis of the convictions of a majority of its members. It is also true that many of the people who would be willing to offer the second argument would also endorse the first, and perhaps not many who would reject the first would be persuaded by the second. Still, there is an important point to the appeal by some liberals, in the style of Rawls, to the second, higher-order argument, which belongs specifically to political rather than overall moral theory. Whether or not it actually commands wide acceptance, the second-order argument tries to appeal to a value which all members of a pluralistic liberal society could reasonably accept even if they disagreed fundamentally in their beliefs about sexual morality. It is not the overriding value of individual personal autonomy, which may be rejected by many religious and other comprehensive views. It is the value of mutual respect, which limits the grounds on which we may call on the collective power of the state to force those who do not share our convictions to submit to the will of the majority.

All government, all society, requires that the state must have such power; the issue concerns only its extent and the admissible grounds of its exercise. The way it defines those limits is one of the most important features of any liberal position – what makes it a liberal theory of democracy rather than mere majoritarianism. As we know from the case of Mill, strict limits on both the extent and the admissible direct grounds for the exercise of state power can be defended directly by appeal to the comprehensive value of happiness and individual human flourishing without relying on any principle of second-order impartiality among comprehensive views. *On Liberty* is a powerful rule-utilitarian defense of liberal principles.

But Rawls wants something else – something that is in a way more difficult and perhaps less likely to persuade in real political argument. He wants a justification for liberty and pluralism that does not rely on the individualistic system of values so many liberals share. Political liberalism should be compatible with religious orthodoxy. Rawls wants this because, when it comes to constitutional essentials, it is insufficiently respectful toward those many members of a liberally governed society who do not share those comprehensively individualistic values to justify the institutions under which we all must live, and the rights which those institutions guarantee, by reference to grounds those individuals cannot reasonably be expected to accept. The reach of a justification for constitutional guarantees of individual freedom must be wider than that even if this means its grip will be more precarious.

Rawls identifies the type of argument he has in mind in his extensive discussions of what he calls "public reason" and its relation to the fact of reasonable pluralism. These concepts are very important in *Political Liberalism* and receive their most developed treatment in a still later essay of 1997.[6] The greatest difficulty in defining such a view is to distinguish between those conflicts of value that belong within the domain of public reason and those that do not. Disagreements outside of the public domain, religious disagreements being the clearest example, should so far as possible be avoided when justifying the design of basic social and political institutions. But disagreements within the domain of public reason can be just as fundamental, yet Rawls believes that those who hold the balance of political power need not hesitate to exercise it on the basis of their views on such questions or to impose the result on those with opposite views. This happens all the time in political debate over issues of war and peace, economic policy, taxation, welfare, or environmental protection, for example. So what is the difference?

Rawls emphasizes that public reason is not to be thought of as an effective decision procedure, guaranteed to produce agreement, but rather as a special kind of disagreement, argument, and counterargument, which tries to use mutually recognized methods of evaluation and evidence, whether these produce consensus or not. Even if we are not convinced by an opponent's arguments about distributive justice, for example, we can recognize them as offering grounds that he thinks would be reasonable for us to accept, simply in virtue of the reasoning capacity that we all share. The same cannot be said for appeals to faith or revelation.

Whether an argument constitutes an appeal to public reason is itself likely to be a contested issue (think of the question of the permissibility of abortion). But the concept of public reason is not put forward by Rawls as a mechanical test for the admissibility of arguments but rather as a characterization of what we should be looking for in an admissible ground for the design of basic institutions. In applying the concept there will be higher-order disagreements, just as there are conflicting arguments within the domain of public reason. But the sense of justice should lead us to try, in good faith, to offer to our fellow citizens grounds for the exercise of collective power that we believe they, from their point of view as fellow reasoners, have reason to accept – even if they do not actually do so. To invoke only our private convictions is, according to Rawls, a violation of the requirement of reciprocity that applies to members of a just society.

In addition to these problems of definition there is the big problem of justification. How can we put aside some of our deepest convictions – convictions about the ultimate ends of life – in deciding how our society should be arranged? It can seem like a betrayal of our values to deliberately refuse, if we have the power, to put everyone on what we believe to be the true religious path to salvation, or on the contrary the true secular path of individual autonomy and self-realization, through the design of the political, social, and educational systems. To base political values on something less than our most comprehensive transcendent values can seem both morally wrong and psychologically incoherent. For how can these narrower political values have the leverage to hold in check transcendent religious values, for example – particularly when the latter are concerned not just with my own interests but with what I take to be the most important interests of everyone, and therefore of my fellow citizens, whatever their own convictions may be? The same question arises about individualistic secular values, which would seem to justify political opposition to orthodox religion.

This is a difficult question of moral theory, lying at the foundation of the idea of individual rights and therefore at the foundation of a liberalism based on rights. The central issue is whether a requirement of mutual respect, operating in the context of the exercise of collective power over the individual members of a society, is strong enough to hold in check not only the unlimited pursuit of the self-interest of the majority at the expense of the minority but also the unlimited pursuit of the ostensibly transcendent values of the majority against the will of the minority who do not share them. Skeptics answer that to base our principles of political right and wrong on something less than our full system of values is to accord those values only superficial importance by comparison with an abstract, almost contentless universality.

Rawls's attempt to answer the question by grounding liberal toleration and freedom on principles of right that are prior to conceptions of the good is one of his most significant contributions. The difficulty of the task is considerable, and the suspicion remains on the part of many critics that such views are a kind of liberal camouflage for much more partisan arguments – that the proposed ecumenical appeal of liberalism is hollow. Some of these critics are themselves liberals who believe it is better to defend liberal ideals by appealing to an explicitly liberal conception of the human good.

But I believe Rawls's alternative is a moral idea of the first importance and that it represents a political ideal worth striving for.

Even if it is much harder to explain and defend than a liberalism based straightforwardly on individualistic and utilitarian values, a Rawlsian political liberalism that could be justified even to those of orthodox religious belief who do not share those values would be preferable as a ground for determining the legitimacy of the exercise of power by a state over all its citizens. Rawls has tried to describe a form of liberalism that can claim the allegiance not only of secular individualists and not only as a modus vivendi or second best. I believe he has identified a source of moral conviction and motivation that does not depend on religious skepticism or an ethic of individual autonomy, and that has an important role to play in the justification of liberal democratic institutions.

## IV

The other great source of controversy in Rawls's moral outlook is his strong egalitarianism, exemplified by the difference principle. Not only the principle itself but various of the claims offered in its support have aroused substantial opposition. He qualifies its status somewhat in *Political Liberalism*, saying that it is part of basic justice but not a constitutional essential and that it is much more difficult to ascertain whether it has been realized than is true of the basic liberties; but it remains a very important part of his overall view.

Rawls defends the difference principle most fully in Chapter 2 of *A Theory of Justice*, arguing that it follows intuitively by a kind of analogy from other principles of equality that are less controversial. His main point is that we cannot be content with equality of opportunity. Even the principle of negative equality of opportunity, which excludes deliberate discrimination, depends on the belief that the social system should not assign benefits or disadvantages solely on the basis of differences between people for which they are not responsible and which they have done nothing to deserve. To exclude qualified candidates from a profession because of their race or sex is to penalize them on grounds that are arbitrary in the worst sense, and a society that permits such a thing is unjust.

This is only a first step, however, because people are no more responsible for the socioeconomic status of the family into which they are born than they are for their race or sex. Yet a system which guarantees only negative equality of opportunity permits class inequalities to develop and accumulate without doing anything to counteract the enormous differences they generate in the opportunities for individuals to acquire the training and background needed to develop their abilities and so to compete for formally open positions. Negative equality of opportunity is therefore not full equality of opportunity. It must be supplemented by positive provision of the resources that will permit each potential competitor to develop his natural abilities and therefore to be in a position to take advantage of his opportunities. That is what Rawls means by fair equality of opportunity.

The same reasoning leads him further. Even under a regime of fair equality of opportunity, undeserved inequalities would continue to arise. Fair equality of opportunity, to the extent that it can be realized, guarantees only that persons of equal natural ability will have roughly equal chances to prosper. But people are not equal in natural ability, and their natural or genetic differences will continue to affect the benefits they gain from interaction with the social and economic order. Yet this too is morally arbitrary, for people are no more responsible for their genetic endowment than for their race or the economic status of their parents. Consequently a just society will counter these undeserved differences in benefit to the extent that it can do so without hurting the very people whose arbitrary penalization it is most concerned to rectify, namely, those who come in last in the socioeconomic race. Hence, the difference principle.

Despite the persuasiveness of these analogies, not everyone is convinced that there is anything unfair about people's benefitting differentially from the employment of their own natural abilities even though they have done nothing to deserve those abilities. Even if they have done nothing to deserve it, their genetic makeup is part of their identity, and it can seem like an assault on the independence of persons to say that they have no right to the benefits which flow from that identity, except insofar as this also benefits others. Such reactions have seized on Rawls's striking remark that "the difference principle represents, in effect, an agreement to regard the distribution of natural talents as a common asset and to share in the benefits of this distribution whatever it turns out to be."[7]

The issue identifies a fundamental cleavage in the liberal tradition between those who identify justice with the fight against any kind of undeserved inequalities that the design of the social system can ameliorate and those who believe the scope of justice is narrower – that society is exempt from responsibility for certain forms of "natural" difference, even if they are in a nonpolitical sense unfair. In this more limited conception, a just society should provide a framework, with fair equality of opportunity and a decent social minimum, in which people can rise by their own efforts to the level to which their natural abilities and efforts are able to take them.

The moral significance of the choice between this vision and Rawls's is quite difficult to characterize. Both are interpretations of the vague idea of relations of mutual respect and cooperation among the separate, autonomous individuals that make up a society. We do not own one another and we want to interact on equal or reciprocal terms in some sense. But in Rawls's conception, we should not want the collectively sustained system of which we are all equally members to allow us to reap benefits on the basis of lucky accidents of fate which we do not deserve, at the expense of others less fortunate who also do not deserve their fate. The fact that one's draw in the natural lottery is undeserved communicates itself morally to what flows from it through the operation of the economy. As Rawls says in another memorable formulation, "In justice as fairness, men agree to share one another's fate."[8]

The opposite view is that we retain more independence than this of the claims of others when we enter a society and do not even metaphorically hand ourselves over to it. Just as basic personal freedom remains protected by liberal equality, so does the right to benefit from one's efforts and one's talents. Our responsibility for one another, as fellow members of a society, is substantial but nevertheless definitely limited by our continued independence.

The moral key to Rawls's more expansive position is in the idea that, because of the essential role of the state, the law, and the conventions of property in making possible the extraordinary productivity and accumulations of a modern economy, we bear collective responsibility for the general shape of what results from the sum of individual choices within that framework. We are therefore responsible for large-scale inequalities that would not have arisen in an alternative framework, and if they are morally arbitrary, we have reason to want to alter the system to reduce them. There is simply something repellent about a joint enterprise in which rewards are apportioned in accordance with genetic endowment – unless there is some further instrumental justification for this apportionment, as there is when an inequality satisfies the difference principle.

Among those who would agree with Rawls in accepting society's responsibility for all outcomes that it permits, and not only for those that it produces deliberately, there is still room for disagreement with the strong egalitarianism of the difference principle. The strict priority given to improvements in the situation of the worst off, in preference even to greater individual and aggregate improvements to the situation of those better off, seems unreasonable – particularly to those drawn to utilitarianism. Utilitarians might agree that social inequalities require justification but that they may be justified because they contribute to the general welfare, not just to the benefit of the worst off.

Even those who would admit some priority to the needs of the worse off over the better off – after all, the better off already *have* what the worse off need – may think the difference principle too absolute. It seems to devaluate the interests of the middle class unreasonably to say that a socioeconomic order will always be more just if it sacrifices them to the interests of the lower class. Such doubts are also voiced at the level of the hypothetical contract: it is often questioned whether the parties in the original position would be rational to adopt the maximin strategy of choice, which leads to the choice of the difference principle, as a way of ensuring that the worst possible outcome will be as good as possible. Rawls's strong egalitarianism displays an exceptionally strong aversion to the generation by social institutions of what he regards as undeserved differences.

In addition to the familiar opposition from his right on the grounds that the difference principle is too egalitarian, there is an interesting criticism from the left to the effect that Rawls is too ready to countenance economic inequalities under the difference principle even if they are the result of acquisitive motives on the part of members of the society – motives diametrically opposed to the ideal of equality.[9] The point is that, in a market economy, it is assumed that inequalities in income and wealth will arise as a result of the wage and profit incentives that drive economic activity. The claim that these inequalities are necessary for the benefit of the worst off depends on the assumption that individuals will not be adequately motivated in their roles as participants in the economy without personal incentives that appeal to the purely individualistic desire to accumulate resources for the discretionary use of oneself and one's family. But the question then arises, Can a society be truly just if there is such a gulf between the egalitarianism that determines the design of its institutions and the individualism that motivates its members when they act in the context of those institutions?

The fact that Rawls accepts this division is a mark of his unqualified attachment to the liberal tradition despite his strong institutional egalitarianism. Political theory is one thing; personal morality is another. Justice is conceived as a specifically political virtue, leaving individuals free to live their lives in pursuit of their own aims and commitments, be these hedonistic or puritanical, libertine or devoutly religious. The special demands of equal respect for the interests of all that justice imposes apply to the sphere of collectively sustained institutions, not to personal life. So liberalism involves a division of the moral territory and leaves individuals free to instantiate a great plurality of forms of life, some of them highly self-absorbed, so long as they are compatible with a just basic structure of cooperation.

## V

This division between the personal and the political, and the assignment of justice firmly to the political category, has come to prominence in Rawls's writings after *A Theory of Justice*, culminating in *Political Liberalism*. He has emphasized that justice as fairness is a freestanding political conception partly in response to criticisms of *Theory* alleging that it relied on a conception of the self as an autonomous, unconstrained subject of choice whose good consisted in forming its own preferences and pursuing their satisfaction, whatever they were. While most of those criticisms depended on misinterpretation, including the gross misinterpretation of attributing to Rawls the view that actual persons were like the stripped-down characters in the original position, the criticisms also threw into relief the difficult question of the coherence of a position that makes political values independent of comprehensive values and capable of dominating them in the political sphere, even if they are concerned with the most important things in life such as salvation and self-realization.

One of the important points Rawls has made is that the alternative, of deriving the political order from a particular comprehensive value system, is often supported by nostalgia for a communitarian past that never existed, in which all the members of a society were united in devotion to their common conception of the good: the Christian world of the middle ages – in fantasy. Rawls points out that the maintenance of orthodoxy of that kind has always required oppression because harmonious agreement over fundamental values does not maintain itself naturally. The Inquisition was no accident; the persecution of heretics and apostates is an inevitable part of the attempt to maintain comprehensive unity and to prevent the outbreak of conspicuous dissent. Pluralism, on the contrary, is the natural result of a regime of basic individual rights and freedoms.

It follows that support for the core of liberalism, the guarantee of basic rights, must be compatible with pluralism. Now admittedly, it would be possible to argue for such rights purely instrumentally on the ground that each party in the plurality of comprehensive views has more to lose from the danger of becoming an oppressed minority than it has to gain from the chance of being the controlling majority. Then liberalism would be adopted as a modus vivendi among parties each of which would prefer, if only it were possible, to impose its comprehensive conception on the others. But Rawls favors the more demanding standard that the equal respect for others expressed by recognition of their rights should be valued for itself and that this should be the highest value in the sphere of political institutions, although not in the conduct of personal life.

The importance of liberal rights depends precisely on the fact that there are things people care about more than the political order but with respect to which a plurality of beliefs and commitments is inevitable. The only way to live together on terms of equality with others with whom we disagree fundamentally about the ends of life, in a framework that imposes its basic shape on all our lives, is to adopt principles for the evaluation of the framework that can be accepted by as many of us as possible. Their basis must therefore be compatible with a wide range of reasonable but mutually incompatible comprehensive views.

That means that some comprehensive views are not reasonable because they do not permit their own subordination to the requirement of reciprocity, that is, to the aim of seeking a collectively acceptable basis of cooperation. Fanatical movements which sub-ordinate the individual to the community depend on comprehensive values that are unreasonable in this sense. But Rawls believes that a wide range of views, forming the plurality typical of a free society, are reasonable and can support the common institutional framework. That is what he means by an "overlapping consensus." Overlapping consensus does not mean the derivability of common principles of justice from all the comprehensive views in the pluralistic bouquet but rather the *compatibility* of each of those comprehensive views with a free-standing political conception that will permit them all to coexist.

There are many forms of liberalism, and there will continue to be. And while the liberal tradition is now in the ascendant politi-cally in economically advanced countries and making considerable inroads elsewhere, it continues to be the object of attack not only from apologists for tyranny and fanaticism but from many others who cannot accept its severe restraints on the legitimate use of gov-ernment power – its insistence that the end, however worthy, does not justify the means. Rawls's advocacy of a specific liberal position and his deep exploration of its foundations in ethical and political theory constitute an enduring contribution to this tradition.

ENDNOTES

1   In S. Collini, ed., *On Liberty and Other Writings* (Cambridge, UK: Cam-bridge University Press, 1989).
2   Rawls, *Political Liberalism* (New York: Columbia University Press, 1993), pp. 5–6 (cited as *"PL"* with page numbers).
3   It has been breached by the policy of affirmative action, which is of course highly controversial in liberal societies, but is probably best un-derstood in Rawlsian terms as an attempt at corrective justice – an attempt to rectify the residual consequences of a particularly gross violation in the past of the first principle of equal rights and liber-ties. Affirmative action therefore does not form a part of what Rawls would call "strict compliance theory" or ideal theory, which is what the two principles of justice are supposed to describe. See *A Theory of Jus-tice* (Cambridge, MA: Harvard University Press, 1971/revised ed. 1999), pp. 8–9/7–8 rev.
4   See the introduction to *PL*, pp. xvii–xx, and pp. xix–xxii in *PL*, 1996 paperback edition.

5   See, for example Joseph Raz, "Facing Diversity: The Case of Epistemic Abstinence," *Philosophy & Public Affairs* 19 (1990).

6   "The Idea of Public Reason Revisited," in John Rawls, *Collected Papers*, ed. Samuel Freeman (Cambridge, MA: Harvard University Press, 1999), 573–615.

7   *TJ*, p. 101/87 rev., sentence rewritten.

8   *TJ*, p. 102/88 rev., sentence eliminated.

9   See G.A. Cohen, "Incentives, Inequality, and Community," in *The Tanner Lectures on Human Values*, vol. 13 (1992), Grethe B. Peterson, ed.; "Where the Action Is: On the Site of Distributive Justice," *Philosophy and Public Affairs* 26 (Winter, 1997): 3–30; *If You're an Egalitarian, How Come You're So Rich?* (Cambridge MA: Harvard University Press, 2000), Lectures 8–9.

# 2    For a Democratic Society[1]

## I. JUSTICE AS FAIRNESS

John Rawls's *A Theory of Justice* tells us what justice requires, what a just society should look like, and how justice fits into the overall good of the members of a just society. But it does not tell us much about the politics of a just society: about the processes of public argument, political mobilization, electoral competition, organized movements, legislative decision making, or administration comprised within the politics of a modern democracy. Indeed, neither the term "democracy" nor any of its cognates has an entry in the index to *A Theory of Justice*.[2] The only traditional problem of democracy that receives much sustained attention is the basis of majority rule, which is itself addressed principally in the context of a normative model of legislative decisions with an uncertain relation to actual legislative processes.[3] This relative inattention to democracy – to politics more generally – may leave the impression that Rawls's theory of justice in some way denigrates democracy, perhaps subordinating it to a conception of justice that is defended through philosophical reasoning and is to be implemented by judges and administrators insulated from politics.[4]

So it comes as something of a surprise when Rawls says, in the preface to the first edition of *Theory of Justice*, that his conception of justice as fairness "constitutes the most appropriate moral basis *for a democratic society*."[5] To be sure, the idea that justice as fairness has a particularly intimate democratic connection is prominent from the 1980 *Dewey Lectures* forward.[6] And in the preface to the revised edition of *Theory of Justice* (dated 1990), Rawls says that the "ideas and aims" of justice as fairness are "those of a philosophical conception

86

*for a constitutional democracy* [emphasis added]," which, he hopes, "will seem reasonable and useful, even if not fully convincing, to a wide range of thoughtful political opinions and thereby express an essential part of the common core of the democratic tradition" (p. xi). But while the idea of democracy (more precisely, as we will see, a family of ideas of democracy) is increasingly in evidence in Rawls's work after *Theory of Justice*, it plays an important role there as well, and in discussing Rawls's conception of democracy, I will not give much attention to the shifts in emphasis or to the broader shifts in outlook from *Theory of Justice* to *Political Liberalism*.[7] Though justice as fairness is not a theory of democracy, and says little about the processes of democratic politics, it is a contribution to democratic thought. It argues that a democratic political regime is itself a requirement of justice – and not simply for instrumental reasons. Moreover, the fundamental aim of the conception of justice as fairness is to present principles that provide the most reasonable norms for guiding the political judgments of members of a democratic society in exercising their responsibilities as citizens.

What, then, does Rawls mean when he says that justice as fairness is "for a democratic society"? How precisely does Rawls fit justice and democracy together?

I begin (Section 2) by explaining three ways in which justice as fairness is a conception for a democratic society. The three ways are connected to three ideas of democracy: *a democratic political regime*, which means a political arrangement with rights of participation, elections, and surrounding rights of association and expression designed to make participation informed and effective; *a democratic society*, which means a society whose members are understood in the political culture as free and equal persons; and *deliberative democracy*, which means a political society in which fundamental political argument appeals to reasons suited to cooperation among free and equal persons, and the authorization to exercise collective power traces to such argument. Justice as fairness is "for a democratic society," then, first because it assigns to individuals an equal right to participate and thus requires a democratic regime as a matter of basic justice. Second, it is addressed to a society of equals, and the content of its principles are shaped by that public understanding. Finally, it is intended to guide the political reasoning and judgment of the members of a democratic society in their exercise of their political rights.

In Section 3, I discuss a few central elements of the conception of political democracy in justice as fairness, exploring in particular why political liberties are basic liberties and how the account of political liberties provides a noninstrumental rationale for a democratic regime.

Finally, in Section 4, I engage more directly with the complaint that justice as fairness, though presented as a conception "for a democracy," inappropriately subordinates democracy – more particularly, the value of political autonomy – to a substantive conception of justice: that the requirements of justice narrow the scope of political debate in ways that deprive democracy of much of its significance. After responding to several variants of the criticism, I suggest that it points to an important limitation on the conception of democracy in *Theory of Justice*. In brief, Rawls is insufficiently attentive there to political disagreement. The fact of disagreement among citizens in a democracy – fostered in part by the organization of mass democratic politics as a competition for political power between candidates and parties – need not lead us to the familiar conception of democracy as nothing more than a struggle to advance interests and partisan ideals by winning political power through elections. But once we acknowledge that disagreement about justice is a permanent feature of democratic societies, then we need to draw a crisper distinction between politics even in an idealized modern democracy and the idealized moral argument that Rawls relies on in *Theory of Justice*.[8]

Before discussing the three interpretations of the claim that justice as fairness is "for a democratic society," I want to make three background points about focus and terminology.

1. As to focus, I will not address the issues of relativism that may be suggested by the phrase "for a democratic society." Thus, it might be said that, in telling us what justice requires in a democratic society, Rawls suggests that the content of justice is always determined relative to a society's political culture. So we could ask what the most reasonable conception of justice is for a democracy, for an aristocracy, or for a community with a shared religious outlook, but not simply ask, What does justice require? Suffice it to say here that no such conclusion follows. In asking what the most reasonable conception of justice is for a democratic society, we answer a question of considerable importance: we address a disagreement among people who all accept an understanding of persons as equals but who dispute the

implications of that understanding. In answering this question, we need not also decide whether the understanding of persons as equals is a compelling cultural assumption, or the most reasonable way to regard people, or a truth of religion or morality.

2. I will use the term "justice as fairness" to name a conception of justice that comprises both principles of justice, and an account of how those principles are to be justified.

The first principle of justice says that each person is to have an equal right to the most extensive total system of equal basic liberties compatible with a similar system of liberties for others. This principle requires stringent protections for liberty of thought and conscience; political liberties (rights of participation); liberty of association; liberty and integrity of the person; and rights and liberties associated with the rule of law. The protection of political liberties under the first principle is expressed in the *principle of participation*, according to which "all citizens are to have an equal right to take part in, and determine the outcome of constitutional processes that establish the laws with which they are to comply" (p. 194). Moreover, political liberty is to be assured a *fair value*: chances to hold office and exercise political influence are to be independent of socioeconomic position (pp. 197–99; *PL*, 327–29).

The second principle – a principle of *democratic equality* – states that socioeconomic inequalities are to be arranged so that they meet two conditions: they are to be attached to offices and positions open to all under conditions of *fair equality of opportunity*, which means that people who are equally talented and motivated are to have equal chances to attain desirable positions, so far as this is consistent with maintaining equal basic liberties; and, according to the *difference principle*, the inequalities attaching to those positions are to operate to the greatest benefit of the least advantaged.

Moreover, the first principle has priority over the second. This "priority of liberty" means that justifications for limiting a basic liberty must show how the proposed limit would contribute to strengthening the system of liberties. To better protect religious liberty, then, it is permissible to limit political liberty by restricting the scope of majority rule and establishing a basic right to liberty of conscience: one liberty is restricted to better protect another basic liberty. But it is impermissible to restrict political liberty to improve the material conditions of the least advantaged; for example, it is not permissible to restrict the voting rights of the better off to improve the economic circumstances of the less well off.

As to the justification of principles, in *Theory of Justice* Rawls sought, as he says, to revive the social contract tradition by carrying the idea of the social contract to a "higher order of abstraction" (p. xviii). Underlying the contract is the fundamental idea of a well-ordered society of persons understood as free and equal who cooperate on fair terms as specified by a conception of justice. According to justice as fairness, principles of justice are requirements of fair cooperation among free and equal persons: the social contract of justice as fairness is framed to present such principles.[9] The contract mediates between the abstract ideal of fair cooperation among free and equal persons and substantive principles of justice, it presents the content implicit in that – as we will see – democratic ideal.

More particularly, the contract is made by rational individuals reasoning about how best to advance their interests under conditions of extreme ignorance. And the most reasonable principles of justice for a society of free and equal persons are "the principles that free and rational persons concerned to further their own interests would accept in an initial situation of equality as defining the fundamental terms of their association" (p. 10). But the fundamental idea is that principles of justice present requirements of fair cooperation among free and equal persons. The agreement by rational individuals concerned to advance their own interests under constraints of ignorance models that fundamental idea and expresses its content. Thus, the fact that certain considerations are irrelevant in an argument about which principles of justice characterize fair conditions of cooperation among free and equal persons is modeled by assuming that those persons are ignorant of the irrelevant conditions: we model irrelevance through ignorance (or restrictions on reasons through limits on information). But the social contract idea models an idea about which considerations are irrelevant in arguments for fair principles for free and equal persons that is given before the construction of the original position.[10]

3. Justice as fairness is a *substantive*, not simply a *procedural*, conception of justice.[11] The substance – procedure distinction is not settled, and for the purposes of discussion here, I will stipulate the content of the distinction. In particular, justice as fairness is a substantive conception of justice in that it comprises standards of justice

for assessing not only processes of collective decision making but also the outcomes of those processes. For example, a just basic structure must protect basic personal liberties, including liberty of conscience. Decisions to restrict those liberties are unjust, even if they are made through a democratic process. In assessing the justice of the basic structure, the principles of justice instruct us to consider directly whether the arrangements protect basic liberties, not simply whether abridgements of those liberties were enacted through a democratic process.[12] A proceduralist, in contrast, rejects standards of justice other than requirements of democratic procedure: the proceduralist says that no norms are binding on a democratic process other than those that emerge through that process. So the democratic proceduralist says that justice requires democratic process and (perhaps) that any outcome of an open democratic process is just.

Virtually all leading theories of justice – whether utilitarian, libertarian, or egalitarian – are substantive according to the account I have just stipulated. Variants of democratic proceduralism are more commonly advanced as theories of political legitimacy (as justifications for the exercise of authority), or as statements of a sufficient condition for political obligation, or as interpretations of the American constitution rather than as theories of justice. So it might be said that democratic etiology suffices to make a regulation legitimate law, or to impose obligations to obey, or that the main aim of the Constitution is to ensure democratic procedures of lawmaking. In any case, justice as fairness affirms that judgments of justice are independent of judgments about such etiology. That justice as fairness is substantive will play a large role in the later discussion about whether justice as fairness subordinates democracy to justice.

## 2. JUSTICE AND DEMOCRACY

Rawls's conception of justice as fairness connects ideas of democracy and justice in three ways. The *content* of the most reasonable conception of justice requires a democratic political system; the *foundation* of the principles lies in the idea of a democratic society, understood as a society of equals, and the content of the principles expresses that idea; and the *role* of the principles is to guide the judgments of members of a democratic society by presenting fundamental norms of public political argument suited to their standing as equals (that is, as members of a democratic society). I will consider these in turn.

## 2.1. Content: Constitutional Democracy

Justice as fairness is "for a democracy," in the first place, because the principles of justice require a democratic political regime. Those principles support a democratic constitution, with a representative legislature, universal political rights (including freedom of speech, assembly, and association), and regular elections in which parties that advance different views of the public good compete for office (pp. 195–6). Such a constitution establishes a political procedure that is just inasmuch as it satisfies the principle of participation (part of the first principle) and that is "imperfect" with respect to advancing other requirements of justice: "the constitution satisfies the principles of justice and is best calculated to lead to just and effective legislation" (p. 173).

The principle of participation states that "all citizens are to have an equal right to take part in, and determine the outcome of, constitutional processes that establish the laws with which they are to comply" (p. 194). It signifies that political liberty is among the basic liberties whose equal assignment to all members is required as a matter of justice. But justice as fairness, as a substantive and not simply procedural conception of justice, also requires protections for nonpolitical liberties, fair equality of opportunity, and a fair distribution (as determined by the difference principle). Rawls's idea is that the nonpolitical liberties will be, in some way, entrenched in a constitution (perhaps in a bill of rights) along with the political liberties and not be up for consideration in normal politics: "The first principle of equal liberty is the primary standard for the constitutional convention. Its main requirements are that the fundamental liberties of the person and liberty of conscience and freedom of thought be protected and that the political process as a whole be a just procedure" (pp. 174–5).

The other requirements of justice provide standards for just legislation, and this leads to the idea that a constitution presents a case of *imperfect procedural justice*. Through its substantive principles, justice as fairness provides the basis for assessing legislation, and political institutions established by the constitution must be designed in part with an eye to generating legislation that gets the right answers – for example, legislation that ensures fair opportunity and promotes the interests of the least well-off group. And within institutions so designed, the legislative process itself must be expressly directed, in the first instance, to ensuring justice, as defined by principles set out in advance, and not simply serve as a forum for fair bargaining among organized social interests. But because the standards of justice are independent of the legislative process, and because the process is not guaranteed to meet the standards – even if the participants conscientiously aim to meet it – we have *imperfect procedural justice*: an independent standard, and no assurance that the process will yield the right results (pp. 74–5, 173). When it comes to constitutions, "The best attainable scheme is one of imperfect procedural justice. Nevertheless some schemes have a greater tendency than others to result in unjust laws." So we are to "select from among the procedural arrangements that are both just [as procedures] and feasible those which are most likely to lead to a just and effective legal order" (p. 173). More precisely, our judgments about the justice of constitutions are to reflect our assessments of what would (or could) be chosen at a hypothetical "constitutional stage" after the principles of justice are on hand and with fuller knowledge than in the original position about the historical circumstances of the society to which the principles are being applied – its resources, level of economic development, and political culture (pp. 172–3). Thus, a constitution is just if and only if it is the constitution that would be chosen – or one of the constitutions that could be chosen – by delegates to a constitutional convention who aim to apply the principles of justice in light of the relevant facts about their society.

In selecting a democratic constitution, then, we need to look in two directions: to the justice of political process and to the justice of outcomes that issue from that process. Justice of process is defined by the rights and liberties included in the first principle; justice of outcomes is assessed by reference to the second principle. In assessing the justice of constitutions, these two directions of consideration converge upon constitutional democracy. The case for political democracy is founded in the first instance on the contents of the first principle – both the principle of participation and the requirement of a process that protects other basic liberties. The second principle reinforces the case for political democracy – at least if we suppose that greater equality of political power means a smaller likelihood of class legislation.

But it would be wrong to suppose that the second principle only has that reinforcing role. Democracy comes in many forms, and the second principle might play a more affirmative role in deciding which form of constitutional democracy to adopt. Thus, consider Arend Lijphart's distinction between consensual and majoritarian (Westminster-style) forms of democracy. The idea of consensual democracy is that laws should have the support of broad coalitions, including each of the major groups in the society. So consensual forms are characterized by multiparty arrangements (typically founded on proportional representation) with executive power sharing among the parties, cooperation between the legislative and executive branches, and coordinated representation of interests; in addition, consensual systems have strong federalism, judicial review, relatively rigid constitutions, strong bicameralism, and independent central banks.[13] Majoritarian democracies differ on each of these institutional dimensions. According to Lijphart, these differences in forms of democratic political arrangement are economically and socially consequential: consensual democracies show higher rates of political representation for women, reduced economic inequality, and stronger welfare states.[14]

I do not wish to assess the evidence for these findings, or whether the consequences Lijphart considers are precisely the right ones for evaluating forms of democracy within justice as fairness, or whether the consensual–majoritarian distinction itself is entirely compelling. Lijphart's view is sufficiently clear and plausible to serve as an illustration. Thus, suppose consensual and majoritarian arrangements are both capable of ensuring basic personal and political liberties and that both perform reasonably well at achieving such democratic values as responsiveness, effectiveness, and accountability.[15] Then we might select a more consensual form of democracy (that is, judge that it would be selected in an ideal constitutional convention) because it appears to be more suited to advancing the requirements of fair equality and the difference principle that fall under the second principle. Making this decision requires believing, as Lijphart does, that the correlation of consensualist institutions and more just outcomes is not spurious: that, for example, consensualism and justice are not both products of a solidaristic culture. Moreover, it must be the case that if participants in the constitutional convention believe that adopting consensual democracy would produce a more solidaristic political culture, and that greater solidarity would in turn enable a society to achieve greater benefits for the least advantaged at a smaller cost in inequality, then those participants would choose consensualism. That is, participants in the constitutional stage must not suppose that they are bound to treat the existing political ethos as a parameter and to pick the constitution that best fits that ethos. They treat the political culture as a fact, not as a binding constraint.[16]

When substantive norms of justice – for example, considerations of distributive fairness – are deployed in assessing types of democratic arrangement, one of two impressions may emerge: first, that the rationale for democracy itself is instrumental. But in the case of justice as fairness, that impression is misguided. While the appropriate form of democracy may be partly determined by judgments about how best to advance substantive justice, the rationale for democracy itself lies in the requirements of the first principle of justice. Second, it might be argued that building substantive standards of justice into the design of democratic arrangements represents an objectionable constraint on the scope of democratic self-government. I will come back to this objection in Section 4.

### 2.2. Foundation: Democratic Society

"Democratic" is sometimes used, as in the previous paragraphs, to characterize a form of government. But it is also used to describe a type of society characterized by conditions of equality. When Tocqueville discusses the democratic revolution in his *Democracy in America* and the replacement of an aristocratic by a democratic society, he has in mind a transformation of the social hierarchy characteristic of feudalism into equality of condition and not the emergence of elected government with widespread suffrage rights. In his review of *Democracy in America*, Mill states:

By Democracy, M. de Tocqueville does not, in general, mean any particular form of government. He can conceive a Democracy under an absolute monarch. . . . By Democracy M. de Tocqueville understands equality of conditions, the absence of all aristocracy, whether constituted by political privileges, or by superiority in individual importance and social power. It is towards Democracy in this sense, towards equality between man and man, that he conceives society to be irresistibly travelling.[17]

Whether a democratic society will be complemented by democratic government – or instead by a centralized despotism – is, for Tocqueville, an open question.

In *Theory of Justice*, Rawls uses "democratic" in this second way as describing a kind of society rather than a political regime when he says, for example, that his two principles of justice express the underlying "democratic conception of society as a system of cooperation among equal persons" (p. 336). Elsewhere, he tells us that the principles of justice express an idea of "democracy in judging each other's aims," meaning that members of a just society do not – "for the purposes of justice" – assess the "relative value of one another's way of life" (p. 388). And when he refers to his interpretation of the second principle of justice as "democratic equality," he also (as I explain pp. 17–19) appears to be using "democratic" to describe a society of equals. Two ideas are essential in the characterization of a society as democratic (as a society of equals): first, each member is understood to be entitled to be treated with the same respect (and therefore is to have the same basic rights) regardless of social position; in contrast, an aristocratic society requires equal respect (and equal rights) within social ranks but differential respect (and rights) across ranks.[18] Second, the basis of equality lies, in particular, in the capacity for a sense of justice: we owe equal justice to those who have a minimally sufficient capacity to understand the requirements of mutually beneficial and fair cooperation, grasp their rationale, and follow them in their conduct. So the basis of equality does not lie in a capacity for self-regulation, or in a generic moral capacity, but specifically in the capacity to understand requirements of justice that provide the fundamental standards of public life. And a democratic society is a society of equals whose members are regarded in the political culture as having that capacity.

These two uses of the term "democratic" – to describe a form of society and a form of political regime – are not founded on mere equivocation. The link, in brief, lies in the fact that a democratic political arrangement expresses, in the design of the highest level of political authority, the idea that the members of the society are equal persons. The connections between a democratic society and democratic regime run in both directions.

Thus, once we have the institutions of political democracy, it is natural to regard the members as equal persons with a claim to equal concern and respect when issues of justice arise, that is, natural to endorse the democratic conception of society. It is natural inasmuch as the conception of members as equal persons, entitled to equal concern and respect in matters of justice, is itself suggested by the practices associated with a democratic regime. For those practices entitle individuals – irrespective of class position or place in the distribution of natural assets – to bring their interests and their judgments of justice to bear on authoritative collective decisions. Thus, Rawls describes the principle that "none should benefit from certain undeserved contingencies with deep and long-lasting effects, such as class origin and natural abilities, except in ways that help others" as a "democratic conception." And this conception is "implicit in the basic structure" of a society that satisfies the first principle and a requirement of fair equality of opportunity.[19]

At the same time, once the members of society are regarded as equal moral persons – once we reject the idea of a fixed aristocratic hierarchy of unequal worth and entitlement where "each person is believed to have his allotted station in the natural order of things" (p. 479) – it is natural to conclude that there ought to be widespread suffrage and elected government under conditions of political contestation with protections of the relevant liberties.[20] For the extension of political (and other) liberties expresses the respect owed to persons as equals in their possession of a basic capacity for a sense of justice (and thus supports self-respect, a matter to which I return later). Thus, in his account of the priority of liberty, Rawls contrasts a society in which mutual respect is secured by establishing the rights associated with equal citizenship from a caste or feudal society in which respect is associated with occupying an allotted social station. And he claims that "when the belief in a fixed natural order sanctioning a hierarchical society is abandoned ... a tendency is set up in the direction of the two principals in serial order. The effective protection of the equal liberties becomes increasingly of first importance in support of self-respect and this affirms the precedence of the first principle" (p. 480). So the emergence of a society that is democratic in Tocqueville's sense fosters the emergence of a political democracy with the basic liberties of citizenship secured for all adult members – fosters, at least in this sense: that it provides a forceful rationale for a democratic regime.

One way in which the idea of a democratic society plays a role in justice as fairness is connected to the original position. Rawls presents the justification for the two principles in terms of a rational choice of individuals under constraints of ignorance. But as I noted earlier, the fundamental idea is that certain considerations are not relevant in arguments about principles of justice. And the relevant–irrelevant distinction embodied in the original position draws on the idea of persons as equals that helps to define a democratic society. The constraints on arguments that are captured by the veil of ignorance are not founded on the concept of morality or the concept of justice but on the democratic conception of persons as free and equal. So the model of justification associated with justice as fairness – unanimous agreement in the original position – expresses a form of normative reflection suited to a democratic society.

Consider, too, how justice as fairness's second principle of justice – comprising fair equality of opportunity and the difference principle – represents an idea of "democratic equality" (pp. 65–73). Let's start with the requirement of fair equality, which condemns inequalities of life chances that owe to differences in social class background. To see the rationale for it, begin with the intuitive and relatively uncontroversial idea that no one should be excluded arbitrarily from attaining a socially desirable position to which special benefits attach (or arbitrarily have their chances of attaining that position reduced). How are we to interpret the notion of an arbitrary exclusion or reduction of chances? In a society with equal political rights, differences of class background are understood as arbitrary, irrelevant differences. If they are irrelevant to a person's standing in the sovereign arena of collective decision making, how could they be relevant to opportunities elsewhere?

In the case of the difference principle, we begin from the controversy about the legitimate extent and sources of inequality fueled in particular by the apparent tension between equal standing as citizens with equal political and personal rights and unequal economic standing. We look for guidance in addressing that controversy. And we try to resolve (or at least reduce) the controversy by drawing out certain ideals that might be regarded as implicit in – by providing the best justification for – democratic institutions and practices and the position of equal citizen within those institutions. Those institutions include the rule of law, the ideal of equality before the law, mass democracy with universal rights of suffrage, individual rights of expression, association and assembly, public education, the separation of church and state, and the universal vulnerability to such burdens as taxation. We arrive in particular at the ideal of a society that treats members as equal moral persons, irrespective of differences of class background and natural endowment; that ideal provides a strong rationale for the equal liberties of citizens. It seems plausible then to use this democratic idea of persons – in effect, the idea that in matters subject to collective decision, differences of class background and natural endowment are not relevant – as a basis for addressing the problem of distributive justice. Whether that idea leads us precisely to the difference principle is another matter, but it seems clear that it leads to some form of egalitarian correction of market distributions, as those distributions do reflect the distribution of natural assets.

To see the force of this strategy of argument, contrast it with a more familiar way of defending social and economic norms on the basis of the idea of democracy. Thus, Dahl distinguishes conditions "integral to democratic process" from conditions that are "external but necessary for democratic process."[21] Rights of political speech, for example, are integral to democracy: the failure to provide those rights directly condemns a regime as undemocratic. Limits on socioeconomic inequality are arguably essential but external. With too much economic inequality, citizens are unlikely to have the equal chances for political influence that is an aspect of democratic process. So while the distribution of income and wealth is not itself a feature of the political process, it influences the extent to which that process conforms to democratic principles. Rawls's extension of democratic ideas to guide judgment about distributive justice is different from (though of course not at all inconsistent with) this political–sociological exploration of external but essential conditions. The idea of democratic equality is to use the most compelling justification of democracy to provide guidance for our judgment about issues of justice other than democratic process, not to work out the conditions that are needed to support a stable and fair democratic process. Thus, where the democratic theorist might say that great inequalities undermine fair democratic process, the Rawlsian says that inequalities in conflict with the difference principle are unjust "in a society that already affirms the other parts of the two principles" because the difference principle "extend[s] to the regulation of these [socioeconomic] inequalities the democratic conception already implicit in the basic structure."[22]

## 2.3. Deliberative Democracy

The principles of justice are intended for the use of citizens in a democracy. This third point about justice and democracy is tied to the practical role of political philosophy. Generally speaking, one of the essential roles of political philosophy is to provide practical guidance: "guidance where guidance is needed" (p. 18).[23] Now in a democracy, final political authority lies in the hands of equal citizens. The principles of justice, then, are intended to guide the judgment of citizens – who, as a group, are the ultimate authority in a democracy – on fundamental constitutional questions and on issues of basic justice and set out the terms of public debate on such matters. Disagreement about fair distribution, for example, is a fundamental feature of modern democratic politics, and the second principle is intended to provide guidance for the judgment of citizens on issues of fair distribution.

Lying behind this conception of the intended practical role of the principles is a deliberative conception of democratic politics. To clarify, let us distinguish four conceptions of democracy, each of which offers an account of the point and purpose of the rights of participation, association, and expression; regular elections; accountability; parties; and public debate that we associate with modern democracy. A first view, commonly called "minimalist," is that democracy is a method for peacefully taming the competitive struggle for power (between elites) – in particular, struggle for control over the state – that defines political life in any society. In a democracy, electoral competition between parties replaces factional intrigue and dynastic struggle as the way to determine who controls the power to punish and to extract resources.[24]

A second, less minimalist conception emphasizes that democracy is not simply a matter of electoral competition but requires broad citizen rights to associate, participate, and express (perhaps through organized groups) interests and opinions – conditions that provide a free and fair background for elections. In this "aggregative" conception of democracy, the underlying democratic idea is to ensure that the exercise of power reflects a fair summation of the interests of citizens: that it gives equal consideration to the interests of each.[25]

A third view is that the arrangements of democracy enable a people – a distinct collective agent, with shared history and sentiments – to govern itself by expressing in law and policy its shared commitments. Though this conception may suggest a plebiscitary form of democracy, it might be argued instead that open discussion is needed to explore how best to advance those shared commitments and to choose governors on the basis of their announced programs.[26]

The fourth view – a deliberative conception of democracy – emphasizes the importance of public debate about law and policy but is skeptical about the existence or importance of a shared culture and sentiments in framing public debate.[27] Instead this conception emphasizes the idea that citizens in a democracy are to defend fundamental laws and policies, and thus the exercise of their collective power, by reference to reasons (say, reasons of the common good), perhaps as expressed in a conception of justice; moreover, the content of the relevant reasons (say, the content of the conception of the common good) must be suited to the equality of citizens.[28] The essential point is that, in this fourth conception, public political argument aimed at authorizing the exercise of collective power is an exercise of the common reason of citizens – more particularly, a form of moral argument, framed by reasons, whose content is suited to the idea of a democratic society (a society of equals). Thus, a political opinion is deemed such not simply by its topic (that it is about institutions, laws, and policies) but by its content; it "concerns what advances the good of the body politic as a whole and invokes some criterion for the just division of social advantages" (p. 229).

Although Rawls says little in *Theory of Justice* about democratic process, he seems there to endorse some variant of a deliberative conception (pp. 199–200, 313–18). In justice as fairness, the justice of laws is defined by reference to an idealized legislative process in which representatives aim to enact just laws (pp. 173–4). Rawls does not explain precisely how this idealized legislative process, which is part of the theory of justice, is connected to an actual legislative process in a just society. But it is clear that actual political processes will not adopt just laws, as defined by the ideal process, unless citizens, representatives, and officials aim to enact just laws (p. 317), and, as in the ideal process, jointly explore how best to achieve that aim (p. 315). Thus, representatives "represent their constituents in a substantive sense; they must seek first to pass just and effective legislation, since this is a citizen's first interest in government" (pp. 199–200). Citizens, in turn, judge their representatives in the first instance by reference to principles of justice and only secondarily by how well those representatives represent other interests than the basic interest in assuring justice. An important part of the account of how people acquire an understanding of justice as fairness is that "principles of justice apply to the role of citizen held by all, since everyone, and not only those in public life, is meant to have political views concerning the common good" (p. 413). In presenting justice as fairness, then, Rawls supposes that he is addressing himself to citizens who hold political opinions (ideas of justice and the common good); acknowledge that they, along with officials and parties, have the deliberative responsibility of presenting public arguments at least about fundamental laws and policies by reference to such opinions; and are uncertain about whether their actual views are the most reasonable political opinions. Recognizing their responsibility, they are looking for guidance on how best to understand justice and the common good in a society of equals (pp. 17–18).

In *Theory of Justice*, Rawls assumes this view of democratic politics as an arena of argument rather than a tamed competition for power, fair aggregation of interests, or expression of shared cultural commitments. And he supposes that his task is to articulate the most reasonable view of justice for citizens and officials to use in their political deliberations – a conception of justice that is for a democracy in that it is intended to guide the judgements of citizens in exercising their deliberative responsibility. While it is common for readers to think that Rawls neglects "politics" in presenting justice as fairness, I suspect that at least part of what fuels the complaint is disagreement with the plausibility of this "reason-giving" picture of politics. If you believe that reasoning from principles could play a substantial role in an attractive form of modern democratic politics, then Rawls's presentation and defense of principles is likely to strike you as engaged with the fundamentals of democratic politics. But if you embrace a more conventional minimalist or aggregative view of democracy, then it is likely to strike you as addressed to political morality rather than real politics.

Now Rawls ties this conception of political deliberation to the idea of a well-ordered society in which there is a consensus on principles of political morality and deliberation takes place among people who share that conception. While members of a well-ordered society have diverse conceptions of the good, they share an understanding of justice given by the two principles: in a well-ordered society, "Political argument appeals to this moral consensus" (p. 232). But the idea of political deliberation does not depend on this demanding ideal of consensus. And in his political liberalism, Rawls embraces the deliberative conception of democratic politics while also accepting that, even under the best circumstances we can reasonably hope for, members of a democratic society will disagree with one another about what justice requires.

But even when Rawls describes political deliberation without a shared conception of justice – when, in *Theory* and in *Political Liberalism*, he imagines citizens endorsing different political conceptions of justice and political parties not acting as "mere interest groups" but instead advancing "some conception of the public good" (p. 195) – he still supposes that politics is, in the first instance, a matter of deliberation: of citizens and representatives defending laws and policies by reference to reasons drawn from a conception of justice that they might reasonably expect others to endorse. Putting the expectation of consensus to the side does not make the need for a conception of justice that is, in this third sense, for a democracy any less pressing.

This conception of politics as an arena of argument may strike us as overly idealized and as underestimating the strategic and competitive side of politics. I cannot address this issue here. Suffice to say that justice as fairness is a conception for a democratic society in part because it is offered as a practical guide for citizens who, as ultimate political authority, are assumed to rely in their political judgments on a conception of justice, to be uncertain about what the best conception is, and to take an interest in defending their views by reference to the most reasonable conception for a society of equals.

### 3. DEMOCRATIC GOVERNMENT

I said earlier that Rawls's first principle of justice includes a principle of participation, which states that "all citizens are to have an equal right to take part in, and determine the outcome of constitutional processes that establish the laws with which they are to comply" (p. 194). Ensuring this equal right almost certainly requires some form of democratic process of collective choice. So in justice as fairness, the rationale for democracy is not exclusively instrumental. The case for democracy is based, in part, directly on the content of the first principle and not simply on a judgment made at the constitutional stage about how best to protect personal liberty or advance other requirements of justice. Why, then, are the political liberties so fundamental?

In his discussion of the priority of liberty, Rawls suggests two lines of argument that might be used to identify basic liberties and argue for their priority. The first line of argument turns on the content of certain "fundamental aims" that are commonly ingredient in determinate conceptions of the good; the second turns on our "highest order interests" associated with our moral powers as citizens (pp. 475–6).[29]

Consider first the argument from fundamental aims. Suppose we are deciding between a conception of justice that ensures stringent protection for liberty of conscience and one that does not. The argument from fundamental aims defends the former on the basis of considerations about the contents of the conceptions of the good, and surrounding moral and religious convictions, that we know people commonly to endorse.

Suppose I consider a choice between a conception of justice that does not guarantee liberty of conscience and freedom of worship to all and a conception that does. If I choose one that does not, then whether or not I receive protection will depend on whether I am in the religious majority or religious minority. If I choose one that does, then I am protected either way. Now reasoning under the veil of ignorance, I have no basis for assigning a likelihood to *my* being in the group whose liberties would be protected rather than in the group whose liberties would be suppressed.

But liberty of conscience is required for me to keep the commitments assigned to me by religious or moral convictions, assuming I have them. Thus, if I have a religious outlook, then I will understand that this view assigns to me as adherent certain basic obligations such as to day and manner of worship. And having religious liberties will be required for the fulfillment of those obligations. To be sure I do not know if I have a religious outlook, but I might have one, or I might have a more secular moral outlook that also assigns me fundamental obligations. And that suffices to make liberty of conscience a fundamental primary good and provide a compelling reason for choosing the conception of justice that ensures its protection.

The crucial point is that I am aware that I may well hold a religious or moral view that in effect says to me: these are your basic obligations. The idea that the obligations are fundamental does not depend on my way of endorsing the view (say the intensity or enthusiasm of my endorsement), it is part of the content of the view itself and thus among the things I believe when I believe the view. Believing a religious view, say, is a matter of believing that I have (for the reasons stated by the view) a set of supreme obligations (say, the obligations are assigned by God as supreme lawgiver). So once I believe it, treating it as basic is not optional because believing it includes believing the parts that say or imply that it is basic. And that the fundamental aims are "nonnegotiable" (*PL*, p. 311) is not a psychological thesis but is part of the content of the religious, philosophical, or moral outlook one may find oneself endorsing: "An individual recognizing religious or moral obligations regards them as binding absolutely" (p. 182) because of the content of religious and moral convictions, not the person's attitude towards them. For this reason, "even granting (what may be questioned) that it is more probable than not that one will turn out to belong to the majority (if a majority exists), to gamble [by choosing a principle that does not ensure equal liberty of conscience]...would show that one did not take one's religious or moral convictions seriously...." (p. 181). And that is so even if the gamble brings some other sort of other benefit. Consider choosing a conception of justice that does not assign priority to liberty of conscience but allows a person's religious liberties to be restricted if that person is compensated with material resources. To make that choice, one would have to accept that "all human interests are commensurable" (*PL*, p. 312). But the person who believes the religious or moral view rejects commensurability because the view itself denies that all goods are commensurable.

So if we choose a conception of justice that does not ensure liberty of conscience, we may find ourselves unable to keep the agreement, because it may require that we violate what we judge to be fundamental commitments and obligations. We cannot, therefore, make a good faith agreement to a conception that does not ensure liberty of conscience.

I have stated the argument from within the original position. But the crucial thesis is that liberty of conscience has special importance, which is not an argument made within the original position: that importance is simply given to the parties. For the rest, we can take the argument about rational choice under ignorance and restate it as an argument about the balance of acceptable reasons once we acknowledge the background concern to find principles of fair cooperation suited to free and equal persons. What the argument brings out is that we can only endorse a public conception of justice that does not provide equal liberty of conscience if we are prepared to let *someone* be subject to conditions to which we would not be prepared to subject ourselves: only if we are prepared to have someone be subjected to conditions that we would reasonably regard ourselves as having compelling reasons to reject. This is an unreasonable failure to treat others as equals and can be seen as such directly.

Rawls says that this reasoning for equal liberty of conscience can be "generalized to apply to other freedoms, though not always with the same force" (p. 181). The other freedoms he has in mind include the political liberties. But he leaves unexplained precisely how this reasoning about fundamental aims generalizes. What are the properties that do carry over from this liberty to other cases? Nor does he explain what limits the force of the generalization.[30]

To extend the argument, we need some way to distinguish certain interests as especially important in the way that religious and moral views present interests in fulfilling their own fundamental requirements as of special importance. But the case for including political liberties among the basic liberties cannot turn on the Aristotelian idea that human beings have a political nature (are political animals): that they realize their true good by exercising their sense of justice and participating in making the collective decisions that are binding on them. Appeal to that idea would violate the requirement that the case for a basic liberty not appeal to a particular view of the best human life. For the same reason, it cannot turn on the Rousseauean or

Kantian idea that autonomy is the supreme good and that we achieve a form of autonomy (call it "public autonomy") when we have equal political liberties.

The proposal, then, is to found the importance of the interests not on a person's basic aims, but on an idea about basic moral powers – in particular, the capacity for a sense of justice. There are three elements of this idea as it figures in the case for political liberty as a basic liberty.

First, as to the content of the idea: citizens understood themselves and one another as having two basic powers: (1) the capacity for a sense of justice, understood as the capacity to form and to act on a conception of fair terms of social cooperation and (2) the capacity for a conception of the good, understood as the capacity for powers of reasoning ("deliberative reason") to form, revise, and actively pursue a system of ends and values. Here, I focus only on the first moral power.

Second, as to the basis of this conception of the moral powers, the official view of *Theory of Justice* (see *PL*, p. xlv) is that this conception is part of a moral doctrine and presents an account of what it is to be a moral agent with the capacity to act on moral principles, to constrain the pursuit of those aims by reference to those requirements, and to achieve moral worth by having a settled disposition to act on those requirements. A second account – suggested in *Theory of Justice* and then more fully developed subsequently – says that the basis for the conception of the person, with the two moral powers, is that it articulates the way that we, as members of a democratic society, understand one another when we are considering matters of political and social justice.

So citizens, according to this view, regard one another as free and equal persons by virtue of their possession of these powers. Citizens regard one another as equals in matters of social and political justice, not because we have an equal right to have our interests (well-being) taken into account, or in being of equal intrinsic worth – much less, in having the same natural endowments or interests – but in that we have, to a sufficient degree, the capacity to understand principles of justice, to offer reasons to others in support of them, and to assess the basic institutions within which we live and that shape our aims and identity in light of those principles.

Third, as to the role of the conception of the person and the moral powers, the development of these powers is connected to the good of persons as free and equal members of a democratic society. How this is so, and what precisely the connection is, needs to be explained, and I will come back to it later. Here I want only to emphasize that the conception of ourselves as free and equal by virtue of the possession of the two moral powers shapes our understanding of our good and of what is needed to achieve it. The underlying idea, modeled in the original position, is that we are to reason about justice by reference to the good (the advantage) of individuals conceived as free and equal members of a democratic society who possess the two moral powers, and whose status as such members is founded on their possession of those powers. The claim is not that the liberties are fundamental to advancing human interests under all conditions (though that may be so), but that they are essential to advancing the good of citizens understood as free and equal persons.

This important idea is not clearly stated in *Theory of Justice*, which originally presented the interest in the liberties (and in other primary goods) in terms of what it is rational for individuals to want to pursue their ends without an idea of the person in the background. Thus, Rawls said that primary goods, including personal and political liberties "are things it is rational to want whatever else one wants. Thus given human nature, wanting them is part of being rational" (p. 223). So the idea seemed to be that, whatever our ends are, we will need the primary goods, including the liberties, in a special place of prominence. Constrained to advance those interests rationally under the veil of ignorance, we get the two principles of justice.

In the revised version of *Theory*, the presentation of primary goods generally – and of the liberties in particular – is modified. Thus, the account of primary goods generally, and of the liberties in particular, is now said to "depend on a moral conception of the person that embodies a certain ideal.... Primary goods are now characterized as what persons need in their status as free and equal citizens, and as normal and fully cooperating members of society over a complete life" (p. xiii).[31]

With those three points as background, we come back now to the political liberties. The central idea is that the argument that political liberty is a basic liberty is tied to the account of the moral powers and the conditions required for their development and expression. The argument is complicated, and I want here to focus on just one piece of it, which connects self-respect with the political liberties, which are understood as favorable conditions for exercising the capacity for a sense of justice.[32]

Thus, self-respect is a fundamental good because it is typically a precondition for the pursuit of our aims (p. 386). Furthermore, because self-respect is so important to a person's good, the social basis of self-respect – essentially, respect from others – is also a crucial good.[33] But to appreciate what is required for others to show us respect (and thus required to support self-respect), it is important to understand how people regard one another, namely, as free and equal moral persons who are free and equal by virtue of their possession of the two moral powers. In particular, we regard one another as equals in that we regard one another as having, inter alia, the capacity for a sense of justice: we take "the two moral powers as the necessary and sufficient condition for being counted a full and equal member of society in questions of political justice" (*PL*, p. 302). Having the capacity for a sense of justice – the capacity to understand and act on fair terms of cooperation – is a fundamental basis of equal status. We regard one another as equals in part because we regard one another as having the capacity to assess the justice of the society: to make reasonable judgments about the rights we should have and about a fair distribution of benefits and burdens. So my self-respect is founded in part on my sense of myself as an equal member who shares responsibility for making the fundamental judgments, with final authority, about social and political issues. When others respect me as an equal, they confirm my sense of my own value. But since the possession of the moral power to form and exercise a sense of justice is the basis of equality, they show that respect by acknowledging and protecting my right to bring my sense of justice to bear on public affairs. And among the conditions required for doing so are the political liberties.

Intuitively, then, the idea is that others show respect for me by expressing their willingness to share responsibility on equal terms for making judgments of justice that provide supreme guidance for collective political life – not simply by recognizing me as an equal in some way, or attributing to me some equal rights regardless of the content of those rights, but as an equal with respect to making the final authoritative judgments about collective affairs. Rawls says: "The basis for self-respect in a just society is not . . . one's income share but the publicly affirmed distribution of fundamental rights and liberties. And this distribution being equal, everyone has a similar and secure status when they meet to conduct the common affairs of the wider society. No one is inclined to look beyond the constitutional affirmation of equality for further political ways of securing his status" (p. 477). The reason that "no one is inclined to look" – or perhaps, does not have good reason to look – is that political equality is understood as equal standing *with respect to making authoritative collective decisions* in light of principles of justice, and ensuring equality with respect to making judgments about these fundamental matters is an especially compelling expression of respect.

Thus, "taking part in political life does not make the individual master of himself, but rather gives him an equal voice along with others in settling how basic social conditions are to be arranged" (p. 205). Moreover, because of that equal voice, "everyone has a similar and secure status when they meet to conduct the common affairs of the wider society" (p. 477). "By publicly affirming the basic liberties citizens in a well-ordered society express their mutual respect for one another as reasonable and trustworthy, as well as their recognition of the worth all citizens attach to their way of life" (*PL*, p. 319). Note that the same importance cannot be attributed to an assurance of equality with respect to other rights. Other rights – to liberty of conscience, or personal property, or privacy – do not have the same connection with the development and exercise of the sense of justice (the basis of equality), nor is there the same showing of respect in acknowledging a right to sovereignty over one's own affairs as there is in acknowledging that right as well as a right to an equal share of sovereignty in determining the conduct of common affairs.[34]

On this account of the nature and basis of the political liberties, the political liberties are not exclusively "protective"; that is, their importance to the bearer of political rights is not exhausted by their role in protecting other rights or advancing our interests: "the effect of self-government where equal political rights have their fair value is to enhance the self-esteem and the sense of political competence of the average citizen. His awareness of his own worth developed in the smaller associations of his community is confirmed in the constitution of the whole society" (p. 205). Because of what they enable us to do – namely, bring our sense of justice to bear on the basic structure and fundamental policies – being assured a right to the political liberties affirms our equal standing as sovereign judges and thereby promotes the fundamental good of self-respect.

Moreover, the case for the importance of the political liberties is not founded on a view about the importance of the exercise of those liberties in the best human life. Instead it is founded on the following ideas:

- A person's having self-respect plays an important role in that person's achieving his or her ends.
- Being respected by others as an equal is important to achieving self-respect.
- The capacity for a sense of justice lies at the basis of our claim to be treated as an equal in matters of justice.

The right to political liberties acknowledges our possession of that moral capacity and enables us to develop and exercise it. What is essential is not so much the good that flows to us from the exercise of the liberties as the affirmation of our equality that comes from acknowledging our right to the political liberties. Martin Luther King, Jr., said that the "great glory of American democracy is the right to protest for right" – that citizens are not simply *able* to advance their *interests* but have the *right* to bring their *sense of justice* to bear on matters of common concern.

### 4. TOO LITTLE DEMOCRACY?[35]

Justice as fairness, then, requires a democratic form of government in which the authorization to exercise political power comes from fair processes of collective choice. This conception expresses a democratic idea of society (a society of equals), and it is meant to guide the judgment and public argument of members of a democratic polity, who are assumed to have a sense of justice and to rely on that sense of justice as the supreme standard for public conduct. Although democracy figures in Rawls's view in these three fundamental ways, it might nevertheless be argued that the idea of democracy does not figure with sufficient prominence in justice as fairness and that Rawls assigns an unacceptable priority of justice to democracy.

This concern about the relative importance of justice and democracy, while important, defies easy specification. One way to state the

concern is to say that justice as fairness subordinates actual democratic politics, including the debate that surrounds it, to the results of
an agreement *made by rational agents reasoning under ignorance.*
But this formulation, with its emphasis on rational choice under
ignorance, does not strike me as the best way to express the fundamental concern. Thus, suppose we adopt what Rawls calls "an
ethical variation of the initial situation," according to which justice
is determined by hypothetical agreement; however, the parties are
not assumed to be rational agents aiming to secure their own good
but reasonable persons defending principles by direct appeal to political values – say, values of reciprocity, fairness, and cooperation on
terms of mutual respect (p. 512). Still, the objection might be raised
that this subordinates actual democratic debate to a hypothetical
agreement – although an agreement among reasonable persons, not
simply rational agents. But even this reformulated objection, with its
emphasis on the actual–hypothetical distinction, does not get at the
heart of the concern. Thus, consider the view that justice is not determined by hypothetical agreement but by balancing a set of reasons
that we find intuitively forceful or by appeal to God's law. These, too,
might be found objectionable even with the appeal to hypothetical
agreement removed completely.

The real concern about the subordination of democracy is that
justice as fairness understands actual democratic politics, and the
debate surrounding it, to be guided and restricted by substantive
principles that we arrive at through reasoning that can be conducted
independently of open public argument between and among citizens.
The point is that justice as fairness assigns too large a role to an exercise of philosophical reason and too small a role to public–political
argument in fixing the fundamental political norms in a democracy.
Even in the ideal constitutional and legislative stages, where a just
constitution and just laws are determined, principles of justice are
set out in advance, and the problem of political life might be seen
as the application of those prior principles, whose content is fixed
prior to argument between and among citizens. Actual democratic
politics – as distinct from idealized constitution and lawmaking –
is even more constrained in that political judgments are supposed
to be guided by beliefs about the judgments of the ideal constitution
makers and lawmakers. Thus, Habermas puts the intuitive objection
with considerable force and clarity when he says that citizens

cannot reignite the radical democratic embers of the original position in the civic life of their society, for from their perspective all of the *essential* discourses of legitimation have already taken place within the theory; and they find the results of the theory already sedimented in their constitution. Because the citizens cannot conceive of the constitution as a *project*, the public use of reason does not actually have the significance of a present exercise of political autonomy but merely promotes the nonviolent *preservation of political stability*.[36]

So justice as fairness conceives of democratic political life as ideally guided by substantive principles of justice set out in advance – principles that are said to articulate the (democratic) idea of society as a scheme of fair cooperation among free and equal persons. But why is this an objection? To be sure, a democratic politics founded on (disciplined by? informed by? guided by?) principles might be less exciting than a more creative, contestative, agonistic, open-ended, edgy, ironic, transformative, everything-up-for-grabs political arena. But while no one wishes for insufferably dull politics, the importance of excitement in political life – unlike stock car racing, slam poetry contests, and bungee jumping – is controversial. In any case, we need some way to clarify precisely what the criticism is once we move away from the idea that it is fundamentally about prudential rationality regulating reasonableness, or the grays of hypothetical agreement regulating life's greens.

The idea that a substantive philosophical theory of justice decides too much in advance of real public argument and claims a kind of authority over actual debate might, then, be understood in at least three ways.

- The point might be that because the conception of justice offers "an independent standard of the desired outcome" (p. 174) – a standard of justice that is independent from the decisions arrived at even through an idealized process of democratic collective decision making – it threatens to *subordinate* those decisions to the judgments of a court, or some other "guardian-like" agent that operates independently from the participation and judgments of citizens. Call this the problem of *institutional subordination*: assigning priority to justice may lead to support for undemocratic arrangements as a better way to achieve justice.

- Alternatively, settling fundamental questions in advance might be interpreted not as inviting political guardianship but as *denigrating* the importance of public argument and political participation. Political life would consist not in making the basic judgments and choices about how to live our collective life – about the fundamental rules that govern us – but in implementing a conception of justice that is already fixed. Politics would not involve any real exercise of autonomy, of self-legislation, through an actual choice of basic ideals and arrangements, or a creative act of initiation (of a kind that Hannah Arendt celebrates and that is characteristic of a new constitutional founding) but would simply determine how best to preserve existing arrangements. Thus, Habermas' remark that "the public use of reason does not actually have the significance of a present exercise of political autonomy but merely promotes the nonviolent *preservation of political stability*." Let's call this the problem of *denigration*: with justice fixed prior to and independently of democratic practice, democratic self-government and politics quite generally are left with the task of implementing first principles rather than specifying their content.
- Or the objection might be that a substantive, philosophical conception of justice is founded on a mistrust of citizens, who need to have their judgments confined by strictures set out in advance. But this mistrust, and the associated effort to cabin judgment, is not only ill-founded but incompatible with a basic idea of the theory: that citizens are equals and are entitled to equal political rights in virtue of having a capacity to live together on mutually acceptable terms. If they are capable of reasoning with others and cooperating on terms of mutual respect, it might be said, then why do they need to have their judgment guided by substantive principles fixed in advance?

If the first two concerns can be addressed, then the suspicion about an underlying mistrust has less force. So I focus here on the complaints about subordination and denigration, both of which express the idea that justice as fairness does not give sufficient weight to the value of political autonomy – that it fails to give self-government its due by depriving people of the authority to decide collectively on the fundamental principles that govern them. Eventually, I will want to embrace a version of the claim that justice as fairness, as presented in *Theory of Justice*, lacks an adequate account of democracy – not, however, because it endorses a substantive conception of justice but because it lacks a plausible account of political disagreement.

### Institutional Subordination

The first concern is that a substantive conception of justice, laid out in advance of democratic practice through rational argument, may lead to a preference for an alternative to democracy in which expert judgment – guided by principles of justice and a knowledge of the relevant facts – determines how best to implement the requirements of justice. If justice is truly what matters most – "the first virtue of social institutions" (p. 3), as Rawls famously says – then perhaps we ought to hand the authority to promote justice to its most reliable institutional proponent. To be sure, the most reliable proponent may be a democratic political arrangement in which citizens and representatives, animated by a sense of justice, discern the demands of justice through public deliberation and debate the constitutional and legislative implications of those demands.[37] But surely democratic decisions may turn out to be unjust, that is the result of acknowledging a political-procedure-independent standard of substantive justice, which makes the issues of constitution and legislation both matters of imperfect procedural justice. No procedure can ensure just results.

That a democracy can make unjust decisions does not of course imply that some alternative to democracy is preferable. After all, no procedure is perfect with respect to justice; judges make mistakes – sometimes large, costly, and hard to undo mistakes. Consider an ideal legislative process in which legislators aim to achieve just laws and make their legislative decisions according to principles of justice on which all agree. Even then, limits on knowledge and failures of reasoning and judgment may lead to unjust regulations (pp. 316–17). The same point applies, a fortiori, to any actual (nonideal) political process whether legislative or judicial (at least some constitutional courts operate by simple majority rule). "We are to decide between constitutional arrangements according to how likely it is that they will yield just and effective legislation. A democrat is one who believes that a democratic constitution best meets this criterion." A democrat need not take the silly position that democracy ensures justice. When unjust laws are passed, "there is no reason why a democrat may not oppose the public will by suitable forms of noncompliance, or even as a government official try to circumvent it.... One does not cease to be a democrat unless one thinks that some other form of government would be better and one's efforts are directed to this end" (p. 261).

These observations are strengthened by the fact that a just constitution must, in the first instance, satisfy the requirements of the principle of equal basic liberties, including the principle of participation. Again, "all citizens are to have an equal right to take part in, and determine the outcome of constitutional processes that establish the laws with which they are to comply" (p. 194). So a constitution with rights of participation is itself a requirement of justice. Because democracy cannot permissibly be restricted to achieve greater economic justice, the only requirements of substantive justice that would provide a case for guardianship are the other requirements of the first principle; that is, the requirement of protecting the nonpolitical liberties.[38] I will come back to this later. For now, it suffices to say that the case for institutional subordination is limited by the priority of liberty.

But suppose we agree that a person is a democrat just in case he or she thinks democracy is best from the point of view of justice. Perhaps he thinks that in part because democratic government is more likely than alternatives to yield just and effective legislation. Democrats, thus understood, do not favor replacing democracy with something else. They might endorse Churchill's estimate that democracy is the worst possible form of government, except for all the others. But a democrat, in the sense now under consideration, might also think that we have an *obligation* to comply with collective decisions, even democratic ones, only when those decisions are just. Let us call such a person a *minimal democrat*. Thus, minimal democrats are *democrats* because they do not favor replacing democracy with something else, but they are *minimal* because they do not think that democratic etiology provides any reason to comply with regulations judged to be substantively unjust.

But justice as fairness does not lead to such minimalism. Keep in mind that the choice of a democratic constitution reflects a judgment about how best to meet the requirements of the principle of participation as well as the other requirements of justice. Suppose we judge that a democratic constitution of a certain kind best meets those demands. That it satisfies the principle of participation will be one important part of the case for that conclusion; the case for a democratic constitution is not founded simply on the claim that it helps to promote just legislation. And suppose we recognize that majority rule is an element of a democratic constitution because decisions with support from a majority, made within a democratic constitution and assumed to be animated by a concern with justice, are more likely to advance justice. Now add that we have a natural duty to support and uphold just institutions, in particular, a natural duty "to comply with and do our share in just institutions" (p. 293) – natural because it binds us irrespective of any voluntary acts on our part. Because a democratic constitution is just and some form of majority rule is an essential part of a democratic constitution, we have a duty to comply with laws that issue from majority judgments within democratic arrangements, even when we judge those laws to be infected by some injustice (p. 311). It is, after all, unreasonable to expect only just laws to issue from any political process. When it comes to reasons for compliance, then, as distinct from justice itself, democracy has a certain priority. More precisely, given the justness of a democratic constitution and the natural duty to comply with just institutions, democratic etiology does make a difference to the case for compliance with laws, even when we judge them to be unjust.

Let us return now to the point I made earlier: that justice requires some form of democratic constitution and that the only considerations of sufficient weight to justify restrictions on democratic process are provided by the other liberties covered by the first principle, say, religious liberties. So justice as fairness is compatible with a system of judicial review of legislation. Not, to be sure, with review that implements the second principle of justice but with review of legislation to ensure the satisfaction of the first principle, that is, the appropriate protection of basic liberties. But such review, it might be said, invites judicial guardianship over the people.[39]

This concern about democracy and judicial review raises a large set of important questions that I can only touch on here. For current purposes, four points are essential.

1. Though justice as fairness is compatible with judicial review, its core ideas do not require protection of basic liberties through an unelected court's review of national legislation to test its constitutionality (*PL*, pp. 234–5).[40] Indeed, it is hard to see how any serious theory of justice – least of all a theory that assumes that citizens in a democracy have, and are animated by, a sense of justice – could issue without considerable additional empirical argument in an institutional conclusion of this kind.[41]

To be sure, justice requires the protection of basic personal and political liberties. But those liberties could in principle be suitably protected by a democratic process in which citizens and elected representatives endorse principles of justice and act with self-restraint within the bounds set by those principles.[42] Some citizens may think that a supreme court should have the role of protecting rights because the political process is unlikely to serve as an appropriate "forum of principle" in which considerations of justice are given due attention. They might observe that the normal responsibility of the political process is not to operate as such a forum and perhaps note that politics in settled democracies continues to be organized to a large extent by competing parties with interests in winning election, not in vindicating principles. And they might urge that a court is well-suited to serve as an "exemplar of public reason" (*PL*, p. 235) that educates citizens and legislators about constitutional principles and thus improves the quality of public debate in part because it is not a party to conventional political bargaining and is not organized by competing political organizations.

But the issue is clearly empirical, and the fundamentals of justice as fairness do not force that conclusion. Indeed, the idea that citizens have a sense of justice and are entitled to basic political liberties as a way to bring that sense of justice to bear on collective decisions suggests that normal politics could, in principle at least, work as a forum of principle.

Whether or not majorities abuse their power depends in part – and perhaps ultimately (*PL*, p. 237) – on the substance and strength of their convictions in political morality and not simply on the presence of institutional constraints on their power.

Of course, if the political traditions of a country assign a supreme court with powers of judicial review a special role in protecting liberties, then citizens may become accustomed to it and assume a division of deliberative labor. Democratic politics, they may suppose, is about interest bargaining, whereas the responsibility of courts is to ensure that such bargaining stays within the bounds of a just constitutional frame. Citizens need not be indifferent to the justice of the constitutional frame; indeed it will be hard for a court to play its role if citizens are indifferent: "Liberty lies in the hands of men and women; when it dies there, no constitution, no law, no court can save it.... While it lies there it needs no constitution, no law, no court to save it."[43] Still, citizens might accept a division of deliberative labor and regard the protection of the constitution as typically the work of a special body – perhaps a constitutional court. And once that conception of the division of labor becomes deeply rooted in the political culture, it may be difficult to ensure the protections of basic liberties through normal political processes.[44] But once again, judgments about the best way to protect basic liberties are not a basic feature of justice as fairness with its commitment to the idea that there are substantive requirements of a just, democratic constitution beyond those of fair political process. Majoritarian and constitutional democrats may well agree on what justice requires but disagree on the kinds of institutions that best serve justice.

2. Judicial protections of rights might be justified not only by reference to nonpolitical liberties that fall under the first principle (say, liberty of conscience) but also by reference to the principle of participation itself. Just as liberty of conscience may not be suitably protected even by a fair democratic process, so, too, rights of political participation may not be so protected. Indeed, one of the major justifications for judicial review is that such review is, in John Hart Ely's

phrase, "representation-reinforcing": it works to prevent majorities from eroding the democratic process itself by depriving people of rights to participate, or to speak freely about political issues, or have their interests duly considered in collective decision making. Indeed, constitutional provisions that assign rights to individuals might, as Alexander Meikeljohn argued, best be understood as conferring powers on citizens that enable them to participate as equals in a fair democratic process – best understood, that is, as provisions that establish or constitute popular sovereignty rather than as protections of individuals from government.[45] So if judicial review is, in some circumstances, the best way to protect individual rights, it need not be seen as reflecting any hostility to democracy, or willingness to assign it an objectionably subordinate position, but might rather be seen as founded on a commitment to it, at least insofar as the rights that are protected are connected to the ideal of democratic process.[46]

3. Justice as fairness, with the principle of participation as part of the first principle of justice, does appear to support, not implausibly, a preference, all else being equal, for protecting basic liberties covered by the first principle through political rather than judicial means. Thus, judicial review does impose a restriction of the scope of decisions governed by majority rule processes and for this reason imposes a restriction on the extent of political liberty (p. 200). If majority rule processes *can* afford adequate protection of political and personal liberties, then justice recommends this political method of protection.[47] If majority rule processes do not provide adequate protection, then justice requires restrictions on majoritarian process, though not a perfectly generalized restriction on democracy – only a restriction when it comes to the protection of basic rights from normal political process. It is hard to see how any reasonable democratic political view could find regulations that require religious uniformity unobjectionable simply because they win the support of the majority in a fair political contest.

4. You might suppose that the commitment to a substantive conception of justice with nonpolitical liberties in the first

principle must, in at least some circumstances, lead to a subordination of democracy to guardian judges. After all, suppose that the people – acting as sovereign through a constitutional amendment process and not simply through normal majoritarian means – seek to amend the constitution and deny religious liberty to some group. It might be thought that justice as fairness holds that it would be permissible for a court to override this judgment, whereas a view that assigned democracy and popular authority a more fundamental role would reject this preemption of popular authority. Justice as fairness would almost certainly reject the amendment as unjust. But the institutional implications are much less clear. Perhaps the right thing to say is not that the court is authorized by the constitution to reject the amendment but that, when the people make such a decision, the constitution has broken down: that two of its fundamental elements – assuring popular authority and assuring liberty of conscience – are at war, and that there is no correct answer within the constitution (*PL*, p. 239).[48]

## Denigration

Consider now the second interpretation of the idea that justice as fairness improperly subordinates democracy to a philosophical conception of justice. This second interpretation claims that justice as fairness denigrates the importance of public argument and political participation: that it subordinates citizens to philosophers. For it says that political life consists not in making the basic judgments and choices about how to live our collective life, and what the rules are that we will be required to comply with, but in implementing a conception of justice whose content is fixed in advance by philosophical reasoning. So in the ideal society of justice as fairness, politics would not, the objection says, involve any real exercise of *political autonomy*. We are politically autonomous when we give ourselves our basic ideals and arrangements. The great moments of political autonomy are the moments of real constitution making. But in the ideal society of justice as fairness, politics would consist simply in determining how best to preserve existing arrangements (assumed to be just) and applying principles determined through an exercise of reason. "The idea of right and just constitutions and basic laws is always ascertained by the most reasonable political conception of justice and not by the result of an actual political process" (*PL*, p. 233).

1. A first response is simply to observe that if this objection comes from a *democratic proceduralist*, then it is deeply misleading. According to the democratic proceduralist, justice requires a fair democratic process but imposes no further constraints on outcomes than that they issue from that process. But the requirement of a fair democratic process itself imposes constraints on politics. Thus, suppose that we say that outcomes are justified if and only if they can be traced to a the fair democratic process. And suppose now that the result of such a process is a series of laws that, if enacted, would unambiguously eliminate the fair democratic process by depriving some group of people of its participation rights or by punishing the advocacy of dissenting political views. Suppose, in short, that democracy, as understood by the democratic proceduralist, kills democracy.

Democratic proceduralists might respond in either of two ways. First, they might object to the regulations and insist that the fundamentals of the fair democratic process be maintained. But a democratic proceduralist who responds this way acknowledges that some norms – those associated with fair democratic procedure – are fixed prior to actual democratic politics. Even the proceduralist, should he or she follow this first track, invokes a standard independent of the outcomes of the democratic process that can be used to rebuke and revoke the results of that process. So the problem cannot be the bare fact of setting such conditions.

Certainly Dahl's democratic proceduralism is of this kind.[49] It is not a majoritarian theory of justice or of legitimacy according to which justice or legitimacy is determined by the judgments of the majority but holds instead that justice requires the equal consideration of interests and that equal consideration demands a fair, democratic process. But if that process produces laws that are incompatible with equal consideration, then the results are unjust and fair process should be preserved.

The second line of response is for the democratic proceduralist to argue that the decision to undermine democracy is legitimate because of its own fair, democratic etiology. If so, it is hard to see how the democratic proceduralist can object to a substantive account of justice on grounds of its denigration of the importance of democracy or political autonomy inasmuch as the proceduralist himself is committed to preserving democracy and political autonomy themselves only if they have the de facto support of a majority.

2. Suppose the democratic proceduralist responds along the first track and thus permits constraints on political decisions when those decisions would undermine democratic process but rejects any other substantive constraints. Then we need to ask about the basis for this distinction, the rationale for drawing such a sharp procedure–substance distinction. One rationale might be to emphasize the importance of the value of collective self-regulation: the fundamental idea that the only legitimate source of law is the collective judgments of a people imposing laws on itself. But appeal to the value of collective self-regulation will not support the intended procedure–substance distinction for reasons suggested in the *fundamental aims* argument for basic liberties.[50]

To see why, consider the importance assigned by equal citizens to basic religious and moral requirements. Given that importance, how could there be *collective* authorization of a regulation that restricts basic religious liberty – authorization by the people as a collectivity of equal members – or collective authorization of a constitutional permission to adopt such regulation? To be sure, a majority, concerned with its group interests, might authorize such a regulation. But that observation simply forces restatement of the question: How could there be collective authorization of an arrangement that empowers a majority to adopt such a regulation? Suppose we interpret the idea of collective authorization as requiring that regulations be backed by appropriate reasons, which is a fundamental notion in a deliberative conception of democracy. And suppose we say that appropriate reasons are those that (very roughly) we can reasonably expect to be acknowledged as acceptable by those to whom the regulations apply (equal members of the political society). Then, no collective authorization of such a regulation is possible because the reasons are bound to be rejected as of insufficient weight given the importance of religious and other moral requirements within the views of those who endorse them.[51] If this is right, then the idea of collective self-regulation carries substantive as well as procedural commitments.[52]

So the argument for drawing a procedure–substance distinction of a kind that only allows constraints on democratic decisions if those constraints can be seen as required to preserve fair democratic process cannot appeal to the value of collective self-regulation – to the principle that a people can be subject to laws if and only if it imposes those laws on itself. For that idea, plausibly understood, does not support democratic proceduralism but a more substantive conception of democracy and political right.

3. The denigration objection suggests that the content of justice is "already fixed" – that it is given prior to political argument – and that politics simply implements prior principles and ensures the stability of just arrangements settled in advance. But this complaint is misleading in at least two ways. In the first place, suppose we interpret "fixed in advance" to mean that, prior to actual politics, citizens have a clear grasp of the requirements of justice and of the rationale for those requirements. The problem with the objection, thus interpreted, is that Rawls presents us with an account of moral learning – about the acquisition of principles of justice – which says that we come to understand the requirements of justice in part by holding the position of equal citizen and by participating in political argument in a society of equals. In particular, we acquire a morality of principles – a direct commitment to principles of justice and desire to be a just person – after first acquiring a morality of association, where the relevant association is the political society comprising equal citizens.

[T]he morality of association quite naturally leads up to a knowledge of the standards of justice. In a well-ordered society anyway not only do those standards define the public conception of justice, but citizens who take an interest in political affairs, and those holding legislative and judicial and other similar offices, are constantly required to apply and to interpret them. They often have to take up the point of view of others, not simply with the aim of working out what they will want and probably do, but for the purpose of striking a reasonable balance between competing claims and for adjusting the various subordinate ideals of the morality of association. To put the principles of justice into practice requires that we adopt the standpoints defined by the four-stage sequence. . . . Eventually one achieves a mastery of these principles and understands the values which they secure and the way in which they are to everyone's advantage. (p. 414)

Thus, one natural interpretation of the claim that principles of justice are given in advance and simply implemented through political participation makes the claim simply false. Politics is understood as in part a process of learning through which the principles and the political values of equality and liberty they articulate are acquired and mastered.

But these observations and suggestions about the acquisition of principles of justice may actually serve to underscore the force of a second interpretation of the objection. Thus, it might be said that, while the principles are mastered in part through political association, their content is given in advance. The content of the principles and the basic structure that satisfies them are given to us, and our role as citizens is simply to internalize the content and preserve the basic structure intact. But our political autonomy is limited by the fact that the content of the principles and corresponding basic structure are given in advance, and not actually chosen by us.

4. The objection just stated seems flawed for two reasons. First, let us suppose – with Rawls – that the institutions of constitutional democracy are just, and let us suppose too that those institutions already exist. Still, their persistence is not guaranteed but requires the work of the current generation. Their reproduction depends on us. Now suppose we reproduce the institutions of constitutional democracy – by complying with the requirements they set on us and supporting them in other ways – because we believe that those institutions are just. Then in at least one sense, we are fully politically autonomous: we give ourselves the institutions that govern us, not, to be sure, by creating those institutions but by sustaining them in light of our own judgments of political morality. Once more, it is worth noting that parallel with the way this issue arises for a democratic proceduralist. Assume that fair democratic procedures already exist. Then citizens cannot choose their own institutions, but they can preserve them for good reasons. So if there is a limit on political autonomy (and I am not sure why there is), it applies with equal force for both views: the substantive view of justice and the democratic proceduralist conception. If there is a limit, it comes from circumstances and not from the content of the view of justice – not, in particular, from its being a substantive conception of justice.

Still, it might be said that, while the institutions persist because we sustain them, in light of our commitment to principles of justice, and to that extent the institutions are not simply given to us, the principles themselves are given to us. Their content is fixed by a philosophical theory and more particularly by their being chosen in a hypothetical original position. But suppose now we accept for the sake of argument both that the principles would be chosen in the original position and that the original position represents a natural way to capture an idea that we already embrace of constraints on arguments for principles of justice *for a democratic society*. Then why should the availability of a good argument for the principles – a compelling case, let us assume, for the conclusion that they are the best articulation of the relevant considerations and restrictions on arguments – lead us to think that our political autonomy is compromised when we act on them? To be sure, we do not give the principles to ourselves in the sense of making the principles up, endorsing them through an act of radical, ungrounded choice, or discovering them for the first time. But the principles are founded on a view of persons as free and equal, and that view is expressed in democratic practices.

Suppose, then, that we follow the argument for the substantive principles and understand the reasons for endorsing them – in particular, that they articulate the idea of a fair system of cooperation among free and equal persons. Then why do we face any restriction on autonomy when we follow the principles? We understand the reasons for the principles, accept them in light of those reasons, and reproduce the institutions because we accept the principles. How could the possibility of presenting the argument as a matter of what people who are free and equal would choose under hypothetical conditions suggest limits on political autonomy once we see the hypothetical choice argument simply as a way to express conditions on arguments for principles addressed to persons thus understood? It is not as though actual persons are being constrained by hypothetical decisions; instead, actual persons are being guided by their own reflective views about reasonable conditions on principles of justice, which are then worked up into an argument for principles through the original position. My autonomy is not restricted, as a general rule, if I act on conclusions that I understand to follow from premises I accept (my autonomy is not limited if I use Bayes's theorem as a constraint on my degrees of belief given that I accept axioms of probability theory). Of course, the principles may not be well supported, but that is a different order of objection. If they are well supported, then concerns about restrictions on political autonomy have uncertain force.

These observations leave vast issues about self-government unresolved. In particular, how can a person, even in a well-ordered society with consensus on substantive principles of justice, be politically autonomous when he or she believes that the laws in force (even elements of the constitution) are not justified by principles on which there is broad agreement and which express democratic ideas of equality? But this question emerges with equal force for a proceduralist view of democracy or justice because there will always be disagreements both about laws and about whether the actual form of democracy in place is the form best suited to ensuring self-government. Moreover, the adherent to the substantive principles can argue that an open democratic process that subjects decision makers to the "full blast of sundry opinions and interest articulations in the society" helps to give us confidence that the laws in force (including the constitution) are among those that could have been adopted in an idealized constitutional or legislative setting.[53] Once more, the absence of actual choice seems not to denigrate democratic self-government.

5. Finally, the denigration objection supposes that justice as fairness reduces political decision making to the implementation of principles given in advance. But this complaint is misguided. To be sure, justice as fairness includes principles of justice that are meant to guide the political judgments of citizens, and in this respect it has a different ambition from democratic proceduralism. Democratic proceduralism presents an account of legitimate collective decision making but does not itself offer any guidance for the judgments of citizens acting within that framework. They may be guided by individual or group interests, or (presumably) by moral or religious views, but nothing in democratic proceduralism corresponds to the conception of democratic equality in justice as fairness.

But the availability of substantive principles of justice does not eliminate political disagreement or the need for political debate and judgment, even if we assume that all citizens embrace the same substantive principles. For example, in applying the difference principle, citizens must already have decided how much to save, and the just savings principle does not dictate a particular savings rate. So disagreements about the extent of obligations to future generations are bound to emerge and inform debates about the requirements of

intragenerational justice as given by the difference principle. Moreover, many political issues do not raise questions of justice as understood within justice as fairness (for example, lots of issues about
environmental protection do not). And when issues of justice are
not in view, there are no prior principles to implement and we have
a politics of interests and values.

Furthermore, the application of the principles of justice themselves calls for judgment, for example, about the kind of constitution
that best ensures the protection of political and personal liberties,
about whether a proposed law infringes too deeply on a fundamental
liberty, or about when efforts to ensure fair equality of opportunity
have gone too far. Consider current debate in the United States about
campaign finance. Translated into the terms of justice as fairness, the
disagreement is about whether and how to restrict a liberty protected
by the first principle – the right to political speech – to ensure the
fair value for political liberty which is also required by the first principle. Adherents of justice as fairness may disagree about the proper
balance[54] as they disagree about every major substantive political
question that has been debated over the past generation in the United
States, including abortion, affirmative action, tax reform, campaign
finance, health care, educational choice and finance, market regulation, and welfare reform. Justice as fairness does not foreclose argument on these issues but proposes terms on which they are to be
debated.[55]

In this respect, justice as fairness is like every other plausible
theory of justice. Millians argue about whether the harm principle
permits regulations of pornography and hate speech, and libertarian
democrats argue about which kinds of education are, to a sufficiently
high degree, public goods to warrant tax support.[56] The availability
of principles to guide judgment does not eliminate the need for judgment and therefore does not eliminate the disagreements that result
when there are (as there often are) conscientious differences of political judgment among people who embrace the same fundamental
principles. Nor does reasonable disagreement among sincere adherents show any failure of principles or reveal their vacuousness. Instead it shows how political principles always operate: they provide a
shared, public terrain of reasoning, that enables mutually respecting
parties to explore their disagreements. Neither apparent nor actual
indeterminacies imply nihilism.

*But ...*

Still, the well-ordered society of justice as fairness is missing something that we associate with democratic politics.[57] And this absence owes, I believe, to the assumption that, in the well-ordered society of justice as fairness, everyone endorses the same conception of justice. "The original position is so characterized that unanimity is possible.... Moreover, the same will hold for the considered judgments of citizens of a well-ordered society effectively regulated by the principles of justice. Everyone has a similar sense of justice and in this respect a well-ordered society is homogeneous. Political argument appeals to this moral consensus" (p. 232). As Rousseau might say, the political society Rawls contemplates in *Theory of Justice* has a determinate general will whose content is given by the principles of justice. Even in *Political Liberalism*, where pluralism about moral, religious, and philosophical doctrines is taken to be a fundamental feature of a democratic society, Rawls seemed to be holding out the prospect of a consensus on a (political) conception of justice among adherents of different comprehensive outlooks (*PL*, p. 35). I say "seemed" because the introduction to the final edition emphasizes that democracies include a plurality of reasonable liberal political conceptions of justice, as well as a plurality of comprehensive doctrines and that social unity and stability cannot be achieved, as a practical matter, through agreement on any specific conception of justice.[58]

Because a well-ordered society is homogeneous in its understanding of justice, democratic politics excludes argument over fundamentals – excludes not by banning such argument (nothing absurd is being said) but by idealizing it away. Thus, suppose we say with Rawls that "it is a political convention of a democratic society to appeal to the common interest" (p. 280). The difference principle gives one specification of the content of this convention, one particular account of when inequalities work to the common advantage: "Since it is impossible to maximize with respect to more than one point of view, it is natural, given the ethos of a democratic society, to single out that of the least advantaged and to further their long-term prospects..." (pp. 280–1). Let us suppose that this account is right. Still, citizens, representatives, and parties can, consistent with endorsing the fundamentals of a democratic constitution, embrace alternative views about how best to understand that convention. If we endorse justice as fairness, we are bound to think that their reasoning is flawed. Nevertheless, other views – for example, "mixed" conceptions of justice that set an acceptable minimum but do not require maximizing the minimum – are not simply unreasonable (pp. 309–10). We can expect such alternatives to flourish in a democratic society and to "compete with one another" (*PL*, p. xlviii). Thus Rawls says that the competing political parties in a constitutional democracy "must advance some conception of the public good" (p. 195). But in a well-functioning democracy we expect different parties to advance different conceptions and not simply different policies animated by a single outlook. We want to see justice enacted and hope that all the major parties are committed to upholding a just constitution. Still, organized debate between competing parties on competing ideas of justice both expresses disagreements among citizens and enables them to fulfill their deliberative responsibilities by presenting reasonable alternatives.[59] Such debate seems to be part of a well-functioning democracy and not a sign of democratic failing.

If we ask what the roots of the problem are in the assumption of unanimity on a conception of justice in a well-ordered society, it is instructive to note what Rawls says in defense of this assumption. Thus, immediately after the passage in which he says that "political argument appeals to this moral consensus," he wonders whether this "assumption of unanimity" is founded on a specifically idealist political philosophy. Rejecting that claim, he notes that the utilitarian philosophies of Hume and Smith, and not simply the idealist views of Kant and Hegel, include the suggestion that "there exists some appropriate perspective from which unanimity on moral questions may be hoped for, at least among rational persons with relevantly similar and sufficient information" (p. 233). And he goes on to say that "the idea of unanimity among rational persons is implicit *throughout the tradition of moral philosophy* [emphasis added]." The ideal of political unanimity on a conception of justice is appropriate, then, because moral thought typically brings with it an expectation of unanimity – at least under idealized conditions of reflection.

But politics and morality are different: moral thought is concerned in part with what *I* should do in a world in which other people do not see eye to eye with me, but democratic politics is concerned with what *we* should do when we do not see eye to eye with one another. As Rawls has argued in *Political Liberalism*, we cannot reasonably demand or even expect a single moral philosophy or doctrine to be embraced by citizens in a democratic society even if we think that some specific view would be endorsed by all under idealized conditions. So it is a mistake to defend the plausibility of an assumption of political unanimity by pointing to the role of expectations of unanimity within moral thought. And once we give up on the expectation of moral unanimity in a democracy, we should also give up on the expectation of political unanimity. It is unreasonable to expect all members to accept the same conception of justice and arguably a virtue of democratic politics that they disagree.

Justice as fairness may be the most reasonable conception of justice for a democratic society. But we cannot expect the most reasonable democratic society to be founded on an agreement about justice. So how might the most reasonable conception of justice be achieved in the most reasonable form of democracy? That question remains open.

ENDNOTES

1  I wish to thank Samuel Freeman for his nearly infinite patience, Tim Scanlon for puzzling with me on and off for several years about what Rawls meant in saying that his theory of justice is "for a democratic society," Oliver Gerstenberg for comments on an earlier draft, and students in my political philosophy seminar during the Spring of 2000 for their comments and questions about earlier versions of this material.

2  Unlike *Justice as Fairness: A Restatement*, ed. Erin Kelly (Cambridge, MA: Harvard University Press, 2001), which has many entries under "democracy," "democratic regime," and "democratic society." The same is true for "citizen," which is not in the index to *Theory of Justice*, but many references to the term appear in *Justice as Fairness* (hereafter *JF*).

3  *Theory of Justice*, revised edition (Cambridge, MA: Harvard University Press, 1999), pp. 313–18. Hereafter, all references to *Theory of Justice* will be included parenthetically in the text and will refer to the revised edition.

4  I associate this important objection with, among others, Michael Walzer, Sheldon Wolin, Benjamin Barber, and Bonnie Honig. But I also hear it, in more intuitive form, from students and colleagues in political

science, and have tried to respond here to the intuitive concern rather than to its theoretical articulation.

5    *Theory of Justice* (Cambridge, MA: Harvard University Press, 1971), p. xviii (emphasis added).

6    In *Collected Papers*, ed. Samuel Freeman (Cambridge, MA: Harvard University Press, 1999), pp. 303–58, esp. 305–7 (hereafter *CP*).

7    *Political Liberalism* (New York: Columbia University Press, 1996). Hereafter, references will be included parenthically in the text, with *PL*. For discussion of the shifts in outlook, see Joshua Cohen, "A More Democratic Liberalism," *Michigan Law Review* 92, 6 (May 1994): 1503–46. Of all the early commentators on *Theory of Justice*, H.L.A. Hart seems to have best understood the democratic background of *Theory of Justice*. Though Hart overstates the importance of an ideal of active participation, he rightly emphasizes the central role in Rawls's view of a conception of democracy. See "Rawls on Liberty and Its Priority" in *Reading Rawls*, ed. Norman Daniels (Stanford: Stanford University Press, 1989), p. 252.

8    Rawls appears to endorse this view in the final edition of *Political Liberalism*, but without developing the implications for the ideal of democracy. See *PL*, xlviii–xlix.

9    I emphasize: not simply principles of fair cooperation among individuals with conflicting interests and values but fair cooperation among persons understood as free and equal. See *TJ*, pp. 11–13. In *JF* (p. 7), this characterization of persons as free and equal is connected to a "democratic conception of justice" founded of how citizens are conceived in a democratic society.

10   It is worth noting that the relevant–irrelevant distinction does not lead us, without further argument, to the idea of justification via prudential-rational choice under ignorance. We could do without a contract altogether and simply assess principles by reflecting on which conception of justice is best supported by the balance of relevant considerations. But even if we model the problem of deliberation among alternative conceptions of justice as a problem of agreement under ignorance, we could simply think of the parties as reasoning under ignorance about irrelevant considerations. But not all ethical norms are irrelevant. So, for example, it is not intuitively irrelevant in assessing a principle of justice that it would permit people to benefit from undeserved assets; awareness of this principle, then, is not excluded simply by the assumption that parties are ignorant about irrelevant considerations. Modeling irrelevance through ignorance does not, then, lead to the original position model of rational choice under ignorance but is fully compatible

with a model of ethical reasoning in the initial situation. See Rawls's remarks on "ethical variations of the initial situation" (p. 512).

11  Joshua Cohen, "Pluralism and Proceduralism," *Chicago-Kent Law Review* 69 (1994).

12  For the sake of simplicity of statement, I am assuming here that we can identify the "democraticness" of the process independent of its protections of all basic liberties. Elsewhere I suggest some difficulties for this view. See "Democracy and Liberty," in *Deliberative Democracy*, ed. Jon Elster (Cambridge, UK: Cambridge University Press, 1998), pp. 185–231.

13  See Arend Lijphart, *Patterns of Democracy: Government Forms and Performance in Thirty-Six Countries* (New Haven: Yale University Press, 1999).

14  See Lijphart, *Patterns*, Chap. 16.

15  Dahl argues that different kinds of democratic arrangement will perform differently with respect to these "democratic values" and that none is perfect "from a democratic point of view." This claim underscores the reasonableness of using considerations of economic and social fairness as a basis for assessing constitutions. See Robert A. Dahl, *On Democracy* (New Haven: Yale University Press, 1998), Chaps. 10–11.

16  For discussion, see my "Taking People As They Are?," *Philosophy and Public Affairs* (forthcoming).

17  See John Stuart Mill, "M. de Tocqueville on Democracy in America," in *John Stuart Mill on Politics and Society*, ed. Geraint L. Williams (Fontana/Collins: Glasgow, 1976), p. 191.

18  See *CP*, p. 116. Tocqueville's own description of the democratic revolution focuses as much on the emergence of greater equality of conditions – social mobility, dispersion of land, spread of education, and associated sentiments and feelings – as on a conception of equality of respect and rights. See, for example, the sweeping summary of French social and political history in *Democracy in America*, trans. and ed. Harvey C. Mansfield and Delba Winthrop (Chicago: University of Chicago Press, 2000), pp. 3–6. For Rawls, an understanding of the lack of social fixity – an abandonment of the "belief in a fixed natural order sanctioning a hierarchical society" – is "part of the background of the theory of justice" (p. 480).

19  See "Reply to Alexander and Musgrave," in *CP*, p. 246.

20  See Dahl, *On Democracy*, p. 10, on the "logic of equality."

21  Robert Dahl, *Democracy and Its Critics* (New Haven: Yale University Press, 1989), p. 167.

22  Rawls, "Reply," *CP*, p. 246.

23   Rawls distinguishes four roles of political philosophy, practical guidance being the first, in *JF*, pp. 1–5.

24   See Joseph Schumpeter, *Capitalism, Socialism, and Democracy* (New York: Harper and Row, 1942), Chap. 22; Adam Przeworski, "Minimalist Conception of Democracy: A Defense," in *Democracy's Value*, eds. Ian Shapiro and Casiano Hacker-Cordon (Cambridge, U.K.: Cambridge University Press, 1999), pp. 23–55.

25   See Robert Dahl, *Democracy and Its Critics.* The literature on democratic transitions often vacillates between Schumpeter's minimalist view and Dahl's more demanding and less narrowly electoralist account. For discussion, see Larry Diamond, *Developing Democracy: Toward Consolidation* (Baltimore: Johns Hopkins University Press, 1999), pp. 7–15.

26   A view of this kind is sometimes associated with Rousseau. The general will and the laws issuing from it are understood to be rooted in prior communal attachments, perhaps shaped initially by a legislator-founder, and subsequently sustained through public rituals. For the attribution to Rousseau, and endorsement of the idea that substantive homogeneity and associated solidarities underlie democracy, see Carl Schmitt, *The Crisis of Parliamentary Democracy*, trans. Ellen Kennedy (Cambridge, MA: MIT Press, 1985), esp. pp. 14–15.

27   The literature on deliberative democracy emerges in the mid-1980s, thus the terminology is not found in *Theory of Justice.* But in my own initial paper on deliberative democracy (written in 1987), I indicated that Rawls had many of the ideas of the deliberative conception, though I was skeptical about how well they fit with the background theory of justice as fairness. See "Deliberation and Democratic Legitimacy," in Alan Hamlin and Philip Petit, eds., *The Good Polity: Normative Analysis of the State* (Oxford: Basil Blackwell, 1989), pp. 17–34. Rawls discusses the idea of deliberative democracy in "The Idea of Public Reason Revisited," in *Collected Papers*, esp. pp. 579–81. For an illuminating exploration of the whole terrain, see Samuel Freeman, "Deliberative Democracy: A Sympathetic Comment," *Philosophy and Public Affairs*, 29, 4 (Fall 2000): 371–418.

28   On the importance of connecting the content of the reasons used in public argument with the democratic idea of persons as free and equal, see Cohen, "Democracy and Liberty"; Rawls, "Reply to Habermas," in *PL*, pp. 430–1; Freeman, "Deliberative Democracy," pp. 402–04.

29   The passage that distinguishes these lines of argument was added in the revised edition and was written in 1975 (xi); it anticipates points that are made more fully in "The Basic Liberties and Their Priority" (1982), which is presented as Lecture 8 of *Political Liberalism.* In the

discussion that follows, I draw on "Basic Liberties," which argues more fully and explicitly than elsewhere that political liberty is among the basic liberties, and indicates, as I suggest in the text, that the strategy of argument cannot simply be a generalization of the argument for liberty of conscience. Still, I think that the two main points – that the capacity or "moral power" for a sense of justice is the basis of equality and that treating political liberty as a basic liberty expresses an essential form of respect – are presented in Sections 77 and 82 of the 1971 edition. Moreover, I think that Paragraph 4 of Section 82 of the 1971 edition suggests the distinction of strategies of argument that I make in the text, So, once more, I will present the argument without worrying over issues about shifts in position.

30  The same observation can be made about the argument in Rawls's 1963 paper on "Constitutional Liberty and the Concept of Justice," *CP*, pp. 73–95. He begins by enumerating a variety of basic liberties, including political liberty, and then focuses exclusively on liberty of the person and liberty of conscience and offers a version of the "fundamental aims" argument sketched above (see esp. *CP*, 86–8). The paper includes no discussion of how the argument for liberty of conscience, which turns on the idea that religious views impose obligations that are "binding absolutely," might be extended to other basic liberties.

31  In *JF*, Rawls offers this change in the account of primary goods to illustrate one of the main kinds of change in the presentation of justice as fairness. The revised account links the primary goods "with the political and normative conception of citizens as free and equal persons" (p. xvi).

32  The argument is developed most explicitly in Rawls, "Basic Liberties," pp. 318–19, though it is also suggested in *Theory of Justice*, pp. 155–6, 205–6, 476–8.

33  For reasons that have to do with the construction of the original position in terms of rational choice under ignorance, Rawls formulates his argument in terms of the good of a person and not in terms of the respect to which a person is entitled. But it is worth noting that the argument for the right to political liberties could be stated in terms of the respect to which persons are entitled in virtue of their possessing the capacity for a sense of justice and not in terms of the contribution of respect from others to self-respect and the contribution of self-respect to a person's own good.

34  Jeremy Waldron makes a case for democratic participation by arguing that the respect that we show to individuals by extending participation rights to them – including the right to participate in debate about the resolution of conflicts of rights – is "continuous with the respect

that rights as such invoke." Waldron thinks that "rights as such" express respect for a person's capacity for moral deliberation; thus, extending a right to participate expresses this respect by entitling the right-bearer to bring that moral capacity to bear on matters of common concern. The failure to extend the right is "insulting" because it treats the person's views (and thus the person himself) as of lesser importance. See *Law and Disagreement* (Oxford: Oxford University Press, 1999), Chap. 11. The line of argument I have attributed to Rawls assigns a more specific moral power to individuals (capacity to cooperate on fair terms) and suggests a more intimate connection between our moral powers and the right to participate. By extending the right to participate we do not simply provide another venue for moral deliberation but, more specifically, ensure that persons can bring their sense of justice to bear on the arena in which issues of justice are under consideration.

35  I have been helped by many conversations with Joshua Flaherty about the issues here.

36  "Reconciliation Through the Public Use of Reason: Remarks on John Rawls's Political Liberalism," *Journal of Philosophy* 92 (March 1995), p. 128.

37  For some suggestive remarks about why a deliberative democracy would be the ideal way to implement substantive norms of justice, see Brian Barry, *Justice as Impartiality* (Oxford: Oxford University Press, 1996), Sec. 16.

38  Though it is permissible, as I noted earlier, to use the second principle in selecting among forms of democracy. See supra, pp. 11–13.

39  Concerns about judicial guardianship and skepticism about the U.S. Supreme Court as a guarantor of rights have been persistent themes in Robert Dahl's work. See his Robert Dahl, "Decision-Making in a Democracy: The Supreme Court as a National Policy-Maker," *Journal of Public Law* 6 (1957): 279–95; *Democracy and Its Critics*, Chap. 13; *On Democracy*, p. 121. For illuminating recent discussion, see Ronald Dworkin, *Freedom's Law: The Moral Reading of the American Constitution* (Cambridge, MA: Harvard University Press, 1996), pp. 1–38; Robert Post, *Constitutional Domains: Democracy, Community, and Management* (Cambridge, MA: Harvard University Press, 1995); Frank Michelman, *Brennan and Democracy* (Princeton: Princeton University Press, 1999); Jeremy Waldron, *Law and Disagreement*, Section III; Cass Sunstein, *One Case At A Time: Judicial Minimalism on the Supreme Court* (Cambridge, MA: Harvard University Press, 1999). A full discussion would require attention to the very different practices in different legal systems that are grouped together as "judicial review." For

discussion of the uncertain democratic status of the specifically "common-law" style of American judicial review, see Antonin Scalia, *A Matter of Interpretation: Federal Courts and the Law* (Princeton: Princeton University Press, 1997).

40 For explanation of the "national legislation" qualification, see Dahl, *On Democracy*, p. 121.

41 Unfortunately, the empirics of judicial review are poorly understood. The same can be said for virtually every major institution of modern constitutional democracies. For discussion of this point, see Joshua Cohen and Archon Fung, "Introduction," *Constitutionalism, Democracy, and State Power: Promise and Performance*, four volumes, eds. Joshua Cohen and Archon Fung (Brookfield, VT: Edward Elgar, 1996).

42 For discussion, see Waldron, *Law and Disagreement*, esp. Part 3. Dworkin believes that if a court decides correctly to overturn legislation that impairs democratic self-government, then that the decision was made by a court imposes no "moral cost" – in particular, no reduced democraticness follows. But he also thinks that judgments about which institutions are best suited to preserving a democratic arrangement are broadly empirical matters. See *Freedom's Law*, pp. 32–5.

43 Learned Hand, *The Spirit of Liberty* (New York: Knopf, 1952), p. 190.

44 For a forceful statement of the concern, see Henry Steele Commager, *Majority Rule and Minority Rights* (New York: Peter Smith, 1943), p. 73. I am grateful to Daniel Munro for this reference.

45 Alexander Meikeljohn, "The First Amendment is an Absolute," *The Supreme Court Review: 1961* (Chicago: University of Chicago Press, 1961): 245–66.

46 To which it should be added that the range of liberties that are suitably connected to an ideal of democratic process is itself a disputed question. Some argue that basic personal liberties are essential to democracy, properly understood. See *Freedom's Law*, pp. 25–6, and Cohen, "Democracy and Liberty."

47 This observation applies straightforwardly to the view in *Theory of Justice*, which says that any restriction on the scope of majority rule is a restriction of political liberty and therefore requires special justification. But it also applies to the position in "The Basic Liberties," which emphasizes the idea of a "fully adequate scheme of basic liberties" (Secs. 8, 9).

48 Rawls's discussion on this issue at *PL* 238–9 draws on Samuel Freeman, "Original Meaning, Democratic Interpretation, and the Constitution," *Philosophy and Public Affairs* 21 (Winter 1992, pp. 41f.).

49 See *Democracy and Its Critics*.

50   See my "Procedure and Substance in Deliberative Democracy," in
     *Democracy and Difference: Changing Boundaries of the Political*,
     ed. Seyla Benhabib (Princeton: Princeton University Press, 1996), and
     "Democracy and Liberty."

51   While the burdened group may be especially keen to raise the objec-
     tion that the burden is inappropriate, others have equally good reason to
     raise it.

52   See my "Democracy and Liberty." For Rawls's doubts about the
     substance–procedure distinction, see "Reply to Habermas," pp. 421–33.

53   See Michelman, *Brennan and Democracy*, esp. pp. 57–60.

54   They are almost certain to reject the idea presented in *Buckley v. Valeo*
     that it is impermissible to restrict the quantity of speech to ensure
     fair political equality For discussion, see John Rawls, "Basic Liber-
     ties," pp. 356–63; Joshua Cohen, "Money, Politics, Political Equality," in
     *Facts and Values*, eds. Alex Byrne, Robert Stalnaker, Ralph Wedgwood
     (Cambridge, MA: MIT Press, 2001).

55   Amy Gutmann and Dennis Thompson make the essential point that
     even agreement on Rawls-like principles of justice leaves consider-
     able room for political disagreement and that a substantive account of
     justice will inevitably (and properly) leave much work for a delibera-
     tive democratic process that brings the principles to bear on laws and
     policy. Moreover, as the campaign finance case illustrates, participants
     in that process will disagree on more than matters of nonevaluative
     fact. See *Democracy and Disagreement* (Cambridge, MA: Harvard Uni-
     versity Press, 1996), pp. 34–7. Gutmann and Thompson misstate Rawls's
     own response, but they are right that Rawls says little about political
     argument in the ideal society of justice as fairness.

56   For the basics, see Friedrich Hayek, *The Constitution of Liberty*
     (Chicago: University of Chicago Press, 1960), pp. 376–94; Milton
     Friedman, *Capitalism and Freedom* (Chicago: University of Chicago
     Press, 1982), pp. 85–98.

57   Rawls acknowledges this concern with particular force in the intro-
     duction to the paperback edition of *Political Liberalism*, pp. xxxviii,
     xlviii–l.

58   See *Political Liberalism*, pp. xlviii–l.

59   For discussion, see Committee on Political Parties of the American
     Political Science Association, "Toward a More Responsible Two-Party
     System," *American Political Science Review* 44 (September 1950),
     Supplement: 1–96; Charles Beitz, *Political Equality* (Princeton: Prince-
     ton University Press, 1989), pp. 114–16, 180–5.

# 3    Rawls on Justification

Rawls offers what might be seen as three ideas of justification: the method of reflective equilibrium, the derivation of principles in the original position, and the idea of public reason. These can appear to be in some tension with one another. Reflective equilibrium seems to be an intuitive and "inductive" method. On one natural interpretation, it holds that principles are justified by their ability to explain those judgments in which we feel the highest degree of confidence. By contrast, the original position argument is more theoretical and more "deductive": principles of justice are justified if they could be derived in the right way, institutions are just if they conform to these principles, and particular distributions are just if they are the products of just institutions. Justifications that meet the requirements of public reason need not have this particular form, but they are limited in a way that an individual's search for reflective equilibrium is not. The idea of public reason holds that questions of constitutional essentials and basic justice are to be settled by appeal to political values that everyone in the society, regardless of their comprehensive view, has reason to care about. This is more restrictive than the idea of reflective equilibrium, since not all of an individual's considered judgments, or even all of his or her considered judgments about justice, need meet this test.

In this Chapter I will examine these three ideas and consider how, in Rawls's view, they are related to one another. I will have the most to say about the idea of reflective equilibrium because it is open to several different interpretations and has been the object of some controversy.

## I

To begin with, there is a question as to whether the method of reflective equilibrium is in fact an idea of justification on a par with the other two I have mentioned. 'Justification' can be understood in two ways. On the one hand, to claim that a *principle* or *judgment* is justified is to say that it is supported by good and sufficient reasons. But we also speak of *a person's* being justified in holding a certain view. To claim that he is is to claim that he holds that view for reasons that he reasonably takes to be good and sufficient. A person can be justified, in this sense, in accepting a principle (for certain reasons) even though the principle itself is not justified because, say, there are other factors (which he could not be expected to be aware of) that undermine the justificatory force of the considerations he takes to be reasons for it. The claims Rawls makes for the original position argument and the idea of public reason are theses about justification in the first of these senses: they purport to describe the kinds of considerations that can *justify* a claim about justice (or about "constitutional essentials"). In the case of reflective equilibrium, however, it may not be clear which sense of justification is involved. A person may be justified in accepting a principle if it accounts for his or her considered judgments in reflective equilibrium and the person has no reason to modify or abandon these judgments. But it does not follow that this *principle* is justified. Whether it is or not will depend on the status of these considered judgments. In order to determine in what sense the method of reflective equilibrium is a method of justification, and to answer other questions about it, I need first to describe this method in more detail.

In broad outline (subject to further refinement) the method of reflective equilibrium proceeds in three stages. One begins by identifying a set of considered judgments about justice. These are judgments that seem clearly to be correct under conditions conducive to making good judgments of the relevant kind; that is, when one is fully informed about the matter in question, thinking carefully and clearly about it, and not subject to conflicts of interest or other factors that are likely to distort one's judgment. The second stage is to try to formulate principles that would "account for" these judgments. By this, Rawls means principles such that, had one simply been trying to apply them rather than trying to decide what seemed to be the case as far as justice is concerned, one would have been led to this same set of judgments. Since one's first attempt to come up with such principles is unlikely to be successful, there is a third stage in which one decides how to respond to the divergence between these principles and one's considered judgments. Should one give up the judgments that the principles fail to account for, or modify the principles, in order to achieve a better fit? It is likely that some accommodation of both of these kinds may be required. One is then to continue in this way, working back and forth between principles and judgments, until one reaches a set of principles and a set of judgments between which there is no conflict. This state is what Rawls calls reflective equilibrium. It should be emphasized that this is not a state Rawls believes we are currently in, or likely to reach. It is rather an ideal, the struggle to attain which "continues indefinitely" (*PL*, p. 97).[1]

Let me turn now to some more specific questions about this process. The first is how the relevant class of "considered judgments" is to be understood. In his 1951 article, "Outline of a Decision Procedure for Ethics," Rawls says that these must be judgments about how conflicts of interests are to be resolved in actual (not hypothetical) cases.[2] In *A Theory of Justice* he takes a broader view: what the principles we seek are to account for are certain judgments "*with their supporting reasons*" (*TJ*, p. 46/41 rev.). The view he takes in his 1974 Presidential Address, "The Independence of Moral Theory," is broader still: we are to seek principles that "match people's considered judgments and general convictions in reflective equilibrium," and he emphasizes that these considered judgments need not be about particular cases but include judgments of all levels of generality (*CP*, p. 289). I will take this last and broadest characterization as the definitive one (and return later to the question of what difference this makes).

A second question concerns the aims of the method itself. Rawls sometimes speaks as if our aims in seeking reflective equilibrium are descriptive. In *A Theory of Justice*, for example, he writes, "Now one may think of moral philosophy at first (and I stress the provisional nature of this view) as the attempt to describe our moral capacity; or, in the present case, one may regard a theory of justice as describing our sense of justice" (*TJ*, p. 46/41 rev.). And he continues on the following page, "A useful comparison here is with the problem of describing the sense of grammaticalness that we have for the

sentences of our native language. In this case the aim is to characterize the ability to recognize well-formed sentences by formulating
clearly expressed principles which make the same discriminations
as the native speaker" (*TJ*, p. 47/41 rev.).

This descriptive interpretation is also suggested by some of
Rawls's remarks in "The Independence of Moral Theory." Distinguishing between what he calls "moral theory" and the broader enterprise of moral philosophy, he writes, "Since the history of moral
philosophy shows that the notion of moral truth is problematical, we
can suspend consideration of it until we have a deeper understanding
of moral conceptions" (*CP*, p. 288). It is clear, he says, that people
appear to be influenced by moral conceptions, so these conceptions
themselves can be made a focus of study. It is in this context that he
mentions the idea of finding principles that "match people's considered judgments and general convictions in reflective equilibrium."
He writes that

one thinks of the moral theorist as an observer, so to speak, who seeks to
set out the structure of other people's moral conceptions and attitudes.... 
We may also include ourselves, since we are ready to hand for detailed self-
examination. But in studying oneself, one must separate one's role as moral
theorist from one's role as someone who has a particular conception. In
the former role we are investigating an aspect of human psychology, the
structure of our moral sensibility; in the latter we are applying a moral
conception, which we may regard (though not necessarily) as a correct theory
about what is objectively right and wrong. (*CP*, p. 288)

These passages may seem to suggest that the aims of the method
of reflective equilibrium can be understood in either of two ways.
According to the descriptive interpretation it aims at characterizing
the conception of justice held by a certain person or group. By contrast, according to what I will call the deliberative interpretation, it
is a method for figuring out what to believe about justice. These two
ways of understanding the method lead to two different rationales for
its structure. On the deliberative interpretation, the rationale for concentrating on *considered* judgments is that these are the most likely
to be correct judgments about their subject matter (morality, or justice). On the descriptive interpretation, the rationale is rather that
these judgments are the most accurate representation of the "moral
sensibility" of the person whose conception is being described. As

Rawls says in *Theory*, they are "those judgments in which our moral capacities are most likely to be displayed without distortion" (*TJ*, p. 47/42 rev.). As this brings out, in the descriptive interpretation, the method of reflective equilibrium does not seem to be a method of justification (or a search for justification) at all, especially when it is applied to other people's considered judgments. Rather, it seems to be a way of arriving at accurate portraits of various possible conceptions of justice, which we may then choose between using some other method. And one might even think that the original position argument offers this method for choosing between different conceptions that we have used the method of reflective equilibrium to describe. As Rawls says (in Section 4 of *A Theory of Justice*), "[O]ne conception of justice is more reasonable than another, or justifiable with respect to it, if persons in the initial situation would choose its principles over those of the other for the role of justice" (*TJ*, pp. 17/15–16 rev.).

We can get a clearer picture of the relation between these interpretations, however, if we consider some questions about the structure of the method of reflective equilibrium, beginning with the idea of a considered judgment.

The characteristics that, according to Rawls, mark out the class of considered judgments fall into three categories. The first have to do with the conditions under which the judgment is made. Considered judgments are ones that are made when a person:

1. Is aware of relevant facts about the issue in question
2. Is able to concentrate on this question: not upset, frightened, etc.
3. Does not stand to gain or lose on the basis of the answer given (cf. *TJ*, p. 48/42 rev.)

The second set of characteristics concerns the way the judgment is held. It must be:

4. One about which the person is confident, that is to say, feels certain rather than hesitant
5. One that is stable over time (and, in the version presented in "Outline," accepted by all competent judges) (*CP*, p. 6)

Finally, at least in "Outline," the judgment must be "intuitive with respect to ethical principles" (*CP*, p. 6). That is to say, it must be arrived at simply by considering what one thinks about the question at hand rather than by consciously applying some principle or

theory. Since this condition seems to be concerned with the independence of considered judgments from the principles that they may be
used to support, rather than with the reliability of the judgments
themselves, I will set it aside. I will also set aside the question of
why we should exclude judgments we endorse only hesitantly or
inconstantly.[3] Ideally, we would want to find principles that explain
these judgments as well as the judgments in which we have stable
confidence. That is, we would want to be able to explain why they
seem at least plausible and, perhaps, to do this in a way that enables
us to resolve our uncertainty about them. At least, it does not seem
part of the method of reflective equilibrium to disavow these aims.
The only problem with them is that they may be too ambitious. The
idea of the method, as I will understand it, is that we should concentrate first on finding principles that account for those judgments
in which we feel most confidence under the conditions listed in the
first category. So I will concentrate on the rationale for the method
so understood.

Each of the conditions in the first category rules out certain judgments as ones we need not consider and rules in others. About each of
these conditions, then, there are two related questions. Negatively,
why should the excluded judgments not be taken into account? And,
positively, why take the judgments that are ruled in – judgments in
which we have confidence under the conditions listed – to have pro-
bative value?

The conditions in the first category fall under the general description of "conditions favorable to the exercise of the sense of justice,
and therefore circumstances in which the more common excuses and
explanations for making a mistake do not obtain." Under such conditions, Rawls says, "The person making the judgment is presumed ...
to have the ability, the opportunity, and the desire to reach a correct
decision (or at least, not the desire not to)" (*TJ*, p. 48/42 rev.). On the
descriptive interpretation, the rationale for these conditions is that,
negatively, the factors they rule out are ones that interfere with the
expression of a person's moral capacity, and, positively, that the judgments they rule in – ones that are not influenced by these factors –
are accurate indications of the nature of that faculty. The positive
part of this rationale can take a stronger or a weaker form. The
stronger form assumes that people have a "moral capacity," a settled
psychological disposition to respond to questions about moral

matters in a certain systematic fashion, and that this is what determines their responses to moral questions insofar as these are not
distorted by factors such as fear, self-interest, haste, fatigue, and so
on. A weaker version of this response would hold merely that we
begin with the *hypothesis* that there is such a capacity. We may then
investigate the behavior of various individuals to see whether, when
distorting factors of the kinds just mentioned are screened out, their
responses to moral questions exhibit the kind of systematic regularity that supports this hypothesis and, if so, what the structure of this
regularity is.

On the deliberative interpretation, the rationale for these requirements is rather that they describe conditions under which a person's
moral judgments are likely to be correct and rule out conditions that
would make them unreliable. The negative part of this answer is
relatively straightforward. Since the rightness or wrongness of an action, or the justice or injustice of an institution, depends on facts
about it, judgments made in ignorance of these facts are unreliable.
Factors such as self-interest and emotional distress also make a judgment unreliable, because these factors can interfere with a person's
assessment of the morally relevant considerations. The positive part
of the answer is more controversial. A direct way of putting it is to
say that the judgments that meet these conditions state those things
that seem to us most clearly to be true about moral matters if anything is, and that unless there is some ground for doubting them
it is reasonable to grant them initial credibility (leaving open the
possibility that they may be revised or rejected later in the process).

It may be objected that this answer "begs the question against
skepticism,"[4] and that the fact that these considered judgments are
open to revision at later stages in the process does not remove this
worry. Suppose, for example, that we were to undertake a process of
reflective equilibrium to render into coherent form the judgments
about astrology in which people felt most confidence, revising many
of these judgments in the process. This would not allay reasonable
doubts about whether astrology is something we should take at all
seriously. The result would not be a set of justified astrological judgments but only, at best, a set of claims that was internally consistent.
Similarly, it may be said, merely subjecting our considered judgments
about morality to scrutiny and possible revision through the method
of reflective equilibrium does not provide an adequate response to

doubts about morality. To respond to those doubts we need to defend
the truth and importance of the considered judgments with which
that process begins. As Richard Brandt says, the idea that the method
of reflective equilibrium leads to beliefs that are justified depends on
the claim that some of the beliefs with which it begins "are initially
credible – and not merely initially believed – for some reason other
than their coherence...."[5]

The force of this objection depends crucially on what doubts about
our considered moral judgments are in question. Broadly speaking,
these doubts might be of either of two kinds. They might be doubts
about morality in general – about whether there are truths about
morality that have the kind of importance claimed for them – or they
may be doubts about whether our particular considered judgments
are morally correct. I will consider doubts of the second kind later,
in discussing the charge of "conservatism." Here I will concentrate
on skepticism about morality in general, which is what is suggested
by the supposed analogy with astrology.

Astrology claims that the sign under which a person is born has
important consequences for his or her personality and fate. It thus is
committed to causal claims – claims about physics and psychology –
that are clearly false. Rendering our astrological judgments internally
consistent would do nothing to allay the reasonable doubts that we
have about it on this score. (To do that, we would need to bring
these judgments into reflective equilibrium with our beliefs about
physics and psychology.) Morality will be in an analogous situation
if, but only if, it too has "external commitments" – that is, only if
the reasonableness of taking moral judgments seriously depends on
claims that go beyond morality itself and lie in, for example, physics,
psychology, metaphysics, or the theory of rational choice.

Rawls holds that morality, or at least justice, has no controversial
empirical or metaphysical presuppositions. Considered judgments
about morality and justice need not, in order to have the importance
claimed for them, be the results of our causal interaction with independently existing moral properties or entities.[6] According to Rawls,
the presuppositions that need to be redeemed to defend morality are
practical rather than theoretical. The kind of objectivity that is appropriate to morality does not require that it should be about independently existing entities but rather that it should be a way of reasoning
about what to do that is distinct from any given individual's point

of view and yields determinate answers in at least many cases. In addition, since a set of arbitrary requirements might have this kind of objectivity, it is crucial to morality that it also be a method of reasoning about what to do that all reasonable individuals have good reason to regard as authoritative and normally overriding.[7] There are thus two kinds of skeptical questions about our considered judgments that need to be rebutted. The first are doubts as to whether what we are aware of when we make such judgments are the requirements of a determinate method of reasoning of the kind just mentioned (and not, for example, mere responses from our own personal point of view.) The second are doubts as to whether this method of reasoning is one that everyone has good reason to regard as authoritative.

The method of reflective equilibrium has a role in answering both of these questions. First, it is by pursuing this method that we can best determine whether and how our moral views can be seen as forming a systematic way of reasoning about what to do. Second, it is only after we have, by using this method, formed a clearer view of what morality, as we can best understand it, is like that we can address the question of the reasons we have for taking it seriously.

When we apply the method of reflective equilibrium to our moral beliefs we begin with the *hypothesis* that our considered judgments represent conclusions about what we should do that are supported by an objective (determinate and person-independent) mode of reasoning that all reasonable people have good reason to regard as authoritative. In trying to decide what our considered judgements are we unavoidably think of them in this way (and not merely descriptively). This does not, however, mean that in pursuing the method of reflective equilibrium we are dismissing skeptical questions of the two kinds just mentioned. These questions are not dismissed but bracketed for the time being because they can only be properly answered by first carrying through this investigation.

What I have been calling the descriptive and the deliberative interpretations of the method of reflective equilibrium are thus not alternatives that are on a par with one another. The deliberative version of the method is primary. Even if our aims in employing the method of reflective equilibrium are understood as descriptive, in order for the method to be carried out, someone – the person whose considered judgments are in question – must be trying to decide what to believe. It does not immediately follow, of course, that someone must be trying to decide this by employing the method of reflective equilibrium. But this conclusion is strongly supported by a more detailed examination of what I earlier termed the third stage of the process, at which conflicts between principles and considered judgments must be resolved.

Suppose that we have found a principle that accounts for many, perhaps most, of the considered judgments with which we began but conflicts with some of these judgments. According to the descriptive interpretation of this process, how are we to decide what to do? It is easier to focus on this problem if we assume, as the descriptive interpretation invites us to, that the judgments in question are not ours but those of another person whose conception of justice we are trying to characterize. According to this interpretation of the process, considered judgments have the standing of data: observed facts about a given person's attitudes. If a given considered judgment does not fit with a principle, this in no way affects its status as a considered judgment; it remains true that this judgment is one that the person has confidence in. Since the standing of a principle depends purely on its ability to account for considered judgments, it may seem that, faced with a conflict between principles and considered judgments, we should decide what to do on a purely quantitative basis. If we can find a principle that accounts for more considered judgments than the one at hand, then we should adopt that principle instead. If we cannot, then we should keep the principle and abandon the considered judgments that do not fit it.

But this is clearly not what Rawls has in mind. He describes the process as involving much more interaction between considered judgments and candidate principles. The fact that a given judgment does not fit with principles that account for most of our other judgments can lead us to change our mind about that judgment itself, and we also may be led to change our mind when we see that the only principles that *do* account for a given judgment are ones that are seen in other ways to be clearly mistaken. Thus, Rawls writes, "Moral philosophy is Socratic: we may want to change our present considered judgments once their regulative principles are brought to light. And we may want to do this even though these principles are a perfect fit. A knowledge of these principles may suggest further reflections that lead us to revise our judgments" (*TJ*, p. 49).[8]

Two important conclusions follow. The first is that the class of considered judgments is not fixed at the first stage, like a set of data, but can at least in principle change constantly throughout the process. What we start with are *judgments* about what is the case, morally speaking, not observations that we, or others, hold certain views. Here it is helpful to bear in mind Rawls's remark that what we begin with are certain judgments *with their supporting reasons*. In the case of empirical observations, we may be convinced that something is the case without having any idea why it is. But moral judgments are not in general like this. Only very rarely is it clear to us (or clear in the way required for a "considered judgment") that something is right, wrong, just, or unjust without our having some idea what makes it so. And even if there are some considered judgments of some level of generality which seem obvious despite the lack of further reasons, the general appropriateness of asking for and giving reasons for such judgments brings out an important aspect of what it is for them to be *judgments*. It is their status as judgments that makes them open to revision as the "Socratic" process of seeking reflective equilibrium proceeds.[9]

The second conclusion, which follows from this one, is that the person whose considered judgments are in question has to be involved in this process – since only that person is in a position to revise his or her judgments – and that for this person it is a constant process of making up his or her mind about what to believe. When we are engaged in the enterprise that Rawls calls moral theory, we may have reason to consider the results of other people's search for reflective equilibrium as well as our own. But the process of seeking reflective equilibrium is something we each must carry out for ourselves, and it is a process of deciding what to think, not merely one of describing what we do think.

This is in my view the best interpretation of Rawls's sometimes seemingly conflicting remarks about the method of reflective equilibrium. Moreover, it seems to me that this method, properly understood, is in fact the best way of making up one's mind about moral matters and about many other subjects. Indeed, it is the only defensible method: apparent alternatives to it are illusory. I will indicate why I think this by considering two commonly heard objections to the method, which I will refer to as the charge of conservatism and the charge of relativism.

The charge of conservatism is based on the plausible idea that an adequate method for deciding what to believe about a subject must provide some standard with reference to which the current beliefs we happen to have can be judged and perhaps found wanting. Reflective equilibrium is too conservative, it is charged, because it is so closely tied to those beliefs themselves. It may be a process through which these beliefs can be made more systematic and internal inconsistencies eliminated, but it lacks the independence that would be necessary to give it real critical or justificatory force.

In response, it can be said first, as I have pointed out, that considered judgments are not taken as fixed but are open to constant revision. Second, it is important that these judgments are not limited to judgments about what is just or unjust in particular cases. If the method of reflective equilibrium were simply a search for principles that made the most sense of the particular judgments we are already inclined to make, then the charge of conservatism would have more force. Even if particular judgments were open to revision, these revisions would be driven simply by the aim of preserving other such judgments. Such a method would shield our particular judgments from other sources of criticism such as criticism in the light of plausible general principles. But this is not the method Rawls describes. As he emphasizes, the class of considered judgments includes judgments of all levels of generality, including general principles and ideas about the function of justice as well as judgments about what is just or unjust in particular cases. This reply is strengthened when we take into account that, according to Rawls, what we are to seek is what he calls "wide" reflective equilibrium. This means equilibrium after we have "had an opportunity to consider other plausible conceptions and assess their supporting grounds. Taking this process to the limit, one seeks the conception, or plurality of conceptions, that would survive the rational consideration of all feasible conceptions and all reasonable arguments for them" (*CP*, p. 289).

This breadth deprives the charge of conservatism of its force. Conservative as opposed to what? It is difficult to imagine what source of criticism or justification is envisaged that the method of reflective equilibrium, so understood, would exclude. This is a strong reply, but its strength may be purchased at a price. If the method of reflective equilibrium held that principles are to be justified simply by their ability to account for our considered judgments about particular questions of justice, then it might be open to a charge of conservatism, but it would at least have distinctive content. But once the method has been broadened in the way just described, so that it includes "the rational consideration of all feasible conceptions and all reasonable arguments for them" it seems to become empty as a methodological doctrine. It becomes simply the truism that we should decide what views about justice to adopt by considering the philosophical arguments for all possible views and assessing them on their merits.

This charge of emptiness seems to me to be largely correct, but nonetheless mistaken in one important respect, and therefore not as damaging as it sounds. The charge is largely correct because the search for wide reflective equilibrium, as Rawls describes it, allows for what might have been seen as alternative methods of justification to be incorporated within it. For example, the possibility that our conception of justice should be founded on self-evident principles is not excluded. All that the method of reflective equilibrium requires is that the self-evidence of these principles be established through that method itself, by their demonstrated ability to carry the day against apparently conflicting judgments and alternative principles. What the method of reflective equilibrium prescribes is, so to speak, a level playing field of intuitive justification on which principles and judgments of all levels of generality must compete for our allegiance. It thus allows all possible sources of justificatory force to be considered. But the method is not vacuous because it is incompatible with some views about these sources. It is incompatible, first, with the idea that any particular class of judgments or principles can be singled out in advance of this process as justified on some other basis and, second, with the idea that any class of *considered* judgments should be left out of this process (for example that "intuitions" about what is just or unjust in particular cases should not be given any weight in justifying general principles but must be derived from them.)

A second charge against the method of reflective equilibrium is that it leads to an implausible relativism. Because the results of the method depend on the considered judgments on which it is based, two people who began with different sets of judgments could arrive at equilibria consisting of different and incompatible principles. The idea that the method of reflective equilibrium is an adequate method of justification leads, it is charged, to the unacceptable conclusion that in such a case the two sets of principles are equally justified. This charge has its greatest plausibility if it is assumed that the set of considered judgments that is chosen at the first stage remains fixed throughout the process, except for some judgments being eliminated because no principle can be found that accounts for them and is otherwise plausible. As I have already mentioned, however, considered judgments are not fixed inputs but are open to constant modification. This reduces the degree to which the results of the method depend on its starting points, and the range of critical reflection included in the search for "wide" reflective equilibrium reduces this dependence still further. But the charge of relativism retains some force, in the form of the following challenge.

Suppose I have carried through the process Rawls describes and found principles that are in reflective equilibrium with my considered judgments. It could still be claimed, not implausibly, that some other person who was equally well-informed might carry through the process just as conscientiously and reach a different result. Is the defender of reflective equilibrium not then committed to the claim that the incompatible sets of principles we have reached are both justified?

The answer is that accepting the method of reflective equilibrium does not commit one to this conclusion. Accepting that method, and accepting that some person is well informed and has carried out the search for reflective equilibrium conscientiously does not even commit one to the conclusion that this person is justified in accepting the principles that result, let alone the conclusion that those principles are justified. Faced with the case of someone who reaches an equilibrium different from my own, I must ask why this divergence occurred. If it occurred because the person began with different considered judgments, then I must ask whether I think, on further reflection, that the judgments that person accepted are correct and whether he or she was correct in rejecting ones that I accepted. If the divergence occurred because the person made different choices at later stages in the process, when faced with the need to revise principles or modify considered judgments, then I need to consider whether these decisions were reasonable and, perhaps, whether I should revise my own decisions in the light of them. Finally, the divergence may be due to our having considered different sets of eligible conceptions of justice, in which case I need to ask whether this shows that there are further possibilities that I must consider in order to have reached wide reflective equilibrium. The reexamination provoked by a case of this kind may disrupt the equilibrium I had reached, but it need not do so. Accepting the method of reflective equilibrium does not commit me to the view that the principles this other person has reached are justified unless I judge that not only that person's starting points but also all of the steps he or she made along the way are sound.[10]

There remains, however, the possibility that I might conclude that that person's starting points and his or her subsequent decisions are sound (or at least, as Rawls puts it, ones that are "reasonable" to accept) and that the same is true of my own. Such a result is not ruled out in advance, but depends on the outcome of the search for reflective equilibrium. As Rawls says,

It is natural to suppose that a necessary condition for objective moral truths is that there be a sufficient agreement between the moral conceptions affirmed in wide reflective equilibrium, a state reached when people's moral convictions satisfy certain conditions of rationality. Whether this supposition is correct, and whether sufficient agreement obtains, we need not consider, since any such discussion would be premature. (*CP*, p. 290)

The fact that the method of reflective equilibrium could lead to a result that called into question the objectivity of our moral beliefs is not an objection to that method. It is, rather, a necessary consequence of the fact that this method does not "beg the question against skepticism."

## II

I mentioned in Section I the possibility that the method of reflective equilibrium might be used simply to characterize different conceptions of justice that we would then choose between using some other method and that the original position argument might be this method. It is clear from what Rawls says, however, that this is not the correct picture of the relation between the two methods. As Rawls makes clear in *A Theory of Justice*, the structure of the original position is itself justified by employing the method of reflective equilibrium. As he says,

In searching for the most favored description of this situation we work from both ends. We begin by describing it so that it represents generally shared and preferably weak conditions. We then see if these conditions are strong enough to yield a significant set of principles.... By going back and forth, sometimes altering the conditions of the contractual circumstances, at others withdrawing our judgments and conforming them to principle, I assume that eventually we shall find a description of the initial situation that both expresses reasonable conditions and yields principles which match our considered judgments duly pruned and adjusted. This state of affairs I refer to as reflective equilibrium. (*TJ*, p. 20/18 rev.)

Considering this process in more detail will illustrate some of the points made in the previous section about the method of reflective equilibrium.

I will begin with Rawls's justification of the original position construction "from above" – that is to say, with the considerations that he appeals to in designing this construction and choosing its particular features. First among these considerations is the idea that the function of a conception of justice is to serve as a publicly shared standard for resolving claims against the basic institutions of society. As Rawls says, the function of a conception of justice is "to regulate all subsequent criticism and reform of [basic] institutions" (*TJ*, p. 13/12 rev.). The second idea Rawls appeals to is that people will have reason to accept a principle as such a regulating standard if it is one that they would have chosen for this role under conditions that were fair. This is the basic idea of "justice as fairness." But what does "fairness" mean here? Conflicting claims against the basic institutions of a society are generally either disagreements about the way it distributes economic goods or disagreements about the opportunities it provides to pursue and promote various "conceptions of the good." So a mechanism for choosing among conceptions of justice will be fair if it is fair between people who stand on opposing sides of such disagreements. The various features of the original position are introduced as ways of fulfilling this requirement.

First, the original position includes all members of the society in question (or their representatives) since it would be unfair to exclude anyone from consideration. Second, it recognizes that these members have interests that may conflict in the ways just described. This recognition is embodied in the specification that the parties are rational – that they want to do as well as possible for themselves or those they represent – and that they are mutually disinterested. This does not mean that they are *self-interested* but that they have distinct aims, perhaps altruistic ones, which they are concerned to advance, and which may conflict. Third, the parties are assumed to be ignorant of their particular economic positions (their talents and the economic circumstances into which they are born) and ignorant of their particular conceptions of the good. This "veil of ignorance" is linked with the idea of fairness since a method for selecting principles of justice would be unfair if it favored some principles over others simply because those principles were beneficial to a certain economic class or religious group. (This is one of our "considered judgments" about justice.) The veil of ignorance prevents this kind of unfairness by depriving the parties of the ability to identify principles that would favor their own particular class or group.

There are, of course, other ways of trying to ensure this kind of fairness. One might, for example, allow the parties full knowledge of their situations but introduce other constraints that would deprive them of the ability to press "unfairly" for principles favoring their particular social position or conception of the good. This might be done by ensuring that the bargaining power of the parties in the initial situation is equal so that they will be unable to force others to accept principles favoring their particular social position or conception of the good even though they would have reason to do this if they could. One problem with this strategy is that it may render the outcome of the initial situation indeterminate. If all we know is that the parties have conflicting interests and equal bargaining positions, what can we conclude about the principles that they will choose? This problem may be solvable, but my present point concerns the way that Rawls seeks to avoid it. The veil of ignorance rules out partisanship while also turning the problem facing the parties into one of a familiar kind – rational choice under conditions of uncertainty – which, he believes, has a determinate solution.

Which of these ideas, appealed to in support of the design of the original position, are considered judgments about justice (albeit, perhaps, ones of a high level of generality)? If by a considered judgment one means a judgment that represents a fixed point in our thinking about justice that is independent of the theory being constructed, then only some of them would seem to fall in this class. This status might be claimed for the idea that the function of principles of justice is to serve as a standard for assessing claims against the basic institutions of a society, and for the idea that the fact that a principle would favor a certain group over others is not in itself a good reason for thinking it a correct principle of justice. Other ideas that I have mentioned seem too dependent on Rawls's rather novel construction to have the status of fixed points in our thinking about justice. For example, the idea that principles of justice are binding if they would be chosen under conditions that are fair has a considerable plausibility, but it does not strike one immediately as a claim about justice that must be true if anything is. Initially at least, this idea has more the status of a plausible hypothesis. Subsequent ideas about the conditions under which such a choice should be made, are, again, too novel and specialized to count as pretheoretical considered judgments, although they derive some support from such judgments. We do not, for example, have a considered judgment that principles of justice should be chosen behind a veil of ignorance or even that this would be the fairest way of choosing them. But it might be one of our considered judgments that if the only people who would have reason to accept a certain principle would be those who belonged to the group that it would favor, then this would count against that principle's claim to be a standard of justice. This gives some support to the veil of ignorance by suggesting that the considerations that it prevents the parties from being influenced by are morally irrelevant. As I have already mentioned, however, the veil of ignorance is only one way to rule out such influence. So the idea that the principles of justice should be identified by asking what principles would be chosen in an original position including such a veil remains at best a plausible hypothesis.

This hypothesis needs to be confirmed by considering how its consequences fit with our considered judgments about what social arrangements are in fact just. (For the purposes of this discussion I will assume that Rawls is correct in his claim about what these consequences are; that is, that his two principles of justice would be chosen in the original position he describes.) A great deal of space in *A Theory of Justice* is devoted to arguing that the two principles are in accord with our considered judgments about justice (or that they are more in accord with these judgments than is utilitarianism, or the perfectionist principle, or other alternative views). Some of this takes the form of pointing out how Rawls's two principles confirm judgments that were already fixed points in our thinking; for example, that they firmly rule out slavery and that they do not permit individual civil and political liberties to be infringed for the sake of other goods. In some other cases the aim is to show that these principles do not lead to results that conflict with our considered judgments; for example, that the difference principle would not lead to a "callous meritocratic society."

But a surprisingly large part – indeed, most – of Rawls's discussion of the implications of his view is devoted to cases in which his two principles seem to conflict with common attitudes about justice, and to arguing that in these cases we should modify or abandon the judgments that seem to conflict with the principles rather than the other way around. So, for example, Rawls argues that we should reject the idea that economic reward should be proportional to moral desert (*TJ*, pp. 103–4/88–9 rev., 310–15/273–77 rev.), or to individuals' marginal contributions to society (*TJ*, pp. 307–8/270–1 rev.), and he argues (in the well-known passage appealing to the idea of arbitrariness from a moral point of view (*TJ*, pp. 71–75/61–65 rev.)) that individuals have no claim of justice to the shares they could command in a free market, and, more generally, that the results of such a market have a claim to be just only so long as the appropriate background conditions are assured. These arguments for modifying judgments that conflict with a principle rather than abandoning the principle itself take just the form that was described in the general account of reflective equilibrium. The fact that so much of Rawls's argument takes this form shows why the charge of conservatism against that method is mistaken.

## III

I turn now to the third idea of justification, the idea of public reason. To see how this idea arises in Rawls's thinking, we should begin with the idea of a well-ordered society, which figures importantly in the argument of *A Theory of Justice*. A well-ordered society, according to Rawls, is one in which "everyone accepts and knows that the others accept the same principles of justice, and the basic social institutions satisfy and are known to satisfy these principles" (*TJ*, p. 454/397 rev.). In a well-ordered society, principles of justice serve as a publicly recognized standard for the assessment of claims about the society's basic institutions. Much of *A Theory of Justice* is devoted to arguing that Rawls's two principles of justice would be chosen by the parties to the original position to play this role, and in particular that they would be preferred over the main alternative conceptions of justice in the philosophical tradition, such as utilitarianism.

But this preference is only provisional until it is confirmed that a society organized around the two principles of justice would be stable. By this Rawls means that "when institutions are just (as defined by this conception), those taking part in these arrangements acquire the corresponding sense of justice and desire to do their part in maintaining them" (*TJ*, p. 454/398 rev.). In particular, principles of justice are stable if children growing up in a society that was well-ordered according to them would come to accept these principles and be moved to act in accord with them. The parties to the original position would not choose a conception of justice that was not stable in this sense. To do so would be fruitless, since such a society would not last over time.

The last two chapters of *A Theory of Justice* are devoted to arguing that his two principles meet this test. Appealing to various principles of developmental psychology, Rawls maintains in Chapter VIII that children growing up in a society that was well-ordered according to these principles would come to have a sense of justice that incorporated them. By itself, however, a purely factual or causal argument is insufficient for his purposes. Rawls wants to show not only that a society based on these two principles would have de facto stability of a kind that might be guaranteed by coercion or indoctrination, but also that it would have what he later calls "stability for the right reasons" (*PL*, pp. xlii, 390, 392). So he needs to show not only that people in a society governed by his two principles would come to have a sense of justice incorporating these principles but also that this sense of justice is something they would have good reason to affirm. As he puts it, he needs to show that having a sense of justice with the content that justice as fairness describes is congruent with our good. This is the task of Chapter IX, entitled "The Good of Justice."

In support of this claim, Rawls argues that someone in a society that was well-ordered in accord with his principles of justice could not "object to the practices of moral instruction that inculcate [this] sense of justice" because "by acting from these principles they are acting autonomously: they are acting from principles that they would acknowledge under conditions that best express their nature as free and rational beings" (*TJ*, p. 515/452 rev.). And later he writes,

But the desire to express our nature as free and equal rational beings can be fulfilled only by acting on the principles of right and justice as having first priority.... It is acting from this precedence that expresses our freedom from contingency and happenstance. Therefore in order to realize our nature we have no alternative but to plan to preserve our sense of justice as governing our other aims. (*TJ*, p. 574/503 rev.)

Rawls later concluded, however, that this argument was inconsistent with what he calls the fact of reasonable pluralism.[11] This is the fact that in any society in which people are free to form their own opinions they will, not unreasonably, come over time to hold a variety of different views on certain fundamental questions such as the meaning and importance of human life, the kinds of freedom that human beings should strive for and are capable of, and the kind of life that is best for human beings to live. An answer to such questions is what Rawls calls a comprehensive view. He believes that in any free society reasonable people will hold many different such views, including not only religions but also secular views such as Kant's and Mill's conceptions of the nature and distinctive value of human life and freedom. This presents a problem for the argument of *A Theory of Justice* because, as I have just mentioned, the reasons given there for holding that people would have good reason to affirm a sense of justice based on Rawls's two principles depend essentially on ideas of autonomy and of what is required to "realize our nature" that are ingredients in a specifically liberal, often distinctively Kantian, comprehensive view.

The main task of *Political Liberalism* is to provide an alternative solution to the problem of stability in order to show that the argument for Rawls's two principles of justice can be completed in a way that is compatible with the fact of reasonable pluralism. Rawls's strategy for doing this lies in the idea of an overlapping consensus. Instead of showing that members of a society that was well-ordered by the two principles of justice would come to have, and would have reason to affirm, a sense of justice based on these principles because they would all come to hold the same (Kantian) comprehensive view, Rawls undertakes to show that people would have reason to affirm a sense of justice based on his two principles no matter what reasonable comprehensive view they come to hold.

This point can be put as follows, using the notion of reflective equilibrium. Suppose that each citizen has both a comprehensive view and a political conception of the standards appropriate for settling questions about the basic institutions of society. We can think of the latter as one component of the former, a "module" within a person's comprehensive view having to do with the assessment of one's political institutions and thus with one important class of relations with one's fellow citizens. If a citizen's views are in wide reflective equilibrium, his or her political conception will be supported by, or at least in harmony with, his or her wider comprehensive view. In a well-ordered society citizens will hold the same political conception even though their comprehensive views may differ. In such a case we can say that there is a wide and general reflective equilibrium with regard to this political conception: the equilibrium is wide in the case of each citizen and general because "the same conception is affirmed in everyone's considered judgments" (*PL*, p. 384, note 16).

So far, I have presented the idea of overlapping consensus entirely as a response to the question of how a well-ordered democratic society could be stable given the fact of reasonable pluralism. The idea of public reason is, at first glance, quite a different notion. It holds, as I have said, that questions of constitutional essentials and basic justice are to be settled by appeal to political values that everyone in the society, regardless of their comprehensive views, has reason to care about. This is a norm of political justification: a specification of the kind of justification that citizens must be able to offer in political discussion when constitutional essentials and questions of basic justice are at issue. So there is a question of how Rawls derives a norm of political conduct from a claim about how democratic institutions could, ideally, be stable in the right way.

The link between the two lies in the fact, mentioned in the preceding paragraph, that a conception of justice is to serve as a public standard of justification with reference to which all questions about the justice of the society's basic institutions are to be settled. The importance of such a public standard has been central to Rawls's thinking from the beginning. He has always stressed the difference between a just society, whose institutions can be justified with reference to a standard that all citizens have reason to accept, and a society whose institutions some people have reason to accept only because they are forced to do so. Already in "Justice as Fairness" (1957) he wrote,

A practice is just or fair, then, when it satisfies the principles which those who participate in it could propose to one another for mutual acceptance under the aforementioned circumstances. Persons engaged in a just, or fair, practice can face one another openly and support their respective positions, should they appear questionable, by reference to principles which it is reasonable to expect each to accept. . . . Only if such acknowledgment is possible can there be true community between persons in their common practices; otherwise their relations will appear to them as founded to some extent on force. (CP, p. 59)

Once the fact of reasonable pluralism is taken into account, however, it follows that a conception of justice that depends on a particular comprehensive view cannot play this important role. Justifications that appeal to it will be ones that some citizens (those who do not share this view) have no reason to accept. This has implications not only for the question of how "stability for the right reasons" may be attained but also for the kind of justifications that citizens should offer one another. Justifications of a society's basic institutions that depend crucially on particular comprehensive views will be reasonably resented by citizens who do not share these views. They will therefore not only be destabilizing but also fail to show proper respect for these citizens, who are owed reasons that they could reasonably accept. Reasons of this sort should therefore not be relied on; if they are offered, reasons appealing to nonpartisan political values must also be available.[12]

This requirement, which is central to the idea of public reason, is what Rawls calls "the criterion of reciprocity." The movement of thought described in the preceding paragraph can be seen as a part of Rawls's pursuit of reflective equilibrium in which he is led, by considering the fact of reasonable pluralism, to refine his earlier ideas of publicity and legitimacy in a way that makes this criterion explicit.

The idea of public reason requires, then, that questions of constitutional essentials and matters of basic justice should be settled by appeal to political values. What are these values? Rawls characterizes them both negatively and, in abstract terms, more positively.

The negative characterization is just that they are not values that are part of some reasonable comprehensive views but not others. His more positive characterization (*PL*, p. 224; *PPR*, pp. 140ff.) is that political values include substantive ideas of justice, including basic rights, liberties and opportunities, and values having to do with public inquiry and debate, such as reasonableness and civility. This positive characterization is extremely abstract. Moreover, when Rawls emphasizes in his later writing that constitutional essentials and questions of basic justice are to be settled by appealing to these "political values," it may seem that his own doctrine, justice as fairness, and his two principles of justice have receded into the background, or perhaps even been replaced. The reason for this appearance has to do with the generality, and hence unavoidable abstractness, of the idea of public reason itself. The idea is that a society should be organized around *some* reasonable political conception of justice (justice as fairness being only one example, albeit Rawls's own preferred choice) and that this conception, rather than any particular comprehensive view, should serve as the basis for settling questions about its basic institutions. Such a political conception will specify particular political values and principles of justice, will order them in a distinctive way, and will specify more fully the standards of political justification. Since he is allowing for the possibility that different reasonable political conceptions will do this in different ways, Rawls does not, *in discussing public reason*, specify fully a set of political values. As he says, "Political liberalism does not, then, try to fix public reason once and for all in the form of one favored political conception of justice" (*PRR*, p. 142). But this does not indicate any withdrawal of commitment to the conception of justice defended in *Theory*.

I have repeated several times Rawls's statement that the requirement of justification by appeal to political values applies only to questions regarding constitutional essentials and matters of basic justice. Some explanation of this limitation is in order. A broader doctrine would impose the same requirement of justification on all legislation, since all legislation involves the exercise of state power in some way – at least through the collection of taxes. Rawls has sometimes been interpreted in this broader way, and some passages in his writings may be open to this interpretation, but he makes clear in his latest work that it is the narrower doctrine that he has in mind (*PL*, pp. 214–15; *PRR*, p. 168). Two reasons for this can be given. The first is that it is the basic structure of a society – to which constitutional essentials and questions of basic justice apply – that requires a special kind of justification. This is a structure that affects citizens' lives and opportunities in fundamental ways and does so not only without their consent but without their being able to have much influence in the matter. By contrast, in a just political order, while citizens do not consent to every piece of legislation (unanimity is not a feasible form of political decision making), they do have a fair opportunity to make their opinions heard and affect the outcome through speaking and voting and through their representatives. If these institutions have the right sort of justification, then this justification also supports legislation enacted through the procedures they define.

The second reason is one of feasibility. As Rawls emphasizes, a political conception must be complete; it must be able to give answers to all, or almost all, of the questions to which it applies. It does not, however, seem plausible that a political conception – which must refrain from taking sides on issues on which reasonable comprehensive views may disagree – could provide the basis for answering all questions that arise in the course of legislation. Consider, for example, the decision whether to build a new highway system. Citizens may disagree as to whether the gains in convenience and efficiency that such a project would bring outweigh the damage to unspoiled wilderness. This is a question that should be open to debate in order to reach a reasonable decision in such a case. But it is difficult to see how there could be a meaningful debate about it if citizens were not allowed to advance their competing reasons for answering this question of value one way rather than another and to try to get their fellow citizens to see the force of these reasons. These will include reasons that reflect their comprehensive views. But if a political system is fair and allows fair opportunity to advance such arguments, then it does not seem to me that those who lose out can claim that the result fails to respect them as free and equal citizens. By contrast, they could have such a complaint against a political system in which the rules of political debate and participation could themselves be justified only on sectarian grounds.

Let me conclude by considering how the claim that an overlapping consensus is possible can itself be established. How could it be shown that all reasonable comprehensive views could, each for its own reasons, accept a certain political conception of justice – for example, that they could all accept justice as fairness? One way to approach this question would be by enumeration – by considering in turn each comprehensive view, or each such view represented in a given society, and arguing that each of these views contains within it good grounds for accepting the political conception in question. This is clearly unfeasible. It would be impossible to survey all possible comprehensive views and inadequate, in an argument for stability, to consider just those that are represented in a given society at a given time since others may emerge at any time and gain adherents.

Rawls's alternative approach is rather to interpret the question in a way that makes the claim of overlapping consensus at least very plausible when considered as a general claim, without examining the distinctive content of particular comprehensive views. One might expect him to do this by a suitable definition of the notion of a reasonable comprehensive view. In part, this is what he does, but in the relevant passages it appears that much of the work is done by relying also on the notion of *a reasonable person* – that is to say, by taking the question of overlapping consensus to be whether a political conception is one that every reasonable person would have reason to support no matter what reasonable comprehensive view he or she held.

Rawls defines the idea of a reasonable comprehensive doctrine by citing three features. Such doctrines (1) involve the exercise of theoretical reason to develop a coherent and intelligible view of the world, (2) involve the exercise of practical reason in identifying certain values as significant and in balancing them when they conflict, and (3) although such views normally belong to some tradition of thought, they evolve over time in response to their adherents' judgments about what they take to be good and sufficient reasons (*PL*, p. 59). Having given this definition, which does not yet seem to provide a basis for assessing the possibility of an overlapping consensus on a political conception, he turns to the idea of a reasonable person. "Since there are many reasonable doctrines," he says, "the idea of the reasonable does not require us, or others, to believe any specific reasonable doctrine, though we may do so." But "reasonable persons will think it unreasonable to use political power, should they possess it, to repress comprehensive views that are not unreasonable, though different from their own" (*PL*, p. 60).

This affects the content of reasonable comprehensive views, insofar as they are views that can be held by reasonable persons. Since reasonable persons do not think that they have good reason to use political power to repress other comprehensive views, they will themselves accept only comprehensive views that do not require this, and if a view they accept seems to require it they will (in accordance with feature (3) above) modify it so that it does not. This leads, Rawls thinks, to the conclusion that reasonable persons (whatever reasonable comprehensive views they may hold) will accept, as a standard for assessing the basic institutions of their society, a political conception of justice which is supported on grounds that do not depend on any particular comprehensive view. Rawls concludes from this that a political conception that is supported by such reasons could be the object of an overlapping consensus among reasonable persons holding diverse reasonable comprehensive views.

Even if this argument is accepted, it may seem to beg the question, or at least to be insufficient, because it does not settle the question of whether any particular comprehensive view (in particular, many of the religious and philosophical views with which we are familiar) is a reasonable view "that could be held by reasonable persons" in the sense that Rawls relies on in this argument. So it seems that the argument needs to be supplemented by something more along the lines of the first strategy I mentioned. And Rawls does indeed offer some supplementation of this kind in a series of long footnotes where he argues that Islam and Roman Catholicism can be understood as such views, although their followers and leaders have not always understood them in this way.[13]

It is often a subject of unresolved tension within a comprehensive view how those who do not accept that view should be treated. On the one hand, as human beings, or children of God, they are "our brothers and sisters"; on the other hand, as nonbelievers they may need to be required to accept the true doctrine. For example, Rawls quotes John Courtney Murray as saying that with Vatican II's acceptance of religious freedom, "a long-standing ambiguity [in the Roman Catholic Church's position] had finally been cleared up" (PRR, p. 167). This is, as I have said, a tension that exists within many comprehensive views, and the account I have attributed to Rawls – of a process in which the view of others that we, as "reasonable persons," come to accept forces a change in the reasons that we think our comprehensive view can endorse – seems a good description of the way in which it may be resolved. It is important to note that Rawls does not exempt his own (earlier) liberal comprehensive view from this description and is therefore not saying simply that *religious* views need to be reformed and become tolerant. After all, the process of thought leading to *Political Liberalism* and subsequent writings was exactly a process of resolving an "ambiguity" within his own liberal view in the way just described.[14]

ENDNOTES

1  In "Reply to Habermas," Rawls says that reflective equilibrium is "a point at infinity we can never reach, though we may get closer to it in the sense that through discussion, our ideals, principles, and judgments seem more reasonable to us and we regard them as better founded than they were before." See John Rawls, *Political Liberalism* (New York: Columbia University Press, 1995, pbk. ed.) p. 385 (cited as *PL* in text).

2  In John Rawls, *Collected Papers*, ed. Samuel Freeman (Cambridge, MA: Harvard University Press, 1999), pp. 1–19 (cited as *CP* in text).

3  Joseph Raz raises this question in "The Claims of Reflective Equilibrium," *Inquiry* 25 (1982), pp. 307–30.

4  See David Copp, "Considered Judgments and Justification: Conservatism in Moral Theory," in D. Copp and M. Zimmerman, eds., *Morality, Reason and Truth* (Totowa, NJ: Rowman and Allenheld, 1985), pp. 141–69.

5  Richard B. Brandt, *A Theory of the Good and the Right* (Oxford, UK: The Clarendon Press, 1979), p. 20. For critical discussion of Brandt's objection, see David Brink, *Moral Realism and the Foundations of Ethics* (Cambridge, UK: Cambridge University Press, 1989), pp. 135–6.

6  See *Political Liberalism*, Lecture III, Section 6, "Objectivity Independent of the Causal View of Knowledge," pp. 116–18.

7  These two points are central to Rawls's discussion of objectivity in Lecture III of *Political Liberalism*. See esp. pp. 111, 119.

8  This passage and the paragraph containing it were omitted in the revised edition of *TJ*.

9  Thus, Norman Daniels writes, "In seeking wide reflective equilibrium, we are constantly making plausibility judgments about which of our considered judgments we should revise in the light of theoretical considerations at all levels." "Wide Reflective Equilibrium and Theory Acceptance in Ethics," *The Journal of Philosophy* 76 (1979), p. 267.

10   Thus, Brandt (see note 4 above) was correct that the justificatory force of an application of the method of reflective equilibrium depends on the credibility of its starting points (and, one might add, of the other judgments made along the way). But this is not an objection to that method.

11   The following discussion summarizes points made by Rawls in his introduction to the paperback edition of *Political Liberalism*. See especially pp. xlii–xliii.

12   See Rawls, "The Idea of Public Reason Revisited," in *The Law of Peoples* (Cambridge, MA: Harvard University Press, 1999), sec. 4. (Referred to as *PRR* in text.)

13   On Islam, see footnote 46 on p. 151 of "The Idea of Public Reason Revisited." On Roman Catholicism, see note 75 on pp. 166–7 and notes 82 and 83 on p. 170 of the same work.

14   Given this fact, it is ironic that that work was criticized by many as an attack on religion, which attempted to deny religious views a role in politics. Much of "The Idea of Public Reason Revisited" is intended to explain why this criticism is misplaced.

# 4   Rawls on the Relationship between Liberalism and Democracy

Rawls and his critics agree on at least this: his theory is liberal. This essay asks, To what extent is it also democratic? Does Rawlsian liberalism denigrate democracy as some critics charge? Despite the enormous literature on Rawls, remarkably little has been written on the relationship between liberalism and democracy in the theory. Critics over the years have suggested that the theory denigrates democracy in one of three ways, which I consider by posing three critical questions about the theory. First, does it devalue the equal political liberty of adults (at any one of three levels of theory formation)? Second, does it devalue the political process of majority rule? Third, does it devalue the kind of civic discourse that relies on more comprehensive philosophies – both religious and secular – rather than on the free-standing political philosophy that Rawls's theory distinctively defends?[1]

In interpreting Rawls's understanding of democracy, I draw upon both *A Theory of Justice* (*Justice*) and *Political Liberalism* (*Liberalism*).[2] The two works diverge at points, which I discuss when the differences bear on Rawls's understanding of the relationship between liberalism and democracy. But together they have more to say about the relationship than either work alone.

In both *Justice* and *Liberalism*, Rawls emphasizes that the subject of justice is the basic structure of society, which he identifies as "major social institutions . . . [that] distribute the fundamental rights and duties and determine the division of advantages from social cooperation" (*Justice*, p. 7/6 rev.). The institutional distribution of fundamental rights, duties, and life chances is the ultimate subject of justice as fairness. But Rawls's theory does not speak directly about the design of democratic institutions, and for good reason. The theory

168

is primarily normative rather than empirical, and it is therefore concerned chiefly with specifying the normative standards – principles and other normative criteria – that democratic institutions must satisfy to be justified. The theory has a lot to say about the ideal of free and equal citizenship. It is this ideal and its principled implications, we shall see, that reveal most about Rawls on the relationship between liberalism and democracy.

To investigate this relationship, I need to begin with a preliminary definition of democracy. Democracy is among the most contested of moral and political concepts. My preliminary definition is therefore stipulative and subject to revision upon further argument. Democracy sometimes is simply defined as majority rule (particularly by its critics). But political philosophy seeks a moral understanding or ideal of democracy, and a moral ideal is forsaken at the start if democracy is defined as majority rule or an alternative decision-making rule or procedure. (Later in this chapter, I pursue other reasons to be skeptical of identifying democracy too closely with majority rule. But the definition with which I begin leaves open the question of what institutions are democratic, depending on the context.)

Basic to the ideal of democracy, as I understand it and as it has commonly been understood in political theory, is equal political liberty. A society is (or is not) a democracy to the extent that it succeeds (or fails) in securing equal political liberty for all its (law-abiding) adult members and in expressing their status as individuals with equal political liberty (or as equal citizens, for short). In Section 1, I suggest why identifying democracy with equal political liberty provides a reasonable starting point for interpreting the relationship between liberalism and democracy in Rawls's theory.

If democracy is identified with equal political liberty, the first question that arises is whether (or to what extent) Rawls's political liberalism devalues equal political liberty by subordinating it to the value that is most often distinctively associated with liberalism, equal personal liberty. The subordination can occur in at least three different levels of theory formation, which I consider in Sections 2, 3, and 4. The theory's most fundamental understanding of what count as the basic liberties may exclude political liberties or clearly value them less than personal liberties (Section 2). Even if the theory includes political liberties among the basic liberties, they may be valued only as means to the ends of personal liberties (Section 3). And even if the theory values political liberties as more than mere means to realizing the personal liberties, it may give priority to personal liberties whenever they conflict with political liberties (Section 4).

Equal political liberty is often closely associated with a defense of majority rule (although there is no logical entailment). Section 5 offers an answer to the second question, Does Rawls's theory devalue majority rule?, by assessing the theory's understanding of the relationship of equal political liberty to majoritarianism.

Citizens who enjoy equal political liberty, one might think, speak their minds about politically relevant issues from any perspective – including their comprehensive philosophies of life – that they reasonably think are most likely to lead to just laws and institutions. Section 6 responds to the third question that arises when we identify democracy with equal political liberty: Does Rawls's theory devalue some kinds of publicly defensible discourse in politics?

## I. EQUAL POLITICAL LIBERTY AND DEMOCRATIC EQUALITY

My task in answering these questions about Rawls's perspective on democracy is unavoidably one of interpretation rather than demonstration. The texts do not explicitly say much about democracy. Were readers to begin by consulting the admirably complete indexes of *Justice* and *Liberalism* for all entries on democracy, they would find only one (not very revealing) entry in *Justice* and not a single entry in *Liberalism*. It would be a mistake, however, to conclude from the few explicit references to democracy that the two books have little to say about the subject. Rather, Rawls implicitly identifies democracy with the same broad ideal of political morality with which he identifies political liberalism: the ideal of all (sane and law-abiding) adult human beings as free and equal members of a fair system of social cooperation.

Attributing to Rawls the identification of democracy with the broad ideal of free and equal membership in a fair system of social cooperation helps explain his definition in *Justice* of "democratic equality," which is the only explicit index entry for democracy. "Democratic equality" is the interpretation of the second ("opportunity") principle that does the most to secure the fair value of liberty for the least advantaged person. The "democratic equality" interpretation joins the difference principle – which maximizes the distribution of primary goods to the least advantaged – with fair equality of opportunity. It therefore does more to express and secure the status of the least advantaged as free and equal members of a fair system of social cooperation than the interpretations of the opportunity principles that Rawls calls "liberal equality," "natural aristocracy," and the "system of natural liberty."

The democratic equality interpretation of the second principle is distinctive among these four interpretations in its aim of ensuring the fair value of personal and political liberty, taken together, for the least advantaged members of society. Democratic equality thereby helps secure for every member of society, not only the more affluent, the actual benefits of personal and political freedoms that are basic to free and equal membership in a fair scheme of social cooperation, not only formal rights. "Taking the two principles [of basic liberty and opportunity] together," as Rawls puts it, "the basic structure is to be arranged to maximize the worth of liberty to the least advantaged of the complete scheme of equal liberty shared by all. This defines the end of social justice" [*Justice*, p. 205/179 rev.]. Rawls views this end of social justice as democratic insofar as it maximizes the capacity of the least advantaged members of society to realize their aims, including their political aims, and is consistent with protecting everyone's equal liberty.

But this interpretation of Rawls's theory still does not face up to the hard questions concerning the relationship between democracy and liberalism. It does not tell us how the theory values political liberties (such as freedom of political speech, political participation, suffrage, and the right to stand for political office) compared to personal liberties (such as freedom of nonpolitical speech, religion, and conscience) within the "complete scheme of equal liberty." This is the first and most fundamental question that must be answered if we are to understand the relationship between democracy and liberalism in Rawls's theory, or indeed more generally.

Before addressing this issue, it is worth noting how the example of "democratic equality" illustrates in microcosm the complexity of interpreting the relationship of the democratic and liberal elements in Rawls's theory. Democratic equality, according to Rawls, does not justify giving less affluent citizens a greater freedom – of speech, for example – as compensation for their lesser income and wealth. Because it maximizes the worth of freedom in general, not just political freedom, to the least advantaged by incorporating the proviso "consistent with protecting everyone's equal liberty," democratic equality is also a liberal principle. "Freedom as equal liberty," Rawls writes in *Justice*, "is the same for all; the question of compensating for a lesser than equal liberty does not arise. The worth of liberty is not the same for everyone.... The lesser worth of liberty is, however, compensated for, since the capacity of the less fortunate members of society to achieve their aims would be even less were they not to accept the existing inequalities whenever the difference principle is satisfied" [*Justice*, p. 204/179 rev.]. This and other liberal features of Rawls's theory are tied to the same ideal of the person that supports the difference principle and political liberty as part of the first principle (of equal liberty). The question distinctively directed to democratic concerns therefore remains unanswered, How does Rawls's theory value political liberty compared to personal liberty? The key to the way Rawls answers this question lies in his emphasis on the similar source of the values of both political and personal liberty in his theory.

## 2. CO-ORIGINALITY OF POLITICAL AND PERSONAL LIBERTY

I therefore turn to Rawls's fundamental ideal of the person as a free and equal member of a fair scheme of social cooperation, which is often identified as "liberal" *rather than* "democratic." The theory is then criticized – or else commended, depending on the perspective of the commentator – for being liberal rather than democratic. But the ideal itself – short of further interpretation and investigation of its implications – cannot tell us whether Rawls's theory is liberal *rather than* democratic, or both. Moreover, it does not help us identify how and why the theory is either liberal or democratic, or both.

The ideal of the person as a free and equal member of a fair scheme of social cooperation is, according to *Liberalism*, political, not metaphysical. What does understanding this ideal politically, not metaphysically, entail? To be a free and equal member of a fair scheme of social cooperation, according to Rawls, requires having a set of liberties that include both personal and political freedoms. This means that to be a free member of a fair scheme of social cooperation, a person must be able to choose among the good lives that are possible within such a scheme of social cooperation. Freedom of choice among good lives requires a set of personal liberties, such as freedom of religion and conscience, freedom of thought and speech, and freedom of association. This might be considered the personal liberty dimension of the ideal. But having freedom of choice among the good lives that happen to be available in one's society is certainly not all that it takes to be a free and equal member of a fair scheme of social cooperation. Although the ideal of course does not imply the impossible – that people can live under laws of their own *individual* choosing – it does imply the need for a fair distribution of political power. Adults should be able to share as civic equals in shaping their institutional context to the extent that this is possible and consistent with the ideal of free and equal membership in their society. This fair sharing of political power among civic equals implies a set of equal political liberties, which has the same source as the set of personal liberties. The personal and political liberties are, to borrow a term used by Jürgen Habermas, co-original.[3]

Equal political liberty is one expression and manifestation of the value of being a free and equal member of a society whose adult members together are self-governing. If the term *self-government* seems misleading, the same idea can be conveyed by saying that equal political liberty entails the right of adult members of a society to share as free and equal individuals in making mutually binding decisions about their collective life. The set of equal political liberties enables adults to share in shaping the context within which each can enjoy the set of equal personal liberties. On this interpretation, which is consistent with what Rawls says in both *Liberalism* and *Justice*, the set of political liberties is as central as the set of personal liberties to the Rawlsian ideal of the person. The first principle of justice – the priority of basic liberty – gives priority to all basic liberties, both political and personal, over the second principle of justice, which governs the distribution of job opportunities, income, wealth, and other primary goods.

This account of the co-originality of the set of basic liberties, both political and personal, parallels Habermas's account of the relationship between private and public autonomy, although Rawls does not rely on a moral ideal of autonomy in *Liberalism*. Instead he relies on what he calls a free-standing political ideal of the person. Despite this difference, on both Rawls's and Habermas's understandings, *neither* the set of basic personal freedoms *nor* those of basic political freedoms has priority over the other. Habermas makes this explicit when he writes, "Thus private and public autonomy mutually presuppose each other in such a way that neither human rights nor popular sovereignty can claim primacy over its counterparts."[4] The same is true in Rawls's theory. To put it in more Rawlsian terms: a liberal democratic ideal is fundamentally committed to securing *both* substantive political and personal liberties. In this sense, Rawls's theory is both democratic and liberal at its core.

The co-originality of basic political and personal liberties in the Rawlsian ideal of the person does not answer the question of how the value of political freedom compares with that of personal freedom when they come into conflict, or when each is more substantively evaluated for the purposes of practical judgment. Co-originality establishes that conflicts between personal and political liberties, between the more distinctively liberal and democratic values, are internal to Rawls's theory itself. These conflicts are part of the condition of human politics – even at its best – rather than an artifact of a misguided politics or an indiscriminate political theory. The theory therefore must suggest a way of adjudicating among conflicts between personal and political liberties without giving either absolute priority at the level of first principle over the other. This still leaves open the possibility that at some other level Rawls's theory subordinates political liberty to personal liberty.

### 3. AN INTIMATE MARRIAGE

Because Rawls's theory incorporates both democratic and liberal values at its core and identifies these values with the same source (a political ideal of the person as a free and equal citizen), it is more difficult than it otherwise would be to distinguish the liberal and democratic elements of his theory. Something similar can be said of Habermas's theory, although he writes more explicitly about the liberal and democratic elements of his theory and sometimes seems to give primacy to the latter. But a close analysis of Habermas's theory, which is beyond the scope of this chapter, would expose a similarly complex understanding of the relationship between liberal and democratic elements. The difficulty of sharply distinguishing the liberal and democratic elements of a political theory is, I think, a necessary part of any theory that takes seriously the basic value of both.

If Rawls and Habermas are right about co-originality, then liberalism, defined as a defense of equal personal freedom, and democracy, defined as a defense of political freedom, are ideally united not merely in a marriage of convenience but more intimately.[5] Neither political freedoms nor personal freedoms are subordinated to the other in a purely means–ends relationship. This is a controversial position for some liberals and for some democrats. Some liberals suggest that the value of equal political liberty, and therefore of democracy, is purely instrumental to a defense of liberal freedoms. For this view to be internally consistent with liberalism, however, liberals must exclude equal political freedom from the list of basic liberal freedoms and create another category of freedoms that are less basic because they are only instrumentally valuable as a means to realizing the other, more basic, personal freedoms. This is precisely what Rawls explicitly refuses to do.

Some democrats reject the idea of an intimate alliance with liberalism for the opposite reason. They think that the personal freedoms valued most by liberals, such as freedom of conscience, speech, and association, are at best instrumentally valuable on democratic grounds. Personal freedoms are instrumentally valuable insofar as they are the preconditions for realizing equal political liberty understood as political autonomy, collective self-government, or popular sovereignty. But for this claim to be consistent with a democratic perspective, the democrat must show why it makes sense to value equal political liberty but not equal personal liberty insofar as both are possible. Democrats who take this position have not offered a compelling response to Habermas's co-originality claim.[6] Valuing the political freedom of individuals, according to Habermas, morally presupposes valuing their personal freedom as well. The relationship between personal and political freedom – for Rawls as for Habermas – is intimate, not only instrumental.

Under conditions of severe oppression, where basic personal freedoms are at risk, it is reasonable to value freedom from cruelty as the overriding end, and political freedom as a necessary means to securing that end for as many oppressed people as possible. Rawls's theory – like Habermas's – asks us to consider the more favorable conditions of a just society, or a nearly just one. A far more intimate relationship then exists between the more distinctively liberal and democratic freedoms connected to the co-originality of their value. Without basic personal freedoms, on the one hand, citizens cannot truly be free to criticize their government or to stand up to a majority in the name of justice. Without basic political freedoms, on the other hand, individuals cannot be as free as possible (consistent with basic personal freedoms) to shape the laws, institutions, and practices within which they can make personal choices about how best to live their own life. It is this kind of intimate relationship that helps account for how "monogamously, faithfully, and permanently married to democracy" liberalism is.[7] Like most intimate relationships, the one between democracy and liberalism is considerably more complex than a marriage of mere convenience.

The marriage of democracy and liberalism is made neither in heaven nor in a metaphysical theory, according to Rawls, but in a socially constructed ideal of people as free and equal members of a cooperative social system. Rawls's claim that his theory is political, not metaphysical, is easily misunderstood. His ideal of the person is not neutral among all metaphysical theories (nor does it claim to be). It rules out some (implausible) metaphysical conceptions of the individual, for example, the person as totally constituted and determined by communally given ends and incapable of identifying and appreciating the value of justice or of a good life.[8] But a political ideal of free and equal persons is compatible with many competing metaphysical conceptions of the person, both religious and secular, and does not presuppose (for example) a Kantian metaphysics.

Although the Rawlsian ideal is socially constructed for the purpose of conceptualizing a just political order, it is no less morally important for that reason. A cooperative social system can be socially constructed for better or for worse. To make it better, we need to ask what would justify a social system that claims the authority to impose the coercive power of the state and man-made law on its members. In *Justice*, Rawls suggests as part of an apparatus of justification the idea of an original position where we all imagine ourselves as free and equal persons without more particular social identities – we do not know whether we are men or women, rich or poor, Christians, Jews, Muslims, or atheists. We then defend principles from this common position. The principles that are defended in the original position satisfy our self-interest, which is in effect the interest of everyone (because none of us while arguing from this position may invoke the particular interests that separate us outside of it).

The idea of the original position helps account for the disagreements between Rawls and Habermas on the relationship between liberalism and democracy. Habermas recognizes that personal and political liberties are co-original in Rawls's theory "at the level of the original position" and at the "first level of theory formation." But he then objects that liberal freedoms gain priority "under the institutional conditions of an already constituted just society."[9] At this second level, Habermas argues, citizens will feel and be constrained because

they cannot reignite the radical democratic embers of the original position in the civic life of their society, for from their perspective all the essential discourses of legitimation have already taken place within the theory; and they find the results of the theory already sedimented in the constitution.[10]

Rawls responds that all levels of thinking – whether in the original position, in order to design a constitution, or after the constitution has been created – are available to every citizen at all times. These levels of thinking are meant to model how citizens may judge the justice of their society, depending on whether they are considering the basic principles, the constitution, or the practices that follow from constitutional (or first) principles [*Liberalism*, pp. 381–96]. The original position therefore does not take away the political liberty of citizens before they even start thinking about the justice of their society. But it does constrain the thinking of citizens so that they do not invoke their comprehensive conceptions when arguing about first principles and constitutional essentials. After all misunderstandings are cleared away, Rawls and Habermas disagree about this feature of the original position as a recommended mode of political discourse. Because political liberalism does not require reasoning from the original position, it dispenses with this particular problem. The remaining question about public discourse, addressed in Section 6, is whether what political liberalism counts as publicly defensible is still too constraining.

In *Liberalism*, Rawls defends the idea that there is a family of ways of justifying a cooperative social system to people who are conceived of as free and equal members of that system [*Liberalism*, pp. 26–8]. The original position is part of this family, no single member of which is privileged by the perspective of political liberalism. Political liberalism therefore asks us to focus on those features of Rawls's theory in *Justice* that are common to the family as a whole and do not require acceptance of the original position. One of these features is the "principle of participation." "All citizens," Rawls writes, "are to have an equal right to take part in, and to determine the outcome of, the constitutional process that establishes the laws with which they are to comply" [*Justice*, p. 221/194 rev.]. Rawls identifies this part of a constitutional democracy with what Benjamin Constant called the "liberty of the ancients."[11] And like Constant, Rawls thinks that the political freedom secured by the principle of participation – although it is only part (and not necessarily the most important part) of what liberty consists in – has been neglected by modern societies to the considerable detriment of its citizens.[12]

Rawls, like Constant, does not advocate the personal liberty of the moderns to the exclusion of the political liberty of the ancients.[13] "If the state is ... to affect permanently men's [and women's] prospects in life," Rawls writes, "then the constitutional process should preserve the equal representation of the original position to the degree that this is practicable" [*Justice*, p. 222/195 rev.]. It remains to be seen, upon further investigation, to what degree equal representation is possible. For Rawls, this judgment is to be made by comparing the value of different liberties when (and if) they compete under specific circumstances.

Rawls absolutely rejects trading off political liberty for something other than another equal liberty, and he also absolutely rejects the general idea that political liberty is of lesser value than personal liberty in modern society and therefore must be subordinated to it. Rawls's first principle of equal liberty, which is preserved in political liberalism, incorporates the protection of *both* personal and political liberties and gives priority to the entire system of basic liberties, not to personal over political liberty, or vice versa.

There are at least three good reasons for giving priority to the complete set of personal and political liberties over other considerations of justice. One reason highlights the important way in which liberalism and democracy are instrumentally related. Political liberties are instrumental in helping people live a good life. Their value is not therefore more contingent than the value of personal liberties. Without personal liberties, people cannot carry out their own purposes unless they happen to have a guardian who will just as reliably carry out their purposes for them. This reason for valuing personal freedoms – that few people can count on unaccountable personal guardians who will serve their interests better than they can do so themselves – is a contingent and instrumental reason for valuing personal liberty. It is a good reason, which helps account for why it makes sense for people to highly prize their personal liberties.

It may be less obvious, but it is no less true that people cannot carry out their own purposes without political liberties. Political liberties serve a more indirect purpose than personal liberties. By exercising political liberties, people collectively create the context within which they can carry out their own (nonpolitical) purposes. The political liberties are instrumental in preserving the other liberties [*Liberalism*, p. 299]. Rawls argues that "to assign priority to these [political] liberties they need only be important enough as essential institutional means to secure the other basic liberties under the circumstances of a modern state" [*Liberalism*, p. 299].

But political liberties are not only important in this instrumental sense, and Rawls's theory helps highlight two distinctively democratic reasons for giving political liberty the same priority as personal liberty. The status of persons as free and equal beings is similarly expressed in public by recognition of the equal rights of law-abiding adults to both personal and political freedoms. If a law-abiding adult born in the United States is denied the right to vote or the right of religious worship, she and we have an equally good reason to think that she is being publicly denied the status of a free and equal person. The public recognition of both personal and political rights *expresses* the standing of individuals as free and equal members of society. When blacks and women were denied the vote in the United States, they were denied the public status of being equal citizens. Expressing our status as equal citizens is an important democratic purpose – call it the *expressive purpose* of political freedoms.[14]

In addition to functioning as instrumental means to securing basic personal liberties and expressing our status as equal citizens, the protection of political liberties serves a third purpose, which is both instrumental and democratic. Political liberties "secure the free and informed application of the principles of justice, by means of the full and effective exercise of citizens' sense of justice, to the basic structure of society" [*Liberalism*, p. 334]. The exercise of citizens' sense of justice is both instrumentally and intimately connected with the exercise of citizens' sense of their own good. This is an important insight of Rawls's theory and the most neglected relationship between liberal and democratic values – one that is simultaneously instrumental and intimate.

If people had no sense of the good that they sought to realize, then justice would have no purpose. It would be hollow, placing constraints (ideally self-constraints) on people's actions for little or no purpose. But if people had no sense of justice, then their pursuit of the good would have far less moral value and therefore be far less admirable. Not only would their actions often conflict with justice, but they would fail to express any commitment to pursuing their own good consistently with the good of others. Our reflective acceptance of justice increases the public value of our pursuit of our own good. As Rawls puts it (borrowing here from Kant), the justice of our actions makes our other accomplishments not only valuable, but admirable and our pleasures good. [*Liberalism*, p. 334]. It does not follow that our sense of justice, and the political freedoms that are means to just actions, are therefore more important than our personal freedoms. Nor that we should devote as much of our time and effort as possible to promoting justice. As Rawls writes with refreshing bluntness, "it would be madness to maximize just and rational actions by maximizing the occasions which require them" [*Liberalism*, p. 334].

What does follow is that, although they serve different purposes, the basic personal and political liberties are both essential to political liberalism. They are intimately as well as instrumentally related. It would weaken the liberal and the democratic nature of political liberalism – which we now have reason to label a liberal democratic theory – to give priority to all personal over all political liberties, or vice versa. From a Rawlsian perspective, the set of basic personal and political liberties, taken as a whole, are on a par in importance even though they serve (some) different purposes. Political and personal liberties, although not substitutable, are co-original and together take priority over other considerations of justice.

## 4. COPING WITH CONFLICTS AMONG BASIC LIBERTIES

This feature of Rawls's theory – a strength from the perspective of valuing political liberty – raises a question which might reveal a potential weakness: How can the theory cope with conflicts among basic liberties, and in particular between political and personal liberties, both of which are basic in principle? If Rawls's theory were simply liberal and not also democratic, then it could clearly give priority in the case of conflicts to personal over political liberties. In the case of conflicts, do political freedoms still end up taking a back seat to personal freedoms? If so, how can this be reconciled with the recognition that both sorts of freedom are fundamental to the ideal of free and equal citizenship? Or is the theory indeterminate? And if so, is this an avoidable weakness?

Rawls is clear and consistent in rejecting the idea that in the case of conflicts political liberties must generally be subordinated to personal liberties. He notes (citing Isaiah Berlin) that "one of the tenets of classical liberalism is that the political liberties are of less intrinsic importance than liberty of conscience and freedom of the person" [*Justice*, pp. 229–30/201–2 rev.]. But he does not endorse this tenet. In any case, even if personal liberties were more *intrinsically* important than political liberties, the question would still remain as to whether their intrinsic value outweighs the instrumental value of political freedoms in overall importance. An intrinsic value is not necessarily greater than an instrumental value. Rawls argues in a different vein that we do not need to assess "the relative total importance of different liberties." He applies "the principle of equal advantage [for all persons] in adjusting the complete system of freedom" [*Justice*, p. 230/202 rev.]. All persons – in order to be treated as free and equal citizens in a fair system of social cooperation – should be equally advantaged or disadvantaged by the trade-offs among particular liberties, including those trade-offs between personal and political liberties.

In the case of conflicts among basic liberties, Rawls's theory is therefore open to arguments that would limit some basic liberties for all citizens for the sake of more fully realizing other basic liberties. It is therefore possible to justify limits on political participation – and the extent of the principle of participation – in order to secure freedom of conscience and religion for all persons more fully. Rawls endorses the possibility that "a bill of rights may remove certain liberties from majority regulation altogether, and the separation of powers with judicial review may slow down the pace of legislative change" [*Justice*, p. 228/201 rev.]. He is careful to say that a bill of rights "may" – not that it "must" – remove certain liberties from majority regulation. A bill of rights may limit political liberty if and only if this can be publicly shown to be a reasonable way of equally protecting the value of the entire set of basic liberties for all citizens.

Rawls's way of proceeding in justifying trade-offs among basic liberties is significantly different from – and far more conducive to protecting political liberty – than giving priority to personal liberties per se over political liberties. That this is so can be seen by the way *Liberalism* is open to arguments about which particular liberties should be given priority in the case of specific conflicts. Rawls makes clear that some political liberties are more valuable than some personal liberties. In *Liberalism*, Rawls uses the same sort of reasoning that he introduced (but did not develop) in *Justice* to conclude that even in a just society "advocacy of revolutionary and even seditious doctrines is fully protected." Why? This particular political liberty is basic to permitting citizens to enlist their capacity for a sense of justice in judging their government. The freedom to enlist one's sense of justice in this way is essential to being able to judge and shape the basic structure of one's society as a free and equal citizen.

By contrast, "libel and defamation of private persons (as opposed to political figures)" is not protected. Political speech is more fully protected than private speech even though it is also potentially far more dangerous. Rawls's argument for protecting revolutionary and seditious doctrines is among the best ever offered for the importance of protecting political speech. The comparison with libel and defamation of private persons highlights the importance that a liberal democratic theory can and should accord to the public use of reason by citizens in judging their government. Unlike the advocacy of revolution, Rawls writes, the libel and defamation of private persons "has no significance at all for the public use of reason to judge and regulate the basic structure, and is in addition a private wrong..." [*Liberalism*, p. 336].

When any two liberties conflict – whether they be political or personal – the method of deciding which should give way to the other depends on an assessment of the relative importance for representative persons of the particular liberties in the overall scheme of equal liberties. It is not to be based on an assessment of the overall importance of political versus personal liberties. The justification for limiting political participation would therefore be to protect the other basic freedoms [*Justice*, p. 229/201 rev.]. This is a justification that can be publicly made by and for free and equal citizens, and it is precisely analogous to the justification that Rawls's theory gives for limiting some personal freedoms for the sake of protecting other more important freedoms. Whether any given limitation of either private or personal freedoms can be justified will depend on its "consequences for the complete system of liberty" [*Justice*, p. 229/201 rev.]. Free and equal citizens can justify limiting some political and some personal freedoms of all for the sake of better securing other freedoms for all. "The priority of liberty does not exclude marginal exchanges within the system of [equal] freedom" [*Justice*, p. 230/202 rev.].

Rawls's defense of permitting restrictions on campaign contributions for the sake of protecting the fair value of political liberty further demonstrates how his theory can avoid indeterminacy without giving priority in principle to either personal or political liberties. His critique of the decision of the United States Supreme Court in *Buckley v. Valeo* [424 US 1, 1976] offers strong support for interpreting political liberalism as democratic as well as liberal in its practical implications, not only in its basic principles. The Court majority in *Buckley* overturned as unconstitutional various spending limits in electoral campaigns by contributors and candidates that Congress put into law in the Election Act Amendment of 1974. The core of Rawls's critique of the majority in *Buckley* is that

the Court fails to recognize the essential point that the fair value of the political liberties is required for a just political procedure, and that to insure their fair value it is necessary to prevent those with greater property and wealth, and the greater skills of organization which accompany them, from controlling the electoral process to their advantage. [*Liberalism*, pp. 360–1]

Three conditions must be met to justify spending restrictions in political campaigns. Rawls argues that (1) there must be no restrictions on the content of speech; (2) there must be no undue or inequitable burdens on various political groups; and (3) the restrictions must further the fair value of political liberty. This example illustrates how "the mutual adjustment of the basic liberties is justified on grounds allowed by the priority of these liberties as a family, no one of which is in itself absolute" [*Liberalism*, p. 358]. While explicitly rejecting the idea associated with classical liberalism that personal liberties generally take priority over political liberties, Rawls's theory does not therefore become completely indeterminate in the face of conflicts among basic liberties. It provides a criterion by which conflicts can be resolved: judge the relative importance of particular liberties in the entire family, whose overall purpose is to permit free and equal citizens to apply principles of justice to their society and to apply deliberative reason to their individual lives. This criterion is as credibly democratic as it is liberal. It offers firm ground for a strong defense of equal political liberty, as Rawls's critique of the Court's decision in *Buckley* suggests.

But the strength of a Rawlsian defense of political liberty importantly depends on our interpretation of the criterion in a critical set of cases – those in which citizens' judgments about the relative importance of particular liberties reasonably differ. As Rawls writes, "different opinions about the value of the liberties will, of course, affect how different persons think the full scheme of freedom should be arranged" [*Justice*, p. 230/202 rev.]. Reasonable disagreements, according to Rawls, are consistent with searching for fair terms of social cooperation with those who are similarly searching for fair terms of social cooperation.[15] Rawls often uses "reasonable" to refer to those parts of comprehensive philosophies of life that are either irrelevant to the principles of justice or part of an overlapping consensus on the principles and therefore pose no problem for political liberalism. But reasonable disagreements over justice can also pose a distinctive problem for political liberalism. Some reasonable disagreements can be both politically relevant and obstacles to an overlapping consensus.

Can pornography be banned for the sake of securing the equal freedom of women? Can restrictions on a woman's basic liberty be justified in the name of respecting the right to life of a second trimester fetus?[16] Can capital punishment be justified? Suppose that, as a citizen, I would argue against capital punishment, against banning pornography, and against outlawing second trimester abortions. Other citizens, however, would (and do) argue in their favor. Do the best arguments on opposing sides of these, or any other political controversies concerning basic liberties, constitute reasonable disagreements? Political liberalism must admit this possibility – even probability. But if there are reasonable disagreements among citizens concerning their basic liberties, then political liberalism faces the challenge of specifying how best to deal with these disagreements, which stand in the way of an overlapping consensus concerning the ordering of our basic liberties. As the examples of pornography, abortion, and capital punishment suggest, there is also reasonable disagreement over whether a disagreement counts as reasonable. It is hard to recognize reasonable disagreements with our own strongly held views and even harder for us to defend a justifiable resolution to these disagreements in the face of both levels of (possibly reasonable) disagreement. These disagreements are all internal to political liberalism but not created by it.

Even (or especially) in the face of reasonable disagreement, political liberalism consistently supports taking one's own side in political arguments and not compromising one's principles. But much more can be said from the perspective of political liberalism about coping with reasonable disagreement than that citizens should take their own principled side in the substantive argument. Although Rawls does not develop this part of political liberalism, his theory has the resources to offer both instrumental and intrinsic reasons for citizens to treat their fellow citizens with mutual respect – or what Rawls calls "civic friendship" [*Liberalism*, li] – when they reasonably disagree, rather than merely to tolerate them (as they should in the face of unreasonable disagreements). Mutual respect entails offering reasons, as Rawls puts it, that our fellow citizens "not only understand – as Servetus could understand why Calvin wanted to burn him at the stake – but reasons we might reasonably expect that they as free and equal might reasonably also accept" [*Liberalism*, p. li].

Reasonable disagreement, then, is characterized by both sides arguing and acting consistently with a civic standard of reciprocity, which is a political ideal of mutually justifying mutually binding laws, not everything important in one's life [*Liberalism*, p. xlvi]. When citizens are guided by reciprocity, even if they do the best they can to find and defend fair standards of social cooperation, they may still disagree over what reciprocity requires of their political institutions and laws. Citizens who are free to think for themselves cannot reasonably expect always to agree about what reciprocity requires any more than they can reasonably expect always to agree about what goodness requires.

But in the midst of reasonable disagreement, which arises within a mutual search for fair standards of social cooperation, citizens can recognize their relationship as one of civic friendship. This relationship is desirable in itself even if we do not desire it as much as more personal forms of friendship. It is also valuable for its educative effects in encouraging fellow citizens to learn from one another and thereby develop better and more mutual understandings of what justice demands. And civic friendship is desirable for its effects in supporting those institutions and laws that protect basic liberty and justice more generally.

This part of political liberalism needs to be developed further in response to the worry that it does not fully face up to the political conflicts caused by reasonable disagreements over matters of justice, which cannot by their very nature be taken off the political agenda. Here I can only briefly suggest some ways in which political liberalism can consistently respond to such disagreements so that citizens are encouraged to make productive use of their equal political liberty. In essence, the idea is that mutual respect – as distinguished from toleration alone – is an important public value, and it is manifest when citizens interact with one another constructively in the midst of reasonable disagreement.

Various modes of constructive interaction are consistent with Rawls's theory even if not fully developed or logically required by it. For example, people who reasonably disagree may demonstrate civic integrity and magnanimity and encourage other people to make productive use of their political freedoms.[17] People with civic integrity explain the publicly defensible reasons for their political positions. They do not hide or distort their views to manipulate or deceive their fellow citizens. People with civic magnanimity recognize the publicly defensible reasons for positions that they oppose. They demonstrate that they respect opposition when such respect is warranted and thereby avoid treating every political controversy as if it were a battle of good against the forces of evil. Although civic integrity and magnanimity may leave reasonable disagreements unresolved at any given time, they are likely to aid in the resolution of those disagreements over time.

A more specific method of manifesting mutual respect in the midst of reasonable disagreement is to economize on moral disagreement with one's political opponents.[18] Citizens who economize on their moral disagreements search for significant points of moral and practical convergence in their positions. They do not compromise their principles or change their views for the sake of agreement. But they do search for ways in which they can accommodate parts of their opponents' reasonable positions without compromising their own. For example, opponents of capital punishment may support the penalty of life imprisonment without parole for the most heinous crimes since they can agree with advocates of capital punishment on the importance of protecting innocent lives. Advocates of capital punishment can support due process guarantees that minimize the chance that the state will sentence an innocent person to death. Were both opponents and advocates of capital punishment to practice an economy of moral disagreement (and both sides must to make the practice work as it should), they probably still would not resolve the reasonable disagreements between them. But economizing on moral disagreement almost certainly would make a positive difference in liberal democratic politics.

The ideas of civic integrity, magnanimity, and the economy of moral disagreement help demonstrate how political liberalism can be developed so that it offers justifiable ways of coping with conflicts among basic liberties that are not resolvable by a general priority principle. These ways are not only consistent with, but also depend upon, a robust defense of political liberty. When developed in this deliberative direction, political liberalism explicitly recognizes that many reasonable disagreements about matters of justice depend for their fair resolution on reciprocity – not only in political theory but also in political action among citizens who enjoy equal political liberty.

## 5. EVALUATING MAJORITY RULE

It is a democratic strength of political liberalism that it ranks political liberties fully alongside of personal liberties and that it is consistent with finding ways in which citizens can respond constructively to reasonable conflicts about matters of justice by exercising their equal political liberties. But is Rawls's political liberalism sufficiently democratic once it is developed in these directions? Doubts remain.

One source of doubt is that political liberalism supports constitutional rather than more popular, majoritarian decision making as a way of resolving disagreements about matters of justice. In *Justice*, Rawls defends those decision-making procedures – whether majoritarian or nonmajoritarian – that are more consistent with protecting the total system of basic liberties. The theory does not assume that a judicial procedure is therefore better than a legislative one. There are two reasons for not assuming this. First, the best-informed people reasonably disagree about when courts or legislatures better protect (which) basic liberties. Second, what constitutes the most justifiable balance among basic liberties is also open to reasonable disagreement. "Those who place a higher worth on the principle of participation," for example, "will be prepared to take greater risks with the freedoms of the persons, say, in order to give political liberty a larger place" [*Justice*, p. 230/202 rev.]. There should be a way under favorable conditions, Rawls continues, to give ample scope to political participation without jeopardizing personal liberties. As we have seen, the theory does not subordinate political freedoms to personal ones, or vice versa.

However, the theory does explicitly subordinate the political procedure of majority rule to "the political ends that the constitution is designed to achieve" [*Justice*, p. 356]. Majority rule is a means to other ends, Rawls writes. The other ends include both political freedoms – such as "freedom of speech and assembly, freedom to take part in public affairs and to influence by constitutional means the course of legislation" – and personal freedoms such as protection of freedom of conscience.

Some form of majority rule is often justified, Rawls also writes, "as the best available way of insuring just and effective legislation. It is compatible with equal liberty and possesses a certain naturalness; for if minority rule is allowed, there is no obvious criterion to select which one is to decide and equality is violated" [*Justice*, p. 356/313 rev.]. Majority rule, according to Rawls, has an instrumental value in achieving "just and effective legislation," a value in being compatible with equal liberty (although not uniquely so), and a value in expressing this compatibility with a "certain naturalness." But, he also writes with admirable directness: "There is nothing to the view ... that what the majority wills is right." (id.) We should judge the outcome of (majority or nonmajority) voting on matters of justice by whether it is compatible with justice.

Does valuing majority rule as a means to realizing just outcomes make Rawls's theory less democratic? To answer this question, we need to ask another. Does the ideal of democracy require that majority rule be considered valuable in itself rather than the generally best means of achieving morally good ends and of expressing political equality? Rawls rejects the definition of democracy as majority rule, but so do most democratic theorists, and for good reason. No one has yet to offer compelling reasons for why defenders of democracy should value majority rule more highly than protecting basic liberties and realizing just legislation. Rawls joins most democratic theorists in not valuing majority rule so highly as to place it above the protection of equal liberty or the realization of just legislation.

Rawls goes a step further. He also suggests that majority rule is not necessarily more democratic in itself than plurality rule or unanimity in all political circumstances. Juries in criminal cases in the United States decide by unanimity. Is this undemocratic or less democratic than a procedure of "let the majority of jurors decide"? A unanimity principle favors the status quo. In criminal cases there are good reasons of justice to favor the status quo. The status quo leaves the defendant free from punishment by the state, whereas there is no similarly strong reason to privilege the status quo in most other political deliberations. To give a minority veto power is morally dangerous in most legislation because considerations of justice argue against privileging the status quo. Even in legislation, however, a divergence from majority rule is not presumptively undemocratic or even less democratic all things considered. Other voting rules may be similarly consistent with expressing and protecting the equal political liberty of citizens and pursuing just legislation.

Some theorists suggest that majority rule, at least in the legislative arena, uniquely respects the equal political authority of every individual, and this equality (at least partly) defines democracy. For them democracy is the form of government that respects the equal political authority of every individual first by counting every person's vote as one, none for more than one, and second by moving the political body in the direction of the larger number of votes. They neglect the other ways of respecting the equal political authority of every individual and expressing that respect publicly. The unanimity rule in jury deliberation respects and expresses this idea as well, if not better, than would majority rule given the public purpose of jury deliberations.

Perhaps juries are insufficiently political bodies to assess the idea that majority rule is inherently more democratic than its alternatives. What about the claim that majority rule is the distinctively democratic principle for voting for representatives, legislation, and constitution making? In some cases, and in some political contexts, plurality rule, proportional representation, or even supermajority rule may offer a greater likelihood of achieving just results and may succeed equally well in expressing the status of citizens and treating them as political equals. Majority rule may be the most common and straightforward way of expressing the equal civic status of citizens who actually have equal political liberties. But it is the expression of equal political liberties that does the moral work in affirming the value of majority rule, not the intrinsic value of majority rule itself.

We need only suppose a situation in which proportional representation or some other procedure rule (consistent with equal political liberty) would lessen the likelihood of passing racially discriminatory laws in a state with a racist majority. To oppose such an alternative to majority rule on the grounds that there is something uniquely democratic about majority rule is to subordinate a defensible political morality committed to treating adults as civic equals to an indefensible claim about the inherent value of majorities' exercising moral authority in politics.

A critic who agrees with this substantive moral judgment may still argue that I am confusing what is right with what is democratic. Why, he may ask, is it not necessarily more democratic to move the political body in the direction of the majority? (It is no argument of course to insist on *defining* democracy as majority rule.) One reason it is not necessarily more democratic to move in the direction of a simple majority is that when the moral merits of the views of voters are held constant, some voters are generally more likely to have a greater chance of constituting a simple majority than others. In a society where there is relatively normal distribution of interests, preferences, and ideals among citizens whose views do not shift randomly over time across this distribution, majority rule cannot be recommended on grounds that it accords equal political authority or influence to each citizen. Yet an alternative procedure may equally respect equal political liberty and be at least as likely to produce justifiable results and to give a fair hearing to the views of all citizens. Under these ordinary circumstances, majority rule per se is not more democratic.

Some other decision-making rules may also better protect the conditions of democracy such as basic political liberties. Majorities can recognize this and agree to bind themselves into the future when they will be tempted to violate minority rights. But majorities also change over time, and it cannot be a necessary condition of justifying every divergence from majority rule that each and every majority consents to the alternative procedure. In practice, this procedural requirement would undermine the very purpose of the protection. Majority rule typically comes into its own, democratically speaking, when it is the best way of either expressing the equal political status of citizens, securing justifiable outcomes, or both. What Rawls says in *Justice* about majority rule is therefore sound and consistent with a conception of democracy that is fundamentally committed to protecting equal political liberty.

Is there a democratic presumption in favor of majority rule (after due deliberation) in the realm of reasonable disagreement? Brian Barry makes a strong case for majority rule in a situation where only one decision needs to be made between only two alternatives, there are no problems of nontransitivity, and none of the outcomes is of "vital importance for the long-term well-being of any of those involved."[19] Imagine that five people in a railway car must decide whether to permit or prohibit smoking. Under these (special) conditions, is there something "natural" about majority rule?[20] Regardless of how we answer this question, it does not follow that majority rule is more democratic under the normal conditions of politics where voting continues over time among more than two alternatives, problems of nontransitivity arise, and (most important) where some outcomes are of vital importance to the basic freedom or well-being of some people. The naturalness of the majority principle in the railway car hypothetical is, as Barry writes, "an artefact of a number of special features either specified or implied in the description of the case."[21] When these features are absent, alternative procedures that respect equal political liberty might be more consistent with a democratic ideal.

Majority rule helps support representative government over time, Barry argues, and representative government protects the basic liberties and well-being of individuals better than any alternative system.[22] This defense of majority rule rejects the idea that it is necessarily more consistent with protecting equal political liberty, or otherwise morally better, than alternative decision-making rules that also respect equal political liberty and support representative government over time. This defense also is consistent with what Rawls's theory says about majority rule. By being open to the possibility of justifying deviations from majority rule for the sake of protecting basic liberties, Rawls's theory is more defensible and no less democratic.

## 6. PUBLICLY DEFENSIBLE DISCOURSE IN POLITICS

But does political liberalism devalue political arguments that invoke a controversial conception of the good life and in this sense also devalue an important part of political liberty? Michael Sandel argues that if there is a "fact of reasonable pluralism" about conceptions of the good, which leads political liberalism to devalue political arguments that invoke a controversial conception of the good life, then the same fact and devaluation should apply to conceptions of justice.[23] If the reason for keeping conceptions of the good out of political argument when matters of basic justice are at stake is respect for reasonable pluralism, then the same argument would seem to hold for keeping controversial conceptions of justice out of politics. But this of course would be absurd, for it would leave no relevant basis on which to decide many of the most morally salient issues of politics. Political liberalism would be hoist with its own petard. It is inconsistent – and undemocratic – in devaluing any political speech that invokes controversial conceptions, and it denies citizens any defensible basis on which to resolve political controversies like abortion, pornography, capital punishment, and welfare reform.

Sandel offers a response on behalf of political liberalism, which he then rejects. The response is that our disagreements over justice are less a matter of fundamental principle than our disagreements about the good life. Many disagreements about the good life revolve around matters as fundamental as whether we must have faith in (which?) God. By contrast, even adversaries in the abortion debate tend to take account of the same fundamental political values: "due respect for human life, the ordered reproduction of political society over time, ... [and] the equality of women as equal citizens" [*Liberalism*, p. 243, n. 32]. This agreement at the level of principle provides a basis for respecting our adversaries as morally reasonable people. No analogous agreement exists at the level of basic principle between some religious and some secular perspectives on the good life.

But citizens often do not agree on basic principles of justice. Some libertarians, for example, reject the idea of liberal egalitarians that we have a duty to help other people in need when our own ability to live a decent (or good) life is not thereby threatened. The rejection by some libertarians of justice as fairness appears to be as deep and fundamental as many disagreements about the nature of a good life. Political liberalism should grant that disagreements about justice can be just as deep and intractable as disagreements about the good life.

There remains a more basic reason for distinguishing between disagreements about justice and the good life. Reasonable disagreements about matters of justice, by their very nature, demand some kind of political resolution, whereas citizens need not adjudicate most of their reasonable disagreements about matters of the good life. Disagreements about matters of the good life that must be adjudicated – the sincere claim by some people that they have a moral duty to impose their ideal of the good life on others – should be adjudicated by the terms of justice, invoking (in this case) the principle of basic liberty. To impose a conception of the good life on other people – in violation of their basic liberty – is an unreasonable demand from the perspective of political liberalism. The argument here is substantive, not formal, concerning the content of basic liberties and the injustice of not respecting someone's basic liberties for the sake of realizing one's own conception of the good life.

Political liberalism offers another argument for why coercion should not be used to implement an otherwise reasonable moral ideal such as perfectionism. People who believe in a reasonable form of perfectionism can freely pursue the ideal in their own lives without imposing their ideal on unwilling nonperfectionists. Rawls allows that a majority can pool its resources and use political means (through the "exchange branch") to overcome coordination problems to implement a perfectionist ideal for all those who subscribe to it. But he argues that taxation against the will of the minority for such

purposes is unjust [*Justice*, pp. 282–4/249–51 rev., 331–2/291–2 rev.].
The same objection to taxing a minority against its will does not
apply to ensuring a decent income for the least advantaged members
of society as long as coercive taxation is a necessary means and the
end is a public obligation.

A final worry remains. Does Rawls's political liberalism unnecessarily devalue political arguments that rely on controversial yet
reasonable conceptions of the good life and that do not threaten the
equal basic liberties or opportunities of individuals? It is true that
some political arguments that rely on controversial conceptions of
the good threaten equal basic liberties or opportunities, and unreasonably so. But not every political argument of this sort does or is
otherwise unreasonable judged by a standard of free and equal citizenship. And some political arguments of this sort – in favor of raising
the social minimum to encourage citizens to perfect their talents –
are directed to what Rawls calls the basic structure of society.[24]

A more inclusive idea of public reason, consistent with political
liberalism, admits that some kinds of perfectionist legislation may
be morally defensible on liberal and democratic grounds. Funding for
the arts in places where it would otherwise be inaccessible, for example, does not threaten equal political (or personal) liberty. Encouraging citizens, without forcing them, to develop their talents is not
an unreasonable or publicly indefensible aim of democratic politics.
Suppose that most citizens freely and reflectively accept these aims
upon due deliberation. Or suppose that most reject it. Why should
their decision either way not prevail and be considered consistent
with public reason even if the decision relies partly upon perfectionist considerations – as long as it is defended democratically and
does not threaten anyone's basic liberties or restrict anyone's basic
opportunities?

Does the more inclusive view of public reason in *Liberalism* allow
for the democratic passage of such legislation? In *Liberalism*, unlike
in *Justice*, comprehensive philosophies per se are not devalued in
the discourse of liberal democratic politics. This difference is both
theoretically and practically significant. The reasons *Justice* offers
[pp. 325–32] against the democratic defense of perfectionist legislation do not hold for all such legislation but only for legislation that
would violate equal basic liberties. Some perfectionist arguments
for funding public theater, dance, music, and art projects in local

communities, for example, do not threaten to coerce anyone into perfecting their artistic talents. What they do propose is (marginally) more taxation, which is coercive. (But taxation per se violates no principle of political liberalism.) Perfectionist arguments of this sort do not threaten basic liberties, and admitting them as legitimate would expand the realm of basic political liberty.

To decide where *Liberalism* stands on the question of whether perfectionist arguments for such legislation can count as part of public reason, let us consider the reason it offers for the more inclusive view, which is an instrumental one [pp. 247–54]. In some historical circumstances, such as the antebellum South, welcoming comprehensive moralities – such as religious conceptions – into constitutional arguments was more likely to achieve just outcomes by the (independent) standards of public reason. This reason needs to be supplemented by two other considerations. The first is that public reason itself may be incomplete and its practical implications indeterminate without the aid of some parts of comprehensive conceptions. The second is that Rawls's idea of public reason, by its own terms, is one of a family of such conceptions which are bound to have different content. I have suggested some reasons to more directly endorse a more inclusive political discourse than *Liberalism*, one that would welcome, for example, perfectionist arguments that do not threaten anyone's basic liberties or opportunities. A more inclusive political discourse would be more democratic to the extent that it broadens the scope of equal political liberty beyond what Rawls explicitly defends in either *Liberalism* or *Justice*.

Some reasonable disagreements about the ordering of basic liberties may be better understood, if not resolved, if citizens publicly discuss all their reasons that are compatible with the search for fair terms of social cooperation and not just those that are part of a freestanding political conception. Some of those reasons – such as the views that a fetus is or is not a constitutional person, or the view that some or all human life is or is not sacred – are part of comprehensive conceptions and are not derivable from a freestanding political conception.[25] For liberal and democratic reasons, it may be a political virtue, even if it is not a necessity, for citizens to include in their political deliberations some disagreements about the good life when those disagreements are politically relevant and reasonable even if not mutually acceptable.

Political liberalism should invite deliberation that includes controversial ideas about the good life when those ideas contribute to the ongoing search for fair terms of social cooperation among free and equal citizens. Rawls opens the door in *Liberalism* to more inclusive conceptions of public reason than *Justice* defends – conceptions that value the contribution of comprehensive philosophies to political discourse for more reasons than Rawls explicitly recognizes in *Liberalism*. More inclusive interpretations of public reason would agree with Rawls that some political discourse unreasonably threatens the basic liberties of individuals. The state and its agents, for example, must not claim the right to restrict people's basic liberty in the absence of any demonstration of harm or threat of harm to others. This argument relies on a substantive moral distinction between a law that does and one that does not threaten to limit basic liberties. It does not rely on a formal distinction between whether or not the arguments offered for the law are politically free-standing or part of a comprehensive conception of the good.

Some comprehensive philosophies threaten to restrict the basic liberties of individuals without good reason, but so do some free-standing political conceptions. Other conceptions in both categories do not. I have offered reasons consistent with Rawls's argument in *Liberalism* for defending a more inclusive version of political liberalism which would welcome those that do not. All of the reasons I have offered are consistent with Rawls's fundamental commitment to protecting the basic liberties of individuals. None of us can claim that a more inclusive political discourse will always increase the chances of protecting the basic liberties. Nor can we claim authoritative knowledge of what our basic liberties should be without opening up political discourse as widely as possible among free and equal citizens to all reasonable views that may thereby be heard in the political forums that influence political decision making. The right of citizens to deliberate about politics is an important part of the equal political liberty that is basic to liberal democracy, but deliberation about politics does not therefore have priority over all other parts of basic liberty.

I have suggested that we can defend a more inclusive public discourse about politics – and to this extent a more democratic conception of justice – than *Justice* provides by further developing the idea of public reason offered in Rawls's more recent writings. Probing Rawls's theory on the relationship of liberalism and democracy affirms that the marriage is intimate. Its enduring internal tensions result not from the wedding of personal and political liberties but rather from the conflicts among basic liberties more generally. To escape those conflicts in the world as we know it would be to escape from freedom, both personal and political.

### ENDNOTES

1  Rawlsian political liberalism, in brief, defends discourse about the basic structure of society that does not depend on (and therefore neither affirms nor denies) the truth of competing comprehensive philosophies of life. Political discourse at its best, according to Rawls, would rely on a relatively free-standing political philosophy whose fundamental ideal is free and equal membership in a fair scheme of social cooperation.

2  John Rawls, *A Theory of Justice* (Cambridge, MA: Harvard University Press, 1971; revised edition, 1999) and *Political Liberalism* (New York: Columbia University Press, 1993; paperback edition 1996).

3  See Jürgen Habermas, "On the Internal Relation between Law and Democracy," *The Inclusion of the Other* (Cambridge, MA: MIT Press, 1998), p. 259.

4  Ibid., p. 261.

5  For the idea that liberalism and democracy are united in a "marriage of convenience," see Judith N. Shklar, "The Liberalism of Fear," in Nancy L. Rosenblum, ed., *Liberalism and the Moral Life* (Princeton, NJ: Princeton University Press, 1989), p. 37.

6  See Habermas, "On the Internal Relation between Law and Democracy," pp. 260–4.

7  Shklar, "The Liberalism of Fear," p. 37.

8  Rawls's theory is not metaphysical in that it does not presuppose or defend a single metaphysical view of the person as I argue in "Communitarian Critics of Liberalism," *Philosophy & Public Affairs* 14 (3) (Summer 1985), 308–22.

9  Habermas, "Reconciliation through the Public Use of Reason," in *The Inclusion of the Other*, p. 69.

10  Ibid., pp. 69–70.

11  Benjamin Constant, "The Liberty of the Ancients Compared with that of the Moderns" [1819], in Benjamin Constant, *Political Writings* (Cambridge, UK: Cambridge University Press, 1988), pp. 309–28.

12    Ibid., pp. 326–7.

13    For Constant, see ibid., p. 327: " ... political liberty is the most powerful, most effective means of self-development. ... Therefore, Sirs, far from renouncing either of the two sorts of freedom ... , it is necessary, as I have shown, to learn to combine the two together."

14    See Shklar, *American Citizenship*, pp. 1–62.

15    On the Rawlsian concept of the reasonable, see Joshua Cohen, "A More Democratic Liberalism," *Michigan Law Review* 92 (6), 1521–43.

16    See Cohen, who says that the opposition to legalizing abortion in the first trimester – as contrasted with the opposition to legalizing pornography – is not reasonable even if it may be right [ibid., p. 1538]. Cohen leaves open the question of whether opposition to legalizing abortion in the second trimester may be reasonable. The relevant consideration here is not whether any particular disagreement should be characterized as reasonable but rather whether political liberalism has resources for dealing with reasonable disagreements, wherever they arise in politics. For a defense of resources based on reciprocity that do not rely on a comprehensive doctrine, see Amy Gutmann and Dennis Thompson, *Democracy and Disagreement* (Cambridge, MA: Harvard University Press, 1996), pp. 73–91.

17    For a more detailed discussion, see Gutmann and Thompson, *Democracy and Disagreement*, pp. 81–5.

18    Ibid., pp. 84–91.

19    Brian Barry, *Democracy and Power, Essays in Political Theory I*, "Is Democracy Special?" (Oxford, UK: Clarendon Press, 1991), p. 30. *Democracy and Disagreement* extends Barry's argument, pp. 27–33.

20    Barry, pp. 29–30.

21    Ibid., p. 59.

22    Ibid., p. 60.

23    See Michael Sandel, "Review Essay on Political Liberalism, by John Rawls," *Harvard Law Review* 107 (7), p. 1776 [pp. 1765–94].

24    Rawls's views have moved in this direction in "The Idea of Public Reason Revisited," in *Collected Papers* (Cambridge, MA: Harvard University Press, 1999), ed. Samuel Freeman, pp. 573–615. But he argues that only public reason understood as a free-standing conception justifies political ends. If citizens rely on part of a comprehensive conception when arguing about adequate income support, for example, this part of their argument must be superseded by an argument that is *independent* of the comprehensive conception. But it is not clear that such a superseding argument is available in some fundamental disputes over even constitutional essentials such as capital punishment and abortion. These disputes cannot be fully resolved without deciding upon the

status of human beings. (Do they have dignity or not, sacredness or not, or inviolability or not and of what sort and under what certain circumstances?) One defensible and moderate revision of Rawls's understanding of public reason is for it to admit arguments, whatever their pedigree, that contribute to mutual justification consistent with the civic ideal of reciprocity.

25 See, for example, Ronald Dworkin, *Life's Dominion* (New York: Knopf, 1993).

# 5 Difference Principles[1]

Few components of John Rawls's political philosophy have proven so epoch-making as what he somewhat oddly called the "difference principle."[2] None has exercised as great an influence outside the circle of academic philosophers. And hardly any has given rise to so many misunderstandings or generated such heated controversies.

The core of the principle is a simple and appealing idea: that social and economic inequalities should be evaluated in terms of how well off they leave the worst off. The idea is simple; it amounts to asking that the minimum of some index of advantage should be maximised. To many, it is also appealing, for the demand that the advantages enjoyed by the least advantaged should be as generous as (sustainably) possible provides a transparent and elegant way of articulating an egalitarian impulse and a concern for efficiency. For it avoids, at the same time, the absurdity of equality at any price and the outrageousness of maximising the aggregate no matter how distributed.

Thus understood, the difference principle bears some undeniable resemblance to the justification of economic inequalities by reference to some notion of the general interest, as in the utilitarian tradition. But aggregate social welfare is not quite the same as the interest of the least advantaged. The idea of using the latter as the benchmark for assessing inequalities had never been given, before Rawls, a powerful explicit formulation that could capture the scholarly imagination. But it had occurred to others before him. For example, the famous Latin fable of the stomach and the limbs is said to have been used by Roman patricians to justify their privileges to the populace: it is in the limbs' interest to feed the stomach through their hard work, for with an empty stomach, the limbs would soon wither.[3] In Anatole France's novel *L'Ile des Pingouins*, a rich farmer argues along the same track "that little should be asked from those who possess a lot; for otherwise the rich would be less rich and the poor would be poorer."[4] Rawls's own single reference to an earlier statement of the idea is to a contemporary passage by George Santayana to the effect that "an aristocratic regimen can only be justified by radiating benefit and by proving that were less given to those above less would be attained by those beneath them."[5]

Once given a bold and careful formulation, the difference principle did so well at arousing the interest of philosophers, economists, and other social scientists that there is not the slightest prospect of this chapter's doing justice to the huge secondary literature this principle generated.[6] Against the background of a succinct presentation of Rawls's main formulations, I limit myself to a clarification of some frequent misunderstandings and a brief discussion of some major difficulties in connection with three central issues: What is the exact content of the maximin criterion? Does the difference principle apply it to outcomes or to opportunities? How widely should one conceive the realm of possibilities over which maximization operates?

## I. THE CRITERION

### A. Rawls's Two Conceptions of Justice

The difference principle is one of the three components of Rawl's "special conception of justice." The latter is distinguished from his "general conception," which applies when, owing in particular to inadequate economic development, "social conditions do not allow the effective establishment of [basic liberties]" (*TJ*, p. 152/132 rev.). According to this general conception,

all social values – liberty and opportunity, income and wealth, and the bases of self-respect – are to be distributed equally unless an unequal distribution of any, or all, of these values is to everyone's advantage. Injustice, then, is simply inequalities that are not to the benefit of all. (*TJ*, p. 62/54 rev.)

The "special conception" is "the form that the general conception finally assumes as social conditions improve." (*TJ*, p. 83/passage omitted p. 72 rev.) The crucial difference is that the special conception assigns strict priority to the equal distribution of basic liberties and to fair equality of opportunities over the demand that other "social values" be distributed "to everyone's advantage."

It is this special conception which is encapsulated in Rawls's famous two principles of justice, which A Theory of Justice first expresses as follows:[7]

First: each person is to have an equal right to the most extensive basic liberty compatible with a similar liberty for others [the "first principle," or "principle of equal liberty"].[8]

Second: social and economic inequalities are to be arranged so that they are both (a) reasonably expected to be to everyone's advantage [the "first part of the second principle," or "the difference principle"], and (b) attached to positions and offices open to all [the "second part of the second principle," or "the principle of fair equality of opportunity"]." (TJ, p. 60/cf. 53 rev.)

Subject to the prior constraint of the other two principles, the difference principle thus requires that one should "arrange social and economic inequalities so that everyone benefits" (TJ, p. 61/53 rev.).[9] Hence, the general conception of justice "is simply the difference principle applied to all primary goods including liberty and opportunity and so no longer constrained by other parts of the special conception" (TJ, p. 83/cf. 73 rev., passage omitted). As used by Rawls and discussed here, the difference principle applies only to a subset of social primary goods – the "social and economic advantages" – and within the confines set by the distribution of the other social primary goods – basic liberties and opportunities – stipulated by the other two principles.

## B. A Theory of Justice's Three Formulations of the Difference Principle

I focus in Section II on the nature of the primary goods contained in this subset but want to concentrate first on the criterion of distribution which the difference principle proposes. What does it mean for social and economic inequalities to be arranged so as to be "to everyone's advantage"? This is an "ambiguous phrase," Rawls notes (TJ, p. 61/53 rev.), which his more explicit "second formulation" is meant to clarify:

Assuming the framework of institutions required by equal liberty and fair equality of opportunity, the higher expectations of those better situated are just if and only if they work as part of a scheme which improves the expectations of the least advantaged members of society. The intuitive idea is that the social order is not to establish and secure the more attractive prospects of those better off unless doing so is to the advantage of those less fortunate. (Rawls *TJ*, p. 75/65 rev.)

In order to spell out the criterion of distribution which emerges from this second formulation, let us first suppose that our society comprises only two categories of people – the "more fortunate" and the "less fortunate" – distinguished by the amount of social and economic advantages the features they possess enable them to expect. Let us further suppose, for the time being, what Rawls (*TJ*, pp. 81–2/71–2 rev.) calls "close-knitness", that is, that changes in the expectations of the better off always affect, negatively or positively, the expectations of the worse off. In this context, we can distinguish the following two jointly exhaustive situations of inequality:

(1) The less fortunate currently enjoy worse prospects than they would under equality.
(2) The less fortunate currently enjoy better prospects than they would under equality.

If the context were zero-sum, that is, if the issue boiled down to dividing an existing cake, then only option (1) could arise, and any existing inequality between the more fortunate and the less fortunate would necessarily be unjust according to the difference principle.[10] But if the context is not zero-sum, that is, if the relevant cakes need to be made and remade and if their size can therefore be affected through some mechanism by how they are divided, then it becomes possible for the better prospects of the better off to improve those of the worst off. How? The most frequently mentioned possibility is that they "act as incentives so that the economic process is more efficient, innovation proceeds at a faster pace, and so on" (*TJ*, p. 78/68 rev.). But this is not the only reason, probably not even the main reason, why maximin may diverge from equality. Inequalities can also be "a way to put resources in the hands of those who can make the best social use of them."[11] The most cogent efficiency-based case for capitalist inequalities (it is sometimes argued) does not rest on the fact that the expectation of huge gains lures entrepreneurs into working hard and taking risks but on the fact that capitalist competition keeps removing wealth, and hence, economic power from those who have proved poor innovators or unwise investors while concentrating it in the hands of those who find and keep finding the cheapest ways of producing the goods that best satisfy consumer demand.[12] This mechanism would be destroyed if profits were redistributed in egalitarian fashion or collected by a public agency. Thus, inequalities of income and wealth may be no less significant as enabling devices than as incentives. This possibility is even more obvious in the case of inequalities of powers and prerogatives attached to social positions.

Both the incentive mechanism and the enabling mechanism make room for possibility (2), that is, for the possibility that inegalitarian schemes may "improve the expectations of the least advantaged members of society" relative to what they would be under equality. According to Rawls's second characterisation quoted at the beginning of the present section, such an improvement provides, subject to the other two principles of justice being satisfied, a necessary and sufficient condition for an inequality between the more fortunate and the less fortunate to be just. In other words, all that is needed to justify an inequality, however large, is some improvement, however tiny, for the worse off, relative to the conceivably very depressed counterfactual situation of total equality between the expectations of the more fortunate and the less fortunate. If this were the end of the story, as implied in many casual interpretations, Rawls's difference principle would be extremely tolerant of social and economic inequality. But it is not. *A Theory of Justice* contains a third and far more demanding formulation of the difference principle, which is also the one Rawls routinely uses with minor variants in later statements:[13] "Social and economic inequalities are to be arranged so that they are both (a) *to the greatest benefit* of the least advantaged and (b) attached to offices and positions open to all under conditions of equality of opportunity" (*TJ*, p. 83/72 rev., my emphasis). This far more stringent condition for just inequalities forces us to distinguish, among situations of type (2), i.e., such that the less fortunate currently enjoy better prospects than they would under equality, the following three mutually exclusive cases:

> (2a) The prospects of the less fortunate could be better than they are now if the prospects of the more fortunate were worse ("unjust").

(2b) The prospects of the less fortunate would be worse than they are now if the prospects of the more fortunate were worse, but they could be better if the prospects of the more fortunate were better ("just throughout").

(2c) The prospects of the less fortunate would be worse than they are now both if the prospects of the more fortunate were worse and if they were better ("perfectly just").

This final formulation involves a shift from the requirement of "some improvement" to the requirement of a "maximal improvement." It thereby opens up the possibility of inequalities which benefit the less fortunate (relative to full equality) but are nonetheless unjust by excess: lowering the expectations for the better off can raise the expectations of the worse off (2a). It also opens up the possibility of inequalities which benefit the less fortunate, which Rawls does not want to call unjust but which he regards nonetheless as suboptimal by default, as being less just than greater inequalities would be: "even higher expectations for the more advantaged would raise the expectations of those in the lowest positions" (2b). Rawls describes schemes which satisfy the latter description as "just throughout, but not the best just arrangement" ("Distributive Justice," p. 138; *TJ*, p. 79/68 rev.). On the continued assumption of close-knitness between the expectations of the more fortunate and those of the less fortunate, it is therefore not enough, for a scheme to be just, that it should satisfy the broad condition (2). Far more restrictively, it must satisfy the disjunction of (2b) and (2c). And for it to be, in Rawls's phrase a "perfectly just scheme" (ibid.), it must satisfy the ever more stringent (2c). In other words, however much a scheme improves the expectations of the less fortunate relative to full equality, it cannot be just if a more egalitarian scheme could sustainably do better for the less fortunate. And it can be just, but not perfectly just, if a more inegalitarian scheme could sustainably do better for the less fortunate.

### C. When Close-Knitness Breaks Down: More and Less Egalitarian Versions of the Difference Principle

What happens when the simplifying assumption of close-knitness breaks down? The possibility then arises that the prospects of the less fortunate may remain unaffected by upward or downward changes in the prospects for the better off. "Perfectly just" schemes, understood as schemes relative to which the expectations of the less fortunate could not be improved, are then no longer necessarily of type (2c). For the expectations of the less fortunate to be unimprovable, it is no longer required that they should be worsened if the more fortunate had less or more than now. Their expectations can also remain unchanged. The following further three cases thereby become possible:

> (2d) The prospects of the less fortunate would be worse than they are now if the prospects of the more fortunate were worse, but they could remain the same as now (though not improve) if the prospects of the more fortunate were better.
>
> (2e) The prospects of the less fortunate would be worse than they are now if the prospects of the more fortunate were better, but they could remain the same as now (though not improve) if the prospects of the more fortunate were worse.
>
> (2f) The prospects of the less fortunate could remain the same as now (though not improve) both if the prospects of the more fortunate were better and if they were worse.

According to Rawls's third and final formulation of the difference principle quoted in the previous section, schemes which satisfy any of these three conditions are as perfectly just as those which satisfy (2c). But room is now made for two more restrictive variants, one more and one less egalitarian than Rawls's "final formulation," each occasionally used by Rawls himself and each matching, under our simple two-class assumption, one of the two main justifications he gives for the difference principle. According to the more egalitarian variant, a necessary condition for perfect justice to obtain is that inequalities should contribute to improving the expectations of the less fortunate.[14] Unlike schemes which satisfy (2c) or (2d), schemes which satisfy (2e) or (2f) are now less than perfectly just since they contain an unused potential for reducing inequality without worsening the fate of the worse off.[15] According to the less egalitarian variant, by contrast, it is not required for perfect justice to obtain that inequalities should contribute to improving the expectations of the less fortunate but only that they should not worsen them. Indeed, perfect justice requires inequalities that improve the prospects of the better off if such improvement does not make the prospects of the worse off any worse. Of the four possible cases, it is now (2c) and (2e) that are perfectly just, while (2d) and (2f) are less than perfectly just, since they contain an unused potential for increasing the prospects of some without worsening the fate of the worse off. Unlike the first variant, this second variant is consistent with efficiency understood as Pareto-optimality or the exhaustion of all possibilities of making some better off without making others worse off. The adoption of this less egalitarian variant is therefore entailed by Rawls whenever he presents the difference principle as consistent with efficiency.[16]

One appealing argument in support of the more egalitarian variant goes as follows. If and only if (2c) or (2d) is satisfied is it possible to legitimise existing inequalities in the eyes of their very victims by telling them, "True, there are undeserved inequalities and you have been unlucky. But under any other feasible scheme you would be even worse off." This argument has been frequently used, including by Rawls himself when presenting the difference principle as a principle of reciprocity or mutual benefit, as a principle that "can be justified to everyone, and in particular to those who are least favored." When the difference principle is satisfied, Rawls writes, the least favoured individual "B can accept A's being better off since A's advantages have been gained in ways which improve B's prospects. If A were not allowed his better position, B would be even worse off than he is" (*TJ*, p. 103/cf. 88 rev. paragraph amended). Phrased in this way, the argument is, however, incorrect. For it should practically always be possible to imagine a feasible scheme under which the particular people who currently form the worst-off group would be made better off. If the absence of any such alternative feasible scheme were required by the difference principle, the latter would be unsatisfiable. But the difference principle is defined by Rawls in terms of anonymous positions, not in terms of proper names. For it to be satisfied, the worse off must not be at least as well off as *they* would be under any other feasible scheme, but at least as well off as *the worse off, whoever they may be,* would be under any other feasible scheme. Hence, when the egalitarian variant of the difference principle is satisfied, one cannot tell the less fortunate, "Under any other feasible scheme your prospects would be even worse." But one can still say, "Under any other feasible scheme someone's prospects would be even worse than yours currently are." The legitimising power of this correct version of the argument, its potential for reducing the "strains of commitment" of the less fortunate, is not quite as great as that of the uncorrected version. But it is not insignificant.

When the less egalitarian variant of the difference principle is satisfied, on the other hand, it is no longer necessarily possible to tell the
victims of inequalities that under any other feasible scheme someone
would be worse off than they are. The difference principle can now
be satisfied even when more egalitarian schemes are feasible under
which no one would be worse off (though some would be no better
off) than the worse off now are. Under this variant of the difference
principle, just inequalities are therefore no longer so safely protected
against their victims' "strains of commitment." On the other hand,
this variant has the advantage of fitting far better into Rawls's other
main argument for the difference principle, the one framed in terms
of the original position. For behind the veil of ignorance, the parties "strive for as high an absolute score as possible. They do not
wish a high or a low score for their opponents, nor do they seek to
maximize or minimize the difference between their successes and
those of others" (TJ, pp. 144–5/125 rev.). They may therefore give
an absolute priority to the level of expected benefit they would end
up with in case they were unlucky enough to be among the least
fortunate. But when comparing two options which are equivalent
on this score, the parties will unambiguously prefer the one that
will give them more in case they turned out to be fortunate after
all.

If applied to situations which are not close-knit, situations in
which it is possible for (some) inequalities to be neither beneficial
nor damaging for the worse off, Rawls's formulations clearly express
two incompatible variants of the difference principle, each of them
called for by one of the main arguments he puts forward in support
of the latter. However, if the assumption of close-knitness does hold,
(2d), (2e), and (2f) never obtain, and both the egalitarian and the lexical variants yield the same selection: (2c). Rawls clearly believes that
this assumption is a reasonable one to make and therefore warns that
he will "always use the difference principle in the simpler form" (TJ,
p. 83/72 rev.), which corresponds precisely to this selection. Once we
exclude the possibility of a tie at the bottom, both the anticipation
of the strains of commitment and the reasoning behind the veil of
ignorance support the choice of a scheme which generates a state of
affairs about which it can be said, "The prospects of the less fortunate would be worse than they are now both if the prospects of the
more fortunate were worse and if they were better."

## D. The Lexical Difference Principle and Its Radical Extensions

Does it follow that the whole issue of what should be done when close-knitness does not hold is of no practical significance? It does if the principle is supposed to operate, as it is by Rawls, within a single generation rather than across generations and within a single people rather than across nations.[17] For it is hard to imagine that any inequality of any importance between social positions in the same national society would not affect, be it slightly, one way or another, the situation of the incumbents of the worse position. If one were to apply the difference principle transgenerationally, or even transnationally, this arguably would be a very different matter. For suppose those with the worst prospects belong to a generation that is no longer around, or live in a country whose situation we cannot hope to affect by our decisions. Then Rawls's "simpler form," which simply demands that inequalities should be to the greatest benefit of the least advantaged, gives precious little guidance: anything goes providing no reachable category is given a deal as bad as the (possibly abysmally bad) fate of the worst-off unreachable one. To get some guidance, we need something like the two variants just discussed.

To see what this guidance could be, we must first work out the two variants for the general case of many categories. In the two-category case, a tie for the worse off required one to make the better off as badly off as possible in the more egalitarian version and as well off as possible in the less egalitarian version. The generalisation of the former is possible, and not altogether absurd, but it raises tricky problems which it would be better to avoid.[18] Instead, the generalisation of the latter is straightforward. It consists in the "lexical difference principle," inspired by Amartya Sen[19] and presented by Rawls (TJ, pp. 81–3/cf. 70–3 rev.) as a natural generalisation of his final formulation: the lexical maximin or leximin ranks situations in which the worst off are equally badly off by looking at the fate of the worst off but one, and so on, in case of successive ties.[20] According to this criterion, inequalities are fine as long as they do not hurt the worst off or, if the worst-off category is unaffected, the worst-off category but one, etc. Like its two-class version, this criterion is consistent with efficiency and fits easily into an original position argument.[21]

In an intergenerational or global context, the lexical difference principle would simply require social and economic advantages to be distributed to the greatest benefit of the worst off among those categories that can be affected by the choice under consideration between alternative schemes.

Rawls has offered various reasons for not using the difference principle across generations and across peoples and for elaborating instead a distinct principle of just savings and a distinct duty of assistance among peoples. This is not the place to present or discuss these. I only note the following paradox. Rawls's alternatives to radical extensions of the difference principle across generations and across peoples are unequivocally less egalitarian than such a radical extension would be. His conception of justice across generations requires that only comparatively poorer generations should make net savings from which richer generations will benefit: "contrary to the formulation of the difference principle, the worst off save for those better off" ("Distributive Justice," p. 146). True, the rate of saving could be chosen in such a way that, as from the second generation, all generations, whether the initial poorer ones or the later richer ones, would benefit relative to a stationary state. But this leaves out the first one, which will unambiguously be made worse off by any positive rate of saving than it would be under (transgenerationally egalitarian) zero growth. Similarly, his conception of justice between nations implies a duty of assistance of poorer nations by richer ones that falls far short of the transnational redistribution which a global difference principle would imply: "The levels of wealth and welfare among societies may vary, and presumably do so; but adjusting those levels is not the object of the duty of assistance" (*LP*, p. 106).

Some may be attracted by Rawls's approach to distributive justice while remaining unpersuaded by his alternatives to a transgenerational and global difference principle in part precisely because of their inegalitarian implications. For them, it is essential to adopt a version of the principle which yields clear and meaningful consequences when extended along these two dimensions. As suggested above (see text to footnote 16), the lexical version of the difference principle is best suited for this task. Paradoxically, it is the less egalitarian variant of the difference principle that offers the best chance of supporting the egalitarian strategy of boldly expanding its scope across both time and space.

## II. THE DISTRIBUENDUM

### A. Outcome Egalitarianism?

After having focused on the distributive criterion for the difference principle, let us now turn to what it is applied to: the distribuendum, which the difference principle – both in Rawls's "final formulation" and in the two variants subsequently explored – requires to be distributed in maximin fashion. Contrary to what some economists still sometimes call the "Rawlsian" criterion of distributive justice, the distribuendum of the difference principle has never been characterised in terms of utility, or welfare, or degree of preference satisfaction, but rather in terms of a subset of primary goods which Rawls calls "social and economic advantages." *Primary goods* were initially conceived by Rawls as "things that every rational man is presumed to want" (*TJ*, p. 62/54 rev., *TJ*, p. 92/79 rev.). They were later redefined as "what persons need in their status as free and equal citizens, and as normal and fully cooperating members of society over a complete life" (*TJ*, revised edition, p. xiii). Whether in the old or the new definition, they fall into two categories: natural and social. *Natural primary goods* include "health and vigor, intelligence and imagination." Although their possession is influenced by social institutions, they are not as directly under the latter's control as social primary goods are (*TJ*, p. 62/54 rev.). It does not follow, however, that inequalities in natural primary goods have nothing to do with social justice. "The natural distribution is neither just nor unjust; nor is it unjust that men are born into society at some particular position. These are simply natural facts. What is just and unjust is the way that institutions deal with these facts" (*TJ*, p. 102/87 rev.). More precisely, social institutions can profoundly affect the consequences of natural inequalities through the distribution of those primary goods which are directly under their control: the *social primary goods*.

Social primary goods include fundamental liberties and opportunities for access to social positions. But in the special conception of justice, the distribution of these goods is governed, as we have seen, by the other two principles to which the difference principle is subordinated. The remaining social primary goods, which are the preserve of the difference principle, Rawls calls *social and economic advantages*. These are defined by a list, whose canonical formulation consists in the following items: income and wealth, powers and pre-rogatives of offices and positions of responsibility, and the social bases of self-respect (see *TJ*, p. 62/54 rev.; *TJ*, p. 93/80 rev.; *PL*, p. 181, etc.). For the maximin criterion, or any other maximization stan-dard, to be applicable, each of these items must be measurable (if only roughly). Even in the case of income and wealth this is not straightforward since some aspects of people's income or wealth (the quality of the physical environment they enjoy, for example) are not self-evidently translatable into monetary magnitudes. And as regards powers and prerogatives, or the bases of self-respect, far more would need to be said for measurement of any kind to get off the ground. Moreover, an overall index would need to be constructed to aggre-gate these various dimensions. Rawls is confident that this can be done – at least for the limited purposes which need to be served. All he needs the index for is to identify the worst-off category in each social state achievable through the operation of some feasible institu-tional scheme consistent with the first two principles and to compare these indexes across such social states. But the strong correlation that tends to prevail between the various dimensions, Rawls argues, makes it unproblematic to identify the worst off (*TJ*, p. 97/83 rev.).

This is not enough to permit comparison across relevant social states, as some schemes may be designed, for example, so as to give a lower income but greater powers to the worst-off category. A mar-ket economy with worker-owned firms may conceivably outperform conventional capitalism in terms of the powers and prerogatives as-sociated with the worst position while doing worse income-wise for everyone.[22] However, appeal to rational prudence from the stand-point of the least advantaged should enable us, Rawls believes, to appropriately weight the various goods to the extent necessary for the sake of applying maximin to the aggregate index (*TJ*, p. 94/80 rev.). Contrary to what Rawls (*TJ*, pp. 91–2/79 rev.) suggests, more is req-uired than intrapersonal comparison, since the worst off need not be the same people in all relevant social states. But the interpersonal comparison involved is arguably unproblematic enough for us to be able to determine in which relevant social state the worst off enjoy the best combination of income and wealth, powers and prerogatives, and the social bases of self-respect.

Let us therefore suppose that these measurement problems are manageable. What we end up with, it seems, is the requirement that we should maximize a synthetic index of the social and economic advantages enjoyed by the worst-off member of the society concerned. Such a slightly clumsy variant of the economists' "Rawlsian" criterion of maximin welfare clearly qualifies as a form of outcome egalitarianism. It involves, however, a deep misunderstanding of Rawls's difference principle. It fails to accommodate, in particular, his repeated emphasis on stating the principle in terms of lifetime expectations of categories of people rather than in terms of particular individual's situations at particular times (see *TJ*, pp. 64/56 rev., 71/62 rev., 73/63 rev., 98/cf. 83–4 rev., passage amended; 99/85 rev., etc.). Adopting such a formulation is not simply, he insists, a convenient way of averaging scores "in order to make this criterion work" (*TJ*, p. 98/cf. p. 84 rev., passage amended). It is a constituent feature of a consistently individualistic approach to justice.

### B. The Least Fortunate and the Incumbents of the Worst Position

How are these classes or categories to be understood? Rawls makes various suggestions. According to one of them, the least advantaged are simply those with least social and economic advantages, the class of people with the most modest "place in the distribution of income and wealth" (*TJ*, p. 96/82 rev.). The characterisation of the worst-off category is then "solely in terms of relative income and wealth with no reference to social positions. Thus, all persons with less than half of the median income and wealth may be taken as the least-advantaged segment" (*TJ*, p. 98/cf. 84 rev.). Rawls does not reject this characterization. On the contrary, he says he supposes that it "will serve well enough" (*TJ*, p. 98/cf. 84 rev. passage amended). Were this characterization to be adopted, however, it would be hard to see what was gained and easy to see what was lost relative to a more fine-grained classification of individuals – eventually into singletons. For example, the category of people with an income less than half the median may have a higher expected income under one scheme, but with a much wider spread of incomes than under another, in such a way that the poorer half of this category has a far higher expected income under the latter scheme than under the former. Why should the former scheme nonetheless be preferred? Settling for a rougher classification can hardly emerge as anything but a handy simplification.

Fortunately, Rawls mentions a second option, which "is to choose a particular social position, say that of the unskilled worker, and then to count as the least advantaged all those with the average income and wealth of this group, or less. The expectation of the lowest representative man is defined as the average taken over this whole class" (*TJ*, p. 98/cf. 84 rev. passage amended). This too, Rawls says, "will serve well enough," even though "certainly not all social positions are relevant. For not only are there farmers, say, but dairy farmers.... We cannot have a coherent and manageable theory if we must take such a multiplicity of positions into account" (*TJ*, p. 96/82 rev.). Do we not face again an irreducible arbitrariness, which gives no more than a pragmatic justification to stopping short of individuals? Moreover, whether the classification is arbitrary or not, is this not some clumsy form of outcome egalitarianism, an attempt to equalise (within the limits of the maximin) the income and wealth associated with social positions which people have come to occupy, at least in part, by virtue of their preferences and efforts?

No, it is not. Properly understood, the difference principle is an opportunity–egalitarian principle, and its being phrased in terms of expectations associated with social positions rather than directly in terms of primary goods is of crucial importance in this respect. How? The basic structure of a society, Rawls writes,

favors some starting places over others in the division of the benefits of social cooperation. It is these inequalities which the two principles are to regulate. Once these principles are satisfied, other inequalities are allowed to arise from men's voluntary actions in accordance with the principle of free association. Thus the relevant social positions are, so to speak, the starting places properly generalized and aggregated. By choosing these positions to specify the general point of view one follows the idea that the two principles attempt to mitigate the arbitrariness of natural contingency and social fortune. (*TJ*, p. 96/82 rev.)

More explicitly:

The least advantaged are defined very roughly, as the overlap between those who are least favored by each of the three main kinds of contingencies. Thus this group includes persons whose family and class origins are more disadvantaged than others, whose natural endowments have permitted them to fare less well, and whose fortune and luck have been relatively less favorable, all within the normal range (as noted below) and with the relevant measures based on social primary goods. (*Collected Papers*, pp. 258–9)

Restriction to the normal range derives from the assumption that "the first problem of justice concerns the relations among those who in the normal course of things are full and active participants in society and directly or indirectly associated together over the whole course of their life." Hence, one should, be it provisionally, abstract from the mentally defective and other "people distant from us whose fate arouses pity and anxiety" (id., p. 259).

Even among people in the "normal range" and even when fair equality of opportunity is realised as much as it can be consistently with the existence of the family, people differ considerably in the natural and social fortune they enjoy. What Rawls calls "liberal equality" is only bothered by inequality rooted in social circumstances. But

there is no more reason to permit the distribution of income and wealth to be settled by the distribution of natural assets than by historical and social fortune. . . . For once we are troubled by the influence of either social contingencies or natural chance on the determination of distributive shares, we are bound, on reflection, to be bothered by the influence of the other. (*TJ*, pp. 74–5/64–5 rev.)

It does not follow, however, that one should adopt the "principle of redress", that is, "try to even out handicaps," to eliminate differences in natural capacities. "There is another way to deal with them. The basic structure can be arranged so that these contingencies work for the good of the least fortunate" (*TJ*, pp. 101–2/87 rev.). How can this be achieved? Precisely by defining a social position that is fully accessible to the least fortunate in this sense and designing the institutions in such a way that the lifetime prospects, in terms of social and economic advantages, of the representative incumbent of this position are as good as they can sustainably be.

What is essential is not that all the least fortunate in this sense should occupy this social position but that they should all have access to it. This can be secured in part through the ban on all discrimination implied by the prior principle of fair equality of opportunity and in part through making the skill requirements so low that anyone "in the normal range," however disadvantaged by nature and upbringing, can be certain to meet them. Occupying that position, rather than another more demanding one, has a major impact on a person's life prospects assessed in terms of an index of income, wealth, powers and prerogatives, and the social bases of self-respect. Among individuals sharing the same social position, however, actual lifetime performance in terms of this index can differ considerably as a result of events which combine chance and choice in varying, generally unassessable proportions: some become chronically sick, others give birth to a handicapped child, some get involved with an incredibly generous partner, others make an unexpected gain when selling their house, some keep buying on credit, others work overtime. Considerable variation in lifetime levels of income and wealth will result. The difference principle does not require us to equalize or maximin these outcomes but only to maximize what the representative incumbent of the worst social position can expect, that is, the average lifetime index of social and economic advantages associated with a position accessible to all the least fortunate (in the normal range). Correctly understood, the difference principle is therefore far more responsibility-friendly (or ambition-sensitive) and hence less egalitarian (in outcome terms) than it is often taken to be.

### C. Guaranteed Income or Wage Subsidies?
### (1) Maximin Scores

This clarification is of crucial importance for the more concrete institutional implications of the difference principle. For in addition to less problematic provisions for the sick, the elderly, and the young, there are at least two importantly distinct ways in which one can think of implementing this principle for the category of people of working age. One, naturally suggested by Rawls's repeated characterization of the worst position as that occupied by "unskilled laborers" (e.g., *TJ*, pp. 78/67 rev., 80/69 rev.), consists in using subsidies to lift the wages of the least productive jobs as much as is durably feasible. A paradigmatic example of such a scheme is Edmund Phelps's proposal of an hourly wage subsidy for full-time workers gradually phased out as the wage rate increases.[23] The second possibility, naturally suggested by Rawls's explicit reference to "a graded income supplement (the so-called negative income tax)" (*TJ*, p. 275/ 243 rev.), consists in introducing a guaranteed minimum income and pitching it at the highest sustainable level.[24] In either case, the very fact that the worst position is accessible to all – "offices and positions are open" and there is in this case no special skill requirement – means that any improvement in the expectations associated with that position will "trickle up", that is, the expectations associated with other low positions will be boosted as the rewards associated with these positions adjust in order to retain an adequate supply of suitably skilled people.[25]

Between some form of employment subsidy and some form of guaranteed income, between these two potential core components of the institutionalization of the difference principle, what should we choose? Perhaps one way of making it easier to come up with a clear-cut answer consists in rephrasing the question as follows: Which scheme will enable us to maximize the income (and hence the other social and economic advantages assumed to be strongly correlated with income) of those with least income? There should be little hesitation about the answer. True, subsidies channelled more narrowly through paid work are likely to depress less the total income to be distributed than would a less discriminating guaranteed minimum income. But this is most unlikely to offset the effect of the basic difference between the two schemes: people who do no work are entitled to the full guaranteed minimum income, whereas they are not entitled to any of the employment subsidy. As phrased so far, the difference principle therefore seems to unambiguously favour a guaranteed minimum income. This is taken for granted, for example, by Richard Musgrave in his early critique of the difference principle,[26] by several "Rawlsian" justifications of an unconditional basic income,[27] and indeed by Rawls himself when expressing his embarrassment at the possibility that his difference principle would end up subsidising Malibu surfers (*PL*, pp. 181–2, fn. 9). It is precisely to block this implication that he proposes making a major change in his list of social and economic advantages, and hence of primary goods, by including leisure in the list.[28] Entitlement to the full subsidy would therefore be restricted to full-time workers since part-time workers already enjoy some form of income in the form of supranormal leisure, and its amount would decline proportionally all the way to zero as working time fell – which is exactly what an hourly wage subsidy would achieve.

In this interpretation, the answer to the question of the institutionalization of the difference principle is unambiguous. Keep the original list of social and economic advantages and you will opt for a guaranteed minimum income at maximum sustainable level. Add leisure to it and you will opt for an employment subsidy, again at maximum sustainable level.

### D. Guaranteed Income or Wage Subsidies?
### (2) Maximin Expectations

This interpretation of the question would be correct, however, only if the difference principle were interpreted, in outcome–egalitarian fashion, as the maximization of the lowest level of income (and other social and economic advantages). But we have seen in Section IIB that what the maximin criterion should be applied to does not consist in actual scores but in the expected score associated with social positions. For the reasons spelled out there, and following Rawls's explicit suggestion, it could be the position of those who, throughout their lives, perform nothing but unskilled jobs, that is, jobs which only require those skills everyone "within the normal range" can be assumed to possess. On the basis of family circumstances and other contingencies more or less independent of one's choice, the lifetime income of people in this position will vary considerably. But, under actual or feasible schemes, it is possible to determine the level of income and of the other social and economic advantages to be expected by people in this position accessible even to the least fortunate, that is, the level its incumbents will achieve on average.

When reinterpreted, as it should be, along such opportunity–egalitarian lines, the original version of the difference principle (which makes no reference to leisure) no longer generates any presumption in favour of a guaranteed minimum income. On the contrary, narrowly targeted employment subsidies are bound to be the winner. Why? One might want to argue that the very fact that paid work is more strongly rewarded, and hence that more paid work will be performed, must increase the surplus available for redistribution and thereby raise, relative to what would be the case under a guaranteed minimum income scheme, the lifetime income of the representative incumbent of the worse position. But this may not hold beyond the short term. For some forms of guaranteed minimum income may be far better than employment subsidies in terms of human capital formation. The latter may be fostered by a scheme more favourable to part-time work and career interruption partly because it affords a greater opportunity to take time off for further training but above all because it makes it less costly for parents to take time off in order to better look after their offspring at crucial periods of their intellectual and motivational development in a way that helps the young grow up into balanced human beings and (partly therefore) effective economic agents. There is, however, a far stronger and more direct argument in support of a presumption for employment subsidies. With a given amount available for redistribution, the very fact that redistribution is focused on employment will induce the "representative man" in the worst social position to do far more paid work than under a work-independent guaranteed income, and will thereby raise his expected income, which is simply the income people in this position will earn on average, not the maximum they "could" earn. Of course, income is not the only item on the list. But wealth is bound to vary in the same direction, probably even in a more pronounced way. And the massive advantage thus gained by employment subsidies looks unlikely to be reversed by any disadvantage one might hope of establishing as regards the other dimensions: powers and prerogatives or the social bases of self-respect.

Thus, it is now employment subsidies, no longer a guaranteed minimum income, which the difference principle appears to clearly favour with the original list of social and economic advantages. But the shift from a maximin of advantages achieved to a maximin of advantages expected by people in a particular social position does not make Rawls's sensible suggestion that leisure should be incorporated on a par with income into the relevant index any less appropriate. Freely chosen time off work is no less important an indicator of the quality of the lifetime prospects of the worst off than their purchasing power. However, if leisure is added to the list, the strong presumption in favour of employment subsidies collapses immediately. For whereas the expected income of the representative incumbent of the worst social position can safely be expected to be higher under the most suitable form of employment subsidies, her expected leisure can equally safely be expected to be more extensive under the most suitable form of guaranteed income. It may still be the case that the aggregate index of income, leisure, and wealth to be expected by the worst-off category is maximized by some form of employment subsidy. But the argument must be based on the differential impact of the two sorts of schemes on overall productivity and hence on the lifetime level of the income–leisure bundles and wealth to be sustainably expected by the worst off. As indicated earlier, which way this differential impact leans is by no means self-evident.

Can this indeterminacy not be resolved by considering the other items in the list of social primary goods whose distribution is governed by the difference principle? Under guaranteed income schemes, the worst-off category will hold fewer jobs and on a more part-time basis than under employment subsidies. Does it follow that there will be fewer powers and prerogatives attached to the position those in the worst-off category occupy? By no means, because the very fact that some of their income does not derive from the jobs the workers hold endows them with a bargaining power which should boost their expected level of powers and prerogatives. What about self-respect, "perhaps the most important primary good," which involves both "a person's ... secure conviction that his conception of the good, his plan of life, is worth carrying out," and "a confidence in one's ability, so far as it is within one's power, to fulfill one's intentions" (TJ, p. 440/386 rev.)? The key social condition for everyone to have access to self-respect in this sense is "that there should be for each person at least one community of shared interests to which he belongs and where he finds his endeavors confirmed by his association" (TJ, p. 442/388 rev.). Although relevant associations are certainly not confined, in Rawls's eyes, to the realm of paid work, the latter is undoubtedly a central component of many people's plan of life, and work relations provide them with the community in which their endeavours are appreciated and recognised. Guaranteed minimum schemes of a sort that lock people into a situation of unemployment are therefore at a strong disadvantage. On the other hand, not all forms of employment relations are equally good at securing self-respect, and employment subsidy schemes which conspicuously mark off the jobs for the unskilled as subsidised (and hence not worth doing if the full cost needed to be paid) would also be defective.

However, not all guaranteed income schemes share the former defect, nor do all employment subsidy schemes share the latter. Does the concern with self-respect generate any general presumption in favour of the most suitable form of either scheme? Employment subsidies are more effective at enlisting unskilled people into jobs in general. However, they need not be better than well-designed, guaranteed minimum income schemes at providing the unskilled with comparatively low-paid jobs which nonetheless provide incumbents with the community of shared interests which the sense of their own worth requires. For some of these schemes, such as a negative income tax or a universal basic income, also amount to implicit employment subsidies. They thereby enable people to buy themselves into a job, while the very unconditionality of the subsidy enables potential workers to be more discriminating and thereby systematically favour those jobs which mean more to the workers than just the pay.

In summary, it is crucial to interpret the difference principle so that it applies to the lifetime prospects of people in the social position with the worst lifetime prospects, which is a position that can be occupied by the least fortunate people ("in the normal range") – those whose innate talents and life circumstances are such that they have access to no other position. This position can be interpreted as the one of those who perform or could perform only those jobs with the least demanding skill requirement. The maximization of the expectations attached to this position does not justify massive means-tested transfers targeted at the poor of the sort characteristic of the welfare state. In Rawls's property-owning democracy, such transfers should be kept marginal – perhaps even confined to people "outside the normal range." Free, effective, and compulsory basic education should do part of the job by reducing the extent to which differences in talents and circumstances translate into inequalities of skills. But beyond that, some systematic channelling of resources towards those who can only occupy the least-skilled jobs is unavoidable. To preserve the social bases of the self-respect of the least fortunate, their receipt of these resources should not be based on their being administratively identified as "needy" but rather should take the form of general subsidy schemes benefitting the less well paid. If leisure is omitted from the index of expectations, we have seen that some sort of employment subsidy scheme is pretty certain to emerge as the most effective embodiment of the difference principle. But as soon as one sensibly assumes, along with Rawls, that the leisure that people in the worst position can expect should also count positively, along with the income they can expect to earn, in the index of expectations, then the strong presumption in favour of suitable employment subsidies melts away and at least some guaranteed income schemes emerge as powerful contenders. Whether someone committed to (the most consistent version of) the difference principle should favour one or the other type of scheme then depends not only on the exact specification of the variant considered but also on the precise weighting of the various components of the index of primary goods (with income and wealth leaning one way, leisure and powers the other way, and self-respect ambivalent) and on an empirical assessment of the magnitude of the steady-state effects to be expected from different schemes along these various dimensions under specific social and economic circumstances.[29]

## III. THE TOOLS

### A. The Constraint of the First Two Principles

We have so far scrutinized the criterion that the difference principle consists in applying and the variable to which it is applied. In its most consistent interpretation, the difference principle requires us to maximize the expectations, in terms of social and economic advantages, including leisure, of the representative incumbent of the social position with the lowest such expectations. Let us now turn briefly to a third and no less important issue. What the difference principle requires remains underspecified if one does not characterize which instruments it has available to help maximize whatever it says one must maximize. Depending on how wide a range of tools can legitimately be used, application of the difference principle may lead to a situation which is more or less favourable to the worst off and more or less close to strict equality.

From the very beginning, Rawls is very clear: the difference principle is meant as a principle for institutions, or practices, rather than for particular actions or persons. An institution is defined as

a public system of rules which defines offices and positions with their rights and duties, powers and immunities, and the like. These rules specify certain forms of action as permissible, others as forbidden; and they provide for certain penalties and defenses, and so on, when violations occur. (*TJ*, pp. 55/47–8 rev.)

More specifically, the realization of the difference principle must concentrate on "the primary subject of justice... the basic structure of society, or more exactly, the way in which the major social institutions distribute fundamental rights and duties and determine the division of advantages from social cooperation" (*TJ*, p. 7/7 rev.). These major social institutions are

> the political constitution and the principal economic and social arrangements. Thus the legal protection of freedom of thought and liberty of conscience, competitive markets, private property in the means of production, and the monogamous family are examples of major social institutions. (ibid.)

Of course, the attempt to realise the difference principle as well as possible does not allow us to shape the basic structure any way we wish but only within the constraints of the other two principles of justice. For example, freedom of thought and the universal right to vote affirmed by the first principle rule out brainwashing as an instrument for boosting citizens' readiness to work as well as disfranchising the rich as a way of making generous redistribution more secure. Even if institutions so shaped could reliably boost the expected level of social and economic advantage attached to the least advantaged position, the priority of the first principle would nonetheless ban them as unjust. Similarly, even if forced labour or a statutory division of roles between men and women could enhance a society's economic performance in such a way that higher expectations could reliably be secured to those confined to the worst-off position, the subordination of the difference principle to the second part of the second principle – fair equality of opportunity, understood as entailing free choice of occupation (*TJ*, p. 275/243 rev.) – would prohibit the discrimination this would involve.

On the other hand, one should not exaggerate the extent to which the operation of the difference principle is constrained in this direct way. For example, "the right to hold (personal) property" (*TJ*, p. 61/53 rev.) constitutes only a very weak constraint on the rules that must govern the ownership and transfer of material goods. This right is perfectly consistent with tax institutions that would spread wealth widely across society. Indeed, this right is even consistent with "liberal socialism" (*TJ*, p. 280/248 rev.), a property regime in which all means of production are publicly owned. This right would only exclude a radical form of communism in which all consumption goods, too, would be held in common.

Similarly, the fundamental liberties do not give individuals an entitlement to the whole of the income which their personal talents enable them to earn on a free market. True, Rawls concedes that, should the question of the ownership of our native endowments arise, "it is persons themselves who own their endowments: the psychological and physical integrity of persons is already guaranteed by the basic rights and liberties that fall under the first principle of justice."[30] Moreover, the difference principle is presented as a principle for the fair distribution of the benefits and burdens of social cooperation, which suggests that whatever people can produce solely by their talents, without relying on social cooperation, should be theirs to keep. But this should not prompt elaborate attempts to work out the residual that is up for redistribution. As regards the taxation of income or external wealth, this constraint is never binding. So much of what anyone can produce is conceivable only due to social cooperation (without which there would not even be language, for example) that the noncooperative output of any individual (so far as that idea makes any sense at all) must shrink into insignificance. Maximin considerations will therefore put a ceiling on the rate at which the income of the more talented is taxed long before the point is reached at which any individual could claim with any plausibility that she could have generated all the remaining net income on her own. Consequently, one is entitled to "regard the distribution of talents as a common asset" (TJ, p. 101/87 rev.) or even to "view the greater abilities as a social asset to be used for the common advantage" (TJ, p. 107/92 rev.).[31] Hence, it seems that there should be plenty of room for institutions to be shaped so as to increase the expectations of the worse off without violating either the fundamental liberties or fair equality of opportunity as understood by Rawls.

## B. No Resources Left for the Difference Principle?

Nonetheless, taken literally, the priority of these two other principles would leave no resources for the difference principle to use. For what does the priority of the first principle mean? "This ordering means that a departure from the institutions of equal liberty required by the first principle cannot be justified by, or compensated for, by greater social and economic advantages" (TJ, pp. 61/cf. 53–4 rev.). Now, the "institutions of equal liberty" cannot reduce to the formal constitutional recognition of a number of fundamental rights. They must encompass those institutions which are required to make these rights effective by protecting them against violation not only by government officials but also by private citizens. The prevention of private violations of physical integrity, for example, is far from fully achieved in any country. Preventing such acts entirely is presumably only possible at the cost of infringing some other fundamental rights and could therefore be blocked by the first principle itself. But within the limits this imposes, far more could no doubt be done to increase the citizens' physical safety, say by allocating more public resources to brighter street lighting, tighter police supervision, or more sophisticated video cameras. As long as such a potential exists, devoting any amount of public resources to the satisfaction of the difference principle, rather than to a more effective protection of people's physical integrity, therefore implies an opportunity cost in terms of fundamental liberties for all and hence a "departure from the institutions of equal liberty."[32]

The same holds, mutatis mutandis, as regards the priority of the principle of fair equality of opportunity – again as soon as the latter does not reduce to requiring a formal ban on discrimination but demands the effective neutralization of the impact of gender, race, or social background on access to social positions. For example, on the background of diverse family settings which give equally talented people greatly different life choices, it would always be possible to pour more money into schools, preschool activities, after-school supervision, free extracurricular activities, and so forth, to further reduce the gap between unequally favored children. Again, a limit may conceivably be imposed by the best interpretation of the principle of fair equality of opportunity itself if making chances more equal ends up making them worse for all through a major shrinking of what they are chances of getting access to. But as long as this limit is not reached, diverting any amount of money into improving the situation of the worst off in any other way would therefore constitute an unequivocal "departure from the institutions of equal opportunity."

This seems to generate an uncomfortable dilemma. Either we stick to the two priority rules, and the conditions under which the difference principle can legitimately guide us are most unlikely ever to be satisfied, or we give up the priority rules and the difference principle as one of the three components of Rawls's special conception of justice vanishes as such and is absorbed into the general conception of justice, which lumps all social primary goods together. Rawls recognizes that "the distinction drawn [between three categories of social primary goods] and the ordering proposed [by the two priority rules] are bound to be at best approximations," but he believes that "under many circumstances anyway, the two principles in serial order may serve well enough" (*TJ*, p. 63/55 rev.). We have just seen that, in any realistic context, they do not serve well enough if the priority rules are taken literally, as implementation of the two principles in serial order would leave the difference principle with nothing to play with, and hence would clash with what Rawls himself would regard as a "reasonable conception of justice."

The only way out of the dilemma involves adopting a milder, but still vigorous, interpretation of what "priority" means: to justify even a small loss as regards a prior principle, one must be able to argue that it is a necessary condition for a major gain as regards a subordinate principle. Resources which would only make a negligible difference in terms of fundamental liberties or equal opportunities can therefore be legitimately devoted to improving the expectations of the least advantaged. Of course, for this milder priority to make sense, it requires, unlike the stricter one, some general metric which applies, be it roughly, across the three categories of social primary goods. But those willing to accept the feasibility of an index of social and economic advantages – without which the difference principle cannot get off the ground – are unlikely to rule out the possibility of such a metric. And there is in any case no other way of escaping the dilemma stated in the preceding paragraph.[33]

## C. The Thick Conception of the Well-Ordered Society

The difference principle is thus, it is hoped, protected against the first two principles' being too greedy. No less threatening is the possibility that the citizens may be too greedy. The difference principle, let us recall, applies to institutions – more specifically the basic structure of society – not to the conduct of individual persons or particular organisations. So, suppose the legal framework mandated by the difference principle is in place. Might citizens driven by their private aims not try to hide as much as possible of their taxable income and wealth? Might the organizations representing the better paid workers not use their bargaining power to ward off any attempt to increase taxation at their expense? Above all, in our globalized

economy, might the owners of financial and human capital not credibly threaten to move away to countries in which the net return on
their assets is higher? And if this is the case, would the amount actually available for redistributive tasks not reduce to precious little,
much of it moreover squandered on control and litigation costs?

Rawls's initial response lies in the full ideal of a society "well-
ordered" by his principles of justice. Such a society is one "in which
everyone accepts and knows that the others accept the same principles of justice, and the basic institutions satisfy and are known
to satisfy these principles" (TJ, pp. 453–4/397–8 rev.). This society's
citizens "have a strong and normally effective desire to act as the
principles of justice require" (TJ, p. 454/398 rev.). More explicitly:
"To accept or to honor the principles agreed to means to apply them
willingly as the public conception of justice, and to affirm their implications in our thought and conduct."[34] Thus, in addition to the
three principles that characterise just institutions, certain principles
for individuals "are an essential part of any theory of justice" (TJ, p.
108/93 rev.).[35] The exact content of these principles can and should
be determined, as in the case of principles for the basic structure, by
adopting the standpoint of the original position. Behind the veil of
ignorance and against the background of the principles selected for
the basic structure, including the difference principle, our concern
to maximise our index of social and economic advantages in case we
end up in the worst position will presumably direct us to make the
following sort of commitment: to willingly disclose all our income
to the tax authorities, to refrain from leaving the country in search
of a more favorable tax treatment, perhaps even (at least if leisure is
not included in the index) to work as hard as possible at the most
productive job we can do.

Clearly, if the conduct of individuals conformed to these principles, application of the difference principle to the basic structure
would lead to a situation with far better prospects for the worst off
and far less unequal expectations than would be the case if individuals were guided by nothing but their self-interest. It has been
argued, in particular by G.A. Cohen, that these would indeed be
the implications of a consistent interpretation of the commitment
to the difference principle characteristic of a well-ordered society.[36]
Unlike the common lax interpretation of the difference principle,
with its exclusive focus on institutions, this strict interpretation

rules out as unjust any inequality deriving from incentive payments, as appropriately committed economic agents will not need to be bribed into doing what is best for the prospects of the worst off.

## D. The Institutional Division of Labour

However, this is not at all the path Rawls wants us to follow. Indeed, according to his own account (*PL*, p. xvi), the most fundamental change in his position since *TJ* precisely consists of the abandonment of a conception of the well-ordered society as the conjunction of "justice as fairness" applying to institutions and "rightness as fairness" applying to individuals. The problem is that in *TJ*'s account, "the members of any well-ordered society... accept not only the same conception of justice but also the same comprehensive doctrine of which that conception is a part, or from which it can be derived" (Restatement, p. 186). But "given the free institutions that conception enjoins, we can no longer assume that citizens generally, even if they accept justice as fairness as a political conception, also accept the particular comprehensive view to which it might seem in *Theory* to belong" (Restatement, p. 187). Whereas a comprehensive moral doctrine is "one that applies to all subjects and covers all values", a political conception "focuses on the political (in the form of the basic structure), which is but a part of the domain of the moral" (Restatement, p. 14). We are thus back to a narrow focus on the basic structure. How does Rawls justify it?

The reason initially given by Rawls is that the effects of the basic structure on people's lifelong prospects "are so profound and present from the start" (*TJ*, p. 7/7 rev.) that the basic structure exerts a "profound and pervasive influence on the persons who live under its institutions" (Restatement, p. 55). This makes sense as a criterion for the inclusion of an institution into the basic structure, but a profound impact is by no means confined to what could readily be described as an institution. The dispositions that govern people's behavioural responses to redistributive schemes would qualify just as easily as many components of the basic structure. Another reason, presented as decisive by Brian Barry, is that the hierarchy of Rawls's principles of justice assigns priority to the freedom of occupational choice over the difference principle.[37] But the question is no longer, as it was in section IIIA, whether in a just society the institutions mandated by the difference principle can restrict occupational freedom, but whether the citizens of a just society must use this freedom to the greatest benefit of the worst off. A third possibility is prompted by Rawls's insistence that "in designing and reforming social arrangements one must, of course, examine the schemes and tactics it allows and the forms of behavior which it tends to encourage" – an approach he associates with Adam Smith's invisible hand and Jeremy Bentham's " artificial identification of interests" (*TJ*, p. 57/49 rev.). Just as the combination of self-interested rational behavior and a battery of lump-sum taxes and subsidies is supposed to enable economists to reach the first-best maximum of their social welfare function, is not also the collaboration of a well-designed basic structure and selfish economic agents an indispensable tool for Rawls' difference principle? Alas not. Because of the priority of the first principle, lump-sum taxation of the better endowed is no part of a Rawlsian's legitimate tool kit, and economic behavior that is less selfish can therefore in principle improve performance in terms of the difference principle.

The most compelling justification for the focus on institutions rather lies in the second reason given by Rawls himself for making the basic structure the primary subject of justice:

Since a public conception of justice needs clear, simple and intelligible rules, we rely on an institutional division of labor between principles required to preserve background justice and principles that apply directly to particular transactions between individuals and associations. Once this division of labor is set up, individuals and associations are then left free to advance their (permissible) ends within the framework of the basic structure, secure in the knowledge that elsewhere in the social system the regulations necessary to preserve background justice are in force. (Restatement, p. 54)

This institutional division of labour is undoubtedly convenient, as it "allows us to abstract from the enormous complexities of the innumerable transactions of daily life and frees us from having to keep track of the changing relative positions of particular individuals" (ibid., p. 54). But does this convenience not come at the heavy cost of letting individual opportunistic behaviour undo what the difference principle attempts to do? In an attempt to avoid the slippery slope leading to a comprehensive moral conception, is one not back to the ever greater risk, in an increasingly secularized and globalized

society, of being left with exceedingly feeble redistributive mechanisms as a result of self-seeking individual conduct by economic
agents?

## E. Motivation-Conscious Institutional Engineering

Here is what I believe to be the most promising line for a Rawlsian
to take in order to avoid this further dilemma. When choosing the
rules that will govern our collective life, it is important that we
should choose rules that are not only simple and intelligible but also
formulated in terms of facts that are objectively verifiable to avoid
arbitrary sanctions. This imposes limits on possible collective rules
that are far narrower than those applying to individual maxims. It
is precisely because of this difference that there is necessarily a gap
between the level of inequality justified by Rawls's "lax" version
of the difference principle and the one justified by Cohen's "strict"
version. However, this gap is greatly reduced if one fully appreciates
that the motivation guiding individual conduct cannot be assumed
to be given exogenously, independently of institutions.

To start with, if the rules can be recognised to be fair by all because
their choice was guided by the ideal of impartiality embodied in the
original position, and if implementation of the rules can be expected
to be fair because of the verifiability of the conditions in terms of
which they are formulated, then citizens will generally have no plausible excuse for infringing them. One can therefore expect citizens
to routinely comply with these rules, not out of fear of sanction, nor
as a direct reflection of a commitment to a particular comprehensive moral conception, but out of allegiance to an institution they
cannot help recognising as fair. This matches the thin notion of a
well-ordered society, defined as a society in which "(nearly) everyone strictly complies with, and so abides by, the principles of justice"
(Restatement, p. 13), which survived Rawls's change of mind between *TJ* and *PL*.

Moreover, there is a wide range of other ways in which the choice
of institutions can affect people's motivation and behaviour in daily
life, and the consequences of this influence for the lifelong prospects
of the worst off need to be factored in when assessing whether a
particular combination of institutions constitutes a just basic structure. For example, legal rules regarding urban planning, health care

provision, or trade union organisation may foster, or instead counteract, segregation between age groups or income classes in such
a way that spontaneous solidarity between these categories is dis-
couraged or nurtured and, consequently, that the expectations of the
worst off are significantly worsened or improved. Similarly, social
policies, labour market legislation, and the regulation of credit and
advertising may conceivably encourage or discourage, to very different extents, an ethos of work and thrift. Of course, as soon as leisure
is included in the index of primary goods, an increased income for
the incumbents of the worst position may be offset by the shrinking
of their leisure. But promoting the work ethos of the more skilled
and affluent is not similarly ambivalent, as part of their greater output, unlike their leisure, can be used to boost the expectations of the
worst off. Most crucially, perhaps, as the world market tightens its
grip and transnational mobility increases, a key feature of a just basic
structure must reside in its ability to generate sufficient allegiance
on the part of the most qualified. In the absence of such allegiance,
countries will need to engage, in order to retain the most qualified, in
a damaging tax competition that will enhance inequality all around
and depress the expectations of the worst off in every country far below what it would have been if no self-serving transnational mobility
of the high-skilled were to be feared.

Thus, there is a Rawlsian alternative to both perfectionism and
vacuity, to both a difference principle incorporated in a comprehensive moral doctrine and one disempowered by individual oppor-
tunism. It can remain exclusively focused on institutions but must
bear in mind that institutions can be a powerful influence on individual motivation. Without overstepping the constraints imposed by
the first two principles, it must not shy away from resolutely designing institutions that foster an ethos of solidarity, of work, indeed of
patriotism – not of course because of the intrinsic goodness of a life
inspired by such an ethos but because of its crucial instrumental
value in the service of boosting the lifelong prospects of the incumbents of society's worst position.

## CONCLUSION

The aim of this chapter has not been to propose a comprehensive
assessment of the difference principle but only to spell out its core

content, to review some of the main objections it has given rise to, and to unfold along the way several distinct interpretations it has received, more or less egalitarian, more or less work-oriented, more or less restricted in scope. Let us briefly reprise the main points.

1. **The criterion.** As characterised by the difference principle, just institutions certainly require far more than that the worst off be better off than they would have been in the absence of any inequality. The inequalities allowed by just institutions must make the worst off as well off as realistically possible. But do just institutions rule out any inequality that does not improve the position of the worst off, or only any inequality that worsens it? Rawls says both, but should say the latter. And if he opted for this less egalitarian version, then radically extending the difference principle across generations and across nations – an option Rawls rules out in favour of far less egalitarian principles – would become far more sensible than it would otherwise be.

2. **The distribuendum.** The metric in terms of which the difference principle is formulated uses an index of social and economic advantages. But what needs to be maximised is not, in outcome–egalitarian fashion, the lowest score achieved, but rather, in opportunity–egalitarian fashion, the expected score of the incumbent of a social position accessible to the least fortunate. With Rawls's initial list of social and economic advantages, the sort of distributive scheme favoured by the difference principle is a guaranteed minimum income if it is understood, as it should not be, in terms of achieved scores. It becomes an employment subsidy scheme if it is understood, as it should be, in terms of expectations. If leisure is added to the list of social and economic advantages, as Rawls later sensibly proposed, then the strong presumption switches from guaranteed income to employment subsidies providing one sticks to the achieved scores interpretation. If instead one adopts, as one should, the interpretation in terms of expectations, the choice between the two types of schemes is crucially dependent on a more precise specification of the index and on some empirical conjectures.

3. **The tools.** Finally, what instruments can legitimately be used to raise the expectations of the worst off? The priority of the other two principles excludes some instruments that would directly clash

with fundamental liberties or the ban on discrimination. But above all, if taken strictly, it makes the resources available for the difference principle shrink into insignificance, as the opportunity cost of these resources, in terms of what could be done to better realise the first two principles, is never zero. Only a milder interpretation of the priority can save the difference principle from practical irrelevance. A second central issue is whether only institutions should be guided by the difference principle or also individual conduct. Rawls's original characterisation of the well-ordered society is arguably conducive to the latter, tighter interpretation. But his more recent writings emphasise the institutional focus. Just institutions will then countenance more inequalities than would otherwise be the case but not quite as many as would be the case if individual dispositions were taken as given.

Thus, the difference principle comes in many variants depending on choices made along many dimensions. Some of these choices are clearly, consistently, and rightly made by Rawls. In other important dimensions, his choices are not so clear, not so consistent, and/or not so clearly right. Depending on what choices are made, one will end up with hardly any just inequality or a tremendous amount. Depending on what choices are made, one also ends up with a principle that does not make much sense if applied on a world scale or one that, instead, as globalisation slowly grinds mankind into one (reasonably pluralistic) people, will become the central reference for discussing global, not just increasingly obsolete national, justice.

ENDNOTES

1 I am grateful to Samuel Freeman, Jeroer Knijff, Frank Vandenbroucke, Andrew Williams and to participants in the Hoover Chair's seminar in social and political philosophy for useful comments.

2 Rawls's first use of the expression is in Rawls, "Distributive Justice," in *Philosophy, Politics and Society*, P. Laslett and W.G. Runciman eds. (Oxford, UK: Blackwell, 1967), 58–82; reprinted in *Collected Papers* [henceforth *CP*], edited by Samuel Freeman (Cambridge, MA: Harvard University Press, 1999), 130–53, at p. 138 to refer to the first part of the second principle "which we may, for obvious reasons, refer to as the difference principle." His motivation for the choice of

the expression is more explicit in Rawls, "Distributive Justice: Some Addenda," in *Collected Papers*, 154–75, at p.163: "All differences in wealth and income, all social and economic inequalities, should work for the good of the least favored. For this reason I call it the difference principle."

3   See, for example, George Santayana, *Reason in Society* (London: Constable & Co, 1905) p. 91; and Jacques Leclercq, *De la communauté populaire* (Paris: Cerf, 1938), p. 53.

4   (Paris: Calmann–Lévy, 1907) pp. 83–4.

5   George Santayana, *Reason in Society* (op.cit.), p. 109, quoted in Rawls, "Distributive Justice," *CP*, p. 151, and *TJ*, p. 74/64 rev., fn12. In the context of his first extensive discussion of the difference principle, Rawls, "Distributive Justice," p. 151, describes this passage by Santayana as "the nearest statement known to [him]" but also mentions Christian Bay, *The Structure of Freedom* (Palo Alto, CA: Stanford University Press, 1958), at pp. 59, 374–5, "who adopts the principle of maximizing freedom, giving special attention to the freedom of the marginal, least privileged man."

6   Comprehensive presentations of the difference principle can be found in Brian Barry, *The Liberal Theory of Justice. A Critical Examination of the Principal Doctrines in "A Theory of Justice" by John Rawls* (Oxford, UK: Oxford University Press, 1973); Tom Beauchamp, "Distributive Justice and the Difference Principle," in *John Rawls's Theory of Justice. An Introduction*, edited by H. Gene Blocker and Elizabeth H. Smith (Athens, OH: Ohio University Press, 1980), 132–61; Thomas W. Pogge, *Realizing Rawls* (Ithaca and London: Cornell University Press, 1989); Walter E. Schaller, "Rawls, the Difference Principle, and Economic Inequality," *Pacific Philosophical Quarterly* 79 (1998): 368–91; Wilfried Hinsch, "Rawls' Differenzprinzip und seine sozialpolitischen Implikationen," in *Sozialpolitik und Gerechtigkeit*, eds. Blasche, Siegfried and Döring, Dieter (Frankfurt, Germany: Campus, 1999), 17–74. Influential critiques include Robert Nozick, *Anarchy, State and Utopia* (Oxford, UK: Blackwell, 1974); Jeremy Waldron, "John Rawls and the Social Minimum," *Journal of Applied Philosophy* 3 (1986): 21–33; Amartya Sen, *Inequality Reexamined.* (Oxford, UK: Oxford University Press, 1992); G.A. Cohen, "Incentives, Inequality and Community," in *The Tanner Lectures on Human Values*, Vol. XIII, edited by G.B. Peterson (Salt Lake City: University of Utah Press), 1992, 261–329, and "Where the Action Is: On the Site of Distributive Justice," *Philosophy and Public Affairs* 26 (1997), 3–30.

7   The labels mentioned between brackets are introduced in subsequent passages of *TJ*.

8 In the revised edition of *TJ* the first principle is amended to read: "Each person is to have an equal right to *the most extensive scheme of equal basic liberties* compatible with a similar scheme of liberties for all." *TJ* 53 rev. (Emphasis added.)

9 This first formulation in *TJ* matches Rawls's first published formulation of the (then still unlabeled) difference principle in "Justice as Fairness," *Collected Papers*, 47–72, at p. 48: "inequalities are arbitrary unless it is reasonable to expect that they will work out for everyone's advantage."

10 I am here assuming that the cake is divisible at will. If not, (2) could obtain even with a given cake, and the difference principle could (trivially) justify inequalities even under zero-sum conditions.

11 Rawls, "A Kantian Conception of Equality," *Collected Papers*, 254–66, at p. 257.

12 See, for example, Jan F. Narveson, "A Puzzle about Economic Justice in Rawls's Theory," *Social Theory and Practice* 4 (1976): 1–27, at p. 10; N. Scott Arnold, "Capitalists and the Ethics of Contribution," *Canadian Journal of Philosophy* 15 (1985): 87–102, at p. 98.

13 See, for example, Rawls, "A Kantian Conception of Equality," *Collected Papers*, 254–66, at p. 258: "Social and economic inequalities [...] must be (a) to the greatest expected benefit of the least advantaged...."; or *Political Liberalism* [henceforth *PL*] (New York: Columbia University Press, 1993), pp. 6–7: "the social and economic inequalities attached to offices and positions are to be adjusted so that, whatever the level of those inequalities, whether great or small, they are to the greatest benefit of the least advantaged members of society."

14 Here are some typical statements: "differences in wealth and income are just only if they are to the advantage of the representative man who is worse off" ("Distributive Justice," p. 163); "According to the difference principle, [this kind of initial inequality in life prospects] is justifiable only if the difference in expectation is to the advantage of the representative man who is worse off..." (*TJ*, p. 78/68 rev.); "Those who have been favored by nature, whoever they are, may gain from their good fortune only on terms that improve the situation of those who have lost out" ("Distributive Justice," p. 140; *TJ*, p. 101/87 rev.); "The two principles are equivalent [...] to an undertaking to regard the distribution of natural abilities as a collective asset so that the more fortunate are to benefit only in ways that help those who have lost out" (*TJ*, p. 179/cf. 156 rev., adding "regard...*in some respects* as a collective asset...").

15 Under the simplifying assumption of two categories (the more fortunate and the less fortunate), it is necessarily the case that making some of the better off better off still, while the fate of the worse off remains

unchanged, increases inequality. With more than two categories, however, inequality could decrease as a result if the better off who are benefited are not among the best off. Applying the criterion would then require a precise index of inequality, and benefiting the worst-off category but one is then likely to be required when the worst-off category cannot be made better off, for otherwise one would be tolerating an inequality which does not contribute to making the worst off better off.

16   For example: "First, the difference principle satisfies the principle of efficiency" (Rawls, "Distributive Justice," p. 163). "The problem is to [. . .] find a conception of justice that singles out one of these efficient distributions as also just" (*TJ*, p. 71/61 rev.); "But it should be noted that the difference principle is compatible with the principle of efficiency" (*TJ*, p. 79/69 rev.); "This is illustrated clearly in the case where there are only two relevant classes; here maximin selects the (Pareto) efficient point closest to equality" ("Reply to Alexander and Musgrave," *Collected Papers*, pp. 232–53, at p. 247).

17   See Rawls, respectively, "Distributive Justice," *Collected Papers*, pp. 145–7; *TJ*, pp. 284–93/251–8 rev., substantially amended; "The Law of Peoples," *Collected Papers*, 529–64, at 558–9; *The Law of Peoples* [*LP*] (Cambridge, MA: Harvard University Press, 1999), pp. 115–19.

18   The generalisation of the more egalitarian variant states that inequalities are fine only if they contribute to improving the fate of the worse off. It does not follow from this criterion that one should level the situation of all reachable categories down to that of the lowest unreachable one. With any plausible index of inequality, improving the situation of the worst-off category but one, or of other categories higher up which are still pretty badly off, is most likely to reduce inequality rather than to increase it, and the criterion amounts, in case of a tie at the bottom, to requiring that inequality should be minimised. A situation which satisfies this criterion will generally not be Pareto-optimal, and its selection cannot be justified from the standpoint of the (envy-free) original position. Nor can it now be said to the worst off, "you can regard existing inequalities as fair because someone would be even worse off than you are now under any other feasible arrangement", but only, "you can regard existing inequalities as fair because someone would be even worse off than you are now under any other *more egalitarian* feasible arrangement". In an intergenerational or global context, the recommendation following from this criterion would be to level down if the only reachable categories are among the best off. But if they include some of the worst off, it may not be very different from what follows from the lexical difference principle to be considered in this paragraph. Secure

prescriptions, however, require a precise specification of the inequality index.

19   See Sen, *Collective Choice and Social Welfare* (Amsterdam: North-Holland, 1979), p. 138.

20   The term *lexical* is motivated by the way in which words are ordered in a dictionary: the rank of the first letter of each word takes strict priority over the rank of its second letter, and so on, when deciding which word should come first.

21   Derek Parfit, *Equality or Priority?*, The Lindley Lecture (University of Kansas: Department of Philosophy, 1995), p. 38, points out this connection between the lexical variant of the difference principle and the original position argument. This lexical variant is the most egalitarian among the principles which fit Parfit's "priority view": "Benefiting people matters more the worse off the people are" (ibid. 19). Unlike the more egalitarian variant of the difference principle (in both its two-class and general form), it does not require any commitment to Parfit's "principle of equality": "It is in itself bad if some people are worse off than others" (ibid. 4).

22   See, for example, Richard Krouse and Michael McPherson, "Capitalism, 'Property-Owning Democracy', and the Welfare State," in *Democracy and the Welfare State*, edited by Amy Gutmann (Princeton, NJ: Princeton University Press, 1988), pp. 78–105.

23   See Edmund Phelps, *Rewarding Work* (Cambridge, MA: Harvard University Press, 1997).

24   Rawls was quick at picking up the idea of negative income tax. Milton Friedman briefly sketched it in his *Capitalism and Freedom* (Chicago: University of Chicago Press, 1962), pp. 191–4, but his first widely available article on the subject ("The Case for the Negative Income Tax," *National Review*, March 7, 1967, 239–41) and the first technical article by James Tobin, Joseph A. Pechman, and Paul M. Mieszkowski ("Is a Negative Income Tax Practical?," *The Yale Law Journal* 77 (1967), 1–27) were published in the same year as Rawls's first article on the difference principle in which the description of the just social structure ends as follows: "Lastly, there is a guarantee of a social minimum which the government meets by family allowances and special payments in times of unemployment, or by a negative income tax" ("Distributive Justice," *CP*, p. 41).

25   See *TJ*, p. 82/71 rev. This instantiates what Rawls calls "chain connection": "if an advantage [for the better off] has the effect of raising the expectations of the lowest position, it raises the expectation of all positions in between" (*TJ*, p. 80/69 rev.).

26   Richard Musgrave, "Maximin, Uncertainty, and the Leisure Trade-Off", *Quarterly Journal of Economics* 88, 1974, 625–32, at p. 632: "Implementation of maximin thus leads to a redistributive system that, among individuals with equal earnings ability, favors those with a high preference for leisure. It is to the advantage of recluses, saints, and (nonconsulting) scholars who earn but little and hence will not have to contribute greatly to redistribution."

27   See, for example, Philippe Van Parijs, "Rawls face aux libertariens," in *Individu et justice sociale. Autour de John Rawls* ( Paris: Le Seuil, 1988), 193–218; reprinted in P. Van Parijs, *Qu'est-ce qu'une société juste?* (Paris: Le Seuil, 1991) and Steven E. Byrne, *A Rawlsian Argument for Basic Income* (University College Dublin: Department of Politics, M.A. thesis, August 1993). The possibility of such a Rawlsian justification of an unconditional basic income is challenged by Eugene V. Torisky, "Van Parijs, Rawls, and Unconditional Basic Income," Analysis 53 (1993), 289–97; Magali Prats, "L'allocation universelle à l'épreuve de *Théorie de la justice*," in *Documents pour l'enseignement économique et social* 106, décembre 1996, 71–110; Georges Langis, "Allocation universelle et justice sociale," in *Cahiers de Droit* 37 (1996), 1037–51; Colin Farrelly, "Justice and a Citizen's Basic Income," in *Journal of Applied Philosophy* 16 (1999), 283–96; François Blais, "Loisir, travail et réciprocité. Une justification 'rawlsienne' de l'allocation universelle est-elle possible?", in *Society and Leisure* 22 (1999), 337–53; Frank Vandenbroucke, *Social Justice and Individual Ethics in an Open Society* Berlin & New York: Springer, 2001, Chapter 3.

28   "While the notion of leisure seems to me to call for clarification, there may be good reasons for including it among the primary goods and therefore in the index as Musgrave proposes." "Reply to Alexander and Musgrave" (1974), in *CP*, pp. 232–53 at p. 253; and

> I shall only comment here that twenty-four hours less a standard working day might be included in the index as leisure. Those who were unwilling to work under conditions where there is much work that needs to be done (I assume that positions and jobs are not scarce or rationed) would have extra leisure stipulated as equal to the index of the least advantaged. So those who surf all day off Malibu must find a way to support themselves and would not be entitled to public funds. (See Rawls, *PL*, pp. 181–2 n. 9, modified version of "The Priority of Right and Ideas of the Good" (1988), in *CP*, 449–72, at p. 455, n. 7.

29   This conclusion is in broad agreement with Schaller ("Rawls, the Difference Principle, and Economic Inequality," op. cit.), who argues that the difference principle provides a strong case for a package of policies – possibly including both general employment subsidies for low-paid work and a low universal demogrant (or basic income) for all adults – that

would "ensure that all working-age persons have an opportunity for at least an above-poverty income without thereby creating significant work disincentives" (p. 379). "If it turned out that the least advantaged representative persons were made worse off because too many people chose to live off their demogrant, then the demogrant would need to be reduced (or even eliminated). But [...] nothing in Rawls's theory appears to prohibit conferring unearned or 'undeserved' benefits on individuals like Smith [who opt for the life of a Bohemian artist]; the only question is whether doing so is in the best interest of the least advantaged representative person" (pp. 380–1). The fact that the best interpretation of the difference principle does not yield a firm justification for an unconditional basic income does not imply that no such justification is possible in a liberal–egalitarian framework. In *Real Freedom for All* (Oxford: Oxford University Press, 1995), I claim to supply one on the basis of a different and more adequate understanding of maximin opportunities.

30   Rawls, *Justice as Fairness. A Restatement* (Cambridge, MA: Harvard University Press, 2000), Sec. 21.3 (referred to as 'Restatement' in text).

31   Here is a much earlier statement of a closely analogous idea: "Every man who possesses natural talents should know that if he shares them with his brothers in need, he possesses them rightly and in accordance with the will, intention and disposition of nature itself. Otherwise he is only a thief and a hoarder indicted by natural law because he holds onto what nature did not create exclusively for him." Juan Luis Vives, *De Subventione Pauperum* [1526]. French translation: *De l'Assistance aux pauvres* (Bruxelles: Valero & fils, 1943), p. 141.

32   In this paragraph, I am assuming that making liberties effective (e.g., guaranteeing people's physical security in the streets through adequate policing) is distinct from ensuring their fair value (e.g., by making sure people are sufficiently fed to be able to walk in the streets). Whereas the latter is governed by the difference principle (except for the "worth of political liberties"), the former is covered by the first one. The high cost of making liberties effective for all (irrespective of securing their fair worth to all) is persuasively illustrated in Douglas Rae, "Democratic Liberty and the Tyrannies of Place," in *Democracy's Edges*, edited by Ian Shapiro, and Casiano Hacker-Cordón (Cambridge, UK: Cambridge University Press, 1999), pp. 165–92.

33   An analogous mild notion of priority could be used to redefine the priority given to the least advantaged by the difference principle itself. This may provide a way of bringing the heavily handicapped under the difference principle without being driven into an "unreasonable" conception of justice, thereby making it possible to get rid of the rather ad

hoc restriction of the difference principle to people "within the normal range."

34  "Reply to Alexander and Musgrave" in *Collected Papers*, pp. 232–53, at p. 250.

35  These principles for individual conduct can be either "natural duties," which apply to everyone, such as the duty "to support and to comply with just institutions that exist and apply to us" (*TJ*, p. 115/99 rev.), or obligations specific to particular positions, such as an obligation of *noblesse oblige* applying to "those who, being better situated, have advanced their aim within the system" (*TJ*, p. 116/100 rev.).

36  See G.A. Cohen, "Incentives, Inequality and Community"; "Where the Action Is"; and most recently *If You're an Egalitarian, How Come You Are So Rich?* (Cambridge, MA: Harvard University Press, 2000); partly anticipated by Thomas C. Grey, "The First Virtue," *Stanford Law Review* 25 (1972): 286–327; Jan Narveson, "A Puzzle about Economic Justice in Rawls's Theory"; Joseph H. Carens, "Rights and Duties in an Egalitarian Society," *Political Theory* 14 (1986): 31–49; and Barry, *Theories of Justice*, op. cit., Appendix C; and critically discussed by, among others, Philippe Van Parijs, "Rawlsians, Christians and Patriots. Maximin Justice and Individual Ethics", *European Journal of Philosophy* 1 (1993): 309–42; David Estlund, "Liberalism, Equality and Fraternity in Cohen's Critique of Rawls," *Journal of Political Philosophy* 6 (1998); Liam Murphy, "Institutions and the Demands of Justice," *Philosophy and Public Affairs* 27 (1998), 251–91; Paul Smith, "Incentives and Justice: G.A. Cohen's Egalitarian Critique of Rawls," *Social Theory and Practice* 24 (1998), 205–35; Andrew Williams, "Incentives, Inequality and Publicity," in *Philosophy and Public Affairs* 27.3 (1998), 226–48; and "In Tax We Trust. Cohen on the Site of Distributive Justice" (University of Warwick: Department of Politics); Frank Vandenbroucke, *Social Justice and Individual Ethics in an Open Society* (op. cit.), and so forth.

37  *Theories of Justice*, op. cit. [Hemel–Hempstead: Harvester-Wheatsheaf, 1989], pp. 399–400.

# 6   Democratic Equality

## Rawls's Complex Egalitarianism

### I. THREE EGALITARIAN CHALLENGES TO DEMOCRATIC EQUALITY

Egalitarianism is not one idea but many, for there are many different kinds and degrees of equality that people can promote and still lay claim to being egalitarians. Rawls's egalitarianism is complex in what it requires, since his "democratic equality" rests on three principles of justice that interact with and limit each other. Democratic equality is also complex in its justification, since it is motivated by several distinct egalitarian ideas that must be integrated in a justifiable way. Our task in what follows is to better understand this complex egalitarian view by considering three challenges to it. First, I present a brief statement of its main ideas.

Democratic equality guarantees citizens equal basic liberties, including the *worth* of political liberties,[1] through Rawls's First Principle. His Second Principle consists of two principles that specify how the benefits of social cooperation are "open to all" and work "to everyone's advantage." Its guarantee of *fair equality of opportunity* requires that we not only judge people for jobs and offices by reference to their relevant talents and skills, but that we also establish institutional measures to correct for the ways in which class, race, and gender might interfere with the normal development of marketable talents and skills. The difference principle (DP) restricts inequalities to those that work maximally to the advantage of the worst-off groups. Rawls gives priority to protecting basic liberties over the other two principles and to equal opportunity over the difference principle. On plausible empirical assumptions, these priorities significantly constrain allowable inequalities.

Because democratic equality permits some inequalities and condemns others, it must include a method of determining when groups are equal or unequal in the relevant ways. For Rawls, the relevant inequalities are between representative members of social groups, such as low-skilled workers or corporate managers, or members of different ethnic or racial groups. The focus on groups reflects Rawls's view that principles of justice govern the "basic structure" of society, that is, its major social institutions such as the "political constitution and the principal economic and social arrangements." These institutions have "profound" effects on people because they "distribute basic rights and duties" and determine the "division of advantages from social cooperation."[2] The emphasis on groups also reflects the historical context of the political struggle for equality, which has always been rooted in the demands of groups, and, through that struggle, has influenced the content of our democratic culture.

Inequalities are measured by an *index of primary social goods*. It includes rights and liberties, powers and opportunity, income and wealth, and the social bases of self-respect.[3] The primary goods may be thought of as the "needs" of citizens.[4] The index allows us to ascertain in a public way people's lifetime expectations of having the all-purpose means – the primary social goods – necessary to develop and exercise their moral powers as persons and to function as citizens. This measure of lifetime expectations is clearly different from the measure of welfare or satisfaction used by utilitarians.[5] To simplify the problem of measuring citizens' needs in the initial construction of his theory, Rawls assumes that all people are fully functional over a whole lifetime.[6] By hypothesis he thus eliminates disease, disability, and premature death as sources of inequality. In Section 3, I relax this assumption and extend the theory so that it addresses these problems of the real world.

Since the three principles of justice were chosen in Rawls's version of a social contract, they constitute terms of cooperation that all can agree are fair and reasonable. Together they assure people that their "needs" as free and equal citizens are met. Meeting some needs of citizens requires the equal provision of certain primary goods, such as basic liberties and opportunity. We may better meet other needs, for example for income and wealth, if some inequalities are permitted, provided they work to the advantage of all and do not undermine protections of liberty and opportunity. When these needs are met, all will have the capabilities to function as free and equal citizens of a democracy.

People have two fundamental capacities or powers by virtue of which they are both rational and reasonable.[7] Their rationality is manifest in their capacity to reflect on, to choose, and to revise their ends or goals in life, as well as to pursue appropriate means for attaining them. They are reasonable in that they have a sense of justice; under normal social conditions people develop skill at judging things to be just and unjust and have a desire to act accordingly and to have others do so as well.[8] Meeting their needs as free and equal citizens means that people will have the capability to exercise and develop fully these moral powers.

Democratic equality is criticized both from the right, for promoting too much equality, and from the left, for promoting too little. For many, it is too egalitarian. A society conforming to its three principles would probably assure people more equality than is provided in any society we see around us today – even the most egalitarian social welfare states. For libertarians, democratic equality unacceptably trades liberty (and the welfare of some) for equality. For many utilitarians, it sacrifices too much welfare for assurances of equality (and liberty).

For others, democratic equality is inadequately egalitarian. Often appealing to some of Rawls's own views, they argue that it fails to protect equality, or the right kind of equality, enough. To improve our understanding of what is distinctive about Rawls's complex account of democratic equality, we consider three important challenges from egalitarian critics in what follows.

The first challenge is to the Second Principle and especially to the difference principle and the inequalities it allows. Though Rawls decries the moral arbitrariness of social and natural contingencies in defending the Second Principle, the difference principle at best only "mitigates" and does not correct for their effects. A more effective egalitarian principle would require compensation for any unchosen unhappiness or disadvantage we may suffer.[9] This appeal to the moral arbitrariness of social and natural contingencies is, however, but one among several egalitarian ideas underlying democratic equality. Properly integrating these ideas leads to Rawls's three principles, while the alternative principle would actually fail to protect the capabilities of citizens.

The second challenge is to Rawls's method of measuring inequality. The index of primary social goods focuses on resources, but people who are ill or disabled, for example, cannot convert those resources into capabilities in the same way others can. By focusing on the wrong "space," that is, on the resources rather than the capabilities (or positive freedom) to do or be what one chooses, the index fails to capture inequalities important to justice.[10] There is, however, a natural way to modify Rawls's primary goods so that his theory can be extended to include disease and disability; doing so also unexpectedly expands the power of the theory in light of recent work on the social determinants of health. With this extension, Rawls's theory and Sen's tend to converge in their focus on the capabilities of citizens.

The third challenge is to the scope of Rawls's principles. It rests on the claim that self-interested market and family choices of individuals will undermine strict compliance with the principles of justice unless we abandon Rawls's view that principles of justice apply only to basic institutions. The full egalitarian force of the difference principle can be realized only if we introduce an "ethos" of justice that governs what for Rawls are private choices and severely limits the demand for self-interested incentives.[11] By leaving individuals the choice space he does, I argue, Rawls properly integrates key ideas that justice must accommodate, and he also leaves us appropriate ways to evaluate the effects of these individual choices.

Each of these challenges – wrong principles, wrong space, wrong scope – addresses a central feature of democratic equality. Each cites some of Rawls's own ideas to show that his position is unstable and should be pushed in a more, or different, egalitarian direction. Defending against these challenges is thus part of an argument in favor of the coherence and adequacy of democratic equality.

## 2. DEMOCRATIC EQUALITY AND MORALLY ARBITRARY CONTINGENCIES

### Why "Democratic" Equality?

Rawls introduces the term "democratic equality" to label, without explaining the modifier, the particular way in which his fair equality of opportunity and difference principles combine two distinct egalitarian concerns, namely, that social positions and their advantages be "open to all" and work to "everyone's advantage."[12] To show that these two principles are neither "bizarre" nor "eccentric" choices made by his rational social contractors but rather fit with our moral convictions, Rawls argues intuitively, from outside the contract situation, that they treat "everyone equally as a moral person" in a way that "does not weight men's share in the benefits of social cooperation according to their social fortune or their luck in the natural lottery."[13] Specifically, he argues that "open to all" is intuitively better captured by *fair* rather than merely *formal* equality of opportunity (or "careers open to talents"), since, by providing public education and other childhood interventions, it better corrects for "morally arbitrary" social contingencies. Similarly, the difference principle, because it gives priority to the interests of the worst-off groups, better corrects for natural contingences, such as the lack of natural talents or skills, than the principle of efficiency, which gives no such priority to those who have the worst luck in the natural lottery.[14]

These crucial passages are subject to two interpretative errors. First, it might seem that we can understand the point of "democratic equality" solely by reference to the Second Principle because Rawls introduces the term to label the two principles comprising it. I believe that is wrong. The point of *democratic* equality requires reference to all three principles of justice, and the modifier cannot be understood without that wider reference. There is nothing specifically "democratic" about the egalitarian content of the Second Principle taken in isolation. That content, however, is functionally important to the exercise of our rights, liberties, and duties as free and equal citizens. Weaker protection of equality than that contained in the Second Principle would interfere with our needs as equal citizens. Rawls remarks that the "end of social justice" is to "maximize the worth to the least advantaged of the complete scheme of equal liberty shared by all."[15] The modifier "democratic" points to the connection between the Second and the First Principles and their joint role in meeting our needs as citizens.

This connection is a striking feature of Rawls's strategy of justification as well. We might contrast a narrow notion of political democracy, focused on certain rights and liberties, with a broader notion reflected in the idea of free and equal citizens agreeing on terms of fair cooperation. Rawls's social contract strategy is aimed at showing that the broad idea not only provides the best rationale for the narrower notion but has specific implications about allowable inequalities that have been the main source of controversy within the liberal political tradition. Democratic equality points to the unity of these ideas.[16]

The second interpretative error is the conclusion that the core idea underlying democratic equality is the rejection of the moral arbitrariness of "brute luck."[17] That inference is also mistaken. No single egalitarian idea plays that role. Moreover, singling out the moral arbitrariness of contingencies from the other egalitarian ideas that Rawls integrates in his contractarian argument for his three principles risks misleading us into thinking that Rawls is committed to an extreme version of the claim about moral arbitrariness that would actually pull us away from democratic equality.

### Democratic Equality Draws on Multiple Egalitarian Concerns

The core idea behind Rawls's social contract, it might be argued, is that the fundamental terms of social cooperation must be acceptable to all citizens. This contractarian idea is itself egalitarian, since even in this general formulation each of us is a lawgiver with veto powers over the principles others propose. Unfortunately, this general formulation of the core idea would be compatible with viewing the contract as a *bargain* that is acceptable to parties who retain their relative threat advantage and bargaining power. Such a bargain would carry into the specification of principles of justice a legacy of entrenched inequalities that would be accepted as a given rather than as needing justification.

To avoid this result, Rawls insists that the terms of social cooperation must be acceptable to all *free* and *equal* citizens, and the contract situation must model or represent that freedom and equality. As I noted in Section 1, Rawls associates two fundamental moral powers or capacities, our rationality and our reasonableness (or sense of justice), with these key democratic ideas. Central to the idea of our freedom is the capacity we each have to form and revise a rational plan of life (or conception of the good). We do so by establishing certain fundamental commitments – our goals and values – and determining the means of carrying out our plan.[18] Central to the idea of our equality is that we each have a capacity for a sense of justice that enables us to "understand, apply, and act from the reasonable principles of justice that specify fair terms of social cooperation."[19] Although we may vary in our specific abilities to reason about justice, we normally have the capacity for a sense of justice in a sufficient degree that we should be granted the rights and bear the duties of citizenship. The egalitarian presumption is that we all have these capacities in a sufficient degree to be counted as equals – to be recognized as, and to participate as, equals – even if there may be variations in our capabilities to reason or deliberate about justice or the good.

A contract among free and equal citizens must, unlike a mere bargain, establish equality as a baseline and justify departures from it. Rawls embodies the idea of equality as a baseline by imposing constraints on the knowledge ("the veil of ignorance") and motivations of contractors. Contractors behind his veil cannot bargain from threat advantage, though they can still rationally pursue arrangements that best meet their needs as citizens. They can rationally accept inequalities only if those inequalities make the worst off better able to meet such needs.

The underlying equality in our relationship as citizens is reinforced when it is made the basis of a *recognitional* component of both the contract and its outcome. A central idea lying behind Rawls's design of the contract and the constraints he imposes on it is that we seek what he calls a "well-ordered society," a society regulated by *public* principles of justice that are the court of final appeal in disputes about the terms of social cooperation.[20] When parties to Rawls's social contract select principles of justice, they must "take into account the consequences of those principles being mutually recognized and how this affects citizens' conceptions of themselves and their motivations to act from those principles."[21]

Because of their interest in recognitional equality, when contractors choose principles they must assure all citizens that the terms of cooperation sustain their sense of self-respect. Self-respect is sustained when there is a basis for each to recognize and respond to others as *equal* citizens. The fundamental importance of protecting the capability of all to participate in democratic processes and public life, and of not simply assuring people formal rights that might be thought empty of real meaning or effect, derives from this concern to protect the recognitional components of equality. Those who are best off must retain the awareness that the worst off are still equal and worthy participants in the democratic regulation of society. Those who are worst off must continue to see themselves as worthy equals – in participation, in opportunity, and in the interest they have in pursuing their ends – or they will not be able to sustain their self-respect and thus their participation. A key reason for insisting that the term "democratic equality" refers to the all three principles of justice, and not just to fair equality of opportunity and the difference principle, derives from the importance of this egalitarian idea about the social bases of self-respect with its echo of Rousseau.[22]

We can now better see the role that Rawls's appeal to moral arbitrariness plays in his argument for democratic equality. It is but one egalitarian idea among several that support his principles, though by no means the sole or dominant underlying idea. Some egalitarian ideas that we have just discussed underlie the contract approach itself or lead to "reasonable" constraints in the contract procedure for selecting principles. In the discussion of democratic equality, the claim about the moral arbitrariness of social and natural contingencies is introduced with a different purpose. It is an intuitive idea, presumably widely held in our democratic culture, that coheres with the Second Principle in "reflective equilibrium."[23] We might have to revise the contract and its argument for that principle if it did not "match" this important moral judgment. The claim about moral arbitrariness also (arguably) plays a background role in helping us determine that there should be a veil of ignorance blinding contractors to how those contingencies actually affect them.

There is no explicit appeal to moral arbitrariness, or other underlying egalitarian ideas, in the contract argument itself. Instead, contractors select one principle over another for only one reason: under the reasonable constraints imposed on their choices, it better improves their lifetime prospects, as measured by the index of primary social goods. Rather straightforwardly, Rawls argues that nonenvious contractors would be acting irrationally if they rejected inequalities that work to everyone's advantage. To show that his contractors would actually choose the difference principle over the principle of efficiency requires more, however. Rawls claims that the deep conditions of uncertainty in the original positions created by the veil of ignorance, as well as the fact that the stakes are so high, namely our lifetime prospects, mean that the appropriate principle of rational choice for contractors is a "maximin" principle. This principle requires maximizing the payoff of the minimum or worst case.[24] If Rawls is right, then the difference principle wins over the principle of efficiency, since it gives priority to making the worst off as well off as possible.

I must ignore here the considerable detail that is present in Rawls' arguments for all three principles, as well as the extensive controversy that surrounds the actual derivation of the three principles, especially the difference principle.[25] My intention is not to evaluate those arguments but to make the modest point that several key egalitarian ideas besides the appeal to moral arbitrariness play a role in the construction of the contract position and the arguments appropriate in it. Democratic equality involves all three principles and in doing so reflects and integrates these several egalitarian ideas. Justice is not *compromised* by this integration; it is *constituted* by it.

### Mitigating the Moral Arbitrariness of Certain Contingencies

Before addressing the criticism that democratic equality only mitigates, but does not eliminate, moral arbitrariness, it is helpful to see how far fair equality of opportunity and the difference principle go in this direction compared with the alternatives Rawls argues against.

What principle would assure us that positions and advantages are open to all in an intuitively appropriate way? As capitalist democracies developed, the feudal idea that birth into a social class should determine opportunity became more and more unacceptable. A first approximation to a better principle governing opportunity calls for "careers open to talents."[26] When careers are open to talents, we judge people for jobs and offices according to the actual talents and skills they display, not irrelevant traits such as their class background, race, gender, sexual orientation, or family connections. This idea is the core of antidiscrimination legislation.

In American society, with its long history of racism, just as in other societies with histories of race and caste discrimination, we know that social practices can lead to the mis- and underdevelopment of expectations, talents, and skills, even after discrimination becomes illegal. The same point is true of gender-biased attitudes, with their long cultural and religious roots. If we then judge people solely on the basis of "careers open to talents," remaining, on the face of it, race or gender "neutral," we may leave in place the strong effects of unfair practices and morally arbitrary social contingencies. Consequently, the very concern that leads us to embrace careers open to talents actually leads us to a stronger principle.

Fair equality of opportunity addresses these worries by requiring compensatory and preventive institutional measures. For Rawls, public education offers one way to minimize the effects of race and class background. Of course, Rawls would have to intend a more uniform or equitable quality of public education than what we see in the United States, where de facto residential segregation and unequal political power lead to basic inequalities between the best suburban schools, serving rich white children, and the worst rural and urban schools, serving poor minority and white children. The effect is that schools end up replicating, not reducing, class and race inequalities.[27] Even if we had more equitable public schools, fair equality of opportunity might also require programs aimed at early educational intervention for preschool children, like Head Start, or comprehensive daycare programs of the sort that exist in some other countries. The day care programs might also be required to provide fair equality of opportunity to women.

Social contingencies, such as class or race position, are not the only morally arbitrary contingencies that can determine our opportunities in life. A natural lottery for talents and skills, including motivational traits, such as determination and diligence, also shapes our prospects in life, even if fair equality of opportunity is assumed. To be sure, we may deserve some credit for the way in which we develop and exercise our marketable talents and skills, and we may acquire legitimate expectations about what we deserve from our talents and skills when we follow the rules set by a social scheme, but we do not deserve (and are not responsible for) the results of the combined social and natural lottery that contributes so much to our capabilities.[28]

Rawls concludes that the same intuition that makes fair equality of opportunity more acceptable than careers open to talents also makes the difference principle more acceptable than the principle of efficiency. The difference principle better mitigates, even if it does not eliminate, the arbitrary effects of the combined natural and social lottery for talents and skills. A strong interpretation of the principle of efficiency would not let us move from an efficient arrangement (even to another efficient one) if doing so would make the rich worse off, whatever the gains to the poor. Obviously the difference principle, which requires that the worst off be made as well off as possible compared with alternative arrangements, better protects those who are likely to have the least marketable skills and talents than this version of the efficiency principle. Even a weaker version of the principle of efficiency that allowed choices among efficient arrangements would not require that we choose the one among efficient alternatives that makes the worst off as well off as possible.

Varying formulations of the difference principle may prohibit, require, or permit gains to other groups that are better off than the worst off, but all share the idea that priority is given to making the worst off as well off as possible. Despite the controversy surrounding these interpretations, and the uncertainty they leave about just how much inequality the difference principle permits,[29] the difference principle means that those who are worst off with respect to talents and skills are as well off as they can be. Rather than supporting a "trickle down" of gains from inequality, the difference principle mitigates the effects of the social and natural lottery by requiring a maximal flow downward.

Rawls remarks that the difference principle treats the distribution of talents and skills as a common asset.[30] He does not mean that society "owns" these talents and skills; individuals "own" them in the sense that they are protected by basic liberties. He means only that the benefits people gain from exercising their talents are determined by a structure of rules that makes that distribution of talents work to everyone's advantage, with priority given to those who are worst off.

Despite mitigation, those with the most marketable talents and skills are likely to end up in the best-off groups, and losers in the lottery are likely to be among those in the worst-off groups. The difference principle falls short of being a "principle of redress" that aims at compensating people for all social and natural contingencies that produce competitive disadvantage; it does not completely level the playing field.[31] If some version of the principle of redress were the sole requirement of justice, which it is not, then the difference principle would compromise what justice requires. The same point about mitigation also holds of the fair equality of opportunity principle. As long as we raise children in families, their opportunities in life will be affected by their family background, unless we unduly interfere with the basic liberties of parents.[32] In this case too we do not compromise what justice requires when we balance various egalitarian considerations. Justice emerges – in this case as mitigation – from the proper integration of multiple considerations.

Even though the fair equality of opportunity and difference principles only mitigate the morally arbitrary influences on prospects in life, the combined force of Rawls's three principles produces a very strong "tendency to equality."[33] First of all, the protection of basic liberties and the worth of political liberties are given priority over the other principles of justice: the distribution of these goods must be assured before other principles are satisfied. Second, fair equality of opportunity is given priority over the difference principle. It, as well as the protection of liberties, must not be compromised by the inequalities allowed by the difference principle. If, however, we have an assurance of fair equality of opportunity, and if people of all groups are guaranteed effective political participation, then the kinds of class privilege we witness in contemporary societies, even egalitarian welfare states, would be significantly diminished. The flood of talent that is produced by giving all groups fair opportunity to develop their talents and skills would undercut the dominance the best-off groups have in replicating their control over economic and social institutions.[34] Under these conditions, the incentives needed to encourage development of socially valuable talents and skills would (arguably) be reduced so that the difference principle itself would authorize lesser inequalities. Thus, even though there is no absolute limit on the amount of inequality allowed by the difference principle, its combination with the other principles and the priority that is given to them suggest that we would see much less inequality in a society governed by democratic equality than it might seem the principle alone would allow.

Later I suggest an unanticipated way in which conformance with democratic equality further reduces inequality, namely, through its effect of lessening health status inequalities between groups.

### Overemphasizing Moral Arbitrariness Undermines Democratic Equality

Integrating various egalitarian considerations into Rawls's social contract yields democratic equality. It mitigates the effects of social and natural contingencies but does not completely eliminate or redress them. With ingenuity and variety, contemporary egalitarians have sought a more complete "leveling of the playing field" through a principle advocating "equal opportunity for advantage": others owe us assistance whenever we suffer a relative disadvantage in our prospects for success or satisfaction in life that arises through no fault or choice of our own. This principle, however, risks undermining important protections of our capabilities as free and equal citizens that are provided by democratic equality.

Before examining the risks of this principle, consider how it emerges from pushing very hard on Rawls's intuitive claims about the moral arbitrariness of social and natural contingencies. We might contrast these elements of "brute luck," which befall us through no fault or responsibility of our own, with the consequences of the choices we make or are responsible for making, that is, with the domain of "option luck."[35] Suppose we examine our talents and decide to develop some of them in order to pursue a certain career. In doing so, we take the risk that we may not be able to sell our skills in an unfavorable market at the price we expect. Such bad "option luck" is, on this view, our own responsibility. No one owes us anything by way of compensation for the choices we have made. If we thought our bad "option luck" imposed obligations on others to assist us, then we would be holding people hostage to our tastes and choices. They would owe us compensation for our wanting to experience or to do or to be things that are very costly. Our bad "brute luck," such as the lack of talents to develop, forces us to compete with others on a playing field that is not truly level. If we have bad brute luck, then social and natural contingencies have made competition between us and others unfair by not giving us comparable "inputs" to the game of life. We have been handicapped in that game through no fault or choice of our own.

Where does this emphasis on choice or responsibility lead us? Suppose I enjoy and cultivate risk-taking through skiing, scuba diving, and hang-gliding. Any medical problems that arise from these choices count as bad option luck and should not give rise to legitimate claims on others for medical assistance, say through ordinary public or private insurance schemes where all health care costs and risks are shared. Similarly, if, as an adult, I learn about the risks of a high-fat diet and yet continue to eat the fatty food that I was raised on and love, then the medical problems I encounter would seem to be the result of my own choices.

Some people accept the implications of this view. They conclude we have claims on others for medical assistance only if we are sick through no fault or choice of our own. Others reject this conclusion. They find abandoning people who are ill to their "chosen" fate a morally unacceptable alternative, concluding that we have obligations to fix the leg broken in the skiing accident simply because the skier can not function normally if we do not. Perhaps they might say that we should share the burden of paying for voluntary risks, since we all take some such risks in order to make life worth living. They may reject "responsibility" tests that would be needed to determine whom we owe medical help. Such tests are intrusive and demeaning (like some welfare eligibility tests), violate concerns about liberty and privacy, and are difficult and costly to administer. The net result is that, even if there is some intuitive appeal to considering responsibility, it is not so central or important that it should not standardly be overridden by other considerations involved in justice.

Some of these problems might be avoided if we clarified what counts as responsibility or fault in these cases and found a more publicly administrable way of addressing them. John Roemer argues that we should divide a population into "types" of people by reference to all their relevant biological and sociological traits and then see if a particular behavior is more or less typical of that type.[36] If it is more typical, the person is less responsible. If it is less typical, the person is more responsible for the behavior. Thus, we might reduce the burden for bad health on those whose ethnic backgrounds led to tastes for fatty food; or we might find biopsychological markers for "risk takers" who thus form a type that should not be held as responsible for their high-risk behavior.

This approach does not capture the relevant notion of responsibility. Atypicality is arguably a poor measure of effort or desert or responsibility. It makes, for example, responsibility depend in large part on what others do, not on what we do. In any case, we still face this sort of outcome: If skiing is a common behavior of the rich but not of poor working people, then the poor skier is more responsible for his or her broken leg in a skiing accident than the rich skier.

Whether or not this appeal to responsibility for bad health troubles us intuitively, putting too much emphasis on it ignores egalitarian considerations central to democratic equality. Our health needs, however they arise, interfere with our ability to function as free and equal citizens. Elizabeth Anderson generalizes the point.[37] To keep people functioning as equal citizens, democratic egalitarians must meet their needs however they have arisen, since capabilities can be undermined through both bad brute and bad option luck. What is crucial is whether needs of the right type are met so that capabilities of the necessary sort are exercisable. Consequently, income transfer schemes that conform with the difference principle should help those whose incomes are diminished by both bad option luck and bad brute luck. Basic institutions should not insist on knowing an individual's history with an eye toward determining who is at fault for the need.

It may be unfair to examine the "equal opportunity for advantage" principle in isolation and then criticize it for failing to protect our needs as free and equal citizens. The egalitarians who defend the underlying intuition and the principle they derive from it do not, however, integrate it with other considerations of justice. In contrast, it is just such a task of integration that characterizes Rawls's argument for democratic equality. This contrast does not make Rawls's version of egalitarianism correct. Still, if it is unfair to criticize "equal opportunity for advantage" in isolation, it is unfair to criticize democratic equality for falling short of equal opportunity for advantage without first integrating that principle into a more comprehensive account of justice.

Because Rawls sees the outcome of the contract as a choice of principles of justice, the principles are taken to reflect what justice requires. They are not compromises with what justice ideally requires. Mitigating the effects of morally arbitrary contingencies – but only mitigating them – is what justice requires. Mitigation is not a pragmatic compromise with the ideal result of completely avoiding the effects of contingencies.

In his later work, Rawls emphasizes that justice is "political" and not "metaphysical."[38] He means by this formula that we must think of a conception of justice as something that is publicly justifiable to all reasonable persons, regardless of their own comprehensive moral views, on a basis that does not compel them to accept the special philosophical and moral views of others. The public justification of democratic equality must draw on elements of a democratic culture that all reasonable people can accept.[39]

Rawls is on fairly safe ground if he claims that it is a widely held feature of our democratic culture that we do not believe the contingencies of birth are things we deserve. He says "it seems to be one of the fixed points of our considered judgments that no one deserves his place in the distribution of native endowments, any more than one deserves one's initial starting place in society."[40] This point, however, falls well short of the claim that we are owed compensation by others for any relative disadvantage we suffer as a result of brute bad luck, but we are owed nothing if we suffer as a result of bad option luck. Without passing judgment on the truth or justifiability of such a view, it seems more likely to be part of a particular comprehensive moral view and not a shared feature of public democratic culture.[41] Someone who held the equal opportunity for advantage view as part of a comprehensive moral view might still be able to endorse the approximation contained in democratic equality, achieving overlapping consensus "for the right reasons."[42]

### 3. PRIMARY SOCIAL GOODS AND THE NEEDS AND CAPABILITIES OF CITIZENS

*Is the Index of Primary Social Goods Insensitive to Important Inequalities?*

A basic challenge to democratic equality is the claim that the index of primary social goods is insensitive to important inequalities that affect our capabilities as citizens. Kenneth Arrow challenged the index by asking who was worse off, the person who is rich but ill or the one who is poor but well?[43] Arrow wanted to show that a satisfaction- or welfare-based measure would answer questions Rawls's index could not. By assuming that all people are fully functional over a normal lifespan, Rawls initially avoids answering Arrow's question, but a usable version of the theory must accommodate health inequalities. Sen, who agrees with Rawls in rejecting the welfare approach Arrow advocated, later argued that people who differ with respect to disease, disability, nutritional needs, or gender will convert the same package of primary social goods into different sets of capabilities; they will remain unequal in ways that matter to justice. It is "fetishist" to focus on resources or inputs rather than on what we really want out of a concern about equality, namely equality in our capability to do or be what we want, our "positive freedom." The challenge to the index is thus part of a broader claim that Rawls seeks equality in the wrong "space" or domain.[44]

### Extending Rawls's Theory to Cover Disease and Disability

To defend Rawls's index of primary social goods, we must show how it can meet all imporant citizens' needs, including health needs.[45] Suppose we view health as the absence of disease, and suppose we think of disease (including the deformities and disabilities that result from trauma) as deviations from the normal functional organization (or normal functioning) of a typical member of a species.[46] In the case of people, of course, our various cognitive and emotional functions are crucial, since normal functioning must permit us to pursue our goals as social animals.

The key to extending Rawls's view is the important relationship between normal functioning and opportunity, one of the primary social goods. Impairments of normal functioning, including early death, reduce the range of opportunity open to individuals in which they may construct or pursue "plans of life." In a given society, with a given level of wealth, technology, and social organization, the *normal opportunity range* is the array of life plans that people in it find reasonable to choose, given their talents and skills. Individuals' fair shares of that societal normal opportunity range are the arrays of life plans it is reasonable for them to choose, given their talents and skills, assuming normal functioning.

Disease and disability thus diminish individual fair shares of the normal opportunity range. The seriousness of the impact on the opportunity range is a crude measure of the relative importance of meeting the health needs that create the problem as compared with others. By promoting normal functioning for a population, comprehensive health care – as well as social institutions and goods aimed at maintaining population health – make a significant, but limited, contribution to the protection of fair equality of opportunity.[47] This approach is not just concerned with inequalities in health status but with improvements in population health because of the importance of normal functioning to the capabilities of citizens in a democracy. Judged from the perspective of Rawlsian contractors, this way of extending the theory seems both reasonable and rational. Contractors have a fundamental interest in preserving the opportunity to revise their conceptions of the good through time. They will thus have a pressing interest in maintaining normal functioning by establishing institutions, such as health care systems, that do just that.

Institutionally, democratic equality will require universal access, without financial barriers, to a system of public health, preventive, acute, and chronic care services. In general, this requires a universal, mandatory national insurance system (but details of organization and financing can vary considerably). Given real resource limits, services will have to be allocated in ways that meet people's needs fairly, since not all health needs can be met. Limits to care should be based on reasons that all can accept as relevant to meeting needs fairly under resource constraints.[48] Inequalities in health status among individuals are addressed by designing institutions that aim in a reasonable and fair way at protecting normal functioning for the whole population. This extension of Rawls's theory accommodates the central examples that Sen (and others) have used to suggest that the target of justice operates in a different space (capabilities, not resources) from the primary social goods.

Does this extension of Rawls's still miss important variations among individuals that are addressed by Sen? It might seem to. By emphasizing normal functioning, the extension draws a reasonably firm line, but not an uncrossable moral boundary, between uses of health-care interventions to prevent and treat disease or disability and other uses, for example, to enhance otherwise normal traits.[49] Disabilities, which can be thought of as medically incurable departures from normal functioning, require "reasonable accommodation" by society, both in the workplace and elsewhere, to create an environment in which the opportunity range of the person with disabilities is reasonably protected.[50] Nevertheless, it might be objected, an opportunity-based account should be just as interested in addressing deficits in capabilities (or opportunity for welfare or advantage) whether they are produced by disease and disability or simply are the result of having talents and skills in the low normal range. For Sen, it might be claimed, it does not matter *why* inequalities in capabilities are present but only that they are and that the inequality can be corrected. This contrast might make Rawls's view seem more insensitive than Sen's to important variations among people.

The contrast is overdrawn. Sen points out that we must address inequalities in capabilities in ways that take into account efficiency, resource limitations, and liberty.[51] Because he does not discuss these constraints on justice in any detail, we do not know what kinds of cases – beyond concerns about disease and disability – would survive a more comprehensive analysis. In addition, on the basis of Sen's account, many variations in capabilities will be "incommensurable," for people will disagree about the value of many sets of capabilities, and we are only required to improve someone's capabilities when all can agree they are worse than those others have. Arguably, the cases where we are most likely to agree will be ones in which people have publicly recognizable diseases and disabilities. If I simply lack a capability in the degree I would prefer, I have no automatic claim on others; others may think the overall package of capabilities I enjoy is no worse than other acceptable packages.[52]

Once we include health status within the notion of opportunity, there is much more convergence between Sen's view and Rawls's than might at first have appeared.[53] The convergence is from both directions. With the extension, Rawls is much more clearly concerned with the capabilities (or positive freedom) of citizens that emerge from meeting their needs, thus entering the same "space" as Sen's account. Similarly, Sen's discussion of capabilities, as Anderson suggests, is most plausibly focused on those capabilities citizens must have to achieve democratic equality – a focus that emerges even more clearly in Sen's most recent work.[54]

### The Social Determinants of Health: Democratic Equality is Good for Our Health

Once we see how to address health through its impact on opportunity, democratic equality turns out to be surprisingly good for citizens' health and conducive to the reduction of health inequalities – and not simply or even primarily because it requires medical services for the sick.[55] Egalitarians, as we shall see, must attend to the "social determinants" of health, since nonmedical institutions have a profound effect on population health and the magnitude of health inequalities between groups. To see this point, it is necessary to state briefly some important recent findings from the social sciences.

We have long known that an individual's chances of life and death are patterned according to social class: the richer and better educated people are, the longer and healthier their lives. Recent studies have clarified aspects of this relationship. If we look across nations, we find that richer nations tend to be healthier than poorer ones, but only up to a certain point. Cuba and Iraq are equally poor (with $3100 gross domestic product per capita), but Cubans have a life expectancy more than 17 years greater than Iraqis. Costa Ricans, whose gross domestic product per capita is $21,000 less than that of Americans, have slightly higher life expectancies than Americans. Clearly something other than absolute differences in wealth matter to population health.

If we look within societies, including relatively wealthy societies with national health insurance schemes, we find a "socioeconomic gradient" of health. British civil servants, for example, have better health and life expectancies the higher their civil service rank. Inequality in health exists not just between the richest and poorest groups but exists across the whole income spectrum. In fact, the more inequality we find within a country – as measured by income distribution or educational differences or differences in political participation – the steeper the health gradient. This means that greater inequality within a society or within geographical regions of that society produces worse health outcomes for middle income groups than would result if there were less inequality but the same aggregate levels of wealth or education. These intrasocietal observations help explain the cross-national differences noted earlier: societies with greater inequality, regardless of level of wealth, have steeper health gradients than societies with less inequality.

All of these studies are, of course, correlational; they identify relationships but do not directly identify causal factors. Still, there is a growing body of evidence suggesting that societies that reduce rather than increase inequalities in income, wealth, education, and political participation are ones that invest heavily and equitably in human and "social capital." They invest in measures that increase social cohesiveness and reduce the sense that some groups are losers, with little control over their prospects in life, shut out of the mainstream. We can expect a complex set of interactive causal mechanisms among the various correlated factors.[56]

Democratic equality would produce a social order with greatly flattened health gradients, for its three principles focus on key social determinants of health identified in these correlational studies. For example, Rawls not only assures people of equal basic liberties but of the effective worth or value of political participation rights. He rejects the claim, for example, that the freedom of speech of the rich is unfairly restricted when we limit rich candidates' personal expenditures on their own campaigns, a limitation the U.S. Supreme Court ruled unconstitutional.[57] The limitation does not unduly burden the rich compared with others, and we must balance the limitation on liberty against the importance of the worth of political participation rights. Since inequality in political participation is a determinant of health inequalities, the institutional protection for political participation required by democratic equality reduces health inequalities and improves population health.

Similarly, the fair equality of opportunity principle would reduce socioeconomic inequalities not only through its regulation of access to health care but also through its implications for education and early childhood interventions aimed at overcoming the negative effects of race and class. Educational levels and educational equality are both identified as key social determinants of health. Finally, the difference principle would ensure that other inequalities were arranged to make the worst off as well off as possible. If my earlier suggestion that conformity with all three principles would produce less inequality than we find in even the most egalitarian welfare states, then the social determinants of health literature suggests the residual health inequalities would be reduced below the relatively flat health gradients that exist in those societies.

Nevertheless, even in a society conforming to the principles of democratic equality, there might be residual health inequalities between social groups. Are these inequalities unjust? Are they acceptable trade-offs – more worse health for more income (and more inequality of both health and income) – from the perspective of justice?

To answer these questions, we must look more closely at how the index of primary social goods is constructed and used. When Rawls introduces the difference principle, he makes the simplifying assumption that we can talk primarily about differences in income and wealth and take those primary social goods as proxies for the rest.[58] Thus, if permitting an income inequality of a certain sort or magnitude made the worst off better off than they would be with lesser inequalities in income, then it would be irrational to reject the improvement, assuming income was a proxy for the other primary social goods.

Income and wealth are not, however, always good proxies for other index items. For example, suppose greater worker control of the workplace improved the social basis of self-respect – or worker health (and thus opportunity) – but turned out to be a less productive arrangement than a more hierarchical workplace.[59] Income is then not a good proxy for opportunity or the social bases of self-respect. If opportunity (or the social bases of self-respect) were weighted more heavily than income in the construction of the index, then the index overall might decrease even though income increased. The priority Rawls gives to the opportunity principle over the difference principles suggests he might well construct the index in this way. If Rawls insists on this priority, then the proper use of the index would tend to constrain income inequalities if they produced significant health inequalities and thus significant opportunity deficits. If Rawls does not give opportunity a higher weight than income, however, he opens the door to more trade-offs between income and health – a trade-off individuals often willingly make. Still, we might accept political decisions trading health for income only if the worst-off groups truly enjoyed effectively equal political participation rights.

If we focus primarily on the difference principle and the rationale for it in isolation from the rest of the theory, it may seem that Rawls is not concerned with *relative* inequality. By ruling out envy and suggesting that rational agents would accept inequalities as long as their absolute level of well-being were improved, he seems to foster this interpretation. But I think the interpretation is misleading in light of the previous remarks about how the index is to be used to measure differences in well-being. If an income inequality produces overall improvement in the index – and not simply greater income – it is rational for the contractors to accept that inequality. But where increased income is not a proxy for the rest of the index, because of the resulting effects on opportunity through health inequalities or because of resulting effects on the worth of political participation rights, then we should not accept the increase in income as rational or as something endorsed by the difference principle. In these cases, income inequality is associated with relative inequalities that do matter because they undercut citizens' needs. Rawls is concerned about relative inequality when that inequality jeopardizes the capabilities of free and equal citizens. (There may also be reason to care about relative inequality above a level at which "sufficient" well-being has been achieved for all groups if the health gradient persists and is steep enough.)

The implications of democratic equality for population health and health inequalities are surprising. Rawls had, after all, initially simplified his theory so that we should think of free and equal citizens as fully functional over a normal life span. His goal was to answer the question, How should we select fair terms of cooperation that all can accept? I have extended his answer to that question by incorporating issues of health within the principles that govern fair equality of opportunity, and I have drawn attention to the correspondence between the key social determinants of health and the primary social goods included in his index and governed by his principles. The consequence is that the theory seems to have application and implications for a broader range of cases than it was originally designed to address. Arguably, this means the theory generalizes on the initial kinds of examples, cases, or evidence for it in a way that provides greater support for it.[60]

Whether or not the extension increases support for the theory, it does increase the claim Rawls makes about its "tendency to equality." Not only does democratic equality produce more equal distributions of the primary goods than, say, alternative utilitarian accounts of justice, but it produces more equality in health – a good it initially did not discuss at all. Since health inequalities formed a central basis for the claim that democratic equality operated in the wrong "space" or domain for justice, that its target was inappropriately focused on inputs rather than outputs, our discussion should suffice to counter at least some of those arguments.

## 4. IS DEMOCRATIC EQUALITY NOT EGALITARIAN ENOUGH?

### Leaving Too Much Leeway to Individuals

In combination, the three principles that constitute democratic equality have considerable egalitarian force. Nevertheless, because of the difference principle, Rawls's view seems less egalitarian than radical or socialist egalitarian views. Whereas "from each according to his ability" says nothing about incentives, perhaps relying instead on fraternal or socialist commitment, democratic equality allows inequality-producing incentives whenever they are necessary to promote productivity or to direct the exercise of talents so they maximally benefit the worst off.[61] Instead of pressing this contrast, G.A. Cohen argues that democratic equality is more egalitarian than Rawls suggests, provided that it is properly interpreted and supplemented with an ethos of justice (see n. 11). I shall argue against both the interpretation and the proposed modification.

Properly or strictly interpreted, Cohen claims, the difference principle allows only inequalities, including incentives, if they are necessary to make the worst off as well off as possible. Since talented individuals could just choose to work harder or to direct their talents at helping the worst off without them, the incentives are not really necessary. Those fully committed to the goals of the difference principle would not demand incentives that fail to maximize the prospects of the worst off. Since these incentives are not necessary, they are not justified. Unfortunately, on the basis of the lax interpretation of the difference principle that Cohen attributes to Rawls, the preferences of incentive-demanders are taken as a given. To reinforce the claim that these incentives are neither necessary nor justifiable, Cohen argues that face to face with those who are worst off, talented individuals would not be able to justify their demand.

Democratic equality faces a second challenge in light of this first one. Its principles govern the basic structure or fundamental institutions of society. Individuals, in their personal choices and their private associations, are free to pursue their conceptions of the good life as they see them, provided that they operate within the bounds set by the principles of justice. For Rawls, this is an important division of responsibility. Society is responsible for regulating the basic structure through principles of justice, assuring that all have the means to develop and exercise their capabilities as citizens. Individuals are responsible for pursuing their ends in ways that comply with and support the principles of justice, but individuals need not (and cannot) evaluate each of their acts to see if it maximizes the well-being of the worst off or directly produces fair equality of opportunity. Among the reasonable constraints on Rawlsian contractors is the limit on their task, namely, that the principles they choose govern the basic structure, not individual motivation or choice.

The second challenge is Cohen's inference that this division of responsibility is fatal to achieving the goals of democratic equality. The division leaves "high fliers" – egotistical but talented individuals – free to demand significant incentives. Similarly, "selfish husbands" can undermine the equal opportunity of their wives and daughters by unfairly dividing domestic chores, regardless of how robustly the institutions surrounding the family try to support the equality of women. Leaving individual market and family choices unregulated by the principles of democratic equality thus produces outcomes that are clearly worse, given the objectives of democratic equality. Yet, Rawls has no way to denounce these choices as unjust, since, by hypothesis, the principles govern only the basic structure.[62]

To avoid these results, Cohen says we must replace Rawls's focus on the basic structure and its accompanying division of responsibility with an ethos of justice that governs individual choices. High flyers and selfish husbands alike would be proscribed by such an ethos; their actions would violate what justice requires. Consequently, the ethos would embody the concern for fraternity that Rawls says is in part captured or "interpreted" by the principles of democratic equality but which is missing in the choices of high flyers and selfish husbands.[63]

### Are the Inequality-Producing Incentives Rawls Permits Unnecessary and Unjustifiable?

The problem case for Rawls, Cohen says, involves the demand for inequality-producing incentives to do a type of work, or work at a level of productivity, that individuals would otherwise honestly refuse to do.[64] Cohen qualifies his claim that all such incentives are unnecessary and unjustifiable by admitting that people need some room for "agent relative prerogatives."[65] They must be given room in which to give reasonable weight to their own interests, the interests of those they care about, and their obligations to those with whom they have special relationships. Otherwise justice becomes an unacceptable form of "moral rigorism" requiring us to be fanatical in our pursuit of justice. Nevertheless, Cohen thinks this concession leaves little room for generating inequality.

To assess the scope of this concession, consider some examples:

SOPHIE.[66] Sophie works as a conceptual artist. The work supports her and is fulfilling despite her modest artistic talent. She would switch to being a commercial artist, a job she would not hate and for which she has much greater talent, only with a very large incentive. Even with the incentive, her work as a commercial artist would produce enough to make the worst off better off than they are when she works as a conceptual artist. If she would switch without the incentive, the worst off would be better off yet.

MAX. Max would work much harder and more creatively teaching and doing research at his university job only if he were paid significantly more – much more than mere compensation for the extra time and effort that would be involved – and were given various "perks" reserved for academic hotshots. He much prefers the contemplative pace of his life as it is, though he would not detest the alternative. With the incentive and his harder work, the worst off will be made better off. If, however, he chose to work as hard at the lower salary as he would at the higher one, then the worst off would be even better off.

BEN.[67] Ben supports his family modestly through an ad agency that he runs from his home. Being self-employed at home allows him to undertake home schooling for his children and to give personal care to his elderly mother, who lives with his family. He would be willing to work outside his home – as he had done with a level of satisfaction others typically enjoy at work – only for an incentive that is much larger than needed simply to cover the costs of care for his mother and tutors for his children. With that much larger incentive, he reasons, he can also provide his children with a much better higher education, or other advantages, otherwise out of reach.

Do the demands for incentives made by Sophie, Max, and Ben fall within their allowable agent-relative prerogatives? Suppose they do. We then not only make room for Max's self-interested choice of the pace of his life but also for the kind of generally admirable dedication Sophie has to her art. We give Ben room to pursue the interests of those for whom he has special affection. We also leave him room to meet the moral obligations, parental and filial, he has toward them. True, he arguably could discharge those obligations by accepting a lesser incentive, one merely covering the costs of hiring others to care for and teach them, but he may believe it is more virtuous or in some other way morally better to discharge them himself. Consequently, as Estlund concludes, significant inequalities can be produced not only by reasonable self-interest, but by affection for others, by moral requirements, and by other moral considerations that are not truly requirements.[68] With agent-relative prerogatives this robust, we exclude explicit cases of greed but not many of the-inequality-producing choices that individuals typically present. The space between Rawls's lax interpretation and Cohen's strict one suddenly shrinks.

Suppose, however, Cohen judges unjust the demands of Sophie, Max, and Ben.[69] Expanding the space between the lax and strict interpretations in this way, however, means it is no longer clear, and may be quite controversial, what agent-relative prerogatives really permit. To the extent that the fine details of preferences and motivations matter, the ethos regulating our choices is likely to fail to meet the publicity constraints that justice requires of institutions.[70]

### What Does a Commitment to the Difference Principle Really Involve?

Leave aside this issue about the scope of agent-relative prerogatives. There is still a problem with the way in which Cohen makes an inference from the fact that citizens under democratic equality accept the difference principle and fair equality of opportunity as principles of justice to his conclusions about their individual commitments and the injustice of individual choices.[71] The problem derives from ignoring the complexity of democratic equality.

Democratic equality, I argued earlier, is a complex view. It involves a commitment to several principles; it rests on varied egalitarian considerations; it derives from integrating them in a particular way – Rawls's contractarian argument. As a result, it gives rise to complex individual commitments.

One commitment that emerges is to a choice space in which to pursue our conceptions of the good life, whatever they turn out to be. We are also committed to pursue that good within the constraints imposed by principles of justice that govern the basic structure of society. We are committed, that is, to the division of responsibility that integrates our rationality and reasonableness in a particular way. These commitments permit us to pursue the means necessary to carry out our plans of life, provided we do not violate the rules that principles of justice impose on the basic structure. Depending on that conception of the good life, we may even pursue more of some goods than others have, provided we do not violate those rules. In resolving disputes about what justice requires of us, we are committed to abiding by what "public reason" tells us about how to interpret the principles and their implications for the institutions around us. Only in this way can we respect the "reasonable pluralism" that emerges under the very conditions of freedom and equality that are involved in democratic equality.

Only with these multiple commitments in mind can we consider what justice requires of us or permits us to do as individuals. Suppose I want to become a priest or rabbi humbly serving a small congregation. Suppose also that I have the rare talents – perhaps I have already demonstrated them – needed to produce technological advances that will make the lives of the worst off much better or to run a corporation that creates great (redistributable) wealth while disseminating those advances. I am free, given my commitments under democratic equality, to become that priest or rabbi, forcing the worst off to forego the advantages I could provide them. Perhaps I would accept no incentive to change my plan; perhaps I put a very high price on changing it. I am free to do either, and my commitment to abiding by the difference principle, which governs the basic structure, leaves me free in these ways.

To suggest that the demands of justice – my commitment to the goals of the difference principle – must outweigh the moral and religious commitments within my life is to pit justice against reasonable pluralism. It is to invoke a substantive conception of how individuals must weigh their moral commitments that goes beyond making justice the prime virtue of institutions and makes it the prime virtue of individual motivations and behavior. It no longer simply constrains individual pursuit of the good; it defines it.

Consider, now, the "face-to-face" test by which Cohen wants to judge the demand for inequality-producing incentives. He imagines talented individuals trying to justify those demands to those who are worst off, asking them to be willing to forego maximal gains in their prospects just because those with talents refuse to work in the right ways without costly incentives. How could someone who accepts the difference principle in a society governed by democratic equality consistently expect those who are worse off to forego such gains?

The fair version of this test assumes that the worst off are also committed to the complex views underlying democratic equality, not simply to getting others to do whatever it takes to maximize their prospects. Minimally, Sophie, Max, and Ben or the would-be rabbi should remind those who are worst off that they too demand reasonable space in their lives to pursue what is valuable to them. If Sophie, Max, and Ben are committed to doing whatever is required of them to make the worst off maximally well off, so too are the worst off themselves. They too must do whatever it takes to produce maximal improvement for the worst-off group. Cohen's test should reveal that was not their commitment either.

### How Should We Evaluate the "Shortfall" from the Ideal Result for the Worst Off?

Let us say that, when people with talents "choose" to make the worst off as well off as possible without demanding incentives, they make an "ideal contribution." Rawls refers to an analogous situation as representing "the ideal of a perfect harmony of interests."[72] His suggestion that there is such an ideal case raises the question how a shortfall from it can be evaluated even when it is not unjust (because the difference principle is laxly satisfied).

There seem to be three main options. Cohen's view, which I have opposed, is that a shortfall from the ideal is unjust and that individual choices that push us below this ideal are themselves unjust. Because Rawls's principles of justice apply only to the basic structure, he cannot (and should not) say the individual choices are unjust.

A second option is that we (and Rawls) can say that some such choices are wrong but not unjust. They might be just plain greedy or selfish, and there is nothing to stop anyone from raising these moral criticisms of such choices. Parents, for example, should try to inculcate a concern in their children for those less fortunate, condemning choices that fail to exhibit such fraternity or benefi- cence. Such elements of background morality obviously support the moral psychology required by just institutions. Consider, however, parents who are raising children in a subculture that encourages strong gender role differentiation. Though struggle will take place in the background culture against gender-biased attitudes, parents also have first-principle liberties to pursue their beliefs even though they may end up constraining the opportunities of their children. Our commitment to multiple principles of justice makes the evaluation of the shortfall in this case more complex.

A third option is that the shortfall is the result of a mix of good and bad, and we should not try to condemn it as morally objectionable (or unjust) even if, from one perspective, it is not ideal. If people are not deeply committed to the diverse projects they have in life, our social lives may be impoverished in various ways. We tell our children to pursue with determination, diligence, and drive what they really find meaningful in life, and we would not advise them instead to drop what they want to do in favor of whatever they are persuaded makes the worst off best off. Rather than condemning the shortfall as either unjust or otherwise morally objectionable, we are better off on the whole to encourage reasonable debate in the background culture about that diversity of goals, values, and commitments to them. This consequence does not challenge Rawls's claim that justice remains the primary virtue of institutions.

## 5. SUMMARY REMARKS

In defending democratic equality against three important egalitarian objections, I have defended both its coherence and adequacy. First, democratic equality is a complex form of egalitarianism. It accommodates concerns about the moral arbitrariness of social and natural contingencies, but it integrates those concerns with others. The result is that we select principles that protect our capabilities as citizens without making responsibility for our needs the central issue it would become on some alternative views.

Second, contrary to those who claim that Rawls's index of primary social goods is insensitive to crucial inequalities among people, there is a natural way to extend it so that it captures such crucial variations as disease and disability. With this extension, democratic equality more explicitly aims at protecting the capabilities (or positive freedom) of citizens. It neither operates in the "wrong space" nor misses the target of justice.

Third, the focus of democratic equality on the basic structure of society does not mean that its goals will be unjustly undermined by the "private" choices of individuals. The commitments we have under democratic equality include a concern that people be able to pursue their diverse goals in life within the limits set by just institutions. A commitment to fair equality of opportunity and the difference principle as principles of justice should not require us to shape our plans of life so the pursuit of the goals of those principles become our primary motivations. Requiring that might yield a world we value less and need not view as more just.[73]

ENDNOTES

1  The worth or value of a liberty can be thought of as the capability to exercise it effectively. See John Rawls, *A Theory of Justice* (Cambridge, MA: Harvard University Press, 1971, revised edition 1999), p. 204/179 rev.; see also John Rawls, *Political Liberalism* (Cambridge, MA: Harvard University Press, 1993), pp. 324–31. Cf. Norman Daniels, "Equal Liberty and Unequal Worth of Liberty," in *Reading Rawls: Critical Studies of A Theory of Justice* (New York: Basic Books, 1975), ed. Norman Daniels, pp. 253–81.

2  Rawls, *Theory*, pp.7–8/6–7 rev.

3  Ibid. p. 62/54 rev.

4  Rawls, *Liberalism*, pp. 180–90.

5  Rawls, *Theory*, p. 94/80 rev.

6  Rawls, *Liberalism*, p. 183; also "Social Utility and Primary Goods," in *Collected Papers*, ed. Samuel Freeman (Cambridge, MA: Harvard University Press, 1999), p. 368.

7  Rawls, *Theory*, p. 19/17 rev.

8  Ibid., p. 46/41 rev.

9  Richard Arneson, "Equality and Equal Opportunity for Welfare," *Philosophical Studies* 54 (1988): 79–95; G.A. Cohen, "On the Currency of Egalitarian Justice," *Ethics* 99 (July 1989): 906–44.

10  Amartya Sen, "Equality of What?" in *Tanner Lectures on Human Values*, Vol. 1 (Cambridge, UK: Cambridge University Press, 1980), ed. S. McMurrin, reprinted in Sen, *Choice, Welfare, and Measurement* (Cambridge, MA: MIT Press, 1982), pp. 353–69; Amartya Sen, *Inequality Reexamined* (Cambridge, MA: Harvard University Press, 1992); Amartya Sen, *Development as Freedom* (New York: Alfred A. Knopf, 1999). Cf. Rawls, *Liberalism*, pp. 182–7.

11  G.A. Cohen, "Incentives, Inequality and Community," *The Tanner Lectures on Human Values*, Vol. 13, ed., G. Peterson (Salt Lake City: University of Utah Press, 1992), pp. 263–329; "The Pareto Argument for Inequality," *Contemporary Political and Social Philosophy*, ed.

Ellen Paul, Fred Miller, and Jellrey Paul (Cambridge, UK: Cambridge University Press, 1995), pp. 16–85; "Where the Action Is: On the Site of Distributive Justice," *Philosophy & Public Affairs*, 26 (1997): 3–30.

12   See Rawls, *Theory*, Sections 12 and 13.

13   Ibid., p. 75/65 rev.

14   Ibid., pp. 67–75/59–65 rev. Rawls uses the "principle of efficiency" interchangeably with the notion of Pareto optimality; a configuration is then efficient when no one in it can be made better off without making someone worse off. A strong formulation of the principle would then prohibit transfers from the rich to the poor even if the resulting arrangement were also an efficient one; a weak formulation would allow choices among efficient arrangements. Choices among efficient arrangements will still not guarantee that the worst off are given priority as the difference principle requires.

15   *Theory*, p. 205/179 rev.; cf. *Liberalism*, p. 326. Rawls does not aim for "positive freedom" as directly as Sen (cf. Daniels, "Equal Liberty"), but his concern for it is manifest in this passage; also see Section 3, p. 351.

16   Joshua Cohen, "Democratic Equality," *Ethics* 99 (July 1989): 727–51.

17   Ronald Dworkin, "What is Equality? Part I: Equality of Welfare," *Philosophy & Public Affairs* 10 (Summer 1981): 185–246; "What is Equality? Part II: Equality of Resources," *Philosophy & Public Affairs* 10 (Fall 1981): 283–345. Cf. G.A. Cohen, "Currency."

18   In part, this capacity is constitutive of our freedom or autonomy (we affirm our commitments); in part, it explains the importance of freedom to us because the freedom to pursue our ends would mean less if we could not choose or affirm them.

19   Rawls, *Political Liberalism*, pp. 103–4.

20   Rawls, *Theory*, pp. 4–5/4–5 rev.

21   Rawls, *Political Liberalism*, p. 104.

22   Joshua Cohen, "Reflections on Rousseau: Autonomy and Democracy," *Philosophy & Public Affairs* 15 (Summer 1986): 275–97.

23   Rationality must be constrained by reasonableness if the contract is to be fair to all and thus preserve the motivating idea of "justice as [ procedural] fairness." See Norman Daniels, *Justice and Justification: Reflective Equilibrium in Theory and Practice* (New York: Cambridge University Press, 1996) for a fuller discussion of reflective equilibrium in both *Theory* and *Political Liberalism*.

24   John Rawls, "Some Reasons for the Maximin Criterion," in *Collected Papers*, pp. 225–31.

25   Some controversy is fed by Rawls's different formulations of the difference principle; some comes from the complexity of other assumptions

involved in his argument, such as "chain connection" and "close-knittedness" ( *Theory*, Sec. 13); some follows from disagreement with giving such strong priority to the worst off regardless of the benefits lost to others and regardless of how well off the worst off are. For a useful discussion, see Andrew Williams, "The Revisionist Difference Principle," *Canadian Journal of Philosophy* 25 (June 1995): 257–82.

26 Rawls, *Theory*, pp. 65ff./57ff. rev.

27 The issue goes beyond the simple financing of schools, for neighborhood characteristics – housing, job prospects, de facto segregation, political power and participation – compound any simple differences in financing local education.

28 Rawls, *Theory*, pp. 103–4; cf. George Sher, *Desert* (Princeton, NJ: Princeton University Press, 1987).

29 Williams discusses several alternatives in "The Revisionist Difference Principle."

30 Rawls, *Theory*, p. 101/cf. 87 rev.

31 *Theory*, pp. 100–1/86–7 rev. The result is a "meritocratic" ordering despite the constraints on rewards imposed by the difference principle. See Daniels, *Justice and Justification*, Chap. 14; cf. Rawls, *Theory*, pp. 106–7/91–2 rev.

32 Ibid., p. 74/64 rev.

33 Ibid., Sec. 17.

34 A key parameter determining the tax rates necessary to produce maximin is the dispersion of talents, which are presumably less under fair equality of opportunity. See Nicholas H. Stern, "Specification of Models of Optimum Income Taxation," *Journal of Public Economics* 6 (1.2 1976): 123–62.

35 See Dworkin, "What is Equality?"; G.A. Cohen, "On the Currency of Egalitarianism."

36 John Roemer, *Equality of Opportunity* (Cambridge, MA: Harvard University Press, 1998).

37 Elizabeth Anderson, "What Is the Point of Equality," *Ethics* 109 (January 1999): 287–337, esp. p. 319.

38 Rawls, "Justice as Fairness: Political not Metaphysical," in *Collected Papers*, pp. 388–414, and *Political Liberalism*, pp. 11–15.

39 Reasonable people will also justify the public conception of justice through seeking "wide reflective equilibrium" with their comprehensive views, but the features of this justification are specific to each comprehensive moral view; see Daniels, *Justice and Justification*, Chap. 8.

40 Rawls, *Theory*, 104/cf. 89 rev., passage amended.

41 Norman Daniels, *Justice and Justification*, Chap. 10.

42 Rawls, *Liberalism*, Lecture IV.

43   Kenneth Arrow, "Some Ordinalist–Utilitarian Notes on Rawls' Theory of Justice," *Journal of Philosophy* 70 (1973): 253ff.

44   Sen, "Equality of What?"; also *Inequality Reexamined*; also *Development as Freedom*. Proponents of the view that we are owed assistance in eliminating all unchosen deficits in advantage or opportunity for welfare also say Rawls puts justice in the wrong space. Cf. Daniels, *Justice and Justification*, Chap. 10.

45   See Norman Daniels, *Just Health Care* (New York: Cambridge University Press, 1985); also see Daniels, *Justice and Justification*, Chaps. 10, 11.

46   I here invoke a narrow "biomedical" model of disease, but the account is not subject to the standard criticism that this view ignores the social determinants of health and well-being, as will be clear shortly. My focus on "normal functioning" need not be tied to any particular controversial philosophical account of the nature of biological functions. A biomedical account allows us to converge through public reasoning on a broad range of the central cases.

47   This extension of Rawls's theory expands the notion of opportunity beyond just access to jobs and offices, for participation in other aspects of a plan of life also are affected by departures from normal functioning. See Daniels, *Just Health Care*, pp. 50–1 ; cf. Rawls, *Political Liberalism*, p. 184 n. 14.

48   Norman Daniels and James Sabin, "Limits to Health Care: Fair Procedures, Democratic Deliberation, and the Legitimacy Problem for Insurers," *Philosophy & Public Affairs* 26 (Fall 1997): 303–50. Also see, Norman Daniels and James Sabin, *Setting Limits Fairly: Can We Learn to Share Medical Resources?* (New York: Oxford University Press, 2002).

49   See Daniels, *Justice and Justification*, Chap. 11. There is nothing in my extension of Rawls's view that would prevent recognizing, on grounds of justice, case by case improvements in the functioning of those with significant deficits in talents or skills either through medical or nonmedical interventions. See Allen Buchanan, Dan Brock, Norman Daniels, and Dan Wikler, *From Chance to Choice: Genetics and Justice* (New York: Cambridge University Press, 2000), Chap. 4.

50   Norman Daniels, "Mental Disabilities, Equal Opportunity, and the ADA," in Richard J. Bonnie and John Monahan, eds., *Mental Disorder, Work Disability, and the Law* (Chicago: University of Chicago Press, 1996), pp. 282–97.

51   Sen, *Inequality Reexamined*, pp. 136–8.

52   See Josh Cohen, "Amartya Sen: Inequality Reexamined," *Journal of Philosophy* 92 (1995): 275–88.

53   Sen expressed a similar view in a seminar at the Harvard Center for Population Studies in 1997–8 and in personal communication.

54  Anderson, "The Point of Equality"; Sen, *Development as Freedom.*

55  In the remainder of this section I sketch the argument developed in Norman Daniels, Bruce Kennedy, and Ichiro Kawachi, "Why Justice is Good for Our Health: The Social Determinants of Health Inequality," *Daedalus* 128 (Fall 1999): 215–51; citations for all statistics and findings noted can be found in the original.

56  Michael Marmot, "Social Causes of Social Inequalities in Health," Harvard Center for Population and Development Studies, Working Paper Series 99.01, January 1999.

57  Rawls, *Political Liberalism*, pp. 359–63.

58  Rawls, *Theory*, p. 78/67–8 rev., 94/80 rev.

59  I owe the example of worker democracy to Josh Cohen (unpublished manuscript and personal communication).

60  See Daniels, Kennedy, and Kawachi, "Why Justice..." pp. 244–6.

61  The incentives that are problematic must go beyond simply compensating for "costs" of training or other labor burdens, for such compensations arguably maintain, rather than create, inequalities. Like G.A. Cohen, I assume Rawls allowed such incentives when he talks about "direct[ing] ability to where it best furthers the common interest" ( *TJ*, p. 311/274 rev.) or "to attract individuals to places and associations where they are most needed from a social point of view" ( *TJ*, p. 315/277 rev.), but compare Smith 1998.

62  Rawls includes the family as part of the basic structure, but the principles of justice still do not regulate individual motivations or choices in the way that is at issue here. See "The Idea of Public Reason Revisited," *Collected Papers*, pp. 595–601 on the family as part of the basic structure.

63  Nozick, in *Anarchy, State, and Utopia* argued that legitimately free choices by individuals, such as fans paying to see Wilt Chamberlain play, would undermine egalitarian distributions. Cohen, who persuasively replied to Nozick's libertarian argument, now complains that choices Rawls leaves individuals free to make undermine egalitarian distributions. Where Nozick complained of state constraints on liberty, Cohen invokes moral constraints. See Cohen, "Where the Action Is."

64  Bluffing – claiming that we would not do the work without the incentive when we really would – implies the incentive really is not necessary and would be condemned by even the "lax" interpretation of the difference principle.

65  Cohen, "Incentives," pp. 302–3. Cohen cites Samuel Scheffler, *Rejection of Consequentialism* (Oxford, UK: Clarendon Press, 1982).

66  The example is from Andrew Williams, "Incentives, Inequality, and Publicity," *Philosophy & Public Affairs* 27 (Summer 1998): 225–47.

67  The example is inspired by David Estlund's Paul and Pauline; Estlund, "Liberalism, Equality, and Fraternity in Cohen's Critique of Rawls," *Journal of Political Philosophy* 6 (March 1998): 99–112.

68  Cf. Estlund, "Liberalism, Equality, and Fraternity." Estlund makes the telling point that we cannot demand fraternity toward all in society without building it out of our fraternal concern for those we are more intimately connected to.

69  Cohen argues it would not be unjust for a gardener who hates doctoring to demand an inequality-producing incentive to take it up, whereas it would be unjust for a gardener who simply strongly prefers doing something else to make such a demand (unpublished manuscript, personal communication, September 1999).

70  See Williams, "Incentives, Inequality, and Publicity."

71  Suppose someone believes that we should accept the difference principle solely or primarily because it (partly) captures his moral belief that brute luck is arbitrary and that we owe each other compensation for unchosen disadvantages (I challenged this interpretative error in Section 2). It might then seem that demanding inequality-producing incentives is directly incompatible with that commitment, making our demand unjust.

72  Rawls, *Theory*, pp. 104–5/89–90 rev. He is contrasting an ideal marginal contribution curve where everyone gains equally (a straight line at a 45° to the origin) with the actual curve produced when people may gain more than others from their contributions even under the difference principle. A shortfall from this 45° line is less than ideal, but it might still reflect a partial harmony of interests (the part of the difference curve that has a positive slope) if no one gains at the expense of others or without some gains to others. I thank Josh Cohen for discussion of this issue.

73  Acknowledgment: I have benefited from discussion of this chapter, or of earlier work on which it draws, with Sudhir Anand, Allen Buchanan, Dan Brock, G.A. Cohen, Josh Cohen, David Estlund, Samuel Freeman, Ichiro Kawachi, Erin Kelly, Bruce Kennedy, Amy Lara, David MacArthur, Lionel McPherson, Fabienne Peter, John Rawls, James Sabin, Amartya Sen, George Smith, Steve White, Dan Wikler, and Andrew Williams. I especially want to thank Josh Cohen and Jerry Cohen for detailed comments on an earlier draft. I have also been supported in part by a Robert Wood Johnson Investigator Award and a Tufts Sabbatical leave.

# 7 Congruence and the Good of Justice

One of Rawls's guiding aims in the development and revision of his work has been to show how a well-ordered society of justice as fairness is realistically possible. Rawls thinks establishing the feasibility, or "stability," of a conception of justice is essential to its justification. My aim is to discuss the role and import of Rawls's stability argument. To do so, I will concentrate primarily on the second part of Rawls's discussion of stability in *Theory of Justice*, the argument for the "congruence of the right and the good." This argument particularly exhibits Rawls's indebtedness to Kant in the justification of his view. After discussing the purpose of congruence (in Sections I and II), I outline in detail what the argument is (III and IV), emphasizing the role of the Kantian interpretation of justice as fairness. Then in Section V, I discuss how problems with the Kantian congruence argument led Rawls to political liberalism.

## I. STABILITY AND CONGRUENCE: OUTLINE OF ISSUES

Rawls's congruence argument has been widely neglected in discussions of his work. Reasons for this neglect are several. First there is sheer exhaustion. The congruence argument begins in Part III of *Theory of Justice* (*TJ*), is developed for over 200 pages, and culminates (in Section 86) at the end of a very long book. Second, there is Rawls's uncharacteristic lack of clarity in setting out the congruence argument: it is interrupted and intertwined with other arguments Rawls simultaneously develops. Finally, there is the feeling among some of Rawls's main commentators that the argument is a failure. As Brian Barry says, Rawls himself seems dissatisfied with the argument, but his dissatisfaction does not seem to me to go anywhere deep enough. The only thing to do is to follow the course followed virtually unanimously by commentators on *A Theory of Justice* and forget about it.[1]

But it would be a mistake to forget about the congruence argument for several reasons. First, it is primarily Rawls's dissatisfaction with congruence that led him subsequently to recast the justification for justice as fairness, culminating in his account of political liberalism. It is then difficult to appreciate *Political Liberalism* without first understanding what congruence is about and Rawls's reasons for dissatisfaction with it.

A second reason to focus on congruence is that it deals with a central problem in moral and political philosophy, a problem which Kant left hanging, or at least failed to resolve, by turning to religion in his account of the Highest Good. The problem is a version of the ancient quandary, whether justice is part of the human good. Rawls argues that under certain social conditions, justice can be part of the human good, and indeed must be if a just social scheme is to be feasible.[2]

Rawls's congruence argument constitutes the second part of his account of the stability of justice as fairness. Concern for social stability is a common feature of social contract views. For Hobbes stability was paramount – the primary subject for a conception of political justice. A just society for Hobbes is nearly identifiable with a stable social order. He conceives of justice as peoples' mutual compliance with the norms and institutions needed to establish peaceful social cooperation. Hobbes argues that nearly absolute sovereignty is needed to secure a stable state of peace. His modern followers think differently; among fully rational agents indifferent to one another and motivated only by their particular interests, there may be little need for coercive political force.[3] Still justice is conceived as the norms and institutions instrumental to achieving a stable state of peaceful and productive cooperation. Moreover, stability is achieved as the result of a practical compromise among essentially conflicting interests. These are two distinctive features of Hobbesian contract views.

The liberal and democratic social contract doctrines of Locke, Rousseau, and Kant conceived of stability differently. Stability does not define the first subject of political justice. For by itself a stable social order, however rational it may be, can be of little moral consequence if it does not rectify but only perpetuates gross injustice. So a conception of justice should be worked out beforehand by relying on independent moral considerations. Then the question of its stability is raised to test the feasibility of a just society conceived along the lines of this conception.[4] What is important is not the stability of cooperation per se but the justice of cooperation and its stability "for the right reasons."[5]

The structure of this argument is articulated by Kant. Kant says that demonstrating how a just constitution is possible is "the greatest problem for the human species."[6] To solve this problem, three things are needed: first, the "correct concept" of a just constitution; second, "great experience during much of the world's course"; and third, "above all else a good will prepared to accept that constitution."[7]

The three parts of Rawls's *Theory of Justice* reflect Kant's framing of these issues. In Part I, "Theory," Rawls sets forth what he sees as the most appropriate conception of justice for the constitution (or "basic structure") of a democratic society. Following the democratic social contract tradition, Rawls contends that a just constitution is possible only if it commands the reasonable agreement of free and rational persons who are equally situated. Appealing to certain moral convictions alleged to be implicit in our sense of justice, Rawls elicits restrictions on arguments for principles of justice to construct this situation of equality, the original position. From there Rawls makes his familiar argument for the principles of justice (the principles of equal basic liberties and fair opportunities, the difference principle, and the natural duties of individuals needed to support just institutions). These provide Rawls's account of the "correct concept" of the principles that define a just constitution.

In Part II of *Theory*, "Institutions," Rawls responds to Kant's second problem. Taking into account the workings of social systems under modern conditions, Rawls provides an account of the democratic institutions satisfying his principles. They are the institutions of a constitutional democracy. They provide for constitutional rights that protect basic liberties, laws guaranteeing fair equality of opportunity, and a "property-owning democracy" (or a liberal socialist scheme) providing a social minimum that enables all citizens to exercise their basic rights effectively and realize fair opportunities, thereby achieving individual independence.

The third of Kant's issues, on the "good will," concerns the feasibility of a just constitution given prominent tendencies of human nature. This subject occupies Rawls throughout Part III, "Ends." The problem is this: Assuming we have accounts of the correct conception of justice, and of the institutions needed to realize it, how are we to motivate rational persons effectively so that they affirm and support these institutions and the conception of justice that informs them? This is not the Hobbesian stability problem of specifying justice by reference to individuals' private wills. If Rawls is correct, justice is already specified in *Theory* Parts I and II by reference to a public will founded on considered moral convictions and knowledge of democratic institutions. Given that these principles and institutions are worked out and already in place, Rawls's stability argument aims to show how these expressions of the public will can engage each individual will – if not ours, then at least the wills of agents living under the idealized conditions of a "well-ordered society" of justice as fairness.[8]

There are at least two problems to deal with here. First, given natural human propensities, how do people come to care about justice to begin with? And second, why should they care about it sufficiently so that they have reason to subordinate pursuit of their ends to requirements of justice? Unless it can be shown that citizens, if not now then at least in a just and well-ordered society, can be regularly motivated to act as just institutions demand, then a just social order is unstable and for this reason utopian.[9]

These two parts of Rawls's stability argument are addressed respectively in Chapters 8 and 9 of *Theory*. In Chapter 8, he sets forth a moral psychology designed to show how people in a well-ordered society of justice as fairness can come to acquire the moral motivation Rawls calls a "sense of justice." Rawls defines the sense of justice as a normally effective desire to apply and to abide by principles of justice and their institutional requirements (*TJ*, p. 505/442 rev.).[10] He advances a social-psychological argument: that individuals in a well-ordered society of justice as fairness will normally come to acquire a settled disposition to support institutions that benefit them. Rawls contends, on the basis of three psychological laws of moral development, the "reciprocity principles," that the sense of justice is continuous with our natural sentiments and is a normal part of human life (at least in a well-ordered society).[11]

Then, in Chapter 9, Rawls further argues how the sense of justice is compatible with, and can even constitute part of, a person's good.

This is the congruence argument proper. Now of this argument, Brian Barry says that it is not only unnecessary but also wrongheaded. It is unnecessary because Rawls has already shown in Chapter 8 how people normally come to acquire a sense of justice to support just institutions. This should be sufficient for stability. The congruence argument is wrongheaded since it stems from Rawls's rejection of the idea that a person can be motivated to do what is right and just out of a sense of duty. To support this reading of Rawls, Barry cites Rawls's rejection of W.D. Ross's doctrine of the "purely conscientious act." Rawls says this doctrine holds

> that the highest moral motive is the desire to do what is right and just simply because it is right and just, no other description being appropriate.... Ross holds that the sense of right is a desire for a distinct (and unanalyzable) object, since a specific (and unanalyzable) property characterizes actions that are our duty.... But on this interpretation the sense of right lacks any apparent reason; it resembles a preference for tea rather than coffee. Although such a preference might exist, to make it regulative of the basic structure of society is utterly capricious.... (*TJ*, pp. 477–8/418 rev.)

Barry responds:

> I am inclined to think that this is a travesty of the thoroughly commonsensical idea represented by saying that people can do their duty out of a sense of duty and not in order to achieve some independently definable end. This does not have to mean that moral action is "utterly capricious," as Rawls has it. We can perfectly well tell a story about motivation that makes acting rightly appear as rational. The story that I would commend is that of T.M. Scanlon. According to this, the moral motive is the desire to act according to rules that could not reasonably be rejected by others similarly motivated.... It is therefore quite natural to say that the thought that something is the right thing to do is what motivates us to act rightly. I take this to be precisely the proposition that Rawls objects to. (Barry, p. 884)

Moreover, it is because Rawls objects to this moral motive that he must make the congruence argument, Barry says:

> Recoiling from "the doctrine of the pure conscientious act," Rawls commits himself in Chapter 9 of *A Theory of Justice* to the ancient doctrine that no act can be regarded as rational unless it is for the good of the agent to perform it. Thus, the problem is one of "congruence between justice and goodness." (id., pp. 884–5)

As Barry would have it then, Rawls, by rejecting the idea that we do what is right and just simply because it is right and just, also rejects the idea that people can normally do their duty out of a sense of duty, or simply for the sake of the duty of justice. And this is why Rawls thinks he must show, in Chapter 9, that justice must promote the human good. How otherwise could people be motivated to do what is right and just given that, for Rawls, (presumably) morality and justice by themselves cannot supply a rational motivation?

This reading misinterprets Rawls on several counts. First, Rawls does not deny that people can act for the sake of duty – quite the contrary. In *Theory* itself Rawls says, simply as a fact about people, that moral principles "engage our affections" (*TJ*, p. 476/416 rev.) and that the sense of justice is "among our final ends" (*TJ*, p. 494/432 rev.). In *Theory* and afterwards he says on numerous occasions that we can act not simply "on" but also "from" our sense of justice and that we can and do act simply for the sake of justice.[12] What Rawls is concerned to deny (in the passage just quoted) is a particular account of moral motivation held by rational intuitionists, like W.D. Ross and H.A. Prichard. This view says that what motivates us in acting morally is our grasping of a simple, unanalyzable, nonnatural moral property, which is by itself sufficient to give rise to a desire to do what is right. It is this motivation, the "desire to do what is right and just simply because it is right, *no other description being appropriate*," that Rawls rejects (*TJ*, p. 477/418 rev., emphases added). For there is an appropriate description for the desire to do what is right. It is, on Rawls's account, the desire to act on principles that rational individuals would agree to from a fair position of equality. Here Rawls agrees with Scanlon.[13] Whereas Scanlon has defined the contractualist moral motivation that Barry himself endorses as "the desire to act according to rules that could not reasonably be rejected by others similarly motivated," Rawls defines the contractualist motivation only somewhat differently as a desire "to live with others on terms that everyone would recognize as fair from a perspective that all would accept as reasonable" (*TJ*, p. 478/418 rev.).[14]

Rawls then does not reject, *pace* Barry, the idea that "people can do their duty out of a sense of duty and not in order to achieve some independently definable end" (Barry, p. 884). But if not, why does Rawls feel it is necessary to say anything more to prove that justice as fairness is feasible? Why the need for the congruence argument?

The reason is that having a sense of justice and acting for the sake of justice still is not sufficient to show that the sense of justice is compatible with human nature or our good – far less so that justice can be part of our good.[15] Having a sense of justice then does not mean people will consistently act justly and that a just society will be stable. It may be that meeting requirements of justice are just too demanding for most people given certain tendencies of human nature. Moreover, justice often conflicts with other primary motives people have, and when it does, what is to ensure that people will not often sacrifice justice for the sake of other primary ends? These issues should come into better focus upon clarification of the structure of the congruence argument.

## II. THE QUESTION OF CONGRUENCE

The question addressed by Rawls's congruence argument is this: Assume that people in a well-ordered society of justice as fairness have an independent sense of justice, and so *do* want to do what is right and just for its own sake. What assurance do we have that they will consistently affirm and act upon this motive and regularly observe requirements of justice? Rawls assumes that people can be expected to act consistently on and from moral motives of justice only if justice is compatible with their good.

What does Rawls mean by a person's good? He formally defines it in terms of what is rational for a person to want under certain ideal deliberative conditions, which accounts for the label, "Goodness as Rationality" (*TJ*, p. 345/347 rev.). Rationality is specified in terms of certain principles of rational choice. Some of these are standard in most any account of practical rationality: taking effective means to one's ends, ranking one's ends in order of priority, and making one's final ends consistent, taking the most probable course of action to realize one's ends, and choosing the course of action that realizes the greater number of one's ends. These "counting principles" as Rawls calls them, are not controversial, and so there is no need to dwell on them.[16] More controversial is Rawls's assumption of the rationality of prudence, or no-time preference – to give equal concern to all the (future) times of one's life. This assumption, taken from Sidgwick, enables Rawls to incorporate the idea of a "plan of life" into the account of rationality, making it part of the formal definition of a person's good. A plan of life consists of a schedule of the primary ends and pursuits a person values, and activities that are needed to realize them, over a lifetime. Each of us can imagine more than one such plan we might be satisfied with. The most rational plan of life for a person satisfies the counting principles and is the plan the person would choose under conditions of "deliberative rationality." These are hypothetical conditions where a person is assumed to have full knowledge of what it is like to live a life pursuing chosen ends, critically reflects upon this plan, and appreciates the consequences.[17] The account of the plan of life a person would choose in deliberative rationality provides Rawls's formal definition of a person's good.

The idea of a rational plan supplies the basis for Rawls's "thin theory of the good." It is presupposed in the argument from the original position; the parties are rational in this sense. With this formal outline of the thin theory in place, we can get a better idea of the congruence problem. There are two ideal perspectives in Rawls's conception of justice: the original position and deliberative rationality. The former provides the foundation for judgments of justice; the latter provides the basis for judgments regarding a person's good. The original position abstracts from all information particular to our situations, including the specific ends and activities constituting an individual's good. In deliberative rationality all this information is restored: judgments of value, unlike judgments of right, are explained relative to individuals' particular ends and situations, and thus Rawls assumes they require full knowledge of one's circumstances. The original position is a collective public perspective[18] – we occupy this position jointly, and judgment is common since we must all observe the same standards of justice. So Rawls characterizes it as a unanimous social agreement. Deliberative rationality, by contrast, is an individual perspective – the "point of view of the individual," to use Sidgwick's terms. Judgments there are made singly, by each individual; because our ends and circumstances differ, Rawls assumes our individual goods must differ. There can be no thoroughgoing agreement on the human good, even under ideal conditions; pluralism of values is a fundamental feature of Rawls's view. Both perspectives are idealizations; neither takes individuals just as they are. Instead, both artificially control the information available and constrain the judgments of those occupying these positions by normative principles: by rational principles in judgments of one's good and by reasonable principles constraining rational judgment in case of judgments of justice. Finally, both perspectives purportedly specify objective points of view, providing a basis for judgments of objective reasons: public reasons of justice applying to everyone from the standpoint of justice, and individual reasons objectively defined for each person from the standpoint of the individual's good.

The congruence argument purports to show that under the ideal conditions of a well-ordered society, the judgments that would be made from these two ideal perspectives coincide. Reasonable principles judged and willed as rational from the common perspective of justice are also judged and willed as rational from each individual's point of view. The basic question of congruence is, Is it rational in a well-ordered society of justice as fairness for persons to affirm individually, from the point of view of deliberative rationality, the principles of justice they would rationally agree to when they take up the public perspective of justice? If so, then it is rational for the members of a well-ordered society to make their sense of justice a regulative disposition within their rational plans, and justice becomes an essential part of each person's good. If Rawls can show this, then he has gone a long way towards resolving Sidgwick's "dualism of practical reason."[19] For then he will have shown that the point of view of the individual, defined by rational principles, and the impartial public perspective of justice, defined by reasonable principles, are not fundamentally at odds, as Sidgwick feared, but are "congruent."

The congruence problem is not to be confused with the traditional question of whether it is rational to be just *whatever* one's desires and situation. On the assumption that rationality involves clarifying one's ends, making them consistent, and taking effective means to realize them, Phillipa Foot, Bernard Williams, and others have argued, following Hume, that there is no necessary connection between rationality and justice. Given their supposition that rationality is taking effective means to given ends, their arguments must be correct. For if it is assumed that people can want most anything and that there may be people with absolutely no moral sentiments, then it is a truism that rationality does not require the pursuit of justice.

Rawls seems to agree (*TJ*, p. 575/503–4 rev.). But this has little bearing on his argument. For Rawls has no interest in showing the rationality of justice whatever people's situations.[20] His argument applies mainly to the favorable situation of a well-ordered society.

And even then, it assumes that everyone in these circumstances already has an effective sense of justice and so has prima facie reason to act on it.[21]

But if congruence already assumes so much, why should it be of any interest? This again is just Barry's objection, namely, that Rawls's argument (in *TJ*, Chap. 8) that members of a well-ordered society normally have a sense of justice is already sufficient to prove stability within Rawls's framework. It is, Barry says, only due to Rawls's faulty moral psychology – his purported belief that it is irrational to do justice for its own sake – that Rawls thinks the congruence argument is needed. I have argued that Rawls is not culpable of the moral psychology Barry ascribes to him. Rather, for Rawls the very fact that a self-sufficient sense of justice is "a normal part of human life" (*TJ*, p. 489/428 rev.) poses the very problem addressed by the congruence argument. For nothing has been said yet which would show that our moral sense of justice is not "in many respects irrational and injurious to our good" (id.).

Several different problems arise once it is assumed that people have a desire to do what is just for its own sake.

1. What is to assure us that our sense of justice is not entirely conventional, a peculiar product of our circumstances with no deeper basis in human tendencies or, what is worse, that the sense of justice may be illusional, grounded in false beliefs covertly instilled in us, either by those in power, or by our circumstances and social relations? People's suspicion that their sense of justice is arbitrary or manipulated in these ways can only cause it to waver and subside, giving rise to social instability. The most forceful criticism of this kind is the Marxian argument that justice is ideological, even incoherent, and based on our affirming false values and living under distorting conditions.

2. Rawls himself concedes (*TJ*, Chap. 8) that justice developmentally has its origins in a "morality of authority" which we acquire from our parents and our upbringing. What guarantees that our sense of justice does not remain anchored in submission to authority and is simply an infantile abnegation of responsibility? Freud argues, for example, that our existing moral feelings may be in many ways punitive, based in self-hatred, and that they incorporate many of the harsher aspects of the authority situation in which these feelings were first acquired (cf., *TJ*, p. 489/428 rev.).

3. Conservative writers contend that the tendency to equality in modern social movements and democratic demands for redistribution are expressions of envy directed against those who are more gifted and successful at managing life and its contingencies. Envy masks a lack of self-worth and a sense of failure and weakness. Here Freud was more evenhanded. The sense of justice, he argued, has its origins not only in the envy of the poor but also in the jealousy of the rich to protect their social advantages. As a compromise, the rich and the poor settle on the rule of equal treatment, and by a reaction-formation envy and jealousy are transformed into a sense of justice. What is to assure us that the sense of justice does not have its source in these undesirable characteristics?

4. In a similar vein, there is the Nietzschean argument that justice and morality are self-destructive sentiments, a kind of psychological catastrophe for us, requiring abnegation of the self and its higher capacities and a renunciation of final human purposes.

5. Finally, most people reflectively affirm the value of sociability and of community. The things that are worth pursuing are not simply private ends done for oneself. Common ends, where we cooperate and aim to accomplish the same object, can be private ends in this sense. But common ends can also be shared – ends that people not only hold in common and achieve jointly but where each person takes enjoyment in the participation of others in the same activity. (Family life, at its best, might achieve these shared ends as can many other joint activities.)[22] Now achieving justice requires a common effort. But even if we want to do justice for its own sake, still for all to act for the sake of principles of justice is not on its face the same as all acting for a shared end. Can justice also be a shared end where each recognizes the good of others as an end and enjoys participating in and accomplishing this joint activity? Is there any value in being a participating member of a just society? How, in other words, can an account of justice account for the values of community?

These are the kinds of problems that any theory of justice needs to address. It may be that we want to do our duty of justice for its own sake; still, if these moral sentiments are grounded in illusions, defeat our primary purposes, prevent us from realizing important human goods, or require ways of acting that are not in our nature consistently to perform, then surely this is relevant to the justification of a conception of justice. This, I am suggesting, is how we should understand the peculiar array of arguments in Chapter 9 of *Theory*. The argument (in Section 78) that justice as fairness allows for the objectivity of judgments of justice is designed to defuse the instability that would result if people thought their moral judgments of justice purely conventional, arbitrary, or grounded in illusion. The argument for autonomy (in Section 78) is supposed to show that justice as fairness is not grounded in a self-debasing submission to authority. The argument (Sections 80 and 81) that feelings of excusable envy will not arise sufficient to undermine a well-ordered society shows how justice as fairness does not encourage propensities and hopes that it is bound to repress and disappoint. And the account of social union (Section 79) aims to show how justice as fairness can account for the good of community. What I will focus on here is a further argument for the congruence of justice with people's good, which responds to the Nietzschean objection mentioned in the preceding list of problems, that justice is a self-destructive moral sentiment.

But first let us return to Barry's claim that there is no need for the congruence argument within a contractualist framework. There is in moral philosophy a phrase deriving from Kant, which says that "ought implies can." Philosophers of all persuasions accept this as a requirement on moral principles yet give it different readings. Hobbesians, like David Gauthier, contend that the Kantian requirement means that we cannot expect people to act on moral rules unless it can be demonstrated that these rules are rational or compatible with people's existing preferences. Otherwise, how could people be motivated to act on these principles? This provides the basis for Gauthier's contractarian account of justice. Justice is the rules of cooperation that purely rational individuals, whatever their ends, would rationally agree to, to satisfy their known preferences.

The congruence argument interprets the requirement that "ought imply can" in a different way. Congruence does not require that moral principles be compatible with given preferences and conceptions of the good. Rather it requires that principles of justice, derived on grounds independent of given preferences, be within the reach of human capacities and be compatible with a human good that affirms our nature. Seen in this way the role of the congruence argument within a contractarian framework comes more clearly into view. For the contractualist account of motivation that Barry himself subscribes to says the moral motive is a desire to justify one's actions to others on terms they could not reasonably reject. But surely others can reasonably reject any moral principles they are not capable of consistently abiding by, given human nature, and which undermine rather than affirm their good even under ideal conditions. If so, then congruence would seem to be a normal feature of a contractualist view.[23]

Return now to the argument that the sense of justice can be a psychological catastrophe. There are different ways to develop this argument. For example, take the claim that moral requirements of justice are overriding; they have priority over all other considerations and aims. In opposition it has been argued that justice requires, it seems, a kind of self-effacement, namely, that we sacrifice pursuit of the ends, commitments, and capacities that define us whenever they conflict with the impersonal demands of justice.[24] To fully respond to this objection it needs to be argued: (1) that justice and exercise of a sense of justice do not have such self-abnegating consequences; moreover, (2) there are intrinsic goods that can be realized only by acting for the sake of justice; and finally (3) justice, rather than being self-destructive, is self-affirming. Rawls advances these three claims by way of several different arguments.[25] Because of its bearing on *Political Liberalism*, my focus here will be upon that part of the argument that invokes the "Kantian interpretation" of justice as fairness.

As background to Rawls's Kantian congruence argument, let us consider briefly a psychological law Rawls puts forward, the "Aristotelian principle" (AP). This principle involves a rather substantial claim about human nature. It says basically that we desire to exercise our higher capacities and want to engage in complex and demanding activities for their own sake so long as they are within our reach.

Other things equal, human beings enjoy the exercise of their realized capacities (their innate or trained abilities), and this enjoyment increases the more the capacity is realized, or the greater its complexity. The intuitive idea here is that human beings take more pleasure in doing something as they become more proficient at it, and of two activities they do equally well, they prefer the one calling on a larger repertoire of more intricate and subtle discriminations. For example, chess is a more complicated and subtle game than checkers, and algebra is more intricate than elementary arithmetic. Thus the principle says that someone who can do both generally prefers playing chess to playing checkers, and that he would rather study algebra than arithmetic. (*TJ*, p. 426/374 rev.)

Rawls does not imagine that the Aristotelian principle states an invariable pattern of choice. It states a natural tendency that may be overcome by countervailing inclinations in various situations such as the desire for comfort and satisfying bodily needs. But it does imply, first, that once a certain threshold is met in satisfying these "lower pleasures," (to use Mill's term), a disposition to engage in activities that call for the exercise of our higher capacities takes over; and second, that individuals prefer higher activities of a kind, the more inclusive they are in engaging their educated abilities.

While this principle, like any psychological law, seems of limited use in explaining people's choices on particular occasions, it is useful in explaining the more general aims and activities about which people structure their lives. Rawls's main contention is that, assuming the Aristotelian principle characterizes human nature, then a plan of life is rational for a person only if it takes this principle into account. It is then rational for persons to train and realize their mature capacities given the opportunity to do so. In conjunction with Rawls's account of a rational plan, this means that the plan of life rational persons would choose under deliberative rationality is one that allows a central place to the exercise and development of their higher abilities. As such, the Aristotelian principle "accounts for our considered judgments of value. The things that are commonly thought of as human goods should turn out to be the ends and activities that have a major place in rational plans" (*TJ*, p. 432/379 rev.). This means that certain valued activities (earlier Rawls mentions knowledge, creation and contemplation of beautiful objects, meaningful work, *TJ*, p. 425/373 rev.) are valued and thought of as human goods largely because they engage and call for the development of aspects of our nature that permit complex development. We enjoy such activities for their own sake; that is what the Aristotelian principle asserts. If so, then the exercise and development of at least some of one's higher capacities will be a part of most anyone's good.

### III. THE GOOD OF JUSTICE AND THE KANTIAN CONGRUENCE ARGUMENT

Now let us turn to Rawls's main argument for the good of justice.[26] A just person has the virtue of justice, which for Rawls is a normally "regulative desire" to abide by reasons of justice in all of one's actions. Rawls's main argument for the rationality of this virtue aims to show that it is an intrinsic good. For the virtue of justice to be an intrinsic good means that exercise of the capacities for justice in appropriate settings is an activity worth doing for its own sake. The primary bases for making such an argument within Rawls's theory derives from the account of rational plans in conjunction with the Aristotelian principle.

How then does the Aristotelian principle fit into Rawls's congruence argument? In *Political Liberalism* Rawls says that, in a well-ordered society, justice as fairness is a good for persons individually because

the exercise of the two moral powers is experienced as a good. This is a consequence of the moral psychology used in justice as fairness. [Note] In *Theory* this psychology uses the so-called Aristotelian principle.[27]

This makes it seem as if the congruence argument involves a straightforward appeal to the Aristotelian principle. The idea here would be that the capacity for a sense of justice is among our higher capacities. It involves an ability to understand, apply, and act on and from requirements of justice (cf. *TJ*, p. 505/443 rev.). This capacity admits of complex development and refinement. Since all have a sense of justice in a well-ordered society, it is rational for each to develop it as part of his or her plan of life.

Consider now two objections to this simplified argument: First, though all may have the same natural capacities, we have them to varying degrees. None of us can develop any capacity to a high degree without neglecting others. The capacities it is rational for people to develop will depend on their natural endowments, their circumstances, their interests, and other factors. All that follows from the Aristotelian principle is that it is rational for each to develop *some* higher capacities. If so, then the range of abilities individuals ought to develop will differ. How then can it be inferred that the capacity for justice should occupy a place in everyone's rational plan?[28] In what way does this higher capacity differ from the capacity for dance or sport, or other highly coordinated physical activity? Some of us might aim to develop these capacities, but others understandably do not.

A second objection is, What warrants making the capacity for justice supremely regulative of *all* our pursuits? Suppose that, consistent with the Aristotelian principle, I decide, like Kierkegaard's aesthete "A," to perfect my capacities for elegance and aesthetic appreciation.[29] I resolve to act in ways that are aesthetically appropriate according to received rules of style and etiquette. Is there anything intrinsic to my sense of justice that would make it regulative of this disposition? Why could I not, consistent with the Aristotelian principle, just as well make my sense of elegance supremely regulative, sacrificing justice when it conflicts with aesthetic norms? More generally, what is to prevent my giving weight to my sense of justice only according to its relative intensity and subordinating it to stronger dispositions, weighing off my concern for justice against other final ends in ordinary ways?

The simplified argument from the Aristotelian principle is not Rawls's argument for congruence. But it is extremely difficult to piece together what his argument is. The best way to uncover his argument is by seeing how he would respond to the two objections just stated. The answers he gives depend on the conception of the person built into Rawls's view.

According to the "Kantian interpretation" of justice as fairness (*TJ*, Sec. 40), and what Rawls later calls "Kantian Constructivism,"[30] justice is construed as those principles that would be justified to, and accepted by, everyone under conditions that characterize them as "free and equal moral persons" (or "free and equal rational beings," in *Theory*, p. 252/222 rev.). The original position specifies these conditions; it is a "procedural interpretation" of our nature as free and equal rational beings (*TJ*, p. 256/226 rev.).[31] Rawls says that, by acting from the principles that would be chosen from this standpoint,

persons express their nature as free and equal rational beings subject to the general conditions of human life. For to express one's nature as a being of a particular kind is to act on the principles that would be chosen if this nature were the decisive determining element.... One *reason* for [acting from the principles of justice], for persons who can do so and want to, is to *give expression to one's nature*. (*TJ*, pp. 252–3/222 rev., emphases added)

Conjoining this conception of the person with the formal account of rationality and the Aristotelian principle, we can identify the focal points of Rawls's Kantian argument for congruence as follows:[32]

1. On the basis of the Kantian interpretation, persons seen as moral agents are by their nature free and equal rational beings (*TJ*, p. 252/222 rev.) (or, the same idea in *Theory*, "free and equal moral

persons" *TJ*, p. 565/495 rev.)[33] Rational agents in a well-ordered society (WOS) conceive of themselves in this way "as primarily moral persons" (*TJ*, p. 563/493 rev.).[34]

2. Rational members of a WOS "desire to express their nature as free and equal moral persons," (*TJ*, pp. 528/462–3 rev., 572/501 rev.). (Rawls evidently sees this as a nonarbitrary rational desire.) Combined with the formal account of a persons's good under the thin theory, this implies,

3. Members of a WOS desire to have a rational plan of life consistent with their nature; which implies, in turn, a "fundamental preference ... for conditions that enable [them] to frame a mode of life that expresses [their] nature as free and equal rational beings" (*TJ*, p. 561/491 rev.).

4. Having a plan of life compatible with the desire to express their nature as free and equal rational beings requires that persons act from principles that "would be chosen if this nature were the decisive determining element" (*TJ*, 253/222 rev.). This is the original position: it specifies conditions that characterize or "represent" individuals as free and equal moral persons in the Kantian interpretation (*TJ*, pp. 252, 515, 528/221, 452, 462–3 rev.).[35]

5. In its standard interpretation, the original position is designed to "make vivid to ourselves the restrictions that it seems reasonable to impose on arguments for principles of justice" (*TJ*, p. 18/16 rev.). It embodies fair conditions of equality that you and I (presumably) find appropriate for an agreement on principles to regulate the basic structure of society.

6. The normally effective desire to apply and act upon principles that would be agreed to from an original position of equality is the sense of justice (*TJ*, pp. 312/275 rev., 478/418 rev.).

7. Taken together, 4–6 suggest that the desire to act in ways that "express one's nature" as a free and equal rational being is "practically speaking" the same desire as the desire to act upon principles of justice acceptable from an original position of equality (*TJ*, p. 572/501 rev.).[36]

8. Thus, for individuals in a WOS to achieve their desire to realize their nature as free and equal rational beings requires that they act on, and from, their sense of justice (*TJ*, p. 574/503 rev.).

9. By the Aristotelian principle, it is rational to realize one's nature by affirming the sense of justice. "From the Aristotelian Principle it

follows that this expression of their nature is a fundamental element of [the] good" of individuals in a well-ordered society (*TJ*, p. 445/390 rev.).[37]

10. The sense of justice is, by virtue of its content (what it is a desire for) a supremely regulative disposition: it requires giving first priority to the principles of right and justice in one's deliberations and actions (*TJ*, p. 574/503 rev.).

11. To affirm the sense of justice is to recognize and accept it as supreme by adopting it as a highest-order regulative desire in one's rational plan.[38]

12. To have justice as a highest-order end is the most adequate expression of our nature as free and equal rational beings and is to be autonomous (cf. *TJ*, p. 515/452 rev.). Autonomy is then an intrinsic good for free and equal moral persons.

The role of the Aristotelian principle here (in 9) is to establish that it is intrinsic to people's good to realize their nature (as free and equal rational beings).[39] Just as crucial, however, are 7, identifying the sense of justice with the desire to realize one's nature, and 10 and 11, establishing the priority of the sense of justice in rational plans. Point 7 is important since, by connecting the sense of justice with our "nature" (I will discuss what this means), 7 establishes that the desire to act justly is not psychologically degenerative. Recall the criticism that the sense of justice is a compulsive desire we subconsciously develop either (a) to mask our weakness (as Nietzsche held), or (b) as an outgrowth of envy and jealously (as Freud held) (cf. *TJ*, p. 539ff./472–3 rev.). Or suppose (c) the sense of justice were nothing more than a disposition furtively instilled in us by those in power to ensure obedience to rules designed to advance their interests (cf. *TJ*, p. 515/452 rev.). In each case, the sense of justice would not be worth affirming as an intrinsic part of our good. It might even be better not to have this desire if we could get along in society without it. But if the sense of justice can be shown to belong somehow to our nature, then Rawls can contend that, by affirming it, we exercise a capacity that is fundamental to our being. And since (by the Aristotelian principle) for persons to express their nature as free and equal rational beings "belongs to their good, the sense of justice aims at their well-being ..." (*TJ*, p. 476/417 rev.).

The crucial question then is, Why does Rawls contend that the sense of justice "belongs to our nature," and what does this obscurity mean? In *Theory* Rawls adopts Kant's position, that persons are, by their nature, free, equal and rational and that in a WOS they publicly conceive of themselves in this way. The "nature" of free, equal, and rational beings is their "moral personality" (*TJ*, Sections 77, 85). Moral personality is defined by the moral powers, which are in effect the capacities for practical reasoning as applied to matters of justice. These capacities include (a) a capacity for a sense of justice (the ability to understand, to apply, and to act on and from requirements and principles of justice) as well as (b) a capacity for a conception of the good (to form, to revise, and to pursue a rational plan of life).[40]

Why are these capacities so important? Rawls's idea is that, from a practical point of view, when acting as agents (and especially in cooperative contexts) we normally see ourselves and each other not just in terms of our particular identities, ends, and commitments; more fundamentally we conceive of ourselves and others as free moral agents capable of determining our actions, adjusting our wants, and shaping our ends – all according to the requirements of practical principles. And, "since we view persons as capable of mastering and adjusting their wants and desires, they are held responsible for doing so."[41]

Now the bases for people's conception of themselves as free and responsible moral agents and as equals are the moral powers.[42] A person without these capacities is not recognized by others as answerable for his or her acts or ends (morally or legally) or deemed capable of taking an active part in social cooperation.[43] Moreover, we do not see our lives as a matter of happenstance simply imposed on us by our situations. Instead, within the limits of the circumstances we confront, we normally see our actions and our lives as under our control. It is by virtue of the capacities for moral personality that we are able to decide what ends and activities we should pursue and can fashion these ends into a coherent and cooperative life plan that accords with principles of rational choice and principles of justice. So it is by virtue of the moral powers as capacities to act upon rational and moral principles that we are able to give "unity" to our lives, and so to our selves, by adopting and pursuing a rational plan of life.[44]

It is because of their central role in making possible our agency that Rawls says that the moral powers "constitute our nature" as moral persons. "Moral person" and "moral personality," terms found in both Locke and Kant, are to be taken here in the seventeenth- and eighteenth-century sense; they refer to agents and their capacities for agency. To say these powers "constitute our nature" means that, when we think of ourselves practically as agents engaged in planning our pursuits in the context of social cooperation, then what is most important to our being an agent for these purposes are the moral powers. Contrast thinking of oneself purely naturalistically as a physical organism or object whose behavior is determined by a combination of forces. This is not how we see ourselves in practical contexts (though some might occasionally think of themselves in this way from a purely naturalistic point of view). That persons are free and responsible agents capable of controlling their wants and answering for their actions is something we just go on from a practical standpoint.[45] This belief provides our orientation in the realm of human activity. And it is hard to see how it could be any other way. For otherwise we must see ourselves and one another as natural objects beyond the realm of responsibility.[46]

So it is the centrality of the capacity for a sense of justice to the self-conception of moral agents that underlies Rawls's claim (in 7) that the sense of justice and the desire to express one's nature are "practically speaking the same desire." And this supports 8, the conclusion that to realize one's "nature" (or practical self-conception) requires acting on, and from, the sense of justice. This addresses (if it does not fully respond to) the first objection (raised at the beginning of this section). This was the question, How can everyone have sufficient reason, even if the Aristotelian principle is assumed, to develop and exercise their capacity for justice? What distinguishes it from other capacities, which we may not have reason to develop, depending on our circumstances? The answer is that development of the sense of justice (along with the capacity for a conception of the good) is a condition of individuals being rational moral agents who are capable of assuming responsibility for their actions and taking part in, and benefiting from, social life. People who do not develop their capacities for music or sports, while they may miss out on worthwhile activities, can nonetheless lead good lives engaged in other pursuits. But those whose moral capacities for justice (and the capacity to be rational) remain undeveloped are not capable of social life. They are not then in a position to achieve the benefits of society and will be hard pressed to learn and pursue most any worthwhile way of life.

## IV. FINALITY AND THE PRIORITY OF JUSTICE

Now turn to the second objection: Even if we assume justice is a good, why should it be regulative of all other values and pursuits? That justice expresses our nature as free and equal rational beings on Rawls's Kantian interpretation (*TJ*, p. 252/222 rev.) should go some way towards responding to this objection. Still, people have ends and commitments they believe are equally, if not more, important than justice or expressing their nature, and often they have more pressing desires to act for these ends. Rawls says, "A perfectly just society should be part of an ideal that rational human beings could desire more than anything else once they had full knowledge and experience of what it was" (*TJ*, p. 477/418 rev.). But given the multiple aims and commitments that people care about, how could this be true?

The problem here is the appropriate position of the sense of justice within rational plans of life of people who are morally motivated and who desire to be just persons. How should the sense of justice be situated in relation to other final ends and within the "hierarchy of desires"? Rawls says that, in drawing up a rational plan, final ends and fundamental desires need to be organized and combined into one scheme of conduct (cf. *TJ*, pp. 410–11/360–1 rev.). And sometimes, after taking into account all relevant reasons and considerations (including the Aristotelian principle), critical deliberation might run out, at which point the rational choice may just be to decide according to the intensity of desire.[47]

The real problem of congruence is what happens if we imagine someone to give weight to his sense of justice only to the extent that it satisfies other descriptions which connect it with reasons specified by the thin theory of the good. (*TJ*, p. 569/499 rev.)

I interpret this passage as follows: Suppose a person is morally motivated by a sense of justice and is trying to decide how to fit considerations of justice into her life-plan. She wants to be a just person yet also aims to be loyal to her family, successful in her career, devoted to her church, and an accomplished amateur musician. These are the primary ends that provide structure to her life. What happens if, after full deliberation, she assigns the sense of justice a position of importance alongside other final ends and weighs it off against them in ordinary ways, sometimes relying on the relative felt intensity of desires to resolve conflicts among her final ends? If people generally reasoned this way, and it were publicly known, then people could not have the kind of assurance regarding others' actions that is needed for a well-ordered society to be stable in Rawls's sense. Ultimately, the congruence argument, to succeed, must show that it is contrary to reason to weigh the sense of justice off against other ends "in ordinary ways." What needs to be shown is that it is rational to give the sense of justice a highest-order position in rational plans. It must have "regulative priority" over all other final ends and parts of rational plans.

One way to argue for assigning priority to a disposition is to establish that it is a desire to be a certain kind of person. Harry Frankfurt has argued that the desire to be a certain kind of person is a "desire of the second or of higher orders"; part of the content of this desire is that a person's first-order desires (desires for particular objects) conform to an ideal that person has set for himself.[48] Here it can be said that, given the content of this desire, one cannot satisfy it if it is balanced off against other desires in the course of practical reasoning. Rawls conceives of the sense of justice in a similar way.

[A]n effective sense of justice ... is not a desire on the same footing with natural inclinations; it is an executive and regulative highest-order desire to act from certain principles of justice in view of their connection with a conception of the person as free and equal.[49]

Still Rawls needs to say more than this. For, so far as Frankfurt's argument go, it could as well apply to the desire to be elegant. That too is a desire to be a certain kind of person, and it would seem compatible with Frankfurt's view that it could also be a highest-order disposition regulative of all one's other desires for someone (for example, Kierkegaard's aesthete) if he or she so chooses. But where does this leave the aesthete who also has a sense of justice? Frankfurt's view seems to imply that which of these two dispositions has primacy is to be settled in the end by that person's radical choice. This cannot be Rawls's view. The very question he aims to raise is, By virtue of what powers are we capable of choice, and what do these capacities reveal about us and how we conceive of ourselves as free moral agents capable of responsible action and social life?

Rawls contends, in effect, that the desire to express one's nature is "highest-order," not because it is a general desire to be most any kind of person but because it is a desire to be a specific kind of person, namely, one who is just. Unlike other desires, there is something special about the desire to be a just person that makes it supremely regulative of all other desires independent of a person's desires or choices.

This is a consequence of the condition of finality: since these principles [of justice] are regulative, the desire to act upon them is satisfied only to the extent that it is likewise regulative with respect to other desires.... This sentiment cannot be fulfilled if it is compromised and balanced against other ends as but one desire among the rest. It is a desire to conduct oneself in a certain way above all else, a striving that contains within itself its own priority. Other aims can be achieved by a plan that allows a place for each, since their satisfaction is possible independent of their place in the ordering. But this is not the case with the sense of right and justice. (*TJ*, p. 574/503 rev.)

As a desire to act on the principles of justice, the sense of justice is subject to the condition of finality that defines these principles. Finality requires that considerations of justice have absolute priority over all other reasons in practical deliberation (reasons of prudence, self-interest, private and public benevolence, etiquette, and so on) (*TJ*, pp. 135/116–17 rev.). Given this condition, persons cannot fulfill their desire for justice if they balance it off against other desired ends, even other final ends, according to their relative intensity or in other ways. To do that would compromise what this desire is a desire for. The sense of justice in effect is a desire that *all* one's desires and their aims conform to the regulative requirements of justice. On its face the sense of justice reveals itself as a supremely governing disposition. We can satisfy what this desire is a desire for only if we assign justice highest priority in our activities. Moreover, given the practical identity of the sense of justice with the desire to express our nature (see 6 in Section III), we cannot "express our nature by following a plan that views the sense of justice as but one desire to be weighed off against others" (*TJ*, p. 575/503 rev.).

Therefore in order to realize our nature we have no alternative but to plan to preserve our sense of justice as governing our other aims. (*TJ*, p. 574/503 rev.)

There is one final claim to consider (12 in Section III), and the congruence argument is complete. What does it mean to realize the conception of the person as a free and equal rational being in one's rational plan? Rawls says,

Kant held, I believe, that a person is acting autonomously when the principles of his action are chosen by him as the most adequate possible expression of his nature as a free and equal rational being. (*TJ*, p. 252/222 rev.; cf. *TJ*, p. 584/511)

In the Kantian interpretation of justice as fairness, Rawls assumes that citizens in a well-ordered society "regard moral personality... as the fundamental aspect of the self" (*TJ*, p. 563/493 rev.); as a result they desire to be fully autonomous agents. Autonomy, in Rawls's Kantian account, requires acting for the sake of principles that we accept, not because of our particular circumstances, talents, or ends, or due to allegiance to tradition, authority, or the opinion of others, but because these principles give expression to our common nature as free and equal rational beings (*TJ*, p. 252/222 rev., p. 515–16/452 rev.). By affirming their sense of justice, members of a well-ordered society accomplish their conception of themselves as free, that is, as moral agents who are free from the eventualities of their circumstances, their upbringing, and their social position. "Acting from this precedence [of the sense of justice] expresses our freedom from contingency and happenstance" (*TJ*, p. 574/503 rev.). And this is what it is to be autonomous. So, "When the principles of justice ... are *affirmed* and acted upon by equal citizens in society, citizens then act with full autonomy."[50] Full autonomy (as opposed to simply "rational autonomy") is then the ultimate consequence of persons realizing their nature by making the sense of justice a highest-order desire in their rational plans. And this means, given the rest of Rawls's argument, that autonomy is an intrinsic good. So Rawls concludes: "[T]his sentiment [of justice] reveals what the person is, and to compromise it is not to achieve for the self free reign but to give way to the contingencies and accidents of the world" (*TJ*, p. 575/503 rev.). It reveals "what the person is" practically, as a moral agent, and so to compromise it is to compromise one's free agency.

Before going on to discuss what Rawls himself sees as problematic about this argument, let us consider a crucial step many will find especially controversial: Rawls's appeal to the finality of considerations of justice.[51] To understand what the controversy over finality might be, we should clarify how Rawls views it. Philosophers often talk about the "overridingness" of moral duties and moral reasons, where this is meant to imply that moral duties and moral reasons outweigh all others. Some have rightly questioned whether duties of justice always must override all other practical considerations. Sometimes it seems perfectly permissible to breach duties of justice, even for the sake of prudential and self-related ends.[52] Rawls's finality condition does not deny this. Finality is not the claim that any specific moral duty or consideration of justice outweighs all other practical norms and considerations on every occasion. Finality, rather, is about the position of considerations of justice in the totality of practical reasons. Considerations of justice taken together are "the final court of appeal in practical reasoning" (*TJ*, p. 135/116 rev.).

Imagine the totality of practical reasons – moral reasons of justice along with other moral reasons (of benevolence, etc.) combined with reasons of prudence, self-interest, law, custom, etiquette, and so on – that bear on the question what we ought to do and their respective weights or degrees of importance. Finality does not say that each and every reason of justice outweighs all other reasons of a different kind. It implies rather (a) that taken together, reasons of justice have a special position in the system of reasons, and (b) that once the course of practical reasoning has reached its conclusion, and all relevant reasons are considered, the question of what one ought to do is settled – no further question about what one within reason ought to do remains to be asked simply because one does not like the conclusion. Thus, when reasons of prudence and self-interest are outweighed by moral considerations, there is sufficient reason, and it is reasonable, to moderate the claims of interest. Likewise, if reasons of interest and prudence outweigh a specific moral duty of justice on a particular occasion, then this is because there is some moral reason that permits that. It is then reasonable, and not simply rational, to act for reasons of prudence or self-interest (e.g., to break a promise to further one's career) under those circumstances.

Finality, then, does not mean that we are always required to sacrifice the ends of the self to the impersonal claims of morality. But if and when morality does not require such sacrifices, and if and when we are sometimes permitted to breach specific moral rules, then this must be because it is justified by the totality of moral reasons. It is not because there are practical reasons of a superior order to the totality of moral reasons. There are no such superior reasons; moral reasons are "the final court of appeal in practical deliberation."

The question now becomes, Why should moral reasons have such a special position in practical reasoning? Consider three kinds of arguments for the finality condition:

1. The finality of moral reasons (or of moral reasons of justice specifically) is part of our understanding of morality (or of justice); some might even say it is "analytic." In any case, it is in the nature of moral reasons (or specifically reasons of justice) that, taken collectively, they cannot be outweighed by other kinds of reasons. To take them into account at all is to give them regulative priority.

2. Finality in the end is a claim about the structure of practical reason of moral agents. For persons who take moral reasons seriously, practical reasoning, appropriately carried through, first involves deciding what is in their best interest by settling their ends and ascertaining what is the rational course of action (according to principles of rational choice and one's rational plan); then secondly, ascertaining whether their rational action (or plan) squares with moral requirements, or what is reasonable. Only deliberations reached in this way are final with respect to all the requirements of practical reason.

3. The finality of moral reasons is connected (in a way represented by, say, Kantian constructivism) with autonomy and the unity of the self as a free and equal moral person. We are able to be free and fully rational agents who give shape and unity to our lives only by virtue of the moral powers. Only if we assign to the moral principles of justice that express these powers a supremely regulative position in our lives can we be fully rational and autonomous.

Some, if not all, of these considerations may play a role in Rawls's finality condition. He may rely on additional considerations, but what these are is just not clear. Rawls initially stipulates that the finality condition is among the "formal constraints of the concept of right." Other than contending that it is reasonable to impose this condition on principles of justice, he has little directly to say about the basis of the finality condition. Rawls does not seem to hold that finality of moral considerations is analytically implicit in the concept of right or that it is part of the meaning of morality. As he says, "The merit of any definition depends upon the soundness of the theory that results..." (*TJ*, p. 130/112–13 rev.). Within his justificatory framework, this means that finality is an appropriate ("reasonable") condition to impose on reasons and principles of justice since the conception of justice that results better fits with our considered moral convictions of justice (in wide reflective equilibrium) than any other theory (surely better than any theory that omits finality). Why this should be the case merits more discussion than I can give the matter here.

## V. THE TRANSITION TO POLITICAL LIBERALISM

Recall that the role of the Kantian congruence argument is to fill out the argument for stability of justice as fairness and to show how a just constitution is realistically possible. If it can be shown that a well-ordered society describes conditions under which justice is an intrinsic good for each person, one that is supremely regulative of pursuit of all other goods, then it has been shown how justice can be supremely rational for each person. Being supremely rational for each, stability has been demonstrated in the strongest possible way, for justice is everyone's best response to his or her circumstances. Does this ambitious argument succeed?

The congruence argument contains many grand and controversial claims. For example, implicit in its conclusion is the Kantian claim that the activity of practical reason in matters of justice is itself an intrinsic good. The argument also implies a Kantian thesis about the nature and constitution of the realm of value: value, including moral principles, has its origin in the activities of practical reason and the principles and ideas it constructs.[53] My concern here is limited to the question of whether the argument succeeds on its own terms.

Assume then that the congruence argument successfully shows that justice is an intrinsic and supremely regulative good for each person in a well-ordered society. Still, what this does not show is that each person in a well-ordered society will in fact recognize and accept justice as an intrinsic good. Unless a sizable proportion of them do, the Kantian congruence argument itself does not significantly advance the case for stability. For only if people believe that justice is an intrinsic good will they be inclined not to compromise justice when it puts significant demands on other aspects of their good.[54] Now it is true that, as part of the justification of justice as fairness, the Kantian congruence argument itself is, under the "full publicity" condition, publicly available and widely known (at least by those interested in this kind of thing.) Given full publicity, part of the public culture of a well-ordered society is the proposition or ideal that justice and autonomy are intrinsic to each person's good. This may be integrated into public education in a variety of ways and accepted by the official culture of a well-ordered society. The problem is that, while these efforts might encourage many to believe that justice is intrinsic to their good, for others it might well have contrary, destabilizing effects.

In *Political Liberalism* Rawls says that there is a "serious problem internal to justice as fairness [arising] from the fact that the account of stability in Part III of *Theory* is not consistent with the view as a whole" (*PL*, pp. xv–xvi). "[T]he serious problem I have in mind concerns the unrealistic idea of a well-ordered society as it appears in *Theory*" (*PL*, p. xvi). What is primarily unrealistic about the account in *Theory*, I conjecture, is the Kantian congruence argument. It fails to appreciate the extent of the "subjective circumstances of justice," or what Rawls later calls "the fact of reasonable pluralism" that characterizes a well-ordered society. These circumstances imply that, while individuals might agree on principles of justice (as the idea of a well-ordered society assumes), under conditions where individuals have freedom of thought, conscience, and association (as liberal principles require), it is unrealistic to expect that they will ever all agree in their religious, philosophical, or ethical beliefs.[55] It is then unrealistic to expect that citizens in a well-ordered society will all agree on the supreme intrinsic good of autonomy, or even the intrinsic good of justice.

Imagine then a well-ordered society of justice as fairness, where there is widespread agreement and support for Rawls's liberal principles of justice. How is this general acceptance possible? Given liberty of conscience and freedom of thought and association, it must be because individuals affirm and support these principles for different reasons and from different points of view. For it is unrealistic to suppose that everyone endorses the principles of justice for reasons specified by the Kantian interpretation. Liberal Thomists then (to take but one example) will affirm liberal principles of justice for their own specific reasons. They are among the natural laws preordained by God and knowable by the natural light of our reason; in following these laws rational beings realize their essence and obtain the final end of their creation, the Beatific Vision.[56] On the basis of this comprehensive religious view, God alone, not human reason, is the ultimate origin of moral standards and the good. Justice and the human good are requirements of our created essence, not of unaided human reason. Moreover, moral autonomy is not an intrinsic good; instead it is a false value which conflicts with what the liberal Thomist sees as the only ultimate intrinsic good, the contemplation and enjoyment of God.[57]

Nothing about a comprehensive religious and ethical view like liberal Thomism is incompatible with compliance with requirements of justice as Rawls construes them. It is then a permissible conception of the good in a well-ordered society and presumably could gain many adherents. But if so, then the content of this (and other) permissible conceptions of the good conflict with the Kantian conception of the good that is a part of public culture according to the Kantian interpretation. This may well have the effect of undermining many people's sense of self-respect, and it might cause resentment since their most basic values are implicitly recognized as false values by the public culture. The problem here is that there is a kind of doctrinal intolerance of non-Kantian conceptions of the good that is built into the public culture of a well-ordered society of justice as fairness. Even if we assume that these religious and ethical views are false (on the assumption that the conclusion to the congruence argument is still sound) they are nonetheless permissible conceptions of the good. Their public rejection can only have the effect of undermining many people's allegiance and support for just institutions.

The problem may go even deeper than this. It may be that, given Rawls's account of a person's good in *Theory* (as the plan of life it would be rational to affirm in deliberative rationality), it cannot be said of non-Kantians that they are mistaken about their good. This would depend on features of Rawls's account of deliberative rationality he does not go into. According to this account, a person's good is the plan of life she would choose if she had full information of "all relevant facts," reasoned correctly, and imaginatively appreciated the consequences of choosing a plan of life. If the full information condition means that a person's good is what she would choose if she had no false beliefs, then we encounter the problem mentioned previously; namely, that many persons in a well-ordered society will have mistaken beliefs (about God's creation of the universe, for example, including the realm of value) and so will not recognize that autonomy is an intrinsic good. If so, then the congruence argument does not ensure the stability of a well-ordered society. But if the full information condition expresses a weaker condition and means simply that everyone has access to all relevant evidentiary information, this would imply that rational plans may be informed by false beliefs (such as God's creation of the realm of value). But if this is the case, then Rawls's Kantian congruence argument would simply fail on its own terms for large classes of people from the outset. For then it would impute to all a conception of the good (to be morally autonomous) which many might not rationally endorse.

The general problem these objections raise is that we cannot expect large numbers of people in a well-ordered society to be motivated to comply with standards of justice for the Kantian reason that they realize their nature as free and equal rational moral beings and are thereby morally autonomous. But this is what the congruence argument sets out to prove in order to show how a well-ordered society can be stable. The only way around this problem is to concede that the Kantian congruence argument is not needed to show the stability of a well-ordered society.[58] But this still leaves the problem the argument was designed to redress, namely, to show the effective rationality of justice in a well-ordered society. Stability then has to be satisfied by other means. This accounts for Rawls's development of the idea of overlapping consensus as well as other ideas central to political liberalism.[59]

Overlapping consensus means that people in a well-ordered society will normally act justly for many different reasons. Given reasonable pluralism, what primarily motivates citizens in a well-ordered society to comply with public principles of justice is not a desire for autonomy or the intrinsic good of justice itself (though many may act justly for these reasons); rather it is the many different values implicit in different comprehensive (or partially comprehensive) doctrines people subscribe to in a well-ordered society. Overlapping consensus is in effect a hypothesis about the kinds of conceptions of the good that will be fostered by a well-ordered society.

It extends the reasoning behind the principles of reciprocity under-lying development of the sense of justice from *Theory* (Chap. 8) so that it applies to reasonable comprehensive doctrines and individuals' conceptions of the good.[60] The crucial assumption is that, as individuals tend to develop a desire to support just institutions that benefit them and those they care for, so too will they incorporate this desire, in some form, into their conception of the good. This means that, from among the many possible religious, philosophical, and ethical doctrines, those that will gain adherents and thrive in a well-ordered society will be reasonable and will endorse (or at least will be compatible with) the public principles of justice, each for their own specific reasons. Unreasonable, irrational, or mad doctrines will not muster sufficient support to gain sizable adherence. There will then be no widely accepted comprehensive view that rejects liberal principles of justice or which assigns an insignificant position to considerations of justice in its scheme of beliefs, values, or moral principles. Assuming that this conjecture holds true in a well-ordered society, all will have sufficient reason to comply with liberal principles of justice for their own specific reasons. Justice will then be rational for each – instrumentally or intrinsically, depending on their particular conception of the good – and society will evince internal stability "for the right reasons" (*PL*, p. 388n.).

Overlapping consensus does not address all of the issues the original congruence argument set out to. It does not claim, for example, that justice as fairness is true or objective according to universal epistemological criteria or that it will be publicly recognized as such. Given different philosophical views, such issues cannot be argued out on the basis of public reasons or resolved as part of the public conception of justice. They are part of ongoing, nonpublic moral and political debate among conflicting comprehensive philosophical views. The important point is that, if an overlapping consensus exists, such disputes should have little effect on the stability of a liberal conception of justice. For whether or not all citizens see liberal principles of justice as objective or true (moral skeptics do not, and they will always be present), all reasonable citizens nonetheless should find these principles the most reasonable principles of justice for persons who conceive of themselves as free and equal moral persons. Moral skepticism and relativism are then effectively neutralized as threats to stability.

Overlapping consensus also does not imply that justice is supremely rational or even an intrinsic good. So far as overlapping consensus goes, justice may be no more than an instrumental good for many people and hence subject to compromise when it conflicts with their final ends. Rawls's thought here may be that, since justice nonetheless occupies a significant position in each person's view, even if only as an instrumental good for many, whatever conflicts with their final ends there are will not be so frequent and entrenched as to undermine stability.

So in a well-ordered society it seems there is no assurance after all that justice will occupy a supremely regulative position in each person's conception of the good. This does not however deprive justice of its finality; rather it shifts finality to a more restricted domain, the political domain of public reasons. Reasons of justice no longer may override all reasons within everyone's conception of the good, but they do override all reasons within the public political domain.[61]

### ENDNOTES

1   Brian Barry, "John Rawls and the Search for Stability," *Ethics* 105 (July 1995): 874–915, at 915, n. 54.

2   Rawls has said (in conversation) that he thinks the congruence argument was one of the most original contributions he made in *A Theory of Justice* and that he is puzzled why it did not attract more comment. This is reason enough to devote attention to the argument.

3   The absence of coercive political institutions is noticeable in David Gauthier's *Morals by Agreement* (Oxford, UK: Oxford University Press, 1984).

4   On different kinds of stability, see Rawls, *Justice as Fairness: A Restatement*, ed. Erin Kelly (Cambridge, MA: Harvard University Press, 2001) pp. 185–6. Rawls refers to the stability of (1) a society or "scheme of cooperation," (2) of a conception of justice, and (3) of "just schemes" of cooperation, or a well-ordered society. Rawls says a scheme of social cooperation is stable when it is "more or less regularly complied with and its basic rules willingly acted upon; and when infractions occur, stabilizing forces should exist that prevent further violations and tend to restore the arrangement" (*A Theory of Justice*, Cambridge, MA: Harvard University Press, 1971, revised edition, 1999, p. 6/6 rev.; referred to in page references in the text as "TJ"). For a scheme to be stable, people need the assurance that everyone else has sufficient reason to comply

with the rules. Hobbes's sovereign is designed to provide this assurance (cf. *TJ*, p. 497/435 rev.), but it comes at the price of justice as Rawls conceives it. Rawls is concerned exclusively with the problem of the stability of a just society. For this reason he applies 'stability' in the first instance to a conception of justice. A well-ordered society is stable when the conception of justice on which it is based is stable and "citizens are satisfied...with the basic structure of their society." *Restatement*, p. 202. Rawls says, "To insure stability men must have a sense of justice or a concern for those who would be disadvantaged by their defection, preferably both. When these sentiments are sufficiently strong to overrule the temptations to violate the rules, just schemes are stable" (*TJ*, p. 497/435 rev.).

5  A term Rawls first uses in "Reply to Habermas." See Rawls, *Political Liberalism* (New York: Columbia University Press, paperback edition, 1996), pp. 388n, 390ff.

6  Here I draw on my paper "Political Liberalism and the Possibility of a Just Democratic Constitution," in *Chicago-Kent Law Review* 69 (1994): 619–68 at 624–5.

7  Immanuel Kant, "Idea for a Universal History," in *Perpetual Peace and Other Essays* (Indianapolis: Hackett, 1983), pp. 33–4.

8  Rawls defines a well-ordered society as an ideal social world where everyone agrees on and accepts the same conception of justice, and this is publicly known; moreover this conception is effectively realized in society's institutions. *TJ*, pp. 4–5/4–5 rev., and Sec. 69. See also *Restatement*, pp. 8–9.

9  Rawls explicitly indicates two parts to the stability argument in *Political Liberalism*, p. 141, though he rephrases the issues there to fit with political liberalism.

10  After *Theory*, particularly in *Political Liberalism* (p. 19), Rawls defines the sense of justice more broadly:

A sense of justice is the capacity to understand, to apply, and to act from the public conception of justice.... a sense of justice also expresses a willingness, if not the desire, to act in relation to others on terms that they also can publicly endorse.

11  See Sections 69–75 of *Theory*, especially 72 and 74. The three reciprocity principles are set forth together at *TJ*, pp. 490–91/429–30 rev. The third says:

Third law: given that a person's capacity for fellow feeling has been realized by his forming attachments in accordance with the first two laws, and given that a society's institutions are just and are publicly known by all to be just, then this person acquires the corresponding sense of justice as he recognizes that he and those for whom he cares are the beneficiaries of these arrangements.

12   See *Theory*, p. 476/416 rev. Also *Political Liberalism*, where the sense of justice is partially defined as a capacity "to act from the public conception of justice," (p. 19) and as a capacity "to be moved to act from fair terms of cooperation for their own sake" (p. 54). Also, Rawls says "Reasonable persons . . . desire for its own sake a social world in which they, as free and equal, can cooperate with others on terms all can accept" (p. 50). This also comes out clearly in Rawls's extended discussion of moral motivation, *PL*, pp. 81–8, where he discusses principle-dependent and conception-dependent desires.

13   Or, more correctly, Scanlon agrees with Rawls, since this is the historical order of influence. See *Political Liberalism*, p. 50, n. 2, where Rawls discusses the kinship of his account of motivation with Scanlon's: "in setting out justice as fairness we rely on the kind of motivation Scanlon takes as basic."

14   Elsewhere Rawls says the sense of justice is "the desire to act in accordance with the principles that would be chosen in the original position." *Theory*, p. 312/275 rev.

15   Scanlon recognizes this problem in "Contractualism and Utilitarianism," in Amartya Sen and Bernard Williams, eds., *Utilitarianism and Beyond* (Cambridge, UK: Cambridge University Press, 1982), p. 106. Scanlon distinguishes two motivational questions. First a theory of morality must make clear the nature of the reasons that morality provides.

> A satisfactory moral philosophy will not leave concern with morality as a simple special preference, like a fetish or a special taste, which some people just happen to have. It must make it understandable why moral reasons are ones that people can take seriously, and why they strike those who are moved by them as reasons of a special stringency and inescapability.

This echoes Rawls's rejection of the purely conscientious act, which Barry criticizes Rawls for by citing Scanlon's account of motivation.
  The second motivational question Scanlon says, is "whether susceptibility to such reasons *is compatible with a person's good* or whether it is, as Nietzsche argued, a psychological disaster for the person who has it. If one is to defend morality one must show that it is not disastrous in this way, but I will not pursue this second motivational question here" (id. emphasis added). Rawls pursues the question, and this is part of the congruence argument. Scanlon then seems to recognizes the same two questions that Rawls does and sees the need for any moral theory to provide an answer to each.

16   See *Theory*, Section 63 for Rawls's account of these principles of rational choice.

17 See *Theory*, Section 64 on "Deliberative Rationality." Rawls says a rational plan of life "is the plan that would be decided upon as the outcome of careful reflection in which the agent reviews, in the light of all the relevant facts, what it would be like to carry out these plans and thereby ascertains the course of action that would best realize his more fundamental desires" (*TJ*, p. 417/366 rev.). Deliberative rationality defines an objective point of view from which to assess a person's good and the reasons he or she has as an individual. The plan of life that a person *would* choose from this perspective is "the objectively rational plan for him and determines his real good" (id.). Perhaps we can never really occupy this position, given its idealizations and uncertainty about the future. But with the information we have, we can determine, Rawls says, a "subjectively rational plan," which defines our apparent good.

18 In *Political Liberalism*, p. xix/xxi, 1996 edition, Rawls distinguishes "the public point of view from the many nonpublic (not private) points of view," which parallels his distinction there between public versus nonpublic reasons.

19 Henry Sidgwick, *Methods of Ethics*, 7th edition (Indianapolis: Hackett, 1981), pp. 404, 506–9.

20 Note however that this does not imply for Rawls that justice is not required by practical reason. According to Rawls's account, not all reasons are desire- or interest-based. See *Political Liberalism*, p. 85n., and the accompanying text on principle-dependent and conception-dependent desires. Nor does the concept of rationality exhaust the kinds of reasons we have on his view. Rawls's account of "the reasonable" implies there are reasons of justice that apply to us, whatever our particular ends or desires. These reasons are established independent of our desires and situations, ultimately by reference to our considered *judgments* and on the basis of our capacities for practical reasoning. This is part of the point of Rawls's Kantian and Political constructivism. See *PL*, pp. 111f., 115 on objectivity and the reasonable; see also "Kantian Constructivism in Moral Theory," in Rawls, *Collected Papers*, Samuel Freeman, ed. (Cambridge, MA: Harvard University Press, 1999), Lecture III, "Constructivism and Objectivity," pp. 340–58.

21 "I am not trying to show that in a well-ordered society an egoist would act from a sense of justice.... Rather, we are concerned with the goodness of the settled desire to take up the standpoint of justice. I assume that the members of a well-ordered society already have this desire. The question is whether this regulative sentiment is consistent with their good." *TJ*, p. 568/497–8 rev.

22 So members of a competitive team might have the common aim, not just of winning but winning with the successful participation of each

teammate; and even members of opposing teams can have a shared end of engaging in a worthy competition and appreciate and even enjoy one another's expertise. Cf, *TJ*, Sec. 79.

23  As Scanlon himself suggests; see note 15 above.

24  The objection does not assume that all other-regarding sentiments are self-destructive. Rather, part of the problem is just that the commitments we have to persons or associations are inevitably compromised by the purportedly overriding and impersonal claims of morality. See Bernard Williams, "Persons, Character, and Morality," in his *Moral Luck* (Cambridge, UK: Cambridge University Press, 1981) pp. 1–19.

25  For example, to show justice is not self-abnegating, Rawls argues in Sections 83–5 that, while self-abnegation might result from a "dominant end" theory like utilitarianism, this charge cannot be leveled against a theory like justice as fairness, which recognizes the heterogeneity of the good and the regulative role of moral principles in constraining the means we adopt to pursue our ends. Section 79, "The Idea of Social Union," constitutes part of the argument for the idea that there are intrinsic goods that can only be realized in acting for the sake of justice. I cannot discuss these arguments here nor go into the complicated Kantian argument in Section 85, "The Unity of the Self," designed to show how just institutions provide background for shaping the unity of the self as a moral agent.

26  Other arguments for the good of justice are suggested in Section 89 of *TJ* and include the argument from social union (Section 79) and an instrumentalist argument (Section 86).

27  *PL*, p. 203 and 203, n. 35.

28  See *Theory*, 567/497 rev., "We should like to know that this desire is indeed rational; being rational for one, it is rational for all, and therefore no tendencies to instability exist." See also p. 568/497 rev. Rawls seems to allow, however, that there may be some in a WOS for whom the sense of justice is not a good (*TJ*, pp. 575–6/504 rev.). Barry notes this apparent inconsistency.

29  See *Either/Or*, Vol. I (Princeton, NJ: Princeton University Press, 1944).

30  See, "Kantian Constructivism in Moral Theory," The Dewey Lectures, 1980, in Rawls, *Collected Papers*, Chapter 16.

31  In "Kantian Constructivism... " Rawls refers to the original position as a "procedure of construction." See *Collected Papers*, p. 340; see also pp. 310–12.

32  Here I interpret the final argument for congruence Rawls suggests in *TJ*, Section 86. See especially p. 572/501 rev., first paragraph, in conjunction with p. 445/390 rev. and then all of Secs. 40 and 85 and other pages cited

in the text. I provide here only the main strands of argument Rawls weaves together without detailed elaboration.

33 "The nature of the self as a free and equal moral person is the same for all" *TJ*, p. 565/495 rev.

34 See also, *Collected Papers*, p. 309.

35 As Rawls makes clearer in "Kantian Constructivism in Moral Theory," the original position can be construed as a "procedural representation" or "modeling" of central features of the conception of moral persons, and thus the principles chosen there are determined by these defining features. See Rawls, *Collected Papers*, p. 308.

36 Rawls says there is a "practical identity" between these two desires (*TJ*, p. 572/501 rev.). Cf. "Properly understood, then, the desire to act justly derives in part from the desire to express most fully what we are or can be, namely free and equal rational beings with a liberty to choose" (*TJ*, p. 256/225 rev.).

37 See also *TJ*, pp. 528/462–3 rev.: "When all strive to comply with these principles and each succeeds, then individually and collectively their nature as moral persons is most fully realized, and with it their individual and collective good."

38 Cf. "These principles are then given absolute precedence . . . and each frames his plans in conformity" *TJ*, p. 565/495 rev.

39 Just why Rawls says this is not clear. Perhaps he takes it as given that it is rational to realize one's fundamental nature. It may also have to do with his argument in Section 85 for "The Unity of the Self." The basic idea here is that it is because of moral personality, the capacities for a sense of justice and a conception of the good, that a person sees himself as a free agent, and is able to shape a plan of life and "fashion his own unity" (*TJ*, p. 561/492–92 rev.).

40 *Theory*, pp. 505/442, rev. 561/491 rev.; "Kantian Constructivism," pp. 312–13.

41 "Fairness to Goodness," *Collected Papers*, p. 284.

42 See *Theory*, Sec. 77, "The Basis of Equality"; see also "Kantian Constructivism," *Collected Papers*, pp. 330–33.

43 "[T]he two moral powers [are] the necessary and sufficient conditions for being counted a full and equal member of society in questions of political justice" (*Political Liberalism*, p. 302).

44 As Rawls contends in *TJ*, Section 85, "The Unity of the Self," pp. 561–3/491–3 rev.

45 Christine Korsgaard makes a similar point in "Personal Identity and the Unity of Agency: A Kantian Response to Parfit," *Philosophy and Public Affairs* 18 (1989): 101–32.

46  Similar considerations underlie Rawls's claim that he is not relying on a metaphysical conception of the person in the argument for justice as fairness. See, "The Independence of Moral Theory," in *Collected Papers*. Perhaps to avoid a misconstrual of the Kantian elements in his view, Rawls, subsequent to *Theory of Justice*, ceases referring to persons' "nature as free and equal rational beings" and substitutes instead the "moral ideal" of "free and equal moral persons." See, "Kantian Constructivism," p. 321.

47  "Sometimes there is no way to avoid having to assess the relative intensity of our desires" (*TJ*, p. 416/365 rev.).

48  In "Freedom of the Will and the Concept of a Person," in *The Importance of What We Care About* (Cambridge, UK: Cambridge University Press, 1988), pp. 11–25.

49  "Kantian Constructivism," *Collected Papers*, p. 320.

50  "The Basic Liberties and Their Priority," Lecture VIII, *Political Liberalism*, p. 305–6. Rawls distinguishes two kinds of autonomy in "Kantian Constructivism," and later in *Political Liberalism*, each of which is associated with one of the moral powers. "Rational autonomy" is acting on a rational plan of life and hence according to principles of rational choice while pursuing ends that are part of the plan of life one would choose in deliberative rationality. "Moral autonomy" is acting on and from the principles of justice. "Full autonomy" involves the combination of these, where justice is given highest-order priority in regulating one's rational plan. In this regard, full autonomy involves the congruence of the right and the good. See "Kantian Constructivism," Lecture I, entitled "Rational and Full Autonomy," esp. p. 308; *Political Liberalism*, pp. 72–81.

51  See, for example, Bernard Williams, "Practical Necessity," in *Moral Luck*, Chap. 10.

52  As Susan Wolf has argued, it may well be permissible sometimes to break an insignificant promise (to meet with a student, say) in order to take advantage of an opportunity that is important to one's career. Or consider what some may think a more serious breach: stealing to prevent one's starvation.

53  Cf. Rawls's discussion in *Political Liberalism*, of Kant's Moral constructivism, pp. 99–101.

54  I am grateful to Milton Meyer for helping me clarify this point.

55  Rawls's reasons for the fact of reasonable pluralism rest on his account of "the burdens of judgment" (*PL*, pp. 54–8), which were implicit in his initial account of the subjective circumstances of justice in *Theory* (*TJ*, 127/110 rev.).

56  See Jacques Maritain, *Man and the State* (1951), pp. 84–101, on natural law, and his *Scholasticism and Politics* (1940), pp. 121–2, on the Beatific Vision.

57  See Maritain, *Man and the State*, at pp. 83–4, where he rejects Rousseau's and Kant's arguments that natural law is based in the autonomy of the will.

58  So here we must partially concur with Barry's criticism that the congruence argument is unnecessary but not for the same reasons he discusses, namely, that having a moral sense of justice is sufficient to prove stability. For reasons discussed in the text, Rawls does not accept this; the problem of showing the rationality of justice still remains.

59  See *PL*, p. xvi, where Rawls says that "all differences [between *Political Liberalism* and *Theory*] are consequences of removing that inconsistency" in the original stability argument. For an account of how overlapping consensus and public reason respond to the problems implicit in the original congruence argument, see my "Political Liberalism and the Possibility of a Just Democratic Constitution."

60  See *TJ*, pp. 490–1/429–30 rev. for a concise statement of the reciprocity principles, and note 11 above for the 3d principle.

61  I thank Gopal Sreenivasan for helping me to clarify this point.

# 8    On Rawls and Political Liberalism[1]

I spoke here approximately five years ago. Then I spoke on Frege and Wittgenstein, [and] so I thought I would continue the series by now talking about Rawls. Some might think there is no connection between Frege and Wittgenstein, on [the] one hand, and Rawls, on the other. For me there is a very close connection, and I hope to bring it out implicitly if not explicitly today.

Everyone knows that in 1971 John Rawls published *A Theory of Justice*, which is very widely considered the most important work in political philosophy and perhaps even in moral philosophy since the end of World War II, and many think the most important work in political philosophy since the writings of John Stuart Mill. But what is not so widely known is that in 1993 Rawls brought out a second book, *Political Liberalism*, which a few of us believe is even more important. This book did not receive much praise upon coming out and has had [much less] attention paid to it. That I should like to change. (As I told Rawls yesterday afternoon just before I came out here, I view myself as an apostle going west.)

Whereas the first book is in the high tradition of at least English-speaking political philosophy, and in the high tradition of liberalism, *Political Liberalism*, the second book, is unique in that it asks a new series of questions about liberalism. That is one reason, I believe, why it has been so poorly received; it has not been sufficiently

*[Editor's Note: Burton Dreben died on July 17, 1999. Before his fatal illness he had intended to convert this public lecture into a more formal contribution for this volume. He was not able to complete this process of conversion. He did however continue to work on and refine this lecture up until the night before his death. It is presented in the form in which he left it.]

recognized that the second book deals with a quite different theme. The first book deals with justice, a much discussed topic; the second book deals with legitimacy, a topic that few contemporary philosophers in the liberal tradition have focused on. (It of course has been dealt with by various so-called political scientists.) The question of legitimacy – that is, under what conditions will someone properly accept a law as legitimate, even if he differs with it, even if he thinks it unjust – is a central question for present-day society. And that is what Rawls is really considering. It grows out of what he considers to be an essential flaw in the first book, a flaw that very few other people ever noted despite the detailed critical discussion to which the book has been subjected. The flaw is this: When you talk about the nature of justice, at least according to Rawls, you are not merely to come up with a theory of justice; you also have to point out why the theory that you are establishing is stable, why the society based on the theory will continue to endure indefinitely. It is not enough to come up with something that will be absolutely good in Plato's heaven; it is quite important to have something that will be good on Plato's earth and will continue to be seen as usable. Hence the last third of the book *A Theory of Justice* deals with this question of stability, or as Rawls comes to call it in much later writings "stability for the right reasons." And the way he argues that the two principles of justice, which the first two-thirds of the book deals with and which are to govern the basic structure of society, are indeed stable, or will create a stable and just society (if you grant certain general conditions about human nature and the environment and so forth), rests on showing that everyone will agree, or at least the vast majority of the society will agree, on these principles of justice. Now what Rawls began to see was that, under the very conditions that satisfy the principles of justice that he worked so hard to establish, reasonable and free and equal people will begin to differ, inevitably and properly so, on those very principles of justice. Hence, from his perspective, the theory of stability that he had set forth in the last third of the book contradicts the first two-thirds of the book.

This leads to a recasting of what he became so world famous for. It is a recasting that raises a whole new series of questions. So let us look first on page 37 of *Political Liberalism*. This will shock you, and should shock anybody who is a well brought-up philosopher:

[A] continuing shared understanding on one comprehensive religious, philosophical, or moral doctrine can be maintained only by the oppressive use of state power.

Let me stop for a moment. Central to Rawls's later thought is the distinction between a comprehensive doctrine and a political conception. This is not a distinction he draws in *A Theory of Justice*, and it is not a distinction that is drawn in general by any political or moral philosopher. But to understand what Rawls has been trying to do for the last twenty years requires making sense of this basic distinction between a comprehensive moral doctrine and a political conception. Much of today will be devoted to working on that distinction. Let us continue on page 37:

If we think of political society as a community united in affirming one and the same comprehensive doctrine, then the oppressive use of state power is necessary for a political community.

Now what this means is that Rawls is saying that even if he could have convinced you that what he wrote in *A Theory of Justice* is right and correct, rational and reasonable, the only way a society based on those principles of justice – Rawls's own principles of justice – could remain stable for the right reasons would be for the wrong reasons. It would entail the use of oppressive state power, which fundamentally contradicts the whole purpose of his work, and certainly contradicts any theory of liberalism that has ever been created. So this is a remarkable assertion. He is asserting that it is inevitable – not inevitable because of some faults in us, but inevitable to the free use of human reason – that reasonable and rational people will inevitably differ on fundamental doctrines. This he calls "The Fact of Reasonable Pluralism." And the only way you could have a community that continues to rest on one doctrine, say Kantian, or Millian, or Rawlsian – we are talking about even liberal doctrines now; that is why this is shocking – would demand oppressive state power. That is what he thought was the flaw in the stability argument of *A Theory of Justice* and which the last twenty-some years of his life have been devoted to trying to rectify. Let us read on a bit.

In the society of the Middle Ages, more or less united in affirming the Catholic faith, the Inquisition was not an accident. The suppression of heresy was needed to preserve that shared religious belief. (*PL*, p. 37)

Now comes the point.

The same holds, I believe, for any reasonable comprehensive philosophical and moral doctrine, whether religious or nonreligious. A society united on a reasonable form of utilitarianism, or on the reasonable liberalisms of Kant or Mill, will likewise require the sanctions of state power to remain so. Call this "the fact of oppression." (*PL*, p. 37)[2]

This, I claim, has never been said before in the history of philosophy. It is a totally radical view.

**1st Questioner:**  One thing I do not understand: How can shared "understanding" be reached by use of political power?

**Dreben:**  What he says is that, even if you have a shared understanding to start with – that is, you read his *A Theory of Justice* and it convinces you – still, through the passage of time, your students at least will not share that understanding. It would take state power, oppressive power, to maintain the primacy of that doctrine. This is something Kant would never have dreamt of saying, nor Mill; nor would Rawls in 1971 have dreamt of saying that. You see, it is really an attack on the traditional view of reason: an attack on the idea that reasonable people can all (or at least sufficient numbers of them) be brought to agree solely through the use of reason on the same philosophical doctrine. Now I said "doctrine"; I did not say "political conception." Look at footnote 39 on this same page 37:

This statement may seem paradoxical. If one objects that, consistent with Kant's or Mill's doctrine, the sanctions of state power cannot be used, I quite agree. But this does not contradict [what I've been saying in] the text, which says that a society in which every one affirms a reasonable liberal doctrine [that is, the same one] if by hypothesis it should exist, cannot long endure. With unreasonable doctrines, and with religions that emphasize the idea of institutional authority, we may think the text correct; and we may mistakenly think there are exceptions for other comprehensive views. The point of the text is: there are no exceptions.

This is what is governing Rawls. I want to emphasize that, whether Rawls is right or wrong, he feels this follows from what he calls in *Political Liberalism* "The Burdens of Judgment." (That is the name of the section on pp. 54–58 of that book.) All I can do today is to point out what for me is deep and important in his later work and then hope you all go home and study it. It is not easy reading. Many people thought *A Theory of Justice* was not easy reading; but compared with the later work, it is much easier reading. There are several stumbling blocks. I shall now note three.

First, the paperback edition of *Political Liberalism*, published in 1996, should be viewed as a second edition of the hardback published in 1993. It contains a twenty-six page Second Introduction (pp. xxxvii – lxii) that modifies and changes the emphasis of the main parts of the text and is the basis for much of what I am saying today. (As part of this paperback, there is the long "Reply to Habermas," which also changes somewhat the main text.[3]

Second, *Political Liberalism* and the subsequent papers connected with it are not always consistent. We shall see some examples of this. They are not deeply or intrinsically inconsistent, but the language is not always consistent because Rawls's ideas are complex and are still being worked out.

Third, the celebrated phrase "justice as fairness" is always a proper name and should be written in such a way that makes this clear. In what I have just called the Second Introduction Rawls makes this explicit:

> I put this phrase [*justice as fairness*] in italics because it is the proper name of a particular account of justice and it is always to be so understood. (*PL*, paperback edition, p. xxxvii., ft. 2)

(I write the phrase with hyphens: justice-as-fairness.) Unfortunately, it is an ambiguous proper name. In the first instance, it is the name of a particular moral doctrine, namely, that worked out in the six-hundred-page book *A Theory of Justice*. But in the book *Political Liberalism*, it has been transformed into a political conception. It is no longer part of a comprehensive moral doctrine, but it is a self-standing political conception. Hence, one of the difficulties in reading the contemporary Rawls is that justice-as-fairness, which was originally conceived as part of a comprehensive moral doctrine, usually stands for, as I just said, a particular political conception. Moreover, in the discussion that we are having this afternoon, the discussion about the paperback *Political Liberalism* and "The Idea of Public Reason Revisited" – which is the best statement of his views, incidentally – "justice-as-fairness" stands for a political conception now used as an example of a liberal political conception. In addition to the fact of reasonable pluralism, there is also "the fact of liberal pluralism": Rawls holds that not only can you not expect citizens to agree on the same comprehensive moral doctrine, but also you can not expect citizens to agree on the same liberal political conception; that would also be unreasonable. So what he has to do is to talk about a "family" of liberal political conceptions – a family, as we shall see, that includes both several political conceptions that today in the United States are called "conservative" and several political conceptions that in Europe are called "social democratic" or even "socialist." The political conception justice-as-fairness is just one member of that family. So when you read him, you have to take into account that what he says about justice-as-fairness is usually being used as an example of something much more general.

**2nd Questioner:** Is the fact of reasonable pluralism to be explained by the fact that a moral doctrine has a certain kind of a status rather than that people have certain kinds of psychologies, like they like to squabble a lot, or something like that?

**Dreben:** I would say it is the result both of the nature of comprehensive doctrines and the nature of free human reason. Rawls points out in the section, "The Burdens of Judgment," that, if you actually think about how people will properly reason with regard to basic questions, you will see it is intrinsic to human reason (and therefore we might call it psychology), that if they are in a free society people will begin to differ. And it is reasonable to differ on these basic questions. It is not "simply the upshot of self- and class interests, or of peoples' understandable tendency to view the political world from a limited standpoint" (*PL*, p. 37). That in part is the point of the idea of public reason. Rawls explicitly distinguishes between being rational and being reasonable:

[T]he reasonable and the rational are taken as two distinct and independent basic ideas. They are distinct in that there is no thought of deriving one from the other; in particular, there is no thought of deriving the reasonable from the rational. (*PL*, p. 51)

If you go back to *A Theory of Justice*, you will see that this distinction is there, but it is never made explicit, and in certain passages it seems to be implicitly denied. But it is always playing a role. For instance, there is no way of correctly understanding what Rawls is doing with regard to his analytical modeling device, what he calls the "original position," unless one understands that the original position (which was presented at first, unfortunately, in the terminology of rational decision theory, which we will soon see he now explicitly forswears) is not in any way an attempt to get the principles of justice solely from the concept of the rational. Rawls says: "To see justice as fairness as trying to derive the reasonable from the rational misinterprets the original position" (*PL*, p. 53). He immediately adjoins a footnote: "Here I correct a remark in *A Theory of Justice*, page 16, where it is said the theory of justice is a part of the theory of rational decision.... this is simply incorrect" (*PL*, p. 53, footnote 7).

Rawls always begins *in mediis rebus*, quite explicitly so. (Hence, I do not write *in medias res*). You start with intuitive moral, political considerations, and then you see what they come to. You can not ground them. And so the original position is always framed under the constraints of the reasonable. The distinction between rational and reasonable is absolutely crucial. It governs everything I am saying and everything Rawls is now saying. The attempt to get as clear as possible about what is rational and what is reasonable is what much of the subject is about. But you can not define these notions. Rawls is quite clear about that; he is a good enough philosopher to know that. To repeat, all you can do is to start with certain intuitive distinctions and see how you can push them and what work they will do.

Look now at page 611 of "The Idea of Public Reason Revisited":[4]

Throughout I have been concerned with a torturing question in the contemporary world, namely: Can democracy [by democracy he always means constitutional liberal democracy] and comprehensive doctrines, religious or nonreligious, be compatible? And if so how?

What Rawls has primarily been doing for the last twenty years is engage in a certain kind of very complex conceptual analysis, namely, he has been investigating the question, Is the notion of a constitutional liberal democracy internally consistent or coherent? Is it conceptually and logically possible to have as an ideal – it's not even a question of how to bring it about – what for him is implicit in the Declaration of Independence, the preamble to the American Constitution, the French Revolution's Declaration of the Rights of Man, the Gettysburg Address, and Lincoln's Second Inaugural. The question of whether it is possible or not arises from the shocking assertion on page 37 of *Political Liberalism*. If, as is indeed the case in the modern world, you will have irreconcilable and conflicting comprehensive doctrines held by the members of the society – that is the given – is it possible for that society to be a constitutional liberal democracy? Thus Rawls is engaged in what he calls "ideal theory": not a theory about nonconflict, but an ideal theory of conflict. In ideal theory you start out with the idea that the reasonable citizen recognizes that his reasonable comprehensive doctrine is probably in irreconcilable conflict with other reasonable citizens' irreconcilable and conflicting reasonable comprehensive doctrines. Then you want to work out whether there can be a coherent conception of a constitutional liberal democratic society, and what are the necessary conditions for such a society.

It is very important to understand that Rawls is a good enough thinker not to argue against those who do not believe in liberal constitutional democracy. Neither in *A Theory of Justice*, nor surely in *Political Liberalism*, nor in any of the other works, is he engaged in the kind of struggle that, say, Locke was engaged in. The outcome of that struggle he takes for granted, just as I think any sensible person should today. You do not argue in political philosophy over the benefits of constitutional liberal democracy; what you try to do is see what that concept leads to, what it entails, what it demands. As he says again and again, you start with the implicit notions and work them out. The key phrases all the time are "working through," "working out." Look at the third and fourth sentences on the top of page 14 of *Political Liberalism*:

In a democratic society [and always you must read that as constitutional liberal democratic society] there is a tradition of democratic thought, the content of which is at least familiar and intelligible to the educated common sense of citizens generally. Society's main institutions, and their accepted forms of interpretation, are seen as a fund of implicitly shared ideas and principles.

For Rawls the task of political philosophy is to work out from this "fund of implicitly shared ideas and principles" an explicit, (and hopefully) coherent liberal political conception. This fund, this "tradition of democratic thought" is the starting point. You do not argue for it. You do not ground it. You see what it leads to.

Rawls is concerned with a genuine question, very relevant today in the United States, also in Israel and in India – three different societies, which all view themselves as constitutional democracies, and in which religion, always a comprehensive doctrine, plays a very big and very troublesome role. That is what is worrying him. And that is a serious question. Or, as he puts it in the third sentence of "The Idea of Public Reason Revisited":

[A] basic feature of constitutional liberal democracy is the fact of reasonable pluralism – the fact that a plurality of conflicting reasonable comprehensive doctrines, religious, philosophical, and moral, is the normal result of its culture of free institutions.[5]

That just sharpens the question on page 37 of *Political Liberalism*. Now, continue on page 574:

Citizens realize that they cannot reach agreement or even approach mutual understanding on the basis of their irreconcilable comprehensive doctrines. In view of this, they need to consider what kinds of reasons they may reasonably give one another when fundamental political questions are at stake. I propose that in public reason comprehensive doctrines of truth or right be replaced by an idea of the politically reasonable addressed to citizens as citizens.

Public reason and its content [are] what this [chapter] is about. This passage demands quite a bit of commentary. What Rawls is saying is that, if you wish to have a coherent conception of constitutional liberal democracy, then on the most basic political questions concerning that society the notion of truth or the notion of right cannot be the governing notion. It must be replaced by a notion of reasonableness, where reasonableness does not entail truth or right. Otherwise you could not possibly hope for agreement between people who hold conflicting comprehensive doctrines; conflicting comprehensive doctrines will have different concepts of truth connected with them. As he goes on to say:[6]

[A]s I said at the beginning, in public reason ideas of truth or right based on comprehensive doctrines are replaced by an idea of the politically reasonable addressed to citizens as citizens.

The point being that any zealous demand for the whole truth as the basis of justification of legitimate law, or of public action, will of course lead to chaos. So one immediate implication of asking the question, How can you have a coherent conception of constitutional liberal democracy? is that the age-old drive to have us all agree on the nature of truth and the nature of right and of righteousness has to be given up. Rawls is making a very radical move, and the force of his recent writings is to try to convince you that move must be made if you can even hope to have a viable liberal constitutional democracy.

Notice that the last three quotations rest on another basic distinction that Rawls draws: the idea of a (moral) person, a key notion of moral thought and of much political philosophy, and indeed a key notion of *A Theory of Justice*, is distinguished from the idea of a (moral) citizen, a key notion of a liberal political conception. For Rawls, you may only hope to have a constitutional liberal democracy if you sharply distinguish between a private sphere and a public sphere, or as he puts it, between the background culture and the public forum. The idea of public reason applies only to the public forum. The same human being is a person in the background culture and a citizen in the public forum. What you do as a citizen for other citizens does not extend to everything you do as a person for other persons. In *A Theory of Justice* you had the person; then in the original position you had the party representing the interests, the good, of the person, and bargaining on behalf of the person, under the constraints of the reasonable, for the best comprehensive principles of justice, with parties representing the different interests of other persons. The party [in the original position] was a purely artificial fiction, an analytical device. In *Political Liberalism* you have to have the person, you have to have the citizen, and then you have the representing party bargaining on behalf of the citizen for the best principles of justice for a liberal political conception. As is also the case in *A Theory of Justice*, the party is purely rational, and, of course, is an abstraction, a fiction.

**3rd Questioner:** But the idea of the citizen is surely not a fiction in the same sense?

**Dreben:** No, very good. The idea of citizen is not a fiction; we are all citizens as well as persons. First look at the top of page 14 of *Political Liberalism*:

Comprehensive doctrines of all kinds – religious, philosophical, and moral – belong to what we may call the "background culture" of civil society. This is the culture of the social, not of the political. It is the culture of daily life.

And then look at footnote 13 on page 576 of "The Idea of Public Reason Revisited":

The background culture includes, then, the culture of churches and associations of all kinds, and institutions of learning at all levels, especially universities and professional schools, scientific and other societies. In addition, the nonpublic political culture mediates between the public political culture and the background culture. This comprises media – properly so named – of all kinds: newspapers, reviews and magazines, TV and radio, and much else.

Rawls tries to clear up another widespread misunderstanding about public reason on page 583 of "The Idea of Public Reason Revisited":

> We must distinguish public reason from what is sometimes referred to as secular reason and secular values. These are not the same as public reason. For I define secular reason as reasoning in terms of comprehensive nonreligious doctrines. Such doctrines and values are much too broad to serve the purposes of public reason.

It is absolutely essential for Rawls that public reason, one of the basic components of political liberalism, *political* liberalism, be neutral with regard to various comprehensive doctrines, various religious doctrines, and so forth. It is not a secular position, if you mean by a secular position something which is a comprehensive doctrine. In no way is what Rawls [is] doing supposed to be part of the so-called Enlightenment project. He is very clear about that; otherwise, the whole enterprise would break down. The whole point of political liberalism is to be as neutral as possible to all comprehensive doctrines. The only comprehensive doctrines it is not neutral toward are those which are unreasonable. A reasonable comprehensive doctrine by no means has to be a liberal comprehensive doctrine. A reasonable comprehensive doctrine can be irrational – you can be like Tertullian and say, "I believe because it is absurd." All a comprehensive doctrine has to do to be reasonable is to endorse a liberal political conception. But outside of that it can hold anything it wants. You are not engaged in the same sort of philosophical battle as Voltaire or anyone like that. This must be grasped, or the whole task is useless.

Remember, I opened up saying this is an enterprise exploring the notion of legitimacy in a liberal constitutional democracy. To say that a law is a legitimate law is not to say that all reasonable citizens agree with it. That is why legitimacy is such a complex and interesting notion in political philosophy. What you really have to worry about in a liberal constitutional democracy is how, when a law is appropriately passed, it is binding on all citizens, even on those citizens who reasonably can differ with it. That is the problem of stability for the right reasons. An example is the problem of abortion, a problem which Rawls discusses in this paper ("Public Reason Revisited," pp. 605–7). It is the problem when, according to your comprehensive doctrine, you view as immoral something that is legal, and yet you are politically–morally bound to obey the law – politically–morally – because the question [of legitimacy] we're always concerned with in political philosophy, as opposed to so-called political science, is not how in fact you get people to agree but how you get them to agree for the right reasons. That is the task of public reason. You are always engaged in a moral enterprise. For Rawls, the notion of the political itself is an intrinsically moral notion. So although a political conception is not a comprehensive moral doctrine because a comprehensive moral doctrine governs or can be extended to govern all aspects of life – background culture and so forth – nevertheless, the fact that you are dealing with a political conception, though limited in one sense, does not mean it is not intrinsically moral. The question of what constitutes a legitimate law is as much an intrinsically moral question as the question of what constitutes a just law, but far more difficult. Because it is unreasonable to assume that, in a liberal constitutional democracy, all reasonable citizens are going to agree on the justice of all laws. That is the height of unreasonableness. And that is what we are concerned about.

**4th Questioner:** I am puzzled by your comments on abortion as an example. I am puzzled by what it means to say that you are politically–morally obligated to follow a negative: that is, a law that says something is permitted.

**Dreben:** Oh no, it does not mean that you are supposed to have an abortion! What it means is that you do not shoot a doctor who performs a legal abortion and claim in defense of such a murder that you acted on behalf of a higher moral principle; or you do not boycott in such a way that a woman who wants to have a legal abortion can not have it.

**4th Questioner:** Okay, but it also can not mean that you are obligated to not try to change the law.

**Dreben:** Oh, absolutely not. You have every right to try to change a law. But you must use reasonable means. If you look in *A Theory of Justice* you will find very few examples of questions that actually excite people, except of course philosophers. Whereas if you look in *Political Liberalism*, you will actually find discussions of the questions that are being discussed today in the Supreme Court, in the Congress, and on the streets, which is what political philosophy should be engaged in. Indeed, there is a whole discussion here about public financing of elections, something that you would not dream of finding in *A Theory of Justice*, but of course is something which is absolutely critical to the whole idea of public reason.

**4th Questioner:** I guess my question is in effect that there is no such thing as a purely reasonable approach to any of these issues. Just as there is room for legitimate disagreement about the abortion laws or the drug laws, because of different rankings of priorities which are derived from religious or other comprehensive doctrines, there will likewise be legitimate room for disagreement on whether we can disagree reasonably. For instance, consider Dostoevsky's benevolent totalitarianism. Now you can say, well okay we're not going to discuss benevolent totalitarianism, but you would have no more right to say that than to say, well we're not going to discuss this side or that side of the abortion laws or the drug laws or. . . .

**Dreben:** Yes, I do have the right, and I shall explain why. To ask me to argue about benevolent totalitarianism, or whatever, is to miss what is basic to the way Rawls now does political philosophy. Neither Rawls nor I am going to argue with Dostoevsky. We feel we have enough problems. I am quite serious. As I said, the genuine problem is to see how one can set up a coherent conception of a constitutional liberal democracy. What Rawls is saying is that there is in a constitutional liberal democracy a tradition of thought which it is our job to explore and see whether it can be made coherent and consistent. That is hard enough to do. We are not arguing *for* such a society. We take for granted that today only a fool would not want to live in such a society. One of the virtues of Rawls is that he does not waste time arguing about autocracy or totalitarianism. He lives in this country, which has many defects, but which has a certain ideal. We start with that ideal. Both Rawls and I know that the American ideal was deeply flawed from the beginning. The Constitution enshrined black slavery, and we are still paying a huge price for that; it is still the source of grave problems in American society. But it is not a problem of American society whether we should be a "benevolent totalitarianism." I do not spend my time or energy arguing against it; I dismiss it. Because it is irrational; it is irrational and unreasonable to want to live in such a society. Now what you could say [is that] it is intrinsic to human nature that the ideal of a liberal constitutional democracy, even if it is internally coherent, can not be brought into effect or can not remain stable except for the wrong reasons. You could argue for such a position – and that very likely was what Dostoevsky was doing – but that is not what [you] are discussing now. Too many philosophers, even today, spend too much of their time trying to argue in the abstract for political liberalism against, say, totalitarianism and so forth. This does not seem to me to be a worthy philosophical enterprise. If one cannot see the benefits of living in a liberal constitutional democracy, if one does not see the virtue of that ideal, then I do not know how to convince him. To be perfectly blunt, sometimes I am asked, when I go around speaking for Rawls, What do you say to an Adolf Hitler? The answer is [nothing.] You shoot him. You do not try to reason with him. Reason has no bearing on that question. So I do not want to discuss it. But what I am perfectly prepared to discuss is whether the idea of liberalism as an ideal, given the burdens of judgment, is contradictory.

**5th Questioner:** So I take it that what you are saying is this distinction between a comprehensive moral doctrine and a political conception is important.

**Dreben:** Absolutely. It is all important.

**5th Questioner:** I guess I am still hung up on that distinction.

**Dreben:** I do not blame you.

**5th Questioner:** One thing you suggested is that the distinction has to do with scope: one is more comprehensive than the other. And the other thing that seems to be suggested is that they apply to different spheres: one applies to the social sphere and one to the political sphere. Is that right?

**Dreben:** Very good, that is an excellent question. Turn to "Public Reason Revisited," page 573, footnote 2:

> I shall use the term "doctrine" for comprehensive views of all kinds and the term "conception" for a political conception and its component parts such as the conception of the person as citizen. The term "idea" is used as a general term and may refer to either as the context determines.

Until this footnote and a very similar one on the first page (footnote 2, p. xxxvii) of the Second Introduction in the paperback *Political Liberalism*, Rawls never explicitly drew these distinctions although he had been implicitly using them for some time, which is one reason why there has been so much misunderstanding. But there are further sources of misunderstanding. Look at footnote 15 on page 14 of *Political Liberalism*:

I comment that I use "ideas" as the more general term as covering both concepts and conceptions.

Rawls thus distinguishes in this footnote – and as he says he already did on page 5 in *A Theory of Justice* – between concepts and conceptions:

Roughly, the concept is the meaning of a term, while a particular conception includes as well the principles required to apply it. To illustrate: the concept of justice applied to an institution means, say, that the institution makes no arbitrary distinctions between persons in assigning basic rights and duties, and that its rules establish a proper balance between competing claims. Whereas a conception includes, besides this, principles and criteria for deciding which distinctions are arbitrary and when a balance between competing claims is proper. People can agree on the meaning of the concept of justice and still be at odds, since they affirm different principles and standards for deciding those matters. To develop a concept of justice into a conception of it is to elaborate these requisite principles and standards.

In these terms, what Rawls was doing in *A Theory of Justice* was working out from the concept of justice, a concept about which he thinks it is easy to get agreement, to a particular conception of justice, justice-as-fairness. It took him about six-hundred pages. And that is what you are to do, he feels, when you are properly engaged in doing moral philosophy and political philosophy. You are to work out from easily agreed upon concepts to particular detailed conceptions. This is what I meant when I said earlier that Rawls is always *in mediis rebus*, in the middle of things.

But now, as the smiles (or frowns) on your faces show, you all see there is a prima facie conflict between the two footnotes in what Rawls says about how he will use the word "conception" (and the word "idea"). The conflict, however, is easily resolved. The word "conception" in the second footnote, which records Rawls's usage until about 1995, is used both for what in the first footnote is referred to as "doctrine" and also for what is referred to there as "political conception". But this verbal play does not get to the heart of what the gentleman was asking: How do you tell whether you are dealing with a comprehensive doctrine or a political conception?

A comprehensive doctrine is something which, traditionally, one would have viewed as an all-encompassing moral position or an all-encompassing religious position. It governs, theoretically, all aspects of your life. Whereas a political conception definitely does not. A political conception does not apply to the background culture at all. Look at page 576 ("Public Reason Revisited"):

> [T]he background culture ... is the culture of civil society. In a democracy, this culture is not, of course, guided by any one central idea or principle, whether political or religious. Its many and diverse agencies and associations with their internal life reside within a framework of law that ensures the familiar liberties of thought and speech, and the right of free association. The idea of public reason does not apply to the background culture with its many forms of nonpublic reason nor to media of any kind.

For instance, the political conception justice-as-fairness is inappropriate for running the internal affairs of a family, of a university, of a classroom, or anything like a standard traditional religious organization, whether in Orthodox Judaism or in Roman Catholicism or in Calvinism, or many associations, or sport teams. All that is part of the background culture. Does this fully answer the question? In particular, does this permit us to clearly distinguish justice-as-fairness as a political conception from justice-as-fairness as a comprehensive doctrine? No! Indeed, much of the criticism of *A Theory of Justice* is the result of not understanding that, even as a comprehensive doctrine, the two principles of justice were to apply primarily to what Rawls called the "basic structure of society."

**5th Questioner:** But in spite of that justice-as-fairness is still a comprehensive doctrine?

**Dreben:** Justice-as-fairness in *A Theory of Justice* is a comprehensive doctrine. Yes. Why? Because, as a comprehensive moral doctrine, or more precisely, as part of a comprehensive moral doctrine, it gives you the comprehensive moral basis for a just society. And part of what Rawls is trying to do in the book *Political Liberalism* is to transform that comprehensive doctrine into a free-standing political conception. It is very misleading in the book, until you read the new introduction, the Second Introduction, and even then. [It is misleading] because the last three chapters of the book are lectures that he gave before he fully grasped what he was doing. For instance, consider the chapter called, "The Basic Structure as Subject." If you read that chapter in *Political Liberalism*, you are apt to be misled, because it does not explicitly use the distinction between doctrine and conception. It was written as a halfway house. Nevertheless, there is a great difference between *Political Liberalism* and *A Theory of Justice*. To repeat, the point of the latter is to present a comprehensive moral doctrine which is to give us a moral basis for what would be a just society. Let us look at Rawls's own assessment at the conclusion of "The Idea of Public Reason Revisited," pages 614–15:

I end by pointing out the fundamental difference between *A Theory of Justice* and *Political Liberalism*. The first explicitly attempts to develop from the idea of the social contract, represented by Locke, Rousseau, and Kant, a theory of justice that is no longer open to objections often thought fatal to it, and that proves superior to the long dominant tradition of utilitarianism. *A Theory of Justice* hopes to present the structural features of such a theory so as to make it the best approximation to our considered judgments of justice and hence to give the most appropriate moral basis for a democratic society. Furthermore, justice as fairness[=justice-as-fairness] is presented there as a comprehensive liberal doctrine (although the term "comprehensive doctrine" is not used in the book) in which all the members of its well-ordered society affirm that *same* [my italics] doctrine. This kind of well-ordered society contradicts the fact of reasonable pluralism and hence *Political Liberalism* regards that society as impossible.

Thus, *Political Liberalism* considers a different question, namely: How is it possible for those affirming a comprehensive doctrine, religious or non-religious, and in particular doctrines based on religious authority, such as the Church or the Bible, also to hold a reasonable political conception of justice that supports a constitutional democratic society? The political conceptions are seen as both liberal and self-standing and not as comprehensive, whereas the religious doctrines may be comprehensive but not liberal. The two books are asymmetrical, though both have an idea of public reason. In the first, public reason is given by a comprehensive liberal doctrine, while in the second, public reason is a way of reasoning about political values shared by free and equal citizens that does not trespass on citizens' comprehensive doctrines so long as those doctrines are consistent with a democratic polity. Thus, the well-ordered constitutional democratic society of *Political Liberalism* is one in which the dominant and controlling citizens affirm and act from irreconcilable yet reasonable comprehensive doctrines. These doctrines in turn support reasonable political conceptions – although not necessarily the most reasonable – which specify the basic rights, liberties, and opportunities of citizens in society's basic structure.

It is time now to get clearer about what constitutes a liberal political conception. On page 583 of "The Idea of Public Reason Revisited" Rawls writes, "Political values," – note he says values – "are not moral doctrines." The operative word is "doctrine." Rawls is certainly not denying that political values are moral values. The key to all of this is the idea that a political conception, which is intrinsically moral, has to be freestanding. You can not use or have a liberal political conception that is going to do the job that public reason demands if it is not freestanding. It is part of its neutrality with respect to comprehensive doctrines that it does not have to depend on any comprehensive doctrine. It has to be intrinsically on its own, although any reasonable comprehensive doctrine, liberal or nonliberal, will be compatible with it. Indeed, by an "overlapping consensus" of differing and even conflicting reasonable comprehensive doctrines Rawls means each such doctrine in its own way endorses or supports the same freestanding, liberal political conception.

Now, [let us return] to page 583–4:

Political values are not moral doctrines, however available or accessible these may be to your reason and commonsense reflection. Moral doctrines are on a level with religion and first philosophy. By contrast, liberal political principles and values, although intrinsically moral values, are specified by liberal political conceptions of justice and fall under the category of the political. These political conceptions have three features:

What follows on page 584 is absolutely crucial for understanding Rawls:

First, their principles apply to basic political and social institutions (the basic structure of society);

That specifies what it is to be a political conception, not necessarily only liberal ones.

Second, they can be presented independently from comprehensive doctrines of any kind (although they may, of course, be supported by a reasonable overlapping consensus of such doctrines);

That is the freestanding character or the autonomy of political conceptions. "Finally," and this is what makes them 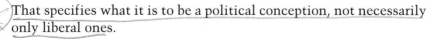liberal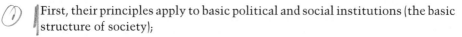

they can be worked out from fundamental ideas seen as implicit in the public political culture of a constitutional [liberal] regime, such as the conceptions of citizens as free and equal persons and of society as a fair system of cooperation.

These are three fundamental criteria that any liberal political conception must satisfy.

Now look on pages 581–2 for a more explicit characterization of what it is for political principles applying to the basic structure to be liberal:

First, [the principles must contain] a list of certain basic rights, liberties, and opportunities (such as those familiar from constitutional regimes);

Second, [the principles must yield] an assignment of special priority to those rights, liberties, and opportunities, especially with respect to the claims of the general good and perfectionist values; and

Third, [the principles must guarantee] measures ensuring for all citizens adequate all-purpose means to make effective use of their freedoms.

This is very important. This is what characterizes Rawls's idea of political liberalism. Certainly, the political conception justice-as-fairness satisfies these three criteria, but so do several other competing political conceptions. Liberal political conceptions will differ primarily on how they satisfy the third criterion. Indeed, as I said earlier, some conceptions that are called "conservative" in the United States today as well as conceptions that are called in Europe "social democratic" are liberal. (However, as Rawls states explicitly on page viii of the Second Introduction, libertarianism is not liberal.) All this looks very abstract. I shall try to be clearer.

Throughout, what is being taken for granted here is that you start with the following basic concepts: a society of people who are free and equal. What Rawls has been trying to do, first in *A Theory of Justice* and then in *Political Liberalism* and subsequent writings, is to work out what these concepts come to. In *A Theory of Justice* he took as his main task, in working these concepts out, the stating of principles which would frame a society which could reasonably and rationally adjudicate between claims arising from each individual's freedom and claims arising from the demand for equality among individuals – claims that will always be more or less in prima facie conflict in a free society, in a liberal society. After all, since the time of the American Revolution and the French Revolution, what has been the fundamental political question of constitutional societies, more or less democratic? Undoubtedly, in such societies the fundamental question of the last two hundred years has been how to deal with the inevitable conflicts arising when claims of the liberties or the freedoms of each individual in the society clash with claims of equality among individuals. In the United States today that is the debate between so-called conservatives and liberals. And the purpose of the particular principles of justice that Rawls first enunciated in *A Theory of Justice* and then re-enunciates – viewed as political principles now, and no longer as comprehensive moral principles of justice – is to provide a structure that will permit in general the rational and reasonable adjudication of these conflicts.

To see what I just said put in a slightly different but equivalent way, look at page 15 from *Political Liberalism.*

[T]he fundamental organizing idea of justice as fairness [= justice-as-fairness, both as a comprehensive doctrine and as a political conception] is that of society as a fair system of cooperation over time, from one generation to the next.

Thus, the most basic notion Rawls begins with, intuitively, is that our society – the only kind of society we are talking about – is ideally a fair system of cooperation that goes from one generation to the next. And the task of political philosophy, starting from that, is to work out what are the fair terms of cooperation. The purpose of the principles of justice, the particular principles that characterize justice-as-fairness – or any other principles that will satisfy the criteria of liberalism stated on pages 581–2 of "Public Reason Revisited" – is to work out the appropriate terms of cooperation. Whereas almost anyone will agree that "Yes, the terms should be fair," the debate comes in with the question, What is fairness? Let me repeat. You start with the idea which Rawls takes for granted; look again at footnote 15 on page 14 of *Political Liberalism,* especially the point about distinctions. To get the full force of what Rawls is doing, ask yourself what is the one cry you constantly hear whenever you see children playing a competitive game?

**Audience:** "That's not fair!"

**Dreben:** Exactly. You rarely hear, That's not just. But you'll always hear, That's not fair. And That's not fair runs very deep. Indeed – I have to be careful now – there is hardly a society, in fact I know of no society that any anthropologist has ever reported on, in which there is not some system for making social decisions that the society views as nonarbitrary. You cannot even have the idea of a society functioning over time – I am not talking just about a liberal society – without some power in the society claiming to be making nonarbitrary decisions among competing claims. When you have a society that is truly arbitrary, it surely collapses. A basic task of political philosophy is to work out the best terms of what would be fair.

**6th Questioner:** Let us suppose that you are right that there is no such society that you have just described.

**Dreben:** Even if there is, it is not ours.

**6th Questioner:** For the sake of argument, I shall agree. But just because every society has to have elements of fairness in it does not mean on its political level – which you're trying to bracket off from the rest of the culture – that fairness has to be the sole consideration. It seems to me that in the preamble to the Constitution the Founders set out a whole slew of objectives such as the creation of a more perfect union, the protection of the general welfare, etc., and then the job of the Constitution is to fulfill these objectives.

**Dreben:** Yes, but all of those are political.

**6th Questioner:** Well, you can argue that they are.

**Dreben:** In fact Rawls does so explicitly in this paper, "The Idea of Public Reason Revisited". Look at page 584:

Examples of political values include those mentioned in the preamble to the United States Constitution: a more perfect union, justice, domestic tranquility, the common defense, the general welfare, and the blessings of liberty for ourselves and our posterity. These include under them other [political] values: so, for example, under justice we also have equal basic liberties, equality of opportunity, ideals concerning the distribution of income and taxation, and much else.

**6th Questioner:** I do not know how you want to parse out the difference between the political and the moral. But it seems to me that if you have a society, it's going to have objectives, and then it is going to choose strategies. Now, is the fairness that Rawls is talking about, in this context, an objective done for its own sake, exclusively?

**Dreben:** No, it is a starting point. Let us look again on these pages 14 and 15 from *Political Liberalism*. It is something he repeats again and again. You start with the idea of a society as a fair system of cooperation over time from one generation to the next. The question is, What content can you give to this idea? What are the worked out fair terms of cooperation? Of course, we are talking about the ideal of our society – I repeat, we are not interested in going beyond the ideal of our society – in which these fair terms are part of a liberal political conception, not a comprehensive doctrine. The overarching problem is how can you have a liberal constitutional democratic society stable for the right reasons in which, say, a vast majority of the citizens hold nonliberal comprehensive doctrines. You must understand that, as a person you can hold almost anything you want, as long as you as a citizen will recognize and endorse liberal principles of justice. This is why one must make the distinction between a comprehensive doctrine and a political conception. Otherwise, there is no way to handle the problem of legitimacy to which we now turn.

Look at the bottom of page 577:

The idea of public reason arises from a conception of democratic citizenship in a [liberal] constitutional democracy. This fundamental political relation of citizenship has two special features: first, it is a relation of citizens within the basic structure of society, a structure we enter only by birth and exit only by death; and second, it is a relation of free and equal citizens who exercise ultimate collective power as a collective body.

Now these two features of citizenship immediately raise the question of legitimacy:

[H]ow, when constitutional essentials and matters of basic justice are at stake, citizens so related can be bound to honor the structure of their constitutional democratic regime and abide by the laws and statutes enacted under it. The fact of reasonable pluralism raises this question all the more sharply, since it means that the differences between citizens arising from their comprehensive doctrines, religious and nonreligious, may be irreconcilable. By what ideals and principles, then, are citizens who share equally ultimate political power [ – that's what makes it a constitutional liberal democracy – ] to exercise that power so that each can reasonably justify his or her political decisions to everyone? (*Collected Papers*, pp. 577–8)

That is the basic problem of political philosophy. How can you justify to someone who does not share your comprehensive moral doctrine, whether liberal or not, the action you have taken as citizen either directly or indirectly through your legislative representatives?

To answer this question we say – this is very tricky because it looks circular. It is circular, but it is a big circle. So that makes it very good philosophy.

> To answer this question we say: Citizens are reasonable when, viewing one another as free and equal in a system of social cooperation over generations, they are prepared to offer one another fair terms of cooperation according to what they consider the most reasonable conception of political justice; and when they agree to act on those terms, even at the cost of their own interests in particular situations, provided that other citizens also accept those terms. (p. 578)

Citizens will differ, I remind you, not only in their comprehensive doctrines, but also in their conceptions of the political liberal principles of justice. But, of course, as citizens, in our kind of society, they will all (or almost all) hold conceptions that satisfy the three criteria of liberalism on pages 581–2 (and hence the three criteria on page 584). To continue:

> The *criterion of reciprocity* [my italics] requires that when those terms are proposed as the most reasonable terms of fair cooperation, those proposing them must also think it at least reasonable for others to accept them, as free and equal citizens, and not as dominated or manipulated, or under the pressure of an inferior political or social position. Citizens will, of course, differ as to which conceptions of political justice they think the most reasonable, but they will all agree that all are reasonable, even if barely so. (p. 578)

What is Rawls saying here? He is saying that the only way we are going to be able to have, even as an ideal, a constitutional liberal democracy is if all citizens, or at least a sufficient number of them (sufficient to keep the rest in check), will agree to reason with each other in terms of liberal political conceptions of justice, that is, liberal principles of justice, which not all citizens will agree are the most reasonable, but all will agree are sufficiently reasonable to be accepted as a justification. That is the hope, and that is the idea he is trying to get at. You will notice, if you compare what is said here with many passages in the book *Political Liberalism*, this goes beyond the book. In *Political Liberalism*, Rawls constantly talks about citizens having different comprehensive doctrines, but they all share the same political conception. That will not do. Rather they are to share the same *family* of liberal principles, although they will differ on the members of the family. Rawls is now trying to grant as much disagreement as possible on the assumption that it is unreasonable to demand too much agreement.

**7th Questioner:** Would it be appropriate to say that all we can reasonably do is to deal with procedural issues?

**Dreben:** No, that is what Stuart Hampshire proposed in that critical review he wrote of *Political Liberalism* and earlier in his book *Innocence and Experience*. For Rawls, the political principles of public reason, since they're intrinsically moral notions, are substantive. Look at page 582:

I assume . . . that these liberalisms [those satisfying the three criteria of liberalism] contain substantive principles of justice, and hence cover more than procedural justice. They are required to specify the religious liberties and freedom of artistic expression of equal citizens, as well as substantive ideas of fairness involving fair opportunity and ensuring adequate all-purpose means, and much else.

And for further documentation, look at footnote 26 on the page 582:

Some may think the fact of reasonable pluralism means the only forms of fair adjudication between comprehensive doctrines must be only procedural and not substantive. This view is forcefully argued by Stuart Hampshire in *Innocence and Experience* (Harvard 1989). In the text above, however, I assume the several forms of liberalism are each substantive conceptions.

What is involved in being reasonable and rational is very difficult to lay out, in fact can never be totally laid out, but you'll see what they come to in practice. They are evolving notions within our constitutional system. Indeed, to truly understand what Rawls is teaching, you have to understand the way the best appellate judges work. Public reason, as he says explicitly, is binding in the first instance on appellate justices and Supreme Court justices, particularly in our kind of system. If you have actually ever read – it is unfortunate that so few Americans do – appellate court decisions and Supreme Court decisions, you will see that what they are always engaged in, when they are at their best, is what Rawls means by public reason. Constantly what you are confronted with in our system is how basic ideas, basic concepts such as freedom and equality, are to be turned into conceptions, how they really are to be applied and developed into workable principles. To be a serious political philosopher, one should understand the development of the common law and what a great judge does; that is the heart of the subject. And that is what is behind Rawls. Perhaps Rawls's greatest contribution is his insistence that you cannot ever completely lay out what it is to be reasonable and what it is to be rational in this political sense. But you can keep listing various criteria, and you can see public reason in action. And these notions will change, because it is imperative that they change, but they change according to implicit development, as you keep working through what is demanded by the fair terms of cooperation of free and equal and rational and reasonable citizens. That is another way in which, without ever emphasizing it, Rawls is engaged in a very substantial shifting of how one does the subject. At times – and this for me is rather unfortunate (he knows I am going to say this) – at times you will find he will seem to base what he calls public reason on Kant's practical reason. This is very misleading. Kant's talk about practical reason is useless for understanding Rawls.

**8th Questioner:** Useless!

**Dreben:** Useless! Indeed, all practical reason can come to in the political sphere is what Rawls is saying about public reason. For me, wherever Rawls has gone slightly astray in exposition has been when he has paid too much lip service to Immanuel Kant. It does not help at all. For instance, look at the footnote to page 48 of *Political Liberalism*.

> The distinction between the reasonable and the rational goes back, I believe, to Kant: it is expressed in his distinction between the categorical and the hypothetical imperative in the *Foundations* and his other writings. The first represents pure practical reason, the second represents empirical practical reason. (*PL*, 48n)

This, I suggest, does not help you at all. But, fortunately, Rawls's better judgment immediately comes into play:

> For the purposes of a political conception of justice, I give the reasonable a more restricted sense and associate it, first, with the willingness to propose and honor fair terms of cooperation, and second, with the willingness to recognize the burdens of judgment and to accept their consequences. (*PL*, 49n)

These are the two virtues of a citizen that permit you to talk about the reasonable. One, the willingness to propose and honor fair terms of cooperation, that means, the willingness to propose and honor political principles of justice in a way that satisfies the criterion of reciprocity. And two, the willingness to recognize the burdens of judgment, and to accept their consequences; and that really means that reasonable citizens are going to differ, irreconcilably differ, on comprehensive moral doctrines, and even on the best reasonable political principles of justice.

For Rawls the idea of the good is not the general good. The good is the individual's own good, the citizen's own good, which he has the capacity always to revise and change, and the citizen's comprehensive doctrine is intimately connected with his idea of his own good. But the idea of the citizen also includes the "equal" part; it has to do with others. This is intrinsic to having a sense of justice; you do not have a notion of justice for yourself alone. If you're going to have a theory of hermits, you do not have to bring in a theory of justice. From the very beginning Rawls is insisting that you do not do political philosophy – indeed you do not do moral theory – for saints or for hermits.

**9th Questioner:** Here is the picture I now have. You started out by worrying about this problem of stability, given the fact of reasonable pluralism. We have this political realm composed of individuals who have different comprehensive doctrines. They also differ on what is the most reasonable of the political conceptions, though they agree on which of them are actually reasonable. Is that the picture of the stable, liberal society?

**Dreben:** It is, provided we make explicit several additional ideas that are essential. To have a well-ordered liberal democratic society is to have one that is effectively regulated by a family of liberal, public principles of justice. And stability for the right reasons comes from the fact that, if you are in such a well-ordered society, your sense of justice will be constantly reinforced. If every citizen knows – this is part of the criterion of reciprocity – if every citizen knows that every other citizen, or a sufficient number of them, will act with regard to principles of justice and justify their political actions by what will be at least reasonable in this family, then stability for the right reasons will endure. What Rawls is arguing against is stability just by a modus vivendi. The idea of tolerance as a political idea was a result of the Reformation and the ensuing Wars of Religion in the sixteenth and seventeenth centuries. Rawls is quite clear about this in *Political Liberalism*. The Catholics could not kill all the Protestants, and the Protestants could not kill all the Catholics. So, after a certain point, each side decided to live with the other, to tolerate the other, but with the hope and expectation that when it would be in a position to do so it would start the killing again. Need I say such a modus vivendi is not a moral notion and does not permit stability for the right reasons? What does permit stability for the right reasons is when each of the comprehensive doctrines, religious and nonreligious, comes to accept, for reasons of its own, as a deep moral virtue that there be genuine diversity in society, that there be conflicting and irreconcilable reasonable comprehensive doctrines represented in society. (It is crucial to note that the grounds or reasons offered by a reasonable comprehensive doctrine for accepting this moral notion of tolerance are internal to the doctrine and need not satisfy the demands of public reason.) A most important example of a nonliberal comprehensive doctrine adopting such a position is Roman Catholicism since Vatican II, when finally, officially, the Roman Catholic Church accepted that, as a moral good, not just as a modus vivendi, there be religious diversity in society. Look at "Public Reason Revisited," page 603, [the] middle of footnote 75:

A persecuting zeal has been the great curse of the Christian religion. It was shared by Luther and Calvin and the Protestant Reformers, and it was not radically changed in the [Roman] Catholic Church until Vatican II. In the Council's Declaration on Religious Freedom – *Dignitatis Humanae* – the Catholic Church committed itself to the principle of religious freedom as found in a constitutional democratic regime. It declared the ethical doctrine of religious freedom resting on the dignity of the human person; a political doctrine with respect to the limits of government in religious matters; a theological doctrine of the freedom of the Church in its relations to the political and social world. All persons, whatever their faith, have the right of religious liberty on the same terms.

A question immediately arises: what role may a reasonable comprehensive doctrine play in public reason? The answer is given by what Rawls calls *the proviso*. Look at page 584:

[T]he content of public reason is given by the principles and values of the family of liberal political conceptions of justice ... To engage in public reason is to appeal to one of these political conceptions – to their ideals and principles, standards and values – when debating fundamental political questions. This ... still allows us to introduce into political discussion at any time our comprehensive doctrine – [and here Rawls goes beyond what is said in the first edition of *Political Liberalism*] – religious or nonreligious, provided that, in due course, we give properly public reasons to support the principles and policies our comprehensive doctrine is said to support. I refer to this requirement as *the proviso*.

So, how is the proviso going to be satisfied? Now here is where you're going to get what you might think is a lot of weaseling, but it is really what I alluded to in mentioning how appellate judges work at their best. Look at page 592:

Obviously, many questions may be raised about how to satisfy the proviso. One is: when does it need to be satisfied? On the same day or some later day? Also, on whom does the obligation to honor it fall? It is important that it be clear and established that the proviso is to be appropriately satisfied in good faith. Yet the details about how to satisfy this proviso must be worked out in practice and cannot feasiblely be governed by a clear family of rules given in advance.

This is Rawls at his best, and many people might say at his least philosophical. For me it is his most philosophical. You cannot do moral philosophy, at any serious level, and certainly you cannot do serious political philosophy, by trying to lay out rules in advance. You have to work out what is implicitly accepted. This is what Hegel saw. He messed it up with his lousy dialectical metaphysics (or metaphysical dialectic), but at least he saw that you have to be *in mediis rebus* and work it through. You cannot do substantial political or moral philosophy in any Cartesian-framed manner or shape of mind whatsoever. That is what Rawls has always seen. That was at the heart of *A Theory of Justice* too. That is the content of what he calls "reflective equilibrium." He continues on page 592:

How they work out is determined by the nature of the public political culture and calls for good sense and understanding. It is important also to observe that the introduction into public political culture of religious and secular doctrines, provided that the proviso is met, does not change the nature and content of justification in public reason itself.

That is, in the end you always have to give answers satisfactory to public reason. No judge qua judge, no legislator qua legislator, no citizen qua citizen can simply say, "Abortion should be legally prohibited because God says it is wrong." Of course any person can do that; the First Amendment guarantees it. You can argue in any way you like in the background culture. But the First Amendment also guarantees that such a reason cannot be the basis of legitimate law. You have to give other reasons as well. Rawls suggests the late Archbishop of Chicago, Joseph Cardinal Bernardin tried to offer such reasons. Look at page 606, footnote 82:

The idea of public order the Cardinal presents includes these three political values: public peace, essential protections of human rights, and the commonly accepted standards of moral behavior in a community of law. Further, he grants that not all moral imperatives are to be translated into prohibitive civil statutes and thinks it essential to the political and social order to protect human life and basic human rights. The denial of the right to abortion he hopes to justify on the basis of those three values. I don't of course assess his argument here, except to say it is clearly cast in some form of public reason. Whether it is itself reasonable or not, or more reasonable than the arguments on the other side, is another mater. As with any form of reasoning in public reason, the reasoning may be fallacious or mistaken.

This is a very important footnote. It makes clear that an argument may satisfy public reason without being either valid or correct, and certainly not compelling. It also makes clear that the requirements of public reason do not (or very rarely) settle by themselves basic social and political questions.

**10th Questioner:** A good citizen, then, must be able and willing to allow public reason to take precedence over what you called the comprehensive.

**Dreben:** On political questions.

**10th Questioner:** Many of these comprehensive doctrines, however, have a definite take on such questions.

**Dreben:** Yes, they do, that is why we have the proviso.

**10th Questioner:** So the question is, how optimistic is Rawls that people are able to allow public reason that sort of precedence?

**Dreben:** That is an interesting question, although not a question in ideal theory, the theory we have been talking about for more than two hours. In answer, all I can say is that Rawls fervently hopes that enough people are able to. Otherwise a constitutional liberal democratic society stable for the right reasons will not exist – even if its conception is logically coherent – since the proviso flows from the criterion of reciprocity, from an essential aspect of what it is for a citizen to be reasonable.

**11th Questioner:** In effect, by reasonable, you mean with the proviso.

**Dreben:** With the proviso, of course. And you should note that there is a difference between how the proviso works in "Public Reason Revisited" (and the Second Introduction) and in the main text of what I am calling the first edition of *Political Liberalism*. Rawls is insisting more and more that nonliberal but reasonable doctrines be expressible in public reason – subject always to the proviso – because of his recognition that as we come to the end of the twentieth century many liberal citizens hold nonliberal comprehensive doctrines.

**11th Questioner:** Could you give an example?

**Dreben:** Yes. A traditional religion (Catholicism, Islam, Judaism, most forms of Protestantism) would, I believe, have to reject the idea of ultimate moral autonomy such as Mill's ideal of individuality or Kant's doctrine of autonomy or Rawls's notion of autonomy in *A Theory of Justice*. Some such idea of autonomy is essential to any liberal comprehensive doctrine. It is a question of ultimate moral authority. But, if the religion is reasonable, it does not reject the idea of "political autonomy, the legal independence and assured integrity of citizens and their sharing equally with others in the exercise of political power."[7]

**12th Questioner:** I have a question about the status of science, or the findings of science. Would that count as a comprehensive doctrine, or would the appeal to the findings of science be allowable in public reason?

**Dreben:** Well it is very clear when Rawls talks about the burdens of judgment that it is part of public reason to use anything that is normally accepted in science. That is common sense. Scientism, however, is a comprehensive doctrine. It might be a secular comprehensive doctrine, but it is still a comprehensive doctrine. But, the fact that you will not get smallpox if you are inoculated permits, in public reason, a judge to order Christian Scientist parents to inoculate their child. It will not permit the judge to order an adult Christian Scientist to take medicine. Unless, of course, the Christian Scientist is carrying a disease that is so dangerous to everyone else that you must at least quarantine him. And this is where public reason comes in. Public reason is common sense, in the best sense of common sense. I mean, you use reason, and you try to keep highfalutin notions to a minimum. There is nothing that is so dangerous to gaining a proper conception of public reason as metaphysics, or Philosophy with a big "P." That is why I said, for me, there is a genuine connection between what I said here five years ago when talking about Frege and Wittgenstein, and now in talking about Rawls.

ENDNOTES

1    An edited version of a talk given to the Philosophy Department at the University of Illinois, Chicago, November 14, 1997. I greatly appreciate the invitation from the Chair and the Department of Philosophy at the University of Illinois at Chicago to give this lecture. They were splendid hosts. I am deeply indebted to Bernard Prusak for the difficult task of transcribing a recording of the original lecture and to Robert Bowditch and Juliet Floyd for urging publication of the transcript. I am even more indebted to Juliet Floyd for editing the transcript to make it worthy of publication. I acknowledge with great pleasure the comments, both critical and supportive, on the edited manuscript, by John Burt, Hillel Chiel, Lynne Cohen, Elizabeth Dreben, William Flesch, Paul Forster, Raya Spiegel Dreben, Samuel Freeman, Warren Goldfarb, Wilbur Hart, Marcia Homiak, Akihiro Kanamori, Anton Kris, Annette Lareau, Andrew Lugg, Hilary Putnam, Ruth Anna Putnam, Laura Quinney, Mard Rawls, Thomas Ricketts, and Sally Sedgwick, as well as the generous support of The Blossom Fund. As the reader will see, I owe an enormous debt to the questioners in Chicago, both at and after the lecture. Finally, obviously, my greatest debt of all is to John Rawls, who has given a compelling vision of liberalism for our time.

2    Rawls has a footnote here in which he says that he has borrowed the term "fact of oppression" from Sanford Shieh.

3    The "Reply to Habermas" first appeared in *The Journal of Philosophy* 92 (March 1995).

4    John Rawls, "The Idea of Public Reason Revisited," in *Collected Papers*, ed. Samuel Freeman (Cambridge, MA: Harvard University Press, 1999) p. 611.

5    See *Collected Papers*, p. 573

6    *Collected Papers*, p. 607.

7    See "Public Reason Revisited," page 586; see also page xliv, *Political Liberalism*.

# 9 Constructivism in Rawls and Kant[1]

## I. THE AMBITIONS OF CONSTRUCTIVISMS IN ETHICS

John Rawls's writings across the last three decades advance the best-known form of Kantian constructivism. During this time his understanding of the terms *constructive* and *Kantian* has changed in various ways, which I shall trace in this chapter and contrast with the form of "Kantian constructivism" which (I argue) can most plausibly be attributed to Kant himself.

The metaphor of *construction* has had a wide use in twentieth-century theoretical and philosophical writing. On a minimal understanding, it is no more than the thought than certain entities are complex, that is, composed out of other more elementary entities. This thought may seem quite neutral about the sorts of things that are elementary and the sorts of things that may be composed out of them. In this very general sense, logical atomism, the procedure of the *Tractatus*, and Carnap's *Aufbau* programme, in which complex statements are constructed from elementary statements of experience, are all forms constructivism. So, too, are many antirealist views of science, theory, and society, which speak, for example, of the social construction of reality (of meaning, of science) or the construction of social identity or the construction of modern France out of more elementary components such as beliefs, attitudes, or interactions.

However, this minimalist understanding of constructivism as ontologically neutral misleads. By and large, the term *constructive* is used by proponents of antirealist views.[2] Realist positions argue that certain facts or properties are features of the world, so need not be based on, or constructed out of, other elements. Of course, realists,

347

too, may think that there are simple and complex facts and properties, but they will not generally be inclined to think of the latter as *constructions* because this would suggest that they are constructed by some agent or agency, a thought which realists reject. However, there is plenty of confusion in the use of the terms *constructive*, *constructivist*, *constructionist*, and their cognates in particular because some antirealist writing on science and society speaks of *facts* as constructed, thus appropriating one of the central terms of realist thought for their own purposes.[3]

Ethical constructivists share the antirealism of many other constructivist claims and positions. Unlike moral realists, they doubt or deny that there are distinctively moral facts or properties, whether natural or nonnatural, which can be *discovered* or *intuited* and will provide foundations for ethics. John Rawls put the point succinctly in 1989 in "Themes in Kant's Moral Philosophy" where he denied that ethical "first principles, as statements about good reasons, are regarded as true or false in virtue of a moral order of values that is prior to and independent of our conceptions of person and society and of the public and social role of moral doctrines."[4] If there were an independent moral order of values, and it could be known, moral realism could be established and constructive approaches to ethics would be redundant.

Antirealism comes in many forms in ethical and political theory, and much of it is not constructivist. Constructivisms are distinctive among antirealist ethical positions, not only in claiming that ethical principles or claims may be seen as the *constructions of human agents* but in two further respects. They also claim that constructive ethical reasoning can be *practical* – it can establish practical prescriptions or recommendations which can be used to guide action – and that it can *justify* those prescriptions or recommendations: objectivity in ethics is not illusory. Ethical constructivists reject not only those nonrealist positions which give up on the entire project of justification (e.g., emotivism) but also those which deploy severely restricted conceptions of justification which are too weak to support strong claims about objectivity in ethics (e.g., relativism, communitarianism, social constructionism applied to ethical beliefs).

Constructivist approaches to ethics are therefore distinctive and ambitious. They hold that, although realist underpinnings are unobtainable, (some) objective, action-guiding ethical prescriptions can be justified. The challenge is to see whether and how this combination of ambitions can be sustained.

## II. THE EVOLUTION OF RAWLS'S CONSTRUCTIVISM

Rawls has consistently advocated a particular constructive procedure, the original position (OP), as the way to justify principles of justice. However, as his work developed he has changed his views of the range of ethical principles that can be constructed, of the justification of OP itself, and of the audiences who can be given reasons to accept OP. Broadly speaking, he has taken an increasingly refined and restricted view of all three. In his earlier work, and in particular in *A Theory of Justice*,[5] Rawls hoped that it might prove possible to justify not only OP, and thereby principles of justice, but also other ethical principles; he offered a coherentist justification of OP, claiming that the principles of justice it endorses are in reflective equilibrium with 'our' considered judgements; and he views this approach as providing reasons for action for a loosely specified 'us', perhaps for anybody. In *Political Liberalism*[6] Rawls qualifies all three claims: he takes a narrower view of the range of claims that can be justified, makes more limited claims about the sharing of justifications, and takes a narrower view about the range of agents who can reason about justice. In the first place, while he still maintains that the constructive procedure of OP can be used to identify principles of justice, he concludes that other moral principles cannot be given a justification that is accessible to all.[7] There can be, and in free societies there will be, a plurality of reasonable comprehensive moral views. Secondly, he holds that the *fundamental justifications* for OP, and thereby for principles and institutions of justice, can be offered by individuals with varying comprehensive moral views and may vary widely: OP is seen as the object of a contingent, overlapping consensus among those with varying fundamental views which do not guarantee any convergence on reasons for affirming those views.[8] Thirdly, Rawls claims that a total lack of shared reasons for accepting OP would undermine political life but that citizens in democratic polities can rely on a more limited range of shared justificatory strategies, which are *political* rather than fundamental. Justice as fairness, he argues in his later work, should be seen as a 'free-standing' conception, which is in reflective equilibrium not only with various comprehensive moral views but with the central ideas within a public democratic culture within which a form of *public reason* may be shared by (and possibly only by) fellow citizens. This conception of public reason provides the common coin used in arguments about justice among fellow citizens, but it provides no universal currency: "Those who reject constitutional democracy ... will of course reject the very idea of public reason."[9]

Although his views changed in these ways, Rawls has at all times maintained not only the view that principles of justice can be constructed but a broadly Kantian view both of substantive political norms and of their justification. His Kantianism amounts to far more than acceptance of a liberal account of justice or rejection of consequentialist ethics. As the title of one of his major works indicates, what he has sought has always been a specifically *Kantian* form of constructivism.[10] A closer look at the stages through which his Kantian constructivism – perhaps Kantian constructivisms – developed is instructive.

In *A Theory of Justice*, Rawls does not speak of constructivism but more broadly of a procedure for agents to identify principles of justice which provide "constructive criteria," that is to say, procedures, for settling moral problems.[11] Here the emphasis is on the *practicality* of a theory that provides constructive criteria or procedures. Rawls contrasts his position with forms of 'intuitionism', which he characterises as impractical because they provide only a plurality of unranked principles and hence no constructive procedures for agents to resolve moral problems. This initial broad conception of ethical construction classifies both Utilitarianism and Rawls's own more Kantian views as constructive: both are contrasted with procedures in ethics which offer no constructive criteria and so are not, or not reliably, practical. Many non-Kantian writers, for example David Gauthier, rightly view their own work as aiming at constructive criteria in this sense even though their approach is in no way Kantian.[12] They are constructivists, but not Kantian constructivists.

By contrast Rawls has always seen his own approach as Kantian as well as constructive. Although in *A Theory of Justice* he describes his specific form of constructivism not as *Kantian* but as *contractarian*, he claims there too that his work is to carry "to a higher level of abstraction the familiar theory of the social contract as found in Locke, Rousseau and Kant."[13] The level of abstraction is presumably higher because OP is a constructive procedure which conceives of the parties who construct principles of justice under particularly abstract descriptions, namely, as lacking all knowledge of their own distinguishing social features.[14]

However, it is far from clear whether the fundamental strategy of justification of *A Theory of Justice* is Kantian. Although Rawls is like Kant in appealing neither to individual preferences nor to a notional hypothetical agreement or social contract, nor to an independent order of moral values, he is unlike Kant in appealing to a conception of *reflective equilibrium* (*TJ*, pp. 20ff.) to justify OP. He characterises OP as a "procedure," a "thought experiment," a "device of representation," and a "model conception"[15] which must be justified by reference to reflective equilibrium between the principles of justice OP generates and "our considered judgements." This approach to justification is *coherentist*:[16] it relies on a certain conception of the *reasonable* (as opposed to the merely, instrumentally rational) – a conception Rawls reworks and develops in the account of public reason in his later work.

In his 1980 *Kantian Constructivism in Moral Theory* Rawls gave the term 'constructivism' a more prominent use. He "specifies a particular conception of the person as an element in a reasonable procedure of construction" (*KC*, p. 304). "Agents of construction" are seen as "free and equal moral persons" who think of themselves as "citizens living a complete life in an ongoing society" (*KC*, pp. 304–5), which constitutes a closed and bounded system (*KC*, p. 323): they draw on "the public culture of a democratic society" (*KC*, p. 306) to argue for principles of justice. Stripped to its essentials, Rawls here maintains that

Kantian constructivism holds that moral objectivity is to be understood in terms of a suitably constructed social point of view that all can accept. Apart from the procedure of constructing the principles of justice, there are no moral facts. (*KC*, p. 307)

In *Kantian Constructivism* Rawls sees Kant's work as closely cognate and deplores the failure of earlier writers to see that Kant offered a constructive rather than a minimally formalist approach to ethics.[17] However, here and elsewhere, he recognises that his constructivism is Kantian but that it is not Kant's. The main difference in method, as Rawls sees it in *Kantian Constructivism*, is that his position assigns "primacy to the social" and specifically that it is designed for citizens, whereas Kant's "account of the Categorical Imperative applies to the personal maxims of sincere and conscientious persons in everyday life" (KC, p. 339)[18]: the OP procedure is quite distinct from the more individualist Categorical Imperative (CI) procedure.

Rawls sees this difference in method as explaining why he and Kant reach different ranges of substantive ethical claims. While Kant hoped to provide a quite general method for addressing ethical issues, including questions of justice, Rawls came to the conclusion that his Kantian constructivism could build an account only of justice: we can construct a reasoned account of the right, but not of the good; of justice, but not of virtue:

Justice as fairness, as a constructivist view, holds that not all the moral questions we are prompted to ask in everyday life have answers. (KC, p. 350)

This emphasis on the limits of his constructivism became even more prominent in Rawls's later writings, where he frequently insists that, since we cannot give a reasoned account of the good, we are bound to be neutral between competing "conceptions of the good" unless they conflict with justice. Constructivism does not provide a comprehensive moral theory, nor do constructive arguments reach all possible audiences: they are based on the shared conceptions of citizens, so provide reasons for action only for those whose most basic commitments they presuppose.

The limits of Rawls's later constructivism are most clearly etched in *Political Liberalism*, whose aim is specifically to "bring out the bases of the principles of right and justice in practical reason" (PL, p. xxx). The conception of practical reason or reasonableness which Rawls advances here is specifically a conception of public reason:

Persons are reasonable when ... they are ready to propose principles and standards as fair terms of co-operation and to abide by them willingly, given the assurance that others will likewise do so. (PL, p. 49)

The others who may share a commitment to "govern their conduct by a principle from which they and others can reason in common" (PL, 49n) are once again envisaged as fellow citizens – specifically as fellow citizens of a democratic society:

[P]ublic reason is characteristic of a democratic people: it is the reason of its citizens, of those sharing the status of equal citizenship... [it is] public in three ways: as the reason of citizens as such, it is the reason of the public; its subject is the good of the public and matters of fundamental justice; and its nature and content is public... (*PL*, p. 213; cf. *PRR*, Part 1)

Fellow citizens are thought of as sharing a bounded and closed society with basic political institutions, including a democratic constitution: democracy and the bounded states in which democracy may exist are evidently presupposed rather than justified in Rawls's theory of justice.

In Rawls's work after 1985, primacy is given not merely to a social (as opposed to an individual) view of reason but very specifically to a political view.[19] He distinguishes his conception of reasonableness from communitarian views, which may count shared social norms as reasons. Since he takes pluralism seriously, he does not assume that social norms will be shared by all fellow citizens, or could provide reasons for action for all. Yet Rawls, too, sees justification between fellow citizens as presupposing a lesser, more political and procedural range of consensus:

[J]ustification is addressed to others who disagree with us, and therefore it must always proceed from some consensus, from premises we and others publicly recognize as true. (*JFPM*, p. 394; cf. *OC*, p. 426)

The form of constructivism that Rawls reached by the time he wrote *Political Liberalism* was deeply political in its focus on justice to the exclusion of other ethical issues, in the role assigned to public reason in justifying principles of justice, and in its insistence that such justification is internal to a bounded society (plausibly, a state) rather than universal or cosmopolitan. Such justification does not address others who are not fellow citizens, who are excluded from or marginalised within a polity, or who do not accept democracy and its constraints. In many ways its resonance is more Rousseauian than Kantian, more civic than cosmopolitan.

## III. RAWLS'S ACCOUNT OF KANT'S CONSTRUCTIVISM

The deepest questions that can be raised about each version of Rawls's constructivism are about the conceptions of reasonableness invoked. Constructive procedures for establishing principles of justice cannot build ethical conclusions from nothing: they aim to build them by justifiable procedures which "agents of construction" can follow. We may quite reasonably ask why we should take "reflective equilibrium with our considered judgements," or "a suitably constructed social point of view that all can accept," or "the public reason of citizens in a democratic society" as constitutive of reasonableness. There are other possibilities, including the form of Kantian constructivism, which Kant himself proposes.

Although much of Rawls's work is quite un-Kantian,[20] his characterisation of his method for establishing principles of justice and of his conclusions as both Kantian and constructivist makes good sense. Yet, as he notes, many commentators have not thought that Kant's method of establishing ethical principles is constructive at all. Some have thought that Kant, despite his disavowals, peddles one more form of rational intuitionism and is a covert moral realist; others, that he offers only a minimal formalism. If those who see moral realism in Kant were right, he and Rawls would share little. If those who see minimal formalism in Kant are right, Rawls's Kantianism would amount to their shared antirealism, their common aspiration to nonrelativist justification in ethics, and their shared liberal views about justice but would not extend to a common ambition to construct a range of ethical conclusions.

Nevertheless, there are good reasons for agreeing with Rawls that Kant's method in ethics is constructive. A background consideration is that Kant combines antirealism with claims to identify objective moral principles: a constructive approach would fit his wider philosophy well. More specifically, there are many junctures at which Kant appeals explicitly to constructive procedures, including his accounts of the justification of theoretical reason and of mathematical reasoning.[21] Finally, and for present purposes most significantly, there are reasons to think that Kant's conception of ethical justification is more radically constructive than the one that Rawls proposes.

Kant's method in ethics clearly resembles Rawls's method in several negative respects. Like Rawls, Kant proposes procedure(s) for justifying ethically important principles of action by appeal to a conception of practical reasoning that does not build on supposed independent moral facts or on actual individual preferences. The procedure(s) envisaged – stated in the various CI formulations – are contrasted with the procedures adopted by proponents of heteronomy in ethics who either support perfectionism by invoking the (illusory) independent values of moral realism or advocate positions such as subjectivism, utilitarianism, or preference-based forms of contractarianism by invoking the (unvindicated) value of satisfying preferences.

Kant's commitment to these negative points is easily established. The best-known version of his procedure of construction, the CI, is the formula of universal law,[22] which enjoins agents to "act only in accordance with that maxim through which you can at the same time will that it become a universal law": agents should reject principles of action which (they take it) cannot be adopted by all.[23] There is no reference here, or in Kant's underlying theory of action, either to any given moral reality or to desires or preferences.

Still, negative points are not enough to show that Kant, too, takes a constructive approach to ethics. Kant can be read as an ethical constructivist only by showing that (despite rejecting rational intuitionism) he proposes a method agents can use to identify specific principles with practical implications and that he justifies this method.

For present purposes I shall take it that the CI procedure(s) have practical implications and can identify at least some ethical principles, for example (but perhaps not only) basic principles of justice.[24] The more demanding question is whether they can themselves be justified without reintroducing some form of moral realism by the back door. Kant evidently takes it that his constructive procedure for ethics is not arbitrary and that it constitutes the weightier aspect of practical reason, or reasonableness. Just as Rawls insists that the rational and the reasonable are both relevant to justifying principles of justice, but that they are distinct, so Kant insists that the principles of the hypothetical and categorical imperatives are both relevant to justifying ethical principles and that they are mutually irreducible.

Yet it is not easy to see why Kant thinks the CI procedures constitute requirements of practical reason or reasonableness. It may be that Kant and Rawls may end up with parallel difficulties, that both propose a constructive procedure for identifying specific practical principles, but both fail to show convincingly that this procedure is grounded in or expresses (an adequate conception of) reasonableness. Their positions may be constructive in the limited sense that they propose procedures which agents can use to establish principles for guiding action but not in the fuller sense of justifying those

procedures and grounding objective normative judgements. If so, neither Rawls nor Kant will justify ethical claims in the stronger sense
to which constructivists aspire.

However, Kant does more than invoke an ungrounded "supreme
principle of practical reason." He holds that an account of practical
reason itself should be susceptible of justification: that ambition is
implicit in the very titles of his major works. Critiques of pure and
of practical reason are critiques not merely of the deployment of
antecedently given uncritically accepted conceptions of reason but
of those conceptions of reason. If Kant can do this, he may offer not a
merely conditional but a deep vindication of ethical principles based
on vindicating a conception of practical reason. If in addition his
vindication of reason were constructive, his constructivism would
be not only deep but also radical.

Rawls explicitly denies this possibility. He holds that Kant does
not and cannot offer a constructive justification for his conception
of practical reason. In *Themes in Kant's Moral Philosophy* he poses
and answers two questions:

First, in moral constructivism, what is it that is constructed? The answer is:
the content of the doctrine ... A second question is this. Is the CI-procedure
itself constructed? No, it is not. Rather, it is simply laid out ... not everything
can be constructed and every construction has a basis, certain materials, as
it were, from which it begins. (*TKMP*, pp. 513–14)[25]

On Rawls's view these materials include Kant's conception of free
and equal persons as rational and reasonable, which is "elicited from
our moral experience" (*TKMP*, p. 514). Ethical reasoning builds on
the basis of these elicited conceptions; practical reason itself is not
justified by any constructive procedure.

In the following section of *Themes in Kant's Moral Philosophy*
Rawls argues that Kant's conception of practical reason is grounded
in his difficult doctrine of the fact of reason, as set out in the *Critique
of Practical Reason*. A quite common view of Kant's discussion of
the fact of reason is that it is to provide the bedrock for all moral
reasoning: practical reason, and thereby the CI procedure(s),[26] are
simply given to human consciousness and hence are not themselves
constructed. This reading suggests that (despite himself) Kant fell
and back on some form of rational intuitionism and even on (moral)
realism.

However, Rawls does not construe Kant's doctrine of the fact of reason as an attempt to offer an unalterable datum (bedrock foundation) for justification in ethics. Although 'the supreme principle of practical reason', alias 'the moral law', alias 'the categorical imperative', cannot be given any deduction, although it cannot be derived from theoretical reason,[27] although it is not a regulative idea (*TKMP*, pp. 521–3), it can be authenticated as the principle needed for "completing the constitution of reason as one unified body of principles" (*TKPM*, p. 523). On Rawls's reading, the second *Critique* confirms that reason is "self-authenticating as a whole" by offering "not only a constructivist conception of practical reason but a coherentist account of its authentication" (*TKPM*, p. 523).

The distinction which Rawls draws here between Kant's constructive use of the CI to establish ethical principles and the merely coherentist justification of CI itself parallels his own strategy in *Theory of Justice*, where the principles of justice are constructed using OP, but OP itself receives only a coherentist justification.[28]

## IV. KANT ON THE CONSTRUCTION OF REASON

Yet when we look at Kant's writing on the vindication of reason, it can seem very natural to read him not merely as arguing that the categorical imperative, the supreme principle of practical reason, coheres with other aspects of his conception of reason but more specifically that it can itself be constructively justified. Towards the end of the *Critique of Pure Reason*, in the initial passages of the *Doctrine of Method*, Kant depicts the edifice of human reason as doomed to failure without a vindication of reason. Although 'materials' in plenty have been assembled in the previous 700 pages of the *Critique of Pure Reason*, the whole project will fail, like that of the uncoordinated builders of Babel, if we cannot find a common plan of reason.[29]

However, there is no independent order of reason which lays down a common plan or procedure that constitutes the principle(s) of practical reasoning: "reason has no dictatorial authority."[30] Since reason is not provided from 'on high', we will either dispose of no more than rationality, or must show how a conception of reasonableness can be constructed out of the capacities and materials which human agents actually have at their disposal. Yet if there is no antecedently given 'plan of reason', no independent, external authority, why should any way of proceeding count as more reasoned than any other? Why should agents who do not enjoy the benefit of a pre-established harmony that orients them to an independently given canon of reason view *any* way(s) of proceeding as requirements of reason, as having an unrestricted authority for organising thinking and doing?

As Kant depicts the matter, the very predicament of a plurality of uncoordinated agents is all we can presuppose in trying to identify principles of practical reason: it is because reason's authority is *not* given that it must be instituted or constituted – constructed – by human agents. Consider the predicament of uncoordinated agents more closely. They cannot take any particular faith or belief, tradition or norm, claim or proposition, in short any arbitrary premise, as having the sort of unrestricted authority which would entitle them to view it as a principle of reason. Yet they need, if they are to organise their thinking and doing together, to find – to construct – some common authority. If they cannot, they will not be in the business of giving and receiving, exchanging and evaluating each other's claims about knowledge and action. How are they to do this? Since all that they have in common is their lack of a given 'plan of reason', all that they can do to is refuse to treat any of the various faiths and beliefs, traditions and norms, claims and propositions they variously adhere to as having an unrestricted authority for organising thinking and doing. However, those who do not regard any specific faith or beliefs, tradition or norms, claims or propositions as having an unrestricted authority for organising thinking and doing in effect adopt the overarching principle of thinking and acting only on principles which they regard as open to, and followable by, all.[31]

This limited discipline of rejecting ways of thinking and acting that cannot be followed by differing others is surprisingly constraining. If thoughts and knowledge claims are to be seen as reasoned, they must at least be followable in thought by others who hold differing views: they must be intelligible to those others. If principles of action are to be offered as reasons for action to others with differing ethical and religious commitments, they must at least be principles that could be adopted by those others and used to organise their action. Agents who accept the 'supreme principle of practical reason' accept that they should adopt basic principles which, they take it, can also be adopted by others who may differ: in short they must accept the principle expressed in the formula of universal law formulation of the CI.

These considerations suggest why we should view the CI as stating a fundamental requirement of practical reason. They have various corollaries. If the discipline of reason requires the rejection of principles which (we take it) not all others can understand or adopt, or view as providing reasons, then any reasonable procedures must be in principle followable by all without restriction. Reason cannot therefore be anchored either in the norms of communities (as communitarians suppose) or in the overlapping consensus of citizens of an ethically diverse polity (as Rawls supposes): it must be accessible in principle even to others with differing norms and differing citizenship: to 'outsiders'. 'Outsiders' would legitimately view any claim that principles of reason are to be identified with the specific beliefs or norms of groups from which they are excluded as fetishising some arbitrary claim (Kant uses the metaphor of an 'alien authority'). Ways of organising thinking and acting that appeal to such spurious 'authorities' – whether the edicts of Church or State, of public opinion or local powers, or the public culture of a particular democratic society – are not ways of reasoning: they are simply arbitrary for foreigners, dissidents, the excluded, and other outsiders. By contrast, where all such 'authorities' are put in question, nobody will be told that some claim that they cannot but view as arbitrary constitutes a reason for them to believe or act.

In a world of differing beings, reasoning is not complete, or we may say (and Kant said) not completely public when it rests on appeals to properties and beliefs, attitudes and desires, norms and commitments which are simply arbitrary from some points of view. In some contexts incompletely reasoned, hence partly arbitrary, stretches of thought are enough to the purposes at hand – but not always. When we seek deep justification that reaches others who are not already like-minded, we can be satisfied only with claims about what to believe and what to do which (we responsibly judge) can be followed by those others. The only strategy that can count as a reason for all is that of rejecting all arbitrary assumptions however respectable, well-trusted, or widely accepted they or their proponents may be.

Organising thought and action on principles that can be followed in thought or adopted in action by differing others may seem a minimal demand and less than the presumptively weighty authority of reason should amount to. Can the universal accessibility of claims about what to think and what to do be *all* that is basic to reasoning? Will this conception of practical reason yield any significant conclusions? Will Kant's constructivist account of reason provide an adequate constructive procedure for ethics (or even for justice)?

These are large questions about the construction of ethics on the basis of Kant's conception of practical reason, which lie rather beyond the scope of this chapter. However, even without complete answers to them, some corollaries of Kant's distinctive construction of practical reason (as opposed to his construction of principles for ethics and politics) can be considered. I list only a few.

1. Kant's vindication of practical reason reveals why he came to view universalisability as 'the supreme principle of practical reason', and why he speaks of it as 'the moral law'. Strikingly his account of practical reason neither claims that there is an 'independent moral order of values' nor presupposes without reason the acceptability of specific social or political structures.

2. His vindication of practical reason is decisively different from the conceptions of reasonableness that Rawls has put forward. In the later versions of his theory of justice, Rawls depicts a conception of democratic citizenship within a bounded society as the source and context of reasoning about justice. By contrast, Kant (although he uses terms such as 'citizenship' and 'public' metaphorically) deploys a conception of practical reason which does not presuppose that those who reason about justice and politics must be linked by common citizenship in a 'bounded society' with a democratic constitution. Kant consequently views state boundaries and the system of states, the exclusions and inclusions which define citizenship in those states, as well as the nature of a just constitution, as problems for justice rather than as presuppositions of justice. As he sees it, basic political institutions do not confer but rather need justification: to invoke them in its absence is to appeal to spurious authorities.[32]

3. In rejecting not only justifications that appeal to shared norms, but those that appeal to shared citizenship, Kant embarks on a construction of justice whose broadest vision is of a cosmopolitan order within which states are to be justified. By contrast, Rawls, who views bounded societies[33] as in part constitutive of reason, must treat international justice as an appendix to domestic justice.

4. The difference between the two conceptions of reasonableness explains why Rawls's fundamentally civic constructivism, while allowing for ethical pluralism within a society, is directed solely

at an account of justice, while Kant's constructivism, which pre-supposes *plurality* but not shared citizenship, can aim at a fuller range of ethical justification (whether it can achieve this is a further matter).

## V. SOME CONCLUSIONS

In this chapter I have said rather little about the practicality either of Rawls's or of Kant's constructivism. Further arguments – there have been plenty – are needed to show the full normative implications of either position. I have concentrated on the question of whether, if practical reason lacks an external or transcendent source, it must reduce either to rationality, or to a contextualised conception of the reasonable that builds on accepted norms or beliefs, powers or institutions. The Kantian constructivisms proposed by Rawls and by Kant himself are highly distinctive in accepting the challenge of showing that ethical justification is possible without presupposing antecedent agreement on specific social norms.

Both go beyond conceptions of justification as anchored in mere rationality or in community norms; both regard such approaches as reaching normative implications only by according value without good reason – whether to actual preferences or to historically contingent configurations of norms and institutions. Both regard such approaches as able to provide no more than incomplete reasons for correspondingly diminished audiences. Yet, despite these similarities, Kant and Rawls have very different conceptions of the reasonable and so of the scope and limits of Kantian constructivism.

The fundamental differences between them lie in their diverging views about the sources, the authority, and ultimately the audiences for practical reasoning. Rawls sees Kant's procedure as "too individualist" because (he claims) it invokes the idea of a domain of individual agents, each of whom reasons on his or her own. This point may or may not be apt if we are considering a use of the CI procedures to test some ethical principle of particular relevance to personal life. But it is inaccurate as a claim about Kant's conception of practical reason. Like Rawls, Kant presupposes a plurality of agents who are coordinated neither by a pre-established harmony nor by the contingencies of shared ideology and norms: but unlike Rawls he also does not assume that they are fellow citizens.

Constructivism for Kant, as for Rawls, begins with the thought that a plurality of diverse beings lacking antecedent coordination or knowledge of an independent order of moral values must construct ethical principles by which they are to live. But Kant takes a more radical view of this lack of coordination: he does not presuppose any determinate social or political structures, not even the nexus of fellow citizens within a bounded, democratic society. Kant's constructivism therefore begins with weaker assumptions than Rawls relies on; it begins simply with the thought that a plurality of agents lacks antecedent principles of coordination, and aims to build an account of reason, of ethics, and specifically of justice on this basis. He thinks of human beings as doers before they become reasoners or citizens.

Although there are many points to be made about what Rawls and others have deemed Kant's individualism in ethics, it is clear that Kant's conception of the construction of reason rests on the view that there are many agents who differ in many ways. The formula of universal law proposes as the test of ethical adequacy simply that agents adopt principles which (they take it) could be adopted by, willed by, all others. It is, as Kant puts it, a conception of the reasonable which addresses "the public in the strict sense, that is, the world,"[34] rather than the restricted public of a particular society or state. Kant's public is not the Rawlsian public, consisting only of fellow citizens in a bounded, liberal democratic society: it is unrestricted. Hence, Kant's conception of ethical method takes a cosmopolitan[35] rather than an implicitly statist[36] view of the scope of ethical concern; correspondingly, he takes a more demanding view of the construction of ethical principles in that he conceives of justification as aiming to reach all others without restriction.

These issues are the key to the different conceptions of the reasonable to be found in Rawls and in Kant and so to the differences between their versions of Kantian constructivism. Rawls, by the time that he wrote *Political Liberalism*, identified the reasonable with the public reason of fellow citizens in a given, bounded, democratic society. Kant was committed to establishing a conception of reasonableness or practical reason (which he too speaks of as *public reason*) that would hold for any plurality of interacting beings. It is this difference that leaves room for Kant, unlike Rawls, to commit himself to a deeply constructive account not only of justice, and more broadly of ethics, but more radically of practical reason itself.

ENDNOTES

1 Earlier versions of this essay were delivered at conferences during 1997 in Riverside, California, and in Munich; I am grateful for pertinent and helpful comments on both occasions and to Samuel Freeman and Catriona MacKinnon for further perceptive suggestions.

2 For discussion of links between antirealism and ethical constructivism, see David O. Brink, *Moral Realism and the Foundations of Ethics* (Cambridge, UK: Cambridge University Press, 1989); Ronald Milo, "Contractarian Constructivism," *Journal of Philosophy* 122 (1995): 181–204; Larry Krasnoff, "How Kantian is Constructivism?," *Kant-Studien* 90 (1999): 385–409.

3 The appropriation is etymologically sound: *facts* are originally *facta* – *done* or *made* by agents rather than *given* to them, as *data* are. Nevertheless the appropriation confuses in that a realist understanding of facts as *given*, *there*, or (as we say) brute – hence not constructed – is now long established. Moreover, social constructionists sometimes slide between the plausible thought that concepts may be (socially) constructed and the controversial thought that truths whose assertion deploys those concepts are all also constructed. Realists, too, can view some concepts as socially constructed.

4 John Rawls, "Themes in Kant's Moral Philosophy" (*TKMP*, 1989), in John Rawls, *Collected Papers*, Samuel Freeman, ed. (Cambridge, MA: Harvard University Press, 1999), pp. 497–528, 511.

5 John Rawls, *A Theory of Justice* (*TJ*) (Cambridge, MA: Harvard University Press, 1971, revised edition 1999).

6 John Rawls, *Political Liberalism* (*PL*) (New York: Columbia University Press, 1993).

7 Rawls's first major arguments against comprehensive moral justification date back to "Kantian Constructivism in Moral Theory" (*KC*, 1980), in Rawls, *Collected Papers*, 303–58.

8 See the post-1980 papers in the *Collected Papers* – in particular "The Idea of an Overlapping Consensus" (*OC*, 1987), 421–48 and "The Domain of the Political and Overlapping Consensus" (*DPOC*, 1989), 473–96 as well as John Rawls's "Reply to Habermas," *Journal of Philosophy*, XCII (1995): 132–79, esp. 143 (also in *PL*, Lecture IX, pbk. ed.).

9 "The Idea of Public Reason Revisited" (*PRR*, 1997) in *Collected Papers*, 573–615, 574. In fact it is not only those who reject democracy but those

who are not citizens of constitutional democracies for whom Rawlsian public reason is inaccessible. The progressive 'politicisation' of Rawls's account of the justification of principles of justice can be traced best in *Political Liberalism*. See also Norman Daniels, "Reflective Equilibrium and Justice as Political" in his *Justice and Justification* (Cambridge, UK: Cambridge University Press, 1996), pp. 144–75.

10    However, it was only midway in his work that Rawls began to use the explicit phrase *Kantian constructivism* – above all in "Kantian Constructivism in Moral Theory" itself.

11    *TJ*, pp. 34/30 rev., 39–40/35–36 rev., 49/43 rev., 52/46 rev.

12    David Gauthier, *Morals by Agreement* (Oxford, UK: Oxford University Press, 1989) views morality as constructed out of rational bargaining or agreement that presupposes the value of satisfying antecedent individual preferences. See also his "Political Contractarianism," *The Journal of Political Philosophy* 2 (1997): 132–48, in which he explicitly labels his own position *constructivist*. In *Morals by Agreement* p. 4, Gauthier attributes a closely similar conception of constructive ethics to Rawls, citing a passage from *TJ*, p. 16/15 rev. in which Rawls claims that the theory of justice is "a part, perhaps the most significant part, of the theory of rational choice." However, in *PL* Rawls explicitly rejects his earlier formulation, pp. 52–3, stating that he no longer holds that the reasonable can be derived from the rational and that his theory of justice is not constructed out of agreement based on individual preferences, pp. 82ff. The gap between Kantian and some non-Kantian forms of constructivism is wide: Rawls contrasts his view with the "Hobbesian liberalism" to be found in the work of Gauthier and others; *OC*, p. 422, n.

13    John Rawls, *TJ*, p. 11/10 rev.

14    Strictly speaking, Rawls's strategy depends not just on *abstract* but on *idealised* conceptions of persons, motivation, and societies: this creates various problems. See Onora O'Neill "Constructivisms in Ethics" in *Constructions of Reason: Explorations of Kant's Practical Philosophy* (Cambridge, UK: Cambridge University Press, 1989), pp. 206–18 and "The Method of *A Theory of Justice*," in Otfried Höffe, ed., *John Rawls: Eine Theorie der Gerechtigkeit* (Berlin: Akademie Verlag, 1998).

15    In *KC*, Rawls labels the original position a *model conception* (308–9); in "Justice as Fairness: Political not Metaphysical" (*JFPM*, 1985), John Rawls, *Collected Papers*, pp. 388–420, he speaks of it as a *device of representation* (402 ff.) (a term also introduced in *KC*, p. 321). Both terms serve to deflect misreadings that treat the original position as Rawls's fundamental justificatory strategy – a reading he would regard as non-Kantian.

16 In appealing to "our considered judgements" Rawls does not smuggle in reliance on any epistemologically privileged way of knowing (a move he criticises in rational intuitionists). He simply takes it that we have pretheoretical moral beliefs and sentiments. See James Griffin *Value Judgement: Improving Our Ethical Beliefs* (Oxford, UK: Oxford University Press, 1996), Chap. 1, for a clear discussion of appeals to intuition by those who are not intuitionists.

17 According to Rawls, Sidgwick and Bradley both mistakenly read Kant's ethics as minimal formalism, while G.E. Moore and W.D. Ross overlook interesting Kantian possibilities because their rational intuitionism, which Kant would have viewed as (perfectionist) heteronomy, claimed knowledge of independent moral truths (*KC*, pp. 341–5, *TKMP*, pp. 510ff.).

18 The difference Rawls notes is explicitly based on contrasting his position with Kant's *Groundwork* rather than with Kant's later writings on justice. There is much more to be said on the respects in which Kant's position is and is not fundamentally individualist.

19 He comments in *JFPM* that he would have done better to title the Dewey lectures not "Kantian Constructivism in Moral Theory" but "Kantian Constructivism in Political Philosophy," *Collected Papers* n. 2, pp. 388–9.

20 For example, his conception of practical reason, his separation of the justification of principles of justice from the justification of other moral principles, his emphasis on political as opposed to wider forms of justification, his assumption that an account of justice may legitimately begin by taking for granted a "bounded society." See Katrin Flickshuh, *Kant and Modern Moral Philosophy* (Cambridge, UK: Cambridge University Press, 2000).

21 For constructivist claims about the vindication of reason and mathematics, see in particular the earlier part of the *Doctrine of Method* in Immanuel Kant, *Critique of Pure Reason*, tr. Paul Guyer and Allen Wood (Cambridge, UK: Cambridge University Press, 1998), pp. A707/B735 onwards.

22 Immanuel Kant, *Groundwork of the Metaphysics of Morals*, tr. Mary J. Gregor, in *Kant's Practical Philosophy* (Cambridge, UK: Cambridge University Press, 1996), 4: 421 (Prussian Academy pagination included in the margins of the translation). I do not mean to suggest that one rather than another formulation of the categorical imperative is favoured by a constructive reading of Kant. The entire picture offered in this chapter could be developed using any of the formulations as illustrative. For a constructivist approach to the formula of the end in itself, see Thomas E. Hill, Jr., "Kantian Constructivism in Ethics," *Ethics* 99 (1989):

752–70, also in his *Dignity and Practical Reason* (Ithaca, NY: Cornell University Press, 1992), pp. 226–50.

23   What this tells us is rather less than some of Kant's critics assume and less critical admirers hope. Kant is concerned with principles that cannot be adopted by all. If his procedure had been to rule out principles that cannot be acted on by all (successfully, at a given time), the critics who have perennially pointed out how implausible such an account of ethics would be would have a highly damaging criticism of Kant.

24   For discussion of the practicality of CI, see Onora O'Neill, *Constructions of Reason*, Part II.

25   Compare Rawls's comment on the limits of his own constructivism: "The conceptions of society and person as ideas of reason are not, certainly, constructed any more than the principles of practical reason are constructed," *PL*, p. 108.

26   I leave open whether the various formulations of the categorical imperative are equivalent or not. My own view is that they are equivalent under a plausible reading; see Onora O'Neill "Universal Laws and Ends in Themselves," in *Constructions of Reason*, pp. 126–44. Thomas E. Hill, Jr., argues otherwise; see his "Humanity as an End in Itself," in his *Dignity and Practical Reason*, pp. 38–57.

27   A strategy whose possibility Kant explored thoroughly before he rejected it. See Dieter Henrich, "Der Begriff der sittlichen Einsicht und Kants Lehre vom Faktum der Vernunft," in G. Prauss, ed., *Kant. Zur Deuting seiner Theorie von Erkennen und Handeln* (Cologne: Kiepenheuer & Witsch, 1973), pp. 107–10.

28   For arguments that, on the contrary, the Fact of Reason itself is constructed, see Pawel Łukow, "The Fact of Reason: Kant's Passage to Ordinary Moral Knowledge," *Kant-studien* 84 (1993): 204–21; Onora O'Neill, "Autonomy and the Fact of Reason in the *Kritik der praktischen Vernunft*," in Otfried Hoeffe, ed., *Immanuel Kant: Kritik der praktischen Vernunft* (Berlin: Akademic Verlag, 2002), pp. 30–41 see also note 25.

29   In this long and suggestive passage Kant writes:

> ...it can be said that in the *Transcendental Doctrine of Elements* we have made an estimate of the materials, and have determined for what sort, height and strength of building they will suffice. Although we had in mind a tower that would reach the heavens, it turned out that the stock of materials was only enough for a house [Wohnhaus] – one just roomy enough for our tasks on the plain of experience and just high enough for us to look across the plain. The bold undertaking had to come to nothing for lack of materials, let alone the babel of tongues that unavoidably set workers against one another and scattered them across the earth, each to build separately following his own design. Our problem is not just to do with materials, but even more to do with plan, since we have

been warned not to risk everything on a favourite but senseless project, which could perhaps exceed our entire resources. Yet we need to erect a solid house, so must build taking due account of the supplies that we have been given and of our needs. Immanuel Kant, *Critique of Pure Reason* (*CPR*), pp. A707/B735 (tr. O. O'Neill)

30  Immanuel Kant, *Critique of Pure Reason*, pp. A738/B766.

31  For consideration of some of the relevant Kantian texts see Onora O'Neill, *Constructions of Reason*, Part I, and "Vindicating Reason" in Paul Guyer, ed., *The Cambridge Companion to Kant* (Cambridge, UK: Cambridge University Press, 1992), pp. 280–305.

32  That Kant does not tie his conceptions of *citizenship* and of *public use of reason* to specific institutional structures is evident in his essay "What is Enlightenment?" (1784) in *Kant's Practical Philosophy*, tr. Mary J. Gregor (Cambridge, UK: Cambridge University Press, 1996), 8: 35–42 (Prussian Academy pagination, included in the margins of the translation), where he speaks of various sorts of civic communication as *private uses of reason* (because they presuppose some 'alien', rationally unvindicated, authority) and of the audience for *public uses of reason* not as the citizens of an already constituted state but as 'the world at large'. His example of such communication – that among men of learning – is perhaps naif, but the point made is clear enough. For closer textual analysis see Onora O'Neill, "Reason and Politics in the Kantian Enterprise" and "The Public Use of Reason," in *Constructions of Reason*, 3–27; 28–50 and "Vindicating Reason" in *The Cambridge Companion to Kant*.

33  He supposes strongly bounded societies that are self-sufficient and whose inhabitants enter by birth and leave by death: in effect states.

34  *What is Enlightenment?*, 8: 38.

35  For recent discussions of Kant's cosmopolitanism see Martha Nussbaum, "Kant and Stoic Cosmopolitanism," *Journal of Political Philosophy* 5 (1997): 1–25; Thomas Mertens, "Cosmopolitanism and Citizenship: Kant against Habermas," *European Journal of Philosophy* 4 (1996): 328–47.

36  It may seem exaggerated to claim that Rawls takes a statist view of public reason since his account of reason presupposes not states but "bounded societies." Yet a conception of justice that is designed to be shared among the citizens of a bounded, closed society assumes that there will be a power that keeps that society closed and bounded: such powers are states, under a standard Weberian definition. For further comments on Rawls's statism, see Onora O'Neill, "Political Liberalism and Public Reason: A Critical Notice of John Rawls, *Political Liberalism*" *Philosophical Review* 106 (1998): 411–28.

# 10    Public Reason[1]

For John Rawls, public reason is not one political value among others. It envelops all the different elements that make up the ideal of a constitutional democracy, for it governs "the political relation" in which we ought to stand to one another as citizens (*CP*, p. 574). Public reason involves more than just the idea that the principles of political association should be an object of public knowledge. Its concern is the very basis of our collectively binding decisions. We honor public reason when we bring our own reason into accord with the reason of others, espousing a common point of view for settling the terms of our political life. The conception of justice by which we live is then a conception we endorse, not for the different reasons we may each discover, and not simply for reasons we happen to share, but instead for reasons that count for us because we can affirm them together. This spirit of reciprocity is the foundation of a democratic society.

Public reason has emerged as an explicit theme in Rawls's writings only after *A Theory of Justice* with his turn to "political liberalism" and the pursuit of a common ground on which people can stand despite their deep ethical and religious differences. But the concept itself has always been at the heart of his philosophy. It runs through his first book in the guise of the idea of publicity, playing an indispensable part in the theory of justice as fairness. The notion of fairness itself, so central to Rawls's thought, denotes that mutual acknowledgement of principles which public reason demands and which forms the real import of the language of social contract he has used to articulate his conception of justice.

Rawls's recent writings about public reason outline a complex model of deliberative democracy, as it is called today,[2] and I examine

368

his account in detail in Sections III and IV. But I begin by unearthing its roots in his earlier idea of publicity and by showing how fundamental is the dimension of Rawls's philosophy to which the idea of public reason gives expression.

## I. PUBLICITY IN *A THEORY OF JUSTICE*

Readers of *A Theory of Justice* ought to wonder more than they do about the contractarian form in which Rawls presents his theory of justice as fairness. Even in the introductory chapter of the book, he does little to explain the need to think about justice in terms of a contract. His notion of an "original position" is meant, like "the state of nature" in the social contract tradition, to describe a situation in which free and rational beings determine the principles that will regulate their subsequent conduct. Yet as Rawls admits (more forthrightly than earlier contract theorists), this initial situation has never existed and never will. The "original position" is a condition in which we imagine choosing principles of justice, not one in which as real people we ever find ourselves. Something needs to be said, therefore, about the reasons to think of principles of justice as the result of an agreement that in fact we never make.

In one passage, Rawls remarks that to understand fair principles of justice as the object of agreement among free and rational persons entails seeing that "the theory of justice is a part, perhaps the most significant part, of the theory of rational choice" (*TJ*, p. 16/15 rev.). This formulation wrongly suggests that fairness derives from the rational pursuit of individual advantage, when in reality it forms an irreducibly moral notion. Of course, the Rawls of *A Theory of Justice* would scarcely have denied this point. Though the parties in the original position are described as deliberating in accord with the principles of rational choice, the conditions he imposes upon their choice (the "veil of ignorance" that denies them knowledge of their class position, assets, and abilities) constitute moral limits on the sorts of information it would be fair for them to utilize. Later Rawls will introduce a distinction between two capacities of reason, the "rational" and the "reasonable," to differentiate these two elements of the original position, and he will disclaim any attempt to derive the reasonable, or the disposition to seek fair terms of cooperation, from the rational (*PL*, pp. 48–53). Still, our question remains, What useful purpose is served by the idea of an original contract, morally defined though it is, if it refers to an agreement which is never really made?

One might suppose that the structure of Rawls's theory would have been clearer had he not made use of this idea. In an insightful review of *A Theory of Justice*, Ronald Dworkin noted that a hypothetical contract, being strictly speaking no contract at all, can have no binding force on the people supposedly subject to it. It is also an idle notion. To claim that certain principles are valid because they would be the object of rational agreement is a roundabout way, he argued, of saying that they are valid because there is reason to accept what they assert. The two principles of justice favored by Rawls have their real basis in the fundamental right to equal concern and respect which they express.[3]

Dworkin's skepticism about contractarian terminology has my sympathy, and I agree that a principle of respect for persons undergirds Rawls's theory of justice. But though the idea of an original contract is, as Rawls will later say, just a "device of representation" (*PL*, p. 24), we need to attend to all the aspects of justice which it serves to represent. In fact, conceiving of the principles of justice as the object of a rational agreement comes to more than saying that each individual concerned has reason to accept them. The language of contract also points to the good in each individual's finding that reason in the reason that others have to accept them as well. This good lies at the core of the ideal which Rawls calls "publicity," and a virtue of the idea of contract, as he observes (*TJ*, p. 16/15 rev.), is that it gives expression to this ideal.

The point is that just as the validity of a contract does not turn solely on the terms agreed to, but also on the fact of agreement, so justice consists in more than the proper distribution of rights and assets. Principles of justice should also be public, each of us affirming them in light of the fact that others affirm them too. More is necessary (we may say to fix terms) than just a *scheme of distributive justice*, even one that each of us has reason to endorse. Equally important is the *publicity* of its defining principles – that our reason for accepting them turns on others having reason to accept them too. When a conception of justice enjoys this kind of common support, it figures in our thinking, as Rawls says a public conception will do (*TJ*, pp. 55f./48 rev., 133/115 rev.), exactly as though it had been the result of an agreement. Even though no formal act of agreement is needed for us to base our reasons on those of others, a "just so" story about a hypothetical contract helps to highlight this public dimension of justice. The contractarian metaphor has the merit of combining in a single image two essential conditions which the principles of justice should satisfy – their justifiability to reason and their publicity. Together these two conditions define Rawls's ideal of a "well-ordered" society, which not only advances the good of its members but does so in accord with a public conception of justice. It is "a society in which (1) everyone accepts and knows that the others accept the same principles of justice, and (2) the basic social institutions generally satisfy and are generally known to satisfy these principles" (*TJ*, p. 5/4 rev.). Justice would not be all that it should be without this shared affirmation.

It is therefore unfortunate that Rawls does not adequately explain why publicity represents so preeminent a value. In *A Theory of Justice*, the "publicity condition" generally enters the discussion from the side, as though merely a further desideratum that principles of justice should possess. It receives no extended treatment of its own. One can easily overlook how central it is to Rawls's very idea of justice, and the contractarian terminology can then appear as otiose as Dworkin claims. Regrettably, too, Rawls's statements about publicity in this book generally equate it with public knowledge, as though it entailed only that citizens know the operative principles of justice and one another's reasons for accepting them. The work he expects from it shows, however, that he has something more ambitious in mind. Publicity really amounts to the demand that the reasons each person has to endorse the principles be reasons the person sees others to have to endorse them as well. It requires that the principles of justice be grounded in a shared point of view.

Publicity's true import becomes evident if we follow the role the concept plays in *A Theory of Justice*. It shapes the ideal of a well-ordered society, as we have seen. But it also acts as a crucial premise in the "stability argument" for the two principles of justice, and to that I now turn. Rawls begins by rejecting those "indirect" forms of utilitarianism that favor maximizing the general happiness by means of encouraging people to act on nonutilitarian principles. Such a system of justice would fail even to be an object of public knowledge (*TJ*, p. 181/158 rev.). However, he next invokes publicity in a deeper sense as he argues that utility, understood as the explicit charter of society, would prove unstable since it would place too great a strain on individual self-esteem (*TJ*, Sec. 29, 69–77). Other things being equal, a conception of justice is better, he holds, the stabler it is, generating its own support so as to outweigh contrary motives. Citizens living under the institutional arrangements it recommends should tend to acquire a commitment to its principles. Stability obtains "when the public recognition of its realization by the social system tends to bring about the corresponding sense of justice" (*TJ*, pp. 177/154 rev.; also 454/398 rev.). The maximization of average utility is thus unlikely to generate its own support since it accords poorly with the facts of moral psychology. Its overriding devotion to efficiency will not inspire the allegiance of those whom it asks to give up their life prospects for the greater good of the whole. Only by calling upon improbable reservoirs of sympathetic identification can utilitarians hope that such a system of justice will endure. By contrast, Rawls argues, his own liberty principle secures the fundamental inviolability of each individual, and his difference principle ensures that everyone benefits from social cooperation. These two principles define a system of justice whose operation is more likely to engage the support of all, even of those who fare worst. Unlike utilitarianism, they exemplify the idea of "reciprocity" (*TJ*, p. 14/13 rev.), an idea rather undeveloped in *A Theory of Justice* but lying at the center of *Political Liberalism* and its doctrine of public reason.

Now this stability argument relies on the inner meaning of publicity, though to see it we must look at the argument somewhat differently than Rawls does himself. One might suppose that it requires principles of justice to be public simply so that everyone may know that they are in force and see what their institutions stand for. However, more must be involved. For stability is said to obtain when the "public recognition of [their] realization", thus the knowledge that others too affirm these principles, fosters everyone's conviction that they are valid and worthy of support. Yet Rawls does not fully explain why people might be moved to espouse certain principles because others espouse them as well. Indeed, he presents this argument in terms of the good which each person will discern in the liberty and difference principles from his own point of view – their guarantee of individual inviolability and their assurance that all will benefit from social cooperation (*TJ*, pp. 177ff./154ff. rev.). But the stability argument has to be different in character. It must show that each person can find reason to embrace these principles in the fact that others embrace them too. It should therefore indicate the good that the public affirmation of the principles may embody.

Halfway through his account of the argument, Rawls takes up a line of thought that suggests what that good is. "The public recognition of the two principles," he writes (*TJ*, p. 178/155 rev.), "gives greater support to men's self-respect and this in turn increases the effectiveness of social cooperation." Respect is indeed the good in question. But note that Rawls's statement asserts not so much that the principles express respect as that their public recognition does so. Thus, the self-respect each person finds confirmed in them has to be part of a mutual respect which their common affirmation displays. Though Rawls is not as clear on this matter as one might wish, his discussion of "the natural duty of respect" here and later in the book entails that the good of mutual respect lies in there being a shared basis for the determination of principles of justice. We respect others as ends in themselves, he holds, when in regard to their claims and interests we act on reasons that we are prepared to explain to them in the light of mutually acceptable principles (*TJ*, pp. 179/156 rev., 337–8/297 rev.). We try to see things as they do, taking our bearings from a point of view that we can all endorse together. Respect for persons implies allegiance to principles that we affirm in the light of others having a reason, indeed the same reason, to affirm them too.

Naturally, respect can mean many things, but in the sense just mentioned it makes up the true nature of the publicity condition. When citizens adopt certain principles of justice for reasons they understand one another to acknowledge, their joint endorsement of the principles amounts to showing one another respect. Their grounds for embracing them do not lie solely in their own, but in a shared point of view. The mutual respect demonstrated by their allegiance to this common basis is then a good which they can regard themselves as having achieved, and that is why the scheme of justice gains in stability. Their society illustrates Rawls's claim that "a desirable feature of a conception of justice is that it should publicly express men's respect for one another" (*TJ*, p. 179/156 rev.). What the publicity requirement really comes to, therefore, is that each person's adherence to the principles of justice should turn on reasons that he understands others to have to affirm them as well. This point remains largely implicit in *A Theory of Justice*, but in several essays published shortly afterwards Rawls spells it out in full detail (see Section II).

Once its full meaning is laid bare, we can better understand why Rawls should attach so great a value to the ideal of publicity. Only principles of justice which citizens affirm on a common basis are ones by which they can show one another respect as persons. The idea that political community should rest on this sort of mutual respect belongs to the heart of Rawls's philosophy. It underlies one of the most telling ways he has of contrasting his view of justice as fairness with utilitarian conceptions (*TJ*, pp. 23–7/20–24 rev., 187–190/163–6 rev.). "Utilitarianism," he observes, "does not take seriously the distinction between persons." It proposes that we adopt for society as a whole a form of practical reasoning appropriate for the single individual: just as the prudent person evaluates his possibilities with an eye to achieving the most good overall, accepting some losses for a greater gain, so a just society regards persons as different lines for an allocation of benefits and burdens that will maximize the net balance of satisfaction as judged by a sympathetic observer. To heed the separateness of persons, by contrast, is to seek principles which they can freely acknowledge before one another – principles, that is, which each can see that others have the same reasons to endorse as he. This mutual acknowledgment of principles is the very essence of what Rawls means by fairness as a conception of justice, though he brought it out better in his earlier and foundational essay "Justice as Fairness" (1958) than in the book, which cloaks it in the language of an original contract.[4] The idea of fairness explains the value of publicity and embodies what Rawls himself calls the natural duty of respect.

One reason for his reluctance to present his theory in these terms may well be the many different meanings "respect" can have. At the end of *A Theory of Justice* (*TJ*, pp. 585–6/513 rev.), he declares that he has not derived the principles of justice from respect for persons because the very notion of respect calls for interpretation, which only a conception of justice can provide. The hermeneutic point is well taken. But it does not rule out the possibility that respect, in a specific sense we grasp perhaps only in the light of his theory as a whole, is a value on which that theory rests. And so, as Rawls goes on to admit, respect for persons plays two roles in his conception of justice. It shapes the two principles themselves with their emphasis on the inviolability of the individual – the role which Dworkin was concerned to lay bare. It also figures in the demand that persons be treated "in ways that they can see to be justified" (id.). That is the role of respect underlying the ideal of publicity.

## II. FROM PUBLICITY TO PUBLIC REASON

In several essays published after *A Theory of Justice*, the notion of publicity receives more systematic attention, and not by accident. Its greater prominence reflects the new direction in Rawls's thinking that leads to *Political Liberalism*. In the course of this transformation the ideal of publicity grows into his doctrine of "public reason."

For instance, Rawls acknowledges more clearly that the importance of publicity in a well-ordered society is not simply a matter of its principles of justice being known to all. They should also be principles that citizens affirm on the basis of a shared rationale. Such is the intent of the distinction introduced in his *Dewey Lectures* (1980) (*CP*, pp. 324–6) and contemporaneous writings (*CP*, p. 293) between three "degrees" or "levels" of publicity.[5] A conception of justice satisfies the "full" publicity condition when its acceptance is not only an object of public knowledge, and not only based upon beliefs to which everyone can assent, but also thereby justified in a manner which all can embrace. In *A Theory of Justice*, Rawls generally used the term "publicity" in a sense equivalent to the first of these levels, the other two being tacitly at work in the way the stability argument capitalizes upon public knowledge of the operative conception of justice. Now the virtue which principles of justice have in being affirmable from a common point of view is made part of the very idea of publicity. Principles public in this strong sense should be our goal, he argues (*CP*, p. 325) because a well-ordered society rests upon fair terms of cooperation to which free and equal persons could agree. Thus, also for the first time, Rawls connects publicity directly (and not just via the metaphor of contract) to the ideal of fairness so that its centrality to his conception of justice comes through more perspicuously than before.

Rawls offers a further argument for the full publicity condition (*CP*, pp. 325–6). Principles of justice should draw on common ground because they apply to institutions having a deep and durable effect on people's lives – not least through the machinery of legal coercion. This transparency in which people can acknowledge before one another the basis of their common life is "a precondition of freedom." Plainly Rawls must mean political freedom or self-rule, where the use of force is involved. For moral principles outside the domain of justice need not, he adds, be public in this strong sense, though their effects on adherents and others alike can be equally profound. Why does Rawls thus limit the scope of the publicity condition? One tacit reason is that coercion differs so significantly from other forms of social influence (namely by its irresistibility) that it ought to be grounded in consensus. Elucidating this moral assumption would require developing the implicit idea of respect, of what it is to treat others as ends in themselves, and this Rawls has never been inclined to do (at least in his political philosophy).

But another reason for the limitation is presented explicitly in the *Dewey Lectures* (*CP*, p. 326). Moral notions distinct from the principles of justice often belong to religious, philosophical, or ethical doctrines on which people in modern societies are unlikely to agree, even as they can find a shared basis for settling questions of political justice. Publicity aims at a freedom of self-determination which citizens can exercise together despite their abiding disagreements. To enjoy this identity-in-difference, they must observe therefore a certain self-discipline, bringing to their deliberations about issues of justice only those convictions which can form part of a common point of view. "In public questions," Rawls writes, "ways of reasoning and rules of evidence for reaching true general beliefs that help settle whether institutions are just should be of a kind that everyone can recognize" (*CP*, p. 326). Here is a first statement of the theory of public reason formulated in response to the doctrinal diversity which will be the chief preoccupation of his emerging political liberalism.

In the transitional essays of the 1980's, Rawls often describes this public form of reasoning in terms of a distinction between justification and proof.[6] Justification is not merely "valid argument from listed premises." Instead, it "is addressed to others who disagree with us, and therefore it must always proceed from some consensus, that is, from premises that we and others publicly recognize as true" (*CP*, p. 394; also pp. 426–7). The contrast is overdrawn, for justification can take many forms, depending on the purpose at hand; sometimes it only consists in showing people how our assertion follows from our own beliefs. But the point Rawls has in mind is obvious. In a well-ordered society, citizens do not determine basic matters of justice by announcing to one another the conclusions they each have derived from their own first principles and then resorting to some further mechanism, such as bargaining or majority voting, to resolve the conflicts. They reason from what they understand to be a common point of view; their aim is to adjudicate disagreements by argument. As we have seen, a public life founded on mutually acknowledged principles is what fairness entails.

This idea of consensus underlies the different notion of an "overlapping consensus," which makes its appearance in his writings of this period.[7] Principles of justice, he argues, ought to be the object of an overlapping consensus among citizens otherwise divided by their comprehensive ethical, religious, and philosophical doctrines. Rawls's point has often been misunderstood. Many have supposed that he means to abandon the claim that his theory of justice is true or correct. If the nature of justice is to be defined by reference to what a society's members happen to agree upon, how can there be any room to argue that current opinion is wrong? And why should we believe that in these matters there is much of substance that people agree upon at all? However, our earlier discussion of publicity explains why these worries are ill-conceived. The basic sense in which principles of justice ought to be the object of consensus is that each person should have both sound and identical reasons to embrace them, for only then does their publicity give expression to mutual respect. Consensus so understood is therefore hardly identical to the extent of agreement about justice that actually obtains in a society. Yet an important question is whether this shared perspective, rooted as it must be in reasons which citizens can acknowledge only by abstracting from their divergent visions of the human good, nonetheless coheres with the comprehensive conceptions to which they are attached. Only if the consensus shaping their public reasoning about justice also forms an overlapping consensus, a common element in their otherwise different points of view, is the structure of their political life likely to endure. The notion of overlapping consensus serves therefore to connect a conception of justice already arrived at, and already marked by a more fundamental kind of consensus, to the question of its stability.

Rawls himself speaks in this regard of two "stages" in his theory of justice as fairness (*PL*, pp. 64, 140ff.). In the first stage the theory aims to describe fair terms of cooperation among citizens, while in the second it considers whether such principles can prove stable. The notion of overlapping consensus comes into play only at this subsequent stage. Clearly principles of justice are not being fixed by appeal to the common denominator of existing opinion. At the same time we should not overlook the idea of consensus that does figure in the initial determination of these principles. Publicity requires that they draw on reasons which all can acknowledge. As Rawls observes (*PL*, p. 64), public reason is a value which the first stage of his argument seeks to respect.

Overlapping consensus became a central notion for Rawls in the 1980s as he realized how much broader is the range of moral outlooks congruent with a commitment to justice as fairness than he had assumed. He became far more alert than before to the fact that in their comprehensive philosophical and religious conceptions of the human good, people have a natural tendency to diverge, not because of prejudice or inadvertence, but because of what he called "the burdens of reason" (*CP*, pp. 475–8) or later "the burdens of judgment" (*PL*, pp. 54–8). The complexity of the evidence, the necessity of weighing together different sorts of considerations, the need for judgment in applying key evaluative concepts, the variety of life experiences in modern society – all these factors conspire to make agreement about the nature of the good life improbable. To be sure, some comprehensive ideals deny the importance of fair terms of social cooperation, and their adherents cannot be expected to endorse Rawls's two principles of justice. But there remain a great many different ethical and religious ideals which share a commitment to fairness. Their proliferation Rawls calls "reasonable pluralism" (*PL*, pp. 36, 63f.), since by reasonableness he means, as I have noted, precisely such a commitment.[8] Reasonable pluralism is the condition we should expect to thrive under free institutions, where in the absence of state power enforcing any particular doctrine the burdens of judgment drive people's thinking in different directions. The principles of justice which citizens embrace from a sense of fairness can therefore prove stable only if they cohere with the various elements of this diversity.

*A Theory of Justice* did not itself approach the problem of stability in this pluralist spirit. Part III of that book laid out a single ethical conception based on regarding an individual's good as the object of a rational plan of life, in the light of which the citizens of a well-ordered society would be moved to act justly. Moreover, this conception, often in so many words but sometimes explicitly (*TJ*, p. 572/501 rev.), displayed the hallmarks of the Kantian ideal of individual autonomy, according to which all our principles of conduct (not just those of justice) should be ones that free and equal rational beings would choose under the ideal conditions of an original position. Such a strategy embodied too narrow a view of the possibilities. Indeed, the multiplication of reasonable views of the human good is something which a modern constitutional democracy is bound to encourage, and thus Rawls's initial solution of the stability problem is caught in an internal contradiction. The way out, he came to see, lies in recognizing that in a free society many disparate comprehensive views of life can still overlap in a public understanding of justice.

It was by taking to heart the fact of reasonable pluralism and seeing the error in his earlier solution to the stability problem that Rawls went on to develop his new theory of "political liberalism" (*PL*, p. xlii). In the classical liberalisms of Kant and Mill, the account of justice had been presented as part of an all-encompassing moral philosophy, and *A Theory of Justice* followed their lead. Yet in fact neither the moral ideal of individual autonomy nor an experimental attitude toward life is an essential ingredient in the rationale for his conception of justice as fairness. What is necessary, Rawls announces in the first essay marking this turn in his thought, is "to apply the principle of toleration to philosophy itself."[9] Justice as fairness, along with the reasons making up the public understanding of its basis, should be regarded as a "freestanding" conception, which people who see a greater value in tradition and belonging than the Kantian and Millian philosophies allow can still embrace.

Political liberalism is not "political" in the sense that, forsaking principled argument, it reduces justice to a compromise among given interests or to the common denominator of existing opinion (*CP*, p. 491). That should now be plain. But it does seek principles of political association which citizens have reason to affirm together despite the religious and philosophical disagreements setting them apart. Moreover, their reasons for embracing the principles must not spring simply from their different perspectives but must also draw upon a common point of view. Only so, as we have seen, can these principles represent fair terms of cooperation that express mutual respect. The shared understanding of principles of justice must therefore be at once reasoned and neutral with regard to the comprehensive conceptions of the good on which citizens disagree. Obviously, it is no small task to work out the character which this common language should have. In the essays of the 1980's and then in *Political Liberalism*, the "full publicity condition" is expanded into a detailed and sophisticated account of "public reason." The idea of public reason has its roots in the notion of publicity employed in *A Theory of Justice*, but Rawls's new concerns have moved this theme from the periphery to the center of his attention.

## III. THE DOMAIN OF PUBLIC REASON

Rawls gives the idea of public reason two extended treatments. The first occurs in *Political Liberalism*, chiefly in Chapter VI, and the second in an essay of 1997, "The Idea of Public Reason Revisited." I center my account around the first while noting the significant revisions in the later essay.

Public reason, Rawls writes (*PL*, p. 217), is an ideal of democratic citizenship, a "duty of civility," which governs the way in which citizens should deliberate together about the fundamental questions of their political life. In seeking to draw up fair terms of cooperation, they should reason from premises which they can all acknowledge. The exercise of public reason will not as a rule mobilize their full thinking about the problems before them, since their comprehensive conceptions of the good and the right are bound to entail distinctive views about other aspects than those having to do with justice. On these matters they may find themselves in deep and irresolvable disagreement. But such differences are set aside when citizens committed to fairness decide questions having to do with the "basic structure" of society – questions which in Rawls's view concern both "constitutional essentials" (the general form of government and the fundamental rights of citizens) and basic matters of social and economic justice (*PL*, pp. 227–30). Similarly, people may well continue to understand these decisions in the light of their various comprehensive doctrines. The demand is only that they see the need for a common perspective and be able and ready to justify their decisions within its terms (*PL*, pp. 241–43).

Why, one might ask, should the domain of public reason be limited to these fundamentals instead of extending to all the political decisions which a community must make? Rawls does not give a clearcut answer to this question (*PL*, p. 215). On the one hand, he suggests that the restriction might eventually be lifted: the sense in focusing on fundamentals is that if the demands of public reason do not apply in this case they can scarcely hold more broadly.[10] On the other hand, he ends his discussion with the thought that citizens might sometimes be right to settle these further issues in a more particularist spirit. Though he gives no example of what he has in mind, one possibility is the present system in the province of Quebec, which guarantees basic rights for all while also giving special protection and support to the use of the French language despite the existence of a sizable Anglophone minority.[11]

Another question is whether the discipline of public reason applies to every kind of political deliberation in which citizens may engage, or only to those deliberations which form part of the official process for arriving at binding decisions that will have the force of law. Certainly when citizens take part in decision making by voting in elections or exercising public office as legislators and officials, Rawls holds that they must base their decisions (again, where matters of basic justice are involved) upon reasoning rooted in a point of view which all can share. Thus, the American Supreme Court, charged as it is with settling questions of constitutional principle, counts as an exemplary organ of public reason (*PL*, pp. 231 ff.). He also emphasizes that in "the background culture" – as members of the particular associations (churches, universities, and professional groups) making up civil society and as adherents of different philosophical and religious conceptions – citizens may discuss among themselves political questions, even of a fundamental sort, according to their own "nonpublic reasons" (*PL*, p. 14; *CP*, p. 576). Political debate rightly shows a greater mix of voices in areas of society other than the circumscribed realm of public reason, and it would be wrong to suppose that Rawls's theory of public reason means to encompass the "public sphere" in this broader sense, which was the topic, for example, of a widely influential study by Jürgen Habermas.[12] Much misdirected criticism has arisen from this confusion.

But to return to our question, Can citizens or particular associations address their comprehensive conclusions about political issues, not only to like-minded souls, but to everyone in the community whatever their persuasion? Can the Catholic bishops, for example, direct their religiously inspired arguments for regarding abortion as murder to believers and nonbelievers alike? Or does the ideal of public reason require that citizens participating in the political debates of society as a whole hold back and speak only in the regimented terms it provides even if they are engaged not in making binding decisions but only in the back and forth of argument? Should they reserve their full-scale views for intramural use?

It may seem that Rawls believes they should. For neither in *Political Liberalism* nor in "The Idea of Public Reason Revisited" does he note the difference between two forms of public debate – *open discussion*, where people argue with one another in the light of the whole truth as they see it, and *decision making*, where they deliberate as participants in some organ of government about which option should be made legally binding. To say, as he does, that public reason concerns the "kinds of reasons [citizens] may reasonably give one another when fundamental political questions are at stake" (*CP*, p. 574) fails to discriminate between the two. Yet the distinction is plain and important. Rawls remarks that there exists a kind of political discourse he calls "declaration," in which citizens make known to one another their comprehensive understandings of the right and the good (*CP*, p. 594; *PL*, p. 249). But he has in mind only their showing one another how their conceptions support the common viewpoint of public reason. Such exchanges do promote mutual trust, as he observes, but they are not the same as a free and open discussion of political questions. Moreover, several times in *Political Liberalism* Rawls places "political advocacy in the public forum" (*PL*, pp. 215, 252) among the activities regulated by public reason. Many have therefore taken him to be claiming that all political debate in society at large, at least when it bears on fundamentals, should not depart from the common ground citizens share.[13]

Now such a view would be unappealing for several reasons. First, it is essential for us to know the different convictions our fellow citizens hold about controversial issues and not only because we need to be reassured that they can nonetheless find in them reason to embrace a common standpoint for political decisions. We also gain a firmer appreciation of the value of that standpoint, seeing how without it so much would tend to drive us apart. Second, unbridled public discussion has the obvious virtue that through it we can come to change our mind. We can find ourselves persuaded by the way some initially unattractive opinion is defended. We can also be impelled to think through more carefully than before our own comprehensive commitments. In fact, the community as a whole may be moved to give a deeper or more nuanced articulation to the common principles by which it orders its political life.[14]

It should be observed, however, that a strait-jacketed view of political debate does not follow from the justification which Rawls himself presents for the ideal of public reason. Its basis, he writes, is "the liberal principle of legitimacy," which holds that "our exercise of political power is proper and hence justifiable only when it is exercised in accordance with a constitution the essentials of which all citizens may reasonably be expected to endorse in the light of principles and ideals acceptable to them as reasonable and rational" (PL, p. 217). This principle captures the thesis advanced in earlier writings, namely, that the terms of political association must form part of a public consensus because of their essentially coercive character. And that thesis in turn, as I mentioned before, gives expression to the value of respect for persons which inspires his thought as a whole, particularly his cardinal ideal of fairness. Rawls has never made clear, it is true, the foundational role of respect, which structures even the freestanding conception of justice he attributes to political liberalism. But that is not our present concern.[15] The pertinent fact is that the ideal of public reason, based as it is upon the principle cited, ought to be understood as governing only the reasoning by which citizens – as voters, legislators, officials, or judges – take part in political decisions (about fundamentals) having the force of law. Rightly conceived, it does not thwart the uninhibited political discussions which are the mark of a vigorous democracy. We can argue with one another about political issues in the name of our different visions of the human good while also recognizing that, when the moment comes for a legally binding decision, we must take our bearings from a common point of view.

Rawls never puts things in this way, and so one cannot be sure that he would agree. But it is what the logic of his position entails. By "political advocacy in the public forum" perhaps he meant (as the context suggests) only the terms in which a candidate for office seeks support, and indeed political campaigns no less than the votes they solicit should adhere to the canon of public reason when constitutional essentials and basic matters of economic justice are at stake. Clarity would have been better served had Rawls given a more complete picture of the kinds of political discussion in a constitutional democracy. Generally, he contrasts the "background culture" with what he calls the "public political culture" (*PL*, pp. 13–14) or the "public political forum" (*CP*, pp. 575–6). Though he defines these latter terms as referring to the institutions and traditions in which citizens or their representatives authoritatively settle fundamental questions of justice, the terms themselves suggest a wider range of political discussion where the rules of public reason do not rightfully apply. I think that at one point Rawls himself may have been misled by this terminology. But to see what I mean, we need first to look more closely, now that the scope of public reason has been defined, at the way that political argument in its jurisdiction ought to proceed.

## IV. THE RULES OF PUBLIC REASON

Obviously, many questions of an ethical or religious character, important though they are to people's self-understanding, will have to be set aside when citizens go about determining the political principles by which they will live, for such questions cannot receive any commonly acceptable answer. But it would be wrong to suppose that for Rawls issues are to be removed from the political agenda just because there exists widespread disagreement about their solution. Public reason does not demand the blanket avoidance of deep-seated conflict as though its highest value were civil peace. On the contrary, public reason embodies the ideal of fairness, and so questions having to do with the fair terms of social cooperation – in other words, matters of basic justice – belong on a society's program of political deliberation, however disputed they may be. Rawls could not be more explicit on this score (*PL*, p. 151). It is hard to see, therefore, how he would have been obliged, as some have charged,[16] to side with Stephen Douglas in the famous Lincoln–Douglas debates of 1858 and regard the issue of slavery as too controversial to be the object of political decision.

Slavery and its abolition constitute one of the formative experiences in American political life. To regard civil war as the worst of political evils and to suppose that differences should always be papered over by a modus vivendi is not a view likely to impress any American thinker, though Europeans of a Hobbesian persuasion often espouse it. One of the benchmarks not just of Rawls's conception of public reason but of his political philosophy as a whole is that basic justice takes precedence over civil peace or, perhaps better put, that it is a precondition for any civil peace worthy of the name. However, the American abolitionists along with the more recent civil rights movement have also inspired a more specific feature of his theory of public reason. William Ellery Channing argued for the emancipation of the slaves just as Martin Luther King, Jr., argued against racial segregation by appealing to the belief that all human beings are equally God's creatures. Clearly they did not do so simply to indicate where they stood personally and to persuade others to share their faith. Their aim was to encourage others to take this religious view to heart as they dealt with those questions in their capacities as voters, legislators, officials, and judges. (Note that I have made clear the involvement of both forms of public debate, which Rawls's own depiction of these movements unfortunately does not distinguish). Did Channing and King therefore overstep the boundaries of public reason? On a straightforward understanding of that concept, they did. But this "exclusive" interpretation is not, Rawls argues (*PL*, 247–54), the only or proper way to think about public reason.

In a well-ordered society, where all citizens affirm together just principles of social cooperation, no one would need in public debate to look outside this common point of view to settle what justice requires. But the situation is different when a society is deeply at odds with itself about constitutional essentials. Then, there exists no generally accepted language of public reason. In such cases, citizens may base their decisions upon comprehensive views that are themselves unlikely ever to form part of public reason, provided they believe or could have believed that thereby the ideal of public reason would be strengthened in the long run (*PL*, pp. 247, 251). Such is the "inclusive" interpretation of public reason as Rawls presented it in the first edition of *Political Liberalism* (1993). Subsequently, however, he has revised his account, though not so as to switch to the opposite position. Rather, he has concluded that even the conditions he had imposed on the appeal to comprehensive views need to be relaxed. Instead of holding that citizens may reach beyond public reason only when their aim is to steer a profoundly unjust society toward greater justice, Rawls now believes that citizens may call upon their full convictions at any time. The sole qualification is what he terms "the proviso": "in due course public reasons, given by a reasonable political conception, [must be] presented sufficient to support whatever the comprehensive doctrines are introduced to support" (*PL*, pp. li–lii). This "wide" view of public reason was introduced in "The Idea of Public Reason Revisited" (*CP*, pp. 584, 591–2), and in the introduction to the second edition of his book (1996) Rawls declares that it represents his considered position.

Nonetheless, I am not convinced that the change is for the better. To begin with, one cannot help but worry about the vagueness of the proviso. On whom does the obligation fall to satisfy it? And how is "in due course" to be defined? Rawls concedes the existence of these difficulties, adding that no hard-and-fast rules but only "good sense and understanding" (*CP*, p. 592) can serve to handle them. That is fine, if the proviso is truly necessary. But it is unclear what advantages favor this more permissive conception in the first place. What need would there be in a well-ordered society to abandon the constraints of public reason? Rawls's answer is that, in invoking their comprehensive views subject to the proviso, citizens make known how their ethical and religious convictions entail commitment to a common idea of justice. As a result, others feel more secure in their own commitment and stability is enhanced – a boon even in the best of circumstances (*CP*, pp. 592–3; *PL*, p. lii).

Certainly, mutual reassurance of this sort is important. But does it have a part to play in the process by which citizens arrive at legally binding decisions in a well-ordered society? When fair principles of justice are mutually acknowledged by all, why should citizens ever cast their nets more widely to establish how a remaining question of constitutional essentials should be authoritatively settled? It cannot be because they have found they disagree or that they feel uncertain about how the question is to be decided in accord with political reason. For, as we shall see, Rawls believes (and correctly so) that even then they should continue to heed the voice of public reason as each of them best understands it. The mutual reassurance which comes from citizens disclosing to one another the comprehensive roots of their commitment to justice really has no place in the deliberations by which they decide what shall have the force of law. But it does have a point in the different sort of public debate I have called "open discussion." Indeed, Rawls's "wide" conception seems motivated by the wish to make room for the freewheeling arguments about political issues that belong to the public life of an energetic democracy. Such arguments are properly part of what he calls "the background culture." To permit them in the "public political culture" as Rawls now proposes (subject to the proviso) is to be misled by what that term suggests as opposed to the way that he himself defined it. In the forum where citizens officially decide the basic principles of their political association and where the canons of public reason therefore apply, appeals to comprehensive doctrines cannot but be out of place – at least in a well-ordered society. The earlier, "inclusive" conception, which allows departures from public reason only when its most elementary ingredients are in wide dispute, appears to be the better view.

So much for the question of how strictly the discipline of public reason applies. Another question concerns how much it should aim to accomplish within its sphere. Ideally, it should set its sights on settling all matters of fundamental justice, for they make up its domain. A political conception of justice, as Rawls says, should aim to be complete. Yet situations arise where citizens, reasoning as best they can from the common ground they endorse as free and equal persons, find that they cannot achieve reasonable agreement on an important issue of justice. The right move may be to put off its resolution, not so much to avoid conflict as to allow more time for reflection and experience to shape deliberation. Suspending judgment can promote democracy.[17] Sometimes, however, a decision cannot be postponed. It would be wrong, Rawls argues (PL, pp. lv f., 240 f.), for citizens then to suppose that, public reason having failed to settle the issue, they may resort to considerations farther afield borrowed from those parts of their comprehensive views on which there is no overlapping consensus.[18] Standoffs requiring a decision are indeed to be handled by a vote, but a vote carried out in the spirit of public reason. Citizens should follow their best sense of what public reason entails despite the disagreement about what that is and the uncertainty they may therefore feel in their own mind. Where possible, they should also seek to minimize their differences by giving extra weight to points of convergence (PL, p. 217).[19]

In fact, disagreements are to be expected within public reason, Rawls declares (*PL*, pp. xlix, lii f., lvi), since its common point of view, rightly conceived, is not defined by any one political conception of justice – not even by the liberty and difference principles in his own theory of justice. This feature of his position has not been widely noted. It first appears in "The Idea of an Overlapping Consensus" (*CP*, p. 427), and after *Political Liberalism* Rawls returns to it in "The Idea of Public Reason Revisited" (*CP*, pp. 581, 583, 605 f.). Rawls has not himself given it the detailed treatment it deserves. But the thesis is exceptionally important. It is his way of dealing with the fact, often adduced against his political liberalism, that justice no less than the good life has been an enduring object of dispute even within liberal societies. It also represents a significant innovation in his thinking since, as we have seen, "publicity" and then "public reason" are notions first worked out as part of his account of the two principles of justice. They are now to be understood in less partisan a fashion.

Public reason, Rawls argues, must be able to welcome a family of liberal conceptions of justice, the essential conditions of a "liberal" conception being that it specify certain basic rights, liberties, and opportunities; that it assign a special priority to these elements of a constitutional regime; and that it aim to provide citizens with the means to make effective use of their freedoms (*PL*, pp. xlviii, 6, 223). These are broad conditions, and citizens may make use of their political traditions and theoretical imagination to flesh them out in various ways. Opposing views are likely to arise, and it is the sign of a vibrant democracy that controversy of this sort should go on and that individuals and social movements should be able to challenge the reigning interpretation of justice – not just in open debate but also in political decision making. Utilitarians, opposed though they must be to Rawls's own principles of justice and wedded instead to the ideal of efficiency, can still conclude that the general happiness is maximized by a scheme of justice satisfying these three conditions.

In their exercise of public reason, citizens may therefore appeal to the different perspectives making up this family of liberal conceptions. Rawls does not explain how they can do so while still heeding the demands of public reason. But it is not difficult to figure out how they have to proceed. In deciding some disputed issue, they must invoke their own views about justice in a form that does not exceed the bounds of the common point of view they share with their fellow citizens. This means that they must present them as ways of formulating more concretely the three conditions constitutive of a liberal outlook. Of course, their different conceptions of justice will also transcend this public rationale, which explains why they are likely to produce contrary interpretations of those basic, but very general, principles embraced by all. But such disputes revolve around the proper understanding of this common point of view and do not call into question the authority of public reason. As Rawls himself remarks in this context (*PL*, pp. xliv, xlix, li; *CP*, pp. 574, 581), citizens having different conceptions of justice have to share a commitment to reciprocity if public reason is to be possible: they must view one another as free and equal citizens and be prepared to offer one another terms of cooperation which all have good reason to affirm. This standard, of course, is tantamount to what Rawls means by fairness, and fairness, as we have seen, forms the core of the ideal of public reason.

Yet precisely when we see this defining feature of public reason for what it is, we may wonder whether Rawls's wish to accommodate a family of liberal conceptions can really be as generous as he supposes. On the one hand, his own two principles of justice are claimed to be one possible view among others that citizens may invoke as they settle basic questions about constitutional essentials and about social and economic inequalities. But on the other, the very exercise of public reason must embody a commitment to fairness. Does not public reason effectively exclude appeal to any idea of justice that does not, like Rawls's, view the distribution of rights and resources as a matter of arranging fair terms of social cooperation? Must not utilitarians, for example, find themselves debarred from speaking their minds? Believing that justice is to be achieved by institutions promoting the greatest net balance of satisfaction, they may well find reason to agree to the three broad principles characteristic of a liberal society. But if they must reason about how to give content to these principles in accord with the ideal of fairness, are they not being expected to switch philosophical allegiances and give up their distinctive way of thinking?

In reality, Rawls's latitudinarian vision of public reason is not the sham that it might seem at first glance. Recall the distinction I mentioned earlier (Section I) between a scheme of distributive justice and the basis – for Rawls, the indispensably public basis – on which the individuals to whom it applies ought to adhere to its principles. The actual import of Rawls's contractarianism, I noted then, lies in aiming to handle both these matters by means of a theory of justice centered on the single notion of fairness. And thus among the liberal conceptions consonant with public reason justice as fairness has a special standing. In this conception, as Rawls himself observes (*PL*, p. 225), "the guidelines of inquiry of public reason . . . have the same basis as the substantial principles of justice." But nothing prevents other members of the group from treating these two topics by separate means. It is not therefore incoherent to consider questions of distributive justice as simply questions of efficiency while admitting that principles of justice, to have the force of law, must satisfy the criteria of public reason. Still, utilitarians who hold such a position will have to give their philosophical doctrine an "indirect" form: they will have to support as the public basis for affirming principles of justice a viewpoint (fairness) different from the one they themselves occupy when judging the ultimate reasons for any moral principles. No doubt Rawls continues to think (as in *A Theory of Justice*) that indirect utilitarianism is therefore inferior to his own liberty and difference principles of justice. But he admits that it can belong to the overlapping consensus of a liberal society and thus take part in the discourse of public reason (*CP*, pp. 433–4). Indeed, he welcomes this fact, given the prominent place of utilitarian thought in the democratic tradition.

## V. CONCLUSION

The loosening of the link between the ideal of public reason and his two principles of justice, the recognition that controversy is an inescapable part of public reason, comprises one of the most interesting developments in Rawls's recent writings. Clearly it involves many complexities, perhaps difficulties too, which have yet to be explored. Yet we should not lose sight of the way in which fairness continues to shape the heart of that ideal. Even though citizens may understand differently the core principles of a liberal society, and even though some may base their views on the idea that maximizing average utility, not guaranteeing the least well off their best prospects (Rawls's difference principle), ought to govern the distribution of resources, they exercise public reason by determining the fundamentals of their political life within a shared and broadly liberal framework. Their adherence to this common point of view is itself a commitment to fairness. And thus the disagreements that mark their deliberations embody at the same time the fundamental sort of respect for one another which fairness involves.

As I showed earlier in Section I, fairness and respect are notions which shape Rawls's thought at the deepest level. Nowhere does he subject them to sustained analysis in their own right. Rather, they are deployed in a variety of ways, sometimes (as with fairness) in the metaphor of the social contract, sometimes (as with respect) more implicitly than otherwise, and sometimes in the guise of cognate notions such as reasonableness and reciprocity. But we will not understand his thought unless we trace their ramifications and perceive the overall conception they define. Fairness and respect inspire the social ideal to which his philosophical work has sought to give systematic expression, an image of society that the early essay "Justice as Fairness" evoked as the "mutual acknowledgement of principles by free persons" (*CP*, p. 59). The essential question is not so much the total good achieved as the relations in which people stand to one another as members of a collective undertaking. To borrow a phrase from the German Idealist tradition, we may say that for Rawls the just society is, first and foremost, a matter of "mutual recognition."

Public reason is the practice in which citizens make this vision a reality. Though an implicit theme already in *A Theory of Justice*, the idea of public reason has assumed its true dimensions only in the "political liberalism" Rawls has fashioned in recent years. The prominence it now enjoys is the fitting culmination of a philosophy devoted to exploring the meaning of fairness for political life.

ENDNOTES

1  References to Rawls's writings are generally given in the text and in accord with the following abbreviations: *A Theory of Justice* (=*TJ*) (Cambridge, MA: Harvard University Press, 1971; revised edition, 1999); *Political Liberalism* (=*PL*) (New York: Columbia University Press, 2nd paperback edition, 1996); *Collected Papers* (=*CP*) (Cambridge, MA: Harvard University Press, 1999).

2  For a theory of deliberative democracy building on Rawls's work, see Joshua Cohen, "Democracy and Liberty," in Jon Elster (ed.), *Deliberative Democracy* (Cambridge, UK: Cambridge University Press, 1998), pp. 185–231.

3  Ronald Dworkin, *Taking Rights Seriously* (Cambridge, MA: Harvard University Press, 1978), Chapter 6 ("Justice and Rights," originally published 1973). For Rawls's reply, see *CP*, pp. 400–401n.

4  See Rawls, "Justice as Fairness," *CP*, pp. 59 and 70, and contrast the less perspicuous, contractarian presentation of the idea of fairness in *TJ*, p. 11.

5  This material is taken up again in *PL*, pp. 66 ff.

6  The distinction goes back to *A Theory of Justice* (*TJ*, pp. 580–1/508 rev.). It also reappears in "The Idea of Public Reason Revisited" (1997), *CP*, p. 594.

7  See "Justice as Fairness: Political not Metaphysical" (1985), *CP*, p. 390 and the two subsequent essays which explore the notion in detail, "The Idea of an Overlapping Consensus" (1987; *CP*, pp. 421–48) and "The Domain of the Political and Overlapping Consensus" (1989; *CP*, pp. 473–96) reworked to form Chapter IV of *Political Liberalism*. The term with a somewhat different sense appears in *TJ*, p. 388/340 rev., whereas the concept itself is at work at *TJ*, pp. 220–1/193–4 rev.

8  "Pluralism" can be a misleading term in this context if it suggests the sort of ethical conception made famous by Isaiah Berlin. Berlin's pluralism is a positive doctrine according to which there are many ultimate, irreducible, and sometimes incompatible ends of life. The pluralism Rawls has in mind might be better described as the existence of reasonable disagreement about the nature of the human good (Berlin's value-pluralism being one of the views in dispute). For more on this distinction, see my book *The Morals of Modernity* (Cambridge, UK: Cambridge University Press, 1996), Chapter 7 ("Pluralism and Reasonable Disagreement").

9  "Justice as Fairness: Political not Metaphysical" (1985), *CP*, p. 388. See also *PL*, p. 10.

10  To this extent, Rawls's thinking moves in the direction of the all-embracing view of deliberative democracy defended in Amy Gutmann and Dennis Thompson, *Democracy and Disagreement* (Cambridge, MA: Harvard University Press, 1996), pp. 34–49.

11  Quebec is the model for the less "procedural," more "communitarian" form of liberalism favored by Charles Taylor, as in "The Politics of Recognition," pp. 242–8 in *Philosophical Arguments* (Cambridge, MA: Harvard University Press, 1995). It is not obviously at odds with Rawls's doctrine of public reason.

12  Jürgen Habermas, *Strukturwandel der Öffentlichkeit* (Darmstadt: Luchterhand, 1962). Rawls notes this terminological difference with Habermas at *PL*, pp. l, 382.

13  Two examples are Michael Sandel in his review of *Political Liberalism* (*Harvard Law Review* 107 (7) (May 1994): 1765–94, particularly at 1789 ff.) and Nicholas Wolterstorff in "Why We Should Reject What Liberalism Tells Us about Speaking and Acting in Public for Religious Reasons," in Paul Weithman (ed.), *Religion and Contemporary Liberalism* (South Bend, IN: University of Notre Dame Press, 1997), pp. 162–81.

14  For reflections along these lines, see Jeremy Waldron, "Religious Contributions in Public Deliberation," *San Diego Law Review* 30 (4) (fall 1993): 817–48.

15  I pursue this subject in "The Moral Basis of Political Liberalism," *Journal of Philosophy* 96 (12) (December 1999): 1–27.

16  Notably, Michael Sandel, in his review of *Political Liberalism*, *op. cit.*, pp. 1779–82; see also his *Democracy's Discontent* (Cambridge, MA: Harvard University Press, 1996), pp. 21–3. Rawls points out the unfoundedness of this charge in "The Idea of Public Reason Revisited" (*CP*, pp. 609–10).

17  This is one of the themes in the "judicial minimalism" of Cass Sunstein, *One Case at a Time* (Cambridge, MA: Harvard University Press, 1999). For Rawls's sympathy with Sunstein's approach, see *CP*, p. 618.

18  For the contrary view, see Kent Greenawalt, *Religious Convictions and Political Choice* (New York: Oxford University Press, 1988) and *Private Consciences and Public Reasons* (New York: Oxford University Press, 1995).

19  Here Rawls alludes to the "principles of accommodation" advocated by Gutmann and Thompson. See their *Democracy and Disagreement*, pp. 79–91.

FRANK I. MICHELMAN*

# 11  Rawls on Constitutionalism and Constitutional Law

*Constitutionalism* – the idea of the subjection of even the highest political authority in a country to limits and requirements having the form and force of law – is a notion of normative political theory. Despite this notion's familiarity to us, theorists continue to puzzle over what, exactly, it means for it to be put into practice or how, exactly, its being put into practice may bear on the moral justifiability of political rulership. Our first general question in this chapter is about John Rawls's contributions to this branch of speculative inquiry.

From a lawyer's standpoint, a "constitution" is an existent law or statute, the country's highest-ranking one, which no other legal enactment, opinion, or decision may contravene. What lawyers call *constitutional law* is a body of learning to be used in specifying the content of this highest-ranking law or statute and applying it to disputed cases. Here, too, we find a field of long-standing debate about how judges and other officials ought to approach their tasks of construing and applying basic-law texts and precedents. The issues prove hard to resolve without getting into speculative questions concerning (a) the ends and reasons for which a country's basic law imposes limits and requirements on ordinary political rule, and (b) the events and conditions by and under which such legal impositions may legitimately be decided and come into force. We may think of judges, lawyers, and their academic kibitzers entering the debates using whatever circulating fund of relevant beliefs and assumptions, concepts and categories, reasonings and teachings may currently comprise the "discourse" of constitutional law. Of course, participants often aim to add to this fund or modify it. Our second general question in this chapter is about how, if at all, Rawls's work may have modified the discourse of constitutional law or may possibly yet do so.

394

## I. RAWLS ON CONSTITUTIONALISM: CONTRACTARIAN LEGITIMACY AND CONSTITUTIONAL ESSENTIALS

### A. Political Liberalism as Constitutional Contractarianism

Rawls has sought to ascertain the conditions of the possibility of political legitimacy in modern, plural societies. He asks how it may be possible that "there [could] exist over time a stable and just society of free and equal citizens profoundly divided by reasonable though incompatible religious, philosophical, and moral doctrines"; or, in terms he interestingly considers equivalent, how "deeply opposed though reasonable comprehensive doctrines may live together and all affirm the political conception of a constitutional regime."[1] Cast in terms of legitimacy, the question is how there can be a moral warrant for enforcement of laws made by majoritarian institutions against individual members of a population of presumptively free and equal persons – how "citizens [in a democracy may] by their vote properly exercise... coercive... power over one another."[2]

Rawls's answer lies in what he calls the *liberal principle of legitimacy*:

Our ... political power is ... justifiable [to others as free and equal] ... when it is exercised in accordance with a constitution the essentials of which all citizens may be expected to endorse in the light of principles and ideals acceptable to them as reasonable and rational.[3]

Rawls thus adopts what we may call a constitutional contractarian mode of political justification. We can distinguish three key components in such a justification as follows:

RATIONAL UNIVERSALISM ("hypothetical contract"). Constitutional contractarianism begins in liberal individualism with the idea that exercises of political power surely are justified when every affected, competently reasoning individual can approve them as in line with his or her own actual balance of reasons and interests.

CONSTITUTIONAL ESSENTIALISM. In modern states, it is beyond imagining that every discrete act of lawmaking could plausibly be portrayed as passing such a demanding test. A hypothetical–contractual standard of political justification can only be meant for application to *constitutional* laws – a restricted set of laws that fundamentally shape, organize, and limit the country's lawmaking system. Constitutional contractarian political justification depends on the view that your finding the constitution acceptably in line with reasons that apply to you, considering your interests, commits you to acceptance of the daily run of lawmakings that issue properly from the constituted system, regardless of whether each and every one of them does or should elicit your agreement.[4] That is the point of Rawls's claim that exercises of political coercion are justifiable insofar as they accord with *"a constitution,* the essentials of which all citizens may be expected to endorse."

Why "the essentials of which"? For starters, we can say because any practically workable constitution is bound, if only for crass political reasons, to contain arbitrary and even irrational matter that could not possibly be said to respond to reasons applicable to everyone in view of their interests. For example, the U.S. Constitution guarantees the "equal suffrage" of every state in the Senate regardless of population. We do not want every such eccentricity to disqualify the constituted regime from contractarian legitimacy as long as its "essential" parts do all satisfy the hypothetical contract test. (We come below, in Parts I(E) and I(f), to the hard question of how it is decided which parts are essential for such purposes.[5])

CIVILITY. But can there really be even an "essential" constitution that is universally rationally approvable in modern conditions of pluralism? Rawls's hope for this depends on a favorable motivational presupposition.[6] Political coercion is justified, Rawls says, when its exercise accords with a constitution whose essentials all may be expected to endorse in the light of principles and ideals acceptable to them not only "as rational" but also "as reasonable." The test is counterfactual, and much is packed into that hypothetical "as reasonable." It means I ought to support the regime and its acts if and only if (a) others generally comply with it, and (b) I can see how its essential parts comply with a set of political ideals and principles that merit mutual acceptance by a competently reasoning group of persons, all of whom suppose each other motivated to find and abide by fair terms of social cooperation in conditions of deep and enduring but reasonable disagreement over questions of the good.[7] Rawls calls a citizen's forbearance from public policy proposals that she cannot sincerely defend in such terms both her "civility" and her submission to a constraint of "public reason."

## B. Political Liberalism's Restricted Universe

Thus a kind of constitutional contractarianism is Rawls's response to the question of the possibility of legitimate government in modern, plural societies. But the response could not have been what it is (it might well have been that there is no discoverable answer to the question) had Rawls not constructed it with a society of a certain kind already in view. No doubt a part of "political liberalism" (Rawlsian contractarianism) is its elaboration of a form of politics in which public, mutually acceptable principles of political justice displace contesting, particular interests and ethics as the framing considerations for public policy debates affecting society's basic structure. But this vision of a publicly reasonable constitutional politics would be blatantly utopian standing by itself. Rawls's philosophy therefore must draw its warrant for the substantial conceivability of a politics of this kind from more elementary considerations, and Rawls proposes no other source for these more elementary considerations than a certain highly general notion of democratic social life that he expects will already have a firm claim on his audience. The vision is "constructed" or "worked out," as Rawls says, from ideal elements – "fundamental ideas" – drawn from "the most deep-seated convictions and traditions of a modern democratic state."[8] In that way, Rawls's contractarian response to the problem of political legitimacy has been specifically shaped to societies already imagined as falling with a certain broad historical tradition of political sensibility.[9] Rawls looks to democratic political culture, broadly viewed, for the makings of a basis for political agreement robust enough to support a democratic constitution even while allowing for the ingrained tendency of constitutional democracy itself to sustain a wide diversity of conflicting moral and religious doctrines.

### C. "Justice As Fairness" (the "Two Principles of Justice") as a Contentious Instance of Political Liberalism

It by no means follows, as some have charged, that Rawls has done nothing but echo back to his circle what it already thinks.[10] By his specific conception of justice "as fairness" (as represented by the famous two principles of justice in their lexical ordering), Rawls means to have produced *one* rational reconstruction of the constitutional–democratic tradition capable, if accepted, of resolving some chronic issues and disagreements internal to that tradition.[11] The line of thought runs approximately as follows: (1) A *political* (as opposed to a sectarian or comprehensive philosophical) conception of justice for the basic structure of a democratic society is worked up from fundamental ideas that can reasonably be "seen as" having been drawn from the culture of such a society. (2) The particular political conception of justice as fairness has been constructed out of a particular set of such fundamental ideas extracted from the public culture of a democratic state. However, (3) there are, presumably, other defensible conceptions of constitutional–democratic justice, each of them perhaps corresponding to a somewhat different "take" on democratic society, a different set of starting-point fundamental ideas that lead to a different conclusion about exactly what "political conception" – what set of principles and ideals for appraising a set of constitutional essentials for a democratic society (on the order of the two principles of justice as fairness) – a reasonable person would endorse.[12] If so, then (4) the failure of constitutional democracies thus far to resolve certain chronic issues of constitutional right and wrong may reflect a plurality of political conceptions, all of which are defensible, if competing, reconstructions of a more abstractly shared and general vision of a democratic society.[13]

Thus, one valid reconstruction might start from a strictly "proceduralist" view of a democratic society as one whose members, respecting each other as free and equal, use no means other than persuasion to resolve disagreements over the basic terms of social cooperation. Such a reconstruction might end in a political conception resembling a Habermasian ideal speech situation. Rawls, by contrast, builds in from the start a substantive dimension of fairness. In his rendition, a democratic culture is one that is committed to basic terms of social cooperation that are *fair*, given that the cooperation is among persons who reciprocally recognize each other as free and equal lifetime associates.[14] From that fundamental idea of social cooperation on fair terms, Rawls develops a "political" conception of persons – as endowed not only with certain moral powers but with corresponding higher-order interests in the exercise of those powers – that go far to explain their moral status of equality in regard to both the making and the content of decisions affecting the basic structure of society.

Rawls maintains that reflection on the fundamental idea of society as a system of fair, lifetime cooperation among free and equal persons leads to the ascription of these powers and interests:

[S]ince persons can be full participants in a fair system of social cooperation, we ascribe to them . . . two moral powers connected with . . . the idea of social cooperation . . .: a capacity for a sense of justice and a capacity for a conception of the good. A sense of justice is the capacity to understand, to apply, and to act from the public conception of justice which characterizes the fair terms of social cooperation. . . . The capacity for a conception of the good is the capacity to form, to revise, and rationally to pursue a conception of one's rational advantage or good. Persons are reasonable . . . when . . . they are ready to [abide willingly by] principles and standards as fair terms of cooperation, given the assurance that others will likewise do so. . . . The rational is . . . a distinct idea . . . and applies to [an agent] with the powers of judgment and deliberation in seeking ends and interests peculiarly its own.[15]

Finally, because "someone who has not developed and cannot exercise the moral powers to the minimum requisite degree cannot be a normally and fully cooperating member of society over a complete life," we ascribe to citizens the "two corresponding higher-order interests in developing and exercising these powers."[16]

It is not, Rawls emphasizes, that we adopt this view of persons as a general scientific account of human vocation. It is rather that these attributions are already salient in the idea of everyone's "taking part in a fair system of social cooperation and seeking and presenting public justifications for their judgments on fundamental political questions" – which is the very notion of a democratic society that the principles of justice as fairness are meant, in a sense, to elucidate.[17] Rawls develops the principles through a work-up of these features of the person into a situation of social choice of principles to govern the basic structure (the "original position") and through the account he gives of the choice that would ensue. The aim is to persuade us (in reflective equilibrium) that these starting points elaborated through this "procedure of construction" capture so well our own sense of the moral core of a democratic society that the resulting prescriptions for the chronic problems and disagreements of constitutional democracy are ones we should accept.

In summary, in a Rawlsian political (as opposed to a sectarian or comprehensive philosophical) conception of justice, a set of values is developed *from* certain fundamental ideas "seen as" inherent in the culture of a democratic society and then transmitted *through* some form of elaboration or demonstration *to* a set of principles (a "political conception" or "conception of justice") to govern the basic structure of a democratic society in conditions of reasonable pluralism, including the main points of its constitution.[18] Built in virtually from the start are key values, which, having been drawn from the public culture of a democratic society, are expected to help recommend the principles to an overlapping moral consensus of the society's differing, reasonable comprehensive views in a wide and general reflective equilibrium. These, then, are "public" or "political" values for the political conception in question, admissible to the public reasoning and argument (over matters of constitutional interpretation or amendment, for example) of all citizens who sincerely hold this conception.[19] Because the starting point fundamental ideas will differ somewhat from one political conception to another, the set of political values will not be exactly the same for every political conception of justice encompassed by political liberalism. In the political conception Rawls defends, justice as fairness, the political values include the fulfillment of the social preconditions to the adequate and full development and exercise by every person of the two moral powers, of the reasonable and the rational, that are presupposed by the very idea – which Rawls equates with that of a democratic society – of lifetime social cooperation on fair terms among human moral equals each with a life to live.[20]

## D. The Categories of Rawlsian Constitutional Analysis

We have mentioned the Rawlsian idea of constitutional essentials but so far have only scratched the surface of it. Before delving deeper, we will need to have before us the full array of Rawlsian constitutional–argumentative categories.

*Constitutional Argument in Justice as Fairness*[21]

| | covered by "the priority of liberty" 1 | covered by public reason contraint 2 | to be resolved as constitutional law 3 | |
|---|---|---|---|---|
| basic governmental structure | yes insofar as it affects the fair value of political liberty | yes | yes | CONSTITUTIONAL |
| securing the core basic liberties (taken severally) | not exactly[22] | yes | yes | ESSENTIALS |
| formal equality of opportunity | no | yes | yes | |
| provision for "basic needs" | yes | yes | yes?[23] | |
| securing a fully adequate scheme of basic liberties | yes | yes | no[24] | MATTERS OF BASIC |
| "fair" equality of opportunity | no | yes | no | |
| effectuation of difference principle | no | yes | no | JUSTICE |
| ALL OTHER MATTERS | no | no | no | |

If we disregard for the moment the column numbered "1," the table speaks plainly enough. The left-most column lists certain classes of matters for political decision. All but the last, residual class of matters is covered by the constraint of public reason (column 2), either as constitutional essentials or as what Rawls calls "matters of basic justice." The constitutional–essential classes are the ones marked "yes" in column 3. They are matters to be resolved at the level of constitutional law, by some combination of constituent lawmaking and judicial or other official interpretation – the point being that these "higher law" resolutions prevail over any contrary action by legislative majorities. The first three listed categories are certainly Rawlsian constitutional essentials, the fourth appears to be one, and the rest are not, but the decisions of legislative majorities regarding all but the bottom category are nevertheless covered – as matters of basic justice – by the constraint of public reason.[25] This information may possibly contain some surprises, but its meaning is at least roughly clear.

Conceptual complication enters with column 1. Not that the idea of the priority of liberty is itself hard to grasp. Rawls holds that, among any set of political values and ideals that together form a conception of political justice that every rational and reasonable citizen of a democracy can accept, some may be seen as specially "preferred" values and ideals, the fullest possible realization of which is not to be traded off against improved realization of any nonpreferred value or ideal.[26] In the Rawlsian political conception of justice as fairness, liberty may not be sacrificed *except* for the sake of liberty. Agree with the claim or not, it is easy enough to grasp.

What may nevertheless seem conceptually puzzling is how any politically decidable matter could be held covered by such an immunity against trade-off and yet not be classed as a matter to be resolved as a part of a country's constitutional "higher" law – or, conversely, why a matter *would* be treated as a constitutional essential even though *not* covered by the immunity against trade-off. A moment's thought shows, however, that such split classifications can make perfectly good sense. Take the case of formal equality of opportunity. Together, the "yes" in column 3 and the "no" in column 1 tell us both that a just constitutional order includes some substantial legal rule or principle of formal equality of opportunity *and* that this principle is shaped with due deference to basic liberties. For example, perhaps a just constitutional order secures persons against express and intentional religion-based discrimination in education and employment but not to the point of seriously impairing any group's religious freedom.[27]

Now take the case of securing for everyone a fully adequate scheme of basic liberties. Together, the "no" in column 3 and the "yes" in column 1 tell us both that – as we will see in Part II(E)[28] – a just constitutional order leaves this task largely open to pursuit by ordinary legislative majorities and that their pursuit of it may permissibly involve some significant circumstantial adjustment or regulation of the exercise or enjoyment of particular basic liberties.

Our table has disclosed a somewhat complex categorial apparatus, including (i) a division of the ideals and principles in a political conception of justice into constitutional essentials and matters of basic justice, (ii) a division of these same items into those that are and are not immunized against being traded off for the sake of the others, and (iii) a decided noncongruence between these two dichotomous divisions. We turn now to considerations motivating this complexity in Rawls's constitutional thought.

## E. Constitutional Essentials and Judicial Review[29]

By "judicial review," let us understand simply a practice of some degree of reliance on an independent judiciary for effectuation of the constitutional essentials in the face of possibly wayward or careless legislative majorities. Rawls apparently believes that provision for some form of judicial review will usually be apt to the purposes of justice. He denies, however, that such provision, in any form, is directly and in all circumstances a requirement of justice.[30] (Since justice does, in Rawls's view, directly and in all circumstances require effective legal recognition of certain constitutional essentials, we can infer that Rawls does not conceptually equate the existence of legal obligation with the availability of judicial "enforcement.")

While arrangements for judicial review are increasingly common among the world's democracies, the choice of how strong a form of them to have (for example, of how easy it should be for popular institutions to override judicial constitutional rulings with their own judgments of constitutional right and wrong) remains a contested one. That is because of a perception that, insofar as important resolutions of the constitutional essentials are committed to the practically final decision of an electorally unaccountable judiciary, there occurs a significant loss of democratic political values – particularly those connected with the political liberties and the development and exercise of citizens' capacities for a sense of justice.[31] Of course, it could still be – opinions differ – that a strong form of judicial review is favorable on the whole to the aim of realizing the most fully adequate total scheme of basic liberties that is practically available. Judicial review might result in a political system's doing better than it otherwise would at optimizing over all of the constitutional essentials including both personal and political liberties.[32] In Rawls's view, that is a judgment call for constitutional framers to settle on a prudential basis in light of their country's historical circumstances.[33]

That said, we must add that an assumption of judicial review's existence seems to hover over some of Rawls's discussions of related matters. In particular, this assumption may play some part in Rawls's sorting – which we are about to examine – of ideals of justice into those that are and those that are not made into constitutional essentials. For example, in the course of explaining his view that the difference principle does not belong among the constitutional essentials, Rawls may be taken to suggest that we probably would not want an independent judiciary dictating, in the constitution's name, all the decisions involved in carrying out its mandate.[34]

## F. Constitutional Essentials and Transparency

In contrast to his presentation of judicial review as an instrumentally contingent feature of just political regimes, Rawls presents the need for a sorting of ideals of justice into those that are and those that are not constitutional essentials as a general feature of such regimes.[35] Is there, then, some further motivation for the sorting beyond the contingencies of judicial review? I suggest there is and that it includes a concern for a relative transparency of application of the constitutional essentials, regardless of who is applying them.

Recall the crucial place of the idea of constitutional essentials in the Rawlsian version of constitutional contractarian political justification. These selected features of the political regime are to bear the full weight of justification in the first instance. Only if the regime's combined resolutions of the constitutional essentials are such as a reasonable citizen can rationally accept, perceiving that others do, can these resolutions ground any presumption of the moral supportability of regime-compliant events of ordinary lawmaking.[36] It follows that, in deciding which basic features of a regime are and which are not to be regarded as constitutional essentials, we have to avoid errors both of under- and overinclusion.

Omission of one or another item from the list of those placed beyond the tender mercies of majorities – liberty of conscience, for example – may render the regime not rationally acceptable to the reasonable. That would be the error of underinclusion, and it is obvious. Less plain is what risk we might pose to legitimacy by placing in the category of constitutional essentials each and every dimension of political justice upon which rational citizens reasonably would insist. If (as in justice as fairness) a commitment to the difference principle is held to be such a dimension, what possibly can be hazardous to legitimacy in writing that commitment into constitutional law? A part of the answer is "nontransparency."

Consider that, in a Rawlsian contractarian view, I can willingly accept the daily run of coercive acts from a constituted regime, despite my aversion to many of them, as long – but only as long – as two conditions are satisfied: (i) I regard this regime as universally reasonably acceptable by the rational, and (ii) I see my fellow citizens abiding by it. But this conjunction of perceptions is possible for me only if I can at all times see what the regime actually *is* that my fellow citizens are abiding by so that I can check whether *that* regime, the one actually in force, does in fact meet the test of universal reasonable and rational acceptability. (That is why interpreters, as Rawls says, must always be seen to be interpreting one and the same constitution.[37]) Now since, according to Rawls, the regime's acceptability to me is given in the first instance by its incorporation of correct settings for a certain minimal set of required features – the constitutional essentials – then (if the fact of this incorporation is to be at all times observable by me) the requirements in the minimal set had better not be either too numerous (hence potentially conflicting[38]) or too opaque to a compliance check by reason of technical complexity of application. Such considerations plainly enter into Rawls's view that basic liberty rights can be constitutional essentials while the difference principle cannot.[39] A concern for transparency of application is doing some of the work here – although, as we are about to see, we must be careful not to overinflate either the moral or the explanatory significance of this concern.

### G. On the Margin: Fair Value of the Political Liberties and Basic Material Needs

If we did, we would disable ourselves from explaining Rawls's unequivocal inclusion among the constitutional essentials of the two requirements that the political liberties of everyone be guaranteed their "fair value" and that citizens' "basic" material needs be met insofar as required to enable them to take effective part in political and social life.[40] "Fair value" of the political liberties means that everyone, regardless of social or economic position, has a "fair opportunity to hold public office and to influence the outcome of political decisions," and Rawls thinks it plain that a political order lacking such a commitment would not be rationally acceptable to every reasonable inhabitant of a constitutional–democratic political culture.[41] He thinks likewise regarding a commitment to secure to every person the minimum material prerequisites for exercise of the basic liberties (especially considering that the basic liberties are classed as such precisely because of their close relation to the development and exercise of a person's moral powers).[42] It is thus not surprising that Rawls would give *prioritized* (nontradeoffable) status to these commitments, and in fact he (strikingly) makes the basic-needs guarantee "lexically prior" even to the so-called first principle of justice as fairness.[43] However, we have seen that the immunity against trade-off of a political value does not, in Rawlsian thought, necessarily suggest the *constitutionalization* of that value.

Is full transparency of application an absolute additional requirement for constitutionalization? If it were, we should have to deny that Rawls could have meant legislation on the constitutional level when he wrote that "there must be legislation . . . to assure that the basic needs of citizens . . . be met so that they can take part in political and social life."[44] And yet he expressly said he was talking there about a constitutional essential. Possibly what Rawls has in mind is a set of broadly couched but particular constitutional guarantees of governmental action to assure everyone of basic subsistence, shelter, health care, and education.[45] Mandates of these kinds have been included in a few contemporary constitutions in the belief that it can sometimes be clear enough that a government is flouting them to provide a transparent reason for judicial intervention.[46] The same may be said of the fair-value-of-political-liberty guarantee, for which Rawls may contemplate a nondetailed constitutional mandate to the government to establish and maintain both some kind of a public financing system for elections and some kind of control on disproportionate spending by corporations and wealthy individuals.[47]

With the full picture now before us, there is no denying the uneasiness of Rawls's insistence on the category of matters of basic justice that are not constitutional essentials – his insistence, that is, on the idea that there are dimensions of basic political justice upon which reasonable citizens would rationally insist but which they would omit from the legal constitution. In effect, Rawls is saying that reasonable and rational citizens would insist on a credible and effective public commitment to the difference principle (say) as a condition of the regime's acceptability to them but that they cannot regard this commitment as a constitutional essential for the very reason that they and others would too often be unable to judge with certainty that it was or was not being met – although, Rawls evidently believes, they *can* make sufficiently certain judgments about commitments to protecting everyone's basic (negative) liberties, to ensuring the fair value of political liberty, and to providing for everyone's basic material needs. It does all make one's head spin, a little. But an appreciable degree of sense can be made here, and Rawls makes it.[48] Reasonable and rational citizens will take their chances, he maintains, as long they can know that (a) at least the "central ranges" of the basic liberties are secure against legislative majorities;[49] (b) and so, to the extent possible, is the guaranteed fair value of the political liberties; (c) and the same for guaranteed satisfaction of everyone's basic material needs; and finally, (d) legislative decision making that bears on further effectuation of the difference principle, of fair equality of opportunity, and of the fullness and adequacy for everyone of the whole scheme of basic liberties,[50] although not strongly controlled by higher law, is at least constrained by public reason.

## II. RAWLS AND AMERICAN CONSTITUTIONAL LAW

### A. "The Law of the Land"

Constitutional law, we said, is a body of learning used to apply the canonical constitution's provisions to specific controversies. In the United States, a common law country where law is always more or less a matter of precedent, constitutional law is largely drawn from the record of past official resolutions of such uncertainties, consisting mainly (for we have strong judicial review here) of opinions written by justices of our national Supreme Court. As of July 4, 1999, a database check showed that no opinion filed by a member of that Court had ever mentioned the name of the philosopher John Rawls.

That proves nothing negative, of course. An absence of Rawls's name from *The United States Reports* is entirely to be expected for reasons that do not impeach his possible sub rosa influence on American constitutional–legal doctrine. (Justices and their law clerks know well the sting of John Hart Ely's famous raillery: "We like Rawls, you like Nozick. We win, 6–3. Statute invalidated."[51]) So it could nevertheless be the case that, as Alan Ryan once suggested, our philosopher's ideas have "crept into the law of the land" thanks to propagation by acolyte law professors writing in law reviews and teaching in classrooms where judicial clerks and future advocates are spawned.[52] But it does not seem likely. *A Theory of Justice* appeared in 1971 in the wake, not the van, of the vaunted Warren Court. Justices such as William Brennan had produced the basic doctrinal ingredients for a liberalized American constitutional law well before they or their law clerks could have heard of Rawls. Their achievement doubtless stood as an exhibit to him. His cannot have stood as a teaching to them.

It is true that a strong egalitarian–liberal current persisted in American constitutional adjudication until well into the 1980s. It is also very probably true that law professors influence law clerks and law clerks occasionally influence judges. But the main inspiration to the liberal professors of the 1970s and 1980s most likely was that of the Warren Court itself. If egalitarian liberalism was flooding the nation's law schools in that period, imitation of the elite judiciary by a professorial vicariate seems a readier explanation than the lucubrations of any philosopher.

So much, then, for Rawls and American constitutional law? No, because "Constitutional law" names more than a body of currently prevalent legal doctrine. It also, as we said at the beginning, names a field of debate having some overlap with normative democratic theory. And that leaves us, as we said, with a general question about what Rawls may have contributed to the "discourse" of that debate.

## B. The Libertarian Core in Constitutional Law

Plainly, he has not contributed the idea of securing everyone against infringement by the state of any of the "basic liberties" covered by the first principle of justice as fairness, including

freedom of thought and liberty of conscience; the political liberties [including the right to vote and to be eligible for public office, together with freedom of speech and assembly and] freedom of association, as well as the freedoms specified by the liberty and integrity of the person [violated, for example, by slavery and serfdom, and by the denial of freedom of movement and occupation]; and . . . the rights and liberties covered by the rule of law [including freedom from arbitrary arrest and seizure].[53]

Any possible conception of justice (on the order of justice as fairness) that does not include this same libertarian core is beyond the pale of constitutional democracy as Rawls conceives it,[54] ipso facto disqualified from figuring in the public reason of the societies with which Rawls is philosophically concerned.[55] Thus, our first, modest conclusion: promotion of constitutional–legal recognition of the core liberties of the first principle cannot, on Rawls's own understanding of his philosophy, be regarded as anything brought or added by that philosophy to the conversation of liberal–democratic constitutionalism.

But what about those unresolved disagreements Rawls hopes justice as fairness can help resolve? There will probably always be specific controversies about how broadly one or another of the various listed basic liberties is to be construed. There are also chronic puzzlements about certain more generalizable issues such as whether the rights in a constitutional bill of rights ought to be regarded as strictly "negative" and "formal" and whether their correlative obligations ought to extend to "private" as well as "state" actors. We want to see whether the political conception of justice as fairness takes definite positions regarding such contested issues of democratic constitutional content and supplies trenchant arguments in support of those positions. If so, the arguments it supplies may well show some distinctive contributions by Rawls to the discursive field of democratic constitutional law.

## C. An Exemplary Case: Same-Sex Marriage

Why is it that Rawls believes the very general and abstract-looking two principles of justice as fairness can be decisive over at least some contested points in constitutional law? In part it is because a statement of the two principles does not exhaust the normative content of the political conception of justice as fairness. That content includes, as well, an expectation about how constitutionally guaranteed basic liberties will have their meanings filled out in application. They are to be construed as expressions of an aim of establishing for all persons the social preconditions of adequate and full development and exercise of the moral capacities – for a sense of justice and a conception of the good – that characterize them as citizens in a democracy and give them their created-equal status in constitutional–democratic thought.[56] It is in this way, Rawls says, that we "connect" the basic liberties with the conception of the person underlying them.[57] Accordingly, a guiding precept for constitutional law is

to specify and adjust the basic liberties so as to allow the adequate development and the full and informed exercise of both moral powers in the [generally prevailing] social circumstances in the . . . society in question.[58]

Consider, in that light, a legal claim that the liberty and equality clauses of the Fourteenth Amendment prohibit states from denying same-sex couples access to marriage on whatever terms the state may set for opposite-sex couples. It has seemed to some thoughtful observers that Rawlsian philosophy, rather than providing support for this claim, screens out of contention the very kinds of considerations to which supportive arguments must appeal. This view is strongly rooted in a perception that marriage in our society is an honorable estate, a matter of gaining not just certain legal exemptions but society's positive endorsement of the partnership's representation of true goods of human life. On the basis of this view, a same-sex couple's claim for admission to the marital estate is one for something more than "bare" or "empty" toleration or a grudging concession of noninterference.[59] It becomes a demand for societal *recognition* of their partnership as an exemplification of a valued way of life, and so leaves those making the claim with the burden of showing something substantively arbitrary – some clear, ethical mistake – in a refusal of such recognition.[60]

On the other hand, the argument continues, theorists of political liberalism insist on excluding substantive views of what is or makes for a good life from debate over what is and is not a basic right.[61] This restriction of the resources of debate over constitutional rights to "public" or "political" values, it is said, can only result in silencing "many" of the ideals that support same-sex marriage.[62] For example, the constraint bars any appeal to the idea of moral autonomy as a component of the good life.[63] As a result, those asserting or proposing a constitutional right of same-sex marriage are left unable to say what is so injurious, unfair, or outrageous about a refusal of it as to justify overriding a fairly counted democratic will.

This is too pessimistic an account of the bearing of political liberalism – specifically, as instanced by justice as fairness – on constitutional claims against exclusion of same-sex couples to the institution of legal marriage as it now exists.[64] In justice as fairness, the political values are not limited to bare toleration and political–procedural fairness. They include the establishment of social preconditions for the development and exercise by all citizens of their moral powers of the reasonable and the rational. It follows that, in justice as fairness, to support a constitutional right to $X$ strictly on the ground that denial of $X$ sets up an unjustified hindrance to the adequate and full development and exercise by everyone of one or the other of the moral powers is to keep strictly within the bounds of public reason. Consider, for example, the following snippet of certified Rawlsian public reasoning about the basic liberties:

... There is no guarantee that all aspects of our present way of life are the most rational for us and not in need of ... revision. [Therefore,] the adequate and full exercise of the capacity for a conception of the good is a means to a person's good, [and insofar as] liberty of conscience, and therefore the liberty to fall into error ..., is among the social conditions necessary for the development and exercise of this power, [liberty of conscience is required.

Moreover,] freedom of association is required to give effect to liberty of conscience; for unless we are at liberty to associate with other like-minded citizens, the exercise of liberty of conscience is denied.[65]

From here, the way is clear to placement of the burden of justification by public reasons on those who support exclusion of same-sex couples from the publicly sanctioned and privileged form of familial association known as marriage. Justice William Brennan marked out most of it – invoking no values or reasons that are not public values and reasons in justice as fairness – in his opinion for the Court in *Roberts v. United States Jaycees*:[66]

The Court has long recognized that, because the Bill of Rights is designed to secure individual liberty, it must afford the formation and preservation of certain kinds of highly personal relationships a substantial measure of sanctuary from unjustified interference by the State.... [W]e have noted that certain kinds of personal bonds have played a critical role in the culture and traditions of the Nation by cultivating and transmitting shared ideals and beliefs; they thereby foster diversity and act as critical buffers between the individual and the power of the State.... Moreover, the constitutional shelter afforded such relationships reflects the realization that individuals draw much of their emotional enrichment from close ties with others. Protecting these relationships from unwarranted state interference therefore safeguards the ability independently to define one's identity that is central to any concept of liberty.

The personal affiliations that exemplify these considerations, and that therefore suggest some relevant limitations on the relationships that might be entitled to this sort of constitutional protection, are those that attend the creation and sustenance of a family – marriage, childbirth, the raising and education of children, and cohabitation with one's relatives. Family relationships, by their nature, involve deep attachments and commitments to the necessarily few other individuals with whom one shares not only a special community of thoughts, experiences, and beliefs but also distinctively personal aspects of one's life.... [R]elationships with these sorts of qualities are likely to reflect the considerations that have led to an understanding of freedom of association as an intrinsic element of personal liberty.

Rawls himself is not so effusive. He simply points out that the political values of justice as fairness easily cover laws and policies reasonably viewed as preconditions to everyone's full development and exercise of the moral powers, as well as those supporting "the institutions needed to reproduce political society over time."[67] To which it would be apt – it may be crucial – to add the point that, in justice as fairness, the "social bases of self-respect" are counted a primary good of which the maximum achievable level is to be assured to those who are most deprived. "The parties in the original position would wish to avoid at any cost the social conditions that undermine self-respect," just because self-respect conditions "a person's sense of his own value, his secure conviction that his good, his plan of life, is worth carrying out" and thus affects the adequacy and fullness of development and exercise of the moral powers.[68]

So we see that, far from being unhelpful to demands for the opening of marriage to same-sex couples as a matter of basic right, the public reason of justice as fairness contains the makings of some impressive supporting arguments.[69] It also contains little or nothing with which to oppose them.[70] Most likely would be a claim that same-sex marriage is bad for the raising and education of children. However, although some claims of that form certainly fall within the bounds of Rawlsian public reason,[71] not all of them do. Consider a concern that children raised by same-sex couples would be likelier than others to grow up nonaverse to same-sex relationships. That cannot itself be a Rawlsian public reason for opposition to same-sex marriage because, as Rawls points out, no political value can inhere in hostility or opposition to same-sex partnership "as such," which can only reflect some religious or otherwise sectarian ethical doctrine.[72] But where else could one take the argument? In what other, nonsectarian way could one plausibly maintain that growing up a child of same-sex married parents is ipso facto dangerous to upbringing? There is, at any rate, no plausible account immediately in sight of how that – any more than growing up in a den of so-called straight people – could significantly hinder the adequacy or fullness of the development or exercise of a person's capacity to discern and adhere to fair terms of social cooperation or to discern, revise, and adhere to a conception of the good.

No doubt there will be some whose passionate convictions are less than fully engaged or assuaged by this restrained political–liberal case for a right against denial of same-sex marriage. Some may ache to base the case on an expectation that exercises of the right will lead to correction of what they believe are bad and wrong ideas about the good life entrenched in heterosexual marriage. As to them, justice as fairness happily notes that they can also freely endorse the moral force of the political case and so be part of an overlapping, political–liberal, moral consensus against the exclusion of same-sex partners from marriage.

But suppose it is widely believed that the hoped-for "corrective" effects on people's ideas about the good life really would ensue from recognition of same-sex marriage. What has justice as fairness to say to those to whom that is an ethically repugnant prospect?[73] It says what all variants of political liberalism are committed to say: that, in a company of free and equal persons divided by a plurality of comprehensive ethical views, it cannot be reasonable to allow any subgroup a privilege of using political authority to shape the basic structure in accordance with that group's special ethical convictions at the cost of equal citizenship for all;[74] that "neutrality of aim" is the only reasonable approach to adjusting the claims to liberty of equally respected citizens whose ethical convictions differ and sometimes collide;[75] that, in sum, a morally defensible answer to the problem of political legitimacy in modern free societies does not come without its price, and the price is the constraint of public reason.

## D. The Basic Liberties: "Formal" or Material?

We come now to two chronic, general issues in liberal–democratic constitutional law. The first is that of a "formal" versus a "material" understanding of a constitutionally protected liberty. Suppose that persons have a Constitutional right to decide their own procreative destinies. Does that comprise only a woman's bare freedom to have a pregnancy aborted according to her own unhindered choice, insofar as she has the means to bring about this result? Or does it also comprise assurance of the means (or of a fair opportunity to obtain the means) required for executing her choice with adequate care and safety? Or what about assurance to all of the material means for exercise of freedoms of thought and association, specifically in the matter of school choice?

Rawls does not doubt that a universally, reasonably acceptable political order must include assurances to everyone of the resources required to give the basic liberties a "fair value" in everyone's hands. That is exactly what the difference principle is about.[76] Nevertheless, the debatability of the measures required by this broad aim disqualifies it, in Rawls's view, from being made a judicially enforceable mandate of constitutional law.[77] So, in justice as fairness, the basic liberties typically guaranteed by constitutional bills of rights are mainly "negative" in import. They obligate certain persons to refrain from acting in certain ways toward others, but they do not require anyone to act. They establish, Rawls says, "a framework of legally protected paths and opportunities."[78]

### E. Application of the Basic Liberties: "Vertical" Only, or "Horizontal" Too?

That brings us to our second, chronic general issue in liberal–democratic constitutional law, that of the "horizontal" application of basic liberty rights – the question of the extent, if any, to which these rights apply against "private" (that is, nongovernmental) actors. How far does a just constitution protect one person's basic liberties against infringement by others exercising their ordinary rights, privileges, and powers as accorded by (we assume) a generally benign body of background law?

A state's ordinary trespass law gives landowners broad rights to decide what activities, conducted by whom, may take place on their lands. Should it be unconstitutional to apply that law in favor of the owners of major shopping malls against persons wishing to pass out political leaflets, nonobstructively, on their sidewalks? How about in favor of owners of small rental properties against unmarried or interracial couples to whom the owners as a matter of conscience do not wish to lease? Or take a slightly different sort of case. Among the equally protected basic liberties of American women is freedom to abort an early pregnancy. Are governments therefore constitutionally obliged (hence permitted) to provide abortion clinic patrons with effective legal protections against noisy, shocking, intrusive, perhaps intimidating forms of expression at clinic entrances? These are among the most vexed and disquieting issues of constitutional law before American society today. (And they show how a certain sort of *positive* obligation can devolve on lawmakers in consequence of a conclusion that the *negative* obligation covers "private" agents.)

Across the world, judges pondering full horizontal application of bill-of-rights guaranties give thought to the possible resulting effects on the basic liberties of citizens.[79] Horizontal application of negative liberties could subordinate a mall owner's freedoms of expression and conscience to the freedom of expression of others whose messages he does not wish to see propagated, especially not with the use of his property; just as it could subordinate the freedoms of association and conscience of a small landlord – not to mention his or her basic-liberty right to use and enjoy personal property – to the liberty and dignity (self-respect) claims of her would-be lessees;[80] just as it could subordinate the freedoms of expression and assembly of abortion clinic protesters to the basic liberties of clinic patrons; and so forth.

How does the ideal constitution prescribe for conflict-of-liberties problems of this kind? Rawls's answer would be "sparingly." His view, apparently, is that a just constitution must reserve to ordinary legislative bodies a wide (not boundless) discretion to make law *either way* for such cases. Before explaining why, let us note that this will be in many settings a controversial response, one with which many contemporary jurists are apt to disagree. As examples we may take both the American judges who apply state bills of rights to prohibit lawmakers from burdening the free expression of leafletters by subjecting them to ordinary trespass law[81] and their critics who conversely maintain that the constitutional rights of owners to control the use of their property, and maybe also their rights of freedom of expression, prohibit lawmakers from requiring accommodation of leafletters in shopping malls.[82] Rawls would say that both sides err in not allowing the legislature discretion to decide what law is best for these conflict-of-liberties cases. (It cannot be a boundless discretion, however. Consider the case of a law requiring mall owners to accommodate, specifically, all leafletters, signature-gatherers, etc., working for campaign finance reform.)

It is very much with conflict-of-liberties cases in mind that Rawls has carefully fashioned the first principle of justice as fairness to provide not that anyone has a right to each of the basic liberties taken separately but rather that all have rights to "a fully adequate scheme of equal basic liberties which is compatible with a similar scheme of liberty for all."[83] Far from condemning substantial legislative curbs on anyone's exercise of any the basic liberties taken singly, this text positively *invites* whatever such curbs are apt to the establishment of a *scheme* of equal basic liberties for everyone that best approximates the standard of full adequacy.[84] In Rawls's thought, it is this best-scheme objective that defines what he calls the priority of liberty, and that notion accordingly has a twofold meaning. It means both (i) that specific basic liberties *are not* curbed for the sake of any social advantage apart from the scheme-of-liberties objective, and (ii) that specific basic liberties *are* curbed as the pursuit of this objective may require. Liberty, Rawls says, *is* to be restricted for, if only for, the sake of liberty – meaning for the sake of a fully adequate scheme of basic liberties for everyone.[85]

Of course, we cannot apply that precept without having at hand some gauge of "adequacy," and justice as fairness provides one: a scheme of basic liberties is adequate insofar as it ensures, for everyone, the social preconditions for the normal, full development and exercise of the moral powers of the reasonable and the rational – an aim that requires the assurance to everyone of certain levels of practical independence and self-respect.[86] In sum, because there are bound to be conflicts among peoples' exercises of the various basic liberties, legislative "adjustment" of them is required to produce a fully adequate overall scheme for everyone.[87]

No doubt this fact gives cause for concern about the determinacy (what I have called the transparency) of the constitutional essentials. (Limiting the number of occasions of conflict requiring adjustment is one reason why Rawls wants to restrict the basic liberties to a relative few.[88]) But we do not have to run this framework of ideas into the ground in order to see that it will not mesh well with a legal doctrine flatly opposed to *all* legislative adjustments of conflicts among basic liberties guaranteed by a constitutional bill of rights. That is exactly why Rawls further says that political liberalism denies us the luxury of a tidily formal public–private distinction. Political liberalism cannot regard

the political and nonpolitical domains as two separate, disconnected spaces, each governed by its own distinctive principles.... A domain so-called, or a sphere of life, is not ... something already given apart from political conceptions of justice. A domain is not a kind of space, or place, but rather is simply the result ... of how the principles of political justice are applied, directly to the basic structure and indirectly to the associations within it. The principles defining the equal basic liberties and opportunities of citizens always hold in and through all so-called domains.[89]

Depending on circumstances of market structure and of the social distribution of wealth, power, and status, private action obviously

418   FRANK I. MICHELMAN

can be gravely detrimental to the development and exercise of the moral powers and to the personal independence and self-respect on which they depend. In a region where malls have completely replaced downtown shopping areas as public gathering places, those whose means are limited may be stymied from the development and exercise of their first moral power by widespread exclusion from mall courtyards and passageways.[90] In a town where there is widespread aversion to interracial or unmarried couples, landlord freedom of choice may lie heavily on both the self-respect and the intimate associations required for development and exercise of the second moral power.

Given all this, why should a Rawlsian conclude that justice as fairness dictates that legislatures should have discretion to decide horizontal application questions *either way*? Why not conclude that justice as fairness makes horizontal application a constitutional requirement? Perhaps because the question of horizontal application is too complexly situation-specific to be aptly resolvable at the level of constitutional law. We have seen how horizontal application is so often a two-way street. The clinic patron's demand for the protester's submission to her procreative liberty right is met by the latter's demand for the former's submission to her expression and assembly rights. The unmarried homeseeking couple's demand for the landlord's submission to their basic rights is met by the landlord's converse demand, and so forth. Horizontal application thus is often a matter of relatively fine adjustment of the reciprocal extents of the liberties in the scheme of basic liberties that is likely to call for more contextual knowledge and finer-grained, more contestable social–causal calculation than Rawls (for reasons we have seen) believes constitutional lawmaking can effectively and legitimately bear. Maybe mall owners should be required to yield, whereas three-decker owners should not. Maybe mall owners should be required to yield in some parts of the state or some moments in history but not others – depending, for example, on how much vitality is left in nearby, old-fashioned town shopping areas. Maybe clinic protesters should be required to leave clinic patrons a fifty-foot square quiet zone around a clinic entrance but not more. And maybe judges of the law should cultivate approaches to their work that leave them ill-suited to drawing these lines under the guise of legal interpretation – especially interpretation of the constitution. For we have seen that Rawls has reasons of political legitimacy for maintaining that constitutional–legal mandates should have relatively clear and uncontroversial applications to the expected run of cases, or at least their applications should be decidable by a demonstrably cogent and transparent – even if elaborate and complex – course of reasoning.

This does not mean, though, that the abstract principles of justice as fairness have nothing to say about horizontal application as a matter of law. What they first and foremost have to say about this question is that constitutional law ought not in any general way to preempt it. They make the question of horizontal application of basic rights a crucial matter of basic justice for a democratic society – not something to take off the table but rather a matter demanding constant, competent, political attention. If the question's sensitivity to context disqualifies it from resolution by constitutional law, then a just constitution must ensure that some subconstitutional lawmaking agency is authorized to address it from time to time.

In South Africa, the Constitution expressly calls on the judiciary at all levels for performance of this responsibility.[91] In the United States, under our prevailing canons of separation of powers and division of institutional labor, the work perhaps cannot mainly be done by courts, but only by legislatures. In a Rawlsian view, therefore, the American judiciary ought to construe the Constitution – assuming no prevailing textual or historical reason to the contrary – to allow a wide latitude for legislative decisions to apply constitutional basic liberties horizontally as a way of optimizing the scheme of basic liberties enjoyed by all.

By this Rawlsian critical standard, the U.S. Supreme Court's performance over the years has been so-so. The Court does permit state legislatures to decide either way the question of a horizontal extension of leafletter free-speech rights at some cost to the exclusionary rights of private property,[92] and of women's antidiscrimination rights at some cost to freedom of all-male association.[93] Under the guise of "time, place, and manner" restrictions, the Court also allows some modest regulation of speech rights for the sake of speech rights.[94] On the other hand, the Court has invoked a Constitutional right against forced association with views with which one disagrees to block a state legislature's attempt to utilize the "extra space" in a major power utility's billing envelopes (referring to the envelopes' capacity to contain additional matter without breaking a postage-rate barrier) for messages from consumer advocate groups[95] – a degree of constitutionalization of the "adjustment" question that Rawlsians might regard as excessive.

Most disturbingly to Rawlsian thought (because it involves the fair value of the political liberties), the Court sweepingly dismisses the very idea of an adequate-scheme-of-equal-basic-liberties rationale for legislative regulation of political campaign spending. "The concept that the government may restrict the speech of some elements in our society in order to enhance the relative voice of others," declares the Court, "is wholly foreign to the First Amendment."[96] In so declaring, Rawls observes, the Court evidently reads the Constitution to "reject altogether" the idea that Congress may work at ensuring a scheme of equal liberties that is fully adequate for all by any means that encroaches on one particularly privileged element in the scheme.[97] Specifically, formal freedom of expression may not be infringed for the sake of the fair value of the political liberties – regardless, it seems, of how persuasive the case for doing so may possibly appear when regarded from the standpoint of securing a fully adequate scheme of liberties to all.

In coming years, the Court will revisit the matter of political campaign regulation, and the results will be evidence of whether Rawls's ideas – his *distinctive* ideas, his ideas where it counts – have indeed crept into the law of the land. What we know already is that Rawls has contributed richly to the fund of ideas we have available for debating and appraising our judiciary's performances in hard constitutional cases.

ENDNOTES

*   Jason Bridges, Ruth Chang, David Charny, Richard Fallon, James Fleming, Samuel Freeman, Linda McClain, and Alec Walen all read drafts and provided very helpful comments.

1   John Rawls, *Political Liberalism* (New York: Columbia University Press, 1996), xx.

2   Id. 217.

3   Id.

4   See Samuel Freeman, "Original Meaning, Democratic Interpretation, and the Constitution," *Philosophy and Public Affairs* 21 (1992): 26 ff., 36 ff., cited approvingly by Rawls, *Political Liberalism* 234 n. 19. Cf.

id. 258–62; John Rawls, *A Theory of Justice* (Cambridge, MA: Harvard University Press, 1999), pp. 195–201 (on "the four-stage sequence"). This means that your finding particular ordinary laws unjust gives you no ground for resort to unlawful force, not that it gives you no ground for denunciation, civil disobedience, or conscientious refusal.

5   Rawls says the constitutional essentials include the "*fundamental* principles" that specify the "*general* structure of... the political process," and the "equal *basic* rights and liberties of citizenship that legislative majorities are bound to respect." Rawls, *Political Liberalism* 227 (emphasis supplied). See Parts I(E), (F).

6   Remarks at Rawls, *Political Liberalism*, 167–8 make clear that the hope is not, in Rawls's mind, a certainty.

7   See Rawls, *Political Liberalism* xliv, xlvi, 226–7; John Rawls, "The Idea of Public Reason Revisited," in *Collected Papers* (ed. Samuel Freeman, Cambridge, MA: Harvard University Press, 1999), pp. 573–615, at 576–9, 581, 605–6.

8   Rawls, *Political Liberalism* 13–14, 300–1.

9   See, for example, Rawls, *Political Liberalism* xl–xli. Cf. Rawls, "Public Reason" 573–4.

10   See John Gray, "Can We Agree to Disagree," *New York Times*, May 16, 1993, §7, at 35 (book review).

11   See, for example, Rawls, *Political Liberalism* 300.

12   See Rawls, "Public Reason" 581–4; Rawls, *Political Liberalism* 227.

13   See, for example, id. 167; Rawls, "Public Reason" 777 n. 35. Unfortunately, beyond the scope of this essay is the important question of how such a capacious view of political liberalism, as presumptively encompassing a plurality of political conceptions of justice, is to be squared with the demand for transparency of constitutional essentials we examine Part I(F). See Rawls, "Public Reason" 585 and n. 35 and, for valuable discussion, Lawrence Solum, "Situating *Political Liberalism*," *Chicago–Kent Law Review* 69 (1994): 549, 576–80; Samuel Freeman, "*Political Liberalism* and the Possibility of a Just Democratic Constitution," *Chicago–Kent Law Review* 69 (1994): 619, 646–58; Kent Greenawalt, "On Public Reason," *Chicago–Kent Law Review* (1994): 669.

14   See Rawls, *Political Liberalism* 259; Rawls, *Theory of Justice* 197–8.

15   Id. 13–14, 18–19, 49–50, 74. See also id. 300–2.

16   Rawls, *Political Liberalism* 74.

17   Rawls, "Public Reason" 607–8. See Rawls, *Political Liberalism* xlv–xlvi, 202–3, 301–2.

18   See id. 304.

19   See id. xlvi, lv.

20  See below, Part II(C).

21  Table created by F.I.M., not John Rawls.

22  See below, Part II(E).

23  See below, Part I(G).

24  See below, Part II(E).

25  See, for example, Rawls, *Political Liberalism* 214–15.

26  See, for example, Rawls, *Political Liberalism* 223, 292–5.

27  Cf. *Corporation of Presiding Bishop v. Amos*, 483 U.S. 783, 795 (1983) (Brennan, J., concurring).

28  Part II(E).

29  For fuller treatment of the bearing of Rawls's thought on the question of judicial review, see Frank I. Michelman, "In Pursuit of Constitutional Welfare Rights: One View of Rawls' Theory of Justice," *Pennsylvania Law Review* 121 (1973): 962, 991–1003 (cited approvingly by Rawls, *Political Liberalism* 339 n. 47); Samuel Freeman, "Constitutional Democracy and the Legitimacy of Judicial Review," *Law and Philosophy* 9 (1990): 327–70; Frank I. Michelman, "On Regulating Practices with Theories Drawn from Them," in Ian Shapiro and Judith Wagner DeCew, eds., *Theory and Practice* (Nomos 38) (New York: New York University Press, 1995), pp. 309, 325–38.

30  See Rawls, *Political Liberalism* 235, 240.

31  See Jeremy Waldron, "A Right-Based Critique of Constitutional Rights," *Oxford Journal of Legal Studies* 13 (1993): 18; Frank I. Michelman , "On Regulating Practices."

32  See Rawls, *Political Liberalism* 232–4; Freeman, "*Political Liberalism*" 660–1.

33  See id. 240; Frank I. Michelman, "In Pursuit of Constitutional Welfare Rights"; Freeman "*Political Liberalism*," 659–60.

34  Compare Rawls, *Political Liberalism* 229 with id. 237. See Rawls, *Theory of Justice* 198–9. Cf. Michael Walzer, "Philosophy and Democracy," *Political Theory* 9 (1981): 379; Lawrence G. Sager, "Justice in Plain Clothes: Reflections on the Thinness of Constitutional Law," *Northwestern University Law Review* 88 (1993): 410, 418–21.

35  See Rawls, *Political Liberalism* 228–30.

36  See id. 229.

37  Id. 237.

38  See id. 296.

39  Such a comparison may be controversial, but it is Rawls's. "We can expect more agreement about whether the principles for basic rights and liberties are realized than about . . . the principles for social and economic justice." Id. 229.

40  Id. 7, 228–9, 338.

41  Id. 327–8.
42  See, for example, id. 308. See above, Part I(C).
43  See id. 7.
44  Id. 166.
45  Cf. Michelman, "In Pursuit of Welfare Rights" 1002–3; Frank I. Michelman, "Welfare Rights in a Constitutional Democracy," *Washington University Law Quarterly* 1979 (1979): 659 (cited approvingly by Rawls, *Political Liberalism* 166 n. 29, 236–7 n. 23).
46  Thus, Rawls remarks that it is not the Court's task to say what arrangements are best but only to check that the legislature does its job. See id. 362. Cf. Frank I. Michelman, "The Constitution, Social Rights and Reason," *South African Journal on Human Rights* 14 (1998): 499 (briefly describing positive economic guaranties in the South African Constitution and related debates).
47  See id. 328, 356–63.
48  See id. 227–30.
49  Id. 295–6.
50  See below, Part II(E).
51  John H. Ely, *Democracy and Distrust: A Theory of Judicial Review* (Cambridge, MA: Harvard University Press, 1980) 58.
52  Alan Ryan, "How liberalism, politics, come to terms," *Washington Times*, May 16, 1993, at B8.
53  Rawls, *Political Liberalism* 291–2, 335.
54  See id. xlviii–ix, 6, 227, 290, 292–3; Rawls, "Public Reason" 768.
55  See above, Part I(B); Rawls, *Political Liberalism* 223; Rawls, "Public Reason" 773–4.
56  See above, Part I(C).
57  Rawls, *Political Liberalism* 293.
58  Id. 333.
59  On "bare" or "naked" toleration, see Linda C. McClain, "Toleration, Autonomy, and Governmental Promotion of Good Lives: Beyond 'Empty' Toleration to Toleration as Respect," *Ohio State Law Journal* 59 (1998): 21, 21–4.
60  See, for example, Carlos Ball, "Moral Foundations for a Discourse on Same-Sex Marriage: Looking Beyond Political Liberalism," *Georgetown Law Journal* 85 (1997): 1875–8.
61  Id. 1878.
62  Id. Cf. Michael J. Sandel, *Democracy's Discontent* (Cambridge, MA: Harvard University Press, 1996), 103–8.
63  Cf. Rawls, "Public Reason" 586; Rawls, *Political Liberalism* xliv–xlv.
64  My aim here is strictly limited to confirming the general receptivity of Rawlsian thought to fundamental complaint against a publicly

and legally privileged form of domestic association that is closed to same-sex partners. I do not address the intriguing question of what this thought has to say about the justifiability of making marriage a publicly recognized, legally consequential status at all, as opposed to a purely "private" matter.

65  Id. 313.

66  468 U.S. 609, 618–20 (1984) (citations omitted).

67  Rawls, "Public Reason" 587.

68  Rawls, *Theory of Justice* 440/386 rev.

69  Compare the liberally disciplined arguments for a right of same-sex marriage offered by McClain, "Toleration as Respect" 77–9, 119–20, 122–4 and David A.J. Richards, *Women, Gays, and the Constitution* (Chicago: University of Chicago Press, 1998), 442–3.

70  See Linda C. McClain , "Deliberative Democracy, Overlapping Consensus, and Same-Sex Marriage," *Fordham Law Review* 46 (1998): 1241, 1249–52.

71  See Rawls, "Public Reason" 587.

72  Id.

73  See also McClain, "Same-Sex Marriage," 1247–52.

74  See Rawls, *Political Liberalism* 226; Rawls, "Public Reason" 613–14.

75  See Rawls, *Political Liberalism* 193–4.

76  See id. 325–6; Rawls, *Theory of Justice* 204–5.

77  See above, Part I(F).

78  Rawls, *Political Liberalism* 325.

79  See, for example, Du Plessis v. De Klerk 1996 (3) SA 850 (CC) (opinion of Ackermann, J.).

80  See Rawls, *Political Liberalism* 298, explaining that the "role" of the basic liberty right to hold personal property is "to allow a sufficient material basis for a sense of personal independence and self-respect, both of which are essential for the development and exercise of the moral powers."

81  New Jersey Coalition Against the War v. J.M.B. Real Estate Corp., 138 N.J. 326, 650 A.2d 757 (1994), cert. denied, 116 U.S. 62 (1995); Robins v. PruneYard Shopping Center, 23 Cal. 3d 899, 592 P.2d 341 (1979), affirmed, 447 U.S. 74 (1980).

82  See, e.g., Richard A. Epstein, "Takings, Exclusivity and Speech: The Legacy of *PruneYard v. Robins*," *University of Chicago Law Review* 64 (1997): 21. The Supreme Court flirted with such a position in Lloyd Corp. v. Tanner, 407 U.S. 551 (1972) but later rejected it in PruneYard Shopping Center v. Robins, 447 U.S. 74 (1980).

83  Rawls, *Political Liberalism* 291.

84  See id. 291, 331–3.

85   See id. 295, 358–9.
86   See id. 332–3.
87   Id. 295.
88   See id. 296.
89   Rawls, "Public Reason" 598–9. Compare Linda McClain's defense of liberalism against feminist objections to an over-formalized "public/private" distinction." See McClain, "Toleration as Respect," 73–6.
90   See New Jersey Coalition Against the War, n. 81 above.
91   See Constitution of South Africa (1996), §§8(2), (3), 39.
92   See PruneYard Shopping Center v. Robins, 447 U.S. 474 (1980); Lloyd Corp., Ltd. v. Tanner, 407 U.S. 551 (1972).
93   See Roberts v. United States Jaycees, 468 U.S. 609 (1984).
94   Cf. Rawls, *Political Liberalism* 341.
95   Pacific Gas and Elec. Co. v. P.U.C., 475 U.S. 1 (1986).
96   Rawls, *Political Liberalism* 360, quoting from Buckley v. Valeo, 424 U.S. 1 (1976).
97   Rawls, *Political Liberalism* 360.

# 12  Rawls and Utilitarianism

In the Preface to *A Theory of Justice*,[1] Rawls observes that "[d]uring much of modern moral philosophy the predominant systematic theory has been some form of utilitarianism" (*TJ*, p. vii/xvii rev.). Critics of utilitarianism, he says, have pointed out that many of its implications run counter to our moral convictions and sentiments, but they have failed "to construct a workable and systematic moral conception to oppose it" (*TJ*, p. viii/xvii rev.). As a result, Rawls writes, "we often seem forced to choose between utilitarianism and intuitionism." In the end, he speculates, we are likely to "settle upon a variant of the utility principle circumscribed and restricted in certain ad hoc ways by intuitionistic constraints." "Such a view," he adds, "is not irrational; and there is no assurance that we can do better. But this is no reason not to try" (*TJ*, p. viii/xviii rev.). Accordingly, what he proposes to do "is to generalize and carry to a higher order of abstraction the traditional theory of the social contract as represented by Locke, Rousseau, and Kant." Rawls believes that, of all traditional theories of justice, the contract theory is the one "which best approximates our considered judgments of justice." His aim is to develop this theory in such a way as to "offer an alternative systematic account of justice that is superior . . . to the dominant utilitarianism of the tradition" (*TJ*, p. viii/xviii rev.).

Rawls sounds a similar note toward the end of Chapter 1, where he observes that "the several variants of the utilitarian view have long dominated our philosophical tradition and continue to do so," and this "despite the persistent misgivings that utilitarianism so easily arouses" (*TJ*, p. 52/46 rev.). This is, he says, a "peculiar state of affairs," which is to be explained by "the fact that no constructive alternative theory has been advanced which has the comparable

426

virtues of clarity and system and which at the same time allays these doubts" (*TJ*, p. 52/46 rev.). Rawls's "conjecture is that the contract doctrine properly worked out can fill this gap" (*TJ*, p. 52/46 rev.).

Rawls's claim to have outlined a theory ("justice as fairness") that is superior to utilitarianism has generated extensive debate. Despite his opposition to utilitarianism, however, it seems evident from the passages I have quoted that he also regards it as possessing theoretical virtues that he wishes to emulate. In particular, he admires utilitarianism's "systematic" and "constructive" character, and thinks it unfortunate that the views advanced by critics of utilitarianism have not been comparably systematic or constructive. This aspect of Rawls's attitude toward utilitarianism has attracted less attention. Yet it marks an important difference between his view and the views of other prominent critics of utilitarianism writing at around the same time, even when those critics express their objections in language that is reminiscent of his. For example, where Rawls says that "[u]tilitarianism does not take seriously the distinction between persons" (*TJ*, p. 27/24 rev.), Robert Nozick, explicitly citing Rawls, says that to sacrifice one individual for the greater social good "does not sufficiently respect and take account of the fact that he is a separate person, that his is the only life he has."[2] And Bernard Williams, developing a different but not entirely unrelated criticism, argues that utilitarianism makes personal "integrity as a value more or less unintelligible."[3] But neither Nozick nor Williams stresses the importance of providing a *systematic* alternative to utilitarianism.

I have said that Rawls's appreciation for utilitarianism's systematic and constructive character has attracted less comment than his claim to have identified a theory of justice that is preferable to utilitarianism. However, a number of critics have argued that Rawls's position has important features in common with utilitarianism – features in virtue of which his view is open to some of the very same objections that he levels against the utilitarian. Whether or not these arguments are successful, they may be seen in part as responses to the emphasis on system that is a feature both of Rawls's theory and of utilitarianism. To the extent that this is so, they can help to illuminate Rawls's complex attitude toward utilitarianism – an attitude that is marked by respect and areas of affinity as well as by sharp disagreements. They can also help us to see that some people may be troubled by Rawls's arguments against utilitarianism, not because they sympathize with those aspects of the view that he criticizes but rather because they are critical of those aspects of the view with which he sympathizes.

In this essay, I will begin by reviewing Rawls's main arguments against utilitarianism. I will then examine an argument by Nozick and by Michael Sandel to the effect that there is a tension between certain aspects of Rawls's theory and his criticisms of utilitarianism. I will explain why I do not regard this argument as persuasive, but will also indicate how it points to some genuine affinities between justice as fairness and utilitarian ideas – affinities that I will then explore in greater depth. My hope is to arrive at a balanced assessment of Rawls's attitude toward utilitarianism. I will conclude by discussing some apparent differences between Rawls's position in *A Theory of Justice* and his position in *Political Liberalism*.[4]

Rawls's criticisms of utilitarianism comprise a variety of formulations which depend to varying degrees and in various ways on the apparatus of the original position. Formally, his aim is to show that the parties in the original position would prefer his own conception of justice – justice as fairness – to a utilitarian conception. Thus, his "official" arguments against utilitarianism take the form of arguments purporting to show that it would be rejected by the parties. Yet the most important of those arguments can also be formulated independently of the original position construction and, in addition, there are some arguments that are not offered from the vantage point of the original position at all.

Rawls gives distinct arguments against two forms of utilitarianism: the classical version and the principle of average utility. Classical utilitarianism, as he understands it, holds "that society is rightly ordered, and therefore just, when its major institutions are arranged so as to achieve the greatest net balance of satisfaction summed over all the individuals belonging to it" (*TJ*, p. 22/20 rev.). It is, according to Rawls, a teleological theory, by which he means that it defines the good independently from the right and defines the right as maximizing the good. The principle of average utility, as its name suggests, "directs society to maximize not the total but the average utility" (*TJ*, p. 162/140 rev.). Although classical and average utilitarianism "may often have similar practical consequences" (*TJ*, p. 189/165 rev.), and although those consequences will coincide completely so long as population size is constant, Rawls argues that the two views are "markedly distinct conceptions" whose "underlying analytic assumptions are far apart" (*TJ*, p. 161/139 rev.).

Rawls observes that the distribution of satisfaction within the society has no intrinsic significance for classical utilitarianism. If a radically inegalitarian distribution – either of satisfaction itself or of the means of satisfaction – will result in the greatest total satisfaction overall, the inequality of the distribution is no reason to avoid it. Of course, as Rawls recognizes, utilitarians frequently argue that, given plausible empirical assumptions, the maximization of satisfaction is unlikely to be achieved in this way. The fact remains, however, that classical utilitarianism attaches no intrinsic importance to questions of distribution and imposes no principled limit on the extent to which aggregative reasoning may legitimately be employed in making social decisions. The losses of some people may, in principle, always be outweighed by the greater gains of other people.

Rawls argues that this commitment to unrestricted aggregation can be seen as the result of extending to "society as a whole the principle of rational choice for one man" (*TJ*, p. 26–7/24 rev.). In other words, we normally think that it is reasonable for a single individual to seek to maximize satisfaction over the course of a lifetime. It is reasonable, for example, to "impose a sacrifice on ourselves now for the sake of a greater advantage later" (*TJ*, p. 23/21 rev.). The classical utilitarian, Rawls argues, reasons in much the same way about society as a whole, regarding it as legitimate to impose sacrifices on some people in order to achieve greater advantages for others. This extension to society as a whole of the principle of choice for a single individual is facilitated, Rawls believes, by treating the approval of a perfectly sympathetic and ideally rational and impartial spectator as the standard of what is just. Since the impartial spectator "identifies with and experiences the desires of others as if these desires were his own," his function is to organize "the desires of all persons into one coherent system of desire" (*TJ*, p. 27/24 rev.). In this way, "many persons are fused into one" (*TJ*, p. 27/24 rev.). In summary, Rawls argues, the classical utilitarian "view of social cooperation is the consequence of extending to society the principle of choice for one man, and then, to make this extension work, conflating all persons into one through the imaginative acts of the impartial sympathetic spectator" (*TJ*, p. 27/24 rev.). This is what leads Rawls to make the claim that this form of utilitarianism "does not take seriously the distinction between persons." This is a decisive objection provided "we assume that the correct regulative principle for anything depends on the nature of that thing, and that the plurality of distinct persons with separate systems of ends is an essential feature of human societies" (*TJ*, p. 29/25 rev.).

It is noteworthy that this argument against classical utilitarianism is developed without reference to the apparatus of the original position and is not dependent on that apparatus. Rawls does, of course, offer an additional argument to the effect that the parties in the original position would reject the classical view. The argument is that the parties, knowing that they exist and wishing only to advance their own interests, would have no desire to maximize the net aggregate satisfaction, especially because doing so might require growth in the size of the population even at the expense of a significant reduction in the average utility per person. This argument is straightforward and appears decisive. At any rate, it has attracted far less controversy than Rawls's claim that the parties would reject the principle of average utility. Yet it is probably fair to say that it has been less influential, as an argument against classical utilitarianism, than the argument offered independently of the original position construction.

Rawls goes on to suggest that if the terms of the original position were altered in such a way that the parties were "conceived of as perfect altruists, that is, as persons whose desires conform to the approvals" (*TJ*, p. 188–9/164 rev.) of an impartial, sympathetic spectator, then classical utilitarianism would indeed be adopted. This leads him to the "unexpected conclusion" that the classical view is "the ethic of perfect altruists," by contrast with the principle of average utility which, from the perspective afforded by the original position, emerges as "the ethic of a single rational individual (with no aversion to risk)" (*TJ*, p. 189/164–5 rev.). Thus, in looking at the two versions of utilitarianism from the standpoint of the original position, a "surprising contrast" (*TJ*, p. 189/165 rev.) between them is revealed. This suggests to Rawls that "even if the concept of the original position served no other purpose, it would be a useful analytic device" (*TJ*, p. 189/165 rev.) enabling us to see the "different complex[es] of ideas" (*TJ*, p. 189/165 rev.) underlying the two versions of utilitarianism. However, the characterization of classical utilitarianism as the ethic of perfect altruists seems puzzling given that the classical view is said to conflate all persons into one. It seems peculiar to suppose that perfect altruists would neglect the distinctness of persons and support the unrestricted interpersonal aggregation to which such neglect is said to give rise. After characterizing classical utilitarianism as the ethic of perfect altruists, moreover, Rawls goes on in the next several pages to ask what theory of justice would be preferred by an impartial, sympathetic spectator who did not conflate all systems of desires into one. In response, he argues that a "benevolent" person fitting this description would actually prefer justice as fairness to classical utilitarianism. But this makes it even less clear why classical utilitarianism should be associated with perfect altruism. If that association is unwarranted, then the contrast between the classical and average views may be less dramatic than Rawls suggests, and the claims of the original position as an illuminating analytic device may to that extent be reduced.

Of course, this is not to deny that the principle of average utility would have more appeal than classical utilitarianism for the parties in the original position. Indeed, whereas Rawls's assertion that the parties would reject classical utilitarianism has attracted little opposition, his claim that his conception of justice would be preferred to the principle of average utility has been quite controversial.[5] Most of the controversy has focused on Rawls's argument that it would be rational for the parties to use the maximin rule for choice under uncertainty when deciding which conception of justice to select. If they do use this rule, then they will reject average utility in favor of his two principles, since the maximin rule directs choosers to select the alternative whose worst outcome is superior to the worst outcome of any other alternative, and the two principles are those a person would choose if he knew that his enemy were going to assign him his place in society. However, as Rawls acknowledges, the maximin rule is very conservative, and its employment will seem rational only under certain conditions. Unless the decision facing the parties in the original position satisfies those conditions, the principle of average utility may be a better choice for the parties even if it is riskier, since it may also hold out the prospect of greater gain (*TJ*, p. 165–6/143 rev.). Yet Rawls argues that the original position does have features that make reliance on the maximin rule appropriate and that the parties would reject average utility as unduly risky.

In general, the use of maximin is said to be rational when there is no reliable basis for assessing the probabilities of different outcomes, when the chooser cares very little for gains above the minimum that could be secured through reliance on maximin, and when the other options have possible consequences that the chooser would find intolerable. Rawls's strategy is to try to establish that the choice between average utility and his two principles satisfies these conditions because (1) the parties have no basis for confidence in the type of probabilistic reasoning that would support a choice of average utility, (2) his two principles would assure the parties of a satisfactory minimum, and (3) the principle of average utility might have consequences that the parties could not accept. Although Rawls first outlines this strategy in Section 26, it is important to emphasize that what he provides in that section is only a sketch of "the qualitative structure of the argument that needs to be made if the case for these principles is to be conclusive" (TJ, p. 150/130 rev.).

With respect to the first condition, Rawls observes in Section 28 that, from the standpoint of the original position, the prima facie appeal of average utility depends on the assumption that one has an equal chance of turning out to be anybody once the veil of ignorance is lifted. Yet Rawls says that this assumption "is not founded upon known features of one's society" (TJ, p. 168/146 rev.). Instead, it is based on the principle of insufficient reason, which, in the absence of any specific grounds for the assignment of probabilities to different outcomes, treats all the possible outcomes as being equally probable. Rawls says that, given the importance of the choice facing the parties, it would be rash for them to rely on probabilities arrived at in this way. This is presumably because the maximization of average utility could, in societies with certain features, require that the interests of some people be seriously compromised. Thus, the excessive riskiness of relying on the principle of insufficient reason depends on the claim about the third condition, that is, on the possibility that average utility might lead to intolerable outcomes. This possibility arises, Rawls suggests, because utilitarianism relies entirely on certain "standard assumptions" (TJ, p. 159/137–8 rev.) to demonstrate that its calculations will not normally support severe restrictions on individual liberties. Given the importance that the parties attach to the basic liberties, Rawls maintains that they "would prefer to secure their liberties straightaway rather than have them depend upon what may be uncertain and speculative actuarial calculations" (*TJ*, p. 160–1/138–9 rev.). The parties would be unwilling to take the chance that, in a society governed by utilitarian principles, a utilitarian calculation might someday provide the basis for a serious infringement of their liberties, especially since they have the more conservative option of the two principles available to them.

If the conclusion that the parties would regard the principle of average utility as excessively risky depends on the claim that, under certain conditions, it would justify the sacrifice of some people's liberties in order to maintain the average level of well-being within the society at as high a level as possible, then Rawls's arguments against average utility are not as different from his arguments against classical utilitarianism as his talk of a "surprising contrast" might suggest. In both cases, the parties are said to fear that their own interests might be sacrificed for the sake of the larger utilitarian goal. And in both cases, this argument from the perspective of the parties corresponds to an independent criticism of utilitarianism as being excessively willing to sacrifice some people for the sake of others.

Defenders of the principle of average utility have challenged Rawls's arguments in a variety of ways. First, they have argued that the "standard assumptions" are sufficiently robust that it would not be excessively risky for the parties to choose average utility even if this meant relying on the principle of insufficient reason. Second, however, they have wondered why, if Rawls believes that it would be unduly risky for the parties to rely on probabilities that are not grounded in information about their society, he fails to provide them with that information. So long as the veil of ignorance prevents the parties from knowing their own identities, providing them with the relevant information about their society need not compromise their impartiality. Third, they have questioned whether Rawls's principles can truly be said to guarantee the parties a satisfactory minimum and whether the parties, who are ignorant of their conceptions of the good, can truly be said to care little for gains above such a minimum. Fourth, they have argued that Rawls's own principles of justice are not altogether risk-free, since the "general conception" of justice as fairness would permit the infringement of basic liberties under extraordinary conditions. Thus, they have maintained, there is less of a difference than Rawls indicates between average utility and his own view in respect of their riskiness. Under normal conditions neither would permit serious infringements of liberty, while under extraordinary conditions either might. Finally, critics have argued that there is a fundamental obscurity in Rawls's account of the way that the parties assess risk. He says that the choice of principles should not depend on the parties' "special attitudes" toward risk, and that the veil of ignorance therefore prevents them from knowing "whether or not they have a characteristic aversion to taking chances" (*TJ*, p. 172/149 rev., sentence amended). Instead, the aim is to show that "choosing as if one had such an aversion is rational given the unique features of . . . [the original position] irrespective of any special attitudes toward risk" (*TJ*, p. 172/149 rev., sentence amended). However, defenders of average utility have questioned whether it makes sense to suppose that there is an attitude toward risk that it is rational to have if one is ignorant of one's "special attitudes" toward risk.

These issues have been extensively discussed, and I will here simply assert that, despite some infelicities in Rawls's presentation, I believe he is correct to maintain that the parties would prefer his two principles to the principle of average utility. In arriving at this conclusion, it is important to guard against an excessively narrow, formalistic interpretation of the "maximin argument."[6] As already noted, Rawls's initial account in Section 26 of the reasons for relying on the maximin rule is merely an outline of what he will attempt to establish subsequently. It should not be interpreted, as it sometimes has been, as the self-contained presentation of a formal decision–theoretic argument which is independent, for example, of the appeals to stability, self-respect, and the strains of commitment in Section 29. The inevitable effect of such an interpretation is to make Rawls's argument seem both more formal and less plausible than it really is.

In fact, Rawls states explicitly that the arguments of Section 29 "fit under the heuristic schema suggested by the reasons for following the maximin rule. That is, they help to show that the two principles are an adequate minimum conception of justice in a situation of great uncertainty. Any further advantages that might be won by the principle of utility . . . are highly problematical, whereas the hardship if things turn out badly are [sic] intolerable" (*TJ*, p. 175/153 rev., sentence amended). In other words, the arguments of Section 29 are intended to help show that the choice confronting the parties has features that make reliance on the maximin rule rational. They are not unrelated arguments.

Indeed, the point goes further. The arguments set out in Section 29 explicitly invoke considerations of moral psychology that are not fully developed until Part III. In other words, Section 29's appeals to psychological stability, self-respect, and the strains of commitment are all intended as contributions to the overarching enterprise of demonstrating that Rawls's principles would provide a satisfactory minimum, whereas the principle of average utility might have consequences with which the parties would find it difficult to live. In slightly different ways, however, all of these appeals are underwritten by the contrast that Rawls develops at length in Part III between the moral psychologies of the two theories. Rawls argues there that because his principles embody an idea of reciprocity or mutual benefit, and because reciprocity is the fundamental psychological mechanism implicated in the development of moral motivation, the motives that would lead people to internalize and uphold his principles are psychologically continuous with developmentally more primitive mechanisms of moral motivation. This means that, in a society whose basic structure was regulated by the two principles, allegiance to those principles would, under favorable conditions, develop naturally out of preexisting psychological materials. By contrast, utilitarianism does not embody an idea of reciprocity. If people are to be stably motivated to uphold utilitarian principles and institutions, even when those principles and institutions have not worked to their advantage, the capacity for sympathetic identification will have to be the operative psychological mechanism. Yet that capacity is, as a rule, not strong enough nor securely enough situated within the human motivational repertoire to be a reliable source of support for utilitarian principles and institutions.

As I have indicated, substantial portions of Part III are devoted to the detailed elaboration of this contrast along with its implications for the relative stability of the two rival conceptions of justice and their relative success in encouraging the self-respect of citizens.[7] Furthermore, Rawls says explicitly that much of the argument of Part II, which applies his principles to institutions, is intended to help establish that they constitute a workable conception of justice and provide a satisfactory minimum (*TJ*, p. 156/135 rev.). The upshot is that the reasons for relying on the maximin rule, far from being fully elaborated in Section 26, are actually the subject of much of the rest of the book.[8,9] In effect, the "maximin argument" functions as a master argument within which many of the book's more specific arguments are subsumed. Viewed in this light, the argument's significance as a contribution to the criticism of utilitarianism is easier to appreciate. By itself, the claim that even the average version of utilitarianism is unduly willing to sacrifice some people for the sake of others is not a novel one. However, by anchoring the parties' unwillingness to accept the sacrifices associated with average utility in a carefully elaborated moral psychology and a developed account of how a workable and efficient set of social institutions could avoid such sacrifices, Rawls considerably strengthens and enriches that familiar criticism. At the very least, his argument challenges utilitarians to supply a comparably plausible and detailed account of utilitarian social and economic institutions and of the processes by which, in a society regulated by utilitarian principles, motives would develop that were capable of generating ongoing support for those institutions and principles. The force of this challenge, moreover, is largely independent of Rawls's claims about the justificatory significance of the original position construction. Even if utilitarians reject the original position as a device for adjudicating among rival conceptions of justice, in other words, this challenge is not one they can easily ignore.

Whereas the maximin argument is presented as a reason why the parties would not choose utilitarianism, Rawls develops another important line of criticism whose ostensible relation to the original position construction is less straightforward.[10] This line of criticism turns on a contrast between those views that take there to be but a single rational good for all human beings and those that conceive of the human good as heterogeneous. We may speak here of a contrast between *monistic* and *pluralistic* accounts of the good. Rawls believes that teleological theories, which define the good independently of the right and the right as maximizing the good, tend also to interpret the good in monistic terms. He thinks this is true of those teleological theories he describes as perfectionist, of certain religious views, and also of classical utilitarianism insofar as its account of the good is understood hedonistically. Nonteleological forms of utilitarianism, such as the principle of average utility,[11] are also monistic if they rely on a hedonistic interpretation of the good. Admittedly, hedonistic forms of utilitarianism recognize that different individuals will take pleasure in very different sorts of pursuits, and so they are superficially hospitable to pluralism in a way that other monistic views are not. For this very reason, Rawls suggests, utilitarianism offers "a way of adapting the notion of the one rational good to the institutional requirements of a modern state and pluralistic democratic society."[12] So long as the good is identified with agreeable feeling, however, the account remains monistic.[13]

Rawls suggests that teleological views may be drawn to monistic accounts out of a desire to avoid indeterminacy in the way the good is characterized, since for teleological views "any vagueness or ambiguity in the conception of the good is transferred to that of the right" (*TJ*, p. 559/490 rev.). He also suggests that part of the attraction of monistic accounts, and of teleological theories that incorporate such accounts, may derive from a conviction that they enable us to resolve a fundamental problem about the nature of rational deliberation. The problem is to explain how rational choices among apparently heterogeneous options can ever be made. Unless there is some one ultimate end at which all human action aims, this problem may seem insoluble. If, however, there is some "dominant end" to which all of our other ends are subordinated, then "a rational decision is always in principle possible, since only difficulties of computation and lack of information remain" (*TJ*, p. 552/484 rev.). Moreover, if there is indeed a dominant end at which all rational human action aims, then it is but a short step to construing that end as the "sole intrinsic good" (*TJ*, p. 556/487 rev.) for human beings. In this way, we may be led to a monistic account of the good "by an argument from the conditions of rational deliberation" (*TJ*, p. 556/487 rev.). And once we have accepted a monistic account of the good, a teleological view directing us to maximize that good may seem plausible. As Rawls says: "Teleological views have a deep intuitive appeal since they seem to embody the idea of rationality. It is natural to think that rationality is maximizing something and that in morals it must be maximizing the good" (*TJ*, pp. 24–5/22 rev.). Furthermore, hedonism is "the symptomatic drift of teleological theories" (*TJ*, p. 560/490 rev.) both because agreeable feeling may appear to be an "interpersonal currency" (*TJ*, p. 559/490 rev.) that makes social choice possible and because hedonism's superficial hospitality to varied ways of life enables it "to avoid the appearance of fanaticism and inhumanity"

(*TJ*, p. 556/487 rev.). Thus, Rawls believes, there is a chain of argument that begins with a worry about the possibility of rational decision and concludes with an endorsement of hedonistic utilitarianism.

Against this line of thought, Rawls argues, first, that there simply is no dominant end: no one overarching aim for the sake of which all our other ends are pursued. Pleasant or agreeable feeling, in particular, cannot plausibly be thought to constitute such an aim. Nor, he maintains, does the irreducible diversity of our ends mean that rational choice is impossible. All it means is that formal principles play a limited role in determining such choices. Rational choice must often rest instead on self-knowledge – on a careful attempt to ascertain which one of a diverse set of ends matters most to us. In making such determinations, we may do well to employ "deliberative rationality" – to reflect carefully, under favorable conditions, in light of all the relevant facts available to us – but there is no formal procedure that will routinely select the rational course of action. And since there is no dominant end of all rational human action, Rawls continues, it is implausible to suppose that the good is monistic. Instead, he says, the "[h]uman good is heterogeneous because the aims of the self are heterogeneous" (*TJ*, p. 554/486 rev.). This drains away much of the motivation for a teleological view. Whereas the idea of arranging social institutions so as to maximize the good might seem attractive if there were a unique good at which all rational action aims, it makes more sense, in light of the heterogeneity of the good, to establish a fair framework of social cooperation within which individuals may pursue their diverse ends and aspirations.

The significance of this criticism is subject to doubts of two different kinds. First, it may seem that the criticism simply does not apply to contemporary versions of utilitarianism which do not, in general, purport to construe the good hedonistically. When such views advocate the maximization of total or average satisfaction, their concern is with the satisfaction of people's preferences and not with some presumed state of consciousness. Yet in "Social Unity and Primary Goods," where he builds on an argument first broached in the final four paragraphs of Section 28 of *TJ*, Rawls contends that even contemporary versions of utilitarianism are often covertly or implicitly hedonistic. For they rely on something like a "shared highest order preference function" as the basis for interpersonal comparisons of well-being, and such a function treats citizens as subscribing to a common ranking of the relative desirability of different packages of material resources and personal qualities – including traits of character, skills and abilities, attachments and loyalties, ends and aspirations. Rational citizens are then assumed to desire an overall package with as high a ranking as possible. This assumption, Rawls argues, implies "the dissolution of the person as leading a life expressive of character and of devotion to specific final ends," and it is only "psychologically intelligible"[14] if one thinks of pleasure as a dominant end for the sake of which a rational person is willing to revise or abandon any of his or her other ends or commitments. If this analysis is correct, then Rawls's argument may apply to a broader range of utilitarian theories than was initially evident.

However, the argument's oblique relation to the original position construction may give rise to doubts of another kind. The argument is not presented to the parties in the original position as a reason for rejecting utilitarianism or teleological views in general. Rather, it appears to play a role in motivating the design of the original position itself. It helps to explain why the parties are denied knowledge of any specific conception of the good, and why they are instead stipulated to accept the thin theory of the good, with all that that involves. Given these starting points, it seems antecedently unlikely that the parties will accept any theory of justice that relies on a hedonistic or other monistic conception of the good. As Rawls says: "The parties . . . do not know what final aims persons have, and all dominant-end conceptions are rejected. Thus it would not occur to them to acknowledge the principle of utility in its hedonistic form. There is no more reason for the parties to agree to this criterion than to maximize any other particular objective" (TJ, p. 563/493 rev.). But this suggests that the parties reject theories of justice that incorporate monistic conceptions of the good because Rawls's argument for pluralism has led him to design the original position in such a way as to guarantee that they will do so. This in turn may cast doubt on the justificatory significance of the parties' choice. And since their choice represents the core of Rawls's "official" case against utilitarianism, one effect of the way he deploys the argument against monism may be to jeopardize that case. In his later writings, Rawls himself expresses misgivings about the role played in TJ by his defense of a pluralistic theory of the good. In "Justice as Fairness: Political not Metaphysical," he describes it as one of the "faults" of TJ that the account of goodness developed in Part III "often reads as an account of the complete good for a comprehensive moral conception."[15] And in *Political Liberalism*, he recasts the argument against monistic conceptions of the good; the point is no longer that they are mistaken but rather that no such conception can serve as the basis for an adequate conception of justice in a pluralistic society.[16]

These considerations implicate some significant general issues – about the justificatory function of the original position and about the changes in Rawls's views over time – which lie beyond the scope of this essay. However, even if the role of the argument against monism in *Theory* raises questions about the justificatory significance of the original position construction, and even if the philosophical character of the argument is in tension with the "political" turn taken in Rawls's later writings, I believe that the argument can stand on its own as an important challenge to utilitarian thought. The same, as I have already suggested, is true of Rawls's claim that utilitarianism tolerates unacceptable interpersonal trade-offs. Indeed, I believe that those two arguments represent his most important and enduring criticisms of the utilitarian tradition.

Despite the vigor of his arguments against utilitarianism, however, some critics have contended that Rawls's own theory displays some of the very same features he criticizes in the utilitarian position. For example, Robert Nozick holds that there is a tension between Rawls's assertion that the difference principle "represents, in effect, an agreement to regard the distribution of natural talents as a common asset and to share in the benefits of this distribution" (*TJ*, p. 101/cf. *TJ*, 87 rev., sentence amended), and his charge that classical utilitarianism does not take seriously the distinction between persons. Nozick suggests that Rawls can avoid this tension only by placing an implausible degree of weight on the distinction between persons and their talents.[17] Michael Sandel, following up on Nozick's point, argues that Rawls has a "theory of the person" according to which talents are merely "contingently-given and wholly inessential attributes" rather than "essential *constituents*" of the self.[18] For this reason, Sandel argues, Rawls does not see the distinctness of *persons* as violated by the idea of treating the distribution of talents as a common asset. However, Sandel believes that the underlying theory of the person suffers from "incoherence"[19] and cannot, therefore, provide Rawls with a satisfactory response to the charge that he too is guilty of neglecting the distinctness of persons.

Sandel maintains that "the only way out of the difficulties Nozick raises" would be to argue that what underlies the difference principle is an "intersubjective" conception of the person according to which "the relevant description of the self may embrace more than a single empirically-individuated human being."[20] This would enable Rawls to say that other people's benefitting from my natural talents need not violate the distinctness of persons, not because my talents are not really part of me but rather because those people may not, in the relevant sense, be distinct from me. Of course, to say this would be to concede that Rawls takes the conventional distinctions among "empirically-individuated human beings" even less seriously than does utilitarianism. Indeed, one of the broad morals of Sandel's analysis is supposed to be that the difference principle is a sufficiently communitarian notion of justice that it requires a thoroughly communitarian conception of the self.

However, I believe that Sandel's analysis raises the metaphysical stakes unnecessarily and that the tension between Rawls's principles and his criticism of utilitarianism can be dissolved without appealing to either of the two theories of the person that Sandel invokes. Classical utilitarianism identifies the good life for an individual as a life of happiness or satisfaction. However, it directs us to arrange social and political institutions in such a way as to maximize the aggregate satisfaction or good, even if this means that some individuals' ability to have good lives – in utilitarian terms – will be seriously compromised, and even though there is no sentient being who experiences the aggregate satisfaction or whose good is identified with that aggregate. In this sense, classical utilitarianism gives (what it regards as) the aggregate good priority over (what it regards as) the goods of distinct individuals. For Rawls, by contrast, the good life for an individual consists in the successful execution of a rational plan of life, and his principles of justice direct us to arrange social institutions in such a way as to protect the capacity of each individual to lead such a life. The idea that the distribution of natural talents should be regarded as a common asset is not the idea of an aggregate good that takes precedence over the goods of individual human beings. Instead, the thought is that a system that treats the distribution of talents as a collective asset under the terms of the difference principle is actually required if each person is to have a chance of leading a good life. In short, utilitarianism gives the aggregative good precedence over the goods of distinct individuals, whereas Rawls's principles do not. In this sense, utilitarianism takes the distinctions among persons less seriously than they do. Since there is, accordingly, no inconsistency between Rawls's principles and his criticism of utilitarianism, there is no need for him to take drastic metaphysical measures to avoid it.[21]

Nevertheless, there are some genuine commonalities between Rawls's conception of justice and utilitarianism, and these commonalities may be partly responsible for the perception that there is a tension between his endorsement of the former and his criticism of the latter. I want to call attention to three of these commonalities. The first, which I have already mentioned, is Rawls's aspiration to produce a theory that shares utilitarianism's "systematic" and "constructive" character. The second is his agreement with the utilitarian view that commonsense precepts of justice have only a "derivative" (TJ, p. 307/270 rev.) status and must be viewed as "subordinate" (TJ, p. 307/270 rev.) to a "higher criterion" (TJ, p. 305/268 rev.). And the third is that both the Rawlsian and the utilitarian accounts of distributive justice are, in a sense to be explained, holistic in character. These three points of agreement, taken together, have implications that are rather far-reaching. They help to explain why it can be tempting to think that Rawls's principles display the very faults for which he criticizes utilitarianism. And although, as I have argued, this temptation should be resisted, they help us to see that Rawls does share with utilitarianism some features that are genuinely controversial and are bound to generate some strong resistance to both views.

Rawls's desire to provide a "constructive" conception of justice is part of his desire to avoid intuitionism. Intuitionism, as Rawls understands it, holds that there is a plurality of first principles of justice which may conflict on particular occasions. Intuitionists do not believe that there are any priority rules that can enable us to resolve such conflicts; instead, we have no choice but to rely on our intuitive judgment to strike an appropriate balance in each case. In this sense, intuitionists deny that it is possible to give a general solution to what Rawls calls "the priority problem," that is, the problem of how to assign weight to conflicting considerations of justice. But "the assignment of weights is an essential and not a minor part of a conception of justice," for if two people differ about the weight to be assigned to different principles, "then their conceptions of justice are different" (TJ, p. 41/36–7 rev.). In effect, then, an intuitionist conception of justice is "but half a conception" (TJ, p. 41/37 rev.). Rawls's aim, by contrast, is to reduce our reliance on unguided intuition by formulating "explicit principles for the priority problem" (*TJ*, p. 41/37 rev.), that is, by identifying "constructive" and "recognizably ethical" (*TJ*, p. 39/35 rev.) criteria for assigning weight to competing precepts of justice. Utilitarianism, of course, achieves this aim by identifying a single principle as the ultimate standard for adjudicating among conflicting precepts. Rawls hopes to show that it is possible for a theory to be constructive without relying on the utilitarian principle, or, indeed, on any *single* principle, as the ultimate standard. Thus, he hopes to produce a solution to the priority problem that offers an alternative to the utilitarian solution but remains a constructive solution nonetheless.

The fact that Rawls agrees with utilitarianism about the desirability of identifying a clear and constructive solution to the priority problem leads more or less directly to the second point of agreement. Both views hold that commonsense precepts of justice must be subordinate to some "higher" principle or principles. For these precepts conflict and, at the level of common sense, no reconciliation is possible, since there is no determinate way of weighing them against each other. Thus, if we are to find a constructive solution to the priority problem, we must have recourse to a "higher principle" to adjudicate these conflicts. In theory, one or more of the commonsense precepts could themselves be "elevated" (*TJ*, p. 305/268 rev.) to this status, but Rawls does not believe that they are plausible candidates. "Adopting one of them as a first principle is sure to lead to the neglect of other things that should be taken into account. And if all or many precepts are treated as first principles, there is no gain in systematic clarity. Commonsense precepts are at the wrong level of generality" (*TJ*, p. 308/271 rev.). Of course, utilitarians believe that the principle of utility provides the requisite higher standard, whereas Rawls believes that his two principles are "the correct higher criterion" (*TJ*, p. 305/268 rev.). But they agree on the need for such a criterion and on the derivative and subordinate character of commonsense precepts of justice.

To illuminate the third point of agreement, we may begin by noting that Rawls calls attention to, and has considerable sympathy with, the broad institutional emphasis that is characteristic of the great writers of the utilitarian tradition. In his early essay "Two Concepts of Rules," for example, he writes: "It is important to remember that those whom I have called the classical utilitarians were largely interested in social institutions. They were among the leading economists and political theorists of their day, and they were not infrequently reformers interested in practical affairs."[22] In the Preface to *A Theory of Justice*, similarly, he deplores our tendency to "forget that the great utilitarians, Hume and Adam Smith, Bentham and Mill, were social theorists and economists of the first rank; and the moral doctrine they worked out was framed to meet the needs of their wider interests and to fit into a comprehensive scheme" (*TJ*, p. vii/xvii rev.). In Rawls's own theory, of course, institutions are made the central focus from the outset, since the basic structure of society, which comprises its major institutions, is treated as the first subject of justice.[23] This in turn leads to the idea of treating the issue of distributive shares as a matter of pure procedural justice (*TJ*, p. 84–5/74 rev.): provided the basic structure is just, any distribution of goods that results is also just.[24] Once the problem of distributive justice is understood in this way, the principles of justice can no longer be applied to individual transactions considered in isolation (*TJ*, p. 87–8/76 rev.). Nor can the justice of an overall allocation of goods be assessed independently of the institutions that produced it. As Rawls says:

A distribution cannot be judged in isolation from the system of which it is the outcome or from what individuals have done in good faith in the light of established expectations. If it is asked in the abstract whether one distribution of a given stock of things to definite individuals with known desires and preferences is better than another, then there is simply no answer to this question. The conception of the two principles does not interpret the primary problem of distributive justice as one of allocative justice. (*TJ*, p. 88/76–7 rev.)

As Rawls emphasizes, utilitarianism does not share his view that "special first principles are required for the basic structure" (*PL*, p. 262), notwithstanding its broad institutional emphasis, nor does it agree that the question of distributive shares should be treated as a matter of pure procedural justice (*TJ*, pp. 88–9/77 rev.). These are important differences between the two theories. The principle of utility, as it has come to be interpreted at least, is a comprehensive standard that is used to assess actions, institutions, and the distribution of resources within a society.[25] Rawls's concentration on the basic structure and his use of pure procedural justice to assess distributions give his theory a greater institutional focus. Yet these differences, important as they are, should not be allowed to obscure an important point of agreement, namely, that neither view is willing to assess the justice or injustice of a particular assignment of benefits in isolation from the larger distributional context. In other words, neither believes that the principles of justice can appropriately be applied to "a single transaction viewed in isolation" (*TJ*, p. 87/76 rev.). The justice or injustice of assigning a particular benefit to a given individual will depend, for utilitarians, on whether there is any other way of allocating it that would lead to an overall distribution with greater (total or average) utility. It will depend, for Rawls, on whether the assignment is part of an overall distribution produced by a basic structure conforming to his two principles. In this sense, both Rawls and the utilitarian take a *holistic* view of distributive justice: both insist that the justice of any particular assignment of benefits always depends – directly or indirectly – on the justice of the larger distribution of benefits and burdens in society.

Holism about distributive justice draws support from two convictions. The first is that all people's lives are of equal value and importance. The second is that the life prospects of individuals are so densely and variously interrelated, especially through their shared participation in social institutions and practices, that virtually any allocation of resources to one person has morally relevant implications for other people. Holists conclude that it is impossible to assess the justice of an assignment of benefits to any single individual without taking into account the larger distributive context of that assignment. In conditions of moderate scarcity, we cannot tell whether a particular person should receive a given benefit without knowing how such an allocation would fit into the broader distribution of benefits and burdens within the society. Nor, to those who find holism compelling, does the project of identifying a putatively natural, presocial baseline distribution of advantages, and assessing the justice of all subsequent distributions solely by reference to the legitimacy of each move away from the baseline, seem either conceptually sound or ethically appropriate. Social institutions structure people's lives in fundamental ways from birth through death; there is no presocial moment in the life of the individual. That being the case, it is not clear what could reasonably count as the "natural" baseline or what the ethical credentials of any such baseline might plausibly be thought to be.[26] Moreover, as the size of the human population keeps growing, as the scale and complexity of modern institutions and economies keep increasing, and as an ever more sophisticated technological and communications infrastructure keeps expanding the possibilities of human interaction, the obstacles in the way of a satisfactory account of the presocial baseline loom larger, and the pressure to take a holistic view of distributive justice grows greater.[27] In their different ways, the Rawlsian and utilitarian accounts of justice are both responsive to this pressure.[28]

Although the case for holism has considerable force, and many of our intuitions about distributive justice are indeed holistic, there are other, nonholistic ideas about justice that also have widespread intuitive support. Often, for example, we seem prepared to say that an individual deserves or has a right to some benefit, and that it is therefore just that he should get it, without inquiring into the larger distributional context. Indeed, according to one familiar and traditional view, justice consists, at least in part, in giving people what they may independently be said to deserve. In other words, there is a prior standard of desert by reference to which the justice of individual actions and institutional arrangements is to be assessed. The basis for a valid desert claim, on this view, must always be some characteristic of, or fact about, the deserving person. In this sense, desert as traditionally understood is *individualistic* rather then holistic. No assessment of the overall distribution of benefits and burdens in society or of the institutions that produced that distribution is normally required in order to decide whether a particular individual deserves a certain benefit. Instead, it is a constraint on the justice of distributions and institutions that they should give each individual what that individual independently deserves in virtue of the relevant facts about him or her.

Neither Rawls nor the utilitarian accepts this view.[29] As is well known, utilitarianism does not regard desert as a fundamental moral notion. Utilitarians may agree, of course, that there are often good reasons for social institutions to allocate benefits and burdens in accordance with publicly announced criteria of merit and demerit. They may also agree that, when an institutional scheme of this kind is in place, individuals who satisfy the relevant criteria can be said to deserve the benefits and burdens in question. But to say this is to treat desert as an institutional artifact rather than as a normative constraint on the design of just institutions. It is not to say that just institutions must give people what they independently deserve. The point is rather that, if just institutions have announced that they will allocate rewards in accordance with certain standards, then individuals who meet those standards can be said to deserve the advertised rewards.

Rawls agrees with utilitarians that individuals who have done what a just institution has announced that it will reward are entitled to receive the rewards in question. Just institutions must honor the expectations they have created, and insofar as talk about desert is just a way of referring to those institutional entitlements, Rawls is happy to agree that just institutions must give people what they deserve. As with utilitarianism, however, desert in this sense is dependent on a prior conception of justice and on the expectations actually established by just institutions. Rawls puts the point as follows:

[I]t is necessary to be clear about the notion of desert. It is perfectly true that given a just system of cooperation as a scheme of public rules and the expectations set up by it, those who, with the prospect of improving their condition, have done what the system announces that it will reward are entitled to their advantages ... But this sense of desert presupposes the existence of the cooperative scheme; it is irrelevant to the question ... [of how] in the first place the scheme is to be designed ... (*TJ*, p. 103/cf. 88–9 rev., passage amended)

Rawls suggests at a couple of points that his view is consistent with the traditional understanding of desert. He says, for example, that there is no conflict between his view of justice and the traditional Aristotelian view. It is true that "Aristotle's definition clearly presupposes ... an account of what properly belongs to a person and what is due to him," but, Rawls argues, "such entitlements are ... very often derived from social institutions and the legitimate expectations to which they give rise," and since there is "no reason to think that Aristotle would disagree with this," the upshot is that there "is no conflict with the traditional notion" (*TJ*, pp. 10–11/10 rev.). Similarly, he thinks he can say "that, in the traditional phrase, a just scheme gives each person his due: that is, it allots to each what he is entitled to as defined by the scheme itself" (*TJ*, pp. 313/275–6 rev.).

These formulations elide the sharp differences between the traditional view of desert and the type of position that both Rawls and the utilitarian appear to endorse. It is true that their view can make room for the claim that a just scheme gives each person what he or she deserves. However, it can do this only by supplying that claim with a very different meaning than it has for the traditionalist. In the traditional view, the claim implicitly relies on an independent and individualistic standard of desert, and what it asserts is that institutions must conform to that standard if they are to be just. For Rawls and the utilitarian, by contrast, the principles of distributive justice, holistically understood, are fixed without reference to any prior notion of desert, and what the claim asserts is merely that just institutions will honor the expectations to which they give rise – expectations that may be expressed, if one likes, using the language of desert.

In summary, then, Rawls agrees with utilitarianism about the desirability of providing a systematic account of justice that reduces the scope for intuitionistic balancing and offers a clear and constructive solution to the priority problem; about the need to subordinate commonsense precepts of justice to a higher criterion; and about the holistic character of distributive justice. Taken together, these three features of his view mean that, like the utilitarian, he is prepared to appeal to higher principle, without recourse to intuitionistic balancing, to provide a systematic justification for interpersonal trade-offs that may violate commonsense maxims of justice. In light of this aspect of Rawls's theory, the temptation to claim that he attaches no more weight than utilitarianism does to the distinctions among persons is understandable. Although I have argued that this temptation should be resisted, it seems fair to say that the Rawlsian and utilitarian approaches to justice have some important elements in common and that these elements run counter to one deeply entrenched tendency in our moral thought.

Within contemporary political philosophy, this tendency receives what is perhaps its most forceful expression in Nozick's work, and it is noteworthy that a resistance to distributive holism appears to be part of what lies behind his objection to "end-result principles."[30] These principles are said to assess the justice of a given distribution (or sequence of distributions) solely by seeing whether the associated distributional matrix satisfies some structural criterion rather than by taking into account historical information about how the distribution came to pass. Significantly, Nozick classifies both the utilitarian and the Rawlsian principles of justice as end-result principles. (Indeed, he claims that the design of the original position guarantees that only end-result principles will be chosen.) As applied to Rawls, this characterization does not seem right, given the lexical priority of his first principle over his second principle and his treatment of the question of distributive shares as a matter of pure procedural justice. It is Rawls, after all, who says that a "distribution cannot be judged in isolation from the system of which it is the outcome or from what individuals have done in good faith in the light of established expectations," and who insists that "there is simply no answer" to the abstract question of whether one distribution is better than another. Yet both the Rawlsian and the utilitarian accounts are indeed holistic, and this may be part of what Nozick finds objectionable about them. For at least part of his complaint is that they exaggerate the significance of the overall distributional context and attach insufficient importance to local features of particular transactions.

This complaint connects up with a more general source of resistance to holism, which derives from a conviction that its effect is to validate a deplorable tendency for the lives of modern individuals to be subsumed within massive bureaucratic structures and for their interests to be subordinated to the demands of larger social aggregates and to the brute power of impersonal forces they cannot control. To accept a holistic account of justice, on this view, is to acquiesce in an erosion of the status of the individual which is one of the most striking features of modern life. Indeed, for some people, this is why Rawls's complaint that utilitarianism does not take seriously the separateness of persons has such resonance. It is ironic, therefore, that the author of that complaint not only is not opposed to holism about distributive justice but in fact is one of its strongest advocates. Nevertheless, once we recognize that, for some people, the words in which Rawls articulates his criticism may serve as a way of expressing resistance to holism, it is understandable why some who have echoed those words have not followed Rawls in seeking to devise a constructive and systematic alternative to utilitarianism. For them, constructiveness, systematicity, and holism may all be symptomatic of a failure to attach sufficient moral importance to the separateness of persons. If so, however, then their ultimate concern is not the same as his, even if it can be expressed in the same words.

This is not to say that their concern is insignificant. Some people understandably abhor many of the tendencies in modern life that create pressure to think holistically about justice and believe that our moral thought, rather than seeking to accommodate those tendencies, should serve as a source of resistance to them. Whatever the merits of this view, however, it is not one that Rawls shares. On this issue, he and the utilitarian are on the same side. Rawls's objection to utilitarianism is not to its holism but rather to the particular criterion it uses for assessing the legitimacy of interpersonal trade-offs. His own theory of justice, one might say, aims not to resist the pressures toward holism but rather to tame or domesticate them: to provide a fair and humane way for a liberal, democratic society to accommodate those pressures while preserving its basic values and maintaining its commitment to the inviolability of the individual. This is something he believes that utilitarianism can never do despite the liberal credentials of its greatest advocates. Some people may think that holism itself undermines liberal values, so that Rawls's aim is in principle unattainable. These people will inevitably conclude that his criticisms of utilitarianism do not go far enough and that his own theory exhibits some of the same faults that they see in the utilitarian view. But, once again, these are not the same faults that *he* sees in utilitarianism, whether or not they can be expressed in the same words.

The fact that Rawls's attitude toward utilitarianism is marked not only by sharp disagreements but also by important areas of affinity may help to explain some otherwise puzzling things he says about the view in *Political Liberalism*. In that book, of course, Rawls' aims are different from his aims in *A Theory of Justice*. His primary goal is no longer to develop his two principles as an alternative to utilitarianism but rather to explain how a just and stable liberal society can be established and sustained in circumstances marked by reasonable disagreement about fundamental moral and philosophical matters. Given his focus on this new task, utilitarianism is relegated largely to the periphery of his concern. One of the few times he has anything substantial to say about it is when he includes classical utilitarianism – "the utilitarianism of Bentham and Sidgwick, the strict classical doctrine" (*PL*, p. 170) – among the views that might participate in an overlapping consensus converging on a liberal political conception of justice, the "standard example" (*PL*, p. 164) of which is justice as fairness. The possibility of such a consensus lies at the heart of his answer to the question of how a just and stable liberal society is possible in conditions of reasonable pluralism.

On the face of it, however, the suggestion that classical utilitarianism might participate in a consensus of this kind is startling. Rawls seems to be proposing that the putatively less plausible of the two versions of the very theory which, in *A Theory of Justice*, he had treated as his primary target of criticism, and as the primary rival for his own principles of justice, might actually join in an overlapping consensus affirming those principles. It is very difficult to see how this might work.[31] For one thing, the participants in the consensus he describes are envisioned as converging not merely on the principles of justice but also on certain fundamental ideas that are implicit in the public political culture and from which those principles are said to be derivable. The most important of these ideas is the idea of society as a fair system of cooperation. Yet Rawls had said quite explicitly in *A Theory of Justice* that classical utilitarianism does not accept that idea (*TJ*, pp. 33/29–30 rev.). Furthermore, the argument from the fundamental ideas to the political conception is envisioned in *Political Liberalism* as proceeding via the original position, which is said to model the relevant ideas (*PL*, Lecture I.4). However, we know that the parties in the original position decisively reject classical utilitarianism. It is, therefore, doubly unclear how classical utilitarianism could participate in the overlapping consensus Rawls envisions; for it rejects the fundamental ideas that form the basis of the consensus, and the arguments that begin from those ideas are said to result in its own repudiation.

To be sure, Rawls does not claim that the political conception is deductively derivable from classical utilitarianism but only that the classical view might support the political conception "as a satisfactory and perhaps the best workable approximation [to what the principle of utility would on balance require] given normal social conditions" (*PL*, p. 171). Yet, as noted above, Rawls explicitly states that an overlapping consensus is "deep" enough to include such fundamental ideas as the idea of society as a fair system of cooperation (*PL*, pp. 149, 158–60, 164–6), and the suggestion that classical utilitarianism might support the political conception as a "workable approximation" does not explain what attitude the utilitarian is now supposed to have toward that idea.[32] Furthermore, this suggestion is ambiguous as between two importantly different attitudes the utilitarian might take toward apparently nonutilitarian principles of justice. The first is to say "that under the conditions of civilized society there is great social utility in following them for the most part and in permitting violations only under exceptional circumstances" (*TJ*, p. 28/25 rev.). When Rawls discussed this attitude in *A Theory of Justice*, he argued that it represented an unacceptably weak commitment to the priority of such principles. The second attitude is to say that utility will actually be maximized if nonutilitarian principles are "publicly affirmed and realized as the basis of the social structure" (*TJ*, p. 181/158 rev., sentence amended). When Rawls discussed this attitude in *Theory*, he argued that it was tantamount to abandoning utilitarianism altogether, since, given the publicity condition, utilitarianism must be "defined" as "the view that the principle of utility is the correct principle for society's public conception of justice" (*TJ*, p. 182/158 rev.). By Rawls's own standards, then, neither of these attitudes would appear to qualify a person *both* as a genuine utilitarian and as a committed participant in an overlapping consensus on a liberal political conception of justice.

If this is correct, then it remains difficult to see how classical utilitarianism could be included in such a consensus. Yet Rawls's willingness to treat it as a candidate for inclusion, which initially seemed startling, may appear more understandable if one keeps in mind the complexity of his attitude toward utilitarianism in *Theory*. I have argued throughout this essay that his undoubted opposition to utilitarianism, and his determination to provide an alternative to it, should not be allowed to obscure some important points of agreement. Perhaps one might even say that it is precisely because he agrees with utilitarianism about so much that Rawls is determined to provide an alternative that improves upon it in the respects in which it is deficient. While there would be no need to provide a better theory if utilitarianism did not have serious faults, the effort would hardly be worth making if it did not also have important virtues. Utilitarianism, in Rawls's view, has been the dominant systematic moral theory in the modern liberal tradition. If he did not himself agree that we need a clear, systematic theory to reduce our reliance on

unguided intuition and provide an adequate basis for liberal, democratic institutions, he would not be so concerned to emphasize utilitarianism's deficiencies or to produce a theory that remedies those
deficiencies while preserving the view's virtues.

Up to a point, then, Rawls and the utilitarian are engaged in a common enterprise, and it is against the background of what they have
in common that Rawls takes utilitarianism as his primary target of
criticism in *Theory*. In *Political Liberalism*, the context of discussion has shifted. The aim now is to show how liberal institutions
can achieve stability in conditions of pluralism by drawing on diverse sources of moral support. In this context, utilitarianism, with
its prominent place in the traditions of liberal thought and its various more specific affinities with Rawls's own view, presents itself as
a natural ally. There is still a problem, of course, given his insistence
in *Theory* that neither classical nor average utilitarianism can put
fundamental liberal values on a sufficiently secure footing. And the
problem becomes more acute, for the reasons given above, when the
overlapping consensus is conceived of as affirming not merely liberal principles in general but Rawls's theory of justice in particular.
Nevertheless, the impulse to treat some form of utilitarianism as a
candidate for inclusion in the consensus, when considered in the context of Rawls's aims in *Political Liberalism* and his sympathy for certain aspects of the utilitarian doctrine, no longer seems mysterious.[33]
Whether or not the tensions between that impulse and his forceful objections to utilitarianism can be satisfactorily resolved, they
provide a salutary reminder of the complexity of Rawls's attitude
toward modern moral philosophy's "predominant systematic theory." At the same time, it is a measure of Rawls's achievement that
utilitarianism's predominant status has been open to serious question ever since *A Theory of Justice* set forth his powerful alternative
vision.[34]

ENDNOTES

1   Harvard University Press, 1971, revised edition 1999. Cited hereafter
    as *TJ* with page references for both the first and revised editions given
    parenthetically in the text.
2   *Anarchy, State, and Utopia* (New York: Basic Books, 1974), p. 33.

3 "A Critique of Utilitarianism," in *Utilitarianism for and against*, eds. J.J.C. Smart and Bernard Williams (Cambridge, UK: Cambridge University Press, 1973), pp. 77–150, at p. 99.

4 Columbia University Press, 1993 (paperback edition, 1996). Cited hereafter as *PL* with page references to the paperback edition given parenthetically in the text.

5 See, for example, Kenneth Arrow, "Some Ordinalist–Utilitarian Notes on Rawls's Theory of Justice," *Journal of Philosophy* 70 (1973): 245–63; Brian Barry, *The Liberal Theory of Justice* (Oxford, UK: Clarendon Press, 1973), Chapter 9; Holly Smith Goldman, "Rawls and Utilitarianism," in *John Rawls' Theory of Social Justice: An Introduction*, eds. H. Gene Blocker and Elizabeth H. Smith (Athens, OH: University of Ohio Press, 1980), pp. 346–94; R.M. Hare, "Rawls' Theory of Justice," in *Reading Rawls*, ed. Norman Daniels (Stanford University Press, 1989), pp. 81–107; John Harsanyi, "Can the Maximin Principle Serve as a Basis for Morality? A Critique of John Rawls's Theory," in *Essays on Ethics, Social Behavior, and Scientific Explanation* (Dordrecht, Holland: D. Reidel, 1976), pp. 37–63; David Lyons, "Nature and Soundness of the Contract and Coherence Arguments," in *Reading Rawls*, pp. 141–67; Jan Narveson, "Rawls and Utilitarianism," in *The Limits of Utilitarianism*, eds. Harlan B. Miller and William H. Williams (Minneapolis: University of Minnesota Press, 1982), pp. 128–43; Robert Paul Wolff, *Understanding Rawls* (Princeton University Press, 1977), Chapter XV.

6 My discussion follows those of Steven Strasnick in his review of Robert Paul Wolff's *Understanding Rawls, Journal of Philosophy* 76 (1979): 496–510, and Joshua Cohen, "Democratic Equality," *Ethics* 99 (1989): 727–51.

7 In *Political Liberalism* (pp. xvii–xx and xlii–xliv) Rawls says that the account of stability given in Part III of the *Theory* is defective because it tests the rival conceptions of justice by asking whether the well-ordered society associated with each such conception would continue to generate its own support over time and, in so doing, this account implicitly assumes that in a well-ordered society everyone endorses the conception on the basis of a shared "comprehensive moral doctrine." In view of the inevitable diversity of reasonable comprehensive doctrines in a modern democratic society, Rawls argues, this is not a realistic assumption, and hence the test of stability is inadequate. Perhaps so, but Rawls should not concede too much here. He may be correct in thinking he needs to show how a society regulated by his conception of justice could be stable despite the prevalence of diverse comprehensive doctrines. Surely, however, if it is true that the well-ordered utilitarian society would not continue to generate its own support even if everyone initially endorsed

utilitarian principles of justice on the basis of a shared commitment to utilitarianism as a comprehensive philosophical doctrine, then that remains a significant objection to the utilitarian view.

8   Thus, I believe it is misleading when Rawls says, at the end of his discussion of relative stability in Section 76: "These remarks are not intended as justifying reasons for the contract view. The main grounds for the principles of justice have already been presented. At this point we are simply checking whether the conception already adopted is a feasible one and not so unstable that some other choice might be better. We are in the second part of the argument in which we ask if the acknowledgment previously made should be reconsidered" ( *TJ*, p. 504/441 rev.). After all, he had said in Section 29, (a) that the stability argument is one of the "main arguments for the two principles" ( *TJ*, p. 175/153 rev.), (b) that it fits "under the heuristic schema suggested by the reasons for following the maximin rule" ( *TJ*, p. 175/153 rev.), and (c) that it depends "on the laws of moral psychology and the availability of human motives," which are only discussed "later on (Sections 75–76)" ( *TJ*, p. 177/154 rev.). These points imply that the discussion in Section 76 is an indispensable part of the presentation of "the main grounds for the principles of justice."

9   In "Justice and the Problem of Stability," ( *Philosophy and Public Affairs* 18 [1989]: 3–30), Edward McClennen acknowledges that a "careful reading of *A Theory of Justice* makes it clear that it would be a mistake to treat the rational choice argument of the analytic construction [i.e., the original position] and the psychological theory pertaining to the sense of justice as completely disjoint" (pp. 6–7). McClennen himself, however, believes that Rawls's conception of justice can best be defended independently of the original position construction by a rational choice argument that makes a more direct appeal to considerations of psychological stability.

10  For helpful discussions of this line of criticism, see Samuel Freeman, "Utilitarianism, Deontology, and the Priority of Right," *Philosophy and Public Affairs* 23 (1994): 313–49; T.M. Scanlon, "Rawls' Theory of Justice," *University of Pennsylvania Law Review* 121 (1973): 1020–69.

11  See *TJ*, p. 66/143 rev., where Rawls says that the principle of average utility "is not a teleological doctrine, strictly speaking, as the classical view is," since it aims to maximize an average and not a sum. Note, however, that under the index entry for average utilitarianism (606/538 rev.), there is a subheading that reads: "as teleological theory, hedonism the tendency of."

12  "Social Unity and Primary Goods," in *Utilitarianism and Beyond*, eds. Amartya Sen and Bernard Williams (Cambridge, UK: Cambridge University Press, 1982), pp. 159–85, at p. 182; also in John Rawls,

*Collected Papers*, ed. Samuel Freeman (Cambridge, MA: Harvard University Press, 1999), pp. 359–87, at p. 384.

13   In light of this assessment of the utilitarian conception of the good and his own defense of a pluralistic conception, Rawls's comment in Section 15 that utilitarianism and his theory agree that "the good is the satisfaction of rational desire" ( *TJ*, pp. 92–3/79–80 rev.) seems misleading at best.

14   "Social Unity and Primary Goods," p. 181.

15   *Philosophy and Public Affairs* 14 (1985): 223–51, at 251n., and Rawls, *Collected Papers*, 388–414 at 414n. See also *PL*, pp. 176–7n.

16   See for example *PL*, pp. 134–5. See also "Justice as Fairness: Political not Metaphysical," pp. 248–9.

17   *Anarchy, State, and Utopia*, p. 228.

18   *Liberalism and the Limits of Justice* (Cambridge, UK: Cambridge University Press, 1982), p. 78.

19   *Liberalism and the Limits of Justice*, p. 79.

20   *Liberalism and the Limits of Justice*, p. 80.

21   There has been extensive discussion and disagreement both about the meaning and about the merits of Rawls's claim that utilitarianism does not take seriously the distinctions among persons. This is partly because Rawls's formulation has appeared to some readers to straddle two or more of the following claims: (1) *a claim of metaphysical error* to the effect that utilitarianism simply fails to notice that persons are ontologically distinct, (2) *a claim of moral error* to the effect that utilitarianism tolerates unacceptable interpersonal trade-offs and thereby fails to attach sufficient moral significance to the ontological distinctions among persons, and (3) *an explanatory claim* to the effect that utilitarianism fails to attach sufficient moral significance to the ontological distinctions among persons because it extends to society as a whole the principle of choice for one person. For pertinent discussion, see Derek Parfit, *Reasons and Persons* (Oxford: Clarendon Press, 1984), Chapter 15; James Griffin, *Well-Being* (Oxford: Clarendon Press, 1986), pp. 167–70; H.L.A. Hart, "Between Utility and Rights," in *The Idea of Freedom: Essays in Honour of Isaiah Berlin*, ed. Alan Ryan (Oxford University Press, 1979), pp. 77–98; Leslie Mulholland, "Rights, Utilitarianism, and the Conflation of Persons," *Journal of Philosophy* 83 (1986): 323–40; Will Kymlicka, "Rawls on Teleology and Deontology," *Philosophy and Public Affairs* 17 (1988): 173–90; Samuel Freeman, "Utilitarianism, Deontology, and the Priority of Right"; Joseph Raz, *The Morality of Freedom* (Oxford: Clarendon Press, 1986): pp. 271–3. I believe that Rawls is not making the first of these claims, that he

is making the second, and that he is also putting forward the third as at least a partial explanation. The question posed by Nozick and Sandel, as I understand it, is whether Rawls's own principles attach any more moral weight to the distinctions among persons than does utilitarianism. My argument in the text is that they do indeed and that their ability to do so is not conditional on Rawls's conceiving of the self either as "unencumbered" or as "intersubjective."

22  *Philosophical Review* 64 (1955): 3–32, at p. 19n.; also in Rawls, *Collected Papers*, 20–46 at 33n.

23  Rawls gives his most extended defense of his emphasis on the basic structure in "The Basic Structure as Subject," which is included in *PL* as Lecture VII. For criticism of this emphasis, see G.A. Cohen, "Where the Action Is: On the Site of Distributive Justice," *Philosophy and Public Affairs* 26 (1997): 3–30; Liam Murphy, "Institutions and the Demands of Justice," *Philosophy and Public Affairs* 27 (1998): 251–91; Nozick, *Anarchy, State, and Utopia*, pp. 204–13. For discussion of the distinctiveness of Rawls's focus on the basic structure, see Hugo Bedau, "Social Justice and Social Institutions," *Midwest Studies in Philosophy* 3 (1978): 159–75.

24  The proviso is essential. Only if the basic structure is regulated by Rawls's substantive conception of justice can the determination of individual shares be handled as a matter of pure procedural justice. Thus, Rawls's reliance on pure procedural justice does not mean that his theory is procedural *rather than substantive*. This is a point that he emphasizes in response to Habermas (*PL*, 421–33), and it explains what he means when he says in the index to *PL* (p. 455) that "justice is always substantive and never purely procedural" – a remark that might otherwise seem inconsistent with the role that *Theory* assigns to "pure procedural justice." For relevant discussion, see Joshua Cohen, "Pluralism and Proceduralism," *Chicago–Kent Law Review* 69 (1994): 589–618, especially fn. 44.

25  Part of Rawls's point, when calling attention in "Two Concepts of Rules" to the interest of the classical utilitarians in social institutions, was to emphasize that the construal of utilitarianism as supplying a comprehensive standard of appraisal represents a relatively recent development of the view: one he associates, in that essay, with Moore. In his later work, however, it is the comprehensive version of utilitarianism that he himself treats as standard and with which he contrasts his own institutional approach to justice. See, for example, Section 2 of "The Basic Structure as Subject," where he associates the comprehensive interpretation with Sidgwick (*PL*, pp. 260–2).

26  See Thomas Nagel, *Equality and Partiality* (Oxford University Press, 1991), pp. 100–2.

27  I have discussed some related themes in "Individual Responsibility in a Global Age," *Social Philosophy and Policy* 12 (1995): 219–36.

28  For related discussion, see Thomas Pogge, "Three Problems with Contractarian–Consequentialist Ways of Assessing Social Institutions," *Social Philosophy and Policy* 12(1995): 241–66. Pogge writes that, in recent decades, there has been a shift from thinking about justice "interactionally" to thinking about it "institutionally." By this he means that there is less emphasis on individual actions and their consequences and more emphasis on the ground rules and practices that structure our social world and supply the framework for our actions. Pogge argues that contractarianism (as exemplified by Rawls's work) and consequentialism are "the two most prominent traditions of institutional moral analysis" and that they "are not as distinct as is widely believed." Indeed, he argues that, when viewed "as guides to the assessment of social institutions, contractarianism and consequentialism are for the most part not competitors but alternate presentations of a single idea: both tend to assess alternative institutional schemes exclusively by how each would affect its individual human participants" (246).

29  Here I draw on my discussion in "Responsibility, Reactive Attitudes, and Liberalism in Philosophy and Politics," *Philosophy and Public Affairs* 21(1992): 299–323.

30  *Anarchy, State, and Utopia*, pp. 153–5.

31  Here I draw on my discussion in "The Appeal of Political Liberalism," *Ethics* 105 (1994): 4–22.

32  This is the flaw in Brian Barry's response to my earlier discussion (in "The Appeal of Political Liberalism") of utilitarian participation in an overlapping consensus. In "John Rawls and the Search for Stability," *Ethics* 105 (1995): 874–915, Barry argues (at pp. 914–5n.) that, because Rawls does not hold that the political conception must be deductively derivable from within each comprehensive doctrine represented in an overlapping consensus, he should not be thought to require that the participants in such a consensus endorse anything more than the principles of justice themselves. However, this overlooks Rawls's repeated remarks about the depth of an overlapping consensus.

33  It is worth noting that, in his earlier paper "The Idea of an Overlapping Consensus" (*Oxford Journal of Legal Studies* 7 (1987): 1–26 at p. 12; also in Rawls, *Collected Papers*, 421–48 at 433–4), Rawls himself had denied that the utilitarianism of Bentham and Sidgwick could belong to an overlapping consensus, but he had suggested that perhaps some form of "indirect utilitarianism" might be able to do so. The latter suggestion

seems more plausible, although even it is not altogether easy to reconcile with the comments in *Theory* I have quoted.

34 Earlier versions of this paper were presented to a philosophy department colloquium at UCLA, a symposium in Stockholm sponsored by the Royal Swedish Academy of Sciences and the Rolf Schock Foundation, and the 2000 Conference of the International Society for Utilitarian Studies, held at Wake Forest University. I am grateful to all of these audiences for helpful discussion. I am also indebted to Samuel Freeman for his comments on a previous draft and to Nicholas Kolodny for valuable research assistance.

# 13   Rawls and Communitarianism

The allegation that liberals neglect the value of community has a long – some would say notorious – history.[1] Rawls's *A Theory of Justice*,[2] immediately acclaimed as the most systematic and sophisticated statement of liberal theory to date, must have confirmed the worst suspicions of those predisposed to believe that liberalism's emphasis on the individual implied its neglect of the formative significance of their social context and the moral significance of relations between them. For Rawls's invocation of a hypothetical contract, whereby rational and disembodied individuals, deprived of all particularity and characterised simply as free and equal, are to agree on principles to regulate the distribution of benefits and burdens in society, seemed perfectly to illustrate the claim that liberalism commits a number of fundamental errors:

- Seeking an unavailable Archimedean point from which to construct an abstract and universally applicable blueprint for society;
- Assuming individuals to be fundamentally self-interested;
- Ignoring the fact that people are socially constituted;
- Positing an incoherent metaphysical essence of the person; and
- Claiming to be neutral while sneaking in strongly individualistic premises.

It is not hard to see why many of Rawls's most influential critics formulated their objections in terms that pointed, in one way or another, to his failure to appreciate the value or significance of 'community', a shared line of attack that, despite important differences, earned them and their critique the label 'communitarian'.

We argue that, despite appearances, Rawls commits none of the theoretical sins with which he has been charged. This defence will not be new to those familiar with the Rawls-inspired literature of the past fifteen or so years.[3] But the communitarian caricature continues to surface often enough to justify another attempt to lay it to rest. With this summary, we hope to put an end to those misunderstandings and misattributions that continue to divert intellectual attention from the real and important issues raised by the communitarian critique. For the debate has by no means been a waste of time. While communitarians may be judged uncharitable in their readings of Rawls, a charitable reading of communitarian texts would regard their objections as pointing to a range of problems and challenges that remain crucial for liberal theory in general, and Rawlsian liberalism in particular.

Moreover, even if some of the misunderstandings have been fostered by communitarian theorists, and some could and should have been avoided, it has only been through being pressed to respond to communitarian objections – whether by rebuttal, accommodation, or the claim that he never held the views objected to – that defenders of Rawls have come to see quite what it is they are defending. The communitarian critique has thus valuably forced a more explicit emphasis on, and perhaps also a clearer self-understanding of, the senses in which liberal theory is underpinned by communitarian concerns. Here, emphasising Rawls's sensitivity to communitarian concerns has particular significance. For while other variants of liberalism, such as the 'new liberalism' of T.H. Green and L.T. Hobhouse,[4] or the more recent 'perfectionist liberalism' of Joseph Raz,[5] wear their 'communitarian' credentials on their sleeve, Rawls's theory is distinctive precisely because it seems so blatantly to commit just those 'individualistic' fallacies to which communitarians take exception. If even Rawls – hypothetical contract and all – can properly be read as a 'communitarian liberal', then disagreement is best understood as being, not between those valuing the individual and those valuing community, but between conflicting visions of community (and of the individuals who inhabit them).

This compatibility of liberalism – even Rawlsian liberalism – and community matters rhetorically because 'community' is an emotive term, a 'feelgood' concept that any political doctrine will want to accommodate. It is important that liberals can sincerely point out that, for all their emphasis on individual freedom and rights, they too value and appreciate the significance of 'community' – particularly at a time when the term 'communitarian' has been adopted by a practical political movement,[6] and major centre-left political parties on both sides of the Atlantic have toyed with the suggestion that 'community' might be their new 'big idea'. It is notable that none of the theorists whose ideas we will be discussing (Michael Sandel, Alasdair MacIntyre, Charles Taylor, and Michael Walzer) have subscribed to Etzioni's 'communitarian platform' (but then again, they have all in different ways moved to distance themselves from the label 'communitarian' altogether!).[7] Nevertheless, it matters that liberals realise that they can argue their corner without abandoning the term 'community' to their political opponents – indeed, we will suggest a sense in which Rawls can make better claim to that term than can his critics.

But the compatibility also matters because it is important that people understand the kind of reason they have to value a liberal society and appreciate that it does not presuppose, or encourage, a view of people as atomised or self-interested individuals, or both. Even if liberal political philosophers were always aware of the sociological, philosophical, and moral underpinnings of their doctrines, it may be that the way in which they presented or argued for them encouraged misunderstanding. This was not helped by the prominence during the 1970s and 1980s of that strand of liberalism that did indeed over-emphasise the individual and promoted what Rawls, no less than communitarians, would regard as an attenuated and morally impoverished conception of the proper relation between the individual and her fellow citizens. The success of the 'neo-liberal' celebration of free-market individualism associated with theorists such as Friedrich von Hayek (Hayek 1960) and Robert Nozick (1974) understandably led some to paint all liberals with the same brush.[8] Our aim is to show that Rawlsian liberalism is quite different, thereby making clear that one does not need to abandon core liberal ideas of individual freedom, rights, and justice in order to avoid the objectionable aspects of 'neo-liberalism'.

That Rawls's position has been something of a moving target has of course complicated our task. How properly to conceive the relation between *A Theory of Justice* and *Political Liberalism*,[9] and to what extent any changes should be read as responses to the communitarian critique, are difficult questions. Nearly all agree that there is at least one crucial difference.[10] In the second book, Rawls's conception of justice is presented specifically as a 'political' conception. As he puts it:

The distinction between a comprehensive doctrine and a political conception is unfortunately absent from *Theory* and while I believe nearly all the structure and substantive content of justice as fairness...goes over unchanged into that conception as a political one, the understanding of the view as a whole is significantly shifted. (*PL*, p. 177)

But this leaves plenty of room for disagreement on other matters. Some see fundamental continuity, reading much of *Political Liberalism* as simply articulating what is not only consistent with, but implicit in, *A Theory of Justice*. Any mention of communitarian theorists or ideas in the later work shows Rawls responding to criticisms in ways available to him all along; such passages do not imply any change in position, let alone any attributable to the communitarian critique. Other commentators argue that his rethinking of his approach involved substantial changes and was influenced (if only in part and unconsciously) by the kind of communitarian criticism levelled against his work in the 1980s. Rawls's own view is clear, if not, as he acknowledges, decisive: "The changes in the later essays are sometimes said to be replies to criticisms raised by communitarians and others. I don't believe there is a basis for saying this" (*PL*, p. xvii). Our own judgement is that there are important changes between the two books (though we would tend to regard these as developments rather than revisions), that some of these yield resources for responding to communitarian objections in ways that were not available in the first book, and that Rawls did indeed conceive these changes as responses to a problem – the problem of stability – internal to justice as fairness. But the way he chose to present those changes and some aspects of the theory that had *not* changed owed much to his desire to show that his position overall was not vulnerable to the communitarian critique.

Although our discussion will, accordingly, pay most attention to Rawls's mature 'political' theory, doing justice both to Rawls and to his critics will require us to refer to both books. The communitarians were writing in criticism of the first, but both it and some subsequent writings that were available to them already provided responses to many of their objections – responses which a more careful reading might have taken into account. It would be quite misleading to suggest that it was *only* by recasting his theory as distinctively 'political' that Rawls was able to avoid or respond to the charges levelled against him. Rawls's attempt to formulate a specifically political conception of liberalism marks a distinctive development within the tradition of liberal thought, and it is one that has itself generated a good deal of controversy. Those who are in general terms sympathetic to the Rawlsian position presented in *A Theory of Justice*, who judge the 'political' framing of that position to be problematic, and who reject the particular senses in which it acknowledges or incorporates communitarian claims, are by no means committed to giving up on 'community' altogether.

## COMMUNITARIAN OBJECTIONS AND RESPONSES

Though each is critical of liberal political theory and practice, the communitarian thinkers whose ideas we will be discussing are engaged in rather different intellectual enterprises and differ markedly in the extent to which Rawls himself is the target of their critique. Recognising that we cannot here do justice to the richness and diversity of their individual projects, it will help consideration of how their various arguments might be applied to Rawls's theory, and how he might respond, if we identify four distinct argumentative strands or themes.

### Conception of the Person

The most familiar way in which the communitarians formulated their general objection to liberalism was in terms of its conception of the person, according to which people are essentially distinct from – their identity fixed prior to – their ends, or values, or conceptions of the good. The fundamental reason for ascribing such a conception of the person to Rawls was, of course, his use of the device of the original position.[11] Rawls appears to argue that a just agreement about the distribution of social goods can be reached only if the participants to that agreement first step behind the veil of ignorance and are thereby stripped of their particularity: their particular natural endowments and social position and their particular conceptions of the good. The communitarians felt that such radical detachment from one's nature and ends was psychologically impossible, that it would anyway deprive the participants of the resources they needed to reason about social justice, and that it ultimately betrayed an incoherent conception of personhood as given prior to particularity and essentially devoid of constitutive attachments.

For Rawls, these charges indicate a serious misreading of the original position. *A Theory of Justice* views the original position as "a purely hypothetical situation" intended solely to help us identify our considered moral judgements about justice (*TJ*, p. 120/104 rev.). Its invocation does not imply that human beings could psychologically or metaphysically survive the stripping away of their talents, social identity, and identification with any particular conception of the good. The original position is rather designed to model the normative claim that it is appropriate to exclude certain considerations or reasons when it comes to thinking about social justice. The constraints of the original position are thus epistemological and moral rather than metaphysical; they reflect Rawls's view that justice requires that people be treated as equal and as free. Respect for their equality is ensured by denying individuals any knowledge of those "morally arbitrary" inequalities resulting from the natural and social lottery, thereby ruling out reasoning that might make reference to such inequalities. Respect for their freedom is ensured by denying individuals knowledge of their particular conception of the good, thereby ensuring that they are motivated not to promote any particular conception but to defend their general capacity to frame, pursue, and revise such conceptions. To Sandel's objection that the original position presupposes an unencumbered subject, a shadowy self detachable from all its ends, Rawls might reply that it simply models the claim that what is important about people from the point of view of justice is their capacity to reflect upon and revise the attachments that they happen to have. One can claim this without holding that people can detach themselves from all their ends at the same time.

This kind of response was available on the basis of *A Theory of Justice* alone. The distinction between comprehensive and political forms of liberalism gives Rawls more to say. The conception of the person at the heart of this theory is of the person qua citizen – one that is implicit in the public political culture of constitutional democracies and that stands free of any particular comprehensive moral or philosophical doctrine. This conception thus applies to the person only insofar as she is a member of the public political realm. It is, Rawls insists, "part of a conception of political and social justice. That is, it characterises how citizens are to think of themselves and of one another in their political and social relationships as specified by the basic structure" (PL, p. 300).

This conception thus need not imply that we can generally step back from each and every one of our ends, or that we are metaphysically detached from them. In fact, Rawls explicitly concedes the validity of Sandel's claim about the phenomenology of our moral experience (PL, p. 31), and he is happy to see such constitutive values and communal attachments flourish in the context of family life, churches, and scientific societies; what he denies is their appropriateness for the realm of politics. For if our identity as citizens turned on whether or not we endorsed a particular conception of the good, coercive political power would be deployed in the service of a particular comprehensive doctrine that could not be publicly justified to all citizens, thereby violating the liberal political ideal or principle of legitimacy (PL, pp. 139–40, 217).

### Asocial Individualism

The second communitarian charge is that Rawls is guilty of asocial individualism – of neglecting the extent to which it is the societies in which people live that shape who they are and the values that they have. The overlap between this charge and the first – particularly evident in Charles Taylor's work – is evident,[12] but we can see more clearly what it adds to the communitarian analysis of liberalism if we distinguish between two importantly different objections that fall under this heading and that tend to be run together – a tendency encouraged by taking too seriously Rawls's use of the classical liberal metaphor of the social contract.[13]

The first objection is the sociological-cum-philosophical point, made by Taylor and MacIntyre,[14] that people necessarily derive their self-understandings and conceptions of the good from the social matrix. Whether stated as a quasi-empirical claim about socialisation processes, or as a conceptual claim about the impossibility of language, thought or moral life outside a social setting, the charge here is that liberalism neglects the way in which the individual is parasitic on society for the very way that she thinks, including the way that she thinks of herself as an individual. This point concerns the necessarily social or communal origin of any individual's ways of thinking, and it applies to any such way of thinking (liberal or otherwise).

The second objection concerns not the source but the content of people's conceptions of themselves and of what makes their lives worthwhile. Here the charge, primarily levelled by Sandel and MacIntyre, is that liberalism fosters a particular understanding of the individual's relation to her community, seeing society as nothing more than a cooperative venture for the pursuit of individual advantage. Conceptions of the good that are communal in content, insisting that relations with others are valuable in themselves, are thereby downgraded. In particular, it is argued, liberalism misunderstands the true value of political community. This strand of thought comes close to a restatement of the first communitarian criticism – that Rawls neglects an individual's constitutive attachments, the ways in which her identity is more closely bound up with her relations to others than a merely associational model of community can allow.

It ought to have been clear from *A Theory of Justice* that Rawls was well aware of the priority of the social matrix to the individual; for there he notes it in passing as a truism.

[S]ocial life is a condition for our developing the ability to think and speak ... No doubt even the concepts that we use to describe our plans and situations ... often presuppose a social setting as well as a system of belief and thought that is the outcome of the collective efforts of a long tradition. (*TJ*, p. 522/458 rev.)

Moreover, one reason for focussing on the basic structure of society as the subject of justice is that "the social system shapes the wants and aspirations that its citizens come to have. It determines in part the sort of persons they want to be as well as the sort of person they are" (*TJ*, p. 259/229 rev.). In *Political Liberalism*, Rawls takes this line of argument further, arguing for what he calls the full publicity condition – the demand that the justificatory grounds of any theory of justice must be publicly available and recognisable to all citizens – precisely because the basic structure shapes "their conceptions of themselves, their character and ends," and a publicly available theory of justice can thereby play an educative role (*PL*, pp. 68, 71). The claim that Rawls neglects the priority of the social matrix to individual self-interpretations cannot be sustained.

More interesting are Rawls's various responses to the second variant of the charge of asocial individualism. Most important, his position does not so much fail to acknowledge communal goods as explicitly deny their legitimacy in any conception of the political realm in modernity:

Justice as fairness does indeed abandon the ideal of political community if by that is meant a political society united on one (partially or fully) comprehensive religious, philosophical or moral doctrine. That conception of social unity is excluded by the fact of reasonable pluralism; it is no longer a political possibility for those who accept the constraints of liberty and toleration of democratic institutions. (PL, p. 201)

What motivates Rawls's concern that his liberalism be distinctively political is precisely the claim that democratic societies are inevitably and permanently characterised by a plurality of reasonable yet different and conflicting comprehensive doctrines, and that the only way to ensure agreement on any one would be by the oppressive use of state power. Rawls's political liberalism is a direct rejection of communitarian demands for political community if this is understood as a political society built around such a doctrine.

But this leaves room for two other kinds of communal goods. First, it is quite acceptable to the political liberal that such goods be realised at the nonpolitical level:

Justice as fairness assumes . . . that the values of community are not only essential but realizable, first in the various associations that carry on their life within the framework of the basic structure, and second, in those associations that extend across the boundaries of nation-states, such as churches and scientific societies. (PL, p. 146, n. 13)

Moreover, political liberalism embodies a vision of the intrinsic value of a properly constituted political community. For, in such a community, politics is not merely instrumental, and society is not merely a private association entered into by presocial individuals for purely personal advantage; members of such a community are committed to a shared goal.

[I]n the well-ordered society of justice as fairness citizens share . . . the aim of ensuring that the political and social institutions are just, of giving justice to persons generally, as what citizens need for themselves and want for one another. It is not true, then, that on a liberal view citizens have no fundamental common aims. Nor is it true that the aim of political justice is not an important part of their noninstitutional or moral identity. (*PL*, p. 146, n. 13)

In other words, a just society is a genuinely social good – and a person's identity as citizen might be described as a constitutive attachment – but it is one based on a purely political rather than a comprehensive conception of that good.

Much of this vision of the common good embodied in a well-ordered society was already laid out in *A Theory of Justice*, which characterises the liberal political community as a "social union of social unions" (*TJ*, pp. 520ff/456ff. rev.). On this account, members of society would participate in any number of different subsocietal social unions; but as free and equal members of the political community within which they would conduct those activities, they would aim at the shared final end of establishing and maintaining just institutions and would prize those institutions as good in themselves. Indeed, in 1971 Rawls was happy to regard the public realisation of justice as a "value of community" – a description now rendered inappropriate only by his somewhat restrictive definition of "community" as "an association of society whose unity rests on a comprehensive conception of the good" (*PL*, p. 146).

### Universalism

Under this heading, Walzer (supported from a very different perspective by MacIntyre) argued that Rawls's theory of justice was designed to apply universally and thus failed to attend to the ways in which different cultures embody different values and practices.[15] Walzer suggested that Rawls's conception of the social resources of which justice demands a principled distribution is conceptually incoherent, for the deliberate abstractness of Rawlsian primary goods – understood as things a person wants, whatever else she wants, and of which she wants more rather than less regardless of her specific life-plan – ensures that any distributive principles appropriate to them will not be usefully applicable to the concrete cases about which we will look to his theory for guidance. Walzer also argued that Rawls's general tendency towards detachment from the particular society of which he is a member, symbolised by the original position, presupposed the aim of establishing distributive principles philosophically superior to the opinions of his fellow citizens and thus implied an undemocratic failure to respect their right to make their own laws and hence their status as culture-producing creatures.

Readers of *A Theory of Justice* could be forgiven for finding plausible at least some elements of this interpretation of Rawls. Quite apart from its conception of primary goods, the book's final paragraph claimed that to see our place in society from the perspective of the original position was to see it *sub specie aeternitatis* (*TJ*, p. 587/514 rev.), and its early claim (*TJ*, p. 16/15 rev.) that justice as fairness was part of a theory of rational choice implies exactly the kind of ahistorical conception of human rationality and human nature to which Walzer objects. According to *Political Liberalism*, however, justice as fairness is the intellectual expression of the public political culture of constitutional democracies and is applicable only to the political sphere of such democracies; the theory is presented as culture and sphere-specific in just the way Walzer desires (albeit, as will be argued later, for quite different reasons). Far from representing an attempt to transcend cultural particularity, the original position is a device for representing an explicitly culture-specific shared understanding. Furthermore, the abstractness of Rawls's notion of primary goods appears less dubious if interpreted as reflecting his sense that the social meaning of our conception of persons as citizens is one that demands that we abstract from their commitment to particular comprehensive conceptions of the good in favour of treating them as equally capable of framing, pursuing, and revising such conceptions. This work of abstraction "is not gratuitous: not abstraction for abstraction's sake. Rather it is a way of continuing public discussion when shared understandings of lesser generality have broken down" (*PL*, pp. 45–6). In Walzerian terms, we might think of this as Rawls's being faithful to our disagreements[16] – as being more Walzerian than Walzer in his sensitivity to the real limits on our shared social meanings in an age of reasonable pluralism.

## Neutrality

A fundamental theme of the communitarian critique evident in the writings of Sandel, MacIntyre, and Taylor was a suspicion of liberal antiperfectionism – of the claim, made by Rawls amongst others, that justice demands that a state should refrain from political action whose justification draws upon elements of conceptions of the good that rightly guide people in their private lives. Such a state might be thought of as being neutral between the different conceptions of the good held by its citizens, whilst not of course entirely eschewing all value judgements (since its neutrality is motivated by a concern for the rights of people understood as free and equal members of the political community); hence, antiperfectionist liberals give priority to the right over the good. Communitarians argue that such antiperfectionism has highly undesirable consequences in that some valuable practices and ways of life simply would not survive unless they were promoted by the state, and that it is fundamentally incoherent in that the distinction between the right and the good upon which it depends smuggles in under cover of "the right" its own particular ideal of the good life for human beings, thereby failing to achieve the neutrality to which it aspires.

It is worth clarifying in what sense this critique of liberal neutrality is "communitarian." After all, challenging the priority of the right over the good, and claiming that Rawls relies upon a thicker conception of the good than might at first sight be apparent, does not in itself make any reference to community.[17] Similarly, not everyone who thinks it is permissible, or even morally required, for the state to act on perfectionist judgements about the value of the ways of life favoured by its citizens need be a "communitarian" – unless they make the further claim that "communal" ways of life are more valuable than solitary ones.[18] Nevertheless, there is a link between community and perfectionism (even the kind of perfectionism that recognises the life of the hermit or artist to be valuable and for that reason worthy of promotion by the state), in that the perfectionist thinks it permissible for the political community to make and act on judgements about what will make the lives of its individual members go better or worse, whereas the antiperfectionist will think that such judgements should be left rather to its individual members, with the state acting merely to provide an appropriately neutral framework within which they are to make and act on those judgements.

Rawls's distinction between political and comprehensive conceptions of the good gives him what seems a very powerful way of responding to the charge that his claims to neutrality are illusory. He argues that the priority of the right over the good allows him to use five different ideas of the good in his overall theory of justice without violating the kind of neutrality he is concerned to achieve. They include the two embodied in what (in *A Theory of Justice*) he called his 'thin' theory of the good – the idea of goodness as rationality and that of primary goods, which together give content to deliberations in the original position – but they go far beyond it (which makes it understandable why communitarians should have thought that his earlier talk of a thin theory of the good misrepresented the full normative presuppositions of his theory). They include a distinction between permissible and impermissible conceptions of the good – the latter being prohibited because their pursuit is not compatible with a respect for the rights of all citizens to do likewise; a conception of the political virtues – those forms of judgement and character that are essential to sustain fair social cooperation over time between citizens regarded as free and equal; and a conception of a well-ordered society – the good that citizens realise in maintaining a just constitutional regime. Presupposing these ideas of the good is, Rawls argues, compatible with a significant degree of neutrality between conceptions of the good because they are purely political values, applying only to the sphere of politics and elaborated from resources available in the public political culture; their affirmation does not presuppose commitment to any particular comprehensive conception of the good but rather builds on the common ground between the range of reasonable comprehensive conceptions held by citizens.[19]

Indeed, for Rawls, as we have seen, political liberalism legitimately embodies a vision of the political community in which its members have common (not merely instrumental) ends: those of supporting just institutions and treating one another justly. Political liberalism can therefore support the classical republican view that the preservation of democratic liberties requires the active participation of citizens in the life of their constitutional regime, whilst denying the legitimacy of the civic humanist view that political participation is the privileged locus of the good life for human beings. If it is to a civic humanist conception of politics that communitarians like Sandel and MacIntyre are inclined, then they are right to think that Rawls excludes it but wrong to imagine that he does so by oversight; rather, he explicitly rejects such a strong conception as a threat to the rights of citizens in a context of reasonable pluralism (*PL*, pp. 205–6).

However, Rawls further argues that his purely political conception of liberalism is not just one way of defending the consistency of liberal neutrality but the only legitimate way of so doing. For the very distinction between political and comprehensive doctrines that permits him, as he thinks, to deflect the communitarian critique of the neutrality of justice as fairness also reveals the validity of that critique as directed against any variant of liberal antiperfectionism which fails to respect that distinction. We can see why by noting that there are two importantly different senses in which political liberalism makes a claim to neutrality. The first has to do with its antiperfectionist substance – Rawls's political view that the state should not act on the basis of judgements as to the relative merits of the various conceptions of the good espoused by its citizens. The second has to do with its purely political form or method – Rawls's political–theoretical view that any justification of his substantive commitment to state antiperfectionism must itself eschew drawing upon elements of a comprehensive doctrine of the good.

We can then think of the communitarian critique as exposing the way in which the standard (i.e., pre-*Political Liberalism*) justifications of liberal doctrines of state neutrality were themselves based upon a strongly nonneutral commitment to a comprehensive liberal conception of the good. Taylor, for example, argued that giving priority to the right over the good presupposed a commitment to the liberal hypergood of autonomy; and Sandel argued that the Rawlsian vision of politics was founded on a highly controversial metaphysical conception of the self. In utilising the distinction between political and comprehensive doctrines to emphasise his own immunity to this line of criticism, Rawls acknowledges that any variant of liberal antiperfectionism based upon a comprehensive liberal conception of the good is not only vulnerable to this charge but runs the risk of violating what for Rawls is the fundamental liberal principle that political power should only be used in ways acceptable to citizens committed to a range of reasonable comprehensive conceptions. Any such version of liberalism (for example, that of Kant, Mill, Dworkin or Raz) would be just another sectarian doctrine seeking to license the exercise of the coercive power of free and equal citizens in ways that could not be justified to those citizens by appeal to their common human reason.

In thus attempting to apply the principle of toleration to philosophy itself, Rawls raises the stakes. He claims to have defined, and to exemplify in his theorising, a more radical and more consistent kind of liberal neutrality and thus to have set a standard against which any liberalism must measure itself.[20] In so doing, he at once endorses the general shape of this criticism, implies that it is well-grounded with respect to many species of liberal political theorising, and claims that, properly understood, his distinctively political conception of liberalism is invulnerable to it.

With respect to the other charge under this heading, that concerning the need for perfectionist state action to prevent the withering away of valuable forms of life, the position put forward in *Political Liberalism* is rather more obscure than that of *A Theory of Justice*. In the earlier book, Rawls was very clear that

the principles of justice do not permit subsidizing universities and institutes, or opera and the theater, on the grounds that these institutions are intrinsically valuable, and that those who engage in them are to be supported even at some significant expense to others who do not receive compensating benefits. (*TJ*, pp. 332/291–2 rev.)

Those who want public goods such as art galleries and museums can get together via their representatives in the exchange branch of government to overcome market imperfections and achieve a level of provision that matches their true aggregate preferences, but such goods are plainly perceived as luxuries to be dealt with only after the claims of justice have been met and the coerciveness of taxation procedures overcome.

*Political Liberalism* presents a rather more qualified view about anti-perfectionist restrictions on support for valuable ways of life. There the values of political liberalism are intended to have priority solely with respect to what Rawls calls "constitutional essentials and questions of basic justice"; and he declares that issues which fall under neither of those headings need not be settled solely by appeal to purely political values.

Many if not most political questions do not concern those fundamental matters, for example, much tax legislation and many laws regulating property;

statues protecting the environment and controlling pollution; establishing national parks and preserving wilderness areas and animal and plant species; and laying aside funds for museums and the arts. (*PL*, p. 214)

It is not clear exactly how to draw the line between such fundamental matters and the rest. The deeper problem Rawls faces is that, since political power is exercised whenever the state implements its decisions, regardless of whether or not they involve constitutional essentials or matters of basic justice (if only because their implementation involves funds derived from taxation), his respect for citizens' rights should apparently entail that all exercises of state power be considered purely in terms of political values, which would mean a return to the stricter or more expansive antiperfectionism of *A Theory of Justice*.[21]

OPEN QUESTIONS

We have argued that Rawls is guilty of none of the charges brought against him by communitarian critics. Nonetheless, as we said in our introduction, the communitarian critique of liberal political theory, and of Rawlsian theory in particular, has been valuable and productive. We have already made good the claim that the communitarian critique has compelled liberals like Rawls to acknowledge and perhaps even to emphasise the extent to which their vision of the good polity depends on substantive and controversial claims about the significance of community. Now we can turn to our suggestion that it has generated several crucial issues that remain unresolved.

## Conception of the Person

In broad terms, Rawls's response to the communitarian's worries under this heading seem sound. The observation that some of us some of the time take our very identity to be bound up with particular religious or ethical doctrines or with our membership in particular communities does not in itself look like a good reason for the state to adopt any particular policies. Nor does it contradict the claims that some people sometimes can exercise their capacity to revise their conception of the good and that that capacity is morally important enough for the state properly to be concerned to protect and promote its exercise.

Nevertheless, the communitarian critique did raise two important points – both concerning not the coherence but the desirability or feasibility of the kind of distancing of oneself from one's values that Rawlsian liberalism demands of some in the realm of politics. First, it calls into question the apparently exclusive liberal preoccupation with the value of autonomy – in Rawls's terms the capacity to frame, revise, and pursue a conception of the good – by pointing out the significance of other aspects of our moral life. Even when liberals such as Rawls point out that they too have room for constitutive attachments of various kinds at the subpolitical level, they remain committed to the priority of autonomy over such attachments whenever they come into conflict. Take, for example, the education of children whose parents are committed to particular religious beliefs, the content of which is such as to downplay the significance of autonomy. Is it the state's task nonetheless to ensure that such children are endowed with what they need to exercise their capacity for autonomy properly – knowledge of their civil rights, of the range of other kinds of life available to them, and so on? Or should the state rather be swayed by, and respect, the moral significance of those religious convictions that, left to themselves, will tend to deprive children of the effective capacity to choose for themselves how they live their lives?[22]

This conflict becomes more complicated when it is claimed, as it is by Kymlicka (1989), that a stable cultural context is itself a condition of individual autonomy.[23] On Kymlicka's view, the valuable contribution of the communitarian critique was to emphasise the significance of a stable cultural identity as a precondition of individual autonomy, but the Rawlsian framework can incorporate this insight by regarding the necessary cultural structure as a primary good. This yields the conclusion that cultural groups should have those "special" rights that are needed to protect and foster such cultural structures; but that raises the difficult questions of precisely which rights are needed for this purpose and how to think about those cases where the group right seems to conflict with the freedom of its individual members.[24] In this sense, the standard liberal problematic concerning the proper relation between the individual and the community reemerges, and is given a distinctively 'communitarian' or 'culturalist' twist by this acknowledgement of the importance of inherently communal factors to individual autonomy itself.[25]

The second point raised by the communitarian critique is closely related. The liberal suggestion that, for the purposes of politics, citizens should be expected to set aside their commitment to conceptions of the good – commitments which they may regard not only as valid but also as constitutive of their very identity – may seem to involve a problematic degree of schizophrenia. Understood as a moral point, the question is whether autonomy is really so important that we should require people who do not judge it so important to ignore their own ethical commitments when deciding proper courses of action for the state. But the point might also be presented as a practical one: is it realistic to advocate a form of politics that postulates and enforces a discontinuity between people's understanding of themselves in private and political life?[26] Can people really be expected to perform the kind of distancing from their own commitments that such a politics involves? In Rawls's view, all reasonable comprehensive doctrines will overlap in affirming political liberalism, thus eliminating such conflicts; but if, as we will argue shortly, this argument embodies a question-begging understanding of what it means to be "reasonable," the difficulty remains.

## Asocial Individualism

We have argued that Rawls is well aware of the sense in which the individual depends on the social matrix for her self-understanding or conception of what makes life worth living, that political liberalism can accommodate a variety of communal goods, both political and nonpolitical, and that it has powerful reasons to deny the legitimacy of the claims of such goods when they presuppose the applicability of comprehensive doctrines in the political realm. A problem nevertheless remains; for Rawls makes no mention of the extent to which his vision of politics relies upon a further hidden premise. Justice as fairness is a theory about how the state should treat its citizens, but it aims to justify such forms of state action in virtue of capacities that individuals possess simply as persons. He thus leaves a significant gap between persons and citizens – between all those human beings who possess the capacity to frame, revise and pursue a conception of the good and the capacity for a sense of justice – and that subset of them who are fellow citizens and who thus can make legitimate claims to civil rights and to a fair share of society's resources. Rawlsian liberalism therefore appears to trade on some criterion over and above these abstract capacities in deciding who is to count as a member of the political community and in drawing boundaries between such communities; and it is difficult to see how any such criterion could avoid embodying a particularistic claim about community and commonality that takes Rawls away from the individualistic premises upon which he claims to be relying.[27]

This presents the point as a matter of justification – what justifies the view that the rights and duties of liberal citizenship apply only to these particular possessors of the capacities that Rawlsian liberals value? But it can also be given a sociological inflection, as an issue concerning the sources of social solidarity. What are the empirical conditions that must obtain if people are to recognise their fellow citizens as having rights of citizenship, especially where these involve distributive claims and thus imply particularly onerous duties? This leads us back to notions of membership and participation that are typically regarded as communitarian rather than liberal. For it may be that what is needed to underpin that feeling of solidarity and identification with particular others upon which even justice as fairness relies is a sense of common identity, history, and culture, and that this can only be sustained if all citizens regard themselves as participating in a shared practice or set of practices that go beyond the mere doing of justice to one another. Even those who accept the Rawlsian conception of the citizen as a free and equal participant in a common political project need to know how and why we have special duties to our fellow countrymen and women, and what kinds of communal life – singing to the flag, watching the same television programmes, participating in collective political deliberation – are required for a society that is grounded in respect for the individual to hold together.[28]

### Universalism

We saw earlier that Rawls's advocacy of a purely political liberalism could blunt the communitarian charge that justice as fairness aspires to a kind of transcultural or universalist conception of justice and its demands. Indeed, Rawls's claim to restrict himself in his theorising to elements derived from the prevailing public political culture makes it possible to present his work as more Walzerian than Walzer's, as more aware of how quickly the 'social meanings' shared by citizens of liberal democracies run out. While illuminating, this way of presenting his position can, however, encourage a misunderstanding of Rawls's motives for turning towards the public political culture.

Rawlsian political liberalism is not at all Walzerian if that means being committed to the idea that justice is the articulation of shared meanings whatever they may be. On the contrary: the respect for public justifiability that drives Rawls's turn towards the resources of the public political culture is motivated by his prior commitment to the conception of the person (as free and equal) that he claims to find there – more specifically, by his belief that coercive state power exercised on behalf of value commitments not publicly justifiable to citizens violates the freedom of those citizens. Rawlsian liberalism thus derives from a normative commitment to the liberal conception of the person rather than to whatever ideas of justice happen to be available in the public political culture. That Rawls has looked to some as if he were attempting merely to articulate ideas to be found in the public political culture of liberal democracies results from the dual role played by this liberal conception of the citizen. On the one hand, this is what leads him – via the liberal ideal of legitimacy – to seek public justifiability in the first place. On the other, it is also part of the public political culture to which he apparently restricts himself when seeking a conception that is indeed publicly justifiable. Emphasising this second role makes it look as if the theory is more relativist than is in fact the case.

Furthermore, there is a crucial ambiguity in what is meant by 'publicly justifiable'. On the one hand, this depends upon what is available in the public political culture: "Since justification is addressed to others, it proceeds from what is, or can be, held in common; and so we begin from shared fundamental ideas implicit in the public political culture in the hope of developing from them a political conception that can gain free and reasoned agreement in judgment ..." (*PL*, pp. 100–1). On the other hand, however, Rawls also has a substantive view about what is and is not publicly justifiable that emerges directly from his category of the "reasonable" – from his understanding of the significance of reasonable pluralism for those who, in accordance with the demands of reasonableness, conceive society as a fair scheme of cooperation between free and equal citizens. But once "the reasonable" takes centre stage, it seems that he has no need to take a detour via the public political culture in order to determine what is publicly justifiable. 'What can serve as a public basis of justification' will then be understood to mean 'what reasonable people have in common,' which will be determined by the consequences of the burdens of judgement for those who view society as a fair scheme of cooperation between free and equal citizens, not by an interpretation of the public political culture. If, for example, we discovered that the public political culture contained an implicit agreement on the overriding importance of some element of a comprehensive doctrine (e.g., the immorality of abortion), that would not, for Rawls, make it reasonable for a state to engage in action predicated on the truth of that view, since (present or future) citizens might reasonably disagree with it. Whereas if we discovered that the public political culture did not embody an implicit commitment to a conception of citizens as free and equal, that would not make such a conception any less reasonable, and no citizen could reasonably refuse to accept the limits it imposes on legitimate state action.

Giving Rawls's category of 'the reasonable' the weight that he seems to want it to bear suggests that, of the three senses in which he thinks of his theory as purely political – its concern with the basic structure of society, its being presentable independently of any particular comprehensive doctrines, and its being elaborated in terms of fundamental ideas viewed as implicit in the public political culture of a democratic society (*PL*, p. 223) – the last is ultimately superfluous. If this is right, then Rawls is far less Walzerian than he may appear to be in that he is under no methodological obligation to restrict his theory of justice to the ideas available in the public political culture. This means that, even when understood as a species of political liberalism, justice as fairness continues to have built into it a rather less culturally specific, and perhaps a rather more universalistic, self-understanding and set of aspirations than it sometimes appears prepared to acknowledge. Whether we think of such an aspiration as a weakness or a strength in a political theory will then depend upon our assessment of the strength of Walzerian and MacIntyrean arguments about its undesirability and incoherence. Rawls's elaboration of the idea of political liberalism does not, in the end, allow him (or us) to avoid confronting that question head on.

## Neutrality

We have already noted some problems with Rawls's response to the communitarian (and more generally perfectionist) worry that anti-perfectionist liberal states will witness the withering away of valuable forms of life. His restricting the scope of the priority of political over nonpolitical values to constitutional essentials and matters of basic justice allows him, in principle, to permit kinds of state action that he once ruled out, but this revised position in turn raises new and awkward questions. Here, we focus on the second strand under this heading, that concerning the consistency of Rawls's claims to neutrality.

We have seen that his response depends upon the distinction he draws between political and comprehensive doctrines, upon his capacity to defend the values of political liberalism without drawing upon any elements of a comprehensive liberal conception of the good. To fulfil this self-denying ordinance, Rawls must find a way of rebutting those who would reject the values of political liberalism, or accord those values less weight than other elements of their comprehensive doctrines, without criticising those doctrines as false. He aims to achieve this by charging such critics with being unreasonable: they invoke elements of a comprehensive doctrine with which other citizens might reasonably disagree and so unfairly utilise the coercive powers of the state. Perhaps the most fundamental open question still remaining over Rawls's response to the communitarians is, What exactly does his notion of the reasonable embody and imply?

The term itself strongly suggests that it registers a purely epistemological or cognitive constraint on evaluative thinking. This suggestion is reinforced by the manner in which Rawls roots the notion in a recognition of the burdens of judgement – sources of disagreement that are compatible with the full reasonableness of all parties involved. On such an interpretation, however, Rawls's response to his comprehensive critic looks at once too strong and too weak. Too strong, because if the burdens of judgement apply to all exercises of human reason with respect to fundamental moral and political matters, they must apply to judgements about purely political issues just as much as to judgements about comprehensive ones, and it would accordingly be illegitimate to impose even a purely political liberal conception of the person upon one's fellow citizens. Too weak, because the burdens of judgement entail only that disagreement about conceptions of the good can be (and perhaps often are) reasonable; they do not and could not show it to be inevitable. To put the point at its most abstract: where reasonable disagreement is possible, so is reasonable agreement. If, however, reasonable agreement were (with however much difficulty) established on an element of a comprehensive doctrine, what would then prevent a state from acting on policies that could be justified by reference to it?

In fact, however, this epistemological reading of the burdens of judgement, and hence of 'the reasonable', misreads Rawls's intentions. For when he introduces the notion of 'the reasonable', he specifies that it has two basic aspects as a virtue of persons. The second is a willingness to recognise and accept the consequences of the burdens of judgement; but the first is elucidated before we are introduced to those burdens and provides the terms in which we must interpret their significance.

> Persons are reasonable in one basic aspect when, among equals say, they are ready to propose principles and standards as fair terms of cooperation and to abide by them willingly, given the assurance that others will likewise do so ... The reasonable is an element of the idea of society as a system of fair cooperation ... Reasonable persons ... desire for its own sake a social world in which they, as free and equal, can cooperate with others on terms all can accept. (*PL*, pp. 49–50)

On Rawls's understanding of the term, then, no one can be reasonable unless he or she accepts the conception of the person and of society that is the irreducible core of political liberalism. As he puts it:

> Observe that here being reasonable is not an epistemological idea (though it has epistemological elements). Rather, it is part of a political ideal of democratic citizenship that includes the idea of public reason. The content of this ideal includes what free and equal citizens can require of each other with respect to their reasonable comprehensive views. (*PL*, p. 62)

The notion of 'the reasonable' does not mark out a set of epistemological constraints that must be respected on pain of irrationality or ignorance of uncontroversial facts; rather, it contributes to the specification of the moral constraints that partly determine what it is to live up to the duties and obligations imposed by participation in a fair system of social cooperation based upon mutual respect. Consequently, neither of the lines of argument mentioned earlier can be valid: for it follows by definition that there simply cannot be either reasonable disagreement over political values or reasonable agreement over elements of comprehensive doctrines. But Rawls's invulnerability to these arguments is based on a manoeuvre that leaves him vulnerable to another, more fundamental, criticism. For the accusation of 'being unreasonable' is Rawls's response to all those whose comprehensive doctrines do not affirm his vision of political society as a system of fair cooperation between free and equal citizens, or affirm it in a way leaving open the possibility that non-political elements of that comprehensive doctrine may, in cases of conflict, sometimes take priority. But it now appears that recognising the burdens of judgement will only result in the right sort of respect for the values of political liberalism if one's comprehensive doctrine endorses a view of political society as just such a system of fair cooperation . In short, his response is entirely circular. By defining 'the reasonable' as including a commitment to a politically liberal vision of society, Rawls defines anyone who queries or rejects that vision as 'unreasonable', but he offers no independent reason for accepting that morally driven and question-begging definition.

In certain places, Rawls even appears to acknowledge that he lacks any non-comprehensive resources for responding to those who question this liberal conception of the proper limits of political action. When, for example, discussing a religious believer who insists that the truth of her comprehensive doctrine (that the religious salvation of a whole people depends upon their conforming to her understanding of the divine will) is so fundamental as to justify civil strife, Rawls declares that "we may have no alternative but to deny this or to imply this denial ..." (1993: 152). He continues to aver that the political liberal need only explicitly assert that such a believer is mistaken in denying the existence of reasonable pluralism and not that her comprehensive doctrine is false.

Nevertheless:

Of course, we do not believe the doctrine believers here assert, and this is shown in what we do. Even if we do not, say, hold some form of the doctrine of free religious faith that supports equal liberty of conscience, our actions nevertheless imply that we believe the concern for salvation does not require anything incompatible with that liberty. Still, we do not put forward more of our comprehensive view than we think needed or useful for the political aim of consensus. (*PL*, p. 153)

Rawls here effectively admits that no one who believed such a religious doctrine would attach the weight that he attaches to the fact of reasonable pluralism, so his supposedly purely political assertion of that fact amounts to an implicit denial of the truth of that doctrine. His own analysis suggests that the significance of reasonable pluralism cannot be determined independently of our comprehensive commitments. It implies that the burdens of judgement do not constitute a value-free, or even a purely political, point of leverage upon comprehensive doctrines that might contest the limits Rawls imposes upon public reason. This means that what, for Rawls at least, makes political liberalism so distinctive and attractive – its claim to have extended the principle of tolerance to philosophy itself, to have discovered a way of defending political anti-perfectionism without invoking controversial value-judgements about the relative worth of competing comprehensive doctrines – disappears. There is, in short, no longer any principled difference between political liberalism and the comprehensive liberalisms it condemned as sectarian – no form of liberal anti-perfectionism that is not founded on a comprehensive and controversial vision of human well-being.

Rawls's stipulative banishing to the realm of the 'unreasonable' those whose comprehensive doctrines conflict with liberal political principles can be viewed in different ways. A charitable reading would see it as an inevitable acknowledgement of the justificatory limits that any political philosophy must ultimately accept. Given the heterogeneity of doctrines about how polities should be organised, it makes no sense to aspire to common ground between *all* of them, and Rawls is to be congratulated for providing such a fully articulated and explicit account of premises of the kind that cannot be avoided by any theorist seeking to justify a particular political system. Even on this interpretation, however, and whatever one's view of the relation between the communitarian critique and the development of Rawls's work between *A Theory of Justice* and *Political*

*Liberalism*, it is surely undeniable that communitarian critics have helped to force those premises into the open.

ENDNOTES

1 For a polemical account stressing the continuity between recent communitarian theorists and earlier antiliberals, see Holmes, Stephen, *The Anatomy of Antiliberalism* (Cambridge, MA: Harvard University Press, 1993).

2 John Rawls, *A Theory of Justice* (Cambridge, MA: Harvard University Press, 1971, revised edition 1999).

3 In addition to Stephen Mulhall and Adam Swift, *Liberals and Communitarians*, 2nd edition (Oxford: Blackwell, 1996), on which this chapter substantially draws, see Amy Gutmann, "Communitarian Critics of Liberalism," *Philosophy and Public Affairs* 14 (3) (1985): 308–322; Will Kymlicka, *Liberalism, Community and Culture* (Oxford, UK: Oxford University Press, 1989); and Alan Ryan, "The Liberal Community," in *Democratic Community*, edited by J. W. Chapman and I. Shapiro (New York: New York University Press, 1993).

4 See, A. Simhony and D. Weinstein, eds., *The New Liberalism: Reconciling Liberty and Community* (Cambridge, UK: Cambridge University Press, 2001).

5 Joseph Raz, *The Morality of Freedom* (Oxford, UK: Clarendon Press, 1986).

6 Amitai Etzioni, *The Spirit of Community: Rights, Responsibilities and the Communitarian Agenda* (New York: Crown Publishers Inc., 1993).

7 As David Miller notes, Taylor and Walzer have both explained and analysed the liberal–communitarian debate in such a way as to evade identifying themselves as communitarians. See Miller, "Communitarianism: Left, Right and Centre," in *Liberalism and its Practice*, edited by D. Avnon and A. De-Shalit (London: Routledge, 1999), p. 171; see also, Charles Taylor, "Cross-Purposes: The Liberal–Communitarian Debate," in *Liberalism and the Moral Life*, edited by N. Rosenblum (Cambridge, MA: Harvard University Press, 1989), and Michael Walzer, "The Communitarian Critique of Liberalism, *Political Theory* 18 (1) (1990): 6–23. MacIntyre explicitly dissociates himself from contemporary communitarianism, whereas Sandel uses the preface to the second edition of his *Liberalism and the Limits of Justice* to register 'some unease' with the application of the communitarian label to the view it advances. See Alasdair MacIntyre, "A Partial Response to my Critics," in *After MacIntyre*, edited by J. Horton and S. Mendus (Oxford: Polity, 1994),

p. 302; Michael Sandel, *Liberalism and the Limits of Justice.* 2nd ed. (Cambridge, UK: Cambridge University Press, 1998), p. ix.

8  Friedrich von Hayek, *The Constitution of Liberty* (London: Routledge & Kegan Paul, 1960); Robert Nozick, *Anarchy State and Utopia* (New York: Basic Books, 1974).

9  John Rawls, *Political Liberalism* (New York: Columbia University Press, 1993) (referred to as *"PL"* in text).

10  But see Brian Barry," John Rawls and the Search for Stability," *Ethics* 105 (4) (1995): 874–915 for the alternative view that *A Theory of Justice* did not, contrary to Rawls's own account, present justice as fairness as premised on a comprehensive doctrine.

11  Michael Sandel, *Liberalism and the Limits of Justice.* Chap. 1.

12  See Charles Taylor, *Philosophical Papers*, vol. 1: *Human Agency and Language* (Cambridge, UK: Cambridge University Press, 1985); *Philosophical Papers*, vol. 2: *Philosophy and the Human Sciences* (Cambridge, UK: Cambridge University Press, 1985); *Sources of the Self: The Making of Modern Identity* (Cambridge, UK: Cambridge University Press, 1989).

13  See Stephen Mulhall and Adam Swift, "The Social Self in Political Theory: The Communitarian Critique of the Liberal Subject," in *The Social Self*, edited by D. Bakhurst and C. Sypnowich (London: Sage, 1995).

14  Alastair MacIntyre, *After Virtue* (South Bend, IN: Notre Dame, 1981).

15  Michael Walzer, *Spheres of Justice: A Defense of Pluralism and Equality* (New York: Basic Books, Inc., 1983).

16  Ibid., p. 313.

17  As Sandel (op.cit. 2nd ed., pp. ix–xi) puts it, this way of tying justice to conceptions of the good is "not, strictly speaking, communitarian. Since it rests the case for rights on the moral importance of the purposes or ends rights promote, it is better described as teleological, or (in the jargon of contemporary political philosophy) perfectionist."

18  George Sher, *Beyond Neutrality: Perfectionism and Politics* (Cambridge, UK: Cambridge University Press, 1997), pp. 156–75.

19  See Rawls, *Political Liberalism*, Lecture V.

20  See also Charles Larmore, "Political Liberalism," *Political Theory* 18 (3) (1990): 339–360.

21  See Steven Wall, *Liberalism, Perfectionism and Restraint* (Cambridge, UK: Cambridge University Press, 1998) for an excellent discussion of this problem. On what liberals can say about state funding of the arts, see also Ronald Dworkin, "Can a Liberal State Support Art?" in *A Matter of Principle* (Oxford, UK: Oxford University Press, 1985); and Harry Brighouse, "Neutrality, Publicity and State Funding of the Arts," *Philosophy and Public Affairs* 24 (1) (1995): 35–63.

22 See Stephen Macedo, "Liberal Civic Education and Religious Fundamentalism: The Case of God v. John Rawls," *Ethics* 105 (3) (1995): 468–96; Eamonn Callan, *Creating Citizens: Political Education and Liberal Democracy* (Oxford, UK: Oxford University Press, 1997); Harry Brighouse, "Civic Education and Liberal Legitimacy," *Ethics* 108 (4) (1998): 719–45.

23 Will Kymlicka, in *Liberalism, Community, and Culture*.

24 Will Kymlicka, *Multicultural Citizenship* (Oxford, UK: Clarendon Press, 1995); and *The Rights of Minority Cultures* (Oxford, UK: Oxford University Press, 1996).

25 Communitarian insights have also informed a good deal of recent writing on multiculturalism. See, for example, Amy Gutmann, ed., *Multiculturalism: Examining the Politics of Recognition* (Princeton, NJ: Princeton University Press, 1994); and Joseph Raz, "Multiculturalism: A Liberal Perspective," in his *Ethics in the Public Domain* (Oxford, UK: Oxford University Press, 1994).

26 The term 'discontinuity' comes from Ronald Dworkin, "Foundations of Liberal Equality," in *Equal Freedom*, edited by Stephen Darwall (Ann Arbor: The University of Michigan Press, 1995), pp. 190–306, which seeks to develop a liberalism that provides 'continuity' between people's ethical and political views.

27 See, Sam Black, "Individualism at an Impasse," *Canadian Journal of Philosophy* 21 (3) (1991): 347–77.

28 See David Miller, *On Nationality* (Oxford, UK: Oxford University Press, 1995); Will Kymlicka, "Social Unity in a Liberal State," *Social Philosophy and Policy* 13 (1) (1996): 105–36.

# 14 Rawls and Feminism[1]

Because John Rawls's work on justice has such fundamental importance, feminists have scrutinized it with particular care and have made many criticisms. Rawls himself has become deeply concerned with these criticisms – in some cases seriously revising his theory in response. In general, he continues to insist, the various feminist objections do not invalidate a liberal approach to the theory of justice: in fact, liberal theories can answer feminist concerns better than other theories. Nor, he believes, is his particular liberal theory wanting: he doubts that it could be shown that justice as fairness does not have the resources to deal with the problems raised by the women's movement.[2] Nonetheless, he concedes, liberal theories of justice have a great deal of work yet to do if they are to make good on this promise, particularly in the area of family justice:

Except for the great John Stuart Mill, one serious fault of writers in the liberal line is that until recently none have discussed in any detail the urgent questions of the justice of the family, the equal justice of women and how these things are to be achieved. Susan Okin's contentions about this in *Justice, Gender and the Family* cannot be denied. Liberal writers who are men should, with whatever grace they can muster, plead nolo contendere to her complaints. (MS, 1994)[3]

In many respects, although not perhaps in all, Rawls is right to say that both his theory in particular and liberal theories of justice more generally have powerful responses to feminist concerns. My aim will be to show the range and interest of the criticisms that have addressed his work from a feminist perspective; to show that some of them rest on misunderstandings and that others can be or have

488

been addressed within his theory; and to point to several problems that seem as yet unresolved.

## I. CARE, EMOTION, AND RELATIONSHIP

One of the most significant areas of feminist philosophical work has been the defense of emotion and relationship as important elements of both ethical and political life. Feminists with these interests have addressed a number of criticisms to Rawls's work.

### A. Seeking Reflective Equilibrium

It is extremely important to distinguish Rawls's account of the reasoning used by those who seek a reflective equilibrium about a political conception from the two distinct forms of reasoning used inside his own conception (the reasoning of the parties in the original position and the reasoning of citizens in the well-ordered society; see *PL*, p. 28). People seeking reflective equilibrium (a state in which our considered judgments and our principles are harmoniously adjusted) occupy, as Rawls recently has put it, "the point of view of you and me" (e.g., *PL*, p. 28).[4] This point of view is one from which we entertain, at times construct, and then assess against our considered judgments a variety of distinct theories of justice, including justice as fairness. If we are striving for narrow reflective equilibrium, we will include only those political conceptions that lie rather close to our considered judgments; if we seek wide reflective equilibrium, we will seek out "all possible descriptions to which one might plausibly conform one's judgments together with all relevant philosophical arguments for them" in such a way that "a person's sense of justice may or may not undergo a radical shift."[5] It is important, then, that the account of our "considered judgments" and of our reasoning as we assess all the different conceptions should not build in assumptions that derive from a specifically Kantian or Rawlsian approach to moral rationality.

Some feminist scholars believe that Rawls has not devoted enough attention to this important question. Obviously, when we embark on the process of scrutiny, we need some account of which judgments are to be regarded as more trustworthy than others, "those judgments in which our moral capacities are most likely to be displayed without distortion" (*TJ*, p. 47/42 rev.). And yet, Rawls's own account urges us to discount any judgments "made with hesitation" and those "given when we are upset or frightened, or when we stand to gain one way or the other" (*TJ*, p. 47/42 rev.). Surely the exclusion of judgments made when we stand to gain is correct. But Held and Nussbaum suggest that any more general discounting of emotion-based judgments (if indeed Rawls intends this) would be inappropriate, the result of a Kantian bias against emotion that should not have been permitted to pervade the "point of view of you and me."[6] Such a bias might have been dispelled by consideration of feminist arguments that show emotions to be intelligent and discriminating ways of considering reality.

Now clearly we do not want to admit any and all emotions to the process. If we hold that emotions are intelligent, this just means that they should be scrutinized the way we scrutinize beliefs, holding that some are more reliable than others. It is very difficult to do this in a way that will be fair to all the major political conceptions: but surely, especially in order to be fair to the more radical among these, we will need at times to consult passions of indignation and love, which can be essential elements in a radical critique of unjust institutions. We must recognize that emotions frequently embed judgments that are the fruits of unjust background conditions.[7] Whole emotion types – for example envy, as Rawls well argues, and perhaps also hatred, and jealousy, and disgust,[8] seem inappropriate for a process of political reflection because they are based on reasons that could not be publicly defended. On the other hand, there are many emotions – forms of love, and compassion, and anger, and fear – that can in principle be fully appropriate and illuminating. We will need to ask in each case whether the emotion in question is based on true or false judgments; thus, forms of anger based upon false beliefs about race or sex should be left to one side. Even love will prove an equivocal, albeit an indispensable, guide when we want to think well about the family and what it contributes to a just society: for our love of our existing ties may often illuminate, but may also blind us to, the need for radical change. The difficulty of deciding which passions to trust, however, is no greater than, and a part of, the difficulty of deciding in general what beliefs and judgments to trust. It is no solution to this difficulty to omit all emotions, any more than it would be to omit all judgments.

When Rawls discusses the moral sentiments in *TJ*, he makes it clear that he rejects a reduction of these to "characteristic sensations and behavioral manifestations" (*TJ*, p. 480/421 rev.), preferring (unlike Kant) a more richly cognitive account. Moreover, he gives these emotions, including indignation and resentment, a significant role in relation to the sense of justice (*TJ*, pp. 488–9/428 rev.). Even though such feelings may be "unpleasant," he argues, "there is no way for us to avoid a liability to them without disfiguring ourselves. This liability is the price of love and trust, of friendship and affection, and of a devotion to institutions and traditions from which we have benefitted and which serve the general interests of mankind" (*TJ*, p. 489/428 rev.). These remarks show that Rawls should be perfectly prepared to admit such emotions into the process of searching for reflective equilibrium as intelligent judgment-containing sources of insight. In *PL* as well, emotions play a significant role: in the account of public reason Rawls makes it clear that speeches expressive of both indignation and compassion (the speeches of the abolitionists and Martin Luther King, Jr.) are good examples of how public reason addresses the evils of a non-well-ordered society.

Moreover, it appears to me that Rawls draws on such emotions in his conversation with the reader. Particularly in the new introduction to *Political Liberalism*, with its reference to "the manic evil of the Holocaust" (lxii), but also throughout the text of that work, with its references to "mad" and "demonic" comprehensive doctrines, we sense the expression of both indignation and fear – emotions that appear quite appropriate to our political reasoning in this era. Indeed it would seem that that the entire text of *TJ*, too, is animated by a high degree of "upset" if we include under that rubric a prophetic passion for radical change in our world and a related love of humanity.

This criticism of Rawls, then, is not a deep one[9]: it just asks him to reconsider his unfortunate use of a dismissive Kantian language about the passions in some methodological contexts in favor of the subtler discriminations he actually exercises in the composition of the text.

## B. The Original Position

An influential area of feminist criticism of Rawls's work concerns the role played by love, care, and relationship in the account of the original position. Noticing that the rationality of the parties in the original position is described as self-interested prudential rationality, and that the parties are characterized as mutually disinterested, unaware of strong ties to others, some feminists have charged that Rawls, like many other thinkers in the liberal tradition, thinks of human beings as basically egoistic, pursuing their own personal ends rather than ends that are shared with others. Annette Baier, for example, simply asserts that, according to Rawls's theory people "have no interest in each other's interests."[10] Alison Jaggar, despite carefully recording Rawls's denial that his theory is egoistic, nonetheless finds egoism in the parties' desire to have more rather than less (for themselves) of the primary goods.[11] Moreover, Jaggar finds in the description of the parties a "metaphysical assumption of abstract individualism" (meaning, apparently, the doctrine that individuals have by nature no strong ties to others) that she takes to be common within the liberal tradition (p. 30). Such theorists charge that, although the informational constraints of the veil of ignorance prevent the parties from preferring self to others in their choice of principles, they are themselves egoists, and Rawls's theory is in that sense an egoistic theory, generating concern for others out of a set of merely external constraints.

This criticism is based on a misreading. But it is not for that reason uninteresting. Indeed, Rawls spends a good deal of time answering Schopenhauer's closely related criticism of Kant's theory, showing that he believes that the charge of egoism must be taken very seriously. The essence of the reply is as follows. Just as Schopenhauer was wrong to suppose that the categorical imperative supplies merely external constraints on the (self-interested) will of a person who agrees to subject her maxims to its test, so too it is mistaken to suppose that the veil of ignorance supplies merely external constraints on persons who are conceived as fundamentally egoistic. For the rationality of the parties in the original position is not meant to be, all by itself, a model of how persons are, or a theory of human nature. It is only together with the veil of ignorance that the account of the rationality of the parties supplies us with a model of something about persons: namely, an account of the moral point of view, a point of view we can try to enter in real life at any time. In the moral point of view, of course, the constraints are internal, not external; the veil of ignorance is thus a model of one part of a person, the part that is capable of being unselfish and caring for others as of equal worth with the self. The rationality of the parties models another part, the part that is concerned with promoting the fulfillment of one's own ends (which, of course, may be ends shared with others).

In effect, as Rawls insists, the entirety of the original position is a model of benevolence. If we ask why we could not model benevolence directly, by imagining the parties as benevolent with full information, Rawls's answer is that the original position comes, in effect, to the same thing, but with a superior economy and clarity given by the fact that we do not have to ask questions such as, How intense is the benevolence and toward whom?, What information precisely?, and so forth (*TJ*, pp. 147–9/127–9 rev.). Thus, benevolence is in the theory but is constructed in such a way as to yield definite results. Furthermore, the difference principle, Rawls insists, exemplifies the important norm of fraternity, namely, "the idea of not wanting to have greater advantages unless this is to the benefit of others who are less well off" (*TJ*, p. 105/90 rev.). (Rawls cites love and care in the family – when things go well there – as one example of this virtue.)

Finally (a point added in the further discussion of Schopenhauer in *PL*, pp. 104–7), the parties, even as parts or aspects of persons, are imagined as trustees for citizens, and thus are not even prima facie egoistic. They are "concerned with securing for the person they represent the higher-order interests we have in developing and exercising our two moral powers and in securing the conditions under which we can further our determinate conception of the good, whatever it is" (*PL*, p. 106). These are good answers to the criticisms as posed.[12]

A related criticism was made by Michael Sandel in a way that has influenced feminist communitarian thought.[13] Noting that the parties in the original position are imagined as isolated from relationships and as ignorant of their conception of the good, Sandel charges that Rawls holds an implausible metaphysical doctrine about the self according to which we are fundamentally isolated individuals for whom relationship, community, and the goals involved in these are posterior to the self and nonnecessary. Once again, the same reply seems warranted: Sandel has mistaken the account of the rationality of the parties for a theory of human nature. Within Rawls's device of representation, the account of the rationality of the parties is simply a model of one part or aspect of a norm of moral reasoning, another crucial part of which is supplied by the veil of ignorance. Only the two taken together model the moral point of view, which, itself, is meant not as a theory of human nature but as a moral norm that forms part of a political conception.

Rawls clearly does think it possible to reflect about social justice without knowing about and pressing the claims of one's own particular conception of the good. In that he may possibly have a genuine difference from some communitarians if the latter think that context and community penetrate our moral reasoning so thoroughly that we can never leave those particular interests aside in order to think fairly and respectfully about the interests of those who have different conceptions of the good. But if they think that, they have not fully argued for that position, and we should not quickly accept such claims since this would put us in a grave and tragic predicament in modern societies characterized by a great diversity of comprehensive doctrines. Rawls's norm of equal respect is an attractive goal for all of us, even if it is very difficult to attain it.

Again, Rawls plainly thinks there is such a thing as human rationality and that it is single. When we take away knowledge of one's concept of the good and one's place in history and culture, we are left with a determinate structure of reasoning, and it appears to be the same for all the parties. In this supposition he may possibly be at odds with some care feminists if they hold, for example, that women have a different style of moral reasoning by biological nature rather than because of social formation. However, it is certain that no such claim has been established, given our understanding of the depth at which cultural influences permeate the formation of thought. Thus, virtually all feminists who hold that men and women characteristically reason differently suspect that these differences are largely the product of differential socialization. Such feminists have no quarrel with Rawls. If we observe existing differences in moral reasoning correlated with gender, we still need to ask what existing form of moral reasoning is the most adequate, normatively, for the job of establishing the basic structure of a just society. Rawls has given one powerful and attractive answer to that question.

Finally, an influential criticism of the original position, pressed by feminists influenced by the discourse ethics of Jürgen Habermas, focuses on the allegedly "monological" nature of the original position: the parties are imagined as basically all alike, and as reasoning on their own, rather than exchanging claims and counterclaims in a dialogue in which different perspectives can be presented and investigated. Feminists such as Seyla Benhabib and Marilyn Friedman hold that "monological" theories that imagine an abstract reasoner and derive conclusions from the thought of that single mind neglect possibilities for political insight available only in interpersonal dialogue where people can explain to one another their experiences and their diverse viewpoints.[14]

It is difficult to compare Rawls's view with Habermasian views for two reasons: first, because the original position is a hypothetical situation, and a device of representation, whereas Habermas focuses on an idealized conception of real social dialogue; second, because Habermas takes the core of social dialogue to lie in the many associations that comprise civil society, whereas Rawls has little to say about civil society (or, as he calls it, the "background culture"), focusing, even in his remarks about dialogue within society, on discussions pertaining to "constitutional essentials and matters of basic justice." Concerning discourse in civil society, Rawls's view is actually less restrictive than Habermas's in the sense that he has no normative view about how it should be carried out and would regard such norms (even the reasonable ones advanced by Habermas) as inappropriate incursions into spheres where individuals and groups may properly speak in accordance with the norms of their diverse comprehensive conceptions. Thus, the authoritarian and the obedient, the mystical and the illogical, are given free play by Rawls in the background culture: the dialogue is an "omnilogue" (PL, p. 383). Moreover, even unreasonable and seditious views are protected by a stringent law of free speech. By contrast, Rawls urges that, in the area of constitutional essentials and matters of basic justice, exchanges be governed by the moral (not legal) norms involved in the wide view of public reason, which does limit to some degree the extent to which it is morally right for individuals to ground their reasoning in their comprehensive doctrines. Here Habermasians tend to feel that Rawlsians are too restrictive.

The precise charge made by Benhabib and Friedman, however, pertains not to public reason but to reasoning within the original position and an alleged absence of diverse voices there. Let us, then, attempt to assess their charge. It would be very difficult to accept their proposal without utterly rejecting the entire strategy of the original position. For parties could not represent diverse social positions as proposed without having knowledge of their era in history, their conception of the good, and much else. But that ignorance of one's own place is a crucial part of Rawls's model of the moral point of view. To what extent, then, do these critics really wish to argue in favor of an altogether different moral ideal?

I believe that they really do not argue in favor of a different norm. In effect, they are asking a different question, namely, how the "purity of heart" Rawls attempts to capture in his device of representation might be achieved in real-world social dialogue. Their answer is that it must be achieved through patient and empathetic listening to diverse perspectives so that we emerge with a full understanding of the experience and point of view of the other. In other words, they rely on empathy and imagination, plausibly, to move us from the narrow sphere of our own goals to a broader and more adequate political perspective. As Okin has pointed out, however, the parties in the original position are required to exercise analogous virtues.[15] They need, that is, to consider the likely experience and fortunes of people in different social positions; their reasoning about the distribution of primary goods must of necessity be guided by an understanding of how different principles of justice would affect people's ability to execute their plans of life, whatever they may be, and so they will need to imagine a wide range of possible distribution patterns – those resulting from different candidate principles – and a wide range of types of life plan in order to be sure that the principles they choose are fair to persons and their conceptions.[16]

I think the real quarrel such critics may have with Rawls is not with the construction of the original position, but, instead, with restrictions on appeals to comprehensive doctrines in the norms of public reason. I address this issue in Section III.

### C. The Well-Ordered Society

Let us now confront a different criticism of Rawls's account of reasoning within the well-ordered society, the claim that Rawls has paid insufficient attention to the emotions as sources of political stability. Even though this criticism has not previously, to my knowledge, been pressed in an explicitly feminist context, it is perhaps one of the more interesting ways in which a feminist perspective on emotion might be applied to the assessment of Rawls's theory, and it grows out of an ongoing body of feminist work criticizing liberal theory for its denigration of emotion.[17]

Rawls, of course, devotes central importance to emotions in his account of moral development. Moreover (see Section IA), he takes a course highly congenial to many feminists when he holds that emotions are not mindless but intelligent and discriminating. He has very interesting things to say about the cognitive content of particular emotions, such as shame, guilt, and love, ascribing to them both complexity and ethical centrality. Even from the start of young children's lives, he holds, love involves a recognition that parents love and seek to benefit them (*TJ*, pp. 463/405–6 rev.) and also the recognition that their love is not conditional on any specific achievements (*TJ*, p. 464/406 rev.). In later childhood years, peer relations are mediated by a complex array of sentiments in which the ability to take up the viewpoint of others and to "see things from their perspective" (*TJ*, p. 468/410 rev.) is crucial. Finally, he argues in a most interesting section (Section 72) that there can be moral sentiments that are "principle-dependent." In the well-ordered society, moral principles themselves engage citizens' affections, forming sentiments whose content cannot be well described without mentioning the principles of justice themselves. In this way, "the sense of justice is continuous with the love of mankind" (*TJ*, p. 476/417 rev.). These sentiments play a major role in Rawls's account of the stability of the well-ordered society in *TJ*, although *PL*, in the spirit of avoiding controversial psychological doctrines, uses a much thinner moral psychology. No feminist could fairly charge that Rawls fails to take the emotions seriously as bonds of society or to respect their contribution to moral and political reasoning.

But some critics have maintained that this role for emotions is insufficient, too closely tethered to reason. Bernard Williams, for example, has insisted, criticizing the views of *TJ*, that the bonds of continuity in a society are emotional, and not (or not merely) principle dependent.[18] Similarly, John Haldane, discussing the nature of constitutional stability in Britain, has argued against Rawls's *PL* that there is a type of quite robust stability that is mediated more by symbol and tradition than by conscious acceptance of rationally justifiable principles.[19] These critics underestimate the role given emotions by Rawls himself. Nor do they sufficiently address the issue of stability for the right reasons. Rawls would be quite unhappy with a British-style stability if indeed this were secured by symbol and tradition merely and not by ideas that citizens can agree to share, ideas that they see as respecting them as free and equal. On this point Rawls seems to me entirely correct: Burkean ideas of stability are dangerous in a world of significant injustice and inequality. They would not offer us stability for the right reasons.

Let us, however, imagine a more subtle form of the critique as follows. Rawls focuses on public political reason and on reason-based moral sentiments as the sources of stability in the well-ordered society. In the process he fails to consider ancillary motives and psychological principles that may actually be essential sources of political stability, including stability for the right reasons. These sources include symbol, poetry, narrative, jokes, and memories.

In order to consider the force of this objection, let me introduce an analogy. When children attend a Passover seder, they are forming emotions that have as their direct object the moral ideas contained in the seder: anger at injustice, love of freedom, compassion for subordinate peoples. They form these emotions, however, not just on account of the propositions concerning freedom embodied in the text. Their emotional responses are mediated by the poetry and the stories and songs, by the presence of beloved family members gathering for a special occasion, by good food and the opportunity to stay up late, by silly jokes and games, and, as time goes on, increasingly by the memory of all these sounds and tastes and the thought of loved people alive and dead. The Haggadah itself (the ritual text) is constructed so as to encourage a type of emotional development that moves in a nonlinear way, backward and forward, between loved particulars and the general ideas that are being conveyed. The stability of the child's resulting moral emotions depends in a significant way on this dialectical process.

Now obviously the whole process of moral instruction would have failed if, as sometimes happens, children only remembered the jokes and not the deeper moral meanings; thus, we usually spend time talking about those meanings and asking children to do so. And the process would have failed in a more egregious way if, as sometimes happens, children learned to have compassion, or a love of freedom, only for Jews; thus we are well advised to spend time talking about other comparable examples of oppression in our own society, and indeed in Israel. Nonetheless, we would not be wise to strip away the songs and the jokes, for in them the essence of moral memory is situated. In that way the authors of the Haggadah were wiser morally than some modern Reform Jews, those who disdained ritual in favor of a pure abstract moral form of discourse. As Proust wonderfully shows, sensory particulars are the vehicle for the continued life of the past.

The critic I imagine urges us to see that the moral emotions of citizens in a Rawlsian well-ordered society are, or should be, like this: that is, fixed on the moral meanings of the political conception but held to those meanings by rituals and narratives of a kind that must be more particular, more uneven, more aesthetic, more tragic, more silly than anything explicitly envisaged in Rawls's text. These rituals and narratives might possibly be confined to what Rawls calls the "background culture" – but on the other hand, inasmuch as they are essential vehicles of public reason, there is no reason to confine them to that role. Candidates for election, legislators, even judges might use such symbols, poetic references, songs, and silly stories if they do so in a way that reinforces and deepens the moral meaning of the political conception. This means that we have the same dangers to face as in the case of the seder: we must be sure that citizens develop a type of patriotic loyalty that is reliably linked to the deeper principles of the political conception, and that does not exalt America (say) above other nations, and that focuses on suffering humanity wherever it occurs. This means that the emotions taught will be less Burkean and more closely allied to political reason than those envisaged by Williams and Haldane. Nonetheless, the critics have raised a significant issue, and one that should lead to a more complicated account of the roots of political stability. I see nothing in Rawls's writing to impede the development of such an account.

## II. JUSTICE IN THE FAMILY

The most difficult problem Rawls's theory faces in connection with women's equality is how to treat the institution of the family. On the one hand, the family is among the most significant arenas in which people pursue their own conceptions of the good and transmit them to the next generation. This fact suggests that a liberal society should give people considerable latitude to form families as they choose. On the other hand, the family is one of the most nonvoluntary and

pervasively influential of social institutions and one of the most notorious homes of sex hierarchy, denial of equal opportunity, and also
sex-based violence and humiliation. These facts suggest that a society committed to equal justice for all citizens, and to securing for
all citizens the social bases of liberty, opportunity, and self-respect
must constrain the family in the name of justice. Most liberal theories (Mill being the honorable exception) have simply neglected this
problem, or have treated the family as a "private" sphere with which
political justice should not meddle. Rawls from the first has denied
this type of public–private distinction by asserting that the family
is part of society's basic structure – ergo one of those institutions
to which principles of justice would apply (*TJ*, pp. 7/6–7 rev.). But,
having granted this, he then has to solve one of the most difficult
of problems. If he has not yet solved it, and I do not think he has, it
does not reflect particular discredit on his theory. It means, rather,
that the solution to this fiendishly difficult problem still eludes us
as philosophers and as people.

We should begin by simply summarizing the development of
Rawls's thinking on this issue because the texts are scattered and
difficult to gather. In *TJ*, Rawls asserted that "the monagamous family" was part of society's basic structure (*TJ*, p. 7/6 rev.). He tells us
that he assumes that the basic structure of a well-ordered society includes "the family in some form" (*TJ*, pp. 462–3/405 rev.), although,
"in a broader inquiry the institution of the family might be questioned and other arrangements might indeed prove to be preferable"
(id.). At several points he recognizes that inequalities of treatment
of children within the family pose obstacles to the full realization
of equality of opportunity within society: even willingness to try requires "happy family circumstances" (*TJ*, p. 74/64 rev., cf. 301/265
rev.). "Is the family to be abolished then?" he asks (*TJ*, p. 511/448
rev.). "Taken all by itself and given a certain primacy, the idea of
equality of opportunity inclines in this direction."

On the other hand, this tentatively radical direction in Rawls's
thought is never pursued, nor are his concerns about family circumstances related to issues of sex hierarchy. Indeed, in many ways
the text of *TJ* was insensitive to emerging feminist criticisms of liberal thought. Rawls never explicitly stated, for example, before 1975
that the parties in the original position are ignorant of their sex[20] –
although one important passage in *TJ* implied as much by saying that

the parties in the original position would see sex discrimination the way they see racial discrimination: as a system of hierarchy that is not only unjust but also completely irrational. They would never entertain the relevant principles because they make sense only as a means of suppression in a society where some already hold a favored position.[21] Rawls also noted that if, in a society, unequal basic rights should turn out to be correlated with "fixed natural characteristics" such as race or sex, the definition of the least well off would need to be adjusted to reflect this fact, and such inequalities, like inequalities of income and wealth, would have to be justified by showing that they were in the interests of the least well off. But such inequalities, he continues, "are seldom, if ever, to the advantage of the less favored" (*TJ*, p. 99/85 rev.).

Such passages suggest that Rawls already saw sex difference as an illegitimate basis for political distinctions, as much as class or race. And yet we have to say that he did little to develop this insight. His deferral of a critique of the family for "a broader inquiry" (in what, as Susan Okin remarked, was far from a narrow inquiry!), his persistent assumption that the parties in the original position are heads of households and trustees for family lines without raising questions about intrafamily distribution, his persistent use of masculine pronouns, his frequent references to "natural sentiments" in the family context, his uncritical acceptance of the the family as being "normally characterized by a definite hierarchy" (*TJ*, p. 467/409 rev.) – all these things led feminists to question the potential of the theory for justice between the sexes.[22]

Susan Okin's important critique led both the prosecution and the defense, arguing that Rawls's theory has great potential for feminist insight – but only if it commits itself to a critique of the family.[23] Okin argues that if justice as fairness is determined to show equal respect for persons, abolishing the political salience of hierarchies of wealth, class, and race, it is simply inconsistent and irrational for it not to question hierarchy based upon sex difference. But questioning this hierarchy requires us to criticize the institution of the family, for it is there, as Mill long ago argued, that hierarchical sex relations are perpetuated.[24] Moreover, it is perfectly reasonable to demand that the political culture shape the family, for the family is already shaped in countless ways by laws and institutions, and is hardly "natural."

Okin concludes that, if indeed the parties in the original position do not know their sex, they will design a society in which sex difference has no more salience, with regard to the basic structure of society, than eye color or race.[25] Sex difference may remain an important fact in citizens' conceptions of the good, but it will not have political salience; and law will counteract inequalities that are found to exist (presumably at the legislative stage): for example, by giving wives who have supported husbands' careers with their own domestic work a claim to half of the husband's income.[26] Like Rawls, Okin assumes that the family in some nuclear form will remain at the heart of a just society and will be its central vehicle for the rearing of children, although she explicitly includes same-sex couples, noting that they may be good models of the equal division of opportunities and responsibilities.

In *PL*, Rawls began to respond to this critique, noting that justice within the family is a major matter omitted in *TJ* (*PL*, p. xxi). Again, he asserts that "the structure of the family" belongs to the basic structure of society (*PL*, p. 258). Although he does not pursue this issue further, he does express his confidence that his principles can ultimately handle the issue of sex inequality. Just as principles worked out for religious difference proved helpful in addressing slavery, so "[t]he same equality of the Declaration of Independence, which Lincoln invoked to condemn slavery, can be invoked to condemn the inequality and oppression of women" (*PL*, p. xxxi). As Okin remarks, this statement needs interpretation, for what seems required is not just any conception of equality but one that involves an end to systematic hierarchy on the basis of a sex, as of race.[27] I think it is evident that this is the idea of equality Rawls has in mind, but he says little in *PL* to show how he would pursue this equality. In fact, some elements of the text cause unease – for example, the distinction (*PL*, p. 137) between the political and "the personal and familial, which are affectional." Similarly, although he recognizes the need to protect some family members against others ("wives from their husbands, children from their parents"), he also insists on the need to protect families "from associations and government" (*PL*, p. 221 n. 8). We are not told how he would balance these concerns.

Finally, in "The Idea of Public Reason Revisited" Rawls published a detailed statement on the question of the family and feminist criticisms. His definition of family is by now somewhat broader: "no particular form of the family (monogamous, heterosexual, or otherwise) is required" so long as it performs the task of caring for children and thus reproducing society stably over time and does not run afoul of other political values.[28] But the family is still assumed to be "a small intimate group in which elders (normally parents) have a certain moral and social authority."[29]

Once again, he asserts that the family forms part of society's basic structure.[30] At the same time, however, he claims that the two principles of justice, while they apply directly to the basic structure, do not "apply directly to the internal life of families."[31] In fact, he continues, the principles apply to families in just the way that they apply to society's many voluntary associations such as churches and universities. That is, the principles supply external constraints on what the associations can do, but they do not regulate their internal workings. A university, for example, cannot violate basic provisions of the criminal law, or of political justice more generally; but it may assign functions in accordance with its own criteria, whatever they are. So too with the family: the principles of justice do supply real constraints by specifying the basic rights of equal citizens. The family cannot violate these rights. "The equal rights of women and the basic rights of their children as future citizens are inalienable and protect them wherever they are. Gender distinctions limiting those rights and liberties are excluded."[32] And yet, citizens are not required to raise their children in accordance with liberal principles; we may have to allow for some traditional, gendered division of labor in families, "provided it is fully voluntary and does not result from or lead to injustice."[33]

In practical terms, Rawls thinks that we cannot make rules for the division of labor in families or penalize those who do not comply. On the other hand, we can, at the legislative stage, introduce laws that protect women's full equality as citizens, for example divorce laws of the sort favored by Okin: "It seems intolerably unjust that a husband may depart the family taking his earning power with him and leaving his wife and children far less advantaged than before... A society that permits this does not care about women, much less about their equality, or even about their children, who are its future."[34]

These proposals certainly go some way to addressing the feminist critique (and see the further defense in Lloyd).[35] But they leave three large problems. First of all, if the family is part of the basic structure, how can it also be a voluntary institution, analogous to a church or a university?[36] The institutions of the basic structure are those whose influence is pervasive and present from the start of a human life. The family is such an institution; universities and churches (except as extensions of families) are not. For adult women, membership in a family may be voluntary (though this is not always clear), and Rawls's protection of their exit options may suffice to ensure their full equality. But children are simply hostages to the family in which they grow up, and their participation in its gendered structure is by no means voluntary. Rawls does not address this deep problem, nor, in talking about civic education, does he comment on the extent to which he would favor compulsory public education when families wish to withdraw their children from the public culture. It is not terribly clear what it would mean to apply the principles of justice to the family as part of the basic structure: for surely the principles apply to the basic structure taken as a whole, and this does not entail that they apply piecemeal to every institution that forms part of the basic structure.[37] And yet the fact that the family is part of the basic structure and institutions such as universities, are not ought to make *some* difference in the way in which the principles apply; Rawls ought to have given us some account of that difference.

Second, Rawls does not acknowledge the parochial character of the Western nuclear family. Surprisingly, he still seems to regard some such unit as having a quasi-natural status; although he has broadened his account to include nontraditional nuclear groupings, he nowhere acknowledges the parochial character of the whole idea of raising children in a nuclear family. Village groups, extended families, women's collectives, kibbutzim, these and other grouping have been involved in the rearing of children; the parties in the original position, not knowing where they are in place and time, should not give preference to a particular Western, predominantly bourgeois, form over other possible forms. They should look at the issues of justice with an open mind, giving favor to those groupings that seem most capable of rearing children with a sense of justice, compatibly with other requirements of justice.

Third, Rawls does not recognize the extent to which, in all modern societies, the "family" is a creation of state action, enjoying a very different status from that of a church or a university. People associate

in many different ways, live together, love each other, have children.
Which of these will get the name "family" is a legal and political
matter and never one to be decided simply by the parties themselves.
The state constitutes the family structure through its laws, defining
which groups of people can count as families, defining the privileges
and rights of family members, defining what marriage and divorce
are, what legitimacy and parental responsibility are, and so forth.
This difference makes a difference: the state is present in the family
from the start in a way that is less clearly the case with the religious
body or the university; it is the state that says what this thing *is* and
controls how one becomes a member of it.[38]

To see this more clearly, let us consider the rituals that define a
person as a member of an association: in the university, matriculation (and, later, the granting of a degree); in a religious body, baptism,
conversion, or some analogous entrance rite; in the family, marriage.
Now it is evident that the state has some connection with university
matriculation and graduation and with religious baptism and conversion: it polices these rites on the outside by defining the institution
as enjoying a particular tax-free status, by preventing the use of cruelty or other illegalities in the ritual, and so forth. But marriage is
from the start a public, state-administered rite. There are state laws
defining it, and these laws restrict entry into that privileged domain.
The state does not simply police marriage on the outside; it marries
people. Other very similar people who do not meet the state's test
cannot count as married even if they satisfy all private and even religious criteria for marriage. (Thus, same-sex couples whose unions
have been solemnized by some religious body still are not married
because the state has not granted them a license.) Similarly, the state
determines who may adopt children and what "natural-born" children are legitimate. All human associations are shaped by laws and
institutions, which either favor or disfavor them and structure them
in various ways. But the family is shaped by law in a yet deeper and
more thoroughgoing way in the sense that its very definition is legal and political; individuals may call themselves "a family" if they
wish, but they only get to be one, in the sense that is socially recognized, if they satisfy legal tests. In short, the political sphere cannot
avoid directly shaping the family structure by recognizing some and
not other groupings as families. Rawls tends to treat the family as
an organization that has an extrapolitical existence and to ask how

far the state may interfere with it. If, instead, he had recognized the foundational character of the state's presence in the family, he might have granted that it makes good sense for principles of justice to rec-ognize and favor whatever units do the jobs of the family in a way that is compatible with political justice.

My feeling is that in this delicate area Rawls has been too ready to recognize what are, in effect, group rights: the right of families to protection against state action. If we really acknowledge the equal worth of all citizens, and the profound vulnerability of children as members of the family structure, we should, I believe, conceive of the liberal dilemma in a subtly different way by thinking how we may balance adult freedom of association, and other important interests in pursuing one's own conception of the good, against the liberties and opportunities of children as future citizens. No group gets special privileges qua group. If we proceed in this way and recognize in addi-tion that there is no group that exists "by nature" and that the family is more a state creation than many other associations, then the nat-ural question will be, What forms of state action, and what forms of privilege given to certain groupings, will best protect the liberties and opportunities of children within limits set by the protection of adult freedom of association and other important liberties?

Using this approach I have argued that a just society might well adopt policies that Rawls would probably consider too intervention-ist, for example, the Indian policies of making dowry illegal and of giving government subsidies to women's collectives as family-like groups that promote the equality of female children.[39] Whether or not the two approaches differ in their concrete recommendations, however, I believe that progress would be made by recognizing (a) that the family is part of the basic structure and not, in the case of children, a voluntary association, and (b) that there is no alternative to public structuring of the family.

One important feminist criticism of Rawls on the family must be treated more briefly. The first feminist criticism to be published is Jane English's critique (1977) of the "heads of households" assump-tion as it applies to the formulation of the just savings principle and the general issue of justice over generations.[40] English, like Okin,[41] is troubled by the provision that the parties in the original position are heads of households and aggregate the interests of family members; she argues that this assumption makes it more difficult for the theory to avoid injustices within the family. Since that device was a crucial part of Rawls's account of savings across generations, English proposes a modification that will enable Rawls to justify a modest rate of saving without the head of households assumption. The modification is to drop the "present time of entry" requirement, in which only presently living persons are represented in the original position (*TJ*, p. 140/121 rev.) and past generations cannot be assumed to have saved.[42] Instead, English proposes that the parties assume that other generations (past and future) save according to just principles too. Since the original position is not an event but a point of view or device of representation, "[o]ur simulating it today is compatible with our predecessors' having done likewise."[43] Rawls has accepted English's proposal (*PL*, 20n, 274n).

### III. RELIGION AND PUBLIC REASON

A controversial part of Rawls's political liberalism is his proposal of constraints on the public role of ideas and reasons drawn from citizens' comprehensive conceptions of the good. According to his most recent view, a moral norm governing public discourse on constitutional essentials and matters of basic justice is that all citizens are to use concepts and reasons internal to the political conception. Comprehensive doctrines may be introduced at any time but only subject to the proviso that "in due course"[44] the utterances be translated into the terms of the public conception either by the speaker or by someone else. (These ideas need, as Rawls recognizes, further specification.) Rawls's idea is that to justify the public use of state coercive power one should use terms that are (potentially, at least) acceptable to all citizens.

Feminists make two objections to this idea. One objection, which they share with many of Rawls's religious critics and with critics from Habermasian discourse ethics, is that such restrictions cut short the public give and take of reasons; a fuller exchange may actually be quite valuable for mutual respect and understanding. This is how I ultimately understand the force of Seyla Benhabib's influential critique.[45] Although it was not articulated with specific reference to Rawls's doctrine of public reason, which had not yet been published, it is in that sphere that Benhabib's concern for wide and unrestricted dialogue has its proper force.

This objection I do not propose to treat at length, since it will surely be discussed elsewhere in this volume. There are certainly many distinct views of what mutual respect and reciprocity require; Rawls is aware that his proposal may meet with sincere objections from reasonable religious conceptions. But the sense of confinement reported by Habermasians should be mitigated by the recognition that Rawls proposes no legal restriction on such speech: it is just a moral norm. And, further, even this norm is suspended once we reach the background culture of civil society, where, as I observed in Section I, Rawls's conception is less normatively restrictive than that of Habermas and much more willing to countenance appeals to faith and authority as sources of reasons perfectly on a par with others. Or rather, to put it more precisely, he has (qua the proposer of justice as fairness) no view at all about how such debates should go and thinks it improper to express one.

A quite different objection is made by Okin, who sees Rawls's norms of public reason as insufficiently restrictive where gender inequality is concerned.[46] She is concerned not with the restrictions faced by all comprehensive doctrines in discussion of constitutional essentials but with the special restrictions attached to "unreasonable" comprehensive doctrines. Okin notes that, according to Rawls, certain comprehensive doctrines are simply "unreasonable," even "mad." Included among these are "doctrines and . . . associated ways of life . . . in direct conflict with the principles of justice . . . [such as those] requiring the repression or degradation of certain persons on, say, racial, or ethnic, or perfectionist grounds, for example slavery in ancient Athens, or in the antebellum South" (PL, pp. 195–6).[47] The proposals made by such groups "can be reasonably removed from the political agenda" (PL, p. 151) and will not come up for majority vote (PL, p. 365); their adherents will not be allowed to pursue those aspects of their comprehensive doctrine (PL, p. 187).

On the other hand, Rawls also supposes, "perhaps too optimistically – that, except for certain kinds of fundamentalism, all the main historical religions [admit an account of free faith] and thus may be seen as reasonable comprehensive doctrines" (PL, p. 170).[48] Okin argues that Rawls is thus flatly inconsistent, for none of the major religions accords with the principles of justice in its treatment of women:

Surely the circumscription of women's roles in life, their segregation in religious life, and their exclusion from important religious functions and positions of leadership – doctrines and practices that are still common to many varieties of religion – render them unreasonable by Rawls's own criteria. There is a serious conflict between freedom of religion and the equality of women.[49]

Therefore, we are to conclude that "Rawls does not apply the same strict criteria of reasonableness to comprehensive doctrines that involve considerable gender inequality that he does to those that treat people differently on racial or ethnic grounds."[50]

Two difficulties stand in the way of this criticism. First, Okin would appear to have the wrong idea about what happens to "unreasonable" comprehensive doctrines in Rawls's society, for she speaks of imposing "restrictions" on such views, implying that their speech will be curtailed or that they will be forbidden to make political proposals. Such a view is plainly at odds with Rawls's account of free speech, which insists that the same view of free speech protects the unreasonable and the reasonable (PL, 343, etc.); no political, religious, or philosophical speech can be censored, in Rawls's view, absent the existence of a grave constitutional crisis "in which free political institutions cannot effectively operate or take the required measures to preserve themselves" (PL, 354). What is at issue, then, is whether certain liberties will be entrenched beyond the reach of majority vote. Rawls favors considerable entrenchment for the enumerated liberties, so it is in that sense that proposals favoring slavery or serfdom will not be able simply to come up for a vote and will in that sense be off the political agenda.[51] But of course anyone who likes may make such proposals unconstrained. If people make such proposals in contexts restricted by the moral norms of public reason, Rawls will hold that they act immorally. If they do so in their private club or their church gathering, he has nothing to say about their conduct except that what they say is in contradiction with the political conception; therefore, the political conception has a right to discourage such views by its own public statements.

But do statements made by the major religions about the status of women fall into this class in the first place? The second difficulty in the way of Okin's criticism is that she does not distinguish between doctrines holding that women should have unequal rights of citizenship and doctrines holding that they are metaphysically unequal or dissimilar in some other respect. In many parts of the world, both religious and nonreligious doctrines do deny the equality of women as citizens: they are held to be incapable of equal rights of travel, contract, property, and so forth, and these proposals are translated into law. Were such doctrines to be found in a society governed by Rawls's principles, they would certainly be "unreasonable," and a liberal state would be entitled to discourage them, though not to suppress their speech. Their proposals would never come up for simple majority vote.

But it seems unlikely that any of the major religions found in our nation currently holds such a doctrine. Unequal assignment of religious functions and inegalitarian normative views about the proper sphere of women's lives can certainly be present in a "reasonable" doctrine – if such a doctrine is prepared to grant the full equal citizenship of women and to impose no barriers to women's exercise of those civic functions, and if, furthermore, women are free, as they always are in Rawls's society, to change religions or to drop religion altogether. Even Southern Baptists, who certainly hold a hierarchical view of women's place in the home, do not propose that women be unequal under the law.[52] Such citizens surely will experience a tension between two aspects of their comprehensive doctrine; and it is in that sense that Rawls foresees that the well-ordered society will indirectly influence comprehensive doctrines, changing some and causing others to fail to gain adherents over time. If people keep hearing about the equality of women as citizens in the public sphere, and if proposals to curtail that equality are off the agenda, then citizens are quite likely to shift or reinterpret their religious doctrine if it is clearly hierarchical – all the more since such doctrines are already questioned by substantial segments within each of the major religions. But to say that there is a tension is not to say that the doctrine is unreasonable.[53] And there is no reason to think that Rawls is treating gender differently from race or ethnicity in this regard. A sexist doctrine that supports equal citizenship is analogous to a racist doctrine that supports equal citizenship, not to a doctrine that favors slavery or serfdom. Both are tolerated as "reasonable," provided that their proponents support fully equal citizenship for women or racial minorities.

Now of course there are significant issues about how far a sexist doctrine, taught early in the home, really is compatible with fully equal citizenship for women (see Section II). In that sense gender is asymmetrical to race, since few African–American children (say) grow up in white supremacist families; the influence of racism, though it may be pervasive in the culture, is likely to arrive at a later date and perhaps (though this is not obvious) to be less deforming as a result. So there may be special worries about sexist comprehensive doctrines; I do not think these worries suffice to make them "unreasonable" when we would not attach that label to a doctrine of metaphysical racism that supported the fully equal citizenship of African–Americans in the public realm.

At bottom, Okin is, I think, basically a comprehensive liberal who finds it insufficient that the state should confine itself to pronouncing on doctrines concerning citizenship without pronouncing on all aspects of the various comprehensive doctrines. It seems to her half-hearted for the state to endorse equal citizenship and not to construct, and vigorously support, the rest of a comprehensive way of life that protects it by teaching a comprehensive doctrine of sex equality. This is a powerful alternative to Rawls's position; many feminists will prefer to follow Okin (and Mill) here. (Mill, for example, suggests that the state would be entitled to cast aspersions on the teachings of authoritarian religions to foster the comprehensive doctrine of liberty.) Certainly we should agree with Okin that there are serious tensions between regarding citizens as self-authenticating sources of valid claims and accepting the teachings of many religions concerning women's subservience. This tension will surely be difficult for the major religions to sort out as they join an overlapping consensus. My own sympathies, however, are with Rawls: the test of toleration is not in the way we deal with views that we like but in the way that we deal with what makes us uncomfortable or even angry. Feminists in a liberal society should treat sexist religious doctrines with respect (provided they endorse equal citizenship); meanwhile, in civil society and personal relations, they may advocate what they consider to be just, working to counteract the influence of such ideas.

## IV. DEPENDENCY AND WOMEN'S WORK

The citizens in Rawls's well-ordered society are "fully cooperating members of society over a complete life" (*PL*, p. 183, et saepe). Real people, by contrast, begin their lives as helpless infants and remain in a state of extreme dependency, both physical and mental, for anywhere from ten to twenty years. At the other end of life, those who are lucky enough to live on into old age are likely to encounter another period of extreme dependency. During the middle years of life, many people encounter periods of extreme dependency, some involving mental powers and some the bodily powers only, but all of which may put them in need of daily, even hourly, care by others. Finally, many citizens never acquire the physical and/or mental powers requisite for independence. Any real society must therefore be a care-giving and care-receiving society and must discover non-exploitative ways to cope with these facts of human neediness. These are central issues for feminism because women traditionally provide the bulk of care for dependents, and this asymmetry is a major source of their more general social inequality.

How does Rawls's theory deal with these questions? And does it deal with them well enough? As Eva Kittay has argued in an excellent discussion, there are five places in Rawls's theory where he fails to confront facts of asymmetrical neediness that might naturally have been confronted.[54]

1. His account of the "circumstances of justice" assumes a rough equality between persons such that none could dominate all the others; thus, we are not invited to consider relations of justice that might obtain between an adult and her infants or her senile demented parents.

2. Rawls's idealization of citizens as "fully cooperating" and so forth puts to one side the large facts about extreme neediness I have just mentioned.

3. His conception of social cooperation, again, is based on the idea of reciprocity between equals and has no explicit place for relations of extreme dependency.

4. His account of the primary goods, introduced, as it is, as an account of the needs of citizens who are characterized by the two moral powers and by the capacity to be "fully cooperating," has no place for the need of many real people for the kind of care we give to people who are not independent.

5. His account of citizens' freedom as involving the concept of being a self-authenticating source of valid claims (e.g., PL, p. 32) fails to make a place for any freedom that might be enjoyed by someone who is not independent in that sense.

Now of course Rawls is perfectly aware that his theory focuses on some cases and leaves others to one side. In the Dewey Lectures he puts the point as follows:

So let's add that all citizens are fully cooperating members of society over the course of a complete life. This means that everyone has sufficient intellectual powers to play a normal part in society, and no one suffers from unusual needs that are especially difficult to fulfill, for example, unusual and costly medical requirements. Of course, care for those with such requirements is a pressing practical question. But at this initial stage, the fundamental problem of social justice arises between those who are full and active and morally conscientious participants in society, and directly or indirectly associated together throughout a complete life. Therefore, it is sensible to lay aside certain difficult complications. If we can work out a theory that covers the fundamental case, we can try to extend it to other cases later.[55]

This reply has several problems. First, it is never altogether clear exactly how many and which cases Rawls means to leave to one side. At times, as in the passage cited (and see also *PL*, p. 272 n. 10), he suggests leaving aside all severe or expensive physical illness as well as all mental disability, whether lifelong or connected to childhood or old age. At other times (e.g., *PL*, p. 302), he plainly regards possession of the two moral powers as a sufficient, as well as a necessary, condition of fully cooperating status. So the example used by Sen to criticize the theory of primary goods – that of a person in a wheelchair – is placed sometimes on one side of the divide, sometimes on another. Surely we should count citizens who have illnesses or physical handicaps as fully cooperating, provided that they have the two mental/moral powers. But then it would appear that such variations in need should, as Sen urges (1979), be taken into account in the very formulation of the account of primary goods and not merely at the legislative stage.[56]

More generally, variations in physical need are a pervasive fact of human life: pregnant or lactating women need more nutrients than nonpregnant persons, and so forth. Even within the clearly recognized terrain of the "fully cooperating," then, the theory of primary goods seems flawed if it does not take such variations into account in determining who is and is not the least well off rather than, as the theory recommends, determining that status by income and wealth alone. So even in order to take account of the physical needs of nondisabled citizens – which the theory seems bound, even on its own terms, to take account of – Rawls will need, I think, to move to an approach more like Sen's in which the primary goods are formulated in a way that permits a good understanding of these variations. The same is all the more clearly true when we add to this group the large number of citizens who are "fully cooperating" in the sense of having the two moral powers but who suffer from a chronic or acute physical disability that affects their ability to convert resources into actual human functioning.[57]

But Kittay's critique cuts deeper. For Rawls's Kantian starting point in reciprocity and regard for personhood discourages him from thinking that justice obtains at all in relations that are seriously asymmetrical on the mental and moral side. Thus, for example, he refuses to grant that we have any duties of justice to animals on the grounds that they are not capable of reciprocity (*TJ*, p. 17/15 rev., 504–5/441–2 rev.); they are owed "compassion and humanity," but "[t]hey are outside the scope of the theory of justice, and it does not seem possible to extend the contract doctrine so as to include them in a natural way" (*TJ*, p. 512/448 rev.). This is true enough, but that might cause us to wonder whether the Kantian contract doctrine offers a complete account of political justice.

The problem is not just one about other species; it is one that pertains to us since we are also animals. Kittay plausibly argues that the issue of care for dependents cannot be left for resolution at the legislative stage, since it affects the design of basic social institutions. If we see citizens as both capable of cooperation and also in need of periods of care, we will naturally include care for extreme bodily and mental needs among the primary goods that are requisite for living a complete life. This will lead to complicated thinking about how to shape basic institutions so that caregiving will not be exploitative and care-receiving will be compatible with self-respect.

### CONCLUSION

John Rawls's work offers important insights for feminists thinking about justice. In many respects, his theory can be adapted to meet the most serious criticisms feminists have made against it. Criticisms based upon issues about emotion and affiliation are, by and large, met already by the theory in its current form or could be met by relatively minor modifications. Criticisms based on the pervasiveness of unequal need and dependency cut deeper. To meet them fully, Rawls would need to make serious modifications both in his account of citizens as fully cooperating members of society over a complete life and also in his account of primary goods. But I see no reason why these modifications cannot be made by a theory basically Rawlsian in spirit.

The criticisms pertaining to the family raise the most difficult and troubling issues, for they seem to threaten the very project of political liberalism. There is no doubt that some of the major comprehensive doctrines oppose the kind of revisionary treatment of family structure that many feminists would see as required by justice. Comprehensive liberals need not be so troubled by this resistance for they are not committed to respecting these diverse views of the good. But Rawls has given good reasons for holding that respect for persons in a situation of reasonable pluralism requires respecting conceptions of the good. It is no accident that in a sphere that is the home both of intimate self-definition and also of egregious wrongdoing the search for liberal justice should encounter difficulties, for liberal justice is committed both to protecting spheres of personal self-definition and to ending the arbitrary and wrongful tyranny of some people over others. But the failure to have a fully satisfactory solution to the difficulties is not a failure of liberal justice because the liberal is right. Self-definition and liberty of conscience are extremely important, and it is also extremely important to end the wrongful tyranny of some over others (in part because it prevents those others from enjoying self-definition and liberty of conscience). I therefore believe that the solution to this problem, if there is one, lies not in the rejection of Rawlsian liberalism but in a deeper and more extensive reflection about alternative liberal principles for its solution. This search would do well to begin by imagining and studying the many ways in which groups of people of many different types have managed, in different places at different times, to raise children with both love and justice.

ENDNOTES

1   I am grateful to Kate Abramson, Marcia Baron, David Estlund, Chad Flanders, Samuel Freeman, Marilyn Friedman, Marcia Homiak, Eva Kittay, Thomas Lynn, Susan Okin, David Strauss, and Cass Sunstein for their helpful comments on a previous draft. Length constraints have

made it impossible for me to respond to all their points as I would have wished.

2  "The Idea of Public Reason Revisited," *The University of Chicago Law Review* 64 (Summer 1997): 765–807, p. 775, n. 28; also in Rawls, *Collected Papers* (Cambridge MA: Harvard University Press, 1999), pp. 573–615

3  John Rawls, 1994, unpublished manuscript cited with permission.

4  John Rawls, *Political Liberalism* (New York: Columbia University Press, 1993, paperback edition 1996), p. 28; cited in text as *PL*.

5  John Rawls, *A Theory of Justice* (Cambridge, MA: Harvard University Press, 1971/revised edition, 1999), p. 49/43 rev. ed.

6  See Held, Virginia, *Feminist Morality: Transforming Culture, Society, and Politics* (Chicago: University of Chicago Press, 1993); Nussbaum, Martha C., "Perceptive Equilibrium: Literary Theory and Ethical Theory," in *Love's Knowledge: Essays on Philosophy and Literature* (New York: Oxford University Press, 1990), pp. 168–94.

7  Nussbaum, Martha C., *Sex and Social Justice* (New York: Oxford University Press, 1999).

8  See Martha Nussbaum, "'Secret Sewers of Vice': Disgust, Bodies, and the Law," in *The Passions of Justice*, ed. S. Bandes (New York: New York University Press, 2000).

9  Insofar as I may have suggested that it was in *Love's Knowledge*, I hereby retract that suggestion.

10  Baier, Annette, "The Need for More than Justice," in *Justice and Care: Essential Readings in Feminist Ethics*, ed. V. Held (Boulder, CO: Westview, 1995), pp. 47–60, at p. 55.

11  Alison Jaggar, *Feminist Politics and Human Nature* (Totowa, NJ: Rowman and Littlefield, 1983), p. 30–1.

12  Baier's criticism is also misdirected when she suggests that Rawls has ignored fraternity in favor of liberty and equality and when she contrasts Rawlsian justice with care defined as "a felt concern for the good of others and for community with them" (Baier, "The Need for More than Justice," p. 48). Nor does her argument rest on solid ground when she invokes the (highly controversial and socially narrow) research of Carol Gilligan to argue that autonomy may not be a norm women can attain (p. 53).

13  Sandel, Michael, *Liberalism and the Limits of Justice* (Cambridge, UK: Cambridge University Press, 1982).

14  Benhabib, Seyla, "The Generalized and the Concrete Other: The Kohlberg–Gilligan Controversy and Moral Theory," in *Situating the Self: Gender, Community and Postmodernism in Contemporary Ethics* (New York: Routledge, 1992), pp. 148–77; Friedman, Marilyn, *What Are*

*Friends for? Feminist Perspectives on Personal Relationships and Moral Theory* (Ithaca: Cornell University Press, 1993).

15  Okin, Susan Moller, "Reason and Feeling in Thinking about Justice," *Ethics*, 99 (1989): 229–49.

16  Friedman will still object that bias can be discerned more readily in an actual dialogue because other parties can notice more readily than a person herself the presence of bias against them in her purportedly unbiased claims. This is a significant point. I am inclined to think, with Okin, that Rawls has done enough to eliminate bias; but other readers may side with Friedman.

17  See Jaggar, *Feminist Politics and Human Nature*, pp. 28–47; Held, Virginia, *Feminist Morality: Transforming Culture, Society, and Politics* and Friedman, *What Are Friends For?* (among others).

18  Williams, Bernard, "Morality and Social Justice," Tanner Lectures given at Harvard University (1983), unpublished.

19  Haldane, John, "The Individual, the State, and the Common Good," *Social Philosophy and Policy* 13 (1996): 59–79.

20  "Fairness to Goodness," *The Philosophical Review* 84 (1975): 536–54 at p. 537; also in *Collected Papers*, 267–85, at p. 268.

21  Finally, if the parties are conceived as themselves making proposals, they have no incentive to suggest pointless or arbitrary principles. For example, none would urge that special privileges be given to those exactly six feet tall or born on a sunny day. Nor would anyone put forward the principle that basic rights should depend on the color of one's skin or the texture of one's hair...Inevitably, then, racial and sexual discrimination presupposes that some hold a favored place in the social system which they are willing to exploit to their advantage. From the standpoint of persons similarly situated in an initial situation which is fair, the principles of explicit racist doctrines are not only unjust. They are irrational. For this reason we could say that they are not moral conceptions at all, but simply means of suppression. ( *TJ*, p. 149)

22  See also, Kearns, Deborah "A Theory of Justice and Love – Rawls on the Family," *Politics* 18 (1983): 36–42.

23  Okin, Susan Moller, "Justice and Gender," *Philosophy and Public Affairs* 16 (1987): 42–72; Okin, Susan Moller, *Justice, Gender, and the Family* (New York: Basic Books, 1989).

24  Mill, John Stuart, *The Subjection of Women* (1869), Ed. with Introduction by Susan Moller Okin (Indianapolis: Hackett, 1988).

25  In Okin, *Justice, Gender, and the Family*.

26  Okin does not restrict this idea to the case of divorce, although Rawls, in accepting it in "The Idea of Public Reason Revisited" (see below) does so restrict it.

27  Okin, Susan Moller, "*Political Liberalism*, Justice, and Gender," *Ethics* 105 (1994): 23–43.

28  *Collected Papers*, p. 596, n. 60

29   Ibid., p. 596

30   Ibid., p. 595

31   Ibid., p. 596.

32   Ibid., p. 599

33   Ibid., p. 599. Rawls understands the fact that it is chosen on the basis of one's religion as a sufficient condition of voluntariness in background conditions that are fair (p. 599 and n. 68); he notes that the question needs a fuller discussion.

34   Ibid., pp. 600–1.

35   Lloyd, S. A., "Family Justice and Social Justice," *Pacific Philosophical Quarterly* 75 (1994): 353–71.

36   See also Cohen, G. A. (1997). "Where the Action Is: On the Site of Distributive Justice," *Philosophy and Public Affairs* 26 (1997): 3–30.

37   See Lloyd, "Family Justice and Social Justice."

38   See Martha Minow's many fascinating examples of how the INS uses definitions of "family" to restrict immigration. Minow, "All in the Family and In All Families: Membership, Loving, and Owing" in *Sex, Preference, and Family: Essays on Law and Nature*, ed. D. Estlund and M. Nussbaum (New York: Oxford University Press, 1997), pp. 249–76. See also, Frances Olsen, "The Family and the Market: A Study of Ideology and Legal Reform," *Harvard Law Review* 96 (1983): 1497–1577; and Frances Olsen, "The Myth of State Intervention in the Family," *University of Michigan Journal of Law Reform* 18 (1985): 835–64.

39   Nussbaum, Martha C., *Women and Human Development: The Capabilities Approach* (New York: Cambridge University Press, 2000).

40   Jane English, "Justice between Generations," *Philosophical Studies* 31 (1977): 91–104.

41   In Okin, *Justice, Gender, and the Family*.

42   See *TJ* 292. This passage has been omitted in the revised edition. See *TJ* 258 rev.

43   English, "Justice between Generations," p. 98.

44   See Rawls, "The Idea of Public Reason Revisited."

45   Seyla Benhabib, "The Generalized and the Concrete Other: The Kohlberg–Gilligan Controversy and Moral Theory"

46   Okin, Susan Moller, "*Political Liberalism*, Justice, and Gender," *Ethics* 105 (1994): 23–43.

47   The two examples at the end of the sentence are not cited by Okin, who ends her citation with "grounds." This makes it possible for her reader to infer, mistakenly, that Rawls proposes to restrict all racist doctrines.

48   Okin remarks that the faith demanded by Roman Catholics and other major religious is not especially free, but I think she misunderstands the

idea of "free faith," which is simply that forced conversion is insufficient for faith, that faith is a matter of assent in the inner world. If she does understand the conception, I am not sure on what grounds she means to deny that the major religious hold this doctrine. Surely the doctrine is not inconsistent with making many nonnegotiable demands of believers or subjecting them to authority in many ways.

49  Okin, "*Political Liberalism*, Justice, and Gender," p. 31.

50  Ibid, p. 31.

51  Could a Constitutional amendment be introduced to reintroduce slavery? Rawls doubts it in the body of the text in *PL*, suggesting that the Supreme Court would be right to reject such an amendment as invalid, given its conflict with the general principles underlying the constitution as a whole (238–9). (This, of course, would be a highly unconventional view as applied to U.S. Constitutional law.) On the other hand, both in that context and in the "Reply to Habermas" he is concerned to distinguish his own view from a natural rights view by insisting that all aspects of the constitution are at some level subject to popular sovereignty of some type.

52  Equality under law is, however, a controversial notion. If, for example, Southern Baptists were to favor repeal of laws making sex discrimination by private employers illegal, that might make their position unreasonable in Rawls's sense if we were to maintain (plausibly) that such antidiscrimination laws are an essential ingredient of full political equality. Moreover, many religions discriminate against lesbians, which is certainly understood by many feminists to be a central form of sex discrimination and integrally related to a more general sexism.

53  Here we encounter an interesting general problem: Rawls does think it necessary that a reasonable doctrine strive for consistency and completeness (*PL* 59). But religious doctrines will have many ways of meeting this requirement; furthermore, it would be inadvisable for Rawls to press the requirement too far or else he will have to hold unreasonable most of the doctrines real people actually hold. Astrology, for example, and New Age doctrines are not paradigms of consistency or scientific rationality, and yet they do not seem to be particularly worth excluding. Given their wide support, a liberal society should probably not define reasonableness in such a way as to put them out of the overlapping consensus.

54  See Eva Kittay, "Human Dependency and Rawlsian Equality," in *Feminists Rethink the Self*, ed. Diana T. Meyers (Boulder, CO: Westview, 1997), pp. 219–66; also Eva Kittay *Love's Labor: Essays on Women, Equality, and Dependency* (New York: Routledge, 1997).

55  "Kantian Constructivism in Moral Theory," in *Collected Papers*, pp. 303–58, at p. 332.

56  Amartya Sen, "Equality of What?", *The Tanner Lectures on Human Values* (Salt Lake City: University of Utah Press, 1979) reprinted in Sen, *Choice, Welfare, and Measurement* (Oxford, UK: Basil Blackwell, 1982), pp. 353–69.

57  See Sen, Ibid.; see also, Nussbaum, *Women and Human Development: The Capabilities Approach*.

# BIBLIOGRAPHY

BIBLIOGRAPHY: THE CAMBRIDGE COMPANION TO JOHN RAWLS

The amount of literature written on Rawls is at least equal to that of any other twentieth-century philosopher. The following bibliography is necessarily selective. Rawls's complete works are first cited. Then follows a list of books and anthologies on Rawls. Most of the bibliography consists of citations of articles in philosophy and other journals. I have not attempted to locate and cite the many important discussions of Rawls that appear in others' books. The two largest divisions of the bibliography list articles on *A Theory of Justice* and *Political Liberalism*. Other divisions reflect topics of special interest which have stimulated discussions of parts of Rawls's work or its implications. Most of the articles listed are in English. (*John Rawls and His Critics: An Annotated Bibliography* by J.H. Wellbank, Denis Snook, and David T. Mason (New York: Garland, 1982) provides abstracts for most of the secondary literature on Rawls prior to 1982. See the bibliography to Thomas W. Pogge's *John Rawls* (Munich: C.H. Beck, 1994) for many works in German.)

WORKS BY JOHN RAWLS

*A Study on the Grounds of Ethical Knowledge: Considered with Reference to Judgments on the Moral Worth of Character*, Ph.D Dissertation, Princeton University, 1950, *Dissertation Abstracts* 15 (1955): 608–9.
"Outline of a Decision Procedure for Ethics." *Philosophical Review* 60 (1951): 177–97.
A review of Stephen Toulmin's *An Examination of the Place of Reason in Ethics*. *Philosophical Review* 60 (1951): 572–80.
A review of Axel Hägerstrom's *Inquiries into the Nature of Law and Morals* (translated by C.D. Broad), *Mind* 64 (1955): 421–2.
"Two Concepts of Rules." *Philosophical Review* 64 (1955): 3–32.

"Justice as Fairness." The first version of this paper, published in the *Journal of Philosophy* 54 (1957): 653–62, was read before the American Philosophical Association, Eastern Division Meetings. An expanded version appeared in *Philosophical Review* 67 (1958): 164–94. It is this version that is most frequently anthologized. Another revised version was translated into French by Jean–Fabien Spitz as "La Justice comme équité" *Philosophie* 14 (1987): 39–69.

Review of Raymond Klibansky, ed., *Philosophy in Mid-Century: A Survey. Philosophical Review* 70 (1961): 131–2.

"Constitutional Liberty and the Concept of Justice," in *Nomos VI: Justice*, eds., C. Freidrich and John W. Chapman, pp. 98–125. New York: Atherton, 1963.

"The Sense of Justice." *Philosophical Review* 72 (1963): 281–305.

"Legal Obligation and the Duty of Fair Play," in *Law and Philosophy*, ed., Sidney Hook, pp. 3–18. New York: New York University Press, 1964.

Review of *Social Justice*, ed., Richard Brandt. *Philosophical Review* 74 (1965): 406–9.

"Distributive Justice." The first version of this paper was published in *Philosophy, Politics, and Society*. Third Series. eds., P. Laslett and W.G. Runciman, pp. 58–82. Oxford, UK: Basil Blackwell, 1967. This essay and the essay "Distributive Justice: Some Addenda" were combined to form a second "Distributive Justice" in *Economic Justice*, ed., E. Phelps, pp. 319–62. London: Penguin Books, 1973.

"Distributive Justice: Some Addenda." *Natural Law Forum* 13 (1968): 51–71.

"The Justification of Civil Disobedience," in *Civil Disobedience*, ed., Hugo Bedau, pp. 240–55. New York: Pegasus, 1969.

"Justice as Reciprocity" (written in 1958) in *Mill: Text with Critical Essays*, ed., Samuel Gorovitz, pp. 242–68. Indianapolis: Bobbs–Merrill, 1971.

*A Theory of Justice.* Cambridge, MA: Harvard University Press, 1971. *A Theory of Justice* has been translated into Chinese, Finnish, French, German, Italian, Japanese, Korean, Portuguese, and Spanish, and eighteen other languages. For the first of these, the German translation of 1975, Rawls made some revisions, which have been incorporated into all of the translations.

*A Theory of Justice*, revised edition, Cambridge, MA: Harvard University Press, 1999 is a publication of the 1975 revised text, which has been used for all translations.

"Reply to Lyons and Teitelman." *Journal of Philosophy* 69 (1972): 556–7.

"Some Reasons for the Maximin Criterion." *American Economic Review* 64 (1974): 141–6.

"Reply to Alexander and Musgrave." *Quarterly Journal of Economics* 88 (1974): 633–55.

"The Independence of Moral Theory." *Proceedings and Addresses of the American Philosophical Association* 48 (1975): 5–22.

"A Kantian Conception of Equality." *Cambridge Review* (1975): 94–9. Reprinted as "A Well-Ordered Society," in *Philosophy, Politics, and Society*, Vol.5, edited by P. Laslett and J. Fishkin (Oxford, UK: Blackwell, 1979) pp. 6–20.

"Fairness to Goodness." *Philosophical Review* 84 (1975): 536–54.

"The Basic Structure as Subject." The first version was published in the *American Philosophical Quarterly* 14 (1977): 159–65 after it was read before the meeting of the American Philosophical Association, Pacific Division, 1977. A revised and expanded version appears in *Values and Morals: Essays in Honor of William Frankena, Charles Stevenson, and Richard B. Brandt*, pp. 47–71. ed., A. Goldman and J. Kim. Dordrecht, Holland: Reidel, 1978.

"Kantian Constructivism in Moral Theory: The Dewey Lectures 1980." *Journal of Philosophy* 77 (1980): 515–72.

"Social Unity and Primary Goods," in *Utilitarianism and Beyond*, ed., Amartya Sen and Bernard Williams, pp. 159–85. Cambridge, UK: Cambridge University Press, 1982.

"The Basic Liberties and Their Priority." *Tanner Lectures on Human Values*, Volume III, pp. 3–87. Salt Lake City: University of Utah Press, 1982.

"Justice as Fairness: Political not Metaphysical." *Philosophy and Public Affairs* 14 (1985): 223–51.

"On the Idea of an Overlapping Consensus." *Oxford Journal for Legal Studies* 7 (1987): 1–25.

"The Priority of Right and Ideas of the Good." *Philosophy and Public Affairs* 17 (1988): 251–76.

"Themes in Kant's Moral Philosophy," in *Kant's Transcendental Deductions*, ed., E. Förster. Stanford: Stanford University Press, 1989.

"The Domain of the Political and Overlapping Consensus." *New York University Law Review* 64 (1989): 233–55.

"Roderick Firth: His Life and Work." *Philosophy and Phenomenological Research* 51 (1991): 109–18.

*Political Liberalism*, New York: Columbia University Press, 1993; the revised paperback edition, 1996, includes an additional preface, and Rawls's 1995 article, the "Reply to Habermas."

"The Law of Peoples," in *On Human Rights: The Oxford Amnesty Lectures, 1993*, ed., Steven Shute and Susan Hurley (New York: Basic Books, 1993), pp. 41–82.

"Reply to Habermas," *Journal of Philosophy*, 93:3 (March 1995).

"Fifty Years after Hiroshima," *Dissent* (Summer 1995): 323–7.

"The Idea of Public Reason Revisited," *University of Chicago Law Review* 64 (Summer 1997): 765–807.

*Collected Papers*, edited by Samuel Freeman, Cambridge, MA: Harvard University Press, 1999.

*The Law of Peoples*, Cambridge, MA: Harvard University Press, 1999, including the paper "The Idea of Public Reason Revisited."

*Lectures on the History of Moral Philosophy*, edited by Barbara Herman, Cambridge, MA: Harvard University Press, 2000.

"Burton Dreben: A Reminiscence," in Juliet Floyd and Sanford Shieh, eds., *Future Pasts: Perspectives on the Place of the Analytic Tradition in Twentieth-Century Philosophy*, New York: Oxford University Press, 2000.

*Justice as Fairness: A Restatement*, edited by Erin Kelley, Cambridge, MA: Harvard University Press, 2001.

*Lectures on the History of Political Philosophy*, edited by Samuel Freeman, Cambridge, MA: Harvard University Press, (Forthcoming).

### BOOKS ON OR SUBSTANTIALLY ABOUT RAWLS

Alejandro, Roberto, *The Limits of Rawlsian Justice*, Baltimore: Johns Hopkins Press, 1998.

Barry, Brian, *The Liberal Theory of Justice*, Oxford, UK: Oxford University Press, 1972.

Baynes, Kenneth, *The Normative Grounds of Social Criticism: Kant, Rawls, and Habermas*, Albany: SUNY Press, 1992.

Bidet, Jacques, *John Rawls et la Theorie de la Justice*, Paris: Presses Universitaires de France, 1995.

Daniels, Norman, *Justice and Justification*, Cambridge, UK: Cambridge University Press, 1996.

Dombrowski, Daniel, A., *Rawls and Religion: The Case for Political Liberalism*, Albany, NY: State University of New York Press, 2001.

Kukathas, Chandran, and Philip, Pettit, *Rawls: A Theory of Justice and Its Critics*, Stanford: Stanford University Press, 1990.

Mandle, Jon, *What's Left of Liberalism: An Interpretation and Defense of Justice as Fairness*, Lanham, MD: Lexington Books, 2000.

Martin, Rex, *Rawls and Rights*, Lawrence, KS: University of Kansas Press, 1985.

Munoz-Darde, Veronique, *La justice sociale: le liberalisme egalitaire de John Rawls*, Paris: Nathan Universite, 2000.

Pogge, Thomas, *Realizing Rawls*, Ithaca: Cornell University Press, 1989.

────── *John Rawls*, Munich: C.H. Beck, 1994.

Sandel, Michael, *Liberalism and the Limits of Justice*, Cambridge, UK: Cambridge University Press, 1982; second edition, 1998.

Schaefer, David, L., *Justice or Tyranny? A Critique of John Rawls's 'A Theory of Justice,'* Port Washington, NY: Kennikat Press, 1979.

Wellbank, J.H., Dennis, Snook and David, T. Mason, *John Rawls and His Critics: An Annotated Bibliography*, New York: Garland, 1982.

Wolff, Robert Paul, *Understanding Rawls*, Princeton, NJ: Princeton University Press, 1977.


ANTHOLOGIES ON RAWLS

Arneson, Richard, "Symposium on Rawlsian Theory of Justice: Recent Developments," *Ethics* 99 (4) (1989): 695–944.

Audard, C., Boudon, R. Dupuy, J.P., et al., *Individu et justice sociale. Autour de John Rawls*, Paris: Le Seuil, 1988.

Blocker, H.G., and Smith, E.H., *John Rawls's Theory of Social Justice*, Athens, OH: Ohio University Press, 1980.

Corlett, J. Angelo, ed., *Equality and Liberty: Analyzing Rawls and Nozick*, New York: St. Martins Press, 1991.

Daniels, Norman, ed., *Reading Rawls*, New York: Basic Books, 1975, reprinted with a new introduction by Stanford Press, 1989.

Davion, Virginia, and Clark Wolf, eds., *The Idea of Political Liberalism: Essays on Rawls*, Lanham, MD: Rowman and Littlefield, 1999.

George, Robert, and Christopher Wolfe, eds., *Natural Law and Public Reason*, Washington, DC: Georgetown University Press, 2000.

Griffin, Stephen, and Lawrence Solum, Symposium on John Rawls's *Political Liberalism*, in *Chicago–Kent Law Review* 69 (3) (1994): 549–842.

Hoeffe, Otfried, ed., *John Rawls: Eine Theorie der Gerechtigkeit*, Berlin: Akademie Verlag, 1998.

——— *Über John Rawls's Theorie der Gerechtigkeit*, Frankfurt am Main, 1977.

Lloyd, S.A., *John Rawls's Political Liberalism*, Special Double Issue of *Pacific Philosophical Quarterly*, 75 (3&4) (Sep./Dec. 1994).

Reath, Andrews, Barbara Herman, Christine M. Korsgaard, eds., *Reclaiming the History of Ethics: Essays for John Rawls*, Cambridge, UK: Cambridge University Press, 1997.

Richardson, Henry, and Paul Weithman, eds., *The Philosophy of Rawls: A Collection of Essays*, in 5 volumes, New York: Garland, 1999.
Volume I: *Development and Main Outlines of Rawls's Theory of Justice*
Volume II: *The Two Principles and Their Justification*
Volume III: *Opponents and Implications of A Theory of Justice*
Volume IV: *Moral Psychology and Community*
Volume V: *Reasonable Pluralism*

Salles, M., and J. Weymark, eds., *Justice, Political Liberalism, and Utilitarianism: Proceedings of the Caen Conference in Honor of John Harsanyi and John Rawls*, Cambridge, UK: Cambridge University Press, 1988.

Stayn, Susan, ed., Symposium on *Political Liberalism*, *Columbia Law Review* 94 (6) (October 1994): 1813–1949.

ARTICLES ON *A THEORY OF JUSTICE*

Ake, Christopher, "Justice as Equality," *Philosophy and Public Affairs* 5 (1975): 69–89.

Arneson, Richard, "Primary Goods Reconsidered," *Nous* 24 (3) (June 1990): 429–54.

Arrow, Kenneth, "Some Ordinalist–Utilitarian Notes on Rawls's Theory of Justice," *The Journal of Philosophy* 70 (9) (May 10, 1973): 245–63.

Baier, Kurt, "Justice and the Aims of Political Philosophy," *Ethics* 99 (4) (July, 1989).

Barber, Benjamin, "Justifying Justice: Problems of Psychology, Politics, and Measurement in Rawls," *American Political Science Review* 69 (1975): 663–74.

Barry, Brian, "Liberalism and Want-Satisfaction: A Critique of John Rawls," *Political Theory* 1 (1973): 134–53.

Bedau, Hugo Adam, "Social Justice and Social Institutions," *Midwest Studies in Philosophy* 3 (1978): 159–175.

———— "Review of Brian Barry's *The Liberal Theory of Justice*," *The Philosophical Review* 84 (1975): 598–603.

Binmore, Ken, "Naturalizing Harsanyi and Rawls," in M. Salles and J. Weymark, eds., *Justice, Political Liberalism, and Utilitarianism*, Cambridge, UK: Cambridge University Press, 1988.

Bowie, Norman, "Some Comments on Rawls's Theory of Justice," *Social Theory and Practice* 3 (1974): 65–74.

Braybrooke, David, "Utilitarianism with a Difference: Rawls's Position in Ethics," *Canadian Journal of Philosophy* 3 (2) (1973): 303–31.

Brock, Dan, "John Rawls's Theory of Justice," *University of Chicago Law Review* 40 (3) (1973): 486–99.

Buchanan, Allen, "Revisability and Rational Choice," *Canadian Journal of Philosophy* 5 (1975): 395–408.

———— "A Critical Introduction to Rawls's Theory of Justice," in *John Rawls's Theory of Social Justice*, H. Gene Blocker and Elizabeth H. Smith, eds., pp. 5–41. Athens, OH: Ohio University Press, 1980.

Chapman, John, "Rawls's Theory of Justice," *The American Political Science Review* 69 (1975): 588–93.

Choptiany, Leonard, "A Critique of John Rawls's Principles of Justice," *Ethics* 83 (January 1973): 146–50.

Cohen, Joshua, "Democratic Equality," *Ethics* 99 (4) (July 1989): 727–51.

Cohen, Marshall, "The Social Contract Explained and Defended," *New York Times Book Review*, July 16, 1972, p. 18.

Corlett, J.A., "Knowing and Believing in the Original Position," *Theory and Decision* 27 (1989): 241–56.

Crocker, Lawrence, "Equality, Solidarity, and Rawls's Maximin," *Philosophy and Public Affairs* 6 (1977): 262–6.

Dworkin, Gerald, "Non-Neutral Principles," *Journal of Philosophy* 71 (August 1974): 491–506, reprinted in N. Daniels, *Reading Rawls*.

Dworkin, Ronald, "The Original Position," *University of Chicago Law Review* 40 (Spring 1973): 500–33, reprinted in N. Daniels, *Reading Rawls*.

English, Jane, "Justice Between Generations," *Philosophical Studies* 31 (1977): 91–104.

Farrell, Daniel, "Dealing with Injustice in a Reasonably Just Society: Some Observations on Rawls's Theory of Political Duty," in *John Rawls's Theory of Social Justice*, H. Gene Blocker and Elizabeth Smith, eds., pp. 187–210. Athens, OH: Ohio University Press, 1980.

Feinberg, Joel, "Rawls and Intuitionism," in Daniels, Norman, *Reading Rawls*.

——— "Duty and Obligation in a Non-Ideal World," *Journal of Philosophy* 70 (1973): 263–75.

——— "Justice, Fairness, and Rationality," *Yale Law Journal* 81 (1972): 1004–31.

Fisk, Milton, "History and Reason in Rawls's Moral Theory," in Daniels, Norman, *Reading Rawls*.

Fiskin, James, "Justice and Rationality: Some Objections to the Central Argument in Rawls's Theory," *The American Political Science Review* 69 (2) (June 1975): 618ff.

Frankel, Charles, "Review of *A Theory of Justice*," *Columbia Human Rights Law Review* 5 (1973): 547–64.

Fried, Charles, "Review of Rawls's *A Theory of Justice*," *Harvard Law Review* 85 (1971–72): 169ff.

Fuchs, Alan, E., "The Concept of Morality in Rawls's Theory," *Journal of Philosophy* 72 (1975): 628–9.

Fullinwider, Robert K., "Hare on Rawls: A Worry About Possible Persons," *Philosophical Studies* 29 (1976): 199–205.

Galston, William, "Defending Liberalism," *American Political Science Review* 76 (September 1982): 621–9.

Gastil, Raymond, "Beyond a Theory of Justice," *Ethics* 85 (3) (1975): 183–94.

Gauthier, David, "Justice and Natural Endowment: Toward a Critique of Rawls's Ideological Framework," *Social Theory and Practice* 3 (1974): 3–26.

——— "Fairness and Cores: A Comment on Laden," *Philosophy and Public Affairs* 22 (1993): 44–7.

Gibson, Mary, "Rationality," *Philosophy and Public Affairs* 6 (1977): 193–225.

Goldman, Alan, H., "Rights, Utilities, and Contracts," *The Canadian Journal of Philosophy*, Supp. Vol. III (Spring 1977).

Goodrun, Craig R., "Rawls and Egalitarianism," *Philosophy and Phenomenological Research* 37 (1977): 386–93.

Gourevitch, Victor, "Rawls on Justice," *The Review of Metaphysics* 28 (1975): 485–519.

Grey, Thomas, C., "The First Virtue," *Stanford Law Review* 25 (1973): 286–327.

Grisez, Germain, "Review of *A Theory of Justice*," *Review of Metaphysics* 26 (1973): 764–65.

Gutmann, Amy, "The Central Role of Rawls's Theory," *Dissent* 36 (1989): 338–42.

Haksar, Vinit, "Rawls's Theory of Justice," *Analysis* 32 (1972): 149–53.

―――― "Rawls and Gandhi on Civil Disobedience," *Inquiry* 19 (1976): 151–92.

Hampshire, Stuart, "A New Philosophy of the Just Society," *The New York Review of Books*, February 24, 1972, pp. 34–9.

Hare, R.M., "Rawls's Theory of Justice," *Philosophical Quarterly* 23 (1973): 144–55, 241–51, reprinted in Norman Daniels, ed., *Reading Rawls*.

Harsanyi, John, "Can the Maximin Principle Serve as a Basis for Morality? A Critique of John Rawls's Theory," *American Political Science Review* 69 (1975): 594–606.

Held, Virgina, "On Rawls and Self-Interest," *Midwest Studies in Philosophy* 1 (1976): 57–60.

Honderich, Ted, "The Use of the Basic Proposition of A Theory of Justice," *Mind* 84 (1975): 63–78.

Hubbard, F. Patrick, "Justice, Limits to Growth, and an Equilibrium State," *Philosophy and Public Affairs* 7 (4) (1978): 326–45.

Hubin, Clayton, "Justice and Future Generations," *Philosophy and Public Affairs* 6 (1976): 70–83.

―――― "Minimizing Maximin," *Philosophical Studies* 37 (1980): 363–72.

Katzner, Louis, I., "The Original Position and the Veil of Ignorance," in *John Rawls's Theory of Social Justice*, H. Gene Blocker and Elizabeth H. Smith, eds., pp. 42–70. Athens, OH: Ohio University Press, 1980.

Keat, Russell, and David Miller, "Understanding Justice," *Political Theory* 2 (1974): 3–31.

Kernohan, Andrew, "Rawls and the Collective Ownership of Natural Abilities," *The Canadian Journal of Philosophy* 20 (March 1990): 19–28.

Klosko, George, "Political Obligation and the Natural Duties of Justice," *Philosophy and Public Affairs* 23 (3) (1994): 251–70.

Kolm, Serge-Christophe, "Equal Liberties and Maximin," in his *Modern Theories of Justice*, pp. 169–208. Cambridge, MA: MIT Press, 1998.

Kymlicka, Will, "Rawls on Teleology and Deontology," *Philosophy and Public Affairs* 17 (1988): 173–90.

—— "Liberal Equality," in his *Contemporary Political Philosophy: An Introduction*, pp. 50–94. New York: Oxford University Press, 1990.

Laden, Anthony, "Games, Fairness, and Rawls's *A Theory of Justice*," *Philosophy and Public Affairs* 20 (3) (Summer 1991): 189–222.

Lessnoff, Michael, "John Rawls's Theory of Justice," *Political Studies* 19 (1971): 63–80.

Levin, Michael, and Margarita Levin, "The Modal Confusion in Rawls's Original Position," *Analysis* 39 (1979): 82–87.

Levine, Andrew, "Beyond Justice: Rousseau against Rawls,"*Journal of Chinese Philosophy* 4 (2) (August 1977): 140.

Lyons, David, "Nature and Soundness of the Contract and Coherence Arguments," in N. Daniels, *Reading Rawls*.

—— "The Nature of the Contract Argument," *The Cornell Law Review* 59 (1973–74): 1064–76.

Mabe, Alan, R., "Review of *A Theory of Justice*," *The Journal of Politics* 35 (1973): 1018–20.

Macleod, A.M., "Critical Notice: Rawls's Theory of Justice," *Dialogue: Canadian Philosophical Review* 13 (1974): 139–59.

MacCormick, Neil, "Justice According to Rawls," *The Law Quarterly Review* 89 (1973): 393–417.

MacIntyre, Alasdair, "Justice: A New Theory and Some Old Questions," *Boston University Law Review* 52 (1972): 330–4.

Marneffe, Peter de, "Liberalism and Perfectionism," *The American Journal of Jurisprudence* 43 (1998): 99–116.

McBride, William, L., "Social Theory *Sub Specie Aeternitatis*: A New Perspective," *Yale Law Journal* 81 (5) (April, 1972): 980–1003.

Mandelbaum, Maurice, "Review of *A Theory of Justice*," *History and Theory* 12 (1973): 240–50.

Margolis, Joseph, "Justice as Fairness," *The Humanist* 33 (1973): 36–7.

McBride, William, L., "Social Theory *Sub Specie Aeternitatis*: A New Perspective," *Yale Law Journal* 81 (1972): 980–1003.

McKenna, Edward, Maurice Wade, and Diane Ziaonni, "Rawls and the Minimum Demands of Justice," *Journal of Value Inquiry* 24 (1990): 85–108.

Meyer, Michel, "The Perelman–Rawls Debate on Justice," *Revue Internationale de Philosophie* 29 (113) (1975): 316–31.

Murphy, Liam, "Institutions and the Demands of Justice," *Philosophy and Public Affairs* 27 (Fall 1998): 151–91.

Nagel, Thomas, "Rawls on Justice," *Philosophical Review* 87 (April 1973): 220–34, reprinted in Daniels, ed., *Reading Rawls*.

Nelson, William, "Special Rights, General Rights, and Social Justice," *Philosophy and Public Affairs* 3 (1974): 411–30.

Nielson, Kai, "The Choice between Perfectionism and Rawlsian Contractarianism, *Interpretation* 6 (1977): 132–9.

——— "Rawls and Classist Amoralism," *Mind* 86 (1977): 19–30.

Norton, David, L., "Rawls's Theory of Justice: A 'Perfectionist' Rejoinder," *Ethics* 85 (1) (1974): 50–7.

Nowell-Smith, P.H., "A Theory of Justice?" *Philosophy of the Social Sciences* 3 (1973): 315–39.

Oberdieck, Hans, "A Theory of Justice," *New York University Law Review* 47 (1972): 1012–28.

O'Neill, Onora, "The Method of *A Theory of Justice*," in Otfried Hoeffe, ed., *John Rawls: Eine Theorie der Gerechtigkeit*, Berlin: Akademic Verlag, 1998.

Orr, D., and W. Ramm, "Rawls's Justice and Classical Liberalism: Ethics and Welfare Economics," *Economic Inquiry* 85 (1974): 50–7.

Pettit, Philip, "A Theory of Justice?" *Theory and Decision* 4 (1974): 311–24.

Pollack, Lansing, "A Dilemma for Rawls?" *Philosophical Studies* 22 (1971): 37–43.

Pritchard, Michael, S., "Human Dignity and Justice," *Ethics* 82 (1972): 299–313.

Rae, Douglas, "Maximin Justice and an Alternative Principle of General Advantage," *The American Political Science Review* 69 (1975): 630–47.

Raphael, D.D., "Critical Notice: Rawls's Theory of Justice," *Mind* 83 (1974): 118–27.

Reiman, Jeffrey, "A Reply to Choptiany on Rawls on Justice," *Ethics* 84 (1974): 262–5.

Ricoeur, Paul, "On John Rawls' *A Theory of Justice*: Is a Pure Procedural Theory of Justice Possible?" *International Social Science Journal* 42 (1990): 553–64.

Ryan, Alan, "John Rawls," *The Return of Grand Theory in the Human Sciences*, Quentin Skinner, ed., Cambridge, UK: Cambridge University Press, 1985.

Scanlon, T.M., "Rawls's Theory of Justice," *University of Pennsylvania Law Review* 121 (May 1973): 1029–69, reprinted in part in Daniels, *Reading Rawls*.

Schaefer, David Lewis, "A Critique of Rawls's Contract Doctrine," *The Review of Metaphysics*, 28 (1974): 89–115.

Scharr, John, "Equality of Opportunity and the Just Society," in *John Rawls's Theory of Social Justice*, H. Gene Blocker and Elizabeth H. Smith, eds., pp. 162–84. Athens, OH: Ohio University Press, 1980.

——— "Reflections on Rawls's Theory of Justice," *Social Theory and Practice* 3 (1) (1974): 75–100.

Scheffler, Samuel, "Moral Independence and the Original Position," *Philosophical Studies* 35 (1979): 397–403.

Schwartz, Adina, "Moral Neutrality and Primary Goods," *Ethics* 83 (1973): 294–307.

Sen, Amartya, "Justice: Means versus Freedoms," *Philosophy and Public Affairs* 19 (1990): 111–121.

Shue, Henry, "The Current Fashions: Trickle Downs by Arrow and Close-Knits by Rawls," *Journal of Philosophy* 71 (1974): 319–27.

―――― "Justice, Rationality, and Desire: On the Logical Structure of Justice as Fairness," *The Southern Journal of Philosophy* 13 (1975): 89–97.

Singer, Marcus, "Discussion Review: Justice, Theory, and a Theory of Justice," *Philosophy of Science* 44 (1977): 594–618.

Sneed, Joseph, "John Rawls and the Liberal Theory of Society," *Erkenntnis* 10 (1976): 1–19.

Sterba, James, "Prescriptivism and Fairness," *Philosophical Studies* 29 (1976): 1411–8.

―――― "In Defense of Rawls against Arrow and Nozick," *Philosophia* 7 (1978): 293–303.

Strasnick, Steven, "Review of Robert Paul Wolff's *Understanding Rawls*," *Journal of Philosophy* 76 (1979): 496–510.

Stuhlmann-Laeisz, Rainer, "Gerechtigkeit und Effizienz: Eine Untersuchung zum Verhaeltnis des Unterschiedsprinzips zu dem der Pareto-Optimalitaët in Rawls's Theorie der Gerechtigkeit," *Allegemeine Zeitschrift fuër Philosophie* 6, (1) (1981): 17–30.

Tattershall, Gerald, "A Rawls Bibliography," *Social Theory and Practice* 3 (1974): 123–7.

Teitelman, Michael, "The Limits of Individualism," *Journal of Philosophy* 69 (18) (October 5, 1972): 545–56.

Thomas, Larry, "To *A Theory of Justice*: An Epilogue," *Philosophy Forum*, (1974–75): 244–53.

Urmson, J.O., "A Defense of Intuitionism," *Proceedings of the Aristotelian Society* 75 (1974–75): 111–9.

Van Dyke, Vernon, "Justice as Fairness: For Groups?" *The American Political Science Review* 69 (1975): 607–14.

Williams, Bernard, "Rawls and Pascal's Wager," in his *Moral Luck*, pp. 94–100. Cambridge, UK: Cambridge University Press, 1981.

Zaitchik, Alan, "Just Enough," *Philosophical Quarterly* 25 (1975): 340–5.

POLITICAL LIBERALISM

Ackerman, Bruce, "Political Liberalisms," *The Journal of Philosophy* 91 (7) (July 1994): 364–86.

Alejandro, Roberto, "What Is Political about Rawl's Political Liberalism?" *Journal of Politics* 58 (1) (February 1996): 1–24.

Arneson, Richard, "Introduction (to a Symposium on Rawlsian Theory of Justice: Recent Developments)," *Ethics* 99 (1999): 695–710.

Baier, Kurt, "Justice and the Aims of Political Philosophy," *Ethics* 99 (1989): 771–90.

Barry, Brian, "John Rawls and the Search for Stability," *Ethics* 105 (4) (July 1995): 874–915.

———— "In Defense of Political Liberalism," *Ratio Juris* 7 (1994): 325–30.

Beggs, Donald, "Rawls's Political Postmodernism," *Continental Philosophy Review* 32 (1999): 123–41.

Brighouse, Harry, "Civic Education and Liberal Legitimacy," *Ethics* 108 (July 1998).

———— "Is There Any Such Thing as Political Liberalism?" *Pacific Philosophical Quarterly* 75 (1994): 318–32.

Charney, Evan, "Political Liberalism, Deliberative Democracy, and the Public Sphere," *American Political Science Review* 92 (1) (March 1998): 97–110.

Cohen, Joshua, "Moral Pluralism and Political Consensus," in *The Idea of Democracy*, eds., David Copp, Jean Hampton, and John Roemer. Cambridge, UK: Cambridge University Press, 1993.

———— "A More Democratic Liberalism," *Michigan Law Review* 92 (6) (May 1994): 1503–46.

———— "Pluralism and Proceduralism," *Chicago–Kent Law Review* 69 (1994): 589–618.

Daniels, Norman, "Reflective Equilibrium and Justice as Political," in his *Justice and Justification*. Cambridge, UK: Cambridge University Press, 1996: 144–75.

Dworkin, Gerald, "Contracting Justice," *Philosophical Books* 36 (1995): 19–26.

Estlund, David, "The Survival of Egalitarian Justice in John Rawls's *Political Liberalism*," *Journal of Political Philosophy* 4 (1996): 68–78.

———— "The Insularity of the Reasonable: Why Political Liberalism Must Admit the Truth," *Ethics* 108, no. 2 (1998): 252–75.

Fischer, Marilyn, "Associations and the Political Conception of Justice," *Journal of Social Philosophy* 28 (1997): 31–42.

Freeman, Samuel, "Political Liberalism and the Possibility of a Just Democratic Constitution," *Chicago–Kent Law Review* 69 (1994): 619–68.

Galston, William, "Pluralism and Social Unity," *Ethics* 99 (1989): 711–26.

Gaus, Gerald, F., "Reasonable Pluralism and the Domain of the Political: How the Weaknesses of John Rawls's *Political Liberalism* Can Be Overcome by a Justificatory Liberalism," *Inquiry* 42 (1999): 259–84.

Gaut, Berys, "Rawls and the Claims of Liberal Legitimacy," *Philosophical Papers* 24 (1995): 1–22.

Griffen, Stephin, M., "Political Philosophy versus Political Theory: The Case of Rawls," *Chicago–Kent Law Review* 69 (1994): 691–708.

Habermas, Jüergen, "Reconciliation through the Public Use of Reason: Remarks on John Rawls's Political Liberalism," *Journal of Philosophy* 92 (1995): 109–31.

Hampshire, Stuart, "Liberalism: The New Twist," *New York Review of Books* (August 12, 1993): 43–6.

Hampton, Jean, "Should Political Philosophy Be Done without Metaphysics?" *Ethics* 99 (1989): 791–814.

—— "The Common Faith of Liberalism," *Pacific Philosophical Quarterly* 75 (Sept./Dec., 1994): 186–216.

Hittinger, Russell, "John Rawls, *Political Liberalism*" *Review of Metaphysics* 47 (1994): 585–602.

Hollenbach, David, "Contexts of the Political Role of Religion: Civil Society and Culture," *San Diego Law Review* 30 (1993): 877–901.

Hurd, Heidi, M., "The Levitation of Liberalism," *Yale Law Journal* 105 (December 1995): 795–824.

Klosko, George, "Political Constructivism in Rawls's Political Liberalism," *American Political Science Review*, 91 (3) (September 1997): 635–46.

—— "Rawls's 'Political' Philosophy and American Democracy," *American Political Science Review* 87 (2) (June 1993): 348–59.

Larmore, Charles, "Political Liberalism," *Political Theory* 18 (3) (1990): 339–60.

—— "Pluralism and Reasonable Disagreement," reprinted in his *The Morals of Modernity*, Cambridge, UK: Cambridge University Press, 1996.

—— "The Moral Basis of Political Liberalism," *Journal of Philosophy* 96 (1999): 599–625.

Lehning, Percy, B., "The Coherence of Rawls's Plea for Democratic Equality, *Critical Review of International Social and Political Philosophy* 1 (4) (Winter 1998): 1–41.

Lloyd, S.A., "Relativizing Rawls," *Chicago–Kent Law Review* 69 (1994): 737–62.

Mandle, Jon, "The Reasonable in Justice as Fairness," *Canadian Journal of Philosophy* 29 (March 1999): 75–107.

Martin, Rex, "Rawls's New Theory of Justice," *Chicago–Kent Law Review* 69 (1994): 737–62.

McCabe, David, "Knowing about the Good: A Problem with Antiperfectionism," *Ethics* 110 (January 2000): 311–38.

Michelman, Frank, "The Subject of Liberalism," *Stanford Law Review* 46 (6) (July 1994): 1807–33.

Mouffe, Chantal, "Political Liberalism: Neutrality and the Political," *Ratio Juris* 7 (1994): 314–24.

Mulhall, Stephen, "Promising, Consent, and Citizenship," *Political Theory* 25 (1997): 171–92.

Neal, Patrick, "Does He Mean What He Says? (Mis)Understanding Rawls's Practical Turn," in *Liberalism and Its Discontents*, New York: New York University Press, 1997.

O'Neill, Onora, "Political Liberalism and Public Reason: A Critical Notice of John Rawls, *Political Liberalism*," *Philosophical Review* 106 (1998): 411–28.

Nickel, James, W., "Rethinking Rawls's Theory of Liberty and Rights," *Chicago–Kent Law Review* 69 (1994): 763–86.

Peffer, Rodney, G., "Towards a More Adequate Rawlsian Theory of Social Justice," *Pacific Philosophical Quarterly* 75 (1994): 251–71.

Raz, Joseph, "Disagreement in Politics," *The American Journal of Jurisprudence* 43 (1998): 25–52.

Rorty, Richard, "The Priority of Democracy to Philosophy," in *Objectivity, Relativity and Truth*, pp. 175–96. New York: Cambridge University Press, 1991.

Sandel, Michael, "Political Liberalism," *Harvard Law Review* 107 (1994): 1765–94.

Scheffler, Samuel, "The Appeal of Political Liberalism," *Ethics* 105 (1994): 4–22.

Simmons, A. John, "Justification and Legitimacy," *Ethics* 109 (1999): 739–71.

Solum, Lawrence, "Introduction: Situating Political Liberalism," *Chicago–Kent Law Review* 69 (1994): 549–88.

Waldron, Jeremy, "Disagreements about Justice," *Pacific Philosophical Quarterly* 75 (September–December 1994): 372–87.

Weinstock, Daniel, "The Justification of Political Liberalism," *Pacific Philosophical Quarterly* 75 (September–December 1994).

Weithman, Paul, "Liberalism and the Political Character of Political Philosophy," in *Liberalism and Community Values*, ed., C.F. Delaney, pp. 189–211. Lanham, MD: Rowman and Littlefield, 1994.

Williams, Bernard, "A Fair State," *London Review of Books*, 13 May 1993.

Wilkins, Burleigh, "A Third Principle of Justice," *Journal of Ethics* 1 (4) (1997): 355–74.

Wolin, Sheldon, S., "The Liberal/Democratic Divide: On Rawls's *Political Liberalism*," *Political Theory* 24 (1) (1996): 97–119.

Young, Iris, M., "Rawls's *Political Liberalism*," *Journal of Political Philosophy* 3 (2) (1995): 181–90.

### RAWLS AND SOCIAL CONTRACT DOCTRINE

Beatty, Joseph, "The Rationality of the Original Position: A Defense," *Ethics* 93 (1983): 484–95.

Browne, D.E., "The Contract Theory of Justice," *Philosophical Papers* 5 (1976): 1–10.

Brudney, Daniel, "Hypothetical Consent and Moral Force," *Law and Philosophy* 10 (1991): 235–70.

Care, Norman, S., "Contractualism and Moral Criticism," *Review of Metaphysics* 23 (1969): 85–101.

Cushing, Simon, "Agreement in Social Contract Theories: Locke vs. Rawls," in Yeager Hudson, ed., *Technology, Morality and Social Policy*, Lewiston Maine: Mellen Press, 1998.

——— "Representation and Obligation in Rawls's Social Contract Theory," *Southwest Philosophy Review* 14 (1) (1997): 47–54.

Diggs, B.J., "A Contractarian View of Respect for Persons," *American Philosophical Quarterly* 18 (4) (October 1981): 273–83.

Eshete, Andreas, "Contractarianism and the Scope of Justice," *Ethics* 85 (1974): 38–49.

Freeman, Samuel, "Reason and Agreement in Social Contract Views," *Philosophy and Public Affairs* 19 (2) (Spring 1990): 122–57.

Gauthier, David, "The Social Contract as Ideology," *Philosophy and Public Affairs* 6 (1977): 130–64.

Gray, John, "Social Contract, Community and Ideology," in J. Gray, *Liberalisms*, London: Routledge, 1989.

Hampton, Jean, "Contracts and Choices: Does Rawls Have a Social Contract Theory?" *The Journal of Philosophy* 77 (6) (June 1980): 315–38.

Johnson, Conrad, "Actual- vs. (Rawlsian) Hypothetical-Consent," *Philosophical Studies* 28 (1975): 41–8.

Keyt, David, "The Social Contract as an Analytic, Justificatory and Polemic Device," *Canadian Journal of Philosophy* 4 (1974): 241–52.

Lessnoff, Michael, "Justice, Social Contract, and Universal Prescription," *Philosophical Quarterly* 28 (1979): 65–73.

Marshall, John, "The Failure of Contract as Justification," *Social Theory and Practice* 3 (1975): 441–59.

Milo, Ronald, "Contractarian Constructivism," *Journal of Philosophy* 122 (1995): 181–204.

Nielsen, Kai, and Roger Shiner, eds., *New Essays in Contract Theory, Canadian Journal of Philosophy*, Supplementary Volume III, 1977.

Rae, Douglas, "The Limits of Consensual Decision," *The American Political Science Review* 69 (1975): 1270–94.

Robins, Michael, H., "Promissory Obligations and Rawls's Contractarianism," *Analysis* 36 (1976): 190–8.

Stark, Cynthia, "Hypothetical Consent and Justification," *The Journal of Philosophy* 97 (6) (2000): 313–34.

Zaitchik, Alan, "Hobbes and Hypothetical Consent," *Political Studies* 23 (1975): 475–85.


### LIBERALISM AND THE PRIORITY OF BASIC LIBERTIES

Barry, Brian, "John Rawls and the Priority of Liberty," *Philosophy and Public Affairs* 2 (1973): 274–90.

Bowie, Norman, "Equal Basic Liberty for All," in *John Rawls's Theory of Social Justice*, H. Gene Blocker and Elizabeth H. Smith, eds., pp. 110–31. Athens, OH: Ohio University Press, 1980.

Brighouse, Harry, "Political Equality in Justice as Fairness," *Philosophical Studies* 86 (1997): 155–84.

DeMarco, Joseph, "A Note on the Priority of Liberty," *Ethics* 87(1977): 272–5.

Daniels, Norman, "Equal Liberty and Unequal Worth of Liberty," in N. Daniels, ed., *Reading Rawls: Critical Studies on Rawls's A Theory of Justice*, (New York: Basic Books, 1975): 253–81.

——— "On Liberty and Inequality in Rawls," *Social Theory and Practice* 3 (1974): 149–59.

Hart, H.L.A., "Rawls on Liberty and Its Priority," *University of Chicago Law Review* 40 (1973): 534–55; reprinted in N. Daniels, *Reading Rawls*.

Kymlicka, Will, "Liberal Individualism and Liberal Neutrality," *Ethics* 99 (1989): 883–905.

Landenson, Robert, F., "Rawls's Principle of Equal Liberty," *Philosophical Studies* 28 (1975): 49–54.

Lessnoff, Michael, "Barry on Rawls's Priority of Liberty," *Political Studies* 4 (1974): 100–14.

de Marneffe, Peter, "Liberalism, Liberty, and Neutrality," *Philosophy and Public Affairs* 19 (Summer 1990): 253–74.

Parijs, Philippe van, "Liberte Formelle et Liberte reelle: La Critique de Rawls par les Libertariens," *Revue Philosophique de Louvain* 86 (1988): 59–86.

Pogge, Thomas, "The Interpretation of Rawls's First Principle of Justice," *Grazer, Philosophische Studien* 15 (1982): 119–47.

——— "Gleiche Freiheit für alle?" in Otfried Hoeffe, ed., *John Rawls: Eine Theorie der Gerechtigkeit*, Berlin: Akademie Verlag, 1998.

Raz, Joseph, "Liberalism, Autonomy and the Politics of Neutral Concern," *Social and Political Philosophy, Midwest Studies in Philosophy* 7, edited by Peter A. French, Theodore, Uehlilng, Jr., and Howard K. Wettstein (1982): 89–120.

Rodewall, Richard, "Does Liberalism Rest on a Mistake?" *Canadian Journal of Philosophy* 15 (1985): 231–52.

Shue, Henry, "Liberty and Self-Respect," *Ethics* 85 (1975): 68–78.

Singer, Marcus, "On Rawls on Mill on Liberty and So On," *Journal of Value Inquiry* 11 (1977): 141–8.

EGALITARIANISM, DISTRIBUTIVE JUSTICE, AND THE
DIFFERENCE PRINCIPLE

Agarwal, Binod Kumar, "In Defence of the Use of Maximin Principle of Choice under Uncertainty in Rawls's Original Position," *Indian Philosophical Quarterly* 13 (1986): 157–76, and in Richardson, H., and Weithman, P., *The Philosophy of Rawls*, Vol. 1, 247–66.

Alexander, Larry, "Fair Equality of Opportunity: John Rawls's (Best) Forgotten Principle," *Philosophy Research Archives* 11 (1985): 197–207.

Althan, J.E.J., "Rawls's Difference Principle," *Philosophy* 48 (1973): 75–8.

Anderson, Elizabeth, "What Is the Point of Equality," *Ethics* 109 (January 1999): 287–337.

Ball, Stephen, "Economic Equality: Rawls versus Utilitarianism," *Economics and Philosophy* 2 (1986): 225–44.

Beauchamp, Tom, "Distributive Justice and the Difference Principle," in *John Rawls's Theory of Social Justice*, H. Gene Blocker and Elizabeth H. Smith, eds., pp. 132–61. Athens, OH: Ohio University Press, 1980.

Buchanan, Allen, "Distributive Justice and Legitimate Expectations," *Philosophical Studies* 28 (1975): 419–25.

Buchanan, James, "A Hobbesian Interpretation of the Rawlsian Difference Principle," *Kyklos* 29 (1976): 5–25.

Clark, Barry, and Herbert Gintis, "Rawlsian Justice and Economic Systems," *Philosophy and Public Affairs* 7 (Fall 1978): 302–25.

Cohen, G.A., "On the Currency of Egalitarian Justice," *Ethics* 99 (July 1989): 906–44.

——— "Incentives, Inequality and Community" in *The Tanner Lectures on Human Values* Vol. XIII, edited by G.B. Peterson, pp. 261–329. Salt Lake City: University of Utah Press, 1992.

——— "Where the Action Is: On the Site of Distributive Justice," *Philosophy and Public Affairs* 26 (Winter 1997): 3–30.

Cohen, Joshua, "Contractualism and Property Systems," in J.W. Chapman and J.R. Pennock, eds., *Nomos 31, Markets and Justice*, pp. 727–51. New York: New York University Press, 1988.

——— "Democratic Equality," *Ethics* 99 (1989): 727–51.

——— "Taking People As They Are," *Philosophy and Public Affairs*, 30, no. 4 (Fall 2001).

Copp, David, "Justice and the Difference Principle," *Canadian Journal of Philosophy* 4 (1974): 229–40.

Daniels, Norman, "Equality of What?: Welfare, Resources, or Capabilities," *Philosophy and Phenomenological Research* 50 (Fall 1990), Supplement: 273–96.

Estlund, David, "Liberalism, Equality and Fraternity in Cohen's Critique of Rawls," *Journal of Political Philosophy* 6 (March 1998): 99–112.

Frohlich, Norman, Joe A. Oppenheimer, and Cheryl L. Eavey, "Choices of Principles of Distributive Justice in Experimental Groups," *American Journal of Political Science* 31 (3) (August 1987): 606–36.

Gardner, Michael, "Rawls on the Maximin Rule and Distributive Justice," *Philosophical Studies* 27 (1975): 255–70.

Goldman, Alan, H., "Rawls's Original Position and the Difference Principle," *The Journal of Philosophy* 73 (1976): 845–9.

Gordon, Scott, "John Rawls's Difference Principle, Utilitarianism, and the Optimum Degree of Inequality," *The Journal of Philosophy* 70 (9) (1973): 275–80.

Gray, John, "Contractarian Method, Private Property, and the Market Economy," in J.W. Chapman and J.R. Pennock, eds., *Nomos 31, Markets and Justice*. New York: New York University Press, 1988.

Hammond, Peter, J., "Equity, Arrow's Condition, and Rawls's Difference Principle," *Econometrica* 44 (1976): 793–804.

Hinsch, Wilfried, "Rawls's Differenzprinzip und seine sozialpolitischen Implikationen," in *Sozialpolitik und Gerechtigkeit*, eds., Siegfried Blasche and Dieter Döring, pp. 17–74. Frankfurt, Germany: Campus, 1999.

Kolm, Serge-Christophe, "Equal Liberties and Maximin: Fairness from Ignorance," in his *Modern Theories of Justice*, pp. 169–208. Cambridge, MA: MIT Press, 1996.

Krouse, Richard, and Michael McPherson, "Capitalism, 'Property-Owning Democracy', and the Welfare State," in *Democracy and the Welfare State*, edited by Amy Gutmann, pp. 78–105. Princeton, NJ: Princeton University Press, 1988.

Mackenzie, Nollaig, "An Alternative Definition of the Difference Principle," *Dialogue: Canadian Philosophical Review* 13 (1974): 787–93.

——— "A Note on Rawls's Decision-Theoretic Argument for the Difference Principle," *Theory and Decision* 8 (1977): 381–5.

MacMahon, Christopher, "The Better Endowed and the Difference Principle," *Analysis* 49 (1989): 213–16.

Martin, Rex, "Poverty and Welfare in Rawls's Theory of Justice," in Kenneth Kipnis, ed., *Economic Justice*, pp. 161–75. Totowa, NJ: Rowmon & Littlefield, 1985.

Michelman, Frank, "In Pursuit of Constitutional Welfare Rights: One View of Rawls's Theory of Justice," *University of Pennsylvania Law Review* 121 (May 1973): 962–1019, reprinted in part as "Constitutional Welfare Rights and *A Theory of Justice*," in Daniels, *Reading Rawls*.

Narveson, Jan, F., "A Puzzle About Economic Justice in Rawls's Theory," *Social Theory and Practice* 4 (1976): 1–27.

Paden, Roger, "Reciprocity and Intergenerational Justice," *Public Affairs Quarterly* 10 (1996): 249–66.

Parijs, Philippe van, "Why Surfers Should Be Fed: The Liberal Case for an Unconditional Basic Income," *Philosophy and Public Affairs* 20 (Spring 1991): 101–31.

——— "Rawls face aux libertariens," in P. Van Parijs, *Qu'est-ce qu'une société juste?*, Paris: Le Seuil, 1991.

——— "Rawlsians, Christians and Patriots. Maximin Justice and Individual Ethics," *European Journal of Philosophy* 1 (1993): 309–42.

Schaller, Walter, E., "Rawls, the Difference Principle, and Economic Inequality," *Pacific Philosophical Quarterly* 79 (1998): 368–91.

Scheffler, Samuel, "What Is Egalitarianism," *Philosophy and Public Affairs*, 31, no. 1 (Winter 2002).

Shaw, Pat, "Rawls, the Lexical Difference Principle and Equality," *Philosophical Quarterly* 42 (1992): 71–7.

Smith, Paul, "Incentives and Justice: G.A. Cohen's Egalitarian Critique of Rawls," *Social Theory and Practice* 24 (1998): 205–35.

Strasnick, Steven, "Social Choice Theory and the Derivation of Rawls's Difference Principle," *Journal of Philosophy* 73 (1976): 85–99.

Torisky, Eugene, V., "Van Parijs, Rawls, and Unconditional Basic Income," *Analysis* 53 (1993): 289–97.

Waldron, Jeremy, "John Rawls and the Social Minimum," in his *Liberal Rights*, Cambridge, UK: Cambridge University Press, 1993.

Weatherford, Roy, "Defining the Least Advantaged, *Philosophical Quarterly* 33 (1983): 63–9.

Weithman, Paul, "Waldron on Political Legitimacy and the Social Minimum," *The Philosophical Quarterly* 45 (1995): 218–24.

Williams, Andrews, "The Revisionist Difference Principle," *Canadian Journal of Philosophy* 25 (June 1995): 257–82.

——— "Incentives, Inequality, and Publicity," *Philosophy & Public Affairs* 27 (Summer 1998): 225–47.

Wolff, Jonathan, "Fairness, Respect, and the Egalitarian Ethos," *Philosophy and Public Affairs* 27 (2) (Spring 1998): 97–122.

Wolff, Robert Paul, "On Strasnick's 'Derivation' of Rawls's Difference Principle," *The Journal of Philosophy* 73 (1976): 849–58.

ON JUSTIFICATION IN MORAL AND POLITICAL PHILOSOPHY:
CONSTRUCTIVISM, REFLECTIVE EQUILIBRIUM,
AND PUBLIC REASON

Audard, Catherine, "The Idea of 'Free Public Reason'," *Ratio Juris* 8 (1995): 15–29.

Baynes, Kenneth, "Constructivism and Practical Reason in Rawls," *Analyse & Critique* 14 (1992): 18–32.

Benhabib, Seyla, "The Methodological Illusions of Modern Political Theory: The Case of Rawls and Habermas," *Neue Hefte für Philosophie* 21 (1982): 47–74.

Bohman, James, F., "Public Reason and Cultural Pluralism: Political Liberalism and the Problem of Moral Conflict," *Political Theory* 23 (1995): 253–79.

Brink, David, "Rawlsian Constructivism in Moral Theory," *Canadian Journal of Philosophy* 17 (1987): 71–90.

Brower, Bruce, "The Limits of Public Reason," *Journal of Philosophy* 91 (1994): 5–26.

Copp, David, "Considered Judgments and Justification: Conservatism in Moral Theory," in D. Copp and M. Zimmerman, eds., *Morality, Reason and Truth*, pp. 141–69. Totowa, NJ: Rowman and Allenheld, 1985.

Daniels, Norman, "Wide Reflective Equilibrium and Theory Acceptance in Ethics," *Journal of Philosophy* 76 (1979): 256–82.

——— "Reflective Equilibrium and Archimedean Points," *Canadian Journal of Philosophy* 10 (1980): 83–103.

——— "Reflective Equilibrium and Justice as Political," in his *Justice and Justification*, pp. 144–75. Cambridge, UK: Cambridge University Press, 1996; revised in *The Idea of a Political Liberalism*, Victoria Davion and Clark Wolf, eds., pp. 127–54. Lanham, MD: Rowman and Littlefield, 1999.

Delaney, C.F., "Rawls on Method," *Canadian Journal of Philosophy*, Supp. Vol. III (1977): 153–61.

DePaul, Michael, "Reflective Equilibrium and Foundationalism," *American Philosophical Quarterly* 23 (1986): 59–69.

Farrelly, Colin, "Public Reason, Neutrality, and Civic Virtues," *Ratio Juris* 12 (1999): 11–25.

Finnis, John, "Abortion, Natural Law, and Public Reason," in Robert P. George and Christopher Wolfe, eds., *Natural Law and Public Reason*, pp. 75–106. Washington, DC: Georgetown University Press, 2000.

George, Robert P., and Christopher Wolfe, "Natural Law and Public Reason," in Robert P. George and Christopher Wolfe, eds., *Natural Law and Public Reason*, pp. 51–74. Washington, DC: Georgetown University Press, 2000.

Greenawalt, Kent, "On Public Reason," *Chicago–Kent Law Review* 69 (1994): 669–89.

Haslett, D.W., "What's Wrong with Reflective Equilibrium?" *The Philosophical Quarterly* 37 (July 1987): 305–11.

Holmgren, Margaret, "The Wide and Narrow of Reflective Equilibrium," *Canadian Journal of Philosophy* 19 (1989): 43–60.

Ivison, Duncan, "The Secret History of Public Reason: Hobbes to Rawls," *History of Political Thought* 18 (1997): 125–47.

Kelly, Erin, and Lionel McPherson, "On Tolerating the Unreasonable," *The Journal of Political Philosophy* 9 (March 2001): 38–55.

Kraus, Jody, S., "Political Liberalism and Truth," *Legal Theory* 5 (1999): 45–73.

Lehning, Percy, "The Idea of Public Reason: Can It Fulfill Its Task?" *Ratio Juris* 8 (1995): 30–9.

Macedo, Stephen, "In Defense of Liberal Public Reason: Are Slavery and Abortion Hard Cases?" in Robert P. George and Christopher Wolfe, eds., *Natural Law and Public Reason*, pp.11–50. Washington, DC: Georgetown University Press, 2000.

Mandle, Jon, "Having It Both Ways; Justification and Application in Justice as Fairness," *Pacific Philosophical Quarterly* 75 (September–December 1994).

Marneffe, Peter de, "Rawls on Public Reason," *Pacific Philosophical Quarterly* 75 (1994): 232–50.

Moore, Margaret, "On Reasonableness," *Journal of Applied Philosophy* 13 (1996): 167–77.

Naticchia, Chris, "Justice as Fairness: Epistemological not Political," *Southern Journal of Philosophy* 37 (1999): 597–611.

Nielsen, Kai, "Our Considered Judgments," *Ratio* 19 (1977): 39–46.

O'Neill, Onora, "The Public Use of Reason," in her *Constructions of Reason*, Cambridge, UK: Cambridge University Press, 1989.

——— "The Method of *A Theory of Justice*," in Otfried Hoeffe, ed., *John Rawls: Eine Theorie der Gerechtigkeit*, Berlin: Akademie Verlag, 1998.

O'Neill, Richard, "On Rawls's Justification Procedure," *Philosophy Research Archives* 2 (1099) (1976).

Raz, Joseph, "Disagreement in Politics," *American Journal of Jurisprudence*, (1998): 25–52.

——— "Facing Diversity: The Case of Epistemic Abstinence," *Philosophy and Public Affairs* 19 (1990): 3–46.

——— "The Claims of Reflective Equilibrium," *Inquiry* 25 (1982), pp. 307–30.

Richards, David, A.J., "Public Reason and Abolitionist Dissent," *Chicago–Kent Law Review* 69 (1994): 787–842.

Sencerz, Stefan, "Moral Intuitions and Justification in Ethics," *Philosophical Studies* 50 (1986): 77–95.

Singer, Peter, "Sidgwick and Reflective Equilibrium," *The Monist* 58 (1974): 490–517.

Snare, Frank, "John Rawls and the Methods of Ethics," *Philosophy and Phenomenological Research* 36 (1975): 100–12.

Solum, Lawrence, "Inclusive Public Reason," *Pacific Philosophical Quarterly* 75 (1994): 217–31.

Wall, Stephen, "Public Justification and the Transparency Argument," *The Philosophical Quarterly* 46 (October 1996): 501–7.

Weithman, Paul, "Citizenship and Public Reason," in Robert P. George and Christopher Wolfe, eds., *Natural Law and Public Reason*, pp. 125–70. Washington, DC: Georgetown University Press, 2000.

Westmoreland, Robert, "The Truth about Public Reason," *Law and Philosophy* 18 (1999): 271–96.

### RAWLS'S MORAL PSYCHOLOGY AND THE STABILITY OF JUSTICE AS FAIRNESS

Agra, Maria Jose, "Justicia, conflicto doctrinal y establidad social en el liberalismo politico de J. Rawls," *Revista Agustiniana* 37 (1996): 999–1048.

Bates, Stanley, "The Motivation to Be Just," *Ethics* 85 (1974): 1–17.

Darwall, Steven, "Two Kinds of Respect," *Ethics* 88 (1977): 36–49.

Deigh, John, "Shame and Self-Esteem: A Critique," *Ethics* 93 (1983): 225–45.

DeLue, Steven, M., "Aristotle, Kant and Rawls on Moral Motivation in a Just Society," *The American Political Science Review* 74 (2) (June 1980), pp. 385–93.

Gibbard, Allan, "Human Evolution and the Sense of Justice," *Social and Political Philosophy, Midwest Studies in Philosophy* 7, edited by Peter A. French, Theodore E. Uehling, Jr., and Howard K. Wettstein, 1982: 31–46.

Giusti, Miguel, "Die liberalistische Suche nach einem 'ubergreifenden Konsens'," *Philosophische Rundschau* 41 (1994): 53–73.

Hill, Thomas, E., Jr., "The Problem of Stability in *Political Liberalism*," *Pacific Philosophical Quarterly* 75 (1994): 332–52.

Hinsch, Wilfried, "Das Gut der Gerechtigkeit," in Otfried Hoeffe, ed., *John Rawls: Eine Theorie der Gerechtigkeit*, Berlin: Akademie, 1998.

Huemer, Michael, "Rawls's Problem of Stability," *Social Theory and Practice* 22 (1996): 375–95.

Klosko, George, "Rawls's Argument from Political Stability," *Columbia Law Review* 94 (1994): 1882–97.

Kohlberg, Lawrence, "The Claim to Moral Adequacy of a Highest Stage of Moral Judgment," *Journal of Philosophy* 70 (1973): 630–46.

———— "Justice as Reversibility," in *Philosophy, Politics, and Society*, Peter Laslett, ed., pp. 257–72. New Haven: Yale University Press, 1979.

Krasnoff, Larry, "Consensus, Stability, and Normativity in Rawls's *Political Liberalism*," *Journal of Philosophy* 95 (6) (1998): 269–92.

McClennen, Edward, F., "Justice and the Problem of Stability," *Philosophy and Public Affairs* 19 (1990): 122–57.

Pritchard, Michael, S., "Rawls's Moral Psychology," *Southwestern Journal of Philosophy* 8 (1977): 59–72.

Sachs, David, "How to Distinguish Self-Respect from Self-Esteem," *Philosophy and Public Affairs* 10 (1981): 346–60.

Scarano, Nico, "Der Gerechtigkeitssinn" in Otfried Hoeffe, ed., *John Rawls: Eine Theorie der Gerechtigkeit*, Berlin: Akademie Verlag, 1998.

Soble, Alan, "Rawls on Self-Respect," *The Journal of Philosophy* 72 (1975): 1–19.

Thomas, Larry, L., "Rawlsian Self-Respect and the Black Consciousness Movement," *Philosophical Forum* 9 (1977–78): 303–13.

## RAWLS AND KANT: THE KANTIAN INTERPRETATION AND THE CONCEPTION OF THE PERSON

Baumrin, Bernard, H. "Autonomy in Rawls and Kant," *Midwest Studies in Philosophy* 1 (1975): 55–7.

———— "Autonomy, Interest, and the Kantian Interpretation," *Midwest Studies in Philosophy* 2 (1977): 280–2.

Buchanan, Allen, "Categorical Imperatives and Moral Principles," *Philosophical Studies* 31 (1977): 249–60.

Darwall, Steve, "A Defense of the Kantian Interpretation," *Ethics* 86 (1976): 164–70.

———— "Is There a Kantian Foundation for Rawlsian Justice?" in H.G. Blocker and E.H. Smith, eds., *John Rawls's Theory of Social Justice*, pp. 311–45. Athens, OH: Ohio University Press, 1980.

Davidson, Arnold, "Is Rawls a Kantian?" *Pacific Philosophical Quarterly* 66 (1985): 48–77.

Daniels, Norman, "Moral Theory and the Plasticity of Persons," *Monist* 62 (1979): 267–87.

Doppelt, Gerald, "Is Rawls's Kantian Liberalism Coherent and Defensible?" *Ethics* 99 (1989): 815–51.

Guyer, Paul, "Life, Liberty, and Property: Rawls and Kant," in his *Kant on Freedom, Law, and Happiness*, pp. 262–86. Cambridge, UK: Cambridge University Press, 2000.

Hill, Thomas, E., Jr., "Kantian Constructivism in Ethics," *Ethics* 99 (1989): 752–70, also in his *Dignity and Practical Reason*, Ithaca, NY: Cornell University Press, 1992.

Hoeffe, Otfried, "Is Rawls's Theory of Justice Really Kantian?" *Ratio* 26 (1984): 104–24.

Johnson, Oliver, "The Kantian Interpretation," *Ethics* 85 (1974): 53–66.

—— "Autonomy in Kant and Rawls: A Reply," *Ethics* 87 (1977): 251–4.

Krasnoff, Larry, "How Kantian Is Constructivism?" *Kant-Studien*, 90 (1999): 385–409.

Levine, Andrew, "Rawls's Kantianism," *Social Theory and Practice* 3 (1974): 47–63.

—— "Capitalist Persons," *Social Philosophy and Policy* 6 (1988): 39–59.

Mason, H.E., "On the Kantian Interpretation of Rawls's Theory," *Midwest Studies in Philosophy* 1 (1976): 47–55.

McCarthy, Thomas, "Kantian Constructivism and Reconstructivism: Rawls and Habermas in Dialogue," *Ethics* 105 (1994): 44–63.

McKerlie, Douglas, "Egalitarianism and the Separateness of Persons," *Canadian Journal of Philosophy* 18 (2) (1988): 205–26.

Piper, Adrian, "Personal Continuity and Instrumental Rationality in Rawls's *Theory of Justice*," *Social Theory and Practice* 13 (1987): 49–76.

Pogge, Thomas, "The Kantian Interpretation of Justice as Fairness," *Zeitschrift für philosophische Forschung* 35 (1981): 47–65.

Scheffler, Samuel, "Moral Skepticism and Ideals of the Person," *Monist* 62 (1979): 288–303.

### RAWLS, JUSTICE, AND INDIVIDUAL DESERT

Ball, Stephen, W., "Maximin Justice, Sacrifice, and the Reciprocity Argument: A Pragmatic Reassessment of the Rawls/Nozick Debate," *Utilitas* 5 (1993): 157–84.

Buchanan, Allen, "Distributive Justice and Legitimate Expectations," *Philosophical Studies* 28 (1975): 419–25.

Gauthier, David, "Justice and Natural Endowment: Towards a Critique of Rawls's Ideological Framework," *Social Theory and Practice* 3 (1974): 3–26.

Goldman, Alan, H., "Real People: Natural Differences and the Scope of Justice," *Canadian Journal of Philosophy* 17 (1987): 377–94.

Mandle, Jon, "Justice, Desert, and Ideal Theory," *Social Theory and Practice* 23 (Fall 1997): 399–425.

Schaar, John, "Reflections on Rawls' Theory of Justice," *Social Theory and Practice* 3 (1) (1974): 87.

Scheffler, Samuel, "Justice and Desert in Liberal Theory," *California Law Review* 88 (3) (May 2000): 965–90.

—— "Responsibility, Reactive Attitudes, and Liberalism in Philosophy and Politics," *Philosophy and Public Affairs* 21(1992): 299–323.

Sher, George, "Effort, Ability, and Personal Desert," *Philosophy and Public Affairs* 8 (1979): 361–76.

Slote, Michael, "Desert, Consent, and Justice," *Philosophy and Public Affairs* 2 (4) (1973): 323–47.

Sterba, James, "Justice as Desert," *Social Theory and Practice* 3 (1) (1974): 101–16.

Steinberger, Peter, J., "Desert and Justice in Rawls," *Journal of Politics* 44 (November 1982): 983–95.


RAWLS, CONSTITUTIONALISM, AND THE RULE OF LAW

Allen, Anita, "Social Contract Theory in American Case Law," *Florida Law Review* 51 (1999): 1–40.

Fallon, Richard, "A Constructivist Coherence Theory of Constitutional Interpretation," *Harvard Law Review* 100 (1987): 1189–286.

Fleming, James, E., "Constructing the Substantive Constitution," *Texas Law Review* 72 (2) (December 1993): 211–313.

——— "Securing Deliberative Autonomy," *Stanford Law Review* 48 (1995): 1–71.

Fleming, James, E., and Linda C. McClain, "In Search of A Substantive Republic", *Texas Law Review* 76 (1997): 509–51.

Foley, Edward, B., " Political Liberalism and Establishment Clause Jurisprudence," *Case Western Reserve Law Review* 43 (1993): 963–81.

Freedman, Eric, "Campaign Finance and the First Amendment: A Rawlsian Analysis," *Iowa Law Review* 85 (2000): 1065–105.

Freeman, Samuel, "Original Meaning, Democratic Interpretation, and the Constitution," *Philosophy and Public Affairs* 21 (1) (Winter 1992): 3–42.

——— "Constitutional Democracy and the Justification of Judicial Review," *Law and Philosophy* 9 (1990–91): 327–70.

Griffin, Stephen, "Reconstructing Rawls's Theory of Justice: Developing a Public Values Philosophy of the Constitution," *N.Y.U. Law Review* 62 (1987): 715–85.

Lipkin, Robert, J., "Beyond Skepticism, Foundationalism, and the New Fuzziness: The Role of Wide Reflective Equilibrium in Legal Theory," *Cornell Law Review* 75 (1990): 811–77.

Michelman, Frank, I., "In Pursuit of Constitutional Welfare Rights: One View of Rawls's Theory of Justice," *University of Pennsylvania Law Review* 121 (1973): 962–1019.

——— "On Regulating Practices with Theories Drawn From Them," In Ian Shapiro and Judith Wagner DeCew, eds., *Theory and Practice* (Nomos 38) New York: New York University Press, 1995, pp. 325–38.

——— "Welfare Rights in a Constitutional Democracy," *Washington University Law Quarterly* 1979 (1979): 659.

Moore, Ronald, "Rawls on Constitution-Making," in *Nomos XX: Constitutionalism*, J.R. Pennock and J.W. Chapman, eds., New York: New York University Press, 1979.

Parker, Richard, B., "The Jurisprudential Uses of John Rawls," in *Nomos XX: Constitutionalism*, J.R. Pennock and J.W. Chapman, eds., New York: New York University Press, 1979.

Richards, David, A.J., *Toleration and the Constitution*. New York: Oxford University Press, 1987.

―――― *The Moral Criticism of Law* Encina, CA: Dickinson Publishing Co., 1977.

Scheltens, D.R., "The Social Contract and the Principle of Law," *International Philosophical Quarterly* 17 (1977): 317–38.

Sullivan, Daniel, "Rules, Fairness, and Formal Justice," *Ethics* 85 (1975): 322–31.

Zuckert, Michael, P., "The New Rawls and Constitutional Theory: Does it Really Taste That Much Better?" Constitutional Commentary 11 (1994): 227.

### RAWLS AND UTILITARIANISM

Ball, Stephen, W., "Choosing Between Choice Models of Ethics: Rawlsian Equality, Utilitarianism, and the Concept of Persons," *Theory and Decision* 22 (1987): 209–24.

Barry, Brian, "Rawls on Average and Total Utility: A Comment," *Philosophical Studies* 31 (1977) 317–25.

Braybrook, David, "Utilitarianism with a Difference: Rawls's Position in Ethics," *Canadian Journal of Philosophy* 3 (1973): 303–31.

Freeman, Samuel, "Utilitarianism, Deontology, and the Priority of Right," *Philosophy and Public Affairs* 23 (4) (1994): 313–49.

Gaus, Gerald, "The Convergence of Rights and Utility: The Case of Rawls and Mill," *Ethics* 92 (1981): 57–72.

Goldman, Holly Smith, "Rawls and Utilitarianism," in *John Rawls's Theory of Social Justice: An Introduction*, eds. H. Gene Blocker and Elizabeth H. Smith, pp. 346–94. University of Ohio Press, 1980.

Hare, R.M., "Rawls's Theory of Justice," in *Reading Rawls*, ed., Norman Daniels, pp. 81–107. Stanford University Press, 1989.

Harsanyi, John, "Can the Maximin Principle Serve as the Basis for Morality? A Critique of John Rawls's Theory," *American Political Science Review* 69 (1975): 694–706.

Kavka, Gregory, S., "Rawls on Average and Total Utility," *Philosophical Studies* 27 (1975): 237–53.

Kymlicka, Will, "Rawls on Teleology and Deontology," *Philosophy and Public Affairs* 17 (1988): 173–90.

Lyons, David, "Rawls Versus Utilitarianism," *Journal of Philosophy* 69 (1972): 535–45.

Miller, Richard, "Rawls, Risk, and Utilitarianism," *Philosophical Studies* 28 (1975): 55–61.

Mulholland, Leslie, "Rights, Utilitarianism, and the Conflation of Persons," *Journal of Philosophy* 83 (1986): 323–40.

Narveson, Jan, "Rawls and Utilitarianism," in *The Limits of Utilitarianism*, eds. Harlan B. Miller and William H. Williams pp. 128–42. University of Minnesota Press, 1982.

Roche, Timothy, "Utilitarianism Versus Rawls; Defending Teleological Moral Theory," *Social Theory and Practice* 8 (1989): 189–212.

Ross, Geoffrey, "Utilities for Distributive Justice," *Theory and Decision* 4 (1974): 239–58.

Taylor, Paul, W., "Justice and Utility," *Canadian Journal of Philosophy* 1 (1972): 327–50.

### RAWLS, ECONOMICS, AND SOCIAL CHOICE THEORY

Arrow, Kenneth, "Rawls's Principle of Just Savings," *Swedish Journal of Economics* 75 (1973): 323–35.

Binmore, Ken, "Social Contract I: Harsanyi and Rawls," *Economic Journal* 99 (1989): 84–102.

———— "Naturalizing Harsanyi and Rawls," in M. Salles and J. Weymark, eds., *Justice, Political Liberalism, and Utilitarianism: Proceedings of the Caen Conference in Honor of John Harsanyi and John Rawls*, Cambridge, UK: Cambridge University Press, 1998.

Blair, Douglas, "The Primary Goods Indexation Problem in Rawls's *Theory of Justice*," *Theory and Decision* 24 (1988): 239–52.

Calvo, C., "Some Notes on Time Inconsistency and Rawls's Maximin Principle," *Review of Economic Studies* 45 (1978): 97–102.

Corrado, Gail, "Rawls, Games, and Economic Theory, in *John Rawls's Theory of Social Justice*, H. Gene Blocker and Elizabeth H. Smith, eds., pp. 71–109. Athens, OH: Ohio University Press, 1980.

Dasgupta, Partha, "On Some Problems Arising from Professor John Rawls's Conception of Distributive Justice," *Theory and Decision* 11 (1974): 325–44.

Gaa, James, "The Stability of Bargains Behind the Veil of Ignorance," *Theory and Decision* 17 (1984): 119–34.

Gibbard, Allan, "Disparate Goods and Rawls's Difference Principle: A Social Choice Theoretic Treatment," *Theory and Decision* 11 (1979): 267–88.

Hammond, P.J., "Equity, Arrow's Theorem, and Rawls's Difference Principle," *Econometrica* 44 (1976): 793–800.

Howe, R., and Roemer, John, "Rawlsian Justice as the Core of a Game," *American Economic Review* 71 (1981): 880–95.

Ihara, Craig, "Maximin and Other Decision Principles," *Philosophical Topics* 12 (1981): 59–72.

Kaye, David, H., "Playing Games with Justice: Rawls and the Maximin Rule," *Social Theory and Practice* 6 (1980): 33–51.

Klevorick, Alvin, K., "Discussion of Rawls Maximin Criterion," *The American Economic Review*, 64 (1974): 158–61.

Mackenzie, Nollaig, "A Note on Rawls's Decision-Theoretic Argument for the Difference Principle," *Theory and Decision* 8 (1977): 381–85.

Maskin, E., "Decision-Making Under Ignorance with Implications for Social Choice," *Theory and Decision* 11 (1979): 319–37.

Mueller, Dennis, D. Tollison, and T.D. Willit, "The Utilitarian Contract: A Generalization of Rawls's Theory of Justice," *Theory and Decision* 4 (1974): 345–67.

Musgrave, R.A., "Maximin, Uncertainty, and the Leisure Trade-Off," *Quarterly Journal of Economics* 88 (November 1974): 625–9.

Rodriguez, A., "Rawls Maximin Criterion and Time Consistency: A Generalization," *Review of Economic Studies* 48 (1981): 599–605.

Sen, A.K., "Rawls versus Bentham: An Axiomatic Examination of the Pure Distribution Problem," *Theory and Decision* 4:301–10, reprinted in Daniels, *Reading Rawls*.

——— "Welfare Inequalities and Rawlsian Axiomatics," *Theory and Decision* 7 (1976): 243–62.

Strasnick, Steven, "The Problem of Social Choice: Arrow to Rawls," *Philosophy and Public Affairs* 5 (1976): 241–73.

Yaari, M., "Rawls, Edgeworth, Shapley, Nash: Theories of Distributive Justice Re-examined," *Journal of Economic Theory* 24 (1981): 1–39.

## RAWLS AND COMMUNITARIANISM

Alejandro, Roberto, "Rawls's Communitarianism," *Canadian Journal of Philosophy* 23 (1993): 75–99.

Baker, Edwin, "Sandel on Rawls," *University of Pennsylvania Law Review* 133 (April 1985): 895.

Benson, Peter, "Rawls, Hegel, and Personhood: A Reply to Sybil Schwarzenbach," *Political Theory* 22 (3) (1994): 491–500.

Bondeli, Martin, "Hegel und die kommunitaristische Kritik an John Rawls's Liberalismus," *Jahrbuch für Hegelforschung* 3 (1997): 29–46.

Buchanan, Allen, "Assessing the Communitarian Critique of Liberalism," *Ethics* 99 (1989): 852–82.

Delaney, C.F., "Rawls and Individualism," *Modern Schoolman* 60 (1983): 112–22.

Gutmann, Amy, "Communitarian Critics of Liberalism," *Philosophy and Public Affairs* 14 (1985): 308–22.

Haldane, John, "The Individual, the State, and the Common Good," *Social Philosophy and Policy*, (1996): 59–79.

―――― "Identity, Community, and the Limits of Multiculture," *Public Affairs Quarterly* 7 (1993): 199–214.

Kymlicka, Will, "Liberalism and Communitarianism," *Canadian Journal of Philosophy* 18 (1988): 181–204.

Larmore, Charles, "Rawls' s Ambiguities and Neo-Romanticism," in his *Patterns of Moral Complexity*, Cambridge, UK: Cambridge University Press, 1987, pp. 118–30.

Lukes, Steven, "No Archidemean Point," in his *Essays in Social Theory*, London: MacMillan, 1978, pp. 187–90.

McCabe, David, "Private Lives and Public Virtues: The Idea of a Liberal Community," *Canadian Journal of Philosophy* 28(4) (December 1998): 557–86.

Mulhall, Stephen, and Adam Swift, *Liberals and Communitarians*, Oxford, UK: Basil Blackwell, 1992.

Narveson, Jan, "Critical Notice of Michael Sandel, *Liberalism and the Limits of Justice*," *Canadian Journal of Philosophy* 17 (1987): 227–34.

Sandel, Michael, *Liberalism and the Limits of Justice*, Cambridge, UK: Cambridge University Press, 1982; revised edition, 1999.

―――― "The Procedural Republic and the Unencumbered Self," *Political Theory* 12 (1984): 81–96.

―――― "The Political Theory of the Procedural Republic," *Revue de Metaphysique et de Morale* 93 (1988): 57–58.

Schwarzenbach, Sybil, "Rawls, Hegel, and Communitarianism," *Political Theory* 19 (4) (November 1991): 539–71.

―――― "A Rejoinder to Peter Benson," *Political Theory*, 22 (3) (1994): 501–07.

Taylor, Charles, "Cross-Purposes: The Liberal-Communitarian Debate," in *Liberalism and the Moral Life*, ed., Nancy Rosenblum, pp. 159–82. Cambridge, MA: Harvard University Press, 1989.

Thero, Daniel, "The Self in the Original Position," *Dialogos* 33 (1998): 159–74.

### RAWLS AND FEMINISM

Baehr, Amy, R., "Toward a New Feminist Liberalism: Okin, Rawls, and Habermas," *Hypatia* 11 (1996): 49–66.

Baier, Annette, "The Need for More than Justice," in *Justice and Care*: *Essential Readings in Feminist Ethics*, ed. V. Held, Boulder, CO: Westview, 1995. pp. 47–60.

Cohen, Joshua, "Okin on Justice, Gender, and the Family," *Canadian Journal of Philosophy*, 22 (1992): 263–86.

Green, Karen, "Rawls, Women, and the Priority of Liberty," *Australasian Journal of Philosophy*, Supplement, 64 (1986): 26–36.

Hampton, Jean, "Feminist Contractarianism," in *A Mind of One's Own: Feminist Essays on Reason and Objectivity*, eds., Louise M. Antony and Charlotte Witt, pp. 227–56. Boulder, CO: Westview, 1993.

Herman, Barbara, "Could It Be Worth Thinking about Kant on Sex and Marriage?" in *A Mind of One's Own: Feminist Essays on Reason and Objectivity*, eds., Louise M. Antony and Charlotte Witt, pp. 49–68. Boulder, CO: Westview, 1993.

Kearns, Deborah, "A Theory of Justice – And Love; Rawls on the Family," *Politics* (Australasian Political Studies Association Journal) 18 (2) (1983): 36–42.

Kelly, Erin, "Justice and Communitarian Identity Politics," *The Journal of Value Inquiry* 35 (2001): 71–93.

Kittay, Eva Feder, "Human Dependency and Rawlsian Equality," in *Feminists Rethink the Self*, Diana Tietjens Meyers, ed., Boulder, CO: Westview Press, 1997, pp. 219–66.

Lloyd, S.A., "Family Justice and Social Justice," *Pacific Philosophical Quarterly* 75 (3&4) (September–December 1994), pp. 353–71.

——— "Situating a Feminist Criticism of John Rawls's *Political Liberalism*," *Loyola (Los Angeles) Law Review* 28 (1995): 1319–44.

Mallon, Ron, "Political Liberalism, Cultural Membership, and the Family," *Social Theory and Practice* 25 (1999): 271–97.

Matsuda, Mari, J., "Liberal Jurisprudence and Abstracted Views of Human Nature: A Feminist Critique of Rawls's Theory of Justice," *New Mexico Law Review* 16 (1986): 613–50.

McClain, Linda, C., "Atomistic Man Revisited: Liberalism, Connection and Feminist Jurisprudence," *Southern California Law Review* 65 (1992): 1171–225.

——— "Toleration, Autonomy, and Governmental Promotion of Good Lives: Beyond 'Empty' Toleration to Toleration as Respect," *Ohio State Law Journal* 59 (1998): 19–132.

Munoz-Darde, Veronique, "Rawls, Justice in the Family and Justice of the Family," *The Philosophical Quarterly* 48 (192) (July 1998): 335–52.

——— "Is the Family to Be Abolished Then?," *Proceedings of the Aristotelian Society* XCIX, part 1 (1999): 37–56.

Nussbaum, Martha, C., "The Feminist Critique of Liberalism," in her *Sex and Social Justice*. New York: Oxford University Press, 1999, Chap. 2, pp. 55–80.

Okin, Susan Moller, "Justice and Gender," *Philosophy and Public Affairs* 16 (1987): 42–72.

——— "Justice as Fairness, for Whom?" in her *Justice, Gender and the Family*. New York: Basic Books, 1989, pp. 89–109.

────── "Reason and Feeling in Thinking about Justice," *Ethics* 99 (2) (1989): 231–5.

────── "*Political Liberalism*, Justice and Gender," *Ethics* 105 (1994): 23–43.

Russell, J.S., "Okin's Rawlsian Feminism? Justice in the Family and Another Liberalism," *Social Theory and Practice* 21 (1995): 397–426.

Schrag, Francis, "Justice and the Family," *Inquiry* 19 (1976): 193–208.

Yuracko, Kimberly, A., "Towards Feminist Perfectionism: A Radical Critique of Rawlsian Liberalism," *UCLA Women's Law Journal* 6 (1995): 1–48.

Zipursky, Benjamin, C., "Self Defense, Domination, and Social Contract," *University of Pittsburgh Law Review* 57 (1996): 579–614.


### THE LAW OF PEOPLES AND INTERNATIONAL JUSTICE

Amdur, Robert, "Rawls's Theory of Justice: Domestic and International Perspectives," *World Politics* 29 (3) (1977): 438–61.

Beitz, Charles, "Rawls's Law of Peoples," *Ethics* 110 (July 2000): 669–96.

────── *Political Theory and International Relations*, Princeton: Princeton University Press, 1979, pp. 127–69.

────── "Justice and International Relations," *Philosophy and Public Affairs* 4 (4) (Summer 1975): 360–89.

Buchanan, Allen, "Rawls's Law of Peoples: Rules for a Vanished Westphalian World," *Ethics* 110 (4) (July 2000): 697–721.

────── "Justice, Legitimacy, and Human Rights," in Victoria Davion and Clark Wolf, eds., *The Idea of a Political Liberalism*, pp. 73–89: Lanham, MD: Rowman and Littlefield, 2000.

Crisp, Roger, and Dale Jamieson, "Egalitarianism and a Global Resources Tax: Pogge on Rawls," in Victoria Davion and Clark Wolf, eds., *The Idea of A Political Liberalism*, pp. 90–101. Lanham, MD: Rowman and Littlefield, 2000.

Danielson, Peter, "Theories, Intuitions, and the Problem of World-Wide Distributive Justice," *Philosophy of the Social Sciences* 2 (1973): 331–8.

DeMarco, Joseph, "International Application of the Theory of Justice," *Pacific Philosophical Quarterly* 62 (1981): 393–402.

Follesdal, Andreas, "The Standing of Illiberal States: Stability and Toleration in John Rawls' Law of Peoples," *Acta Analytica* (1997): 149–60.

Hinsch, Wilfried, "Global Distributive Justice," *Metaphilosophy* 32 (January 2001): 58–78.

McCarthy, Thomas, "Two Conceptions of Cosmopolitan Justice," in *Reconstituting Social Criticism*, I. MacKenzie and S.O'Neill, eds., New York: St. Martins Press, 1999.

────── "On the Idea of a Reasonable Law of Peoples," in, J. Bohman and M. Lutz-Buhmann, eds., *Perpetual Peace: Essays on Kant's Cosmopolitan Idealism*, pp. 201–17. Cambridge, MA: MIT Press, 1997.

Moellendorf, Darrel, "Constructing a Law of Peoples," *Pacific Philosophical Quarterly* 77 (2) (June 1996): 132–54.

Naticchia, Chris, "Human Rights, Liberalism, and Rawls's Law of Peoples," *Social Theory and Practice* 24 (3) (Fall 1998): 345–74.

Paden, Roger, "Reconstructing Rawls's Law of Peoples," *Ethics and International Affairs* 11 (1997): 215–32.

Pogge, Thomas, "An Egalitarian Law of Peoples," *Philosophy and Public Affairs* 23 (3) (Summer 1994) 195–224.

———— "Human Flourishing and Universal Justice," *Social Philosophy* 16 (1) (1999).

Tan, Kok Chor, "Liberal Toleration in Rawls's Law of Peoples," *Ethics* 108 (1998): 276–95.

Wenar, Leif, "Contractualism and Global Economic Justice," *Metaphilosophy* 32 (1) (January 2001): 79–95.

Wicclair, Mark, "Rawls and the Principle of Non-intervention," in H. Gene Blocker and Elizabeth H. Smith, eds. *John Rawls's Theory of Social Justice*, pp. 289–308. Athens, OH: Ohio University Press, 1980.

### RAWLS, MARX, AND LEFT CRITICISM

Buchanan, Rupert, "Investment Income in Rawls's *Theory of Justice*," *Dialogue* 22 (1983): 539–42.

DeMarco, Joseph, P., "Rawls and Marx," in H. Gene Blocker and Elizabeth H. Smith, eds., *John Rawls's Theory of Social Justice*, pp. 395–430. Athens, OH: Ohio University Press, 1980.

DiQuattro, Arthur, "Rawls and Left Criticism," *Political Theory* 11 (1983): 53–78.

Francis, Leslie, P., "Responses to Rawls from the Left," in H. Gene Blocker and Elizabeth H. Smith, eds., *John Rawls's Theory of Social Justice*, pp. 463–93. Athens, OH: Ohio University Press, 1980.

Howard, Michael, W., "Contradiction in the Egalitarian Theory of Justice," *Philosophy Research Archives* 10 (1984): 35–56.

Kung, Guido, "The Marxian Critique of Rawls," in James J. O'Rourke, ed., *Contemporary Marxism*, pp. 237–44. Boston: Reidel, 1984.

MacPherson, C.B., "Rawls's Models of Man and Society," *Philosophy of the Social Sciences* 3 (1973): 341–7.

Miller, Richard, "Rawls and Marxism," *Philosophy and Public Affairs*, 3 (Winter 1974): 167–91, reprinted in Daniels, *Reading Rawls*.

Moulin, Herve, and John Roemer, "Public Ownership of the External World and Private Ownership of Self," *Journal of Political Economy* 97 (2) (April 1989): 347–67.

Nielsen, Kai, "On the Very Possibility of a Classless Society: Rawls,

MacPherson, and Revisionist Liberalism," *Political Theory* 6 (1978): 191–208.

——— "Capitalism, Socialism, and Justice: Reflections on Rawls's Theory of Justice," *Social Praxis* 7 (1980): 253–77.

Reiman, Jeffrey, H., "The Labor Theory of the Difference Principle," *Philosophy and Public Affairs* 12 (2) (Spring 1983): 133–59.

Schweickart, David, "Should Rawls Be a Socialist?" *Social Theory and Practice* 5 (1978): 1–27.

Wolff, Robert Paul, *Understanding Rawls*, Princeton: Princeton University Press, 1977.

Young, Iris, M., "Toward a Critical Theory of Justice," *Social Theory and Practice* 7 (1981): 279–302.


CONSERVATIVE AND LIBERTARIAN CRITICISMS

Bloom, Allan, "Justice: John Rawls vs. the Tradition of Political Philosophy," *The American Political Science Review* 69 (1975): 648–62.

Bork, Robert, "Justice Lite," *First Things* 37 (November 1993): 31–2.

Flew, Anthony, "Rawls's Theory of Justice," in H.D. Lewis, ed., *Contemporary British Philosophy*, London: George Allen and Unwin.

——— "Social Virtue and Blind Justice: On Rawls's Theory of Justice," *Encounter* 41 (1973): 73–6.

George, Robert, "Public Reason and Political Conflict: Abortion and Homosexuality," *The Yale Law Journal* 106 (1997): 2475–504.

Goldman, Alan, H., "Responses to Rawls from the Political Right," in H. Gene Blocker, and Elizabeth Smith, eds., *John Rawls's Theory of Social Justice*, pp. 431–62. Athens, OH: Ohio University Press, 1980.

Hospers, John, "A Review of Rawls's *A Theory of Justice*," *The Personalist* 55 (1974): 71–7.

Mack, Eric, "Distributivism vs. Justice," *Ethics* 86 (2) (1976): 145–53.

Nozick, Robert, "Distributive Justice," in his *Anarchy, State, and Utopia*. New York: Basic Books, 1974, Chap. 7, pp. 149–231.

Nisbet, Robert, "The Pursuit of Equality," *Public Interest* 35 (1974): 103–20.

Rand, Ayn, "An Untitled Letter," *Ayn Rand Letter* 2 (9) (1973).

Rasmussen, Douglas, "A Critique of Rawls's *Theory of Justice*," *Personalist* 55 (1974): 303–18.


RAWLS AND RELIGION

Beckley, Harlan, "A Christian Affirmation of Rawls's Idea of Justice as Fairness," Parts I and II, in *Journal of Religious Ethics* 13 & 14 (1985, 1986).

Fern, Richard, "Religious Belief in a Rawlsian Society," *Journal of Religious Ethics* 15 (1987): 33–58.

Franklin, Robert Michael, "In Pursuit of a Just Society: Martin Luther King, Jr, and John Rawls," *Journal of Religious Ethics* 18 (1990): 57–77.

Jackson, Timothy, "To Bedlam and Part Way Back: John Rawls and Christian Justice," *Faith and Philosophy* 8 (1991): 423–47.

Jones, Gregory, "Should Christians Affirm Rawls's Justice as Fairness?" *Journal of Religious Ethics* 16 (1988): 251–71.

Macedo, Stephen, "Liberal Civic Education and Religious Fundamentalism: The Case of God v. John Rawls?" *Ethics* 105 (3) (April 1995): 468–96.

O'Neil, Patrick, "The Fate of Theological Facts in the Original Position of Rawls's *A Theory of Justice*," *Dialogue* 28 (1986): 45–56.

Papa, Edward, "Kant's Dubious Disciples: Hare and Rawls," *American Catholic Philosophical Quarterly* 65 (1991): 159–75.

Proudfoot, Wayne, "Rawls on the Individual and the Social," *The Journal of Religious Ethics* 2 (2) (1974): 107–28.

Quinn, Philip, L., "Political Liberalisms and their Exclusions of the Religious," *Proceedings and Addresses of the American Philosophical Association* 69 (2) (1995): 35–56.

Solum, Lawrence, B., "The Religious Voices in the Public Square: Novel Public Reasons," *Loyola (Los Angeles) Law Review* 29 (June 1996): 1459–85.

Sterba, James, "Reconciling Public Reason and Religious Values," *Social Theory and Practice* 25 (1999): 1–28.

Waldron, Jeremy, "Religious Contributions in Public Deliberation," *San Diego Law Review* 30 (4) (Fall 1993): 817–48.

Weithman, Paul, "Taking Rites Seriously," *Pacific Philosophical Quarterly* 75 (1994): 272–94.

———— "Rawlsian Liberalism and the Privatization of Religion: Three Theological Objections Considered," *Journal of Religious Ethics* 22 (1994): 3–28, with replies by David Hollenbach, Timothy Jackson, and John Langan, S.J.

Wilkins, Burleigh, "A Third Principle of Justice," *Journal of Ethics* 1 (1997): 355–74.

Wolterstoff, Nicholas, "Why We Should Reject What Liberalism Tells Us About Thinking and Acting in Public for Religious Reasons," in Paul Weithman, ed., *Religion and Contemporary Liberalism*, pp. 162–81. South Bend, IN: Notre Dame Press, 1997.

DISCUSSIONS AND CRITICISMS OF RAWLS'S EARLY WORKS

Burkholder, L., "Rule-Utilitarianism and 'Two Concepts of Rules'," *The Personalist* 56 (1975): 195–8.

Care, Norman, "Contractualism and Moral Criticism," *The Review of Metaphysics* 23 (1969): 85–101.

Chapman, John, "Justice as Fairness," *Nomos VI: Justice,* eds., C.J. Friedrich and John Chapman, New York: The Atherton Press, 1963, pp. 147–69.

Hall, Everett, "Justice as Fairness: A Modernized Version of the Social Contract," *The Journal of Philosphy* 54 (1957): 662–70.

Mardiros, Anthony, M., "A Circular Procedure in Ethics," *Philosophical Review* 61 (1952): 223–5.

Margolis, Joseph, "Rule-Utilitariarism," *Australasian Journal of Philosophy* 43 (1965): 220–5.

McCloskey, H.J., "Two Concepts of Rules – A Note," Philosophical Quarterly 22 (1972): 344–8.

Murrary, John Courtney, Jr., "The Problem of Mr. Rawls's Problem," in *Law and Philosophy,* Sidney Hook, ed. New York: New York University Press, 1964, pp. 29–34.

Nagel, Ernest, "Fair Play and Civil Disobedience, *Law and Philosophy,* Sidney Hook, ed., New York: New York University Press, 1964, pp. 72–6.

Nozick, Robert, "Moral Complications and Moral Structures," *Natural Law Forum* 13 (1969): 1–50.

Quinn, Michael Sean, "Practice Defining Rules," *Ethics* 86 (1975): 630–47.

Ransdell, Joseph, "Constitutive Rules and Speech Act Analysis," *The Journal of Philosophy* 68 (1971): 385–400.

Rempel, H.D., "Justice as Efficiency," *Ethics* 79 (1969): 150–5.

Rosen, Bernard, "Rules and Justified Moral Judgment," *Philosophy and Phenomenological Research* 30 (1970): 436–43.

Runciman, W.G., and A.K. Sen, "Games, Justice, and the General Will," *Mind* 74 (1965): 554–62.

Schwyzer, Hubert, "Rules and Practices," *The Philosophical Review* 78 (1969): 451–67.

Wolff, Robert Paul, "A Refutation of Rawls's Theorem on Justice," *The Journal of Philosophy* 63 (1966): 179–90.

MISCELLANEOUS DISCUSSIONS AND REVIEWS

Daniels, Norman, "Rights to Health Care and Distributive Justice, Programmatic Worries," *Journal of Medicine and Philosophy* 4 (1979): 174–91.

Elliott, Robert, "Rawlsian Justice and Non-Human Animals," *Journal of Applied Philosophy* 1 (1984): 95–106.

Hill, Thomas, Review of John Rawls's *Collected Papers, Journal of Philosophy,* 98(5) (May 2001): 269–72.

Larmore, Charles, "Lifting the Veil," *The New Republic,* February 5, 2001,

Issue No. 4490, pp. 32–7 (a review of Rawls's *Lectures on the History of Moral Philosophy*).

Moskop, John, "Rawlsian Justice and a Human Right to Health Care," *Journal of Medicine and Philosophy* 8 (1983): 329–38.

Nagel, Thomas, "The Rigorous Compassion of John Rawls," *The New Republic* (October 25, 1999): 36–41 (Review of *Collected Papers*, *The Law of Peoples*, and *A Theory of Justice, Revised edition*).

Newey, Glen, "Floating on the LILO: John Rawls and the Content of Justice," *Times Literary Supplement* (September 10, 1999): 9–10 (a Review of Rawls's *Collected Papers*).

Nussbaum, Martha, "The Enduring Significance of John Rawls," *The Chronicle of Higher Education*, July 20, 2001 issue.

Pogge, Thomas, "A Brief Sketch of Rawls's Life," in Henry S. Richardson, ed., *The Philosophy of Rawls*, Vol. I: *Development and Main Outlines* of *Rawls's Theory of Justice* (New York: Garland, 1999) pp. 1–15.

Rogers, Ben, "Behind the Veil," *Lingua Franca* 9 (5) (July–August 1999): 57–65.

Schneewind, J.B., "What's Fair is Fair," *The New York Times Book Review*, June 24, 2001, p. 21 (a review of Rawls's *Justice as Fairness: A Restatement*).

Thero, Daniel, P., "Rawls and Environmental Ethics: A Critical Examination of the Literature," *Environmental Ethics* 17 (1995): 93–105.

VanDeveer, Donald, "Of Beasts, Persons, and the Original Position," *Monist* 62 (1979): 368–77.

Waldron, Jeremy, "The Plight of the Poor in the Midst of Plenty," *London Review of Books*, 21, no. 14 (15 July, 1999): 3–6 (review of Rawls's *Collected Papers*).

# INDEX

Abortion: 184–5, 192–3; and public reason, 42, 59–60 n75, 198 n24, 327, 343, 382; reasonable disagreement over, 195, 328; formal vs. material right to, 414; and trespass law, 415, 418

Abstract individualism: feminist criticism of Rawls on, 492

Adoption: state control of, 505

Advertising: regulation of as a factor in social ethos, 231

Affirmative action: 84 n3

Agency: Kantian conception of, 8; and the moral powers, 28, 295–6

Agent-relative prerogatives: 265

Aggregate social welfare: and the least well off, 200

Altruism: and the original position, 430, and classical utilitarianism, 430–1; and distinctions among persons, 432; and sympathetic spectator, 431

American Revolution, the: 335

Anderson, Elizabeth: 255, 259

Animals: outside realm of justice on Rawls's account, 514

Anti-perfectionism: liberal, 470–1; and priority of right over good, 471; non-communitarian criticisms of, 471; Rawls's support of state doctrine of, 473; Rawls's defense of, 484

Anti-realism: as a constructivist doctrine, 347

Arendt, Hannah: on autonomy, 114

Aristotle: on justice and desert, 447

Aristotelian principle: defined, 25, 289–90; and congruence of justice and

the good, 26, 291; as a psychological law, 289; and sense of justice, 291, 293

Arneson, Richard: 271 n9

Arnold, N. Scott: 235 n12

Aron, Raymond: 62

Arts: funding for, 194, 486 n21; justifiable grounds for state support of, 474

Arrow, Kenneth: 454 n5; on sensitivity of primary goods as an index, 256

Autonomy: 26, 288; and moral powers, 5; moral, 28; and Kantian constructivism, 28; rejected by Thomism, 29, 305; as basis of comprehensive liberalism, 74; rejection of, 96–7; cannot serve as basis for including political liberties among basic liberties, 107; and political action, 114; political, 121; and preservation of social institutions, 125; and good of justice, 159; public and private, 173–4; as an intrinsic good, 294, 300; and acting for the sake of justice, 300; and fact of reasonable pluralism, 304; rational and moral distinguished, 314 n50; full, 314 n50; Kantian ideal of in TJ, 379; as a liberal hypergood, 473; liberal emphasis on questioned, 476; priority of in political sphere, 476; disputes over importance of, 477

Background culture: contains comprehensive doctrines, 325; and civil society; 325, 331; elements of, 326; contrasted with public political

557

Ely, John Hart: 408; on judicial review, 119–20

Emotion: importance of for ethics emphasized by feminists, 489; intelligence of, 490; and unjust background conditions, 490; Rawls acknowledges role of in search for reflective equilibrium, 491; use of in public reason, 491; as source of stability, 496, 497; Rawls on cognitive content of, 497

Emotivism: contrasted with constructivism, 348

Empathy: role of in social dialog, 496

Employment subsidies: see wage subsidies

Ends: common and shared, 287; plurality of, 438

English, Jane: on heads of households assumption, 506; on just savings principle, 507

Enlightenment project: Rawls's project as distinct from, 326

Environmental protection: not fully covered by justice as fairness, 128; provision of, 475

Envy: and lack of self-worth, 287; excusable, 288

Epstein, Richard A.: 424 n82

Equal citizens: and sense of self-respect, 23; importance of role of in moral education, 124; see also, Equality; Free and equal citizens

Equal consideration: demands a fair democratic process, 122

Equal liberty: institutions of, 224–5; see also, Basic liberties

Equal opportunity for advantage: as alternative to democratic equality, 253; and moral arbitrariness of social and natural contingencies, 253; fails to protect needs of free and equal citizens, 255; as part of comprehensive doctrine, 256

Equal political liberty: fundamental to democracy, 169, 173; relationship to equal personal liberty, 169; seen as merely instrumentally valuable by some liberals, 175

Equal respect: as highest political value, 83; and basic rights, 96; and political democracy, 97; see also, Mutual respect

Equality: and liberalism, 64, 65; socioeconomic, 65; and second principle of justice, 89; and democratic society as society of equals, 96; basis in sense of justice, 96, 247; relationship to sense of justice, 109; as baseline for contract among free and equal citizens, 247; tendency towards, 252; Conservatism and, 287; and rejection of sexual hierarchy, 502; under law, 519 n52; and sex discrimination, 519 n52

Equality of opportunity: different interpretations of, 68–9; and influence of the family, 69; not sufficient for equality, 69; and natural abilities, 79; formal, 79, 245; and affirmative action, 84 n3; covered by constitutional law, 401; and deference to basic liberties, 402; see also Fair equality of opportunity

Estlund, David: 240 n36, 267, 276 n67

Ethical constructivism: contrasted with moral realism, 348; distinguished from moral anti-realism, 348; and justificatory role of ethics, 348; and objectivity, 348–9; see also, Contructivism; Kantian Constructivism

Ethos of justice: question of need for in democratic equality, 264; as alternative to Rawls's focus on basic structure, 265; G.A.Cohen on, 265–9

Etzioni, Amitai: 462

Exchange branch: use of to achieve perfectionist ends, 193

Fact of reason: in *Critique of Practical Reason*, 356; Rawls's account of, 357

Fair equality of opportunity: defined, 69, 89; its priority over the difference principle, 72, 252; vs. formal equality of opportunity, 79, 245; rationale for, 98; role of in difference principle, 215; difficulties in implementation of, 225; and race, class, and gender, 241; role of education in, 245, 250; as requiring